Male, Female

Male, Female

The Evolution of Human Sex Differences

DAVID C. GEARY

American Psychological Association
Washington, DC

First printing September 1998
Second printing February 1999

Published by
American Psychological Association
750 First Street, NE
Washington, DC 20002

Copies may be ordered from
APA Order Department
P.O. Box 92984
Washington, DC 20090-2984

In the U.K., Europe, North Africa, and the Middle East, copies may be ordered from
American Psychological Association
3 Henrietta Street
Covent Garden, London
WC2E 8LU England

Typeset in Goudy by EPS Group Inc., Easton, MD

Printer: Data Reproductions Corp., Auburn Hills, MI
Cover designer: Design Concepts, San Diego, CA
Technical/production editor: Marianne Maggini

Library of Congress Cataloging-in-Publication Data
Geary, David C.
    Male, female : the evolution of human sex differences / David C. Geary.
       p.   cm.
    Includes bibliographical references and index.
    ISBN 1-55798-527-8 (hardcover : acid-free paper)
    1. Sex differences. 2. Human evolution. I. Title.
QP81.5.G43 1998
155.3'3—dc21   98-26961
                                            CIP

British Library Cataloguing-in-Publication Data
A CIP record is available from the British Library.

Printed in the United States of America

CONTENTS

v

FIGURES AND ILLUSTRATIONS

PREFACE

Men are not from Mars and women are not from Venus, although there are many times when both sexes seem to be from different planets. The behavior of members of the opposite sex and the misunderstandings that often arise when men and women try to negotiate relationships have been a source of mystery and confusion throughout the ages. If one has ever been baffled by the behavior of members of the opposite sex, or even by one's own behavior in relating to members of the opposite sex, then this book will be of interest to you. The book is not, however, a guide to creating (or fixing) relationships with members of the opposite sex, but rather it is an attempt to explain and understand differences in the social behavior of boys and girls and men and women, as well as many other sex differences.

More precisely, the purpose of this book is to explain the different ways in which men and women pursue one of the most fundamental goals of life, to reproduce, and to describe how the accompanying reproductive strategies are related to a wide array of physical, behavioral, social, emotional, cognitive, and neural sex differences. The book is written from the perspective of evolutionary selection—life, death, and reproduction—and follows Darwin's principles of sexual selection.[1] These basic principles provide a unifying theme around which the evolution and development of human sex differences can be understood. In short, the principles of sexual selection and the accompanying patterns that have emerged in many other species are used as the theoretical framework for attempting to organize and make sense of the vast literature on human sex differences.

As should become apparent in this book, many human sex differences are readily understandable from this perspective, including sex differences during the course of human evolution (e.g., differences in the physical

[1] As found in *The Descent of Man, and Selection in Relation to Sex*, published in 1871.

xi

size of the human being's male and female ancestors), the pattern of parental care, sexual behavior and the attributes preferred in mates, the nature of social aggression, social motives and patterns of emotional expression, physical development, play preferences, social development, brain and cognition, and many others. The implications of these sex differences, as they relate to modern society, are explored in the final chapter of this book.

Within these chapters I obviously attempt to cover a wide range of human sex differences and try to do so within a single theoretical framework. Given this, the book should provide a provocative, but hopefully convincing, discussion of the origins of human sex differences and a discussion of the mechanisms that influence how these differences are expressed from one culture or context to the next. In other words, the presentation should be of interest to nearly anyone who has a professional or personal interest in the topic—psychologists, biologists, anthropologists, and the informed laypublic—whether or not one believes that sexual selection is the theoretical perspective that should guide the study of human sex differences.

In writing the book, I contacted—by phone or by electronic mail (and occasionally in person)—experts in a number of fields to ensure that I had not missed an important study or simply to just ask questions. I would like to thank all of these individuals for responding to my queries: Jamie Arndt, Janet Astington, Scott Atran, Ann Bettencourt, Sandra Bosacki, Napoleon Chagnon, John Colombo, Larry Davis, Frans de Waal, Uta Frith, Doreen Kimura, Eleanor Maguire, Barbara Malt, Ken Pugh, Sheldon Solomon, and Henry Wellman. I would also like to thank the many individuals who commented on drafts of one or more chapters: Dave Bjorklund, Chuck Borduin, Lynne Cooper, Mark Flinn, Jeff Gilger, Glen Good, Carmen Hamson, P. Paul Heppner, Mary Hoard, Dave MacDonald, Joshua Schwartz, Ken Sheldon, Melanie Sheldon, Scott Saults, Fred vom Saal, and Carol Ward.

Special thanks are due to Martin Daly and Kevin MacDonald for reviewing the entire manuscript, Christopher Nadolski for his work and patience in preparing many of the illustrations found throughout the book, the Research Council of the University of Missouri—Columbia for providing the leave necessary to write this book, Tom DiLorenzo (Chair, Department of Psychology, University of Missouri—Columbia) for providing an additional class release to finish the project, and Judy Nemes and Marianne Maggini for their work on many aspects of the final production of the book, including a thorough review of the entire manuscript. Finally, I thank my wife, Leslie, for tolerating my many musings and an occasional rant during the 16 months that it took to write this book. Of course, the conclusions drawn here are my own and are not those of any of the above-mentioned individuals.

Male, Female

1

BEGINNINGS

Sex differences in brain, behavior, and cognition are inherently interesting to the scientist and to the layperson alike. In fact, some level of interest in sex differences would be expected for nearly all individuals of any sexually reproducing species, given that one of the most fundamental goals of life—to reproduce—necessarily involves negotiating some type of relationship with at least one member of the opposite sex. Not surprisingly, research on sex differences has occupied biological and social scientists for more than a century, but, with a few notable exceptions (e.g., Buss, 1994; Daly & Wilson, 1983), the research programs in these two broad areas have largely developed independently of one another. In recent years, biologists have used Darwin's (1871) principles of sexual selection (explained in chapter 2) to provide a coherent theoretical framework for the study of sex differences across hundreds of studies and across scores of species (Andersson, 1994).

At the same time, social scientists have, for the most part, been studying sex differences from a completely different theoretical perspective, gender roles (e.g., Eagly, 1987). The gist is that most nonphysical human sex differences are the result of the culturally mediated social roles that are adopted by boys and men and by girls and women. In many cases, the belief that human sex differences are the result of the adoption of such roles is accepted, it seems, without a critical evaluation of this perspective. The goal of this book is not to provide such a critical evaluation—

3

although associated discussion can be found in chapter 6 and in chapter 7—but rather to approach the issue of human sex differences from the same theoretical perspective that is used to study sex differences in all other species—sexual selection. In fact, it is the thesis of this book that human sex differences can never fully be understood without an appreciation of sexual selection and an understanding of how the associated processes are manifested in other species. The basic structure of the book is overviewed in this chapter, following a brief introduction to the mechanisms of evolutionary selection (see Buss, Haselton, Schackelford, Bleske, & Wakefield, 1998; Dennett, 1995; and Weiner, 1995, for extended and accessible discussion of the mechanisms of evolutionary selection).

THE MECHANISMS OF EVOLUTIONARY SELECTION

Any process, event, or ecological condition that in any way influences life, death, and reproduction is a potential selection pressure. Any such pressure acts on individuals, but not in a random fashion; although random or chance events do occur and can influence evolutionary processes (Mayr, 1983). Rather, for nearly all features of physiology, body structure, or behavior, individuals of the same species will differ to some degree. In many cases, these individual differences are unrelated to life, death, and reproduction. In other cases, even slight differences can determine which individuals will live and reproduce and which individuals will die. It is in these cases that evolutionary selection is occurring (Darwin, 1859).

The result of such selection is that those individuals that happen to have a somewhat shorter beak or a somewhat larger body size—or whatever characteristic influences survival and reproduction—will survive in greater numbers than their peers. If these characteristics are inherited, then the survivors will produce offspring that also have a somewhat shorter beak or a somewhat larger body size than other members of the same species (i.e., conspecifics). If these characteristics continue to influence life, death, and reproduction in the offspring's generation, then the process will repeat itself. Over generations and sometimes in a single generation, there is a change in the selected characteristic, such that the average individual in the population now has a shorter beak or a larger body size than the average individual did several generations earlier.

It is this process—natural selection—that shapes species to their ecology. All that is required for natural selection to occur is that the trait dealing in life, death, and reproduction varies across individuals and that some portion of this variability has a genetic basis (Mayr, 1983). Under these conditions, selection will occur, whether the trait is physical, physiological, or behavioral.

> If evolution of behavior proceeds like the evolution of structural or molecular characteristics, then, according to the Darwinian interpretation, it must have two characteristics. First, in order to be able to respond to selection pressures, such behavior must at least in part have a genetic basis, and secondly, the genetic basis must be somewhat variable, that is, it must be able to supply the material on which natural selection can act. Behavioral characteristics thus would share, whenever they evolve, the two most important aspects of evolving structural characteristics: variability and a genetic basis. (Mayr, 1974, pp. 653–654)

Thus, heritable individual differences provide the grist for evolutionary selection. Given that nearly all features of human anatomy, physiology, behavior, and cognitions show individual variability that is partly heritable, they are all potentially subject to selection pressures (e.g., Bouchard, Lykken, McGue, Segal, & Tellegen, 1990; Farber, 1981; Finkel & McGue, 1997; Plomin & Petrill, 1997). The issue is complex, however (Kirkpatrick, 1996; Waxman & Peck, 1998). Selection pressures can reduce or eliminate heritable variability; thus, many traits that have undergone strong selection in the past no longer show heritable variability (e.g., all genetically normal human beings have two legs, an inherited but nonvariable characteristic; Daly, 1996). Some traits that show heritable variability have not been subject to selection pressures at all (S. J. Gould & Vrba, 1982; e.g., reading ability, which is discussed in chapter 9), and other traits that show heritable variability are only subject to selection pressures under certain conditions. Selection pressures can vary from one generation to the next or from one geographical region to the next. At times—when food is abundant and predators and parasites are scarce—selection pressures are weak, and, thus, most individuals survive and reproduce (i.e., individual differences are not especially important under these conditions).

The process of evolutionary selection and change can be illustrated by the work of Rosemary and Peter Grant (e.g., Grant & Grant, 1989, 1993); this research is nicely captured in Weiner's (1995) Pulitzer Prize winning narrative. For several decades the Grants have been studying the relation between ecological change on several of the Galápagos islands—Daphne major and Genovesa—and change in the survival rates and physical characteristics of several species of finch that reside on these islands, often called *Darwin's finches*. One of these finches, the medium ground finch (*Geospiza fortis*), resides on Daphne major, and ecological change on this island has been shown to result in changes in the average beak size of individuals of this species from one generation to the next (Grant & Grant, 1993). Figure 1.1 shows that individual medium ground finches naturally vary from one another in beak size and in other physical characteristics.

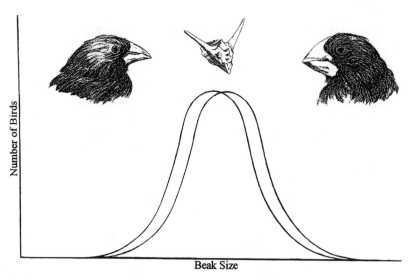

Figure 1.1. Cross-generational change in average beak size in the medium ground finch (*Geospiza fortis*). Illustration by Christopher Nadolski.

On the left side of the figure is an illustration of an individual with a relatively small beak, and on the right side is an individual of the same age and sex with a relatively large beak. The distributions show that the beak size of most individuals will be in between these two extremes.

For the medium ground finch, and in fact for all of Darwin's finches, the size and shape of an individual's beak determine which foods can be eaten and which foods cannot. When food sources (e.g., seeds, insects, and so forth) are plentiful and varied, there is little relation between beak size and survival and reproductive rates. Under these conditions, most of Darwin's finches—within and across species—survive and reproduce. When foods are scarce, individual birds tend to specialize in one food source (e.g., seeds) or another (e.g., insects), depending on the size and shape of their beak. Under these conditions, some food sources are usually more plentiful than others. Individuals that are able to specialize—because of beak size and shape—in a relatively abundant food source (e.g., a particular type of seed) survive and reproduce in greater numbers than individuals whose beak size and shape force them to specialize in a scarce food source.

To illustrate, there was very little rain on Daphne major in 1973. The result of this drought was an 84% decline in the quantity of foods available to Darwin's finches and a sharp increase in finch mortality rates (Weiner, 1995). For Darwin's finches, life or death depended greatly on beak size. One of the foods that was still relatively plentiful during this time was the seeds of the caltrop plant (*Tribulus cistoides*). These seeds are encased in mericarps (shown in the center of Figure 1.1), which are armored with spikes and are relatively large, at least for a finch. Some medium ground finches, or *fortis*, were able to exploit this food source, whereas others were not.

> *Fortis* with bigger beaks can crack the mericarp and gouge out the seeds faster than those with smaller beaks. Tiny variations are everything. A *fortis* with a beak 11 millimeters long can crack caltrop; a *fortis* with a beak only 10.5 millimeters long will not even try. "The smallest grain in the balance" can decide who shall live and who shall die. Between a beak big enough to crack caltrop and a beak that can't, the difference is only half a millimeter. (Weiner, 1995, p. 64)

During this time, medium ground finches with relatively large beaks survived in greater numbers than conspecifics (recall, members of the same species) with relatively small beaks. To make matters worse, survivors with relatively small beaks were at a mating disadvantage. It appears that short-beaked males were weaker than their better fed large-beaked peers, which appeared to result in a difference in the vigor of the courtship displays of small- and large-beaked finches. Female medium ground finches chose mates on the basis of the vigor of their courtship display and thus preferred large-beaked males. The combination of differential survival rates and female choice—a feature of sexual selection discussed in chapter 2—resulted in a measurable shift in the next generation's average beak size (beak size is heritable), as illustrated in Figure 1.1. The leftmost distribution represents the beak size characteristics of medium ground finches before the drought, and the rightmost distribution represents these characteristics after the drought. Just after the drought, individual differences in beak size were still evident, but the average beak size had increased and there were fewer individuals with extremely small beaks and more individuals with extremely large beaks.

For the medium ground finch, having a beak that is larger than average is not inherently better than having a beak that is smaller than average; it is only beneficial during periods of drought. Several years after the drought, in 1982–1983, an especially strong El Niño event resulted in a 14-fold increase in rainfall on Daphne major (Grant & Grant, 1993). After this heavy rainfall, the number of caltrop plants and their mericarps decreased significantly, and the number of smaller seeds available on the island increased significantly. "Mechanical efficiency of handling small seeds appears to be a feature of finches with small beaks" (Grant & Grant, 1993, p. 114). The result was that small-beaked individuals survived in greater numbers than large-beaked individuals and that small-beaked males were preferred as mating partners (presumably because of more vigorous courtship displays). The survival and reproductive advantages of small-beaked individuals were evident for at least 6 years following the El Niño event. After several generations, the average beak size of medium ground finches was now smaller than it was just after the drought—the distribution had shifted back to the left.

An equally important finding was that these selection pressures affected only beak size and not other physical characteristics (e.g., leg length; Grant & Grant, 1993). In other words, under difficult conditions—those resulting in strong selection pressures—evolutionary selection can act quickly (sometimes in one or a few generations) and selectively (affecting only those traits that directly influence survival and reproduction). The process of relatively fast evolutionary selection and change is not restricted to Darwin's finches. It has also been demonstrated with a number of other species (e.g., Reznick, Shaw, Rodd, & Shaw, 1997; Seehausen, van Alphen, & Witte, 1997), including, perhaps, humans (Holliday, 1997). On the basis of change in relative bone size (e.g., femur—that is, thigh bone—length), comparing fossils dating from 6,000 to 30,000 years ago to modern populations, Holliday concluded "that the current patterns of body form in Europe go back no farther than 20,000 years" (Holliday, 1997, p. 444).

OVERVIEW OF THIS BOOK

To comprehend and appreciate human sex differences fully, an understanding of the evolutionary, hormonal, and ecological conditions that underlie sex differences in other species is essential, as noted earlier. In fact, a full understanding of human sex differences requires that I begin with a consideration of the evolution of sexual reproduction itself. This is so because the grist of evolutionary selection is heritable individual differences, and the ultimate source of this variability—and the first topic addressed in chapter 2—is sexual reproduction. In relation to asexual reproduction, sexual reproduction appears to provide a number of benefits, including elimination of harmful mutations (Crow, 1997), ecological adaptation (G. C. Williams, 1975), and generation of a complex and varied immune system (Hamilton & Zuk, 1982). In all of these cases, the result is greater variability, or individual differences, within sexually reproducing species than within asexually reproducing species.

Once sexual reproduction evolved, an essential feature of the life history of all individuals of sexually reproducing species was to find a mate or mates. To further complicate this life task, the individual variability that results from sexual reproduction will ensure that all potential mates are not equal, which, in turn, results in competition for the most suitable mate or for the most mates. The process associated with choosing and competing for mates is sexual selection (Darwin, 1871), the fundamentals of which are the topic of the second section in chapter 2. Sexual selection is a dynamic process that is influenced by a host of factors, including sex differences in the relative costs and benefits of reproduction (Trivers, 1972) and the ecology of the species (Emlen & Oring, 1977), among others. These dynamics are most typically expressed in terms of female choice of mating partners and male–male competition over access to mates or for control of those resources that females need to rear their offspring (Andersson, 1994), the nuances of which are detailed in chapter 2. Following the discussion of the dynamics of female choice and male–male competition, the focus shifts to discussion of the mechanisms that influence the expression of the associated sex differences in brain, behavior, and cognition (i.e., sex hormones).

Chapter 3 brings the reader one step closer to human sex differences and focuses exclusively on sexual selection in nonhuman primates and on the apparent pattern of sexual selection in our hominid ancestors. The research reviewed in this chapter reveals that nearly all of the sex differences found in humans are evident in many other primate species. As an example, one of the more thoroughly studied aspects of primate social behavior is male–male competition. For many species of primate, including humans in many contexts, males compete by means of physical attack and physical threat to establish social dominance over other males. The position within the resulting dominance hierarchy oftentimes has rather dramatic reproductive consequences for individual males. In many contexts, only the most dominant, or alpha, male sires offspring (e.g., Altmann et al., 1996). The achievement of social dominance is complex, however. In some species, social dominance is achieved through one-on-one physical contests, in other species it is more dependent on the coalitional activities of groups of males, and in still other species it is influenced by the social support of females in the group (Dunbar, 1984; Goodall, 1986; Smuts, 1985). All of these different patterns, and many other features of male–male competition in primates, are described in chapter 3.

With the exception of humans, female choice has not been as systematically studied in primates as male–male competition or female choice has been in other species (e.g., birds). The research that has been conducted clearly indicates that females in many, if not all, primate species prefer some males to others as mating partners (Smuts, 1985). The bases for female choice appear to vary with social and ecological conditions but are often influenced by infanticide risks and the social support that a male partner might provide (Hrdy, 1979). For instance, in the olive baboon (*Papio anubis*), females prefer as mating partners those males that provide social protection (e.g., from other males) and other forms of care to them and to their offspring (Smuts & Gubernick, 1992).

Female–female competition is also evident in most, if not all, primate species. However, unlike male primates, female primates more typically compete for access to high-quality food and not for access to mates (Silk, 1993). Access to high-quality food has important reproductive consequences for these females and their offspring, as females that have access to this food are larger, healthier, and have more surviving offspring than their undernourished peers. Male choice is also evident in many species of primate and appears to be based on the nature of the relationship between the male and individual females and on implicit reproductive concerns. All other things being equal, male primates prefer to mate with females that are currently fertile (this is typically signaled through a swelling of the sexual organs) and that have borne one or more offspring (Silk, 1987).

One of the more consistent consequences of male–male competition in primates is larger and more aggressive males than females (Plavcan & van Schaik, 1997b). The more intense the male–male competition, the larger the sex difference in physical size, although these differences are somewhat less pronounced in species in which male–male competition is coalition based, as in a cousin of *Homo sapiens*, the chimpanzee (*Pan troglodytes*; Goodall, 1986). The consistent relation between physical sex differences and the intensity of male–male competition allows inferences to be drawn about the likely nature of male–male competition in human beings' ancestors. Beginning with the *Australopithecine* ancestors and continuing to modern humans, males are physically larger than females. When these patterns are combined with the patterns of male–male competition and female choice that are evident in extant primates, inferences can be —and are in the final section of chapter 3—drawn about the potential pattern of sexual selection during the course of human evolution (Foley & Lee, 1989).

Beginning in chapter 4 and continuing throughout the remainder of the book, the focus is on sexual selection in modern human populations. Chapter 4 focuses specifically on paternal investment. In most mammalian species, males provide little if any direct investment in offspring (Clutton-Brock, 1989). As a result, the reproductive effort of males tends to be largely focused on mating effort and the associated male–male competition, and the reproductive effort of females tends to be largely focused on parental effort and the associated female choice (e.g., to get the best genes for their offspring). The dynamics of sexual selection are much more of a complication for species—which includes humans—in which males show some level of direct parental investment. When both the mother and the father invest in offspring and there are individual differences in the quality of care or genes that parents provide to these offspring, then female–female competition and male choice become important features of sexual selection, in addition to male–male competition and female choice (G. A. Parker & Simmons, 1996). Chapter 4 provides a contrast of maternal and paternal investment, documents the pattern of paternal investment across cultures and across species of primate, and, finally, provides an overview of the relation between paternal investment and the physical and social well-being of children.

Chapter 5 provides a review of the dynamics of sexual selection in modern humans (i.e., female choice, female–female competition, male–male competition, and male choice). As with other primates, the dynamics of sexual selection in humans is complex and can vary from one culture or context (e.g., different historical periods within a culture) to the next. For instance, men throughout the world compete for cultural success (Irons, 1979); that is, they compete for control of culturally important resources and for the establishment of social status. Cultural success can be achieved in many different ways, ranging from obtaining the head of one's competitor to securing a high-paying job. However it is achieved, successful men typically have more wives and children, or at least more mating opportunities, than their less successful peers (Chagnon, 1988; Irons, 1993; Pérusse, 1993). In other words, in chapter 5 there is not only discussion of sexual selection in humans but there are also numerous illustrations of how these dynamics are expressed in different cultures, during different historical periods within cultures, and how they are modified by social ideologies.

Chapter 6 provides the foundation for later discussion of developmental sex differences (chapter 7) and sex differences in brain and cognition (chapter 8) and is one of the more unique features of this book. The goal of chapter 6 was to develop a unified framework for understanding sex differences in the motivational, emotional, cognitive, neural, and developmental processes and systems that underlie the sex differences in reproductive strategies described in chapter 4 and chapter 5. The basic thesis is that the fundamental motivation of human beings, and all other complex organisms, is to achieve some level of control over the social (e.g., other people), biological (e.g., food), and physical (e.g., territory) resources that support life and allow one to reproduce (Geary, 1998; Heckhausen & Schulz, 1995). Or stated otherwise, the motivational, emotional, behavioral, and brain systems that make up the human mind have been shaped by evolutionary selection to organize and guide attempts to control the social, biological, and physical resources that support survival and reproduction. Childhood is the portion of the life span during which these systems become adapted (e.g., through play) to local ecologies.

In this view, sex differences that are evident during development should be a reflection of later sex differences in reproductive strategies. The evidence for this thesis is provided in chapter 7. More specifically, the chapter covers sex differences in physical development, during infancy, play patterns, social development, and parenting influences—all from the perspective of sexual selection. As an example, for primate species characterized by relatively intense male–male competition, males are not only larger than females, but they also show a different pattern of physical development (Leigh, 1996). The most general pattern is for males to mature later than females and to show a longer growth spurt during puberty (this contributes to their larger size). For species in which there is relatively little male–male competition and a monogamous mating system, males are the same size as females, and males and females show nearly identical growth patterns (Leigh, 1995). Sex differences in human physical development follow the pattern found in species with relatively intense male–male competition (Tanner, 1990) and clearly support the position that male–male competition has been an important social dynamic during the course of human evolution.

In chapter 8, sex differences in brain and cognition are approached by using a proposed system of evolved cognitive modules developed in chapter 6, a system of modules corresponding to the motivation to control social, biological, and physical resources. Social modules, for instance, are divided into individual-level cognitions—such as language, facial processing, and theory of mind (i.e., the ability to make inferences about the intentions, emotional states, and so on of other people)—and group-level cognitions—such as the formation of in-groups and out-groups. The use of this theoretical framework provides a unique organization to the research on human sex differences in brain and cognition and reveals patterns that are consistent with the view that many of these sex differences have been shaped by sexual selection. As an example, although girls and boys and women and men readily classify other human beings in terms of favored in-groups and disfavored out-groups (Stephan, 1985), there appear to be sex differences in the dynamics of in-group and out-group formation. In comparison to girls and women, boys and men appear to place more social pressures on in-group members to conform to group mores and appear to develop more easily agonistic attitudes and behaviors toward members of an out-group, especially during periods of competition or conflict. The sex difference in the dynamics of in-group and out-group formation can readily be understood in terms of the evolution of coalition-based male–male competition.

The final chapter (chapter 9) provides a discussion of how sex differences that appear to have been shaped by sexual selection might indirectly be related to sex differences that are important in modern society (Geary, 1996), including sex differences in academic competencies (e.g., reading achievement), violence, accidental death and injury rates, the experience of anxiety- and depression-related symptoms (e.g., sad affect) and disorders, eating disorders, and occupational interests and occupational achievement. To illustrate, girls and women obtain higher average scores than boys and men on reading achievement tests in elementary school, junior high school, high school, and in the general population of adults (Hedges & Nowell, 1995). Reading is almost certainly not an evolved cognitive competency, and thus the advantage of girls and women in this area is not directly related to past selection pressures (Geary, 1995a; Rozin, 1976).

Nonetheless, the advantage of girls and women in reading achievement might be indirectly related to more primary (i.e., evolved) cognitive sex differences. For instance, girls and presumably women appear to have a more elaborated theory of mind than same-age boys and men (Banerjee,

1997; chapter 8). Girls and women appear to be more skilled, on average, than boys and men in making inferences about the emotional state, intentions, and so on of other people, which, in turn, appears to contribute to their advantage on tests of reading comprehension. The sex difference, favoring girls and women, on tests of reading comprehension is largest for social themes and smallest for themes that do not involve people (Willingham & Cole, 1997). In other words, theory of mind might facilitate reading comprehension through skill at mentally representing the plots and subplots that unfold in the narrative, and girls and women appear to have an advantage over boys and men in generating these mental representations.

2

PRINCIPLES AND MECHANISMS OF SEXUAL SELECTION

The focus of this chapter is on the power and the eloquence of Darwin's (1871) principles of sexual selection for understanding how sex differences can emerge over the course of evolution and for understanding how any such differences are expressed in each new generation. I begin with discussion of the evolution of sexual reproduction, because an understanding of the factors that led to the evolution of sexuality and distinct sexes is needed to understand the persistence of variability among individuals, in general, and the dynamics of sexual reproduction, in particular. An introduction to the processes of sexual selection then follows and includes discussion of the roles of parenting, female choice of mating partners, and male–male competition in the evolution and proximate (i.e., here and now) expression of sex differences in reproductive strategies. The chapter concludes with an overview of the ways in which sex hormones induce many of the sex differences described in this chapter and the ways in which sex hormones appear to influence sensitivity to environmental conditions.

WHY SEXUAL REPRODUCTION?

A principal advantage of asexual reproduction is that one does not have to mix one's genes with another individual to produce offspring. That

15

is, barring mutations, offspring are genetically identical to the parent. With sexual reproduction, in contrast, there is only a 50% overlap, on average, between the genes of offspring and each of their parents (Bulmer, 1994; Ridley, 1993; G. C. Williams, 1975; G. C. Williams & Mitton, 1973). Given this, for sexual reproduction to be a viable alternative to asexual reproduction, the benefits of the former must be more than double the benefits of the latter (G. C. Williams, 1975). Despite the clear, short-term genetic advantage, there are a number of long-term costs to asexual reproduction that result in important evolutionary disadvantages. Most generally, models of the advantages and disadvantages of sexual and asexual reproduction, respectively, have focused on the deleterious effects of mutations, the ability of offspring to adapt to their ecology, and the resistance to parasites. Each of these models is briefly discussed in the respective sections below.

Mutations

Genetic mutations result primarily from mistakes in DNA repair and replication (Crow, 1997). Although the frequency with which these mutations occur is currently debated, it is clear that a small number of mutations, and sometimes a single mutation, can affect the individual's behavior or physiology; that is, the individual's phenotype (Keightley & Caballero, 1997; Kondrashov, 1988; Peck & Eyre-Walker, 1997). Those mutations that do affect the phenotype are almost always harmful, although most of these mutations result in only small reductions in life span and in the number of offspring contributed to the next generation (Crow, 1997). In most cases, it is the accumulation of mildly harmful mutations that eventually results in the affected individuals being unable to reproduce at all and thus being eliminated from the population.

Asexual reproduction results in a faster accumulation of harmful mutations over generations than sexual reproduction does (Kondrashov & Crow, 1991; Muller, 1964; Vrijenhhoek, 1993). More precisely, with sexual reproduction, some individuals have only a few mutations, whereas other individuals have many mutations. Those individuals with many mutations are less likely to survive and to reproduce than their cohorts with fewer mutations (Crow, 1997). The net result is that relatively harmful mutations are eliminated from sexually reproducing populations, without endangering the entire population. With asexual reproduction, harmful mutations that arise in one generation will necessarily be passed on to all members of the next generation, which, in turn, will eventually result in the accumulation of a large number of harmful mutations over many generations. Muller (1964) explained the process in terms of a ratchet—now called *Muller's ratchet*—whereby the number of mutations from one generation to the next necessarily ratchets up, or increases. Ridley (1993) likened the process to photocopying:

> Muller's ratchet applies if you use a photocopier to make a copy of a copy of a document. With each successive copy the quality deteriorates. . . . Once the original is lost [through mutations], the best copy you can make is less good than it was before. (p. 48)

In addition to providing a mechanism, as noted earlier, that can eliminate harmful mutations without affecting the entire population, sexual reproduction appears to afford a number of other advantages over asexual reproduction (Crow, 1997; Kondrashov, 1988). With the genetic recombination associated with sexual reproduction, many offspring will have fewer potentially harmful mutations than their parents; others will, of course, have more. In addition, when DNA is damaged, having two copies of the same gene—one from each parent—appears to facilitate DNA repair, if one of these genes is damaged (see Bernstein, Hopf, & Michod, 1989).

Ecological Adaptation

Other models have focused on differences in the genetic and phenotypic variability of asexual and sexual species and the consequent ease with which the associated lineages can adapt to ecological change (Bell & Maynard Smith, 1987; B. Charlesworth, 1993; G. C. Williams, 1975; G. C. Williams & Mitton, 1973). With sexual reproduction, offspring are different from one another because, in most species, they share only 50%, on average, of the same genes. The offspring generated from asexual reproduction, in contrast, differ only as a result of mutations, which will always involve considerably less than 50% of the individual's genes. The result is greater genetic and phenotypic variability in the offspring of sexually reproducing species, compared with asexual species.

Greater variability, in turn, allows for adaptations to ecologies that change from one generation to the next and allows for adaptations to highly competitive environments (Darwin, 1859; Reznick et al., 1997; G. C. Williams & Mitton, 1973). In this view, asexual reproduction is favored when the ecology of the parent and that of the offspring are essentially the same. The parent is obviously adapted—the phenotype of the parent enabled it to survive and to reproduce—to this ecology, and given that the offspring are genetically identical to the parent, except for mutations, they too will be well adapted to the ecology of their parent. However, if the conditions that support survival change from one generation to the next, then the characteristics that enabled the reproduction and survival of the parent may or may not be well suited to the new ecological conditions, the conditions in which the offspring must survive and reproduce. Sexual reproduction ensures variability in offspring and thus increases the chances that at least some of the offspring will survive and reproduce under the new ecological conditions.

G. C. Williams (1975) explained this process in terms of a lottery analogy. The ecological conditions that support survival and reproduction represent the winning number. Asexual reproduction is like having 100 lottery tickets, all with the same number. With sexual reproduction, you get fewer tickets—50 in this case—but they all have different numbers. If you do not know the winning number in advance—that is, if the ecological conditions that support survival and reproduction frequently change—then sexual reproduction, although more costly (you cannot buy as many tickets), is more likely to result in a winning number. That is, sexual reproduction results in at least some offspring that are well suited to the new ecological conditions.

Another potential advantage to variability in offspring is represented by the elbow-room model (Bulmer, 1994). The basic premise is that offspring that differ to some extent, genetically and phenotypically, do not compete for identical environmental resources. In other words, offspring that differ from one another—those resulting from sexual reproduction— are better able to seek different niches within the same environment and thus are better able to reduce the intensity of competition among themselves (Dawkins & Krebs, 1979; Segal & MacDonald, 1998). With asexual reproduction, the primary competitors for survival are often one's more or less identical siblings. Even in relatively stable environments, competition among siblings can be severe if resources are limited (G. C. Williams & Mitton, 1973). Thus, intense competition favors niche seeking (Dawkins & Krebs, 1979), which, in turn, is made possible through phenotypic variability. Within species, phenotypic variability is most readily achieved through sexual reproduction.

Parasite Resistance

One of the more intensely studied models of the evolution of sexuality focuses on the coevolution of hosts and parasites (Hamilton, 1980, 1990; Hamilton, Axelrod, & Tanese, 1990; Hamilton & Zuk, 1982; Ives, 1996; Møller, 1990b, 1997; Read, 1987, 1988; Sorci, Morand, & Hugot, 1997). Parasites such as viruses, bacteria, and worms are ubiquitous and often negatively affect the fitness of the host. Nearly all organisms are under constant threat from a variety of these potentially harmful parasites, which, in turn, creates strong selection pressures for the evolution of antiparasite adaptations, such as immune responses to viruses or bacteria (G. Beck & Habicht, 1996; A. V. S. Hill et al., 1991). However, because parasites generally have shorter life spans than their hosts, the parasite lineage is often able to adapt—for instance, through selection acting on advantageous mutations—to the host's antiparasite adaptations. The result is that the host's adaptations to these parasites are less functional, at least in the short term.

With asexual reproduction, the antiparasite defenses of the parent and the offspring are nearly identical, differing only as the result of mutations. Any such mutations are unlikely to result in an effective long-term defense against the more rapidly evolving adaptations of the parasites (Hamilton et al., 1990). Thus, once adapted to the defenses of the parent, the parasites are equally well adapted to the defenses of the offspring. In such situations, harmful parasites will quickly reduce the viability of, or even eliminate, the lineage (Hamilton, 1980).

In this view, the principal function of sexual reproduction is to create a highly variable antiparasite defense system, one that can respond to a variety of different parasites and that can be changed, to some extent, from one generation to the next. If the parasites have specifically adapted to the defenses of the parent, then a change in these defenses will typically benefit their offspring. The parasites will then make adaptations to these new defenses, which, in turn, will be reconfigured in the next generation of the host. The process of successive adaptations creates a coevolution between parasites and the host's defenses against these parasites (Dawkins & Krebs, 1979). The coevolution of hosts and parasites is reciprocal, however. It does not lead to any particular end point, such as permanent immunity, but rather to a potentially never-ending pattern of resistance and susceptibility to parasites (Ridley, 1993). Van Valen (1973) illustrated this concept by means of Lewis Carroll's (1871) Red Queen. "The Red Queen is a formidable woman who runs like the wind but never seems to get anywhere: . . . [She states to Alice], you see, it takes all the running you can do to keep in the same place" (Ridley, 1993, p. 64). Stated otherwise, the coevolution of hosts and parasites ensures that there is constant change and individual variability, at least for the characteristics, such as the immune system, that are the focus of this coevolution, but the mean viability of the host does not necessarily change.

The immune system provides an excellent illustration of the evolution of a system of defense against parasites (other defense systems include, for example, the chemical defenses of many plant species). The genes that code for specific immune responses—genes from the major histocompatibility complex (MHC)—are the most variable family of genes ever identified (Nei & Hughes, 1991), in keeping with the prediction that variability is the key to keeping one step ahead of parasites. There are specific MHC immune responses to specific parasites, and thus natural selection should favor individuals with a varied MHC, given that almost all organisms are potentially threatened by more than one parasite (Ploegh, 1998; Takahata & Nei, 1990). Within populations, natural selection will ensure that the genes that code for specific immune responses will increase or decrease in frequency across generations, depending on the parasites in the particular region (A. V. S. Hill et al., 1991). The overall variability of the immune system is maintained, however, even with such selection pressures (A. V. S. Hill et al., 1991; Howard, 1991).

Although mutations contribute to the maintenance of MHC variability, the overall variability of this family of genes appears to be most readily achieved, at least in some species, through sexual reproduction, specifically, disassortative mating—the mating of individuals with differences in their MHC (MHC differences appear to be detected by olfactory cues, or odor). In one related study, Potts and his colleagues (Potts, Manning, & Wakeland, 1991) examined the relation between mating patterns in mice (*Mus musculus domesticus*) and MHC disparity between mating partners. Females largely control choice of mating partners in this species and consistently choose males with an MHC different from their own. Moreover, Potts et al. (1991) found that "females seek extraterritorial matings with males that are relatively more MHC-disparate than their own territorial mate" (p. 620). Recent research also suggests that MHC disparity might have an important influence on human mate choices (e.g., Wedekind, Seebeck, Bettens, & Paepke, 1995; see the *Female Choice* section of chapter 5) but might not be involved in mate choice in some other species (e.g., Soay sheep, *Ovis aries*; Paterson & Pemberton, 1997).

Nevertheless, the results of the Potts et al. (1991) and many other studies (e.g., Hamilton et al., 1990; Møller, 1990b; Wedekind et al., 1995) are consistent with the view that the evolution of sexuality was driven, at least in part, by the benefits associated with maintaining a diverse and ever-changing system of defense against parasites. This model of host–parasite coevolution does not preclude the earlier described influence of mutations or facility of adaptation to changing ecologies on the evolution of sexuality (Hamilton et al., 1990; Kondrashov, 1988). In fact, all of the models make many of the same predictions. In particular, the central feature of both the ecological adaptation and the host–parasite coevolution models is that the principal function of sexual reproduction is to maintain genetic and phenotypic variability (i.e., individual differences), at least for those traits under selection pressures (Andersson, 1994; Darwin, 1859; Wilcockson, Crean, & Day, 1995).

Individual differences in any such traits, in turn, ensure that all potential mates are not equal. Thus, once evolved, sexual reproduction not only required that one find a mate but also created pressures to find the most suitable mate or, in some cases, the most mates. The processes associated with mate choice and competition for mates is called *sexual selection* (Darwin, 1871), and the following section provides an introduction to the basic principles of sexual selection and illustrates many of the associated sex differences (for a more complete discussion, see Andersson, 1994; Cronin, 1991; J. L. Gould & Gould, 1996).

SEXUAL SELECTION

The discussion begins with a distinction between the pressures associated with natural selection and those associated with sexual selection, beginning with Darwin (1859, 1871). Darwin (1859) viewed survival and reproduction as a struggle for existence, a struggle against parasites, predators, ecological change, and even members of one's own species (i.e., conspecifics).

> Owing to this struggle for life, any variation, however slight and from whatever cause proceeding, if it be in any degree profitable to an individual of any species, in its infinitely complex relations to other organic beings and to external nature, will tend to the preservation of that individual, and will generally be inherited by its offspring. The offspring, also, will thus have a better chance of surviving, for, of the many individuals of any species which are periodically born, but a small number can survive. I have called this principle, by which each slight variation, if useful, is preserved, by the term of Natural Selection. (Darwin, 1859, p. 115)

Sexual selection, in contrast, is not a struggle for existence per se but rather "depends on the advantage which certain individuals have over other individuals of the same sex and species, in exclusive relation to reproduction. When the two sexes differ in structure in relation to different habits of life . . . they have no doubt been modified through natural selection" (Darwin, 1871, Vol. I, p. 256). Thus, for Darwin, natural selection was the principal evolutionary force that shaped the behavior and physiology of the species, including many sex differences (Ghiselin, 1974, 1996). Sexual selection was largely restricted to characteristics that were directly related to and influenced mate choice and competition for mates, although, as illustrated below, natural and sexual selection are not mutually exclusive (Andersson, 1994; Darwin, 1871; R. A. Fisher, 1958; Pomiankowski & Iwasa, 1998).

Current descriptions of sexual selection are often more inclusive—including "habits of life"—than those proffered by Darwin (Cronin, 1991), but the means by which sexual selection operates, intersexual choice of mating partners and intrasexual competition over access to mating partners, remains unchanged. In most species, these dynamics are expressed through female choice of mating partners and male–male competition, each of which is illustrated in later sections. But first, consider the likely basis for the evolution of female choice and male–male competition—a sex difference in the level of parental care (Trivers, 1972; G. C. Williams, 1966).

Parental Care

Although Darwin (1871) identified and defined the basic principles of sexual selection (e.g., mate choice), he did not elaborate on the evolutionary origins of these principles. In fact, the issue of the origins and even the issue of the existence of sexual selection were debated, sometimes vigorously, in the 100 years or so following publication of Darwin's (1871) *The Descent of Man, and Selection in Relation to Sex* (Cronin, 1991). It is only recently that some level of consensus has been reached regarding the origins of intersexual choice and intrasexual competition. Early contemporary models of the origins of these forms of sexual selection were provided by G. C. Williams (1966, 1975) and Trivers (1972) and focused on sex differences in parental care, specifically sex differences in the relative costs and benefits of producing offspring.

> It is commonly observed that males show a greater readiness for reproduction than females. This is understandable as a consequence of the greater physiological sacrifice made by females for the production of each surviving offspring. A male mammal's essential role may end with copulation, which involves a negligible expenditure of energy and materials on his part, and only a momentary lapse of attention from matters of direct concern to his safety and well-being. The situation is markedly different for the female, for which copulation may mean a commitment to a prolonged burden, in both the mechanical and physiological sense, and its many attendant stresses and dangers. (G. C. Williams, 1966, pp. 182–183)

Trivers (1972, 1985) formalized these observations in his model of parental investment and sexual selection. In this model, each individual's overall reproductive effort is a combination of mating effort (e.g., time spent searching for mates) and parental effort, or parental investment, as shown in Figure 2.1. *Parental investment* is any cost (e.g., time or energy) associated with raising offspring that reduces the parent's ability to produce or to invest in other offspring (see also Trivers, 1974; but see Dawkins, 1989, for a critique). Given that some level of parental investment is necessary for the *reproductive success*—the number of offspring surviving to the next

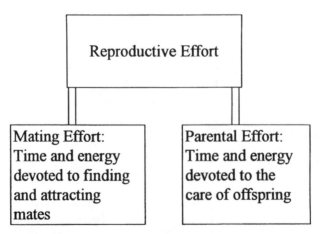

Figure 2.1. An individual's reproductive effort is divided, although not evenly, between mating effort and parental effort.

generation—of both parents, the nature of the parental investment provided by females and males creates the basic dynamics of sexual reproduction and sexual selection. In Trivers's words, "The sex whose typical parental investment is greater than that of the opposite sex will become a limiting resource for that sex. Individuals of the sex investing less will compete among themselves to breed with members of the sex investing more" (Trivers, 1972, p. 140).

Stated somewhat differently, if one sex provides more than his or her share of parental investment, then members of that sex become an important reproductive resource for members of the opposite sex (Dawkins, 1989). Basically, the reproductive success of members of the lower investing sex is more strongly influenced by the number of mates that can be found than by investing in the well-being of individual offspring; whereas the reproductive success of members of the higher investing sex is more strongly influenced, in most cases, by investment in offspring than in finding mates. In this view, the dynamics of sexual selection are influenced by the ways in which each sex distributes its reproductive effort across mating and parental effort (Clutton-Brock, 1991), which, in turn, is influenced by a variety of factors, including the potential reproductive rates of males and females, the operational sex ratio (OSR), and the mating system of the species. All of these factors are interrelated but are briefly discussed in separate sections (Andersson, 1994).

Reproductive Rates

Any sex difference in the potential rate of reproduction can create a sex difference in the relative mix of mating and parental effort. In such species, the sex with the higher potential rate of reproduction typically invests relatively more in mating effort than in parental effort, whereas the sex with the lower rate of reproduction invests relatively more in parental effort than in mating effort (Clutton-Brock & Vincent, 1991). This is so because, after mating, members of the sex with the higher potential rate of reproduction can rejoin the mating pool more quickly than members of the opposite sex, and it is often in their reproductive best interest to do so (G. A. Parker & Simmons, 1996), particularly when biparental care is not necessary for the viability of offspring (Clutton-Brock, 1991; Maynard Smith, 1977). In many, though not all, species, males have a higher potential rate of reproduction than females because of sex differences in the time and cost associated with the production of sperm and eggs and because of any cost associated with gestation and postnatal care (Bateman, 1948; Clutton-Brock, 1991; Johnstone, Reynolds, & Deutsch, 1996; G. A. Parker & Simmons, 1996; Trivers, 1972; G. C. Williams, 1966).

For species with internal gestation and obligatory postnatal female care (e.g., suckling with mammalian species), the rate with which females can produce offspring is considerably lower than the potential reproductive rate of conspecific males (Clutton-Brock, 1991). At the same time, internal gestation and the need for postnatal care necessarily result in more maternal than paternal investment (Trivers, 1972) and create a sex difference in the benefits of seeking additional mates. Males can benefit, reproductively, from seeking and obtaining additional mates, whereas females cannot (Maynard Smith, 1977). Thus, the sex difference in reproductive rates, combined with offspring that can effectively be raised by the female, creates the potential for large female–male differences in the mix of mating and parental effort, and this potential is often realized in nature, if other conditions are also met (see below).

For instance, in more than 95% of mammalian species, females can effectively provide all of the parental care and in fact do so; notable exceptions are the carnivore and primate orders, in which some level of paternal care is evident in 30% to 40% of the genera (i.e., groups of highly related species; Clutton-Brock, 1991). Female care, in turn, frees males to invest in mating effort. In most mammalian species, the reproductive effort of males is indeed almost exclusively focused on mating effort, typically in the form of male–male competition, as described later. The pattern of a higher potential reproductive rate in males is not universal. However, exceptions—which always occur in species with external development of the zygote (i.e., the fertilized egg)—to this pattern seem to prove the main point (Andersson, 1994).

As an example, consider the mating system of the red-necked phalarope (*Phalaropus lobatus*), a polyandrous shorebird (i.e., females potentially have more than one mate; Reynolds, 1987). In this species, males provide most or all of the parental care, specifically, the building of the nest and the incubation of the eggs; the fledglings fend for themselves once hatched (i.e., they are precocial). The high level of paternal care makes it possible for the female to pursue other mating opportunities, and she typically does: Once the clutch is laid, the female often leaves in search of another male. The crucial feature of this mating system is that females are ready to produce another clutch about 1 week after laying their first clutch, whereas the incubation time for males is close to 3 weeks. The result is that the effective rate of reproduction is potentially higher in females than in males because females can produce about two clutches of eggs for every single clutch of eggs that can be incubated by a male. The limiting factor in the number of offspring that can be produced by females is thus the number of unmatched males.

In theory then, the females of this species should show many of the characteristics that are typically associated with the males of species in which males compete for mates (see the *Male–Male Competition* section later in this chapter; Trivers, 1972). In fact, this "sex-role reversal" is found in the red-necked phalarope (for other examples, see Andersson, 1994;

Clutton-Brock & Vincent, 1991; Oring, Lank, & Maxson, 1983; Owens, Burke, & Thompson, 1994; Petrie, 1983; Reynolds & Székely, 1997). Red-necked phalarope females are slightly larger than males, have a brighter plumage, fight with other females for access to males, and, once paired, guard their mates against competitors (Reynolds, 1987). Males, in contrast, rarely threaten or attack one another, although they will guard their mate until the eggs are laid; across species, *mate guarding* by males is very common and functions to ensure that any offspring are indeed the individual male's; that is, it ensures *paternity certainty* (Andersson, 1994).

Not only are the behavioral sex differences in red-necked phalaropes similar, though reversed, to those found in species in which male–male competition is prevalent but the consequences of this competition are also similar. The most important of these evolutionary consequences—and the principal force governing the evolution of female–female competition—is that the reproductive success of females is more variable than the reproductive success of males. Some females produce two clutches per breeding season, each with a different male, and many other females go unmated; unmated males, in comparison, are rare. In short, females that capitalize on the high level of paternal care of offspring will produce more offspring than females that assist the male in clutch incubation. As long as the male can effectively incubate the eggs himself, evolution—through differential reproduction—will favor females that pursue and are successful in gaining additional mates (i.e., females that invest more in mating effort than in parental effort).

However, why do males show more parental care than females in polyandrous species? For polyandrous shorebirds, such as the red-necked phalarope, it is likely that paternal care was preceded evolutionarily by monogamy and biparental care (Temrin & Tullberg, 1995). One possibility is that evolution from monogamy to polyandry was related to high mortality rates of offspring, for example, through predation (Emlen & Oring, 1977), combined with offspring that require little postnatal care (Temrin & Tullberg, 1995). Predation, or other causes of high mortality, would favor females that could produce one or more replacement clutches in a breeding season or that could produce several clutches in succession. The latter is possible only if there is a high level of paternal care, or at least male incubation of the clutch. In this view, high levels of paternal care and serial polyandry benefit both the males and the females of the species, although this scenario is far from certain (Clutton-Brock, 1991; Reynolds & Székely, 1997); for discussion of alternative models of polyandry, see Birkhead and Møller (1996) and Zeh and Zeh (1997).

Operational Sex Ratio

The OSR is defined as the ratio of sexually active males to sexually active females in any given breeding area at a given point in time and is related to the rate of reproduction (Emlen & Oring, 1977). For instance, in a population in which there are as many sexually mature females as there are sexually mature males—an actual sex ratio of 1:1—any sex difference in the rate of reproduction will skew the OSR toward the sex with the potentially faster rate of reproduction. For the red-necked phalarope, the OSR is skewed toward females; that is, there are more unmated females than males in the breeding population at any given point in time (Reynolds, 1987). The net result, as described earlier, is a shortage of unmatched males, for which females vigorously compete (see also Oring et al., 1983; Owens et al., 1994). The OSR is influenced by a number of other factors as well, including sex differences in the time of arrival at breeding sites, the degree of synchrony–asynchrony in female sexual receptivity, and the spatial distribution of resources and mates (Emlen & Oring, 1977).

As an example of the importance of time of arrival at the breeding site, consider the spotted sandpiper (*Actitis macularia*), another polyandrous shorebird in which males provide most of the parental care. One way in which female spotted sandpipers compete is to arrive at the breeding site before the males, which leads to a highly skewed OSR; that is, there are more unmated females than males. As males arrive at the breeding site, females fight among themselves, sometimes to the point of injury, for access to these males. As with the red-necked phalarope, there are considerable reproductive benefits to successful females, despite the cost of competition (i.e., risk of injury), as early breeders are more likely to produce additional clutches than later breeders are (Oring et al., 1983).

The degree to which female sexual receptivity is synchronized can also have an important influence on the OSR, as can the ecological distribution of potential mates. If all females are sexually receptive at the same time and for a limited amount of time, then males are severely limited in the number of females with whom they can mate (Emlen & Oring, 1977). Under these conditions, the OSR would mirror the actual sex ratio, and if this ratio were close to 1:1, monogamy—if biparental care is necessary—and little male–male competition are predicted. Asynchronous or prolonged female receptivity creates the potential for polygyny (i.e., the potential for males to mate with more than one female) and results in a shift in the OSR, so that there are more unmated males than females in the mating pool. Males then compete for access to the females. However, whether the potential for polygyny, or polyandry for that matter, is realized depends on the ecology of the mating system, as discussed in the next section.

Ecology of the Mating System

The basic premise of the just-described models is that any sex difference in the rate of reproduction or OSR—both of which are influenced by a sex difference in parental effort—creates the potential for individual members of one sex to monopolize the reproductive effort of more than one member of the opposite sex. Sex differences in the rate of reproduction or OSR are not enough, however, to result in polygamy (i.e., either polygyny or polyandry). The ecology of the species must have the potential to support polygamy, a potential that is determined by the extent to which "multiple mates, or resources critical to gaining multiple mates, are economically defendable . . . [and on] the ability of the animals to utilize this potential" (Emlen & Oring, 1977, p. 215).

In keeping with Trivers's (1972) model, the ability of animals to utilize any environmental potential "depends in large part on the degree of parental care required for successful rearing of young" (Emlen & Oring, 1977, p. 216), in particular, the freeing of one sex from parental care. Such emancipation is a necessary prerequisite for polygamy because only then do members of the emancipated sex have the time and energy to devote to mating effort. Even this is not enough. For polygamy to be realized, the resources that support the species need to be clustered in space (except perhaps for lekking species, see below), and, in most cases, members of the higher investing sex need to be sexually receptive at different times and need to be clustered together. If resources or potential mates are sparsely distributed, sexual receptivity is limited to a very short window of time, or both, then there is little opportunity for members of one sex to monopolize the reproductive efforts of members of the opposite sex. In these situations, monogamy and high levels of biparental care, if necessary, are expected, as is found in many species of bird. In many of these species, resources are sparsely distributed, and, as a result, biparental care is often needed to raise nestlings successfully (Clutton-Brock, 1991; Rees, Lievesley, Pettifor, & Perrins, 1996). If the spatial distribution of resources and the temporal distribution of potential mates coalesce, then there is a potential for polygamy, different forms of which are described in Table 2.1.

With *resource defense polygyny*, males compete for control of the highest quality territory, and males controlling these high-quality territories are often able to attract more than one mate: Territorial quality is usually determined by some combination of food sources, nesting sites, and predation risk (Andersson, 1994). *Female defense polygyny* is often found when females aggregate. Aggregation is typically related to reduced risk of predation or limited birthing sites (Andersson, 1994; Clutton-Brock & McComb, 1993) and is common in many ungulates (i.e., hoofed mammals) and pinnipeds (e.g., seals, sea lions, and so forth). An example of the latter is the northern elephant seal (*Mirounga angustirostris*), in which a very small number of males control large numbers of females (i.e., harems) that cluster on relatively confined beaches during the breeding season (Le Boeuf, 1974; Le Boeuf & Peterson, 1969).

The elephant seal also provides an excellent example of *male dominance*

TABLE 2.1
An Ecological Classification of Mating Systems

Classification	Description
Monogamy	Neither sex has the opportunity of monopolizing additional members of the opposite sex. Fitness often maximized through shared parental care.
Polygyny	Individual males frequently control or gain access to multiple females.
Resource defense polygyny	Males control access to females indirectly, by monopolizing critical resources.
Female (or harem) defense polygyny	Males control access to females directly, usually by virtue of female gregariousness.
Male dominance polygyny	Mates or critical resources are not economically monopolizable. Males aggregate during the breeding season, and females select mates from these aggregations.
Polyandry	Individual females frequently control or gain access to multiple males.
Resource defense polyandry	Females control access to males indirectly, by monopolizing critical resources.
Female access polyandry	Females do not defend resources essential to males but, through interactions among themselves, may limit access to males.

Note. From "Ecology, Sexual Selection, and the Evolution of Mating Systems," by S. T. Emlen and L. W. Oring, 1977, *Science, 197,* p. 217. Copyright 1977 by the American Association for the Advancement of Science. Adapted with permission.

polygyny and is discussed in greater detail in the *Male–Male Competition* section in this chapter. Another common form of male dominance polygyny is illustrated by behavior on the lek (Emlen & Oring, 1977). Here, males aggregate in one location and compete for dominance or position on the lek. Competition can be direct, as in energetic displays, or indirect, as in ornamentation (e.g., bright plumage; Andersson, 1994). In most lekking species, females choose their mates, which typically results in a small number of males fathering most of the offspring. After copulation, females leave the lek to nest elsewhere, and the male remains to court other females.

In lekking species in which the male provides most or all of the parental care, such as the Eurasian dotterel (*Charadrius morinellus*), females compete for access to males, as predicted by the parental investment model of sexual selection (Trivers, 1972). Once the dotterel female has chosen a potential mate, she courts the male and attempts to isolate him from the lek. At this point, other females typically interrupt the courtship, and fighting then ensues between the two females, with additional females often joining the fray (Owens et al., 1994). This form of female–female competition provides a good illustration of female access polyandry, whereas the spotted sandpiper provides an example of resource defense polyandry. As noted earlier, female spotted sandpipers arrive at the breeding site before the males arrive and compete for control of nesting territories. Successful females are able to attract one or more males to these territories, whereas unsuccessful females remain unmated. As with the Eurasian dotterel, male spotted sandpipers provide most or all of the parental care (i.e., nest building and egg incubation).

Summary

The dynamics of sexual selection are created as each individual pursues her or his reproductive self-interest (Dawkins, 1989). With sexually reproducing species, these pursuits necessarily involve the opposite sex and oftentimes result in sex differences in the degree to which reproductive efforts are distributed between mating effort and parental effort. Initial differences in the time and cost associated with the development of sperm and ova often create a female bias toward parental effort, which, in turn, often—but not always—allows males to invest more in mating effort (Clutton-Brock, 1991). The female bias toward parental effort and the male bias toward mating effort are most evident in species with internal gestation and some form of obligatory female care of young, as with mammals, although this pattern is also common in insects, reptiles, fishes, and birds (Andersson, 1994).

In some species with external development of the zygote, the roles can be reversed, with males biased toward parental effort, and females toward mating effort (Andersson, 1994). Whether it is males or females that provide more care to young, the same basic factors appear to be operating (Clutton-Brock & Vincent, 1991; Emlen & Oring, 1977; Trivers, 1972). Members of the sex that can produce offspring more quickly compete among themselves for access to members of the opposite sex, if the OSR is biased and if the ecology of the species results in the clustering of resources and potential mates, combined with the ability to control these resources or mates (Emlen & Oring, 1977).

Although these same basic factors appear to capture the dynamics of sexual reproduction across species, the specifics of sexual selection are expressed in many different ways and can take many different forms (see Andersson, 1994); and, of course, there is considerable variability within species (vom Saal & Howard, 1982; alternative mating strategies are discussed in chapter 3 and chapter 5). The two most general forms, as noted earlier, involve female choice of mating partners and male–male competition for the establishment of social dominance or for the direct control of resources or mates. These most basic forms of sexual selection and a number of illustrative examples are presented in the following sections.

Female Choice

Although many naturalists readily accepted the notion of male–male competition, Darwin's (1871) proposal that female choice was also a potent force in the evolution of sexually selected traits was met with more skepticism (Cronin, 1991). Today, the issue is not so much whether females choose mating partners—female choice has been demonstrated in many polygynous, monogamous, and polyandrous species—but rather the proximate and ultimate bases of their choice (Andersson, 1994); males are generally less choosy in their mate choices than females are, although males are very choosy in some monogamous species with high levels of paternal care and in some species in which there are large individual differences in female fecundity (e.g., Andersson, 1994; Choudhury & Black, 1993). Following early debates between Darwin and Wallace, the central issue became whether females choose mating partners for reasons of aesthetics (Darwin's position) or whether they choose for more practical features, those that aid or predict offspring survival (Wallace's position; e.g., Wallace, 1892, although his view on sexual selection vacillated). Overviews of these respective "good-taste" and "good-genes" versions of female choice are presented in the following subsections, followed by a brief consideration of recent research on social learning and female choice of mating partners.

Good Taste

One of the more important insights presented in *The Descent of Man, and Selection in Relation to Sex* (Darwin, 1871) was that many physical dimorphisms between males and females of the same species cannot be attributed to natural selection or differences in "habits of life." In fact, the bright and oftentimes rather large plumage of the males of many species of bird (as illustrated in Figure 2.2) likely increase risk of predation. As a result, these sex differences cannot be explained in terms of natural selection and might in fact be eliminated by natural selection if some other process were not operating. Darwin argued that this other process is sexual selection; in particular, female choice of aesthetically pleasing males.

For Darwin (1871) and later R. A. Fisher (1958), the evolution of good-looking males could occur if females simply preferred more colorful or more elaborated males to their less flamboyant peers. Any such preference might initially result from a female sensory bias for certain color patterns or the brightness of certain colors that "may serve as a charm for the female" (Darwin, 1871, Vol. II, p. 92; Ryan & Keddy-Hector, 1992). Once such a preference is established—even if it is completely arbitrary or somewhat deleterious with respect to natural selection—it can become exaggerated if the male feature and the female preference for that feature are genetically linked (R. A. Fisher, 1958; see Ritchie, 1996, for a possible example). Such a link can occur, and can be perpetuated, if daughters inherit a preference for the sexually selected features of their father and if sons inherit these same features. Any such "sexy son" will—especially in polygynous species—enjoy greater reproductive success than the sons of less elaborated males, as long as the female preference for this exaggerated

Figure 2.2. Female and male hummingbirds (*Spathura underwoodi*). From *The Descent of Man, and Selection in Relation to Sex* (Vol. II, p. 77), by C. Darwin, 1871, London: John Murray.

trait does not change (Andersson, 1994) and as long as this trait does not become so exaggerated that it reduces the viability of the males (e.g., through predation; R. A. Fisher, 1958; Pomiankowski & Iwasa, 1998).

In this way, a relatively arbitrary female preference could, in theory, result in the evolution of many of the secondary sex differences described by Darwin (1871), such as the elaborate plumage of the males of many species of bird. In practice, however, it is often difficult to determine exactly what is driving female choice of mating partners (Cherry, 1993; L. S. Johnson, Kermott, & Lein, 1994; Kirkpatrick & Ryan, 1991; Pribil & Picman, 1996; Weatherhead, 1994). Moreover, as described in the next section, sexy fathers and their sexy sons are often healthier, more resistant to parasites, and generally more vigorous than their duller cohorts, suggesting that choice of aesthetically pleasing males may make good sense for a number of reasons.

Good Genes

The basic assumption of good-genes models is that female mate choice is based on physical health, behavioral competence, or genetic superiority of the female's selected mates and that sexually selected characteristics, such as the bright plumage of the males of many species of bird, are a reliable indicator of these qualities (Andersson, 1982; Hamilton & Zuk, 1982; Iwasa & Pomiankowski, 1994; Møller, 1997; Zahavi, 1975). The basic premise is that the state of male secondary sexual characteristics is condition dependent; that is, the degree of coloration, vigor of courtship displays, quality of male song, and so on is sensitive to genetic and phenotypic health and, given this, provides essential information to the female about suitor quality (see Andersson, 1994, for a list of sexually selected traits, Table 6.A). Zahavi argued further that many sexually selected characteristics were a "handicap," in the sense that the development and the maintenance of such characteristics incur some cost to the male. Selection would favor the evolution of any such handicap because only superior males could incur such costs, or, stated differently, inferior males would not be capable of deceiving potential mates by faking good health, for instance (Folstad & Karter, 1992). Handicaps are thus "honest" signals of the male's genetic and phenotypic condition.

If so, then the quality of these male characteristics should vary directly with the genetic and phenotypic health of the male, and females should use these characteristics in their choice of mates. Although these issues are not entirely settled, field work and experimental studies generally support such models (Borgia, 1986; Hamilton & Zuk, 1982; G. E. Hill, 1991; Møller, 1993, 1997; Møller & Thornhill, 1998; Owens & Hartley, 1998; Sheldon, Merilä, Qvarnström, Gustafsson, & Ellegren, 1997; von Schantz, Wittzell, Göransson, Grahn, & Persson, 1996; Zuk, Thornhill, & Ligon, 1990). Hamilton and Zuk proposed one of the more influential of these models and argued that the condition of many sexually selected traits is dependent on parasite load. If one of the primary selection pressures for the evolution of sexual reproduction is resistance to parasites, as described earlier, then it follows that mate selection should be influenced, at least in part, by indicators of the degree to which a potential mate is free of parasites. Hamilton and Zuk argued, for instance, that the bright plumage of the males of many bird species varied directly with degree of parasite infestation, with infected males sporting duller displays than their healthier counterparts.

In an experimental test of this hypothesis, Zuk et al. (1990) infected a group of male red jungle fowl chicks (*Gallus gallus*) with a parasitic worm (*Ascaridia galli*) and compared their growth and later success in attracting mates with a group of unaffected males. Affected males grew more slowly than their healthy peers, and, in adulthood, their sexually selected characteristics were more adversely affected by the parasitic worm than were other physical characteristics. For instance, the comb of affected males was smaller and duller than that of unaffected males, but many other physical characteristics, such as ankle length, did not differ across these groups. A mate-choice experiment demonstrated that unaffected males were preferred 2:1 to their affected cohorts and that female choice of mates was related to sexually selected features, such as comb length, but not to other features, such as ankle length (Sheldon et al., 1997; Zuk et al., 1990).

In another test of the model, von Schantz et al. (1996) examined the relations among a sexually selected male characteristic, spur length (a projection on the wing of the male), male viability, and MHC genotype in the ring-necked pheasant (*Phasianus colhicus*). Spur length varied with MHC genotype, and both were significantly related to the likelihood of survival to 2 years of age. Specifically, longer spur lengths were associated with a higher likelihood of survival. Equally important, males with longer spurs were preferred as mating partners by females and fathered offspring with higher survival rates than their cohorts with shorter spurs (von Schantz et al., 1989; von Schantz, Grahn, & Göransson, 1994). Discussion of how parasite infestation might affect the expression of male ornaments is presented in the *Sex Hormones and Parasites* section (see also Folstad & Karter, 1992).

These and other studies (e.g., Møller, 1994a; Wedekind, 1992) support Hamilton and Zuk's (1982) position that the quality (e.g., brightness) of many of the secondary sexual characteristics of males varies with degree of parasite infestation, and, given this, these characteristics are good indicators of the genetic and phenotypic quality of the male, as indexed by the survivability of the male and his offspring. These studies also suggest that females use these characteristics in their choice of mating partners, as predicted (Hamilton & Zuk, 1982). However, other research indicates that male quality and female mate choice are not simply related to parasite resistance and, in some cases, might not be related to parasite resistance at all. Female mate choice is often related to other factors, such as male provisioning of the female and her offspring, that may or may not be influenced by parasite load (e.g., Borgia, 1986; G. E. Hill, 1991; Kirkpatrick & Ryan, 1991; Petrie, 1994; Petrie, Halliday, & Sanders, 1991; Read & Weary, 1990).

Borgia (1986), for instance, examined the relation between parasite infestation and female mating preferences for the satin bowerbird (*Ptilonorhynchus violaceus*). Overall infestation rates were low, but those males that were infected were less likely to hold a courtship arena (i.e., a bower) than those males that were not infected. There was very little infestation for bower-holding males, but females still strongly discriminated between these males, indicating that although parasite load might influence the ability to acquire or to keep a bower, additional factors were influencing female choice (see the *Male–Male Competition* section). In a study of the monogamous house finch (*Carpodacus mexicanus*), G. E. Hill (1991) found that females preferred brightly colored males and that degree of coloration was a good predictor of the male's later level of parental investment. Brighter males provided more food to their mate during clutch incubation and more food to the nestlings than duller males did. Moreover, in relation to these relatively drab males, brighter males were more likely to survive from one year to the next and to father sons with a brighter plumage. The latter and other findings suggest that bright plumage is not simply the result of better feeding or other environmental conditions but is also attributable to a genetic component (e.g., Møller, 1990b, 1991; Petrie, 1994).

Of course, the plumage coloration of the house finch might be influenced by parasite resistance (C. W. Thompson, Hillgarth, Leu, & McClure, 1997). The point is that these studies indicate that it is not simply physical health that is predicted by secondary sexual characteristics. In addition, these characteristics are often signals of behavioral (e.g., parental investment) and genetic qualities of the male that are beneficial to the female or her offspring. In other words, the dynamics of mate choice are often rather more subtle than simply choosing the most disease-resistant mate and, in fact, often involve the balancing of a mix of potential costs and benefits (Andersson, 1994). Some of the costs and benefits of female mate choice are nicely illustrated in an impressive series of field and experimental studies of the monogamous barn swallow (*Hirundo rustica*; Møller, 1988, 1989, 1990a, 1991, 1994a, 1994b).

Female mate choice in barn swallows is determined, in large part, by the length and symmetry of the male's tail feathers, as shown in Figure 2.3 (Møller, 1988, 1991, 1993), although the quality of the male's song also influences mate choice (Møller, Saino, Taramino, Galeotti, & Ferrario, 1998). Males with relatively long and symmetrical tail feathers obtain mates more quickly, are more likely to sire a second brood during any given breeding season, and obtain more extrapair copulations than their conspecifics with relatively shorter or asymmetric tail feathers (Møller & Tegelström, 1997; Saino, Primmer, Ellegren, & Møller, 1997). Moreover, these longer tailed males mate with higher quality females, as indexed by the level of female parental investment, specifically, the quantity of food provided by the females to their offspring (Møller, 1994b). This level of parental investment, in turn, contributes to the greater reproductive success of these longer tailed males. From this, it can be concluded that the evolution of the length and symmetry of the tail feathers of the male barn swallow has been influenced by female mate choice (i.e., sexual selection) and, in any given generation, influences individual differences in male mating and reproductive success (Møller, 1994a).

However, what benefit do females obtain by choosing males with relatively long tail feathers? In the barn swallow, feather length detrimentally

Figure 2.3. Two pairs of male (longer tail) and female barn swallows (*Hirundo rustica*). From *Sexual Selection and the Barn Swallow* (p. 159), by A. P. Møller, 1994, New York: Oxford University Press. Copyright 1994 by Oxford University Press. Reprinted with permission.

affects foraging, and, thus, relatively long tail feathers are a cost to both the male and the female with whom he mates (Møller, 1994b). Thus, unlike the house finch (G. E. Hill, 1991), this sexually selected trait is not a good indicator of later paternal investment in offspring, but rather it indicates lower than average paternal investment. Despite this cost, females appear to obtain both direct and indirect benefits from mating with males with longer tail feathers. This is so because tail-feather length does appear to be a good indicator of parasite resistance and general physical viability (Møller, 1990a, 1991; Saino, Bolzern, & Møller, 1997). The direct benefit is reduced risk of parasite infestation during mating (an analogue of a sexually transmitted disease).

Moreover, the parasite resistance and general physical vigor indicated by the length of tail feathers are heritable and thus convey indirect benefits in terms of more viable offspring. In one cross-fostering (i.e., "adoption") study, nestlings with fathers that had shorter or longer tail feathers were switched so that one half of the nestlings were raised by their biological parents and one half by foster parents and one half of all nest sites were infected with a common parasite (Møller, 1990a). In infected nests, parasite resistance was strongly correlated with the biological father's tail-feather length, whether or not the nestling was raised by biological or foster parents. In contrast, the rearing father's tail-feather length was not related to the parasite resistance of his foster nestlings. Field studies also indicate that the length of a male's tail feathers is a heritable indicator of the likelihood of survival from one year to the next (Møller, 1991, 1994a).

The expression of these heritable characteristics, however, is condition dependent; that is, not simply reflecting genes for longer tail feathers (Møller, 1994a). Condition-dependent selection means that the expression of the genes that govern the development of sexually selected traits is influenced by the physical condition of the male (e.g., parasite load and nutrition). As noted earlier, lower genetic-quality males are more strongly affected by poor environmental conditions than their higher genetic-quality conspecifics are (see also Potti & Merino, 1996; Saino, Bolzern, et al., 1997); that is, individual differences among males are more evident under harsh environmental conditions (e.g., many parasites, less food, and so forth) than under conditions with weaker selection pressures (e.g., few parasites, plentiful food, and so forth). For instance, experimentally elongating tail feathers (by gluing on an additional section) resulted in greater costs—in terms of foraging ability and survivability—for naturally shorter than longer tailed males (Møller, 1989), indicating that long tail ornaments can only be maintained by the most vigorous males. Long tails are indeed a handicap (Zahavi, 1975). Stated otherwise, only genetically and phenotypically superior males can develop long and symmetric tail features.

Møller's (1994a) studies of the barn swallow illustrate the exquisite relation between male ornamentation and female choice of mating partners and, at the same time, provide important insights into the evolution and expression of sex differences. Female mate choice focuses on those physical features (secondary sexual characteristics) that provide information on the genetic, behavioral, or physical qualities of potential suitors. Evolutionary selection operates not simply on the phenotypic development of these physical characteristics but rather on the sensitivity of these characteristics to the physical and genetic condition of the male. Males of low genetic quality (e.g., those with MHC genotypes that are not resistant to local parasites) do not develop the same quality of ornamentation that their more resistant peers do. The male ornaments are barometers that are strongly affected by the condition of the male, and female mate choice reflects the evolution of the female's ability to read these barometers.

Social Learning

In an intriguing series of studies, Dugatkin and his colleagues have demonstrated that female mate choice in the guppy (*Poecilia reticulata*) is influenced, in part, by social learning, in particular by imitation (Dugatkin, 1992, 1996; Dugatkin & Godin, 1992, 1993; Kirkpatrick & Dugatkin, 1994). Under some conditions, females of this species follow the lead of other females in choosing their mates. In the first series of studies, Dugatkin (1992) placed two males of similar size and coloration in Plexiglas containers at different ends of an aquarium. A focal female was placed in a Plexiglas canister at the center of the aquarium and watched another female, the model, court with one or the other male. The question was whether the model's choice would influence the choice of the focal female after she was released from the canister. It apparently did; 85% of the time, the focal female chose the male preferred by the model.

Follow-up experiments ruled out a number of alternative explanations, such as simply copying the location preferred by the model rather than her mate choice, and indicated that imitation occurred only if the model and her chosen male displayed courtship behaviors (Dugatkin, 1992). Subsequent studies indicated that focal females will often change their mate choice, if they observe the model court with a male that they had previously rejected (Dugatkin & Godin, 1992). Imitation is not random, however. Females will only imitate same-age or older, and presumably more experienced, females; older females do not imitate the preferences of younger models (Dugatkin & Godin, 1993).

In a more recent experiment, the genetic preferences of the female, specifically its preference for orange-colored males, were pitted against the mate choice of another female (Dugatkin, 1996); orange coloration is a sexually selected trait in this species. Here, imitation was assessed under four conditions: The male courted by the model (the model had no choice and was forced to be close to this male by a Plexiglas barrier) was paired with another male with equal orange coloring or with a small (12%), moderate (24%), or large (40%) advantage in the proportion of orange coloration. Under control conditions, in which no model was present, females chose the more colorful male 85% to 90% of the time. When the focal female observed the model courting with a less colorful male, she chose the less colorful male about 80% of the time when the coloration differences between the two males were small to moderate. With large coloration differences, in contrast, the focal female did not imitate the model.

A similar form of imitation has been demonstrated in at least one other species of fish (Schlupp, Marler, & Ryan, 1994), and possibly in some lekking species (Andersson, 1994), but it does not appear to occur in many other species (Clutton-Brock & McComb, 1993; Jamieson, 1995). For instance, female fallow deer (*Dama dama*) tend to join males with large harems. Such behavior might indicate that the females are imitating the mate choice of other females. Clutton-Brock and McComb, however, demonstrated that this behavior is due to a preference for herding with other females and is not due to an imitation of mate choice. Similarly, in three-spined sticklebacks (*Gasterosteus aculeatus*), males construct the nest and care for offspring, and females prefer to deposit their eggs in nests that already contain eggs. However, this preference appears to be more strongly related to the presence of other eggs rather than to imitating the mate choice of another female per se (Goldschmidt, Bakker, & Feuth-De Bruijn,

1993). Nonetheless, these behaviors do influence male reproductive success and might therefore be considered an indirect form of mate choice (Wiley & Poston, 1996).

The research of Dugatkin and his colleagues suggests that, in some species, mate choice might directly be influenced by nongenetic "cultural" factors. Imitation might even be favored by natural or sexual selection. Dugatkin and Godin (1993) suggested that female imitation might be beneficial—and thus potentially influenced by selection pressures—if it reduced the costs associated with finding a suitable mate, such as risk of predation or lost foraging time. Imitation might also result in sexy sons, as described earlier. Either way, these studies provide a potentially important twist to traditional models of female choice.

Male–Male Competition

In addition to the greater ornamentation of the males of many species, relative to conspecific females, Darwin (1871) also noted that in some species males were larger than females and, at times, sported some type of armament; physical sex differences, such as these, are called *physical dimorphisms*. Darwin argued that some of these physical dimorphisms—as with the horns of the male antelope (*Oryx leucoryx*) shown in Figure 2.4 —evolved as the result of male–male competition. For other species, it was argued that these male armaments—as with the male chameleon (*Chamaeleon bifurcus*) depicted in the same figure—were a form of display and simply affected female mate choice (Darwin, 1871). Subsequent research has shown that armamentation is rarely for display. Rather, armaments are almost always used in direct physical competition among males for the establishment of social dominance or for the direct control of mating territories or the mates themselves (Andersson, 1994).

Although female–female competition over mates occurs occasionally, as with the red-necked phalarope, it is relatively rare in comparison to male–male competition. Male–male competition determines which males will reproduce and which males will not and thus, like female mate choice, has been and continues to be an important feature of sexual selection. In this section, two examples of male–male competition are highlighted: one illustrating direct physical competition among males, and the other indirect (behavioral) competition.

Physical Competition

The dynamics and consequences of direct male–male competition are nicely illustrated with studies of the northern elephant seal (Clinton & Le Boeuf, 1993; C. R. Cox & Le Boeuf, 1977; Haley, Deutsch, & Le Boeuf, 1994; Le Boeuf, 1974; Le Boeuf & Peterson, 1969). Like many mammalian

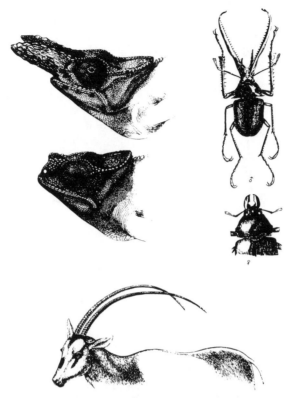

Figure 2.4. Examples of sexually selected characteristics in males. To the upper left are the male (top) and female (bottom) of the *Chamaeleon bifurcus*; to the upper right are the male and female of the beetle *Chiasognathus grantii*; and at the bottom is a male *Oryx leucoryx*, a species of antelope. From *The Descent of Man, and Selection in Relation to Sex* (Vol. II, p. 35; Vol. I, p. 377; and Vol. II, p. 251, respectively), by C. Darwin, 1871, London: John Murray.

species (Clutton-Brock, 1991), the reproductive life histories and the degree of mating and parental effort associated with reproduction differ for male and female northern elephant seals. Male northern elephant seals become sexually active around 8 years of age, as compared with 3 years of age for females, provide no parental care, and differ considerably among themselves in terms of the number of offspring they sire. For the northern elephant seal and many other mammals, the principal factor governing differences in the reproductive success of different males is differences in the number of females with whom they mate (Clutton-Brock, 1988; Clutton-Brock, Albon, & Guinness, 1988; Le Boeuf & Reiter, 1988). Individual differences in the reproductive success of males is directly and strongly related to the outcomes of male–male competition: For the northern elephant seal, this competition is one on one; although in some other species, competition can be among coalitions of males (e.g., Clutton-Brock, 1989; Packer et al., 1988).

During the breeding season, female northern elephant seals aggregate on relatively confined beaches, and their male conspecifics compete physically with one another for sexual access to these females, as shown in Figure 2.5.

> These encounters consist of two males rearing up on their foreflippers and trumpeting individually distinct calls . . . at one another. In most cases, one of the males retreats at this stage; if neither male submits, a fight ensues. The two males approach one another and push against each other chest to chest, while delivering open mouth blows and bites at each other's neck, flippers and head. (Haley et al., 1994, p. 1250)

Success in these bouts is related to physical size, age, and residency (i.e., established males as opposed to newcomers) and determines social dominance. Social dominance, in turn, strongly influences reproductive outcomes (Haley et al., 1994; Le Boeuf, 1974; Le Boeuf & Peterson, 1969). For instance, less than 1 out of 10 males survives to age 8 years, less than one half of these survivors mate at all. For those males that do mate, mating is largely monopolized by socially dominant individuals. The net result of mortality and male–male competition is that less than 5% of the males sire between 75% and 85% of the pups (Le Boeuf & Peterson, 1969; Le Boeuf & Reiter, 1988).

One consequence of intense male–male competition is that selection favors the evolution of characteristics that aid males in their quest for social dominance. One of the most important of these characteristics, at least for northern elephant seals, is physical size (Haley et al., 1994), which, in turn, has resulted in the evolution of a very large sex difference in the size of male and female northern elephant seals. For the northern elephant seal, mature males weigh between three and nearly eight times as much as mature females (Le Boeuf & Reiter, 1988).

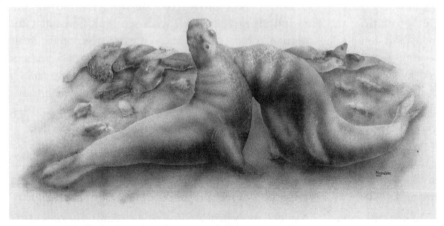

Figure 2.5. Physical competition between two male northern elephant seals (*Mirounga angustirostris*). Illustration by Christopher Nadolski.

Although the physical dimorphism of the northern elephant seal is on the extreme side, it is by no means uncommon. Differences in the physical size or armament of males and females are a common feature of those mammalian species in which males physically compete for social status, territory, or direct access to females (e.g., Clutton-Brock et al., 1988; Clutton-Brock, Harvey, & Rudder, 1977; Darwin, 1871; Mitani, Gros-Louis, & Richards, 1996; Packer et al., 1988). Nevertheless, as with the barn swallow, reproduction and sexual selection are rather more complicated in the northern elephant seal, and in other mammals, than implied by the focus on male–male competition. For instance, smaller and socially subordinate male northern elephant seals sometimes father offspring by "sneaking" into harems and mating with females, which is possible because they resemble females (Le Boeuf, 1974).

Moreover, C. R. Cox and Le Boeuf (1977) suggested that female northern elephant seals may exert some choice in determining which male will sire their pups. These females will often "protest" (e.g., through threat vocalizations) the sexual advances of males. These protests, in turn, typically incite male-on-male aggression, effectively disrupting the mating attempt. Protests are much more common, however, for low- than high-ranking males, and when protests are issued they are much more likely to result in mating disruption for low- than high-ranking males. The net effect of female protest is an increase in the likelihood that a socially dominant male will sire her offspring. In other words, female northern elephant seals also influence the dynamics of sexual reproduction, even though male–male competition is the most conspicuous feature of reproductive effort in this species (see Wiley & Poston, 1996).

The development of social hierarchies and same-sex aggression is not limited to males, even in species in which male–male competition is an important feature of sexual reproduction (Clutton-Brock, 1988). Female elephant seals often bite one another or one another's pups, but this form of aggression appears to be largely due to overcrowding and not to competition over mates (Baldi, Campagna, Pedraza, & Le Boeuf, 1996). Like male northern elephant seals, male red deer (*Cervus elaphus*) physically compete for social dominance, which, in turn, influences access to females (Clutton-Brock et al., 1988). Female red deer form dominance hierarchies as well, but not to secure access to males. Rather, the dominance hierarchies of female red deer influence access to food. During feeding, dominant females are less likely to be interrupted by other females than subordinate females are, and, thus, dominant females tend to be better nourished than subordinate females. Better nourishment, in turn, appears to increase the survival rate of the dominant female's offspring, especially sons; because of sex differences in physical size and metabolic rate, poor nutrition generally affects males more severely than females (Clutton-Brock, Albon, & Guinness, 1985; Trivers, 1972).

In addition, the focus on male–male competition—which is understandable given the often dramatic nature of this competition—and the resultant variability in the reproductive success of different males should not be taken to mean that there is not important variability among females. There is. For northern elephant seals, red deer, and probably all species, there are crucial differences in the survivability of offspring born to different females. In most species, individual differences in the reproductive success of females appear to be related to a host of factors, including maternal age, social dominance, and genetics but, importantly, not to access to mates (Clutton-Brock et al., 1988; Le Boeuf & Reiter, 1988). However, for species in which male–male competition is a central feature of sexual reproduction, reproductive variability among females is not as large as that found among males (Clutton-Brock, 1988).

Stated more directly, even when both males and females behave aggressively toward members of the same sex, form social hierarchies, and are similar in other ways, it cannot be assumed that the same evolutionary selection pressures have created these similarities. In red deer, for instance, the establishment of social hierarchies serves different purposes for males than it does for females, that is, access to mates for males and access to food for females (Clutton-Brock et al., 1988; Trivers, 1972). On the other hand, male–male competition not only affects the size of males but also appears to affect the size and reproductive strategies of females (Carranza, 1996; Clutton-Brock et al., 1977). Across species, as males size increases, female size increases as well, although not to the same degree as males, and females tend to have fewer offspring per litter. Both the increase in female size and the change in number of offspring produced per breeding season appear to be necessary to accommodate larger male offspring.

Thus, for species in which physical competition between males is a salient feature of sexual reproduction, the dynamics and consequences of sexual selection can be complex. Nevertheless, it is clear that any such male–male competition has resulted in important sex differences, favoring males, in physical size, strength, and aggressiveness (Mitani et al., 1996).

Behavioral Competition

Sexual selection can create behavioral, as well as physical, sex differences. The bower-building activities of the males of most bowerbird species (about 3 out of 4 of the 19 species build bowers; Gilliard, 1969) provide an intriguing, and perhaps unique nonhuman, example of a complex suite of behaviors that appears to have evolved by means of sexual selection. Bowers are structures that are typically built from twigs and leaves; are decorated with flowers, shells, bones, and other objects; and serve as a courtship arena. An example of such a bower, for the satin bowerbird, is provided in Figure 2.6.

Figure 2.6. The bower, or mating arena, of the male satin bowerbird (*Ptilonorhynchus violaceus*). Illustration by Christopher Nadolski.

At least for some species, the construction of a bower is, in a sense, a behavioral manifestation of the bright plumage of the males of many other bird species or the long tail feathers of the barn swallow (Gilliard, 1969; Lenz, 1994). Across species, bowerbirds with the most complex bowers tend to have the dullest plumage (Lenz, 1994; but see Kusmierski, Borgia, Uy, & Crozier, 1997), suggesting that

> the forces of sexual selection in these birds have been transferred from morphological characteristics—the male plumage—to external objects . . . these objects have in effect become externalised bundles of secondary sexual characteristics that are psychologically but not physically connected with the males. [Moreover], once colourful plumage is rendered unimportant, natural selection operates in the direction of protective colouration and the male tends more and more to resemble the female. (Gilliard, 1969, p. 55)

As the focus of sexual selection moves from physical to behavioral competition, as illustrated by bower building, it appears that many of the physical differences between males and females lessen, but, at the same time, certain behavioral differences—those that directly affect reproduction—emerge. Studies of bower birds thus reveal a rather different form of female choice and male–male competition than is the case in northern elephant seals.

In many bowerbird species, the quality of the bower built by the male appears to provide a good indicator of overall male quality (e.g., health) and is the primary determinant of female choice of mating partners (Borgia,

1985a, 1985b, 1995a, 1995b; Borgia, Kaatz, & Condit, 1987; Borgia & Mueller, 1992; Frith, Borgia, & Frith, 1996), although parasite resistance indirectly influences female choice as well, as noted earlier (Borgia, 1986; Borgia & Collis, 1989). Bower quality is related to overall symmetry of the structure and to the types of objects used to decorate the bower. For instance, in an extensive series of studies of the satin bowerbird, Borgia found that 16% of the males fathered most of the offspring and that their success in attracting females was strongly related to the symmetry of their bower, the overall density of construction (i.e., number of sticks), and the decoration with relatively rare blue flowers and snail shells (e.g., Borgia, 1985b).

Skill at constructing and maintaining high-quality bowers is related to a number of factors, including age, social learning, social dominance, sex hormones, and the activities of other males; that is, the frequency of bower destruction by competitors (Borgia, 1985a; Borgia & Wingfield, 1991; Collis & Borgia, 1992; Pruett-Jones & Pruett-Jones, 1994). As with the male northern elephant seal, male bowerbirds generally become sexually active at a later age than their female conspecifics (Collis & Borgia, 1992). The relatively delayed maturation of male bowerbirds appears to allow them to develop the skills necessary to build quality bowers. Juveniles often visit the bowers of mature males, imitate their displays and bower building, and practice these displays and bower building in the years before they reach sexual maturity.

In addition to social learning, androgens (i.e., male hormones) also influence bower-building activities, but in ways that complement social learning (Borgia & Wingfield, 1991; Collis & Borgia, 1992). Borgia and Wingfield found that testosterone levels were strongly related to the quantity of bower decorations (e.g., number of sticks in the bower) but were not related to bower quality, such as symmetry. Male sex hormones thus appear to influence the energetic features of bower building (i.e., gathering materials), but experience, which comes from age and practice, influences the overall quality of the construction. Sex hormones also appear to influence which males are able to construct and maintain a bower and which are not; bower-holding males have higher testosterone levels than males that do not hold bowers and tend to be socially dominant over these males (Collis & Borgia, 1992).

For bowerbirds, social dominance is determined by the outcomes of male–male threats and other agonistic behaviors at communal feeding sites and influences an important form of male–male competition—the destruction of one another's bowers and the stealing of rare objects (Borgia, 1985a; Borgia & Mueller, 1992; Lenz, 1994; Pruett-Jones & Pruett-Jones, 1994). Bower destruction and decoration stealing lower the quality of their competitor's bowers and thus reduce the likelihood that these competitors will find mates (Pruett-Jones & Pruett-Jones, 1994). In studies of the satin bowerbird, Borgia (1985a) found that socially dominant males were more likely than less dominant males to destroy their neighbor's bowers. The bowers of socially dominant males were just as likely to be attacked as those of their less dominant peers—attacks almost always occur when the male is not at the bower—but attackers spend less time at the bowers of dominant, relative to subordinate, males. "Threat posed by more aggressive males may cause destroyers to avoid long visits at their bowers, thereby reducing the possibility of the destroyer being caught in the act of destruction" (Borgia, 1985a, p. 97). The net result is that less damage is inflicted on the bowers of socially dominant birds, which, in turn, yields an important advantage in attracting mates.

The dynamics of sexual reproduction are obviously rather complex in bowerbirds, involving a mix of female choice and male–male competition. The most intriguing feature of these dynamics is that male–male competition is not primarily based on physical prowess, although physical threats and occasional attacks do influence social dominance, but rather is based on skill at constructing relatively complex structures and on strategic raids of competitors' bowers. Most important, research on bowerbirds illustrates that sexual selection can act to create systematic behavioral differences between males and females. In the *Sex Hormones, Cognition, and Brain Development* section, several illustrations of how sexual selection can also create cognitive and neural sex differences are provided.

Proximate Mechanisms and Consequences of Sexual Selection

Although sexual selection operates through differential reproduction and thus explains the evolution of sex differences across generations (Darwin, 1871), any such evolved difference must be expressed in each and every new generation. The "here-and-now" or proximate expression of sex differences is largely mediated by sex hormones (e.g., testosterone) and the ways in which the effects of these hormones interact with environmental conditions (Sandnabba, 1996), although more direct—that is, nonhormonal and genetic—influences on sex differences are also possible (Arnold, 1996). The hormonal changes that create differences between males and females appear to be initiated by one or a few genes on the Y chromosome (Koopman, Gubbay, Vivian, Goodfellow, & Lovell-Badge, 1991), and it appears that males and females of the same species are otherwise very similar genetically (Gaulin, 1995). One important implication is that sex hormones act to modify the physical, behavioral, cognitive, or brain systems of males or females and do not create completely different systems. Stated otherwise, many of the hormone-mediated differences between males and females are a matter of degree, not a matter of kind.

Nevertheless, a complete understanding of sex differences requires an understanding of how sex hormones modify the physical, behavioral, cognitive, and brain systems of males and females. The sections below provide examples of some of these modifications. The first focuses on sex hormones, parasite resistance, and the expression of secondary sexual characteristics; whereas the second section illustrates the relations among sex hormones and sex differences in behavior, cognition, and brain development. The final section briefly illustrates how sex hormones promote similarities in the behaviors of males and females in monogamous species.

Sex Hormones and Parasites

Although Hamilton and Zuk (1982) predicted a relation between parasite resistance and the expression of secondary sexual characteristics, such as the bright plumage of the males of many species of bird, they did not discuss the mechanism by which parasite infestation can affect the expression of such characteristics. Folstad and Karter (1992) have recently described such a mechanism (see also Folstad & Skarstein, 1997; Hillgarth, Ramenofsky, & Wingfield, 1997). A simplified version of their model is presented in Figure 2.7. At the core of the model is the reciprocal relation between sex hormone levels, especially testosterone, and overall competence of the immune system, although the relation between hormones and immunocompetence is complex and not yet fully understood (see McEwen et al., 1997, for a thorough review).

Infestation with parasites will lead to an increase in immune system activity, which, in turn, can suppress the secretion of testosterone (Folstad & Karter, 1992; Saino & Møller, 1994; Saino, Møller, & Bolzern, 1995; Zuk, 1996; Zuk, Johnsen, & Maclarty, 1995). The resulting decline in testosterone levels will then result in poorly developed secondary sexual characteristics. Moreover, increases in testosterone levels, as are necessary for the development of secondary sexual characteristics in males, can suppress the effectiveness of the immune system, which then increases risk of dis-

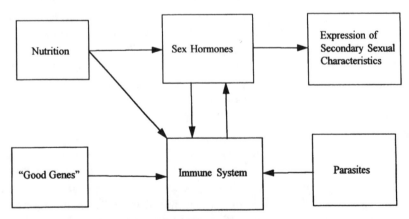

Figure 2.7. Hypothesized relations among sex hormones, immune functioning, parasites, and expression of secondary sexual characteristics.

ease. However, experimental and field studies indicate that high testosterone levels only selectively—affecting some males more than others—increase risk of infestation by parasites (e.g., Saino et al., 1995; Zuk, 1996; Zuk & McKean, 1996). Specifically, immunosuppression is more evident in low-quality than in high-quality males, as would be expected if secondary sexual characteristics were a condition-dependent indicator of male quality and the focus of female choice of mating partners.

Saino and Møller's studies of testosterone levels and immune system competence in the barn swallow illustrate the main point (Saino, Bolzern, et al., 1997; Saino & Møller, 1994; Saino et al., 1995). As described earlier, the primary secondary sexual characteristic in the male barn swallow is length of tail feathers (see Figure 2.3). In natural conditions, long tail feathers are associated with higher testosterone levels and lower rates of parasite infestation (Saino & Møller, 1994), which, at first blush, would appear to be inconsistent with the model. However, experimental studies show that testosterone implantation suppresses the immune system of males with shorter tail feathers more severely than males with longer tail feathers and results in increased parasite loads and higher mortality rates in shorter tailed than in longer tailed males (Saino, Bolzern, et al., 1997; Saino et al., 1995). The pattern indicates that males with long tail feathers can support high testosterone levels—and thus more effectively compete with other males—without compromising their immune system, suggesting that their immune system (e.g., MHC genes) is well adapted to local parasites and they are in better general physical condition than males with short tail feathers. Indeed, males with relatively short tail feathers paid a heavy cost, usually death, when testosterone levels were experimentally increased (Saino, Bolzern, et al., 1997; Saino et al., 1995). The data are consistent with the view that the expression of secondary sexual characteristics cannot be faked; that is, these characteristics are an honest signal of male quality (Zuk, 1996).

The model presented in Figure 2.7 is more complex than implied by the previous discussion. Nutritional status, for example, also interacts with sex hormone levels, immune system functioning, and expression of secondary sexual characteristics (Folstad & Karter, 1992). A poor nutritional state will often result in lower testosterone levels and immunosuppression. Moreover, the development of secondary sexual characteristics (e.g., larger size) typically places higher nutritional demands on males than on females. Thus, not only are males compromised by a testosterone-mediated suppression of the immune system but they are also often more sensitive than females to fluctuations in the quantity and quality of food sources; this is why poor nutrition is often associated with greater mortality in males than in females (e.g., Clutton-Brock, Albon, & Guinness, 1981; Clutton-Brock et al., 1985; Trivers, 1972).

Basically, the relations among environmental factors, such as nutrition and parasites, the immune system, and sex hormones, appear to result in greater male than female sensitivity to harmful environmental conditions, which, in turn, creates greater phenotypic and genetic variability within groups of males than within groups of females, at least for traits in which expression is influenced by male hormones (e.g., Potti & Merino, 1996; Rowe & Houle, 1996). Of course, when sexual selection operates more strongly in females than in males, as with the red-necked phalarope, the prediction is greater variability within groups of females. Despite these complexities, the basic features of the model appear to capture the essential elements governing the relation between female mate choice, expression of secondary sexual characteristics, and parasite resistance.

Sex Hormones, Cognition, and Brain Development

Sex hormones not only influence reproductive behaviors, sensitivity to environmental conditions, and expression of sexually selected traits but they also have a clear and sometimes substantial influence on the organization of the brain systems that supports sexually selected behaviors and cognitions (e.g., Arnold & Gorski, 1984; DeVoogd, 1991; E. Gould, Woolley, & McEwen, 1991; Healy, 1996), although the development of many of these brain regions is also sensitive to environmental influences and might involve more direct nonhormonal influences (e.g., Arnold, 1996; Juraska, 1991). These relations are extensive, and a full discussion is beyond the scope of this book, but are briefly illustrated with bird song and mating patterns of monogamous and polygynous voles.

Social monogamy is common in passerine birds (small perching song birds), but sexual fidelity is not (Birkhead & Møller, 1996; Zeh & Zeh, 1997). In many of these species, extrapair copulations are frequent and largely controlled by female choice (i.e., males court and females choose). In some species, female choice of mating partners is influenced by the complexity of the male's song, which appears to be an indicator of male quality; males often have two distinct features embedded in their song, one that influences female choice (females tend to prefer males with complex song) and one that signals dominance and territorial control to other males (Andersson, 1994; Ball & Hulse, 1998). In a number of species, bird song is thus related to individual differences in the reproductive success of males, and given this, there is little doubt that male song is a sexually selected behavior in these species (Andersson, 1994; Saino, Galeotti, Sacchi, & Møller, 1997).

Moreover, it is now clear that the development and the expression of bird song are controlled by an interconnected system of brain areas and that in many species the development and the functioning of these areas are influenced by sex hormones (DeVoogd, 1991; Nottebohm, 1970, 1971; Rasika, Nottebohm, & Alvarez-Buylla, 1994). In a number of passerine species, several of these areas (e.g., higher vocal control center and *robustus archistriatalis*) are three to six times larger in the male than in the female, although, for some species, the magnitude of these differences changes seasonally, becoming most pronounced during the breeding season (Nottebohm, 1981). Furthermore, Nottebohm (1980) showed that testosterone implants greatly increased the size of these same areas in females and induced malelike song, whereas male castration reduced the size of these areas and impaired song production. Other research, reviewed by DeVoogd (1991) and Ball and Hulse (1998), suggests that in some species sex hormones influence the ways in which these sex-dimorphic areas respond to early environmental cues (e.g., father's song) and song expression in adulthood. In other words, the learning of complex song often requires both early exposure to song (e.g., Petrinovich & Baptista, 1987; M. J. West & King, 1980) and exposure to male hormones (DeVoogd, 1991), although the relative influence of hormonal and environmental factors varies across species (Marler, 1991).

The research of Gaulin and his colleagues provides another important illustration of the sometimes complex relations between sex hormones and sex differences in behavior, cognition, and certain brain areas (Gaulin, 1992, 1995; Gaulin & Fitzgerald, 1986, 1989). Gaulin's approach to the study of sexually selected characteristics is to compare evolutionarily related species—those with a recent common ancestor—of voles (small rodents, *Microtus*), some of which are monogamous and some of which are polygynous. By comparing evolutionarily related species of monogamous and polygynous voles, Gaulin and his colleagues have been able to study the effects of sexual selection—which will operate more strongly in polygynous than in monogamous species (Darwin, 1871)—on sex differences in spatial cognition and at least one underlying brain region.

In the polygynous meadow vole (*Microtus pennsylvanicus*), males compete with one another by searching for and attempting to mate with females that are dispersed throughout the habitat. Prairie and pine voles (*Microtus ochrogaster* and *Microtus pinetorum*), in comparison, are monogamous, and males do not search for additional mates, once paired. These differences in mating strategies create sex differences in the size of the home ranges of meadow voles but not in that of prairie and pine voles (Gaulin, 1992). An illustration of how male competition for access to dispersed females might result in a sex differences in the area of the home range is provided in Figure 2.8. The top of the figure indicates that polygynous males will court five or six females. In such situations, sexual selection, through differential reproduction, will favor males that court the most females, which is possible only through an expansion of the home range. The bottom of the figure shows a rather different situation, in that monogamous males and females share the same range.

Field studies of polygynous and monogamous voles indicate that they

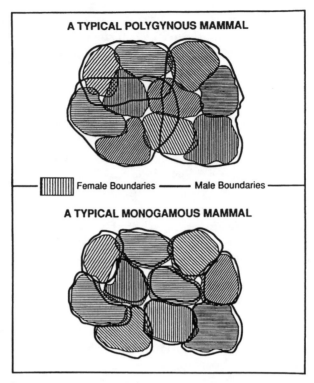

Figure 2.8. A general representation of sex differences in the home ranges of polygynous and monogamous mammals, where the polygynous males compete by courting ecologically dispersed females. From "Does Evolutionary Theory Predict Sex Differences in the Brain," by S. J. C. Gaulin, 1995, in M. S. Gazzaniga, editor, *The Cognitive Neurosciences* (p. 1215), Cambridge, MA: MIT Press. Copyright 1995 by MIT Press. Reprinted with permission.

do indeed follow the pattern shown in Figure 2.8. In the polygynous meadow vole, males have home ranges that cover four to five times the area of the home ranges of females, but only during the breeding season and only in adulthood (Gaulin, 1992; Gaulin & Fitzgerald, 1986); the same pattern of seasonal variation in spatial abilities is found in the male polygynous deer mouse (*Peromyscus maniculatus*; Galea, Kavaliers, Ossenkopp, Innes, & Hargreaves, 1994). The latter pattern indicates that the sex difference in the size of the home range is indeed related to the reproductive strategy of the male (i.e., searching for females) and suggests that this difference is mediated by sex hormones. As predicted, the home ranges of male and female prairie and pine voles overlap and do not differ in size (Gaulin & Fitzgerald, 1986).

These patterns lead to a very important prediction: Male meadow voles should have better developed spatial abilities—those abilities needed for navigation (Shepard, 1994)—than female meadow voles and male prairie and pine voles. Moreover, there should be no sex differences in the spatial abilities of monogamous prairie and pine voles. A series of laboratory and field studies confirmed these predictions. The polygynous male meadow vole shows better navigational skills than conspecific females and better navigational skills than the males of monogamous species (Gaulin, 1992; Gaulin & Fitzgerald, 1986, 1989). An equally important finding is that this same pattern of differences is found for the overall and relative volume of the hippocampus, which supports spatial cognition, among other cognitive abilities (Jacobs, Gaulin, Sherry, & Hoffman, 1990; Sherry, Vaccarino, Buckenham, & Herz, 1989). The hippocampus of male meadow voles is larger than that of female meadow voles and larger than that of male prairie and pine voles. As would be expected for a sexually selected trait, the development of the hippocampus is influenced by sex and other hormones (Gould et al., 1991).

Although some earlier studies failed to find sex differences in spatial maze learning (e.g., Juraska, Henderson, & Müller, 1984), more recent and better controlled studies of the polygynous laboratory rat also suggest a hormonally mediated male advantage in spatial learning (Seymoure, Dou, & Juraska, 1996; C. L. Williams, Barnett, & Meck, 1990; C. L. Williams & Meck, 1991). For instance, C. L. Williams et al. found that normal males and testosterone-treated females outperformed castrated males and normal females on spatial tasks. Moreover, normal males and hormonally treated females relied primarily on the three-dimensional geometry of the environment to navigate, whereas castrated males and normal females used a combination of landmark and geometric cues to navigate. The latter finding suggests that, at least in some species, the sex difference in spatial cognition is related to hormonally mediated differences in strategic approaches to navigating.

An illustration of the use of geometric and landmark cues for navigating is presented in Figure 2.9. Navigation by means of landmarks is based on the relative location of objects in the environment, such that finding A would be based on its proximity to the tree and B by its proximity to the rock. Geometric-based navigation depends on the overall pattern of cues in the environment, as illustrated by the triangle in the figure. The use of geometric cues would allow one to navigate easily from the current position to A and then to B, even though B is obscured by the rock when viewed from Position A. The use of landmark cues would make finding B from Position A more difficult, in comparison to the use of geometric cues (Gallistel, 1990; J. L. Gould, 1986). It appears that geometric cues are useful for navigating in novel ecologies and landmarks for familiar ecologies. Thus, the males' reliance on geometric cues, at least in polygynous mammals, might reflect selection for expanding their home range into the less familiar home range of other males. It should be noted, however, that sexual selection does not predict that males in all species will have better developed spatial abilities than conspecific females. A sex difference in

Figure 2.9. An illustration of the use of landmark and geometric cues for navigation. (See text for description.) Illustration by Christopher Nadolski.

spatial cognition should only be found when the reproductive activities of males and females differ and only when these activities require that males and females have different home ranges or use those ranges differently (e.g., different foraging patterns; Gaulin, 1995). Studies of the brown-headed cowbird (*Molothrus ater ater*) nicely illustrate this point (Sherry, Forbes, Khurgel, & Ivy, 1993). Brown-headed cowbirds are brood parasites; that is, females lay their eggs in the nests of other species that then hatch and feed the cowbird nestlings. Female cowbirds must utilize the home range in more complex ways than male cowbirds because the females must locate suitable hosts for their eggs. Moreover, many hosts will only accept cowbird eggs after they have started laying eggs of their own. Thus, female cowbirds not only need to locate potential hosts, they also must remember their locations and return to them at suitable times. The sex difference in the spatial demands of reproduction should then result in a larger hippocampus in female relative to male cowbirds. This is exactly the pattern found by Sherry et al. (1993). As with voles, no sex differences in hippocampal size were found for species of monogamous birds—when males and females share a home range—that are evolutionarily related to the cowbird (e.g., red-winged blackbirds, *Agelaius phoeniceus*).

In addition to sex hormones, the development of the hippocampus and other brain areas that appear to support spatial cognition is influenced by environmental conditions, and the pattern of sex differences often varies, in complex ways, across these conditions (Juraska, 1986, 1991). For instance, for the laboratory rat, certain regions of the visual cortex—which appear to contribute to spatial cognition (M. C. Diamond, 1991; M. C. Diamond, Johnson, Young, & Singh, 1983)—are larger for males than for females. However, these brain differences are often only found for males reared in socially and environmentally complex environments; no sex differences were found for rats reared in social isolation (Juraska, 1991). Juraska (1991) detailed many other complex interactions between environmental rearing conditions and the pattern of sex differences in brain development and noted that any such differences are not always mirrored at the behavioral level. For instance, Seymoure et al. (1996) found a male advantage in spatial learning, whether or not the rats were reared in enriched or isolated environments.

Although there is much to be learned, it appears that the expression of sex differences in brain development and cognition is not simply related to sex hormones. Rather, as with the earlier described expression of sexually selected traits (*Sex Hormones and Parasites* section), the expression of any such sex difference appears to involve an interaction between hormonal influences and the environments to which the individuals are exposed. Perhaps the expression of some sex differences in brain development and cognition is also condition dependent (i.e., only evident under optimal physical, genetic, and environmental conditions).

Sex Hormones, Monogamy, and Parenting

Sex hormones do not always create sex differences. They are sometimes implicated in promoting similarities in the behaviors of males and females and would be expected to do so in monogamous species (Gaulin, 1995). For instance, two hormones—oxytocin and vasopressin—appear to be involved in promoting and maintaining the long-term social affiliation between male and female prairie voles and in promoting parental care in male prairie voles (Carter & Getz, 1993; Winslow, Hastings, Carter, Harbaugh, & Insel, 1993). Similarly, another hormone—prolactin—appears to promote parental behavior and cooperative social behavior in some socially monogamous birds (e.g., Schoech, Mumme, & Wingfield, 1996). In particular, the research by Schoech and his colleagues suggests that prolactin promotes male provisioning of the female while she incubates their clutch and later promotes feeding of the nestlings by both parents, although prolactin has many other behavioral and physiological effects (de Vlaming, 1979).

SUMMARY AND CONCLUSION

The chapter began with a brief consideration of the factors that appear to have been involved in the evolution of sexual reproduction. Even though many of the associated issues are still debated, there is consensus that one of the principal benefits of sexual reproduction is the maintenance of individual differences in those traits that affect survival and reproduction (Kondrashov, 1988). Variability among individuals is, of course, the grist on which evolution works and provides several benefits, in relation to asexual reproduction. Among these benefits are cross-generational adaptations to changing ecologies, niche seeking in socially competitive environments, and an ever-changing system of defense against rapidly evolving parasites (Apanius, Penn, Slev, Ruff, & Potts, 1997; Dawkins & Krebs, 1979; Hamilton & Zuk, 1982). These benefits affect the overall survival of the species but should not be interpreted to mean that evolution is for the good of the species (Dawkins, 1989; Hamilton, 1964). Rather, individual variability largely determines which individuals within the species, or sex, survive and reproduce and which do not (e.g., Packer & Pusey, 1997).

Once sexual reproduction evolved, the finding of a mate or mates then became a central issue in the life history of individuals. In fact, variability in the quality of potential mates sets the stage for the dynamics of sexual reproduction and thus the evolution of sex differences, that is, sexual selection (Darwin, 1871). The dynamics of sexual reproduction are typically played out through female choice of mating partners and male–male competition for social dominance, control of resources, or direct control of mates, each of which can influence which males sire offspring and which do not (Andersson, 1994). The specifics of female choice and male–male competition can vary widely across species and ecologies (Emlen & Oring, 1977), but the general dynamics appear to be the same (Andersson, 1994).

Across species, female choice tends to focus on those characteristics that are an honest (i.e., not easily faked) signal of male quality (Zahavi, 1975). These signals, in turn, are expressed through the male's secondary sexual characteristics, which can range from the brightly colored plumage of the males of many species of birds, to male song, to the complex suite of behaviors necessary to build and to maintain bowers (Hamilton & Zuk, 1982). The expression of these characteristics is typically at a cost to the male, however. In most cases, it appears that only the most genetically and physically fit males can develop the quality of secondary sexual characteristic necessary to attract mates and therefore sire offspring (e.g., Møller, 1994a). The net result of female choice is that in many species only a minority of males sire offspring.

Male–male competition typically has the same effect as female choice: A few males sire most of the next generation, and most males leave no offspring. In many cases, males compete for access to females; for example, through the attainment of social dominance or through the control of the resources females need to reproduce (e.g., Clutton-Brock et al., 1988). In other cases, males compete on those dimensions that females use in their choice of mating partners, as illustrated by the bower-building activities of the males of most bowerbird species (e.g., Borgia, 1995a). Whether the dynamics of sexual reproduction center on female choice, male–male competition, or some combination, the result is typically large individual differences, within the most competitive sex, in the number of offspring represented in the next generation.

In summary, sex differences have evolved for characteristics associated with differences in the reproductive activities of males and females but only for those characteristics that ultimately influence individual differences in reproductive outcomes (Darwin, 1871; Gaulin, 1995). Any such differences can be evident in females, males, or both and can involve physical, behavioral, or cognitive characteristics and are often associated with sex differences in the structure and functioning of the brain (Ball & Hulse, 1998; DeVoogd, 1991). Whatever the characteristics, the expression of many of the associated sex differences is mediated by sex hormones and the ways in which sex hormones influence sensitivity to environmental conditions (Juraska, 1991).

3

SEXUAL SELECTION IN PRIMATES AND DURING HUMAN EVOLUTION

Now that the general features of sexual selection have been described, I turn to the dynamics of sexual selection in nonhuman primates and to the likely pattern of sexual selection during the course of human evolution. The argument is not that human social systems (e.g., mating systems) and human sex differences will be identical to those found in related species. Rather, the examination of the pattern of sexual selection (e.g., degree of male–male competition) across primate species provides useful constraints on the types of patterns that were likely evident during the course of human evolution (Foley & Lee, 1989; Rodseth, Wrangham, Harrigan, & Smuts, 1991) and demonstrates that many of the sex differences in reproductive strategies found in modern humans (described in chapter 5) are evident in many other species of primate. In all, this chapter consists of two general sections. The first overviews the dynamics of sexual reproduction in primates; the second focuses on the implications of these patterns, combined with the fossil record, for drawing inferences about the influence of sexual selection over the course of human evolution.

THE DYNAMICS OF SEXUAL REPRODUCTION IN PRIMATES

The general mating systems of different species of primate include monogamy–polyandry (hereafter *monogamy*), polygyny, and the combination of high levels of polygyny and polyandry (polygyny–polyandry; Clutton-Brock, 1989). Monogamous primates tend to be arboreal (i.e., they live in trees) and show few sex differences in physical size or in the pattern of physical development (Clutton-Brock et al., 1977; Leigh, 1995). For species with polygynous or polygynous–polyandrous mating systems, in contrast, there tend to be distinct physical differences between females and males. The most notable of these are dimorphisms in body and canine size (i.e., teeth used in threat displays and in biting), both of which tend to favor males (Gaulin & Sailer, 1984; Harvey, Kavanagh, & Clutton-Brock, 1978a, 1978b; Mitani et al., 1996; Plavcan & van Schaik, 1992, 1997a, 1997b). The sex differences in body and canine size appear to be related to a number of factors, including predation risk and the degree of intra-sexual competition (Harvey et al., 1978a; Manning & Chamberlain, 1993; Plavcan, van Schaik, & Kappeler, 1995).

In these species, male–male competition often consists of threat displays and physical attack, both of which are facilitated by larger body and canine size in species with intense one-on-one competition and both of which are also important, but less so, in species in which competition is between coalitions of males (Manson & Wrangham, 1991; Plavcan et al., 1995). In both cases, the male-on-male aggression is often related in one way or another to mating competition, and, given this, the associated sex differences in physical and canine size have been shaped, to a large degree, by sexual selection. In addition to these physical dimorphisms, sex differences in the pattern of physical development are common in primate species with polygynous and polygynous–polyandrous mating systems and also appear to have been shaped by male–male competition (Darwin, 1871; Leigh, 1995, 1996; see the *Physical Development* section of chapter 7).

The pattern of sex differences in physical size and physical development across primate species is important because this pattern allows inferences to be drawn about the mating system and, therefore, the dynamics of sexual reproduction over the course of human evolution. Sex differences in physical size and development, as well as some other physical differences, in modern humans and over the course of human evolution— as described later in this chapter—are consistent with the view that the evolutionary history of humans is polygyny (Alexander, Hoogland, Howard, Noonan, & Sherman, 1979; Dixson, 1993; Marshall, 1978; A. R. Rogers & Mukherjee, 1992). An examination of the dynamics of reproduction and sexual politics in polygynous, as well as in polygynous–polyandrous, primate species will therefore provide important insights into the evolution and current expression of sex differences in humans (Buss, 1994; Smuts, 1995). The consideration of primates with polygynous–polyandrous mating systems is important, because these include the two species that are most closely related to humans: the chimpanzee (*Pan troglodytes*) and the bonobo (*Pan paniscus*; e.g., Mountain, Lin, Bowcock, & Cavalli-Sforza, 1993).

The following sections provide overviews of the general features of sexual selection in such species, specifically male–male competition and female choice of mating partners. I begin with a discussion of male–male competition, because this is one of the more intensely studied aspects of primate social behavior and, thus, relatively more is known about this feature of sexual selection than about female choice (Gray, 1985; Smuts, 1987b). In addition, a brief discussion of the dynamics of female–female competition and male choice of mating partners is presented at the end of this section. Although female–female competition and male choice of mating partners do not appear to be as central to sexual reproduction in primates as male–male competition and female choice, they are common in many primate species, including humans, and therefore merit discussion (Buss, 1994; L. Ellis, 1995; Silk, 1987).

Male–Male Competition

One of the traditional hallmarks of sexual selection is physical male–male competition for establishing social dominance, gaining control of the resources needed for survival and reproduction, or gaining control of mates themselves (Darwin, 1871; Emlen & Oring, 1977). In most primate species, males are unable to control the resources that support survival and reproduction. As a result, male–male competition often focuses on attempts to influence or control the mating activities of other males and the mating activities of sexually receptive females (Smuts, 1995). The relative success at achieving such control is influenced, among other things, by the individual male's social rank or social dominance, as described in the first section below. The second section provides a discussion of the relation between sex hormones and social dominance, and the third section focuses on coalition-based male–male competition. The fourth and final section describes the mating strategies of males that do not appear to be dependent on social dominance (Smuts, 1987b).

Social Dominance

In chapter 2, a prototypical example of the establishment of social dominance through physical contest—physical attack or threat of attack—was presented for the northern elephant seal (*Mirounga angustirostris*). Recall that studies of this species have revealed that socially dominant males sire the majority of the offspring born in any given generation (Le Boeuf, 1974; Le Boeuf & Peterson, 1969). The establishment and the maintenance of social dominance appear to follow a similar pattern in some primate species; however, for other species, the overall relation between social dominance and reproductive outcomes is not as straightforward as that found in the northern elephant seal (e.g., L. Ellis, 1995; Goodall, 1986; Riss & Goodall, 1977; van Lawick-Goodall, 1971). This is so because in many species, a male's rise to social dominance, or not, can be influenced by the social support of the dominant females within the group and because the influence of social dominance on reproductive outcomes varies with the social and ecological conditions of the group, such as group size, OSR (recall, operational sex ratio), and so on (Dunbar, 1984; Raleigh & McGuire, 1989; Smuts, 1995). Nevertheless, all other things being equal, the establishment and the maintenance of social dominance often have important reproductive consequences for individual males (L. Ellis, 1995).

As an example, consider the mandrill (*Mandrillus sphinx*), for whom the relation between social dominance and reproductive outcomes appears to be similar to that found in the northern elephant seal. Of the mandrill, shown in Figure 3.1, Darwin (1871) proclaimed that no "other member of the whole class of mammals is coloured in so extraordinary a manner as

Figure 3.1. The male mandrill (*Mandrillus sphinx*). From *The Descent of Man, and Selection in Relation to Sex* (Vol. II, p. 292), by C. Darwin, 1871, London: John Murray.

the adult male mandrill. The face at this age becomes of a fine blue, with the ridge and tip of the nose of the most brilliant red" (Vol. II, p. 292). In addition to this sexually dimorphic color pattern, males are two to three times the weight of conspecific females and compete by means of physical attack and threat of attack (e.g., aggressive facial and canine displays) to establish social dominance over other males (Dixson, Bossi, & Wickings, 1993; Wickings, Bossi, & Dixson, 1993).

The importance of a male's position within the resulting dominance hierarchy was demonstrated in an extensive 5-year study of a colony of free-ranging—that is, captive but living in a seminatural environment—mandrills. In this study, Dixson and colleagues examined the relations among male social dominance, testosterone levels, and reproductive success, as measured by DNA fingerprinting (Dixson et al., 1993; Wickings et al., 1993). Dominant and subordinate males did not differ in age or body weight but differed considerably in testosterone levels and in the degree of facial and sexual-organ coloration; only the most dominant males showed the coloration characteristics described by Darwin and, at the same time, had much higher testosterone levels than their subordinates.

The two most dominant males—of the six males old enough to father offspring—sired all 36 offspring born during the 5-year period. Moreover, the number of offspring fathered in any given year was related to the relative dominance of these two males. During the first 3 years of the study, the most dominant male (the alpha male) sired 17 of the 18 offspring born during this time, whereas the second-ranked male (the beta male) sired the other offspring. During the fourth year of the study, the ranking of these two males switched; the formerly second-ranked male was now the alpha male and remained the alpha male through the fifth year of the study. However, the new alpha male only sired 2 offspring during the fourth breeding season, whereas the former alpha male (now the beta male) sired 4 offspring. This pattern indicates that change in social dominance and change in reproductive outcomes are not perfectly correlated, perhaps because of female choice. Nevertheless, the new alpha male fathered 9 of the 12 offspring born during the fifth year of the study, and the beta male sired the 3 remaining offspring (Dixson et al., 1993).

Observation of the mating activities of colony members indicated that these two males achieved their reproductive success by dominating the sexual activities of females during the female's most fertile time; this time frame is signaled by the swelling of sexual organs (see Hauser, 1996, for a general discussion). In other words, all males copulated with females, but only the dominant males copulated during the time frame when the female was most likely to conceive (i.e., during estrus; Wickings et al., 1993), and this exclusionary relationship was achieved by means of mate guarding (see Andersson, 1994). The dominant males monitored the activities of sexually receptive females and disrupted the mating attempts of other males.

As with the mandrill, males—and oftentimes females—tend to form dominance hierarchies in many other polygynous and polygynous–polyandrous primate species (de Ruiter & van Hooff, 1993; L. Ellis, 1995; Hayaki, Huffman, & Nishida, 1989; Ohsawa, Inoue, & Takenaka, 1993). However, the relation between dominance rank and mating and reproductive success in these primate species is not always as strong as that found in the mandrill. In fact, in some studies, no relation is found between a male's social rank and his reproductive success (de Ruiter & Inoue, 1993), and some scientists have argued that many of the studies that have found a relation are methodologically flawed (e.g., Bercovitch, 1986, but see Cowlishaw & Dunbar, 1991). The different pattern of results across studies is related, in part, to whether captive, wild, or free-ranging groups have been studied and to the complexities of social relationships within these groups.

Studies that find little or no relation between social dominance and reproductive success are often based on captive groups, with studies of wild and free-ranging groups more often finding a positive relation (de Ruiter & van Hooff, 1993). In other words, the social dynamics that emerge within groups of captive primates often differ from the pattern of social relationships that form in wild settings (de Waal, 1982). One result is that in captive groups, socially dominant males are less able to control the social and sexual behavior of other group members, which, in turn, often leads to a weaker relation between social dominance and reproductive outcomes. Female choice, inbreeding avoidance, and alternative mating strategies of nondominant males (see the *Alternative Mating Strategies* section later in the chapter) also appear to reduce the relation between social dominance and reproductive outcomes. For instance, females tend to avoid mating with older, but still dominant, males that have copulated with their mother (Perloe, 1992) and sometimes prefer males that have recently joined the group and are therefore of low rank (Smuts, 1987b).

Although many issues associated with the relation between social dominance and reproductive outcomes are still contested, studies that use DNA fingerprinting to establish paternity and that involve long-term observation of wild or free-ranging groups should eventually bring some resolution to the question. Fortunately, in addition to the just-described research on the mandrill, a number of other DNA fingerprinting studies have already been conducted. These studies indicate that across species, the relation between a male's social dominance and his reproductive success ranges from slight to substantial (see L. Ellis, 1995, for an extensive review).

In one 11-year study, Altmann and her colleagues used DNA fingerprinting and behavioral observation to assess the relation between social dominance and reproductive outcomes, among other things, in a group of wild savannah baboons (*Papio cynocephalus*; Altmann et al., 1996). Of the 20 adult males that were members of the group at one time or another, a single individual, Radi, sired a disproportionate number of offspring, 44%. During a 4-year reign as the alpha male, Radi sired 81% of the 27 offspring born during this span. In contrast, during the years before and after his reign, Radi sired less than 20% of the offspring. Similar findings—again using DNA fingerprinting to establish paternity—have been reported for groups of wild long-tailed macaques (*Macaca fascicularis*; de Ruiter & van Hooff, 1993; de Ruiter, van Hooff, & Scheffrahn, 1994). Across three groups, the alpha male sired between 52% and 92% of the offspring, whereas low-ranking males sired, as a group, between 2% and 9% of the offspring. For the chimpanzee, several DNA fingerprinting studies also suggest that socially dominant males sire more offspring than their subordinate cohorts (Ely, Alford, & Ferrell, 1991; Sugiyama, Kawamoto, Takenaka, Kumazaki, & Miwa, 1993). As with the mandrill, for the baboon, the long-tailed macaque, the chimpanzee, and many other primate species (e.g., rhesus macaques *Macaca mulatta*; Manson, 1996), alpha males influence these reproductive patterns through mate guarding, that is, by attempting to monopolize the sexual activities of females during the time frame when the females are most likely to conceive.

A somewhat different pattern of results has been reported for some groups of Japanese (*Macaca fuscata*) and rhesus (*Macaca mulatta*) macaques (Inoue et al., 1993; Inoue, Takenaka, Tanaka, Kominami, & Takenaka, 1990; D. G. Smith, 1993, 1994). Inoue and colleagues found a strong relation between social dominance and mating behavior in the Japanese macaque but a much weaker, although generally still positive, relation between social dominance and paternity, as determined by DNA fingerprinting. For the rhesus macaque, D. G. Smith found a relation between social dominance and reproductive outcomes, but unlike the mandrill, baboon, long-tailed macaque, and chimpanzee, high reproductive success preceded the rise to social dominance. It appears that female choice was involved, with females preferring to consort with midranked males that would later rise to be dominant (Huffman, 1992; see *Female Choice* section later in the chapter). However, these studies were based on captive—although in some cases free-ranging—groups, and it is not clear how this affected the social and sexual dynamics within these groups (Berard, Nürnberg, Epplen, & Schmidtke, 1993; de Ruiter & van Hooff, 1993; Ely et al., 1991; A. Paul, Kuester, Timme, & Arnemann, 1993; Segesser, Scheffrahn, & Martin, 1994).

In all, these early DNA fingerprinting studies confirm Darwin's (1871) position that male–male competition affects reproductive outcomes and that it is an important feature of sexual selection in primates. However, the achievement and the maintenance of social dominance and the associated reproductive consequences are sometimes more complex than originally envisioned by Darwin. For instance, for some species, a male's social rank often affords benefits above and beyond the number of offspring sired each year, and one of the most important of these benefits is the avoidance of infanticide of his offspring (Böer & Sommer, 1992; L. Ellis, 1995; Hrdy, 1979; but see Bartlett, Sussman, & Cheverud, 1993).

Under some conditions, when one male or a coalition of males from outside of the group displaces the residing male or males, the new alpha male will attempt to kill any suckling infants; suckling females are unable to sire offspring because suckling suppresses ovulation. Females often resist the attacks of the new alpha male on her infant. However, when infanticide does occur, the female often becomes sexually receptive to the new alpha male and often has offspring with this male (Hrdy, 1979). In these situations, male infanticide is thus a reproductive strategy, at the expense of the recently deposed male, the female, and of course the infant (see also vom Saal & Howard, 1982). The threat of infanticide indicates that the maintenance of social dominance can influence not only the number of offspring sired but, under some conditions, also the number of offspring surviving to maturity (L. Ellis, 1995). In many species, it is therefore in the best interest of the male—and oftentimes the females with whom he has sired offspring—to attempt to maintain social dominance past his peak physical and reproductive years (Hrdy, 1979; Smuts, 1987a).

Sex Hormones and Social Dominance

It is of interest to consider whether the achievement of social dominance in male primates is related in any way to male quality, such as disease resistance or general physical health, as it appears to be in many of the nonprimate species described in chapter 2. In wild primate groups, injured or sick males typically experience a drop in social rank and presumably a drop in the number of offspring they sire (Bygott, 1979; Goodall, 1986; Riss & Goodall, 1977; Sapolsky, 1993). In one study of a captive population, Bercovitch and Nuernberg (1996) found that dominant male rhesus macaques not only sired a disproportionate number of offspring, as indicated by DNA fingerprinting, but they were also larger and in better physical health than their subordinate peers. On the basis of these findings, the Folstad and Karter (1992) model of parasite resistance, immune suppression, and the testosterone-mediated development of secondary sexual characteristics (see the *Sex Hormones and Parasites* section of chapter 2), a relation among testosterone levels, physical health, and social dominance might be expected in primates.

Indeed, the research of Sapolsky and his colleagues (Ray & Sapolsky, 1992; Sapolsky, 1993) indicates that there is a relation among sex hormone levels, immune system activity, and social dominance in primates, but these relations are rather complex. In wild olive baboons (*Papio anubis*), for instance, dominant males in stable social hierarchies have relatively low levels of stress hormones, are in better physical condition, and appear to have better functioning immune systems than subordinate conspecifics. Testosterone levels are not any higher than those of subordinates, except during agonistic or other stressful events, such as a challenge to a dominant male's social position. Under these conditions, the testosterone levels of dominant males rise more quickly than those of subordinate males. Moreover, once the stressful event is over, testosterone and stress hormone levels quickly return to baseline levels in dominant males, but the stress hormone levels of subordinate males remain elevated. These relations suggest that dominant males have finely tuned hormonal and general endocrine functions, as might be expected from the Folstad and Karter (1992) model.

However, it appears that social position influences testosterone and stress hormone levels, rather than hormone levels strictly influencing social position (Coe, Mendoza, & Levine, 1979). In other words, changes in social position appear to result in parallel changes in indexes of male quality. A striking example of this process is provided by the aftereffects of losing a harem in male gelada baboons (*Theropithecus gelada*; Dunbar, 1984); the primary mating system of this species is harem defense polygyny (Emlen & Oring, 1977; see Table 2.1). "Defeated harem-holders literally age overnight. Their chest patches fade from the brilliant scarlet of a harem male to the pale flesh-color typical of juveniles and old animals, their capes lose their luster and their gait loses its bounce. The changes are both dramatic and final" (Dunbar, 1984, p. 132). A similar pattern has been found in many species of New World monkey (i.e., *Callitrichidae*). When dominated by other males, subordinate males experience a severe drop in the level of those hormones (e.g., luteinizing hormone) responsible for testicular development and the maturation of sperm, which effectively results in a socially induced sterility (Abbott, 1993).

Of course, many of these factors probably influence one another. Illness will compromise a male's physical condition, which his competitors will quickly take advantage of, that is, use as an opportunity to establish dominance over the ill male (Goodall, 1986). A drop in social position, in turn, can further compromise the male's health and reproductive capabilities (Sapolsky, 1993). At this point, it appears that male quality, such as physical size and health, facilitates the achievement of social dominance but that social dominance also facilitates physical health. Future research will undoubtedly clarify the relations between social position and physical health and provide insights into whether the rise to social dominance or the development of secondary sexual characteristics, such as those found in the mandrill, are in any way related to the good-genes models (e.g., parasite resistance) described in chapter 2 (see also Hauser, 1996).

Social Dynamics and Coalitions

Nearly all primates live in relatively complex social systems (Foley, 1996). The activities of individuals within these systems include a wide range of social behaviors and biases, all of which should be familiar. Included among these are parental—primarily maternal—care of offspring, sibling rivalry over parental attention, preferential social support and affiliation with friends, preferential treatment of one's kin, and aggressive and at times lethal interactions with conspecifics (Altmann et al., 1996; de Waal, 1982; Dunbar, 1986; Goodall, 1986; McGrew, 1992). The fluidity and the complexity of these behaviors suggest that many primates are considerably more sophisticated, cognitively and socially, than many people would imagine. A full discussion of these topics is beyond the scope of this book, but, fortunately, excellent treatments are available elsewhere (see, for instance, Byrne, 1995; de Waal, 1982; Goodall, 1986; Smuts, Cheney, Seyfarth, Wrangham, & Struhsaker, 1987).

The focus here is on the complexities of male–male competition within the context of primate social systems, with an emphasis on the chimpanzee (see Wrangham & Peterson, 1996, for an engaging discussion). The social system of the chimpanzee is of particular interest because it shows a number of potentially important similarities to the most common social structure found in preindustrial human societies (Manson & Wrangham, 1991; Rodseth et al., 1991). In human societies, men tend to stay in their natal, or birth, group, whereas women typically emigrate from their birth group once married (e.g., Ember, 1978; Pasternak, Ember, & Ember, 1997; Rodseth et al., 1991); in situations in which men leave their birth group, they tend to reside near their male kin, that is, the wife's residence is often in the same community—or in a neighboring community—as the man's parents. This same pattern is found in the three species of primate most closely related to humans—the chimpanzee, bonobo, and gorilla (*Gorilla gorilla*)—but is found in only a few other primate species (e.g., the hamadryas baboon, *Papio hamadryas*; Colmenares, 1992; Ghiglieri, 1987; Sigg, Stolba, Abegglen, & Dasser, 1982). More technically, in these species, males are the *philopatric* sex—the sex that stays with the birth group. In most other primate species, females are the philopatric sex; that is, males emigrate and females stay with their birth group (Wrangham, 1980).

The presence of related males within larger communities is important because it appears to be a precondition for the formation of stable male coalitions (Rodseth et al., 1991). The formation of such stable kin-based coalitions is common in the chimpanzee (Goodall, 1986) and in humans. For the chimpanzee, these coalitions form the nucleus of larger communities and actively maintain the borders of these communities (Goodall, 1986; Riss & Goodall, 1977). Within these communities, different coalitions—the composition of which will vary somewhat from one encounter to the next—are often in competition with one another but may unite in response to conflicts with other communities (de Waal, 1982, 1993; Goodall, 1986). These patterns are similar to those seen in most preindustrial human societies, as is described in chapter 5. In these societies, groups of related men occupy relatively well-defined territories and form coalitions in response to competing coalitions within the community and in response to potential threats from neighboring communities (Rodseth et al., 1991).

This is not to say that the behavior of chimpanzees is the prototype from which human evolution should necessarily be viewed. Indeed, relative to the chimpanzee, the bonobo, which is also closely related to humans, appears to show less intense intergroup aggression and less stable male–male coalitions (see *Female Coalitions* section for further discussion; Furuichi & Ihobe, 1994; D. A. Hill & van Hooff, 1994; Ihobe, 1992; Kano, 1992; Nishida & Hiraiwa-Hasegawa, 1987; van Hooff & van Schaik, 1994; Wrangham, 1986). Moreover, women maintain ties with their kin, even when they leave their natal group, unlike female chimpanzees (Rodseth et al., 1991). Nevertheless, discussion of the chimpanzee is important because it illustrates that long-term patterns of human aggression, particularly male-on-male aggression, are not uniquely human (Daly & Wilson, 1988a; Keeley, 1996; Manson & Wrangham, 1991) and because it illustrates the dynamics of coalition formation as a feature of male–male competition in social primates (see also Sigg et al., 1982).

Chimpanzee communities consist of up to 100 or so adult males, adult females, and their offspring, although the typical community consists of 35 to 40 individuals (Bygott, 1979; Goodall, 1986). Within such communities, groups of males define a territory that contains the smaller territories of a number of females and their offspring (Goodall, 1986; Wrangham, 1979). Of particular interest here is the cooperative behavior of coalitions of males, as related to the sexual politics of intra- and intercommunity relationships (de Waal, 1982; Goodall, 1986); that is, as related to the achievement of social dominance within communities and maintaining or expanding the community's territory at the expense of neighboring communities.

For the chimpanzee, social dominance is achieved in much the same way as was described for the mandrill, through physical displays or physical attack, with one important difference: Male chimpanzees typically form coalitions to improve or maintain their position within the dominance hierarchy (Goodall, 1986). As a result, the achievement and the maintenance of social position are not only related to physical strength and aggression but are also influenced by social skills and intelligence (Riss & Goodall, 1977). The establishment of coalitions is often, but not always, related to kinship (i.e., brothers are often coalition partners) and is maintained through affiliative behaviors, such as grooming (Byrne, 1995; Riss

& Goodall, 1977; Wrangham, 1986). In competition with other males, the behavior of coalition partners ranges from the mere physical presence of one male while the other threatens or attacks another male, to joint displays, and, occasionally, to joint attacks. Goodall (1986) described the dynamics of an encounter between two such coalitions:

> Goliath arrives in camp alone, late one evening. Every so often he stands upright to stare back in the direction from which he has come. He seems nervous and startles at every sound. Six minutes later three adult males appear on one of the trails leading to camp; one is high-ranking Hugh. They pause, hair on end, then abruptly charge down toward Goliath. But he has vanished silently into the bushes on the far side of the clearing. For the next five minutes the three crash about the undergrowth, searching for the runaway. . . .
>
> Early the next morning Hugh returns to camp with his two companions. A few minutes later, Goliath charges down, dragging a huge branch. To our amazement, he runs straight at Hugh and attacks him. The two big males fight, rolling over, grappling and hitting each other. It is not until the battle is already in progress that we realize why Goliath, so fearful the evening before, is suddenly so brave today: we hear the deep pant-hoots of David Graybeard. He appears from the undergrowth and displays his slow, magnificent way around the combatants. He must have joined Goliath late the evening before, and even though he does not actually join in the fight, his presence provides moral support. Suddenly Goliath leaps right onto Hugh, grabbing the hair of his shoulders, pounding on his back with both feet. Hugh gives up; he manages to pull away and runs off, screaming and defeated. (p. 313)

The development and the maintenance of coalitions, such as that between Goliath and David Graybeard, are common features of chimpanzee politics within communities, as is the formation of larger groups of males—including an occasional female—for patrolling the border of their territory and for making incursions into the territory of neighboring chimpanzee communities (Goodall et al., 1979). "A patrol is typified by cautious, silent travel during which the members of the party tend to move in a compact group. There are many pauses as the chimpanzees gaze around and listen. Sometimes they climb tall trees and sit quietly for an hour or more, gazing out over the 'unsafe' area of a neighboring community" (Goodall, 1986, p. 490). When members of such patrols encounter one another, the typical response is pant-hooting (a vocal call) and physical displays on both sides, with the smaller group eventually withdrawing.

At other times, meetings between patrols from one group and members of neighboring communities are deadly. Goodall (1986) described a disturbing series of such attacks, one of which is illustrated in Figure 3.2, by one community of chimpanzees on its southern neighbor. Over a 4-year period, the southern group was virtually eliminated, one individual at a

Figure 3.2. Coalition-based aggression in the chimpanzee (*Pan troglodytes*).
Illustration by Christopher Nadolski.

time, by the northern community, which then expanded its territory to
include that of the now extinct southern group. As an example of the
ferocity of such attacks, consider the fate of Goliath—a member of this
southern group—that was attacked 12 years after the just-described inci-
dent with Hugh:

> Faben started to attack, leaping at the old male and pushing him to
> the ground, his functional hand on Goliath's shoulder. Goliath was
> screaming, the other males giving pant-hoots and waa-barks and dis-
> playing. Faben continued to pin Goliath to the ground until Satan
> arrived. Both aggressors then hit, stamped on, and pulled at the victim
> who sat hunched forward. Jomeo, screaming, joined in. . . . The other
> males continued to beat up their victim without pause, using fists and
> feet. . . . Faben took one of his arms and dragged him about 8 meters
> over the ground. Satan dragged him back again. . . . Eighteen minutes
> after the start of the attack, Jomeo left Goliath, followed by Satan and
> Faben. . . . In the attack (Goliath) was, inevitably, very badly hurt.
> He had one severe wound on his back, low on the spine; another
> behind his left ear, which was bleeding profusely; and another on his
> head. Like (most other members of the southern group), Goliath, de-
> spite intensive searching by all research personnel and field staff, was
> never seen again. (Goodall, 1986, pp. 508–509)

The just-described pattern of patrolling males attacking individuals
from neighboring communities has been reported in other chimpanzee
groups that are geographically isolated from the Gombe groups studied by
Goodall and her colleagues, as has the systematic pattern of attacks between members of other neighboring chimpanzee communities within the

Gombe (Nishida, 1979; Nishida & Hiraiwa-Hasegawa, 1987). For instance, once the northern group moved into its defeated neighbor's territory, the members of the group began to experience incursions by patrolling groups from a larger, more southern community. During the ensuing conflict, the northern group eventually lost its newly acquired territory and a portion of its original territory to this larger group (see Goodall, 1986). Of course, the intentions of the individuals perpetrating these attacks are not known, but they appear to be related to a general fear of unfamiliar individuals, the acquisition of prime feeding areas, and the recruitment of females into the community (Goodall, 1986; Manson & Wrangham, 1991; Nishida, 1979).

These descriptions of intra- and intercommunity aggression should not be taken to mean that chimpanzee communities are continually in conflict or that individual chimpanzees are continually fighting with one another. Rather, interindividual and intercommunity aggression are features of chimpanzee social life that reflect extreme modes of resolving conflicts of interest. In most cases, such conflicts are resolved through elaborate display and other social signals, and only when these signals do not result in conflict resolution (e.g., one male signaling submission to another) do conflicts escalate to physical aggression (de Waal, 1989; Goodall, 1986). Moreover, these descriptions should not belie the fact that chimpanzees show a whole suite of social behaviors, including the nurturing of young; friendly social affiliation; and, as described below, the formation of individual male–female consortships.

Alternative Mating Strategies

Recall that for male northern elephant seals, mating and reproductive success are largely determined by the establishment of social dominance and the maintenance of a harem. An alternative mating strategy, used by some subordinate males, involves sneaking into harems and attempting to mate with females (Le Boeuf, 1974). Like the northern elephant seal, alternative mating strategies are common in many different primate species (e.g., Dunbar, 1986; Smuts, 1987b; Tutin, 1979). In some cases, as with the northern elephant seal, alternative mating strategies are, in a sense, forced onto subordinate males because of the monopolization of females by dominant males. In these situations, the strategy used by dominant males typically results in a higher reproductive success than the alternatives used by other males. In other cases, however, alternative mating strategies truly are alternative strategies; that is, each is relatively effective in terms of siring offspring (see Smuts, 1987b).

Although it was noted earlier that the mating system of the chimpanzee is polygynous–polyandrous, several alternative mating relationships have been observed (Goodall, 1986; McGinnis, 1979; Tutin, 1979). The most frequent form of mating is indeed polygynous–polyandrous, in which a female will mate with many males, and males will attempt to mate with many mature females. During these mating episodes, there is typically little male-on-male aggression. However, during the time frame when the female is most likely to conceive (which is signaled by sexual-organ swelling), males actively compete to mate with the female, and dominant males or coalitions of males aggressively attempt to prevent the female from mating with other males (i.e., they mate guard). In fact, the mating guarding of estrous females is the primary mating strategy of dominant males. The third mating strategy involves the consortship (Tutin, 1979).

Consortships are restricted to a male–female pair, are initiated by the male, but typically, although not always, require female cooperation (i.e., female choice). These consortships are often preceded by a period of time during which the male affiliates with, grooms, and shares food with the female (Tutin, 1979). Tutin also found that the formation of consortships was not related to the dominance rank of the male, except that, in her study, the two most dominant males did not appear to form consortships; rather, as was just noted, their mating strategy centered on the mate guarding of estrous females (but see McGinnis, 1979). Once the pair is formed, they separate from the community and spend anywhere from several hours to several weeks in isolation at the periphery of the community.

The most interesting and potentially most important finding of this and related studies is that these different mating strategies result in very different conception rates (Goodall, 1986; Tutin, 1979). In Tutin's study, 73% of the matings were polyandrous, 25% resulted during mate guarding by dominant males, and 2% occurred during consortships. Despite the low frequency of consortship matings, it was estimated that roughly 50% of the offspring born during the study period were conceived during such a consortship; most of the remaining offspring were likely conceived by dominant males. Social affiliation with individual females and formation of an exclusive consortship thus appear to be features of a viable male mating strategy that is not dependent on social dominance.

Female Choice

Although female choice of mating partners has received less systematic study than male–male competition, it is now clear that such choice is evident in nearly all primate species and is an influential feature of the dynamics of sexual reproduction in these species (Gagneux, Woodruff, & Boesch, 1997; Gray, 1985; Huffman, 1992; Perloe, 1992; Smuts, 1987b). In the two respective sections below, brief overviews of the pattern of female choice and the apparent bases for such choices are provided.

Pattern of Female Choice

Across species, females can directly choose their mating partners by soliciting or refusing copulations or they can indirectly choose mating partners by influencing which males can and cannot enter the group (Smuts, 1987b; Wiley & Poston, 1996). An example of the former is provided by Tutin's (1979) just-described research on consortships in the chimpanzee, in which, in many cases, the development of a consortship is dependent on female cooperation. In most cases, if the female does not wish to accompany the male on a consortship, she simply needs to alert other group members, which, in turn, will disrupt the unwanted male's solicitations. In other cases, however, males appear to coerce the "cooperation" of isolated females through threat displays or physical aggression (Goodall, 1986), although it should be noted that forced copulations are uncommon in non-human primates, except in the orangutan (*Pongo pygmaeus*; Rodman & Mitani, 1987).

Despite male coercion, in many primate species—including the chimpanzee—females actively rebuff, sometimes quite aggressively, the sexual interests of some males and initiate sexual activities with other males (Dunbar, 1984; Kano, 1992; Smuts, 1985). Examples of female-initiated sexual activities are quite clear in the bonobo: "A female sat before a male and gazed into his face. When the male responded to this invitation, she fell on her back, elevated her buttocks and presented her genitals. In this case they copulated ventro-ventrally" (i.e., "missionary style"; Kano, 1980, p. 255). A more recent study suggests that female chimpanzees also initiate consortships (Gagneux et al., 1997). In this study, DNA fingerprints indicated that just over one half of the group's offspring was sired by males in neighboring groups. Although the degree of extragroup paternity is probably higher in this particular group of chimpanzees than for chimpanzee communities in general, the overall pattern suggests that the females in this group were seeking sexual relationships with extragroup males; males in this particular group appear to be under attack from a neighboring group, and, thus, it is in the females' best interest to develop relationships with the would-be insurgents (Wrangham, 1997).

Another example of female choice is provided by Smuts's (1985) extensive studies of female–male relationships in the olive baboon. In this species, as with most other species of primate, male–male competition over access to estrous females is an important feature of reproductive activities. In species in which stable female–male relationships have been studied, such as the olive baboon, females generally favor the development of such relationships with more dominant males (Smuts, 1985). Nonetheless, although they often do so, female olive baboons—and females in most other primate species—do not always accept mating partners on the basis of the outcome of male–male competition (Perloe, 1992; D. G. Smith, 1993;

Smuts, 1985, 1987b). Female olive baboons often reject the mating attempts of males that have displaced—through male–male competition—a preferred male. An illustration is provided by Smuts's (1985) field notes:

> At noon, Delphi, a young adult female, is in consort with Zim, an older, resident male. During an aggressive encounter, Zim loses Delphi to Vulcan, a young natal male about the same age as Delphi. Zim, Alex, and Boz, three older residents, immediately begin to follow the consort pair. Delphi looks back at them and Vulcan nervously herds her away. He tries to groom her, but she pulls away and begins to feed. At 1256 Vulcan approaches Delphi and begins to mount her. She jumps away, and he watches her as she resumes feeding. At 1258 he tries to mount her again, placing his hands on her back. Delphi walks away and Vulcan follows, still holding on to her. He maintains this "wheelbarrow" position for several steps, but then Delphi swerves sharply to one side and he falls off. He approaches her again 1 minute later, but she moves behind a large bush before he reaches her. . . . They circle the bush in alternate directions for several minutes, until finally Vulcan catches Delphi. He tries to mount, but Delphi pulls away. . . . During the 3 hours we followed them Delphi refused 42 copulation attempts. (pp. 170–171)

Moreover, females can sometimes influence the outcomes of male–male competition. In several species of baboon, for instance, males are more likely to displace a male that is attempting to consort with a female, if the female is not responding to the male's gestures (e.g., Bachmann & Kummer, 1980; Smuts, 1985). In other cases, females actively attempt to leave a consortship with one male, in favor of another male. Again, Smuts (1985) provides an illustration:

> Lysistrata and Dante are feeding close together. Lysistrata looks up and surveys the area. She glances at Dante, who has his back to her and is still feeding. Then she suddenly dashes off to chase a lower-ranking female feeding about 20 m away—an atypical act. During the chase, she runs directly past Sherlock, and he immediately cuts in between Lysistrata and Dante, who, after a moment of confusion, is now pursuing his partner. When Sherlock catches up to Lysistrata, she stops chasing the female and a new consortship is formed. (pp. 179–180)

In still other cases, coalitions of females act to influence which males are able to enter the group and which are not. One of the clearest examples of this is provided by the dynamics of harem acquisition in the gelada baboon (Dunbar, 1984). Gelada baboons are organized into harems consisting of a single male and between 1 and 10 females and their offspring. Males have two general strategies for acquiring a harem. In the first, the male follows the group as a peripheral and subordinate (to the harem-holding male) member and begins to develop relationships, through grooming, with the juveniles in the group and gradually with individual females.

In many cases, the females will eventually desert, usually as a group, the harem-holding male in favor of the follower.

The second strategy involves a hostile takeover attempt, with the intruder provoking and attacking the harem-holding male. The ensuing fights can last for several days, on and off, and can result in severe injury to one or both of the males. Nevertheless, in most cases, "what is crucial to the outcome is the behavior of the females. It is they who decide, by what amounts to a collective decision, whether to desert en masse to a new male or to retain their existing harem male" (Dunbar, 1984, p. 132). Before the final decision is made, the females often fight among themselves, with some females attempting to prevent other females from interacting with the interloper. Apparently, the females often "disagree" about which male is to be preferred. Each individual female's degree of loyalty to the existing male appears to be determined in large part by the amount of time the male has spent grooming, or affiliating, with the female.

Bases for Female Choice

In relation to female choice in many species of bird (see chapter 2), much less is known about the bases of female choice in primate species, except, of course, humans (see chapter 5). For instance, it is not known whether the bright coloration patterns of the dominant males of some primate species, such as the mandrill or gelada baboon, are an indicator of male quality and a basis for female choice or whether they are largely dominance-related signals to other males. Similarly, in some primate species, male control of breeding territories is an important feature of male–male competition, but it is not clear whether female choice of territory is also involved (Goodall, 1986; Sigg et al., 1982). Finally, the male's ability to provide food to the female and her offspring is the basis of female choice in some nonprimate species (e.g., G. E. Hill, 1991), but it does not appear to be involved in most nonhuman primates, with a few minor exceptions; for instance, male chimpanzees and apparently male bonobos will often share food with estrous females (Goodall, 1986; Kano, 1980; McGrew, 1992).

For the most part, it appears that female choice of mating partners is influenced by the dynamics of social and sexual relationships within the group, especially the frequency and intensity of aggressive encounters (Smuts, 1987a, 1992). In some species, female choice appears to involve selecting males that will provide protection for them and their offspring from the agonistic behaviors of other group members (e.g., Altmann, 1980; Smuts, 1985, 1987b; Smuts & Gubernick, 1992). Sometimes female choice of mating partners is influenced by threat of infanticide. Recall that a distinct threat of infanticide is found in some species when the group's alpha male is displaced by a new male or by a coalition of males (L. Ellis,

1995; Hrdy, 1979). Hrdy has argued that the polyandrous mating patterns found in many of these species and the tendency of females to mate with unfamiliar males—those at the periphery of the group and therefore candidates to displace resident males—are features of an evolved strategy to counter the threat of infanticide. This is so because males are much less likely to attack infants, if they have copulated with the infant's mother. Moreover, in many species, males that have copulated with a female will provide some form of investment (e.g., carry) in her offspring, even if he is not likely to be the father; the male's behavior, in these cases, is better understood as mating effort rather than as parental effort (see Smuts & Gubernick, 1992; Whitten, 1987).

In species that live in multimale–multifemale groups, a more everyday threat comes from other members of the group. Goodall (1986), for instance, found that adult-male chimpanzees directed one and one-half aggressive displays toward adult females for every single aggressive display directed toward adult males and physically attacked females nearly twice as often as they physically attacked males. In keeping with the earlier discussion on male–male competition, male-on-male aggression was primarily related to the establishment and the maintenance of social dominance. Male-on-female aggression was found in a variety of contexts, including disputes over food (especially meat), sexual encounters, and displaced aggression (i.e., a male attacking a nearby female after an aggressive encounter with a more dominant male). Female-on-female aggression is also common in the chimpanzee and primarily involves disputes over food and protection of offspring, as discussed below (see the *Female– Female Competition and Male Choice* section).

In the olive baboon, adult males direct aggressive displays toward females five times a week, on average, and physically attack females once a week (Smuts, 1985). Moreover, individual females are, on average, severely attacked—leaving wounds that require weeks or months to heal— about once a year. Infants are also frequently physically harassed (e.g., pulled out of mother's grasp) or attacked by other group members, both male and female. These patterns of aggressive display and physical attack are found in many other primate species and represent a major feature of social life for these species. Female choice of mating partner in the olive baboon, and in at least several other primate species (e.g., rhesus macaques), appears to involve a social strategy to counter these threats (e.g., Altmann, 1980; Dunbar, 1984; Sigg et al., 1982; Smuts, 1987a).

In particular, this strategy involves the development of personal relationships, or friendships, with one or two males (Smuts, 1985). As with many other primates, olive baboons show distinct preferences for some members of the opposite sex and will flirt and solicit other forms of affiliative interactions (e.g., grooming) with these individuals. In many cases, these affiliations develop into long-term friendships or pair-bonds, with individual males and females showing preferential treatment of their friend or friends in comparison to other members of the opposite sex (see also Sigg et al., 1982), although these friendships are not the most common form of relationship between males and females. In olive baboons, friends often travel, feed, and sleep together, as shown in Figure 3.3 (Smuts, 1985).

> What made Friends special was, most of all, the unusual quality of their interactions. Female baboons, in general, are wary of males. This is understandable: Males sometimes use their larger size and formidable canines to intimidate and bully smaller troop members. Females, however, were apparently drawn to their male Friends, and they seemed surprisingly relaxed around these hulking companions. The males, too, seemed to undergo a subtle transformation when interacting with female Friends. They appeared less tense, more affectionate, and more sensitive to the behavior of their partners. (Smuts, 1985, p. 61)

Despite the special nature of these relationships, the development of friendships entails both costs and benefits to males and females. As stated earlier, the primary benefit to females is the protection that her friend provides her and her infant from other members of the group. The tendency for females to favor the development of these relationships with more dominant males might reflect the ability of these males to better control the dynamics of social conflict than their more subordinate peers

Figure 3.3. Male and female friends, in the olive baboon (*Papio anubis*). Photo by Barbara Smuts/Anthrophoto. Printed with permission.

might. In any case, Smuts's (1985) observational studies of group behavior indicated that when a female, or her offspring, was attacked and defended, the defender was the female's friend roughly 90% of the time. Moreover, in more than four out of five female–male friendships, the male spent a considerable amount of time affiliating with the female's offspring (e.g., grooming and playing)—even if he was not the father—but only rarely affiliated with the offspring of other females (Altmann, 1980; Smuts, 1985; Smuts & Gubernick, 1992): Male relationships with infants were not always affiliative, however, as infants were often used as buffers in agonistic encounters with other males. There are costs to the female as well—attacks by friends; nonfriends attacked females three to four times more frequently than friends did. The reasons for male attacks on their female friends were not clear but appeared to involve displaced aggression and resulted from her straying too far from him. The latter was interpreted by Smuts as jealousy-related mate guarding (see Smuts, 1985).

The principal benefits to males were in terms of their sexual relationships with female friends and their support during the males' conflicts with other group members. The sexual relationship between friends was not exclusive. Nevertheless, males copulated with their female friends about twice as often as would be expected on the basis of the overall pattern of sexual activity within the troop. Male preferences for specific females are also evident in gelada baboons, and in this species, males are 50% more likely to ejaculate when copulating with their preferred female partner than when copulating with other females in their harem. These patterns, combined with Tutin's (1979) findings, suggest that males are more likely to sire offspring with female friends than with other females. If so, then, in many cases, the formation of a friendship will not only increase the males' chances of siring offspring but will also result in males investing in and protecting their own offspring. The principal costs to males were the time and energy as well as the physical risks associated with defending their friends and their friends' offspring.

Although there is much to be learned, it is clear that females in many, if not all, primate species prefer some males over others as mating partners and that these preferences oftentimes, but not always, conflict with the mating priorities associated with the outcomes of male–male competition (Perloe, 1992; D. G. Smith, 1993). As a result, female choice of mating partners appears to be more entwined with the social and sexual politics of the larger community than is apparently the case with female choice in most nonprimate species (see chapter 2). In many cases, these choices involve the development of selective relationships with one or a few males that are preferred as mating partners and that provide support during social conflict.

Female–Female Competition and Male Choice

The earlier section on male–male competition might have created an impression that female primates are generally nonaggressive, in relation to their male conspecifics. This is not the case: Female-on-female aggression is quite common across primate species (Silk, 1987, 1993). In fact, across species, there appears to be no consistent sex difference one way or the other in the frequency of aggressive encounters. In some species, females are relatively more agonistic than males, and in other species, males are relatively more agonistic than females (Smuts, 1987a). Nevertheless, there are consistent sex differences—across species—in the pattern, severity, and focus of aggressive encounters.

In a review of sex differences in aggression, Smuts (1987a) found that male-on-male aggression resulted in more severe wounds (e.g., open gashes) than female-on-female aggression in all 16 primate species for which information on intrasexual aggression was available for both males and females. In relation to female-on-female aggression, and again across species, male-on-male aggression also tends to be more ritualized (i.e., it involves more stereotyped social displays, presumably because of the costs of escalation) and more frequently related to mating (Silk, 1993; Smuts, 1987a). Although females do, at times, compete for mates, particularly in species with high levels of paternal care, female-on-female aggression is most frequently related to disputes over food (Trivers, 1972; Wrangham, 1980).

Despite these differences, like male-on-male aggression, female-on-female aggression is often coalition based and results in the formation of dominance hierarchies within and between groups. The first two sections below provide overviews of the pattern of coalition-related aggression in females and the formation of female dominance hierarchies, respectively. The final section provides brief discussion of the bases for male choice of mating partners.

Female Coalitions

Sex differences in the formation of coalitions are strongly related to which sex stays in the natal group and which sex emigrates (Ghiglieri, 1987; Wrangham, 1980). When they are formed, coalitions are almost always among members of the philopatric sex (as a reminder, the sex that stays in the birth group) and are formed on the basis of kinship, as in mother–daughter coalitions. Except for the earlier noted, and a few other, species, females are almost always the philopatric sex in primates. These are sometimes called *female-bonded species*, and the formation of coalitions is common in these species (e.g., the rhesus macaque; Sade, 1967). Unlike males, in which coalitional activities are related one way or another to sexual access to females, the formation of competing coalitions in females is more typically related to the defense of high-quality food sources (e.g., fruit trees; Silk, 1987; Trivers, 1972; Wrangham, 1980; see Sterck, Watts, & van Schaik, 1997, for an extended discussion).

Access to high-quality foods has important reproductive consequences for females. For instance, wild primate groups that have been provisioned (by humans) with high-quality foods typically show rapid population growth (e.g., Mori, Watanabe, & Yamaguchi, 1989). This rapid population growth is achieved through the improved nutritional status of females, which, in turn, results in earlier sexual maturation (and thus a longer reproductive life span), shorter intervals between births, and lowered mortality of offspring (Silk, 1987; Wrangham, 1980). In nonprovisioned groups, coalitions of related females often compete over high-quality food sites, with the larger group typically displacing the smaller—and therefore subordinate—group and enjoying reproductive benefits, such as more births, as a result (Wrangham, 1980).

In many primate species, females also form coalitions as a within-group social strategy—in particular, to counter male-on-female aggression—for the protection of their offspring (e.g., infanticide avoidance) or in response to feeding disputes (Hrdy, 1979; J. R. Kaplan, 1977; Parish, 1996; Smuts, 1992). In many of these species, coalitions of females, and occasionally individual females, are often able to dominate (e.g., during feeding disputes) larger males (Smuts, 1987a). This pattern contrasts sharply with the pattern found in most of the species in which males are the philopatric sex. In these species, individual males are almost always dominant over individual females, and unrelated females typically do not form coalitions to counter male-on-female aggression or male domination (Ghiglieri, 1987; Goodall, 1986); although female chimpanzees do appear to form coalitions in captive settings (de Waal, 1982).

One intriguing exception to this pattern is the bonobo, in which males are the philopatric sex and are physically larger than females, but females still form coalitions (de Waal & Lanting, 1997; Parish, 1996; F. J. White & Burgman, 1990); the larger size of males is likely due to male–male competition (Kano, 1992; Kano & Mulavwa, 1984). In a study of three captive populations of bonobos, Parish found that female–female affiliations (e.g., sexual contact and cofeeding) were much more common than male–male affiliations or male–female affiliations. Moreover, coalitions of females were able to dominate individual males, and they used this domination to control high-quality feeding sites and apparently to exercise female choice in mating situations (e.g., refuse male initiated consortships).

In these populations, male-on-female aggression was rare, but female-on-male aggression was common. "Most often, the attacks have taken the form of several females holding the male down while biting him in the extremities (fingers, toes, ears, and testicles), although severe attacks by single females have also occurred" (Parish, 1996, p. 77). Some instances of female coalitions attacking males have been reported in wild populations as well, although male-on-male aggression is by far the most common form of agonistic behavior in wild settings (Furuichi, 1989; Kano, 1992). Moreover, in wild populations, the extent of female–female affiliations appears to vary with group size, although they are still common, and it appears that male–female affiliations predominate, including frequent mother–son affiliations (Kano, 1980; F. J. White & Burgman, 1990).

Female Dominance Hierarchies

Females commonly form dominance hierarchies in female-bonded species and appear to form more subtle hierarchies in species in which males are the philopatric sex (Ghiglieri, 1987; Parish, 1996; Pusey, Williams, & Goodall, 1997; Silk, 1993; Wrangham, 1980). Just as a male's position in the male dominance hierarchy can have reproductive consequences, a female's position within the female hierarchy can also have reproductive consequences (Silk, 1987). A female's position within the hierarchy is related to the outcomes of agonistic interactions between individuals, the rank of her mother, and the size and rank of her kin-based coalition (de Waal, 1996; Mori et al., 1989).

Although the relation between dominance rank and female reproductive success varies from one group to another and from one species to another, across groups of baboons, macaques, and vervets, high dominance rank "is positively correlated with age at menarche, age at first conception, age at first birth, probability of conceiving in a given year, number of sterile years, interbirth intervals, length of postpartum amenorrhea, number of offspring produced, and infant survival" (Silk, 1993, p. 65). More recently, Pusey et al. (1997) demonstrated that high-ranking female chimpanzees have a higher lifetime reproductive success than low-ranking conspecifics. The offspring of these high-ranking females had lower mortality rates and matured more quickly than the offspring of low-ranking females. Although some of the differences in early mortality appear to be due to the tendency of some high-ranking females to kill the infants of low-ranking females, the bulk of the differences (e.g., age at maturation) between the offspring of high- and low-ranking females appears to be related to access to high-quality food (e.g., fruit). Whatever the cause, dominance rank is thus one important contributor to individual differences in the reproductive success of females (Dunbar, 1986; Fairbanks, 1993; Mori et al., 1989; Smuts & Nicolson, 1989).

Within groups, differences in the reproductive success of higher and lower ranking females appear to be strongly related to the dynamics of social behavior, in addition to access to high-quality foods. Basically, higher ranking females consistently harass their lower ranking conspecifics. The resulting stress, in turn, appears to disrupt the hormonal systems associated with ovulation and the maintenance of pregnancy (Smuts & Nicolson, 1989). The most extreme form of this is found in marmoset and tamarin monkeys (*Callitrichidae*), in which dominant females can completely suppress the mating behavior of subordinate females and nearly completely inhibit the secretion of the hormones (e.g., luteinizing hormone and presumably follicle stimulating hormone) that induce ovulation (Abbott, 1993). This socially induced infertility appears to be related to social conflict and to pheromone control (i.e., a chemical signal in the dominant female's urine).

Moreover, it appears that dominant females are often better able to control the dynamics of social interactions than their less dominant conspecifics are, which is to their reproductive benefit (see *The Motivation to Control* section of chapter 6). In vervet monkeys (*Cercopithecus aethiops*), for instance, high-ranking females allow affiliations between offspring and other females more frequently than lower ranking females do (Fairbanks, 1993; Fairbanks & McGuire, 1995). This *alloparenting* (a form of "babysitting") reduces the cost, such as reduced foraging efficiency, of parental care for high-ranking females, which, in turn, shortens the birth interval (see also Trivers, 1974). Alloparenting, however, can be risky, as other females will often injure or not protect (e.g., from predators) these infants (Nicolson, 1987). In vervets, high-ranking females can easily retrieve their infants from allomothers, whereas low-ranking females cannot. Thus, the risks of alloparenting are lower for high-ranking than for low-ranking females, and the consequent ability to use allomothers yields reproductive benefits to these high-ranking females.

Male Choice

As with females, individual preferences appear to influence the mating activities of males in some primate species (e.g., the gelada baboon; Dunbar, 1984). In addition to individual preferences, males, more generally, prefer to mate with those females that are the most likely to conceive and that are the most likely to rear offspring successfully (Altmann et al., 1996; Dixson et al., 1993; Goodall, 1986; Manson, 1996; Tutin, 1979). In many primate species, the fertility of the female is signaled by sexual-organ swelling and changes in sexual-organ coloration. During this fertile period, males show a preferential treatment of (e.g., food sharing) and a desire to mate with these females and, of course, are most likely to fight among themselves for mating privileges with these females (e.g., Goodall, 1986).

In some species, males also prefer older females that have borne one or more offspring to adolescent females that have not yet given birth (e.g., the chimpanzee; Silk, 1987). In addition to demonstrated fertility, older females tend to be more skilled mothers than their younger peers, and, as a result, their infants are more likely to survive (Nicolson, 1987; Smuts &

Nicolson, 1989). Moreover, males often prefer high-ranking to low-ranking females as mating partners (Robinson, 1982). The preference for high-ranking females is understandable, given the just-described relation between social dominance in females and reproductive outcomes in many species. Finally, male choice and female–female competition might be expected in species in which males provide a considerable level of parental investment, as is the case in many—but not in all—monogamous primates (Goldizen, 1987; Leighton, 1987; Nicolson, 1987; G. A. Parker & Simmons, 1996; Smuts & Gubernick, 1992; Trivers, 1972).

SEXUAL SELECTION AND HUMAN EVOLUTION

In this section, the pattern of physical sex differences, or sexual dimorphisms, found in our hominid ancestors is considered in light of the pattern of sexual dimorphisms found in living primates. Examination of the pattern of physical dimorphisms across human evolution provides unique information on the likely nature of sex differences in our ancestors—such as the degree of male–male competition—and the evolution of any such differences (Foley & Lee, 1989). The first two sections below provide a skeletal summary of the major species in our evolutionary past and the pattern of physical sex differences across these species, respectively. The third section provides discussion as to how these patterns —when considered in combination with the pattern of sex differences found in primates—were potentially related to male–male competition, female choice of mating partners, and, more briefly, female–female competition/male choice during the course of human evolution.

Origins

The study of human origins is an exciting and fluid enterprise. The fluidity of this endeavor results from new fossil discoveries and refinements in the ways in which our ancestors are classified (e.g., Bermúdez de Castro et al., 1997; Leakey & Walker, 1997; Swisher et al., 1996). As a result, there is some variation across the classification systems for the genus *Homo* and our predecessor genus *Australopithecus* (e.g., Delson, 1985; Howell, 1978; McHenry, 1994b; B. Wood, 1992). Debates often revolve around the evolutionary succession of one species to another and whether the fossil record attributable to one species represents a single or several species. For instance, one of the earliest identified and more extensively studied hominid species (hominids walk upright)—*Australopithecus afarensis*—includes individuals that vary considerably in size. These large differences have led some scientists to conclude that the associated fossils actually represent two species, whereas others have argued that these fossils represent a single, highly sexually dimorphic species. Recent evidence supports the position that *A. afarensis* is indeed a single but highly sexually dimorphic species (Aiello, 1994; Richmond & Jungers, 1995).

The goal here is not to discuss these nuances but rather to provide a stepping stone to the later discussion on sexual dimorphisms across species of *Homo* and *Australopithecus*. A relatively crude representation of the major species, and their apparent time of appearance, across these two genera is presented in Figure 3.4 (McHenry, 1994b; Vrba, 1985). Despite the nature of the representation in Figure 3.4, it is not certain that there is a simple linear succession—*H. habilis* evolving from *A. africanus*, which, in turn, evolved from *A. afarensis*—across these species (Strait, Grine, & Moniz, 1997; B. Wood, 1992). For instance, it is not entirely clear if *A. africanus* was the evolutionary intermediate between *H. habilis* and *A. afarensis* or whether *A. africanus* represents the beginnings of a now defunct evolutionary path that diverged before the emergence of *Homo*. Moreover,

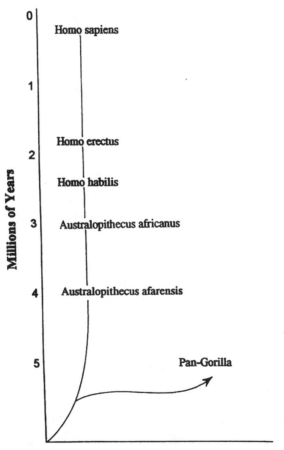

Figure 3.4. Evolutionary tree of our hominid ancestors. Illustration by Christopher Nadolski.

these is some question as to whether the fossils classified as *H. habilis* represent one or two species (B. Wood, 1992). As a result, the pattern described in the *Sexual Dimorphisms* section for *H. habilis* needs to be interpreted with some caution. Despite these difficulties, the pattern shown in Figure 3.4 represents a reasonable, although simplified, representation of the evolutionary tree of our hominid ancestors (McHenry, 1994a; Vrba, 1985; B. Wood, 1992), and, given this, the pattern of physical dimorphisms across these species provides important clues as to the nature of sexual selection during the course of human evolution.

Sexual Dimorphisms

It was noted earlier in the chapter that sex differences in primate canine and body size are good indicators of the pattern of male–male competition and the mating system of the species (Plavcan & van Schaik, 1997a; Plavcan et al., 1995). Across primate species, the male advantage in both body weight and size of canines tends to increase as the intensity of male–male competition increases. Given this, the pattern of sex differences in canine and body size can be used to make inferences about the likely nature of male–male competition and the mating system of our *Homo* and *Australopithecine* ancestors, as discussed in the first section below. In the second section below, evidence for more recent—over the past 300,000 or so years—changes in the degree of sexual dimorphisms is briefly discussed.

Sex Differences in Canine Size and Body Weight

As one might imagine, the study of sex differences on the basis of the fossil record is a rather complicated matter. Central issues involve determination of the sex of the fossil, determination of whether the pool of fossils under study represents one or multiple species, and determination of the most appropriate method for making body size estimates on the basis of partial remains (e.g., Armelagos & Van Gerven, 1980; Feldesman, Kleckner, & Lundy, 1990). Because of these complications, disagreements about the magnitude of sexually dimorphic traits are relatively common. For instance, there is some variability in the estimates of the body weight of male and female *A. afarensis*, although there is more general agreement that in this species males were moderately to considerably larger than females (e.g., Aiello, 1994; Lovejoy, Kern, Simpson, & Meindl, 1989; Richmond & Jungers, 1995).

The study of fossilized canines is somewhat less complicated than the study of other bones, given that teeth are more likely to be preserved as fossils than other bones and, as such, are relatively abundant (M. H. Day, 1994). The determination of sex is still difficult, however, and, given this, interpretations of any sex differences in canine size must be made with some caution (Wolpoff, 1976). Moreover, across *Australopithecus* and *Homo* species, the pattern of sex differences is different for body weight and canine size. Although this research suggests that males were both physically larger and had larger canines than females in all of our hominid ancestors, the body weight differences are consistently larger than the canine size differences (Plavcan & van Schaik, 1997a).

The pattern suggests that male–male competition was an important feature of our evolutionary history, but, according to Plavcan and van Schaik (1997a), it does make judgments about the intensity of this competition uncertain. Wrangham and Peterson (1996), in contrast, argued that the reduced canine size in hominids reflects an increased reliance on arms and hands, as in hitting, in the context of male–male competition and the emergence of weapons, rather than a reduced intensity of this competition, as suggested by Plavcan and van Schaik (1997a). As described later, evidence with modern humans supports Wrangham and Peterson's position (e.g., *Play* section of chapter 7 and the *Physical Modules* section of chapter 8).

In living primates, sex differences, favoring males, are evident in the breadth of canines, and similar differences are evident in all of the *Australopithecus* and *Homo* species represented in Figure 3.4 (Frayer & Wolpoff, 1985); male canines also tend to be longer than female canines (Plavcan & van Schaik, 1997b). The relative degree of the sex difference in canine breadth is shown in Figure 3.5. All values over 100 represent larger male than female

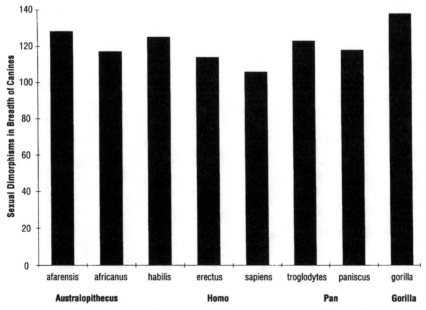

Figure 3.5. Sexual dimorphisms in breadth of canines across hominid and related species. Values greater than 100 indicate larger male than female canines (see text).

canines. As an example, it has been estimated that in A. *afarensis*, male canines were 128% of the size of female canines. This degree of dimorphism is in between that of living chimpanzees and gorillas, as shown in the right-most section of the figure. The middle section of the figure clearly shows a decline in the degree of canine dimorphism across the three species of *Homo*—that is, *H. habilis*, *H. erectus*, and *H. sapiens* (i.e., modern humans) —although a small male advantage in canine breadth is still evident in modern humans (Frayer & Wolpoff, 1985).

The physical size of our ancestors can be estimated on the basis of the relation between the size of certain bones (e.g., the femur, or thigh bone) and overall body size and weight in living humans and other primates (e.g., McHenry, 1991). In other words, human body weight can accurately be predicted on the basis of the size of these bones. The equations used to predict human (or other primate) body weight are then applied to fossil bones to yield estimates of the weight and size of *Australopithecus* and extinct *Homo* species. Different methods yield somewhat different estimates, but the pattern of sex differences is generally the same. For instance, some methods suggest that A. *afarensis* males were more than twice the weight of A. *afarensis* females, whereas other methods yield a more moderate sexual dimorphism for this species (McHenry, 1991; Richmond & Jungers, 1995; Wolpoff, 1976).

In one of the more extensive analyses of these relations, McHenry (1991, 1992, 1994a) found evidence for a male advantage in body weight in all *Australopithecus* and *Homo* species, as shown in Figure 3.6. On the basis of

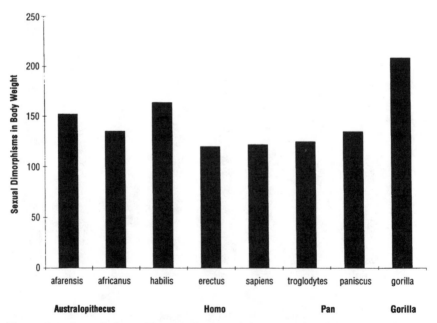

Figure 3.6. Sexual dimorphisms in body weight across hominid and related species. Values greater than 100 indicate heavier males than females (see text).

these estimates, it would appear that *A. afarensis* and *H. habilis* were the most dimorphic of our ancestors and that they were more dimorphic than the chimpanzee and the bonobo but less dimorphic than the gorilla; the predecessor of *A. afarensis*, *A. anamensis*, appears to have been at least as sexually dimorphic as *A. afarensis* (C. Ward, personal communication, July 1997). Our most recent ancestor, *H. erectus*, shows a degree of dimorphism that is comparable to modern humans.

In addition to evolutionary change in the pattern of sexually dimorphic traits, models of human evolution are also enhanced by a consideration of evolutionary change in brain volume, among other things (see McHenry, 1994a). Methods similar to those used to estimate body weight and size can be used to estimate cranial size and from there brain volume across *Australopithecine* and *Homo* species. McHenry's (1994a) estimates are shown in Figure 3.7. Other methods have yielded somewhat higher estimates (e.g., Howell, 1978; McHenry, 1994b), but, again, the pattern is the same regardless of which method is used. It can be seen that the brain volume estimates for *A. afarensis* and *A. africanus* are comparable to the chimpanzee but are considerably lower than *Homo*. Note that the large reduction in body weight dimorphism from *H. habilis* to *H. erectus* parallels a large increase in brain volume and presumably a parallel increase in cognitive competencies (Barton, 1996; Rushton & Ankney, 1996).

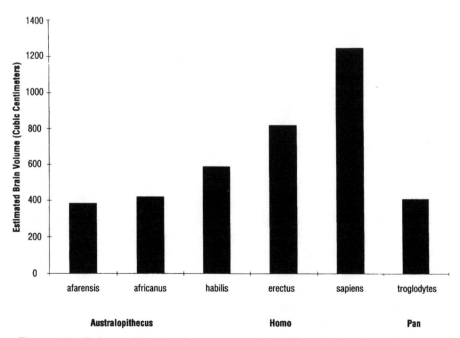

Figure 3.7. Estimated brain volume across hominid and related species.

More Recent Evolutionary Change

The same methods described earlier have been used to estimate changes in canine and body size dimorphisms over the past 300,000 years in *H. sapiens*. Some of these studies suggest continued reductions in these physical sex differences (Brace & Ryan, 1980; Frayer, 1980; Frayer & Wolpoff, 1985; Ruff, Trinkaus, & Holliday, 1997). With these studies, it appears that any more recent decreases in the magnitude of sexual dimorphisms are largely related to decreases in canine and body size in men, as opposed to a relative increase in the size of women (e.g., Brace & Ryan, 1980; Ruff et al., 1997).

Another recent study, in contrast, found little change in the physical size differences between modern men and women and differences evident in human fossils from 200,000 to 300,000 years ago (Arsuaga et al., 1997). These recent findings—combined with A. R. Rogers and Mukherjee's (1992) analysis suggesting that sexually selected physical dimorphisms tend to show very slow evolutionary change—suggest that there has been little change in the physical size differences comparing men and women since the emergence of modern humans. Nonetheless, final resolution of this issue must await further analyses of the fossil record.

Evolutionary Models

Reconstruction of the evolution of social behavior on the basis of the fossil record is at best an educated guess, and any such model needs to be treated as such. The patterns evident in the fossil record, when combined with what is known about living primates, do nonetheless allow the field of possibilities to be narrowed (Foley & Lee, 1989). In the sections that follow, the field of possibilities is narrowed with respect to male–male competition, female choice of mating partners, and female–female competition/male choice, respectively. The section ends with a consideration of the relation between sexual selection and the sexual division of labor.

Male–Male Competition

One of the most striking patterns described earlier is the male advantage in physical and canine size for all species of *Australopithecus* and *Homo*, although the magnitude of the sex difference is larger for physical than canine size. Recall that for primates, a male advantage in physical and canine size is almost always related to one-on-one or coalition-based male–male competition and is associated with a polygynous or a polygynous–polyandrous mating system (e.g., Plavcan & van Schaik, 1997a, 1997b; Plavcan et al., 1995). Given this, it is almost certain that male–male competition was a central feature of the evolutionary history of humans and that the associated mating system was not monogamy (Ghiglieri, 1987; but see Lovejoy, 1981). However, the pattern of sex differences in physical and canine size does not inform researchers about the intensity of male–male competition or whether the mating system of our ancestors was polygynous or polygynous–polyandrous (Plavcan & van Schaik, 1997a).

With respect to the latter issue, several current features of human sexuality suggest polygyny (Alexander et al., 1979). First, in most primate species with frequent polyandrous matings, the sexual receptivity of females is signaled through the swelling of and coloration change in sexual organs, whereas such changes are less common in monogamous or one-male (i.e., harem-holding) mating systems (Hauser, 1996; but see Hrdy, 1979, 1997). The concealed ovulation of women is thus most consistent with either a monogamous or polygynous (i.e., one male), but not a highly polyandrous, mating system (Symons, 1979). Second, polyandrous mating systems tend to be associated with a rather large testicle size in males, relative to body weight. The testicle size of men is smaller than would be expected for a highly polyandrous mating system, such as that found in the chimpanzee (e.g., Dixson, 1993), but is larger than would be expected for a completely monogamous species; this pattern suggests that female hominids likely had more than one mating partner but did not have the high number of partners found in species with frequent polyandrous matings (see the *Female Choice* section of chapter 5). Finally, although most human mating systems are functionally monogamous, about five out of six human societies allow polygyny (Murdock, 1981).

In addition to a more or less polygynous mating system, at some point in our evolutionary history, complex multimale–multifemale communities emerged with males as the philopatric sex (Foley, 1995, 1996; Foley & Lee, 1989; Ghiglieri, 1987; Rodseth et al., 1991). Whether this occurred with A. *afarensis* or later is not clear. As noted earlier, some estimates suggest that A. *afarensis* males might have been twice the size of conspecific females, a size difference that is typically found with intense one-on-one male–male competition, as is found with the gorilla (Fossey, 1984; Wolpoff, 1976). Intense one-on-one competition is most consistent with either single-male harems or solitary males that controlled territories that encompassed the territories of several females (Ghiglieri, 1987). Either way, it seems likely that the emergence of multimale–multifemale communities was followed by the emergence of coalition-based male–male competition within and between these communities, as was illustrated earlier with the chimpanzee, whether it occurred with A. *afarensis* or later (Rodseth et al., 1991).

An alternative explanation is that human sexual dimorphisms in general, such as larger men than women, reflect the emergence of a sexual division of labor, in particular, hunting in males and food gathering and child care in females (e.g., H. E. Fisher, 1982; Lovejoy, 1981); these issues are discussed more fully below but merit brief consideration here. Although it is likely that hunting was an important feature of human evolution (K. Hill, 1982), it is not likely to be the ultimate source of the earlier described sexual dimorphisms. For instance, the teeth of A. *africanus* appear to be primarily adapted for grinding grains and roots (Wolpoff, 1973). Although this, of course, does not preclude meat eating, it does suggest that the male advantage in physical size preceded the evolutionary emergence of hunting as a major feature of human subsistence and further supports the position that the larger size of males than females in all of our ancestor species is the result of male–male competition.

Female Choice

Sexual dimorphisms across *Australopithecus* and *Homo* species indicate less about female choice than about the pattern of male–male competition. Nevertheless, on the basis of the earlier described pattern in living primates, it seems likely that female choice was an important feature of the sexual dynamics of our ancestors (Darwin, 1871; Gagneux et al., 1997). Studies of living primates and modern hunter–gatherer societies suggest that some scenarios for the evolution of female choice are more likely than others. With primates, the most interesting comparison species include those that are most closely related to humans—the chimpanzee and the bonobo—and other primates that live in multimale–multifemale communities. This is not to say that female choice in our ancestors was the same as that found in these species. Rather, the pattern of female choice in these species provides useful information on the range of alternative bases of female choice in our ancestors. Of the chimpanzee and bonobo, the bonobo might provide a more appropriate model of male–female relationships because stable male–female affiliations are more evident in the bonobo than in the chimpanzee and because such male–female bonds are found, to some degree or another, in all human societies and are clearly related to reproduction (Betzig, 1989; see chapter 5).

Smuts's earlier described research on the olive baboon provides the most extensive research available on the formation of female–male relationships and female choice of mating partners for primates that live in multimale–multifemale communities (Smuts, 1985; Smuts & Gubernick, 1992). On basis of Smuts's studies and patterns found in preindustrial societies, the possibility that the evolution of female choice in hominids was influenced by the formation and the maintenance of more or less stable, though not sexually exclusive, female–male relationships should be considered. As with the olive baboon, any such affiliation would have presumably provided some degree of protection and social support for females and their offspring during periods of intragroup conflict; although this might have initially been mating effort rather than parental investment on the part of the male (Smuts & Gubernick 1992). The possibility that hominid females preferred relatively dominant males also needs to be considered, given this tendency in the olive baboon and in several other primate species, including humans, in which long-term female–male relationships are formed (Smuts, 1985; see *Female Choice* section of chapter 5). Presumably, such a preference would have been beneficial to females, given the ability of dominant males to better control the dynamics of social conflict more than the subordinate males could.

If such choice did indeed evolve in hominids, then female–male affiliations would have been maintained through sex and perhaps pair-bonding, in keeping with studies of the olive baboon, wild bonobos, and modern humans (MacDonald, 1992; Smuts, 1985). In bonobos, for instance, male–female affiliations are common throughout the female's cycle and appear to be supported by near continuous sexual receptivity in the female and by less obvious changes, in relation to the chimpanzee, in sexual-organ swelling associated with estrous females (Goodall, 1986; Kano, 1980). In this view, the evolution of concealed ovulation in hominid females might be interpreted as reflecting an adaptation that increased the length of sexual receptivity, which, in turn, increased the stability of male–female affiliations and perhaps male provisioning, as discussed below (K. Hill, 1982; E. M. Miller, 1994; but see J. Diamond, 1992); concealed ovulation would have also allowed women to more easily find extrapair partners, given that this concealed ovulation makes the mate guarding by men more difficult (see the *Female Choice* section of chapter 5). As is apparently the case with other primates, it is not unreasonable to assume that in our ancestors, the development of such friendships provided reproductive benefits to the male. These benefits would have likely included preferential sexual relationships with his female friends, a higher likelihood of siring offspring in the context of these relationships, as contrasted with more casual sexual relationships, and more direct investment in his offspring.

Alternative evolutionary models have focused on a female preference for males that are able to provide material resources—especially meat obtained through hunting—to her and her offspring (e.g., K. Hill, 1982; Lovejoy, 1981; E. M. Miller, 1994). Indeed, in the chimpanzee and in the bonobo, females often preferentially mate with males that provide them with high-quality food, especially meat (Goodall, 1986; Kano, 1980; McGrew, 1992). These models are based also on patterns found in hunter–gatherer societies (Ember, 1978; Symons, 1979), in which—as described in chapter 5—men typically provision their families with meat obtained through hunting.

The argument that provisioning emerged as an important consideration in female choice of mating partners in no way invalidates Smuts's

(1985) position that female choice was more strongly related to the development and maintenance of female–male affiliations. In fact, during the course of human evolution, female choice might have been influenced by both the male's ability and willingness to provision and the degree of pair-bonding, although, as described in chapter 5, the relative importance of pair-bonding and provisioning as bases for female choice varies across cultures. For instance, in harsh resource-limited habitats, female choice appears to be more strongly related to the man's ability to provision for her and her children than on the development of personal intimacy.

Female–Female Competition and Male Choice

As described in chapter 5, female–female competition over mates would be expected in situations in which males differed in the degree to which they could invest in females and their offspring and when males were limited in the number of females in whom they could invest, as illustrated in chapter 2 with the red-necked phalarope (*Phalaropus lobatus*). Any such competition would have presumably focused on those features that females preferred in mates, such as the nature and quality of their social support or provisions provided to them and their offspring.

As with modern humans and all other living primates, male choice of mating partners would almost certainly have focused on those features that signaled fertility and the likelihood of successful rearing of offspring, although individual preferences seem likely as well (Buss, 1994; Smuts, 1985). Again, concealed ovulation would obscure obvious signals of fertility and thus promote greater male–female affiliations than might otherwise be the case.

The Evolution of Sex Differences and the Sexual Division of Labor

It was argued earlier that sexual selection is more likely to be the ultimate source of many human sex differences than the sexual division of labor, even though a division of labor is found to some degree or another in arguably all human cultures (Murdock, 1981); a sexual division of labor is in fact common in many species, including many socially monogamous species (Black, 1996; Clutton-Brock, 1991; Gaulin & Boster, 1992; Ruff, 1987; Wolfe & Gray, 1982). The implications of this argument are important, because the conceptualization of sex differences on the basis of a division of labor suggests the evolution of more or less complementary roles and relatively little male–female conflict (e.g., Lovejoy, 1981; see Ghiselin, 1974).

In contrast, if sex differences are the result of sexual selection, then these differences largely reflect the dynamics of intrasexual competition and intersexual choice of mating partners, and such dynamics would manifest frequent conflicts of interest, whether they are between males and females,

males and males, and females and females, as described in chapter 5. A sexual division of labor might emerge from such dynamics (e.g., male provisioning based on female choice), but any such division of labor is not likely to be the ultimate source of most human sex differences. In this view, the physical, behavioral, and cognitive sex differences often ascribed to the division of labor are in fact due to natural and sexual selection and not to the evolution of cooperative maternal and paternal investment in offspring: In fact, physical sex differences are uncommon in species in which males and female invest equally in offspring, even though a division of labor is found in many of these species (e.g., Clutton-Brock, 1991; Leighton, 1987).

For instance, there is no reproduction-related sexual division of labor in the chimpanzee, but the sex difference in the pattern of hunting and foraging found in many hunter–gatherer societies is found in the chimpanzee (Goodall, 1986; Kawanaka, 1982; McGrew, 1992). Although both male and female chimpanzees hunt, male hunting is more organized, systematic, and efficient than female hunting. Because of their greater size and aggressiveness, male chimpanzees are also able to capture a wider range of prey (e.g., other primates) than females are. As a result of these differences in hunting efficiency, meat represents a relatively larger portion of the diet for males than for females. The female diet, in contrast, consists of a much higher proportion of ants and termites than the male diet. The ants and termites are found in fixed locations that are frequently surveyed, and, given this, their acquisition appears to be similar to foraging patterns found in humans (Silverman & Eals, 1992; see chapter 8—*Physical Modules* section—for implications for human sex differences).

The reliance of female chimpanzees on ants and termites as sources of food and their foraging strategies for obtaining these foods have almost certainly been shaped by natural selection. Similarly, the larger size and aggressiveness of the male chimpanzee are almost certainly related to male–male competition and are shaped by sexual selection (Goodall, 1986). Nevertheless, this advantage in size and aggressiveness, and the tendency to form coalitions, make male chimpanzees relatively efficient hunters, both individually and in cooperation with other males. In other words, in the male chimpanzee, the physical and behavioral tendencies that have been shaped by sexual selection are coopted—or used for a purpose for which they were not originally designed—for hunting (S. J. Gould & Vrba, 1982).

Hunting then provides a valuable resource (high-calorie meat) that is used for survival as well as to enhance mating opportunities. Once meat is systematically used to enhance mating opportunities, it can potentially become a source of male–male competition, particularly if males differ in their hunting abilities (Symons, 1979). In this view, the sexual division of labor likely emerged from preexisting sex differences—shaped by natural and sexual selection—and not originally as a form of cooperative parental investment (see Frost, 1998, for an alternative explanation). Or stated otherwise, the emergence of male provisioning of a woman and her offspring, for instance, was—and still is in many cases—a form of mating effort and did not necessarily reflect the evolution of paternal care in children (but see Lovejoy, 1981).

Nevertheless, in many societies, the ability of men and women to perform roles associated with the traditional division of labor influences mate selection and retention choices. In an extensive cross-cultural review of marital relationships, Betzig (1989) noted the following:

> Inadequate support is reported as cause for divorce in 21 societies and ascribed exclusively to the husband in all but one unspecified case. . . . An interesting thing about these economic factors is that they are so clearly segregated according to sex. Husbands are divorced for failing to provide material means, wives for failing to process them. (p. 664)

These cross-cultural patterns suggest that success at performing the tasks associated with the sexual division of labor likely influences mate-choice decisions, and, given this, relative success in these areas is now likely under the influence of sexual selection. For instance, male provisioning is now a form of male–male competition and is a feature of female choice in many cultures. However, the sex differences that enable males to provide certain resources more efficiently (e.g., meat through hunting) or to compete more aggressively than females to obtain these resources did not appear to originally evolve for cooperative child rearing. Rather, these sex differences more likely emerged from male–male competition, although today, the net effect is, in many cases, cooperative child rearing, particularly in infancy (Crano & Aronoff, 1978). Regardless, the ultimate source of most human sex differences appears to be sexual selection and not the sexual division of labor or other economic or cultural patterns that are—from an evolutionary perspective—relatively recent phenomena.

SUMMARY AND CONCLUSION

There is little question that most primates live in complex social systems and that the dynamics of social relationships within these communities are strongly influenced by the different ways in which males and females pursue their reproductive interests. In most, if not all, nonmonogamous primate species, male–male competition is probably the most conspicuous feature of social dynamics in these communities, and, given this, it is not surprising that male–male competition is one of the more fully studied features of primate social behavior (Smuts, 1987a). In these species, competition among individual males or coalitions of males is consistently related to the reproductive strivings of these individuals and is based on physical contest—physical display or physical attack—and, in a few species, on the ability to form and to maintain coalitions with other males: In almost all cases, the result is larger and more aggressive males than females (Plavcan et al., 1995).

However it is achieved, the outcome of such competition is the establishment of a dominance hierarchy, and, in most species, the male's position in this hierarchy has important reproductive consequences (e.g., Dixson et al., 1993). The most frequent consequence is that dominant males attempt to and are often successful at controlling the social and sexual behavior of other group members, both male and female. Dominant males achieve the latter by means of mate guarding or by restricting the sexual behavior of females at those times when the female is most likely to conceive. Studies that have used DNA fingerprints to establish paternity indicate that the mate guarding of dominant males consistently provides them with a reproductive advantage in comparison to their subordinate peers. In some cases, dominant males effectively prevent their competitors from siring a single offspring (e.g. Altmann et al., 1996).

Male striving for social dominance is not the whole story, however. The alternative mating strategies that are used by less dominant males combined with female choice often undermine the reproductive strivings of dominant males (e.g., Perloe, 1992; Smuts, 1987b). One such male strategy appears to be based on female preferences (i.e., female choice) and involves the formation of one-on-one male–female relationships and, in some cases, relatively long-term friendships (Dunbar, 1986; Smuts, 1985; Tutin, 1979). For the female, the development of friendships with one or more males appears to be a strategy designed to elicit male support during times of social conflict and to elicit male investment in her offspring (Hrdy, 1979; Smuts & Gubernick, 1992). For the male, the development of such relationships increases the likelihood of siring offspring and, in some cases, results in direct investment in these offspring.

In many cases, females seem to prefer to develop these friendships with relatively dominant males, presumably because these males are better able to control the dynamics of social conflict than subordinate males are (Robinson, 1982; Smuts, 1985). In other cases, the mating priorities established by means of male–male competition and female choice conflict, and, in many of these cases, it appears that female choice prevails (Gagneux et al., 1997). Male primates also show preferences in their choice of mating partners, although they are not as particular as females. Most generally, males prefer to mate with females that are the most likely to conceive and that are the most likely to rear offspring successfully, although, as just mentioned, individual preferences based on personal relationships are also important in some species (Dunbar, 1986; Smuts, 1985). In cases in which males provide individual benefits to a female and her offspring, some level of female–female competition over affiliations with such males is expected; any such competition, however, is almost never as severe as that found with male–male competition (Robinson, 1982; Smuts, 1987a).

The combination of the reproductive strategies evident in living primates, the associated sex differences in physical size, and the pattern of physical dimorphisms evident in our hominid ancestors allow inferences to be drawn about the nature of sexual dynamics over the course of human evolution. The pattern of physical dimorphisms in our ancestors (e.g., larger males than females) is consistent with the view that male–male competition was a prominent feature of human evolution and was most likely a feature of a more or less polygynous mating system (Ghiglieri, 1987). Furthermore, it is very likely that the tendency of men to form coalitions in competition with other coalitions of men (e.g., Keeley, 1996) has a long evolutionary history and is—and has always been—related to reproductive competition (Daly & Wilson, 1988a; Ghiglieri, 1987; Goodall, 1986; Sigg et al., 1982).

The evolution of female choice is more difficult to reconstruct, but patterns of female choice found in related primate species and in other species that live in complex multimale–multifemale communities—as our more recent ancestors likely did—allow the range of possibilities to be narrowed (Foley, 1996). Most likely, female choice of mating partners was based, at least in part, on the social or material benefits that the male (or males) could provide (K. Hill, 1982; Smuts, 1985); other possibilities involve features associated with the good-genes models of female choice (see chapter 2 and chapter 5). Social support would have likely involved some form of protection of the female and her offspring during periods of conflict, as well as care of her offspring. More likely than not, a female preference for material support—such as meat provided through hunting—emerged only after the evolution of a female preference for social support, given that these social preferences are evident in species in which males provide little or no material resources to the female or her offspring. In either case, it has been argued that human sexuality—in particular concealed ovulation and the more or less continuous sexual receptivity of women— evolved as an adaptation to increase the stability of female–male pair-bonding and facilitated paternal investment in offspring (H. E. Fisher, 1982; MacDonald, 1992), the topic of the next chapter.

4

PATERNAL INVESTMENT

As we learned in chapter 2, there is a strong cross-species relation between sex differences in reproductive activities and the degree to which males and females invest in the well-being of their offspring (Johnstone et al., 1996; G. A. Parker & Simmons, 1996; Trivers, 1972). When females provide most or all of the parental care, males focus their reproductive efforts on mating, which, in turn, typically results in intense male–male competition for access to mates or for control of the resources that females need to raise their offspring with. In these species, the mating effort of females is largely restricted to female choice of mating partners (Clutton-Brock, 1991; Darwin, 1871; Trivers, 1972). The situation is more complicated, however, in those species in which both parents provide some level of care to their offspring: When both parents invest in their offspring, and there are individual differences in the quality of care (or genes) provided by both parents, then sexual selection generally involves female–female competition and male choice, in addition to male–male competition and female choice (Johnstone et al., 1996; G. A. Parker & Simmons, 1996; Pérusse, Neale, Heath, & Eaves, 1994).

Given this, the dynamics of sexual selection in humans and the associated sex differences in mating strategies (discussed in chapter 5) will strongly be influenced by the extent to which fathers invest in the well-being of their children. Thus, the current chapter provides a review of human paternal investment and in doing so also provides the background needed to understand sexual selection in humans, particularly female–female competition and male choice. The discussion of paternal investment begins with a comparison of the cross-cultural pattern of paternal and maternal care in the first section below. The second section provides an overview of the level of care provided by men in comparison to males of other primate species, and the third section provides discussion of individual and cultural differences in the level of paternal care. The influence of fathers on the well-being of children is discussed in the fourth and final section.

PATERNAL VERSUS MATERNAL INVESTMENT

Issues centered on the nature and extent to which mothers and fathers invest in their children are socially and scientifically contentious and always will be (e.g., Silverstein, 1991; Travis & Yeager, 1991). Scientifically, assumptions about the mother–infant relationship, for instance, influence the types of child-development research questions that are asked and the types of studies that are conducted (see Silverstein, 1991). Socially, differences in the nature and extent of maternal and paternal care are often a source of marital conflict, at least in industrial nations (Eibl-Eibesfeldt, 1989; Kluwer, Heesink, & Vandevliert, 1996; Parke, 1995; Scarr, Phillips, & McCartney, 1989). The goal here is not to consider the social implications of the pattern of sex differences in parental care (these are briefly addressed in chapter 9) but to examine the research literature on the pattern of maternal and paternal care found across human populations. These patterns are described in the first section below, whereas hormonal influences on parenting behavior are described in the second section.

Cross-Cultural Patterns

The pattern of biparental care found in humans needs to be first considered in terms of the most general pattern found in mammals. As was mentioned in chapter 2, internal gestation and postpartum suckling, among other things, make mammalian reproduction different from that which is found in birds, fishes, and reptiles (Andersson, 1994; Clutton-Brock, 1991; Pryce, 1992). In particular, these features result in obligatory female investment and in an important sex difference, favoring males, in the potential rate of reproduction (see the *Reproductive Rates* section of chapter 2; G. A. Parker & Simmons, 1996; Trivers, 1972). The combination of these factors—and the fact that paternity is never certain (see the *Female Choice* section of chapter 5)—contributes to the general pattern of relatively little paternal care in more than 95% of mammalian species (Clutton-Brock, 1991). From this perspective, the question then becomes why do human males contribute to the care of offspring at all (Clutton-Brock, 1989), as contrasted with the question of why don't men and women contribute equally to the care of their children (Silverstein, 1991).

In keeping with the general pattern found with mammals, greater maternal than paternal availability for and engagement with children is found across human cultures (Belsky, Rovine, & Fish, 1989; Eibl-Eibesfeldt, 1989; Hewlett, 1992a; M. M. West & Konner, 1976; Whiting & Edwards, 1988; Whiting & Whiting, 1975). Whiting and her colleagues' extensive cross-cultural studies of children's social behavior and development provide numerous examples of this sex difference. In one study of the social behavior of 3- to 6-year-olds in Kenya, India, Mexico, the Philippines, Japan, and the United States, it was found that children of this age were in the proximity of or in contact with their mother 32% to 47% of the time in five of the six cultures and 9% of the time in the sixth (a rural village in Japan); the estimate for the latter is biased, however, because observations were not taken in the household (Whiting & Whiting, 1975). In these same communities, children were in the proximity of or in contact with their father between 3% and 14% of the time. Across these cultures, children were in the presence of their mother 3 to 12 times more frequently than in the presence of their father, as shown in Figure 4.1 (see Whiting & Whiting, 1975).

A similar pattern was found in follow-up studies of communities in Africa, South Asia, South America, Central America, and North America (Whiting & Edwards, 1988). Here, 4- to 10-year-old children were found to be in the presence of their mother two to four times more frequently than in the presence of their father. Observation of 5- to 7-year-olds in Kenya, Guatemala, Peru, and the United States indicated that children were much more likely to be directly engaged in activities with women (mother, grandmother, aunt, etc.) than with men. The smallest difference was found in the United States, where children of this age were found to be directly engaged in activities with women two and one-half times more frequently than they were engaged in activities with men. The pattern differed somewhat for boys and girls, however. Girls spent relatively more time interacting with women than boys did, and boys spent relatively more time interacting with men than girls did. Nevertheless, the extent of these sex differences varied across cultures, and this pattern was not as pronounced as the overall difference in the frequency with which mothers and fathers interacted with their children (Eibl-Eibesfeldt, 1989; M. M. West & Konner, 1976; Whiting & Edwards, 1988).

The sex difference in parental care is even more pronounced for infants and toddlers (i.e., the first 3 years of life; Crano & Aronoff, 1978). Breast-feeding is, of course, the domain of mothers and in many preindustrial societies continues until the child is 3 to 4 years old (Eibl-Eibesfeldt, 1989). Mothers not only breast-feed infants and young children but also provide most of the child's daily care, such as bathing. In observational

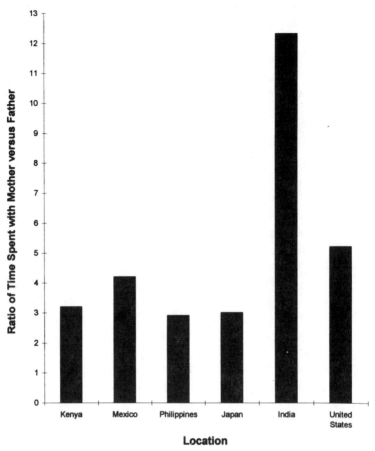

Figure 4.1. Ratio of maternal to paternal care. For instance, in the study site in Kenya, children were in the presence of or engaged in activities with their mother 3.2 times as often as with their father.

studies of families in Liberia, Kenya, India, Guatemala, and Peru, it was found that fathers were rarely or were never engaged in the care of infants (i.e., children younger than 1 year of age; Whiting & Edwards, 1988). In the United States, it was found that fathers provided relatively more care to their infants than fathers in these other settings did, although U.S. fathers still provided considerably less care than the infants' mothers (see also Belsky et al., 1989; Harkness & Super, 1992). The same cross-cultural pattern was found for toddlers (i.e., 2- to 3-year-olds) and, in fact, for children and adolescents (Parke, 1995; Whiting & Edwards, 1988).

The sex difference in the extent to which mothers and fathers provide care to their offspring cannot be attributed to a general inability of men to care for infants and young children. When fathers do interact with infants and young children, they show many of the same characteristics as mothers (e.g., they switch to baby talk) and can provide competent routine care (Belsky et al., 1989; Eibl-Eibesfeldt, 1989; Lamb, 1981; Parke, 1995), although there is some indication that custodial fathers (after divorce) monitor the activities of their children less diligently, on average, than custodial mothers (Buchanan, Maccoby, & Dornbusch, 1992). Nor can this sex difference be attributed to father absence, for instance, because he is away hunting or working outside of the home. In an extensive longitudinal study of family interactions after the birth of the first child, Belsky, Gilstrap, and Rovine (1984) found that when both parents were present, U.S. mothers engaged their infants one and one-half to two times more frequently and provided routine care three to four times more frequently than their husbands.

The same result was found in similar studies conducted in Sweden and Israel (Lamb, Frodi, Hwang, & Frodi, 1982; Lampert & Friedman, 1992). In the Swedish study, home observations of maternal and paternal interactions with infants were conducted for traditional and nontraditional families (Lamb et al., 1982). Nontraditional families were those in which the father had taken leave from work to care for the infant and had expressed a desire to be the primary caregiver of the infant. Indeed, on a self-report measure, nontraditional fathers rated parenthood more highly than did nontraditional mothers; the opposite pattern was found for traditional families. Despite differences in expressed attitudes toward child care, the mother was the primary caretaker in all of the traditional and nontraditional families. In fact, traditional and nontraditional fathers differed little in the ways in which they interacted with their infants; the primary difference being that traditional fathers were more likely to play with their infants than nontraditional fathers were.

Observation of parental care in preindustrial societies, such as the !Kung San (Botswana), revealed essentially the same pattern of sex differences as those found in the United States, Sweden, and Israel (Flinn, 1992; Griffin & Griffin, 1992; M. M. West & Konner, 1976). Studies of the !Kung San are particularly interesting because their social customs center on equality among group members and because they have sometimes been described as being representative of the type of social structure in which human beings evolved (Eibl-Eibesfeldt, 1989). Despite the social norm of equality, observational study of the amount of time spent in caregiving activities—for children younger than 2 years of age—indicated that !Kung San fathers provided less than 7% of this care, with the majority of the remaining care provided by the mother (see M. M. West & Konner, 1976). In another hunter–gatherer society in Central Africa, the Aka pygmies, fathers provide more direct care to their infants and children than fathers in any other society that has been studied do (Hewlett, 1988, 1992b). For instance, one observational study indicated that when they were in camp, Aka fathers held their 1- to 4-month-old infants 22% of the time, on average. Nevertheless, during the course of the day "the father would on average hold his infant for a total of 57 minutes while the mother would hold the infant 490 minutes" (Hewlett, 1988, p. 268).

The sex difference in the level of parental investment is reflected also in the frequency with which mothers and fathers abandon their children, such as after a divorce (Betzig, 1989; H. E. Fisher, 1989). The pattern of parental involvement with children after divorce has been studied extensively in industrial societies, and these studies have indicated that the majority of noncustodial fathers are not actively involved in the day-to-day raising of their children (Amato & Booth, 1996; Fox, 1995; Furstenberg, 1990; Furstenberg & Nord, 1985). In one large-scale nationally (United States) representative study, it was found that about three out of five children had not seen their noncustodial father during the past year, four out of five had never slept at his house, and the majority of these fathers exerted little effort to maintain any type of contact (such as through phone calls) with their children (Furstenberg & Nord, 1985). In all, it was found that only one out of six children had any type of regular contact with their biological father. The same pattern was found in a more recent national (United States) longitudinal study of parent–child relationships (Amato & Booth, 1996). These findings cannot simply be attributed to the fact that fathers are much more likely to be the noncustodial parent (greater than 85% of the time; Furstenberg, Peterson, Nord, & Zill, 1983) than mothers, as both of these studies found a very different pattern when the mother was the noncustodial parent (see Emery, 1988, for a review).

Furstenberg and Nord (1985) noted that in comparison to noncustodial fathers, noncustodial mothers "tend to maintain a much more active role in childrearing ... are distinctively more likely to visit with their child on a regular basis, have overnight visits, and have more indirect contact by phone and letter" (p. 896). Amato and Booth (1996) concluded that "divorce does not appear to weaken mothers' affection for their children" (p. 364) but leads to a deterioration in the relationship between fathers and their children. The pattern of relatively less paternal than maternal investment in children is often more evident for children who are born to unmarried couples (Fox, 1995), although many of these fathers do remain in periodic contact with their children (Parke, 1995). In addition to relatively little direct involvement with their children, about one half of the biological fathers who are not living with the mother (because of divorce or lack of marriage) fail to monetarily support their children, and those who do provide support, even when it is in full compliance with court orders, invest relatively little in their children, in comparison to the mother and fathers in intact families (Fox, 1995; Furstenberg, Morgan, & Allison, 1987; Maccoby, Buchanan, Mnookin, & Dornbusch, 1993).

Although these patterns are more prevalent in the United States than in most other industrial nations—because of national differences in the rate of divorce—the pattern of relatively little paternal involvement with children after separation from the children's mother is found in other industrial as well as in preindustrial societies. Basically, fathers invest more in their children when are they residing with their children and the children's mother (Brunelli, Wasserman, Rauh, Alvarado, & Caraballo, 1995; Draper, 1989; Flinn, 1992; Furstenberg et al., 1983; Hewlett, 1992b; K. Hill & Hurtado, 1996; M. M. West & Konner, 1976). For instance, in an observational study of parent–child social interactions in a Caribbean village, Flinn found that resident fathers were much more likely to provide some level of care to their children than nonresident fathers were, especially after the nonresident father or the mother remarried (see also Draper, 1989; Furstenberg et al., 1983). The same pattern of paternal disengagement after remarriage is evident in industrial societies (Emery, 1988) and indicates that the level of paternal investment after divorce is influenced by a number of social factors (remarriage, nature of the relationship with his ex-spouse, and so on) above and beyond the inherent differences in maternal and paternal investment.

In summary, in all regions of the world, across subsistence activities, and across social ideologies (e.g., degree to which stated social norms are egalitarian), *observational* studies have indicated that mothers invest more time and energy in the direct care of their children than fathers do; however, *self-report* measures sometimes have shown a more equal participation of men and women in "domestic labor" (e.g., Greenstein, 1996; Russell, 1982). The sex difference in parental care is especially pronounced during infancy and toddlerhood but generally continues into childhood and through adolescence (e.g., Belsky et al., 1989; Parke, 1995; Whiting & Edwards, 1988). The cross-cultural pattern of sex differences in parental care is consistent with the view that human parental investment follows the general pattern found in most mammalian species; that is, mothers are relatively more invested, on average, in the well-being and development of their children than fathers are (Irons, 1988; Trivers, 1972). The only deviation from this pattern is that human fathers show relatively more parental investment than that which is found in most other mammals (Clutton-Brock, 1989).

Hormonal Influences

In those mammalian species in which hormonal influences have extensively been studied, it is clear that maternal behavior—such as responding to infant distress vocalizations—is influenced by the hormonal changes that occur during pregnancy (e.g., changes in estradiol and progesterone levels) and by the hormonal changes associated with the birthing process and with suckling (e.g., release of oxytocin and prolactin; Corter & Fleming, 1995; Pryce, 1992, 1993, 1995). However, in many of these species, maternal caretaking is also influenced by previous experience with infants (e.g., play parenting before maturation), characteristics of the infant (e.g., facial expressions), the degree of conflict within the group, and the availability of resources in the general environment, among other things (Bard, 1995; Nicolson, 1987; Pryce, 1995). Although female hormones appear to make primate mothers more sensitive to infant characteristics (e.g., vocalizations), influence them to respond to infants in ways that facilitate mother–infant interactions, and more generally influence their motivation to attend to infants, these are by no means fixed, reflexive responses—they are sensitive to contextual and developmental factors (see Lee & Bowman, 1995; Pryce, 1995).

Hormonal influences on the behavior of human mothers are very likely, given that many of the just-noted effects appear to be common to mammals (Fleming, Ruble, Krieger, & Wong, 1997; Pryce, 1995; Rosenblatt, 1995). Nonetheless, the relatively few studies that have been conducted with humans indicate that the hormonal, social, and contextual influences on parental behavior are very complex and are not completely understood at this point (Belsky, 1993; P. W. Berman, 1980; Corter & Fleming, 1995; Fleming, Corter, & Steiner, 1995). As an example, mothers recognize the cry of their infant within the first 2 days following the child's birth (Formby, 1967) and respond with greater physiological arousal—as indicated by heart rate acceleration—to the cry of their infant in comparison to unfamiliar infants (Wiesenfeld & Klorman, 1978). There is some evidence that this pattern of maternal response to crying infants is related to the increase in cortisol levels that typically accompany the birth of a child (Fleming et al., 1995); high cortisol levels have also been found to be related to first-time mothers' attraction to infant odors (Fleming, Steiner, & Corter, 1997).

After the birth of a child, many fathers also show increased cortisol levels and increased arousal to the cry of their infant, suggesting that the just-described maternal response might not directly be related to circulating female hormones per se (Fleming et al., 1995; Frodi et al., 1978). Fleming, Ruble, et al. (1997), in contrast, found that estradiol levels during pregnancy were related to mothers' postpartum attachment to their children —the higher the estradiol levels relative to progesterone levels, the stronger the feelings of attachment. Moreover, females who have not had a child also show heart-rate acceleration to crying infants, but single males do not (Eibl-Eibesfeldt, 1989; Furedy et al., 1989), and there is some evidence that fathers' sensitivity to newborns and infants might be related to a drop in testosterone levels (Corter & Fleming, 1995); cortisol tends to suppress testosterone secretion (Folstad & Karter, 1992; Sapolsky, 1993). If so, then paternal sensitivity to infants might decline as testosterone increases to levels found before the birth of the child.

Either way, studies of the influence of prenatal exposure to sex hormones also suggest an influence of androgens on parenting behaviors. In an extensive review of the influence of sex hormones on human sex differences, Collaer and Hines (1995) concluded that prenatal exposure to androgens had masculinizing and defeminizing effects on girls. For instance, girls with congenital adrenal hyperplasia (CAH)—which results in prenatal exposure to high levels of androgens—show, on average, less interest in infants and dolls and less interest in play parenting than their unaffected sisters or other matched controls (see the *Play* section of chapter 7).

The overall pattern paints a very complex and not well-understood picture of hormonal (prenatal and circulating), contextual, and developmental influences on parental behavior. For instance, these studies suggest that prenatal exposure to male hormones and high levels of circulating male hormones might decrease sensitivity to and interest in children and that estradiol levels during pregnancy might influence later maternal attachment to the child. Even if these hormonal influences prove to be the case, it is also clear that there are individual differences in both men and women in responsiveness to infants and children (e.g., Pérusse et al., 1994). Indeed, despite the general pattern of sex differences, it is clear that not all mothers relate to their infants and children in ways that facilitate nurturing mother–child relationships and that there are clearly many high-investment fathers (Belsky, 1993; Daly & Wilson, 1981, 1985; Deater-Deckard, Scarr, McCartney, & Eisenberg, 1994; Lamb, 1981).

PATERNAL INVESTMENT ACROSS PRIMATE SPECIES

Across primate species, the relationship between adult males and infants and juveniles ranges from intensive caregiving to general indifference (Whitten, 1987). Intensive caregiving is found primarily in monogamous New World primates and especially in those species in which the mother typically gives birth to twins (e.g., the saddleback tamarin, *Saguinus fuscicollis*; Goldizen, 1987). "Males of these species share all parental duties except nursing, and although the extent of participation is quite variable within species, they are generally the major caretakers of infants" (Whitten, 1987, pp. 343–344). In these species, paternal care extends anywhere from 1 month to 1 year and includes holding, grooming, feeding, and protecting the infant.

In many other primate species, the relationship between males and infants and juveniles is best described as affiliative (Bard, 1995; Whitten, 1987). In these species, males do not typically provide intensive caretaking, but they are often in the proximity of infants, particularly during periods of rest and foraging (Whitten, 1987). Close proximity to males is associated with male protection of infants—especially if the male has developed a friendship with the infant's mother—and with greater access to food for the infant (Smuts, 1985; Smuts & Gubernick, 1992). Males may also carry infants, play with them, and groom them, although the extent of these activities varies across species.

The level of affiliation between human fathers and their children is similar to that found in the olive baboon (*Papio anubis*)—described in chapter 3 (see the *Pattern of Female Choice* section)—but is higher than that found in the two species most closely related to humans: the chimpanzee (*Pan troglodytes*) and the bonobo (*Pan paniscus*; Bard, 1995; Ghiglieri, 1987; Goodall, 1986; Smuts, 1985; Whitten, 1987). In a review of male–infant relationships across nearly 50 primate species, Whitten (1987) concluded that

> human males more closely resemble the males in "affiliative" nonhuman primate species than the males in the "intensive caretaking" species. Only in their provision of food do human males resemble the intensive caretakers. However, since subsistence is typically provided to the mother rather than directly to the offspring, even this parental investment is inextricably linked to mating efforts and interests. (p. 348)

INDIVIDUAL AND CULTURAL DIFFERENCES IN THE PATTERN OF PATERNAL INVESTMENT

As noted previously, there are considerable individual differences in the extent to which men provide direct and indirect care to their children. The factors that contribute to these individual differences are not fully understood, but what is known suggests that a combination of genetic, contextual, and societal influences affects whether and to what extent men contribute to the well-being of their children (Draper, 1989; Jain, Belsky, & Crnic, 1996; Katz & Konner, 1981; Parke, 1995; Pérrusse et al., 1994). Basically, the question addressed in this section is what are the conditions that moderate the level and nature of human paternal investment? The first section below focuses on genetic and social influences on individual differences in paternal investment, and the second focuses on the wider cultural and ecological conditions that are associated with these differences.

Genetic and Social Influences

In a unique, but therefore preliminary, study of the genetic and environmental contributions to two features of parental investment—care (e.g., sensitivity to the child's emotional state) and protection (e.g., keeping the child in close proximity)—Pérusse et al. (1994) found evidence for modest genetic contributions to individual differences in both paternal and maternal investment. For fathers, genetic models explained between

18% and 25% of the individual differences on these dimensions of parental investment and between 23% and 39% of the individual differences in maternal investment. These same models suggest that unique environmental effects account for the majority of the within-sex individual differences in both paternal and maternal care and protection (see Emlen, 1995, and Reiss, 1995, for a related discussion).

One apparent social influence on parental investment and parenting style is the nature of the spousal relationship (Belsky, 1993; Belsky et al., 1984; Brunelli et al., 1995; Feldman, Nash, & Aschenbrenner, 1983; Lamb, Pleck, & Levine, 1986; Scher & Mayseless, 1994; Simons & Johnson, 1996). Although quality of the spousal relationship—for instance, degree of confidential communication, level of conflict, and so on—has been shown to be related to the ways in which both mothers and fathers interact with their children (Amato & Keith, 1991; Belsky, 1993; M. J. Cox, Owen, Lewis, & Henderson, 1989; Davies & Cummings, 1994; Howes & Markman, 1989), "paternal parenting is more dependent on a supportive marital relationship than maternal parenting" (Parke, 1995, p. 37). For instance, a number of observational studies of parent–infant and parent–child interactions have found a significant sex difference in the relation between marital satisfaction and parental engagement with children (Belsky et al., 1984; Feldman et al., 1983; Lamb & Elster, 1985).

In all, "the quality of the marital dyad, whether reported by the husband or wife, is the one most consistently powerful predictor of paternal involvement (with his infant) and satisfaction (with the parenting role)" (Feldman et al., 1983, p. 1634). Belsky et al. (1984) and Lamb and Elster (1985) also found that fathers' engagement with their children was related to the quality of the marital relationship, but, at the same time, they found little relation between the level of marital interaction (e.g., degree of communication) and mothers' involvement with their children. Basically, it appears that marital conflict results in the father's withdrawal (emotional or physical) from his children and his spouse (e.g., Christensen & Heavey, 1990; Gottman, 1998), although this withdrawal is sometimes more pronounced for daughters than for sons (Kerig, Cowan, & Cowan, 1993).

In addition to the quality of the marital relationship, direct paternal involvement with children appears to be related to the nature of the father's work and his personal ambition; the latter is often implicitly related to mating effort (see the *Male–Male Competition* section of chapter 5). For instance, Feldman et al. (1983) found that fathers in demanding jobs were less involved in infant caretaking and were less playful with their infants than fathers in less salient occupations. Lamb et al. (1986) suggested also that there is a trade-off between family involvement and commitment to work. In comparison to men who were more focused on work than on family, "family-oriented accommodators ... [were] more professionally passive and less successful professionally. They also tended to be in less prestigious jobs ..., although it is not clear whether this was a cause or an effect of the family-oriented accommodative strategies" (Lamb et al., 1986, p. 79).

A similar relation has been found between a man's relative success in culturally important endeavors and direct paternal investment with the earlier mentioned Aka pygmies and with the Ache, a hunter–gather society in Eastern Paraguay (Hewlett, 1988; K. Hill & Hurtado, 1996; K. Hill & Kaplan, 1988). For Aka pygmies, high-status men—those with large kin networks and therefore high hunting success—hold their infants less than one half as frequently as other men, who typically have few kin, do: Men without kin (i.e., brothers) hunt either alone or with their wife and are generally less successful hunters in comparison to men who hunt in larger kin-based groups. The less direct care provided by these high-status men appears to be balanced by the provisioning of their families with diets that consist of a high proportion of fat and protein (Hewlett, 1988). Thus, it appears that as indirect paternal investment—such as income or meat obtained through hunting—increases, direct paternal investment—such as caretaking—often decreases.

Cultural and Ecological Influences

Wider cultural and ecological factors also influence the nature and extent of paternal investment in children. On the basis of an assessment of the frequency of father–infant proximity across 80 preindustrial cultures, M. M. West and Konner (1976) concluded that fathers are more available for their children "where gathering or horticulture ... is the primary mode of subsistence and where combinations of polygyny, patrilocal residence, the extended family, or patridominant division of labor are absent" (pp. 202–203). In a similar analysis, Draper and Harpending (1988) characterized human cultures as tending to be father absent or father present, reflecting differences in the relative emphasis of men on mating effort and parental investment, respectively (see Figure 2.1 and the *Parental Care* section of chapter 2).

Father-absent societies are characterized by aloof husband–wife relationships, a polygynous marriage system, local raiding and warfare, male social displays—verbal and with ornamentation—and little or inconsistent direct paternal investment in children (Draper & Harpending, 1988; Hewlett, 1988; Whiting & Whiting, 1975). These conditions "are particularly prevalent in so-called middle-range societies, i.e., those where agriculture is practiced at a very low level" (Draper & Harpending, 1988, p. 349) and in resource-rich ecologies. In the latter, women can often provide adequate care to their children (e.g., through small-scale agriculture) without the direct contribution of the fathers (Draper, 1989; E. M. Miller, 1994), and, thus, it is likely that paternal investment does not affect child mortality rates in these ecologies to the same extent as it does in other ecologies (refer to discussion below).

In these societies, the reproductive strategies of men are primarily focused on mating effort, as noted earlier. Basically, men compete with one another for the establishment of social dominance or for the control of those material resources (e.g., land and cattle) that women need to raise their children with (e.g., Borgerhoff Mulder, 1990). The establishment and the maintenance of social dominance, in turn, influence the number of women the man can marry and the number of surviving children (e.g., Chagnon, 1988; Irons, 1993), as is found in many other primate species (e.g., Altmann et al., 1996; see the *Male–Male Competition* section of chapter 5).

Father-present societies, in contrast, are more commonly found in harsh or unstable ecologies and in industrial, or other relatively large, stratified societies (Draper & Harpending, 1988). These societies are generally characterized by ecologically or socially imposed monogamy (Flinn & Low, 1986). Under harsh ecological conditions, the vast majority of men are unable to acquire the resources (e.g., meat obtained through hunting) needed to support more than one wife and family. The reproductive aspirations of these men are thus ecologically restricted to monogamy, with high levels of paternal investment often being necessary to ensure the survival of their children. In many industrial societies, monogamy is socially imposed (i.e., there are formal laws that prohibit polygynous marriages). Although the factors that have led to the cultural evolution of socially imposed monogamy are not fully understood (see Betzig, 1995, and MacDonald, 1995a, for discussion), the net result is a relative shift in men's reproductive efforts, from mating effort to parental effort. Whether monogamy is ecologically or socially imposed, these father-present societies are generally characterized by high levels of spousal affiliation and intimacy, low levels of warfare or a professional military, which results in fewer men being socialized for intergroup aggression (Keeley, 1996), and relatively high levels of men's provisioning of their spouse and children (Draper & Harpending, 1988; Whiting & Whiting, 1975).

There are, however, important individual differences within both father-absent and father-present societies. For instance, even though direct paternal investment in children tends to be lower in cultures that allow polygynous marriages, in comparison to cultures in which monogamy is ecologically or socially imposed, most of the men (greater than 80%) in most polygynous societies are monogamously married (Murdock, 1981). Even so, there is some indication that in cultures that allow polygyny, monogamously married men often divert social and material resources from the family to their mating efforts, that is, their attempts to attract and to obtain a second wife (e.g., Hames, 1992); this, of course, occurs in monogamous societies as well. Moreover, under some conditions, high-status polygynously married men are able to invest more material and social resources in their many children than are low-status and monogamously married men. On the Ifaluk islands, in the Western Pacific, chiefs tend to have more wives (serial monogamy in this case) and children than lower status men have, but they associate with their children twice as often as these lower status men (Betzig & Turke, 1992). This is possible because high-ranking men receive tributes from other families and receive relatively more food from communal fishing than low-ranking men do. The net result is that chiefs spend less time working than other men and have more material resources and time to invest in their children.

PATERNAL INVESTMENT AND THE WELL-BEING OF CHILDREN

The earlier described differences in the extent of maternal and paternal investment in children should not be interpreted as indicating that fathers have little effect on the well-being of their children. The finding that human males show higher levels of affiliation with their children than males in the two primate species most closely related to humans is consistent with the position that paternal investment has increased since the emergence of *Australopithecus afarensis* (see chapter 3), and this finding suggests that any such investment can have important consequences for children. The importance of paternal investment varies widely, however, across cultures and across contexts.

In some cases, father presence appears to have little or even an adverse effect on the well-being of children (e.g., with chronic unemployment), whereas, in other cases, paternal investment significantly affects child mortality rates (K. Hill & Hurtado, 1996; Lancaster, 1989; McLoyd, 1989). In most cases, paternal investment has more subtle effects on children's social, psychological, and physiological functioning (Cherlin et al., 1991; Flinn, Quinlan, Decker, Turner, & England, 1996; Furstenberg & Teitler, 1994). The first and second sections below focus on the relation between paternal investment and the physical and social well-being of children. The third and final section provides a contrast of the effects of paternal versus maternal investment on the well-being of children.

Physical Well-Being

The importance of paternal investment for the well-being of children is implicitly or explicitly acknowledged in many societies. For instance, lack of paternal support is a common justification for infanticide in many cultures (e.g., Bugos & McCarthy, 1984). Daly and Wilson (1988a) found 112 expressed rationales for infanticide gleaned from the ethnographies of 60 societies. In 6 of these societies "infants were said to be killed when no man would acknowledge paternity or accept an obligation to provide for the child. ... In addition, the mother's unwed status was offered as grounds for infanticide in 14 societies ... presumably [due to] lack of reliable paternal support for the children" (Daly & Wilson, 1988a, p. 52), and in one society (the Baganda, Africa), high levels of spousal conflict was listed as a justification for infanticide. In a study of a random sample of 300 35- to 45-year-old American women, Essock-Vitale and McGuire (1988) found that "pregnancies were significantly more likely to end in a voluntary abortion if the woman was unmarried or, if married, was not certain that the husband was the father of the child" (Essock-Vitale & McGuire, 1988, pp. 230–231).

K. Hill and Hurtado's (1996) extensive ethnography and demography of the Ache provide a clear illustration of a more direct influence of the father on child mortality rates. For forest-dwelling Ache, about one out of three children die before reaching the age of 15 years, with highly significant differences in mortality rates for father-present and father-absent children. Father absence—because of death or divorce—triples the probability of child death because of illness and doubles the risk of being killed by other Ache or being kidnapped—and presumably killed or sold into slavery—by other groups (Hurtado & Hill, 1992). Overall, father absence at any point before the child's 15th birthday is associated with a mortality rate of more than 45%, as compared with a mortality rate of about 20% for children whose father resides with them until their 15th birthday.

Death because of sickness is related, in part, to the adequacy of the child's diet, and in many preindustrial societies, including the Ache, paternal provisioning provides an important component of this diet. Even though the Ache share the proceeds from hunts among all members of the group and thus fathers do not directly provision for their children, the children of skilled hunters have lower mortality rates than the children of less skilled hunters (K. Hill & Kaplan, 1988; see also Symons, 1979). It appears that the children of skilled hunters are generally better treated by group members than are the children of less skilled hunters. According to K. Hill and Kaplan (1988), this better treatment likely involves a greater tolerance "of food begging by the children of good hunters" (p. 283), a greater willingness of band members to stay in one location to nurse the ill child of a good hunter, and greater alloparenting (e.g., baby-sitting) of these children. The Ache, however, are not generally willing to invest in the well-being of genetically unrelated children and, as noted previously, will often kill children whose father has died or left the group after divorce (see K. Hill & Hurtado, 1996).

In many other preindustrial societies, fathers directly provision for their children, typically with meat obtained through hunting, and a man's skill at providing this resource can significantly influence child mortality rates (e.g., Blurton Jones, Hawkes, & O'Connell, 1997). Griffin and Griffin

(1992) provided one poignant example from the Agta, a hunter–gatherer society in the Philippines:

> Sinebo . . . was a loving father but was plagued by the all-too-frequent problem (as the Agta view it) of seeing most of his children die. His two wives had managed to keep only one daughter alive. Others died of malnutrition, illness, and bad luck. Although the observation period was too brief to be certain, Sinebo may have been less than a skillful hunter. He hunted frequently but his catches were poor. (p. 315)

In industrial societies and in other contexts in which food and health care are more or less readily available, child mortality rates are very low, in comparison to the 40% to 65% range (across societies) often found in hunter–gatherer societies (K. Hill & Hurtado, 1996). For instance, Ache living on reservations have much lower child mortality rates than forest-living Ache (except during the initial contact period). Health care is available on the reservation, and families are able to engage in small-scale gardening, work for wages, and accumulate material resources. Even with lower overall mortality rates, paternal investment still influences the survival rate of children, especially infants. Over the course of about 25 years, considerable—fivefold—variation has emerged in the net worth (i.e., value of all personal property) or socioeconomic status (SES) of families living on the reservation, and K. Hill and Hurtado (1996) have found that "a man's SES is a strong predictor of his offspring's survival to adulthood" (p. 303).

The relation between SES and the physical well-being of children is in fact found throughout the world. In a review of the literature on the relation between SES—defined as a composite of income, educational level, and occupational status in industrial societies—Adler et al. (1994) concluded that "individuals in lower social status groups have the highest rates of morbidity and mortality within most human populations. Moreover, studies of the entire SES hierarchy show that differences in social position relate to morbidity and mortality even at the upper levels of the hierarchy" (p. 22). The relation between SES and health holds for all members of the family, not just for the primary wage earner, and is not simply related to access to health care or to differences in health-related behaviors (e.g., smoking). In addition, SES appears to influence how well one is treated by other individuals and the degree to which one can control the activities of everyday life, which, in turn, appear to influence physical health (Ray & Sapolsky, 1992; see *The Motivation to Control* section of chapter 6). Across industrial societies, paternal income and occupational status are an important, and sometimes the sole, determinant of the family's SES, and, given this, paternal investment in the family can affect the physical well-being of the children in important ways (see Irons, 1979, for an example in a preindustrial society).

A recent study by Flinn and his colleagues provides some intriguing clues as to the potential relation between paternal investment and the physical well-being of children (Flinn et al., 1996). In this 8-year study, the family environment and cortisol and testosterone profiles were assessed for children and adults in a rural village in Dominica, in the West Indies. Among other things, it was found that the presence or absence of father was related to the cortisol and testosterone levels of boys, but not of girls. In comparison to boys residing with their biological father, father-absent boys and boys living with a stepfather had either unusually low or highly variable cortisol levels and weighed less. An analysis of adults who grew up in father-present or father-absent households also revealed significant differences: As adults, father-absent men had higher cortisol levels and lower testosterone levels than their father-present peers. The endocrine profile of father-absent men suggests chronically high stress levels, which can significantly increase the risk for a number of physical disorders (e.g., Sapolsky, 1986, 1991, 1993). In all, it was concluded that the "early family environment has significant effects on endocrine response throughout male life histories" (Flinn et al., 1996, p. 125; see also Flinn & England, 1995, 1997).

The results of a 70-year longitudinal study (United States) of mentally gifted individuals also suggest that there are long-term consequences to the stability of the early family environment (Friedman et al., 1995; J. E. Schwartz et al., 1995). Here, it was found that "children of divorced parents faced a one third greater mortality risk than people whose parents remained married at least until they reached age 21" (Friedman et al., 1995, p. 71). For both men and women, this mortality risk translated into a 4-year gap in the life span of children from divorced and intact families, although mortality rates were higher for people from divorced families at all ages in adulthood. For instance, men whose parents had divorced were three times more likely to die by age 40 years than men whose parents had not divorced. The early death of a parent, in contrast, had little effect on life span, suggesting that the relation between parental divorce and later mortality risks is mediated by the social stressors often associated with divorce (Tucker et al., 1997).

On the basis of an analysis of fossil records from several prehistoric populations, Goodman and Armelagos (1988) also found that systemic stress during childhood, which can be assessed on the basis of the enamel development of teeth, was related to a 6- to 10-year reduction in longevity. These results are consistent with the view that parental conflict or other social stresses have important consequences for the well-being of children (e.g., Amato & Keith, 1991). Or stated otherwise, children living in stable social and home environments and with both biological parents appear to be in better health and apparently enjoy a longer life span, on average, than children living in other situations (see also Belsky, 1997; Daly & Wilson, 1981, 1985, 1988b; Flinn & England, 1997).

Social Well-Being

In contexts in which child mortality rates are low, paternal investment appears to provide more subtle social–competitive advantages to children. As noted earlier, social competitiveness, as indexed by SES in industrial societies for example, is consistently related to morbidity and mortality risks in most human populations and is likely to be particularly important during periods of high society-wide stressors (e.g., famine). In other words, paternal investment that increases the social competitiveness of children likely provides a buffer—reducing mortality and morbidity risks—against unforeseen large-scale social stressors, given that such stressors will affect less socially competitive individuals (e.g., lower SES families) more harshly than more socially competitive individuals.

In industrial societies, one indicator of paternal investment is divorce, as described earlier. Divorce and the many effects often associated with divorce, such as marital conflict, father absence, and change in SES, appear to have social and psychological effects on children, although many of the differences between children from divorced and intact families can be traced to differences in family functioning before any such divorce (Cherlin et al., 1991; Furstenberg & Teitler, 1994). Nonetheless, some differences between children from intact and divorced families remain, after controlling for predivorce levels of family conflict and other potentially confounding variables (Cherlin et al., 1991). In particular, it appears that divorce results in a small-to-moderate increase in aggressive and noncompliant behaviors, particularly in boys, as well as in an early onset of sexual activity and lowered educational achievement for adolescents and young adults (both men and women), respectively, although the dynamics associated with divorce and these outcomes are not fully understood (Amato & Keith, 1991; Belsky, Steinberg, & Draper, 1991; Rothbaum & Weisz, 1994; Stevenson & Black, 1988).

The finding that divorce, which typically results in lower levels of paternal investment (both direct and indirect), results in earlier sexual activity and lower educational achievement in adolescents and young adults is consistent with the view that paternal investment in industrial societies is associated with improvements in children's later social competitiveness, as contrasted with increased survival rates in preindustrial societies (Belsky et al., 1991; K. Hill & Hurtado, 1996). In other words, given that child mortality rates are low in industrial societies (at least during the last few generations) with or without paternal investment, paternal investment in these societies is not as important for children's survival as it is in many preindustrial contexts. However, given the strong

relation between educational outcomes and later SES in industrial societies, paternal investment that increases educational outcomes will likely
result in children having a social–competitive advantage, on average, over
children whose fathers did not provide the same level of investment; early
sexual activity is also associated with lower educational outcomes. Moreover, should wider social conditions change and become more harsh (i.e.,
should stronger selection pressures arise), this social–competitive advantage would likely result in a reproductive advantage, given that high-status
parents typically have more surviving children (or more surviving grandchildren) under these conditions than low-status parents (e.g., Irons, 1979,
1993).

There is also evidence for more direct paternal effects on the social
and psychological functioning of children (Parke, 1995), both positive and
negative. Paternal psychopathology (e.g., substance abuse) has been associated with aggressive, noncompliant behaviors and depression and anxiety in children, possibly reflecting a combination of genetic and environmental influences (Phares & Compas, 1993; Reiss, 1995). On a more
positive note, paternal involvement in play, especially rough-and-tumble
play and play in which the child is able to control or influence the dynamics of the episode, is associated with children's skills at regulating their
emotional states and their social competence later. For instance, boys and
girls who have fathers who regularly engage them in physical play are more
likely to be socially popular (i.e., chosen as preferred playmates by their
peers) than children who do not regularly engage in this type of play
(Carson, Burks, & Parke 1993; Parke 1995). Again, this pattern suggests
that paternal investment improves, on average, the social–competitiveness
of children.

Paternal Versus Maternal Investment

In all, although there are some circumstances in which fathers' involvement in the family has little or adverse effects on children, it is more
generally the case that direct and indirect paternal investment improves
the well-being of children. The importance of paternal investment is particularly evident in harsh environments, as with the Ache, in which such
investment often has a significant influence on the likelihood of children
surviving to adulthood; it is conditions such as these that likely mirror the
selection pressures that led to the evolution of paternal investment. In
contexts in which childhood mortality is low, indirect (e.g., contribution
to family income) and direct (e.g., care) paternal investment has more
subtle effects, generally improving children's physiological, social, and psychological functioning (Emery, 1988).

At the same time, it should be noted that the relative influence of
maternal investment is generally larger than the influence of paternal in-

vestment. With the Ache, for instance, death of the mother doubles the risk of child mortality in comparison to death of the father; mortality rates are 100% for children whose mother dies before the child reaches the age of 2 years (K. Hill & Hurtado, 1996). K. Hill and Hurtado's findings are not restricted to hunter–gatherer societies, as Voland (1988) found the same pattern—increased child mortality rates with paternal or maternal death but higher mortality rates with maternal death—in an analysis of birth and death records from seventeenth- to nineteenth-century Germany.

Flinn et al. (1996) noted that "permanent absence of mother during infancy is associated with abnormal cortisol profiles for male and female children" (p. 146), whereas father absence was associated with abnormal cortisol profiles in boys but not in girls, as described earlier. Even with boys, the influence of mother absence is larger in comparison to father absence. Finally, the quality of the mother–child relationship appears to have a stronger influence on the social and psychological functioning of children than the quality of the father–child relationship (e.g., Rothbaum & Weisz, 1994), possibly because mothers spend more time with their children than do fathers (Parke, 1995).

SUMMARY AND CONCLUSION

When considered in terms of mammalian reproduction, it is unremarkable that—throughout the world—mothers show a much greater availability for and engagement with their children than fathers do. This is because internal gestation and suckling necessarily result in higher levels of maternal than paternal investment (Andersson, 1994). Under these circumstances, the cross-species pattern is for the reproductive strategies of females to be biased toward parental effort and the reproductive strategies of males to be biased toward mating effort, as described in chapter 2 (Trivers, 1972). The most noteworthy feature of human parental care is that many fathers show some degree of direct and indirect investment in their children. Although the level of paternal care is far from noteworthy for those individuals who call for equal maternal and paternal investment in their children, it is nonetheless remarkable in comparison to the little paternal care found in the two species most closely related to humans and in terms of the more general pattern found with mammals (Clutton-Brock, 1989; Whitten, 1987). The combination of results is entirely consistent with the view that level of paternal investment has increased considerably since the emergence of A. *afarensis* (see chapter 3).

Although the evolutionary sequence of events cannot be known with certainty, the emergence of paternal investment in humans most likely resulted from the coevolution of the reproductive strategies of women and of men (Alexander, 1990; Darwin, 1871; Dawkins, 1989; E. O. Wilson, 1975).

In comparison to industrial societies, the social and ecological conditions in hunter–gatherer societies are almost certainly more similar to the social and ecological conditions within which humans evolved (Tooby & Cosmides, 1995), and living under such conditions greatly increases the risk of child death because of disease, malnutrition, and, in some cases, homicide. Under these circumstances, the investment that men can provide to children becomes a potentially important resource to women, in their quest to keep their children alive and healthy (e.g., K. Hill & Hurtado, 1996).

Given this, it is likely that at some point after the emergence of *A. afarensis*, female choice of mating partners became increasingly contingent on the male hominid's willingness and ability to provide social protection or material resources to her children, whether or not they were his children (E. M. Miller, 1994; Smuts & Gubernick, 1992), as shown at the top of Figure 4.2. Simply stated, a female hominid that made sexual access contingent on male investment in her children likely had more surviving chil-

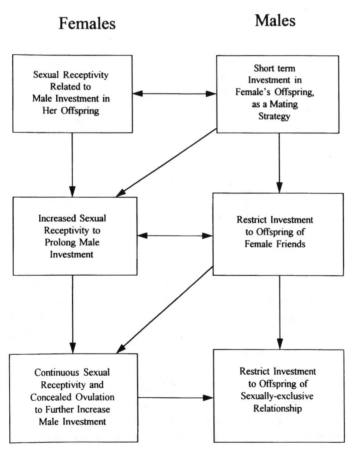

Figure 4.2. Sketch of one potential sequence of "events" leading to the evolution of paternal care in humans.

dren than a female hominid that did not demand such investment. In keeping with this position is the finding that the pattern of male care found in other primates (as described in chapter 3) is primarily related to mating effort and not to parental effort. In other words, the initial evolution of paternal investment was more likely to have been related to female choice of mating partners that invested in her children than a male-initiated shift from mating to paternal effort (see Lovejoy, 1981; Smuts & Gubernick, 1992). When male investment provided a female hominid with an important reproductive advantage (i.e., more surviving children), it seems likely that selection would favor the evolution of an increase in the duration of sexual receptivity (perhaps similar to that seen in the bonobo), which, in turn, would have further increased the level of male investment in her offspring.

Higher levels of male investment result in an opportunity cost of mating with fewer females and would thus be maintained only if males restricted this investment to offspring that were more likely than not to be theirs; perhaps resulting in a situation similar to that seen in the olive baboon (Smuts, 1985). Male investment, in turn, not only increased the chances of offspring survival but probably also provided these offspring with a competitive advantage—through an increase in the sophistication of the competitive skills acquired during a longer and longer developmental period (Alexander, 1990; see the *Physical Development* section of chapter 7). Stated somewhat differently, male investment likely enabled the evolutionary emergence of a period of protracted development, which, in turn, enabled slow-developing offspring to acquire skills that provided them with an advantage, in adulthood, over their faster maturing conspecifics. A long developmental period likely increased the need for male investment, which, in turn, would favor the evolution of other female strategies— concealed ovulation and near-continuous sexual receptivity—to further increase this investment. Under these conditions, male hominids that only invested in offspring that were almost certainly their biological offspring were likely at a reproductive advantage, relative to male hominids that invested in the children of other males (e.g., Daly, Wilson, & Weghorst, 1982). Basically, as the level of paternal investment increases, the male concern over paternity certainty increases as well.

In this view, the evolution of parental investment is the result of the coevolution of the female's strategy to increase the quantity and quality of resources provided to her offspring and the male's counterstrategy to only provide these resources to his biological offspring. Nonetheless, only under extreme conditions, in which a lack of paternal investment always resulted in the death of the offspring, would monogamy and equal levels of maternal and paternal care evolve; less than 100% paternity certainty also militates against equal levels of maternal and paternal investment (see the *Female Choice* section of chapter 5). Under less severe conditions—as is found in most traditional societies today—paternal investment often improves the chances of the children surviving to adulthood, but, at the same time, many children who are abandoned by their biological father survive, yet not at the same rate as children who are not abandoned by their father. Given this, it seems likely that during the course of human evolution, paternal investment resulted in only a conditional, and not an absolute, improvement in the survival rate of children. Under conditions such as these, men who adopted a strategy of selective investment in some women and their children and little or no investment in other women and their children would very likely have a reproductive advantage over men who invested in only a single woman and her children, as well as an advantage—in many circumstances—over men who showed little investment in any of their children (Draper & Harpending, 1988). The fact that paternal investment results in an improvement in the well-being of children under some conditions, but not under other conditions, means that men's parental investment is not obligate (i.e., it is optional in many contexts, in that it is not always needed to ensure the survival of their children), which, in turn, creates the dynamics of sexual selection in humans, as described in chapter 5.

5

SEXUAL SELECTION IN
CONTEMPORARY HUMANS

In most mammalian species, sexual selection is driven primarily by male–male competition and female choice (Andersson, 1994). However, the relatively high levels of paternal investment described in chapter 4 change the dynamics of sexual selection in humans, in comparison to most other mammals. In theory and in practice, the dynamics of human mating involve female–female competition and male choice, in addition to male–male competition and female choice (Johnstone et al., 1996; G. A. Parker & Simmons, 1996; Perper, 1989). To complicate matters further, the dynamics of these features of sexual selection can vary considerably from one culture to the next, and especially across cultures that have different marriage systems (Flinn & Low, 1986). As a result, a complete understanding of sexual selection in humans requires consideration of the sociopolitical context within which mate choices are made.

A brief overview of these contexts is provided in the *Marriage Systems* section below. The social, contextual, and psychological features of the four basic dimensions of sexual selection (female choice, female–female competition, male–male competition, and male choice) are summarized in the four sections that follow the *Marriage Systems* section. The chapter closes with a brief discussion of cultural and historical variability in the ways in which these features of sexual selection are expressed, as related to those ecological variables—such as the OSR (recall, operational sex ratio)—

that result in variation in the mating strategies of other animals (see chapter 2).

MARRIAGE SYSTEMS

A variety of marriage systems are found across human populations, including monogamy, female defense polygyny, resource defense polygyny, and, in a few cases, polyandry (see Table 2.1; Alexander, 1979; Emlen & Oring, 1977; Flinn & Low, 1986). The social and ecological conditions that account for these differences in marriage system are not yet fully understood, although some general patterns have emerged (Flinn & Low, 1986). As mentioned in chapter 4 (see the *Individual and Cultural Differences in the Pattern of Paternal Investment* section), monogamy is most common in those societies living in harsh, resource-limited ecologies and in large politically and economically stratified societies. For the former, monogamy is ecologically imposed; that is, the efforts of both parents are needed to raise their children successfully, men are unable to acquire the social or material resources needed to attract and to support a second wife and family, or both (Alexander et al., 1979). In many politically stratified societies, monogamy is socially imposed, that is, there are formal laws that prohibit polygynous marriages (see the *Cultural and Historical Variability in Mating Dynamics* section at the end of the chapter). However, monogamy —whether ecologically or socially imposed—is the central marriage system in only about one out of six human societies (Murdock, 1981).

Polygyny is found in nearly all other societies. Female defense polygyny is often found in societies in which the accumulation of material resources is difficult but also in which there are differences in the social and political power of individual men (Flinn & Low, 1986). Within these societies, men from large kin groups are often able to form politically powerful coalitions, which work to control the social and mating activities of individuals within the larger group, much like the chimpanzee coalitions described in chapter 3. Also, dominant men within these coalitions often have many wives (e.g., Chagnon, 1974, 1977, 1979, 1988). Resource defense polygyny is common in societies in which material resources can be accumulated and polygynous marriages are not prohibited. An apparently universal feature of these societies is the emergence of differences in the extent to which individuals (almost always men) or kin-based coalitions control the material resources of the society (e.g., L. Ellis, 1993). Within these societies, wealthy men generally have many wives and tend to use their wealth to control the social and sexual behavior of their wives, as well as other men (Betzig, 1993; Flinn & Low, 1986). Polyandry occurs in less than 1% of human societies and is found where the economic activities of two men (typically brothers) are required to support a family (Flinn & Low, 1986).

The just-described variability in human mating systems indicates that the specifics of sexual selection—such as the relative importance of female choice or the intensity of male–male competition—are influenced by a host of ecological and social factors and that individual preferences are almost always constrained, to some extent, by such factors. Given this, a full discussion of the mechanisms of sexual selection in human populations requires consideration of mating activities at two levels: the social and ecological contexts that influence mating decisions and the preferences that emerge in the absence of any constraints imposed within these contexts. The latter is thought to reflect the evolved psychological mechanisms that, when fully expressed, would optimize the individual's reproductive success (Buss, 1994; Cosmides & Tooby, 1994; Tooby & Cosmides, 1990). Discussion of the motivational, emotional, and cognitive systems that appear to make up these evolved psychological mechanisms is presented in chapter 6 (*The Motivation to Control* section; Geary, 1998). The four sections that follow provide discussion of the dynamics of sexual selection in terms of actual mate choices and in terms of the preferences that emerge in the absence of social and ecological constraints on these choices.

FEMALE CHOICE

As with females in other species with slow developing (i.e., altricial) offspring, the implicit and explicit reproductive decisions of women are influenced by the quantity and quality of resources needed to raise their children successfully (Clutton-Brock, 1991; Darwin, 1871; Trivers, 1972). As described in chapter 4, paternal investment can substantially enhance the well-being of children, and, thus, the nature and quality of the social and material resources that individual men can provide to offspring are in theory—and in practice—an important consideration in female choice of marriage partners, as discussed in the first section below. The second section provides a description of the personal and behavioral attributes that women prefer in prospective marriage partners, and the third section provides an overview of the physical and possibly genetic, such as MHC (as a reminder, major histocompatibility complex) compatibility, attributes that appear to influence female choice. A brief discussion of alternative mating strategies is presented in the fourth and final section.

Social Status

In those primate species in which relatively long-term female–male relationships develop, dominant males are often preferred over less dominant males as mating partners. This is so because these dominant males can provide greater protection from conspecifics and because affiliation with these males often increases access to high-quality foods (e.g., Smuts, 1985; see the *Female Choice* section in chapter 3). Similarly, the social status of men is an important, although certainly not the only, consideration in women's choices of and preferences for marriage partners (Buss, 1994), although for humans the markers of social status vary somewhat across societies (Irons, 1979). In societies in which material resources are not easily accumulated, social status is often determined by coalition formation and other sociopolitical activities (e.g., Chagnon, 1988). In other societies, social status is determined by the accumulation and control of material resources, in addition to sociopolitical activities (which are typically focused on the distribution of these resources). Thus, the specifics of women's social-status preferences are likely to vary from one culture or context to the next. Nonetheless, the common theme across these contexts is that women generally prefer mates who can and will help them to organize social and material resources in ways that enhance the well-being of their children (see *The Motivation to Control* section of chapter 6).

In many cultures, however, women's marriage preferences are often confounded by the economic and political priorities of their kin. In these societies, the choice of marriage partner often results from the competing financial and political interests of the woman's kin and her individual preferences, although her preferences and the interests of her kin often coincide (Small, 1992). Such conflicts of interest are especially evident in societies in which young women are an economic asset to their families; that is, in those societies in which bride-price (i.e., material resources) or bride-service (i.e., labor) are required of prospective suitors. In an analysis of the dynamics of marriage across 860 societies, Daly and Wilson (1983) found that the bride's kin required a substantial bride-price or bride-service in 500, or 58%, of these societies and a less substantial bride-price in 53 other societies. In another 27 societies, men from different kin groups often acquire wives through a direct exchange of daughters, thus circumventing female choice (Hrdy, 1997). In only 205, or slightly less than 1 out of 4, of these societies are the women's marriage preferences relatively untethered by the priorities and preferences of their kin (but see Small, 1992). Nonetheless, even in these societies, kin often attempt to influence the marriage choices of their children: both women and men (it is their genes too; e.g., Flinn, 1988b; Trivers, 1974). In all, this analysis indicates that in 2 out of 3 societies, young women are an economic asset to their kin and are sometimes treated as such. The result is that their ability to exercise their preferences for marriage partners is often constrained, to some extent, by kin influences.

An example of the dynamics of female choice and kin influence is provided by the marriage patterns of the Kipsigis, a pastoral group in Kenya.

At the same time, these marriage patterns illustrate the female preference for mates who control material resources (Borgerhoff Mulder, 1988, 1990). In this society, access to land and cattle, which are controlled by men, has important reproductive consequences for women. "Land access is correlated with women's reproductive success, and may be an important causal factor contributing to reproductive differentials, given the greater availability of food in the homes of 'richer' women and the lower incidence of illness among them and their offspring" (Borgerhoff Mulder, 1990, p. 256).

Choice of marriage partners is technically made by the young woman's kin and is influenced, in part, by the man's bride-price, or bride wealth offer, in addition to his social reputation and his political influence. In some cases, the preferences of the woman and the best interest of her parents strongly conflict, and in these cases, female choice is sometimes circumvented by the priorities of the woman's kin. Here, "parents reported having given their daughters to men who were patently poor because, they said, 'the bridewealth offer was so good'" (Borgerhoff Mulder, 1990, p. 261). In most cases, however, the parents' decision is influenced by their daughter's preference, and these joint decisions are strongly influenced by the amount of land made available to her and her future children (and her parents' grandchildren).

Across an 18-year period, Borgerhoff Mulder (1990) found that the two men (the alpha and beta males) offering the most land to prospective brides were chosen as husbands by 13 of 29 brides and their families, and either one or both of these men were married in 11 of the 15 years in which one or more marriages occurred. The two lowest ranking men, in contrast, were chosen as husbands in only 1 of these 15 years. Moreover, a husband was chosen only 10 times from the group of men—sometimes as many as 10 men in a given year—offering less than an average amount of land. In addition to the material resources offered by the prospective mate, female choice in the Kipsigis is also influenced by the number of co-wives the man has, if any, and by the number of surviving offspring of any co-wives. For suitors with one or more wives, those men with more surviving children are preferred as husbands. However, all other things being equal, women's choices suggest that they prefer bachelors (i.e., monogamous marriages). In theory, a preference for a monogamous marriage would reflect the woman's desire for her husband to invest all of his resources in her children, which should improve the well-being of these children. Indeed, monogamously married women, or women married to wealthier men with only one co-wife, had more surviving children than women married to men with many co-wives (Borgerhoff Mulder, 1990; Daly & Wilson, 1983); however, note that the relation between polygyny and the reproductive outcomes of women is complex and not fully understood (Borgerhoff Mulder, 1997; D. R. White, 1988).

With the Kipsigis, female choice is thus intertwined with the material and political interests of the woman's kin, but in most cases, these interests largely coincide with her preferences. Basically, mate choice in Kipsigis women is influenced by the quantity and quality of resources that will be made available to the woman and her future children, which, in turn, will influence the health and survival rate of these children (see also K. Hill & Hurtado, 1996; Irons, 1979).

A woman's preference for a marriage partner who will provide material resources to her and her children is, in fact, found throughout the world, at least in those societies in which material resources can be accumulated or in which men provide a high-quality but perishable resource, such as meat obtained through hunting (Betzig, 1997; Symons, 1979, 1980). In the United States, for instance, "in any given year, the men whom women choose to marry earn 50% more income than comparably aged men whom women do not marry" (Buss, 1996, p. 12). These patterns not only are reflected in marriage choices but also influence decisions to divorce (Betzig, 1989; Buckle, Gallup, & Rodd, 1996). In the most extensive cross-cultural study of the pattern of marital dissolution ever conducted, Betzig (1989) found that "inadequate support is reported as cause for divorce in 21 societies and ascribed exclusively to the husband in all but one unspecified case" (p. 664).

In societies in which material resources are not readily accumulated, female choice is often influenced by the social status of prospective marriage partners, as exemplified by studies of the Yanomamö Indians of Venezuela (Chagnon, 1974, 1977). The Yanomamö are characterized by frequent raiding and small-scale warfare among different villages (Chagnon, 1988). Under these conditions, men who are skilled at political negotiations (e.g., organizing across-village feasts), who are fierce warriors (i.e., having killed one or more people), or both enjoy a higher social status than other men, although they generally do not differ from other men in terms of control of material resources (Hames, 1996). In comparison to other men, these high-status men have more wives—marriage appears to reflect a combination of female choice and negotiations among male-kin groups—and they receive more food tributes from other families in their village, as is found with the Ifalukese (Betzig & Turke, 1992; Hames, 1996). The net result is that women (and their children) who marry these men do not suffer nutritionally in comparison to monogamously married women, and they may be better treated by other group members, as a consequence of their marriage (Hames, 1992, 1996; K. Hill & Kaplan, 1988). Of course, many of these women might prefer to be monogamously married to these high-status men but are not able to achieve this end because of the competing reproductive interests of their husbands.

In other words, for the Yanomamö and all other human beings, except perhaps ruthless despots (see Betzig, 1986), one's preference for a marriage partner (or partners) and one's actual marriage partner might not be the same. Because of this, social–psychological studies of explicit preferences for marriage partners are an important adjunct to the above-described research on actual marriage choices, as these studies appear to more clearly capture the processes associated with any evolved social and psychological mechanisms involved in reproductive behaviors (e.g., Buss, 1996; Buss & Schmitt, 1993; Cosmides & Tooby, 1994; see the *Psychological Control Mechanisms* section of chapter 6). In other words, social–psychological studies provide insights into the mate-choice preferences that would be expressed when such choices are unencumbered by the realities of social life.

Research on marriage preferences has been conducted throughout the world and supports the position that female choice is influenced by the quantity and quality of resources that might be provided by a prospective husband. The most extensive of these studies was conducted by Buss (1989b). Here, 37 samples of men and women—totaling more than 10,000 people—across 33 countries, six continents, and five islands were administered a survey on their mate-choice preferences. Most relevant to the current discussion is the pattern of sex differences for items associated with the prospective mate's financial prospects and the associated psychological and behavioral indicators (i.e., ambition and industriousness). Women rated "good financial prospect" higher than men did in all 37 cultures, although the differences were not statistically significant in one sample (Spain). In 29 samples, women's ratings of the importance of the "ambition and industriousness" of a prospective mate were significantly higher than men's ratings, and higher, but not significantly so, in 5 other samples. In only 1 sample were men's ratings significantly higher than those of women's, the Zulu of South Africa. Buss suggested that this finding reflected the high level of physical labor (e.g., house building) expected of Zulu women.

Hatfield and Sprecher (1995) found the same pattern for groups of college students in the United States, Japan, and Russia. In all three cultures, women valued a prospective mate's potential for success, earnings, status, and social position more highly than men did. A meta-analysis of research conducted in this area from 1965 to 1986 revealed the same result (Feingold, 1992a). Across studies, it was found that about three out of four women rated SES as being more important in a prospective mate than the average man did: Or stated otherwise, only about one out of four men rated the SES of a prospective mate more highly than the average woman did. Studies conducted before 1965 support the same conclusion (e.g., R. Hill, 1945), as does a more recent study of a nationally (United States) representative sample of unmarried adults (Sprecher, Sullivan, & Hatfield, 1994). In this study, it was found that—across age and ethnic status (Black and White)—women preferred husbands who were better educated than they were and who earned more money than they did.

Wise preferences, it seems. A recent study of more than 1,800 Hungarians who were 35 years of age or older, and thus not likely to have more children, indicated that women who had married older and better educated men had, on average, more children, were less likely to get divorced, and reported higher levels of marital satisfaction than women who married younger, less educated, or both, men (Bereczkei & Csanaky, 1996; see also Brown & Hotra, 1988). In yet another study, it was found that for college women, the minimally acceptable earning potential of a prospective husband was the 70th percentile—on the basis of earning potential alone, 70% of men were eliminated from the pool of potential marriage partners. The corresponding figure for college men was the 40th percentile—the pool of potential mates included women with a below average earning potential (Kenrick, Sadalla, Groth, & Trost, 1990).

The female preference for relatively high-status marriage partners is also found in studies of singles ads and in the themes that emerge in popular fiction novels (e.g., Greenlees & McGrew, 1994; Whissell, 1996). As an example, in a study of the content of 1,000 "lonely hearts" advertisements, Greenlees and McGrew found that women were three times more likely than men to seek financial security in a prospective partner. Studies of the themes in classic and popular works of fiction provide a window into the psychological control mechanisms (see chapter 6) that motivate reproductive activities, mechanisms that are largely unencumbered by the dynamics of actual mate choices. Free-market choices indicate that, on average, women prefer romance novels and men prefer adventure novels, those involving male–male competition and uncommitted sex. Whissell found the same themes across 25 contemporary romance novels and 6 classic novels that have traditionally appealed to women more than to men, including two stories from the Old Testament—written about 3,000 years ago. In these stories, the male protagonist is almost always an older, socially dominant, and wealthy man who ultimately invests his resources in the woman protagonist and her children.

Personal and Behavioral Attributes

Although female choice is influenced by the social status and the wealth of a prospective husband, these in and of themselves are not typically enough. In fact, socially dominant men are often arrogant, self-serving, and generally inclined to pursue their own reproductive interests, which often involve a preference for multiple mating partners rather than investment in a single woman and her children (Betzig, 1986; Pratto, 1996). The personal and behavioral characteristics of prospective husbands then become an important consideration in the ultimate choice of a marriage partner, as these characteristics provide information on the ability and the willingness of the man to make a long-term investment in the woman and their children (Buss, 1994).

Across a wide array of personal and behavioral attributes, except for age and physical attractiveness, women are generally more selective in their preferences for marriage partners than men are (e.g., Feingold, 1992a; Hatfield & Sprecher, 1995; Kenrick et al., 1990), which is in keeping with the prediction that the sex that invests the most in offspring will choose mates more carefully than the sex that invests the least (G. A. Parker & Simmons, 1996; Trivers, 1972). In addition to ambition, industriousness, and social dominance, women rate the emotional stability and the family orientation of prospective marriage partners more highly than men do. There are, however, a number of attributes that are rated highly by both women and men, in particular whether the prospective mate is kind and understanding as well as intelligent. In fact, Buss (1989b) found that women rated a prospective mate who was "kind–understanding" and "intelligent" more highly than a prospective mate who was neither of these, but who had high earning potential. These patterns suggest that women prefer mates who are socially dominant but also intelligent, sensitive, and willing to invest in a family (Buss, 1994).

Ache women seem to have similar preferences, indicating that they desire handsome, kind, and strong (i.e., men of good character) husbands (Feingold, 1992a; K. Hill & Hurtado, 1996). An interview with an Ache woman illustrates these preferences:

KIM HILL: Achipura, what kind of man could get many women, what kind did women love, the kind who could easily find a wife?

ACHIPURAGI: He had to be a good hunter.

KIM HILL: So if a man was a good hunter he could easily find a wife?

ACHIPURAGI: No, not just a good hunter. A good hunter could find a wife, but a man needed to be strong.

KIM HILL: When you say strong, do you mean a man who could beat up others in a club fight?

ACHIPURAGI: No, women don't like those men. Women don't like men who love to hit others. I mean a strong man. One who would walk far to hunt, one who would carry heavy loads. I mean a man who would work hard when everyone was tired, or build a hut when it was cold and rainy. I mean a man who was strong. A man who could endure and not get tired.

KIM HILL: Did women love big men then [i.e., men of large body size]?

ACHIPURAGI: No, they would love a small man or a large man, but he had to be strong.

KIM HILL: What other men would be able to acquire a wife easily?

ACHIPURAGI: A man who was "a good man."

KIM HILL: What does it mean, "a good man"?

ACHIPURAGI: A good man is one who is handsome [attractive face]. One who is nice and smiles and tells jokes. A "good man" is a man whom women love. (K. Hill & Hurtado, 1996, p. 228)

Many women also prefer men with whom they can develop an intimate and emotionally satisfying relationship (Buss, 1994; MacDonald, 1992), although this preference appears to be more common in middle-class and upper-middle-class Western culture than in many other cultures or, in fact, in the working-class of Western societies (Argyle, 1994). "Emotional satisfaction is central to white middle-class Euroamerican marriages because the Euroamerican family is so mobile, nucleated, isolated, and far away from relatives so that emotionally close relationships are hard to come by. . . . Husband–wife emotional satisfaction is not as critical for the Aka as it is for Euroamericans" (Hewlett, 1992b, p. 170). This is not to say that emotional satisfaction, or the development of a pair-bond, is not important or not preferred by Aka women, or for women in other cultures, but that it is not as high a priority in mate-choice decisions as it is in Western culture (MacDonald, 1992). In many other contexts, women are more focused on keeping their children alive than on developing intimacy with their husbands.

Nevertheless, studies of sex differences in the pattern of jealousy reactions suggest that emotional commitment is an important aspect of a long-term relationship for many women (Buss, Larsen, & Westen, 1996; Buss, Larsen, Westen, & Semmelroth, 1992; Geary, Rumsey, Bow-Thomas, & Hoard, 1995; but see DeSteno & Salovey, 1996; C. R. Harris & Christenfeld, 1996). These studies indicate that women, more than men, show greater self-reported and physiological distress to a partner's emotional infidelity—developing an attachment to another women—than to his sexual infidelity; whereas men, as a group, show the opposite pattern. The results of a more recent study suggest that women's tendency toward emotional jealousy varies across the menstrual cycle (see Figure 8.1 and the associated text for related discussion). When estrogen levels are relatively low (during menstruation), women appear to be relatively more sexually jealous (i.e., they show the same pattern that is found in men). When estrogen levels are relatively high, in contrast, women, on average, are relatively more emotionally jealous than sexually jealous (Gaulin, Silverman, Phillips, & Reiber, 1997), suggesting that the strength of the desire for intimacy with one's mate might be moderated by sex hormones.

Although the degree of the sex difference in the tendency toward emotional and sexual jealousy varies across contexts (see Geary et al., 1995), and apparently across the menstrual cycle, it is consistent with the finding that for many women intimacy is required before the development of a sexual relationship (Oliver & Hyde, 1993). Buss (1994) has argued that in many contexts, intimacy can be used to predict the likelihood of the man's future commitment to a woman and her offspring. At the same time, the delay of sexual relations until intimacy has developed can often discourage men who are primarily interested in short-term sexual relationships; that is, men who will not invest in any resulting children (Buss, 1994; Buss & Schmitt, 1993; L. Paul & Hirsch, 1996; Symons, 1979).

Physical Attributes and Parasite Resistance

Ache women are not alone in their preference for handsome husbands. In the earlier noted examples of classical literature and romance novels, the male protagonist is almost always socially dominant, wealthy, and handsome (e.g., Whissell, 1996). Indeed, a female preference for an attractive mate makes biological sense (Betzig, 1997; Gangestad, 1993). Not only are handsome husbands more likely to sire "sexy sons," they might also be healthier, be more disease resistant, and have had fewer difficulties during their physical development (Gangestad, Thornhill, & Yeo, 1994; Grammer & Thornhill, 1994; Singh, 1995b; Thornhill & Gangestad, 1993, 1994; however, see D. Jones & Hill, 1993). Although it is not certain, it appears that the physical attributes that women find attractive in men might be condition-dependent indicators of the man's physical and genetic health, just as the long symmetric tail feathers of the male barn swallow (Hirundo rustica) or the comb length of the male red jungle fowl (Gallus gallus) are indicators of their genetic and physical qualities (Møller, 1994a; Thornhill & Møller, 1997; Zahavi, 1975; Zuk et al., 1990); of course, women are not explicitly aware of this relationship (see the Architecture section of chapter 6 for discussion of implicit and explicit knowledge).

Figure 5.1 presents an illustration of the physical and facial features that most women would prefer in a marriage partner, all other things being equal. Basically, it appears that physically attractive men are somewhat taller than average and have an athletic (but not too muscular) and symmetric body shape, including a 0.9 waist-to-hip ratio (WHR) and shoulders that are somewhat wider than their hips (creating a V shape; Barber, 1995; S. P. Beck, Ward-Hull, & McClear, 1976; Cunningham, Barbee, & Pike, 1990; Gangestad et al., 1994; Hatfield & Sprecher, 1995; Pierce, 1996; Singh, 1995b; Thornhill, Gangestad, & Comer, 1995). The facial features

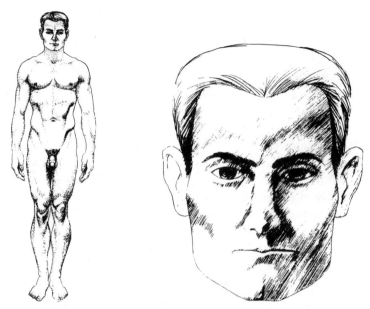

Figure 5.1. Illustration of the physical and facial attributes of men that are rated as attractive by women. Illustration by Christopher Nadolski.

that women rate as attractive include somewhat larger than average eyes, a large smile area, and prominent cheekbones and chin (Barber, 1995; Cunningham et al., 1990).

Symmetric body and facial features, along with prominent cheek-bones and masculine chin, appear to be good indicators of genetic varia-bility (which is important for disease resistance), lack of illness during development, and current physical health (Barber, 1995; Thornhill & Gangestad, 1993). For instance, the development of prominent cheek-bones and a masculine chin is related to androgen levels during puberty (Tanner, 1990). Chronic illness during this time can suppress androgen secretion, which, in turn, would result in the development of less promi-nent cheekbones, a more feminine-looking chin, and, as a result, lower rated physical attractiveness (Thornhill & Gangestad, 1993; see Figure 2.7 and the *Sex Hormones and Parasites* section of chapter 2).

Shackelford and Larsen (1997) found that men with less symmetric facial features were less physically active, manifested more symptoms of depression and anxiety, and reported more minor physical problems (e.g., colds, headaches, gastrointestinal problems, and sleeping problems) than their peers with more symmetric faces. Men with asymmetric faces and body features also have higher basal metabolic rates, somewhat lower IQs, and fewer sexual partners than their more symmetric peers (Furlow, Armijo-Prewitt, Gangestad, & Thornhill, 1997; Gangestad & Thornhill, 1997; Manning, Koukourakis, & Brodie, 1997; Thornhill & Møller, 1997). Nevertheless, facial attractiveness is not always a reliable indicator of physical health. Kalick and his colleagues found that rated physical attractiveness was correlated with physical health but only for individuals in the midrange of attractiveness (Kalick, Zebrowitz, Langlois, & Johnson, 1998). The physical health of relatively unattractive people tended to be underestimated, whereas the physical health of very attractive people tended to be overestimated.

Several other lines of evidence are consistent with the position that physical indicators of disease resistance and general health influence human mate choices. In one approach to this issue, Low (1988, 1990) argued that living in environments with high levels of parasites would increase variability in the health of men and thereby create considerable individual differences in physical attractiveness. Differences in attractiveness, in turn, would reduce the number of acceptable male marriage partners and thereby increase the degree of polygyny. In keeping with this prediction, an analysis of 186 cultures revealed a strong relation between the number of parasites the population is exposed to, or degree of pathogen stress, and degree of polygyny (Low, 1990): As the degree of pathogen stress increases, the number of unmarried men increases. Gangestad and Buss (1993) found that women and men in these same regions of the world rated the importance of the physical attractiveness of a prospective mate more highly than individuals living in regions of the world with lower levels of pathogen stress did, a pattern consistent with the view that physical attractiveness is oftentimes an indicator of physical and perhaps genetic health (Thornhill & Gangestad, 1993).

There is also some evidence that female mate choice is based on MHC dissimilarity, in keeping with the position that one function of sexual reproduction is to create a variable immune system (Hamilton & Zuk, 1982); recall that MHC includes the genes that code for certain immune responses (see the *Why Sexual Reproduction?* section of chapter 2). In fact, the finding that women are, on average, considerably more sensitive than men to pheromonelike odors, which appear to provide information on MHC genotype, and that sensitivity to these odors increases with increases in estrogen levels but decreases with increases in androgen levels is consistent with the view that the evolution of female choice in humans is related, in part, to the ability to detect implicitly the MHC genotype of potential mating partners (Apanius et al., 1997; Herz & Cahill, 1997; Velle, 1987).

Indeed, Wedekind and his colleagues found that women who were not taking oral contraceptives—oral contraceptives appear to change body odor preferences—rated the body odors of MHC-dissimilar men as more pleasant and sexy than the odors of MHC-similar men (Wedekind et al., 1995). Moreover, odors from MHC-dissimilar men were more likely to remind these women of their husbands or ex-husbands than the odors from MHC-similar men. In a 5-year prospective study of fecundity (i.e., the capacity to bear children) in Hutterite couples, Ober and her colleagues found evidence for MHC-based disassortative mating (i.e., mate choices based on MHC differences) and that MHC-dissimilar couples were able to conceive more quickly (in 2 months vs. 5 months) and tended to have fewer spontaneous abortions than MHC-similar couples (Ober, Elias, Kostyu, & Hauck, 1992; Ober et al., 1997).

Hedrick and Black (1997), in contrast, found no evidence of MHC-based disassortative mating in 194 couples from 11 South American Indian tribes. Hedrick and Black's results are difficult to interpret, however. The marriage systems varied greatly across these 11 tribes, and, as a result, the overall degree to which female choice influenced marriage patterns was not clear. In other words, MHC-based disassortative mating might only be found in human populations in which women exercise considerable freedom in choosing a marriage partner and might not be evident in populations in which female choice is suppressed by dominant men.

Although the research conducted thus far has not provided a definitive answer to the question, it is consistent with the view that female choice of mating partners is sensitive to indicators of the physical and, perhaps, the genetic health of prospective mates, as reflected, in part, in the man's physical attractiveness (Thornhill & Gangestad, 1993). A series of studies by Graziano and his colleagues qualifies this pattern of female choice, however (Graziano, Jensen-Campbell, Shebilske, & Lundgren, 1993). Here, it was found that women's ratings of the physical attractiveness of men, but not men's ratings of women, were somewhat moderated by the ratings of their peers, especially if the rating was negative. Other studies suggest that women's ratings of the physical attractiveness of men were also influenced by their perceived social dominance (e.g., Townsend, Kline, & Wasserman, 1995). Thus, women's ratings of the attractiveness of men appear to be influenced by social comparisons or other social processes, above and beyond men's actual physical characteristics (see the *Social Learning* section of chapter 2).

Alternative Mating Strategies

Under some conditions, women can benefit by engaging in a sexual relationship with a man other than their social or marital partners or by engaging in serial relationships (i.e., practicing polyandry). With respect to the former, extrapair sex is in fact common, even in species in which males and females are socially monogamous. With the monogamous barn swallow, for instance, females will often engage in extrapair copulations with males that are of a higher quality—those with long and symmetric tail features—than their mate (Møller, 1994a); recall that offspring sired by males with long and symmetric tail feathers have higher survival rates than offspring sired by other males (see the *Female Choice* section of chapter

2). Birkhead and Møller (1996; see also Westneat & Sherman, 1997) estimated that across 20 socially monogamous species of bird, in which male provisioning improved offspring survival rates but was not absolutely essential for offspring survival, about 15% of nestlings were sired by extrapair males.

For humans, the definitive study of cockoldry rates has not yet been conducted, although it is clear that cockoldry does occur in our species. In the earlier mentioned (chapter 4) study conducted by Essock-Vitale and McGuire (1988), it was found that about one out of five American women reported engaging in at least one extramarital affair and that at least some of these affairs resulted in pregnancy. Bellis and Baker (1990) found that female-initiated infidelity often occurred around the time of ovulation and within a few days of a sexual relationship with the husband or boyfriend; the timing of these encounters, in turn, would promote competition between the sperm of these two men (Baker, 1996). Moreover, the extrapair copulations were less likely to involve the use of contraceptives than the copulations with the main partner were. The overall pattern indicates a greater than 50% chance of any resulting child being sired by the extrapair partner. Other studies suggest that men are cuckolded (i.e., raise the child of another man) anywhere from 1% of the time to more than 25% of the time, depending on the population under study (e.g., Bellis & Baker, 1990; Betzig, 1997; Flinn, 1988a; Gaulin, McBurney, & Brakeman-Wartell, 1997; Potthoff & Whittinghill, 1965), although these estimates should be interpreted with caution.

Whatever the cockoldry rate, male sexual jealousy makes women's extramarital affairs potentially dangerous, and, thus, these affairs are likely to be engaged in only if they result in some benefit to the woman or her children (Daly et al., 1982; Hrdy, 1997). The finding that women rate physical attractiveness and social dominance as relatively more important in a short-term than in a long-term sexual relationship suggests that women might sometimes engage in extramarital affairs to enhance the genetic quality (and variability) of their children and, perhaps, to promote competition between the sperm of different men (Bellis & Baker, 1990; Buss & Schmitt, 1993; Campbell, 1995; Gangestad & Simpson, 1990; Kenrick, Groth, Trost, & Sadalla, 1993; Schmitt & Buss, 1996; Townsend et al., 1995).

Under other conditions, a woman having multiple mating partners can result in increased social and material support for her children (Buss, 1994). The clearest example of this is found with the Ache, in which children whose father has died or left the group are often killed by other group members. As an apparent counterstrategy to reduce this risk, Ache women will often have sexual relations with several men. In other words, having several mates appears to be a strategy to confuse paternity, as appears to be the case with many other primate species in which infanticide is a risk (Hrdy, 1979, 1997). Any man with whom the women has had an affair just before or during the pregnancy is called a *secondary father*. K. Hill and Hurtado (1996) found that the mortality rate of children with one secondary father was roughly one half the mortality rate of children with no secondary father or two or more secondary fathers. Apparently, if paternity is too uncertain, as is the case with many secondary fathers, men will not protect children. The sexual behavior of Ache women thus appears, at least in part, to be a social strategy designed to enlist men to help to protect their children in a risky social environment (see also Smuts, 1985, 1995).

Under conditions in which most men do not have the material or social resources to support a family, many women appear to adopt a strategy of developing relatively short-term relationships with a number of these men, each of whom provides some type of investment (e.g., money or child care) during the course of the relationship (Buss & Schmitt, 1993; Campbell, 1995). In essence, these women are practicing polyandry. In recounting a study conducted in the Dominican Republic, Lancaster (1989) noted that in comparison to women monogamously married to men with low incomes,

> women who excluded males from the domestic unit and maintained multiple liaisons were more fecund, had healthier children with fewer pre- and post-natal mishaps, were able to raise more children over the age of five, had better nourished children (as measured by protein per capita), and had better psychological adjustment (as measured by self-report and lower maternal blood pressure). (pp. 68–69)

FEMALE–FEMALE COMPETITION

It was noted in chapter 3 that female-on-female aggression is quite common across primate species, although this aggression is almost never as intense (that is, injury inflicting) as male-on-male aggression (Silk, 1993; Smuts, 1987a). In most of these species, female–female competition is over access to high-quality food, not access to mates (see the *Female–Female Competition and Male Choice* section of chapter 3). The situation is more complicated for women, however. Given that men in many societies strive to restrict the access of women to those resources needed to raise their children successfully and that they more generally compete with one another for resource acquisition and control, men, in a sense, become potential "resource objects" to women (Buss, 1994; Hrdy, 1997). In other words, women are expected to compete for access to resource-holding men, just as other female primates compete with one another for the resources needed to survive and to raise their offspring.

Although women sometimes seek and might compete for short-term mating partners (Gangestad & Simpson, 1990), the intensity and focus of female–female competition appears to be for marriage partners (Schmitt & Buss, 1996). In middle-class Western culture, female–female competition involves a combination of presenting themselves in ways that mirror the attributes associated with male choice of mating partners, such as physical attractiveness, and derogating these same attributes in potential competitors (Buss, 1988; Cashdan, 1993; Schmitt & Buss, 1996; S. Walters & Crawford, 1994). Buss and Shackelford (1997) found that the same tactics used to attract mates were often used to keep them. For instance, women married to ambitious men with relatively high incomes (i.e., men of high mate value) used more mate retention tactics, such as enhancing her appearance and monitoring his activities, than women married to less prosperous men.

Other studies indicate that female–female competition also involves indirect forms of aggression (i.e., relational aggression), which include gossip and other tactics that attempt to exclude the competitor from the social group (Bettencourt & Miller, 1996; Björkqvist, Lagerspetz, & Kaukiainen, 1992; Crick & Bigbee, 1998; Crick & Wellman, 1997; Geen, 1990; Grotpeter & Crick, 1996). A sex difference, favoring girls and women, in the use of relational aggression is evident during the preschool years but appears to become especially prominent during early and midadolescence (Crick, Casas, & Mosher, 1997; Crick & Wellman, 1997; Galen & Underwood, 1997; see Campbell, in press, for related discussion). The increase in the magnitude of the sex difference in relational aggression at the time of puberty is important, because intrasexual competition, as related to sexual selection, is almost always most intense during the initial mate-finding period of the life span (Daly & Wilson, 1988a).

Moreover, Van Goozen and her colleagues found that male-to-female transsexuals—who were administered antiandrogens and estrogens—reported a decrease in direct forms of aggression (e.g., physical assault) and an increase in indirect forms of aggression after 3 months of hormonal treatments (Van Goozen, Cohen-Kettenis, Gooren, Frijda, & Van de Poll, 1995). Female-to-male transsexuals, in contrast, were administered testosterone and showed an increase in levels of direct aggression 3 months into the hormonal treatment. The relation between sex hormones and styles of aggression, combined with the increase in the magnitude of the sex difference in relational aggression at around the time of puberty, is consistent with the view that this form of female–female competition is related to sexual selection (Campbell, 1995, in press).

In this view, social gossiping and social exclusion might be an implicit tactic designed to increase social stress, which, as noted in chapter 3, can have adverse reproductive consequences (see the *Female–Female Competition and Male Choice* section; Abbott, 1993; Smuts & Nicolson, 1989). In addition, gossip about competitors often focuses on their sexual fidelity,

which, when in question, can make a woman an undesirable marriage partner. In fact, Campbell (1995) found that in some situations—particularly
those in which there are few men with resources—being called a "slut" is
"fightin'" words for some young women, as illustrated below:

> She started spreading rumors about me saying that I used to sneak out
> in the middle of the night in my night-dress and meet ten boys or
> something, really stupid. . . . Well we were arguing with each other
> about the rumor mainly and she was saying she didn't say it . . . and
> then she started calling me names like that and then she started to
> walk off across the road and she said "I'll get you some time, you
> fucking bitch." And that made me mad because if she was going to
> get me she was going to get me there and then, I mean there was no
> point in getting me later and so I kicked her in the back and she fell
> flat on her face . . . and we started fighting. (Campbell, 1995, pp.
> 115–116)

Campbell (1995) also noted that in "China and Zambia . . . female aggression is principally driven by competition over resources and often includes men. The degree of female economic and social dependence on men
is related to the intensity with which women are prepared to fight to secure
high-status men" (p. 116).

Finally, in some parts of the world, female–female competition appears to involve material resources, such as a dowry (Dickemann, 1981;
Gaulin & Boster, 1990). Although bride-price or bride-service are common, the use of a dowry—in which the bride's family provides resources
to the couple or to the groom's family—occurs in less than 6% of human
societies (Daly & Wilson, 1983; Murdock, 1981). Gaulin and Boster demonstrated that the use of the dowry is found primarily in highly stratified
societies with socially imposed monogamy. Under these conditions, wealthy
men will invest the bulk of their resources in a single woman and her
children, as contrasted with the tendency of wealthy men to invest their
resources in many wives and families in societies in which monogamy is
not socially imposed. The net effect is that the mate value of wealthy men
is much higher in societies with socially imposed monogamy than in polygynous societies. Gaulin and Boster argued that dowry usage is a form of
female–female competition to attract these high-status men as marriage
partners. Similarly, in other societies with socially imposed monogamy, a
woman's financial prospects might contribute to her overall attractiveness
as a marriage partner. In the United States, men do indeed rate the financial prospects of a potential marriage partner as important, although not
as important as her physical attractiveness and not as highly as women
rate the financial prospects of men (Kenrick et al., 1990).

Thus, in relatively affluent contexts—in which monogamy is socially
imposed and many men have the resources to invest in a family—female–
female competition is largely manifested in terms of tactics designed to

attract the attention of men and to derogate potential competitors. These tactics typically center on the women's and their competitors' physical, social (e.g., fidelity), and, in some cases, financial prospects. In these contexts, female–female competition also involves attempts to exclude competitors from the social group, which is achieved by means of relational aggression (e.g., gossiping). As the number of resource-holding men decreases, the intensity of female–female competition over these men increases accordingly and can become quite physical, although not as frequently deadly as male–male competition.

MALE–MALE COMPETITION

Male–male competition and female choice are in some respects different sides of the same coin. As implied in the *Female Choice* section, men will often compete on those dimensions that women desire in marriage partners (i.e., in terms of the acquisition of social and material resources; Buss, 1994; Symons, 1979). More broadly, male–male competition often takes the form of the acquisition of those skills and resources that define success within the wider culture. Indeed, in those preindustrial societies in which male–male competition has been studied, it has consistently been found that a man's cultural success is directly related to his reproductive success (Betzig, 1986; Casimir & Rao, 1995; Irons, 1979, 1993; Klindworth & Voland, 1995). However, it is not always the case that men compete on the basis of those dimensions that women prefer in marriage partners. In many societies—and arguably throughout human evolution—men have competed for sociopolitical power and, when possible, for material resources, and they have used their power to control the sexual behavior of women and other men, independent of female choice (Chagnon, 1979; Hrdy, 1997; Smuts, 1995). An overview of this aspect of male–male competition, as it is expressed in preindustrial societies, is discussed in the first section below, whereas the second section presents a discussion of male–male competition in industrial societies.

Competition in Preindustrial Societies

Like male chimpanzees, men clearly have the capacity for intense and oftentimes deadly one-on-one, as well as coalition-based, competition, although men are not mindlessly driven to physical aggression nor are they biologically destined to physical combat. As with other primates, physical aggression is used only when social displays or other social rituals fail to resolve issues of social dominance or other social conflicts. "Even the most bellicose societies did not award the best warriors or captains their highest positions of status or leadership. Instead, these rewards were reserved for men who, although they were often expected to be brave and skilled in war, were more proficient in the arts of peace" (Keeley, 1996, p. 144). Nonetheless, the potential for aggression and violence by men can be neither denied nor underestimated (Daly & Wilson, 1990; Wrangham & Peterson, 1996).

At times, coalition-based male-on-male aggression appears to be related to natural disasters or other factors (e.g., drought) that diminish the ability of social groups to survive in their current ecology. These groups then move into the territory of neighboring groups, which, in turn, will sometimes lead to deadly conflict (Keeley, 1996). Under these conditions, male aggression is influenced more by natural than sexual selection. Under many other conditions, however, male-on-male aggression—whether one on one or coalition based—is related to the establishment and the maintenance of social dominance, the acquisition of the resources needed to support reproduction (e.g., stealing cattle to pay bride-price), or the direct capture of women. Such conflict often has reproductive consequences for both men and women and is thus directly related to sexual selection.

As with other primates and other mammals in general, in preindustrial societies, the reproductive risks and rewards of intrasexual competition are far greater for men than for women (Chagnon, 1979; Daly & Wilson, 1983, 1990; Trivers, 1972). In the Yanomamö, for instance, the single most reproductively successful man, Shinbone, had 43 children, as compared with 14 children for the single most successful woman. Shinbone's father "had 14 children, 143 grandchildren, 335 great grandchildren and . . . 401 great-great grandchildren" (Chagnon, 1979, p. 380); the two latter estimates are low because many of the descendants of Shinbone's father are still in their reproductive years. At the same time, other Yanomamö men have had few or no children (see also Jaffe et al., 1993). The pattern of greater reproductive variance for men than for women is especially evident in societies in which ecological or social conditions (e.g., laws that prohibit polygynous marriages) do not limit the potential of individual men to sire offspring with many women. Under these conditions, male–male competition has a potentially profound influence on the reproductive success of individual men (Daly & Wilson, 1983).

Given this, it is not surprising that one-on-one and coalition-based male-on-male aggression is a common feature of traditional hunter–gatherer, horticultural, pastoral, and agricultural societies. Ambushes, raids, and occasional larger scale battles among fraternal kin groups from neighboring villages or bands are common features of social life in about 90% of these societies (Ember, 1978; Keeley, 1996); many of the remaining societies are relatively isolated or politically subjugated to larger groups (Keeley, 1996). In more than one half of these societies, intergroup conflict occurs more or less continuously (i.e., at least once a year) and ultimately results in the death of about 30% of the group's young men, on average (Chagnon, 1988; Keeley, 1996; D. R. White & Burton, 1988). Across societies, motives for these conflicts include "blood revenge" (i.e., retaliation for the killing of a member of the kin group), economic gain (i.e., land, booty, and slaves), capture of women, and personal prestige. The latter typically involves the accumulation of culturally important trophies, such as the scalps or the heads of competitors, that influence the man's reputation and social status within the community, which will, in turn, influence his desirability as a marriage partner.

The pattern of intergroup aggression cannot be attributed to interference from modern societies, as warfare is typically less frequent after contact with modern societies (Keeley, 1996). Nor can this pattern be considered a relatively recent phenomenon, as archaeological evidence suggests frequent intergroup aggression over at least the past 20,000–30,000 years (see Keeley, 1996).

> For example, at Crow Creek in South Dakota, archaeologists found a mass grave containing the remains of more than 500 men, women, and children who had been slaughtered, scalped, and mutilated during an attack on their village a century and a half before Columbus's arrival (ca. A.D. 1325). The attack seems to have occurred just when the village's fortifications were being rebuilt. All the houses were burned, and most of the inhabitants were murdered. This death toll represented more than 60 percent of the village's population, estimated from the number of houses to have been about 800. The survivors appear to have been primarily young women, as their skeletons are underrepresented among the bones; if so, they were probably taken as captives. (Keeley, 1996, p. 68)

The capture of women and the murder of competitors have nothing to do with female choice—it is simply men pursuing their reproductive interests at the expense of other human beings (D. R. White & Burton, 1988). That men sometimes benefit from such aggression is clear. In many preindustrial societies and throughout human history, coalition-based aggression is often associated with personal gain, including more wives, larger territories, the acquisition of slaves, and, most important, higher reproductive success. Betzig (1993), in fact, has argued that in every one of the first six civilizations—ancient Mesopotamia, Egypt, Aztec (Mexico), Inca (Peru), and imperial India and China—"powerful men mate with hundreds of women, pass their power on to a son by one legitimate wife, and take the lives of men who get in their way" (p. 37; see also Betzig, 1986). The same is true, although on a much smaller scale, in many regions of the world today. In the Yanomamö, about two out of five men have participated in at least one murder, and those who have killed have a higher social status than men who have not killed, and two and one-half times as many wives, and about three times as many children, on average (Chagnon, 1988). In the Ache, about one out of five men has participated in at least one murder and has more surviving children than men who have not murdered (K. Hill & Hurtado, 1996; see also Betzig, 1986).

Reproduction-related male-on-male aggression is even evident in societies that do not routinely engage in coalition-based intergroup warfare. The Gebusi of New Guinea, for instance, are described as being primarily a gatherer society (with some hunting) with male social life "markedly devoid of male status rivalry. Instead, there is a pronounced aura of diffuse male friendship and camaraderie" (Knauft, 1987, p. 460). Yet, the Gebusi have one of the highest per capita murder rates in the world, including a precontact homicide rate that was estimated to be more than 10 times that found in most major U.S. cities. Although Knauft argued that Gebusi murders are related to superstition (i.e., sorcery) and psychological factors and not to reproduction, he nonetheless concluded that "sorcery homicide is ultimately about male control of marriageable women" (Knauft, 1987, pp. 465–466). Similar patterns are found in other so-called peaceful societies (Daly & Wilson, 1988a; Ember, 1978; Keeley, 1996; Knauft, 1987).

Finally, there is some evidence to support the position that the pattern of male aggression is influenced by sex hormones, although the relation between hormonal levels and patterns of behavioral aggression is far from consistent (Archer, 1991, 1994; J. A. Harris, Rushton, Hampson, & Jackson, 1996; Reinisch, 1981). Testosterone levels, for instance, are sometimes found to be correlated with aggression, particularly with antisocial behavior and other people's ratings of aggressive behavior (as contrasted with self-reports), but this relationship has not always been found (Archer, 1991; J. A. Harris et al., 1996; Susman et al., 1987). The overall relation between testosterone and behavioral aggression appears to be mediated by a more complex set of relations among social dominance, past history of aggression, and current contextual factors (e.g., the outcome of competition), among other things (C. T. Halpern, Udry, Campbell, & Suchindran, 1993; Sapolsky, 1993; Schaal, Tremblay, Soussignan, & Susman, 1996). At this point, it appears that testosterone is more strongly related to male— but apparently not to female—dominance seeking than to behavioral aggression per se, although dominance seeking can, at times, involve male-on-male aggression (Mazur & Booth, in press).

Competition in Industrial Societies

In relation to the pattern found in many preindustrial cultures, the level of male-on-male physical violence is low in industrial societies (Daly & Wilson, 1988a; Ember, 1978; Keeley, 1996). When male-on-male aggression does escalate to homicide in industrial societies, the precipitating events are often centered on sexual jealousy or male status competition, as is the case in preindustrial cultures (Daly & Wilson, 1988a; M. Wilson & Daly, 1997). Nonetheless, in industrial societies with socially imposed monogamy, male–male competition is most generally focused on the acquisition of social and material indicators of cultural success. Or stated otherwise, in modern society, middle- and upper-middle-class men typically compete to acquire those social and material resources (e.g., SES) that influence female choice of mating and marriage partners.

Before wide-scale industrialization, it appears that the relation between cultural success and reproductive success was the same in modern nations as is currently found in preindustrial cultures (Betzig, 1995). On the basis of extensive parish and government birth, marriage, and death records between 1760 and 1810, Klindworth and Voland (1995) were able to reconstruct the relation between social status and long-term reproductive outcomes for Krummhörn men in northwest Germany. Information from tax records indicated that there were large differences in the wealth (land and cattle ownership) held by different families. In comparison to other men, the wealthiest Krummhörn men had sired more children— primarily because they married younger wives—and had more children survive to adulthood. Most important, across generations, non-elite men were four times more likely to experience an extinction of their lineage (i.e., reach a point at which there were no surviving direct descendants) than their elite cohorts.

However, in industrial nations today there is little or sometimes a negative relation between cultural success (i.e., SES) and reproductive success (e.g., H. S. Kaplan, Lancaster, Bock, & Johnson, 1995). Men with higher earnings and all of the trappings of cultural success, such as a college education and a professional occupation, do not sire more children than their less successful peers. This pattern has led some investigators to argue that any evolved tendencies associated with male–male competition are no longer relevant in technologically advanced societies (Vining, 1986). Pérusse (1993, 1994), in contrast, argued that the combination of socially imposed monogamy and contraception obscures the relation between cultural success and mating success in these societies.

A study of the relation between SES and the sexual behavior of more than 400 men from Quebec supported this position (Pérusse, 1993, 1994). Here, cultural success was defined in terms of income, educational level, and occupational status (i.e., SES), and sexual behavior in terms of the number of reported sexual partners and the overall frequency of coitus. The combination of the number of sexual partners and frequency of coitus was used to derive an estimate of the likelihood of paternity, in the absence of birth control. For unmarried men 30 years of age and older, SES was strongly and positively related to individual differences in the likelihood of paternity, explaining as much as 63% of the individual differences on this measure (see also Pérusse, 1994). As in other human societies and with most other primates, higher status men reported more sexual partners and more overall sexual activity than their lower status peers. This relationship was somewhat lower, but still positive, in younger unmarried men, as might be expected, given the length of time needed to acquire indicators of cultural success in modern societies (e.g., higher education).

Thus, men in industrial societies compete in terms of the indicators of success in these cultures—primarily in terms of educational and occupational status (e.g., Pratto, 1996; Pratto, Stallworth, Sidanius, & Siers, 1997)—just as men in other societies compete in terms of the dimensions of cultural success in their societies (e.g., control of cattle or having had murdered). Similarly, across societies, a man's cultural success influences his ability to attract and retain mates (Irons, 1993). It appears that in terms of male–male competition, the primary difference between industrial societies and other societies is that the combination of socially imposed monogamy and birth control in the former eliminates the relation between cultural success and reproductive success in industrial societies (see also Townsend et al., 1995).

MALE CHOICE

Although men do not typically invest as much in the well-being of children as women do, they do invest considerably more than males of most other mammalian species (Clutton-Brock, 1989). In this view, men should show more selectivity in their choice of mating and marriage partners than is evident in most other mammals, and this is indeed the case (Trivers, 1972), especially in societies with ecologically or socially imposed monogamy (Frost, 1998). In these societies, men and women are more similar than different in the criteria they use in selecting a marriage partner (Kenrick et al., 1990). Sex differences are most evident in the desire for and the effort devoted to finding short-term or casual mating partners, as described in the first section below. The second section presents a description of the personal and behavioral attributes that men prefer in marriage partners, and the third, and final, section describes the physical attributes of women that men find attractive.

Alternative Mating Strategies

It was noted earlier that women will often pursue short-term sexual relationships, most typically in situations in which the resources or social support of more than one man is needed to raise their children successfully. For many men, in contrast, the pursuit of short-term sexual relationships is an end in itself, as men who pursue such relationships often benefit reproductively (G. C. Williams, 1966). The issue is not one of polygyny versus monogamy, it is one of paternal investment. Men pursuing a long-term relationship, whether it is a polygynous or monogamous marriage, are typically signaling that they will invest in their children. Men pursuing a short-term relationship invest little, if anything, in their children. Basically, men, more than women, have a mixed reproductive strategy, pursuing short-term, low-investment relationships with some women and long-term, high-investment relationships with others (Buss & Schmitt, 1993; Draper & Harpending, 1988; L. Paul & Hirsch, 1996; Symons, 1979; Townsend et al., 1995; G. D. Wilson, 1997).

The extent of the sex difference in the preference for short-term mates is demonstrated by studies of attitudes toward sexual behavior and sexual fantasy (Symons, 1979). In a meta-analysis of 177 studies conducted in the United States and Canada—representing the responses of more than 125,000 people—on sexual attitudes and sexual behavior, Oliver and Hyde (1993) found rather large sex differences in the attitude toward casual sex and the frequency of masturbation; the latter reflects, in part, a disparity between sexual appetite and the number of sexual partners. About four out of five men had more positive attitudes about casual sex than the average woman, and about six out of seven men reported masturbating more frequently than the average woman. More moderate differences were found, favoring men, in the reported frequency of intercourse and in the number of sexual partners. Women, in contrast, more strongly endorsed the double standard—that premarital sexual activity is less acceptable for women than men—and reported more anxiety and guilt over sex than men did, although these differences were not large.

Moreover, it was found that the sex difference for attitudes toward casual sex did not differ for studies conducted in the 1960s, 1970s, or 1980s, suggesting that this is a relatively stable difference (see also Symons, 1979). Other aspects of sexual behavior and sexual attitudes did change across decades, indicating that many aspects of sexuality are influenced by cultural mores (see also Buss, 1989b). The largest change was found in attitudes toward sexual relationships for couples who are engaged to be married, with women more likely to endorse this type of relationship in the 1980s than in the early 1960s. Thus, as social prohibitions against female sexuality lessened in the United States, the attitudes of women toward sexual relationships showed only selective changes. Women's preference to avoid casual sexual relationships, in comparison to men, remained unchanged, but their willingness to engage in a sexual relationship with a man who had committed to a long-term relationship, and thus future support of their children, increased greatly.

The sexual fantasies of men and women also show some large differences, as exemplified by a study conducted by B. J. Ellis and Symons (1990). In this study, it was found that men were twice as likely as women to report having sexual fantasies at least once a day and were four times as likely to report having fantasized about sex with more than 1,000 different people (8% of women vs. 32% of men). Although there were no sex differences in feelings of guilt over sexual fantasies, men and women differed considerably in the content of their fantasies. Women were two and one-half times more likely than men to report thinking about the personal and emotional characteristics of their partner, whereas men were nearly four times as likely as women to report focusing on the physical characteristics of their partner. Moreover, women were twice as likely as men to report fantasizing about someone with whom they are currently romantically involved with or had been involved with, whereas men were three times as likely to fantasize about having sex with someone they were not involved with and had no intention of becoming involved with.

The sex difference in preferences for short-term mating partners is also illustrated by Kenrick et al.'s (1993) study of the minimally acceptable characteristics of a partner for the following: single date, one-night stand, sexual relations, steady dating, and marriage. Sex differences were smallest for steady dating and marriage—presumably situations in which the man will invest in any children—and largest for a one-night stand. In all, the standards of men dropped considerably for a one-night stand relative to a steady dating or marriage partner; for most attributes, women's standards dropped only slightly for a one-night stand. An example of this pattern is shown in Figure 5.2 for the minimally acceptable level of a partner's intelligence (data from Kenrick et al., 1993, Study 2), although it should be noted that the pattern of sex differences for a one-night stand might well be larger in populations in which birth control is not readily available to women.

Finally, sex and adrenal hormones have been found to be related to sexual interests, behavior, and fantasy (e.g., McClintock & Herdt, 1996; Sherwin, 1988). As an example, for men whose testicles do not produce much testosterone, testosterone replacement therapy has repeatedly been shown to result in increases in sexual activity and sexual fantasy (e.g., Gooren, 1987). Similarly, testosterone implants have been shown to increase, at least over the short term, the sexual fantasies and sexual activity of postmenopausal women (see Sherwin, 1988). Recent research also suggests that adrenal hormones, which include some testosterone (as a metabolite), are involved in sexual attraction to members of the opposite (sometimes the same) sex (McClintock & Herdt, 1996).

Of course, it is not surprising that sex hormones influence sexual interests. The point is that the sex differences in sexual behavior, attitudes, and fantasies are related to the sex differences in exposure to sex and adrenal hormones and thus almost certainly to the sex difference in reproductive strategies, although social mores also influence the sexual behavior of men and women (Dunne et al., 1997).

In all, the pattern of sex differences across studies is consistent with the view that sexual activity is influenced by the costs of reproduction (Trivers, 1972). In situations in which the individual (man or woman) intends to invest in children, a pattern of relatively high mate-choice stan-

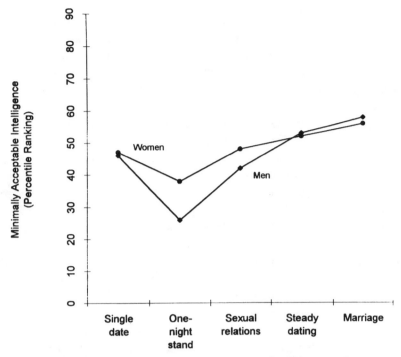

Figure 5.2. Sex differences for the minimal level of intelligence of a partner across a variety of social and sexual situations. This figure is based on data from "Integrating Evolutionary and Social Exchange Perspectives on Relationships: Effects of Gender, Self-Appraisal, and Involvement Level on Mate Selection Criteria," by D. T. Kenrick, G. E. Groth, M. R. Trost, and E. K. Sadalla, 1993, *Journal of Personality and Social Psychology, 64*, p. 960. Copyright 1993 by the American Psychological Association. Reprinted with permission of the authors.

dards and constrained sexual relations is found (see L. Paul & Hirsch, 1996). In situations with relatively low costs, which can only be achieved by men who will not invest in offspring, rather lower mate-choice standards and less constrained sexual attitudes are found. Men, but not women, thus have the option of reproducing with and without investment in offspring (Perper, 1989), and this sex difference appears to drive the extent to which men and women pursue short-term mating opportunities.

Personal and Behavioral Attributes

When choosing a marriage partner, the personal and behavioral attributes that men prefer in women are very similar to the attributes that women prefer in men, although men are not as selective, on average, as women (e.g., Buss, 1989b). Basically, in many societies, all other things being equal, men prefer intelligent marriage partners and ones with whom a compatible and cooperative relationship can be developed. Kenrick et al. (1990), for instance, found that men rated the personality, friendliness, and sense of humor of a potential marriage partner very highly, and just as highly or even more highly than her physical attractiveness (see also Kenrick et al., 1993). Buss also found that—across cultures—both men and women rate intelligence, kindness, and understanding as very important attributes of a marriage partner, and for many men these are relatively more important than her physical attractiveness (see Buss, 1989b).

One area in which men and women differ is the importance of their partner's sexual fidelity, although this is, of course, a relative and not absolute difference. As mentioned earlier, men respond with greater self-reported and physiological distress to a partner's imagined sexual infidelity than women do, and such reactions appear to capture an important aspect of male sexual and proprietary jealousy (Buss et al., 1992; Daly et al., 1982; Dickemann, 1981; Geary et al., 1995). In fact, male sexual jealousy appears to be a near universal influence on the dynamics of male–female relationships, including male-on-female aggression and male attempts to control the social and sexual behavior of their partners. The sex difference in jealousy reactions, in turn, reflects differences in maternity and paternity certainty: Maternity is certain, paternity is not, as noted earlier. From this perspective, male sexual jealousy then functions to ensure that men invest in their biological offspring (e.g., Andersson, 1994; Buss & Schmitt, 1993; Daly & Wilson, 1988a; Daly et al., 1982; A. J. Figueredo & McCloskey, 1993; Flinn, 1988a).

The dynamics of male sexual jealousy are nicely illustrated by Flinn's (1988a) extensive observational study of mate guarding in a rural Trinidadian village. In this village, "13 of 79 (16.4%) offspring born . . . during the period 1970–1980 were putatively fathered by males other than the mother's coresident mate. Clearly, mate guarding could have significant effects on fitness" (Flinn, 1988a, p. 10). Indeed, mate guarding by men, but not by women, was found to be a common feature of male–female relationships, although such guarding varied with the fecundity of the man's partner. For instance, men monitored the activities less diligently and had fewer agonistic interactions with pregnant and older wives than they did with younger and nonpregnant wives. Moreover, men courting the same woman had roughly three times the number of agonistic interactions, such as cussing or fighting with a broken bottle, than male dyads that were not in competition, in keeping with the earlier discussion on male–male competition.

Sexual jealousy not only influences the dynamics of male–female relationships but also is an instigating factor in the dissolution of many of these relationships, as illustrated by Betzig's (1989) cross-cultural study of divorce. In this study, it was found that—except in cases of sterility—adultery was the most common cause of marital dissolution across cultures. "In 25 societies, divorce follows from adultery by either partner; in 54 it

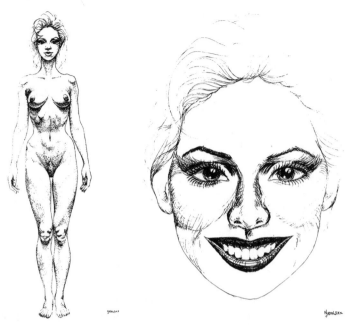

Figure 5.3. Illustration of the physical and facial attributes of women that are rated as attractive by men. Illustration by Christopher Nadolski.

follows only from adultery on the wife's part and in 2 only from adultery on the husband's. If marriage qualifies as near universal, so must the double standard" (Betzig, 1989, p. 658). More seriously, Daly and Wilson's (1988a) seminal study of homicide indicates that one of the most common motives—across cultures—for a man killing his wife is her sexual infidelity, her suspected sexual infidelity, or her "desertion" of him.

Physical Attributes and Fecundity

Although both women and men prefer sexually attractive to unattractive partners, this preference is consistently found to be stronger in men than in women (e.g., Buss, 1989b; Feingold, 1990; Hatfield & Sprecher, 1995). Men's ratings of women's physical attractiveness have been found to be related to a number of specific physical features, including WHR (recall, waist-to-hip ratio), facial features that signal a combination of sexual maturity but relative youth, body symmetry, and age (Buss, 1994; Cunningham, 1986; D. Jones, 1995; D. Jones & Hill, 1993; Kenrick & Keefe, 1992; Møller, Soler, & Thornhill, 1995; Singh, 1993a, 1993b, 1995a; Singh & Young, 1995). This combination of features (illustrated in Figure 5.3) appears to provide an indicator of female fecundity.

It was noted in chapter 3 (*Male Choice* section) that male primates generally prefer to mate with older females, presumably because these females have more surviving offspring than younger females. For humans, the situation is more complicated, as fecundity is not linearly related to age. For women, fecundity is relatively low in the teen years, peaks at about age 25, and then gradually declines to near zero by age 45; the fertility of men declines with age as well but not as sharply as is found with women (Crow, 1997; Menken, Trussell, & Larsen, 1986; J. W. Wood, 1994). Given this pattern, men's mate choices should be relatively more sensitive to age than women's mate choices and more sensitive to age than the mate choices of other male primates, in which conspecific females do not experience menopause. Moreover, men's age-related preferences should be for marriage and mating partners in the age ranges that have the highest fecundity, moderated by issues of compatibility, as noted in the previous section.

Buss's (1989b) earlier described 37-culture study, as well as a number of other studies, support this position (e.g., Buckle et al., 1996; Buss & Shackelford, 1997; Kenrick & Keefe, 1992; Kenrick, Keefe, Gabrielidis, & Cornelius, 1996; Sprecher et al., 1994). Across all 37 cultures, men preferred marriage partners who were younger than themselves. An analysis of marriage patterns in 30 of these cultures indicated that these preferences were put into practice. Across these cultures, brides were, on average, 3 years younger than their grooms. Kenrick and Keefe demonstrated this same pattern across samples from the United States, Germany, Holland, and India. Examination of marriage patterns earlier in this century in the United States and Poro—a small Philippine island—revealed the same pattern, men married women younger than themselves. The marriage patterns also revealed that as men aged, they tended to marry younger and younger women (Buckle et al., 1996; Kenrick & Keefe, 1992). For instance, in 1923, the typical American man in his 20s married a woman who was about 3 years younger than himself, as did the typical Filipino man between 1913 and 1939. In contrast, the typical man in his 60s married a women who was about 15 years younger than himself in the United States and 20 years younger in Poro. A more recent study suggests that these patterns cannot be attributed to a social norm that "men should marry younger women, and women should marry older men." Kenrick et al. (1996) found that the most attractive dating partner for teenage males was a woman about 5 years older than they were (i.e., a woman with higher fecundity than adolescent females the same age or younger than these adolescent males).

The facial features shown in Figure 5.3 portray a combination of relative youth (e.g., large eyes), sexual maturity (e.g., prominent cheek bones), and emotional expressiveness (e.g., large smile area; e.g., Cunningham, 1986; D. Jones, 1995), whereas the body features reflect a combination of health, age, and fecundity (Singh, 1993a). Of these features, the WHR appears to be a particularly important criterion used in men's assessment of the physical attractiveness of women (but see Tassinary & Hansen, 1998). Across age and ethnic and racial status, men rate women of average weight and with a WHR of 0.7 as more attractive than thinner and heavier women with a 0.7 ratio and women of any weight with ratios different than 0.7 (Singh, 1993a, 1993b, Singh & Luis, 1995); the attractiveness of the relative thinness of women varies across cultures and historical periods within cultures (Feingold & Mazzella, 1998), but the preferred WHR appears to be invariant. The WHR, in turn, appears to be an honest indicator of women's health and fecundity. For instance, women with ratios greater than 0.85 are at risk for a number of physiological disorders and appear to have greater difficulty conceiving than women with lower ratios (Singh, 1993a; Zaadstra et al., 1993).

Overall facial and body symmetry also appear to be important influences on men's ratings of women's physical attractiveness, although symmetry appears to be more important for the rated attractiveness of men than women (e.g., Shackelford & Larsen, 1997). One possible exception is breast symmetry. The breasts of nonsuckling women are relatively larger—for no apparent physiological reason—than those found in other primates, suggesting that breast size is a sexually selected characteristic in women (e.g., Barber, 1995; J. Diamond, 1992; E. M. Miller, 1994). There are in fact a number of studies consistent with this view, although they should be considered suggestive and not definitive at this point. Singh (1995a) found that women with asymmetric breasts were rated as less attractive by men than women with symmetric breasts, and Scutt and Manning (1996) found that many asymmetries tend to be lower at the time of ovulation relative to other points in women's cycle; any reduction in asymmetries would, in turn, increase female attractiveness and therefore male sexual interest. Møller and his colleagues found that breast asymmetry was negatively related to fecundity in samples of women from Spain and the United States; that is, women with large breast asymmetries had fewer children, on average, than other women (Møller et al., 1995). Manning, Scutt, Whitehouse, and Leinster (1997) found the same pattern for women in England.

CULTURAL AND HISTORICAL VARIABILITY IN MATING DYNAMICS

At this point, it should be clear that there is not one reproductive strategy for women and another for men, as the strategies adopted by women and by men often vary across contexts and across historical periods (see Hurtado & Hill, 1992, for an illustration). Such variability indicates that for humans—and in fact for many other species (Andersson, 1994)—the reproductive strategies adopted by males and females are sensitive to a host of ecological and social conditions. For humans, the OSR (recall, operational sex ratio, see chapter 2), the proportion of young men in the population, the ecology within which the social group lives, and cultural ideology appear to be particularly important influences on reproductive strategies (MacDonald, 1995a; Mesquida & Wiener, 1996; Pedersen, 1991; Secord, 1983; D. R. White & Burton, 1988).

The OSR is reflected in the proportion of marriage-age men to marriage-age women in the local population, and imbalances in the OSR appear to influence the reproductive strategies adopted by women and men. In industrial societies, one factor that skews the OSR is the population growth rate, with expanding populations yielding an "oversupply" of women. An oversupply of women results from the earlier noted preference of women for slightly older marriage partners and of men for slightly younger marriage partners. With an expanding population, the younger generation of women will be selecting marriage partners from a smaller cohort of older men. The resulting imbalance in the numbers of marriage-age men and women appears to have a profound influence on a number of general social patterns, including divorce rates, sexual mores, and levels of paternal investment, among other things (Guttentag & Secord, 1983; Pedersen, 1991; Secord, 1983). "Sex ratios by themselves do not bring about societal effects, but rather that they combine with a variety of other social, economic, and political conditions to produce the consequent effects on the roles of men and women and the relationships between them" (Guttentag & Secord, 1983, p. 137).

Whatever the cause, during periods when there is an oversupply of women, such as from 1965 through the 1970s in the United States, men are better able to pursue their reproductive preferences than women are. This is so because an oversupply of women decreases the intensity of male–male competition and increases the intensity of female–female competition, so that women, on average, are not in a position to exert their preferences. In comparison to other historical periods, these periods are generally characterized by liberal sexual mores (i.e., many sexual partners for both men and women), high divorce rates, increases in the number of out-of-wedlock births and the number of families headed by single women, increases in female participation in the workforce, and generally lower levels of paternal investment (see Guttentag & Secord, 1983). Basically, during these periods, men, on average, are able to express their preference for a variety of sexual partners and relatively low levels of paternal investment (Pedersen, 1991). A very different pattern is associated with historical periods in which there is an oversupply of men (Guttentag & Secord, 1983). Here, women are better able to enforce their preferences than men are. As a result, these periods are generally characterized by conservative sexual mores and by an increase in the level of commitment of men to marriage, as indexed by declining divorce rates and greater levels of paternal investment (Pedersen, 1991).

Wider population characteristics also appear to influence the dynamics of sexual selection. Mesquida and Wiener (1996) found that populations with a relatively high proportion of young men (15–30 years of age) are characterized by relatively severe levels of coalition-based aggression, as indexed by war-related death rates, although this pattern appears to be moderated by the overall prosperity of the community. Male-on-male aggression is most deadly in populations or segments of a population with relatively scarce resources; that is, in those contexts in which only a minority of men can control enough resources to be a desirable mating or marriage partner (Daly & Wilson, 1988a; M. Wilson & Daly, 1997). Under these conditions, the reproductive potential (e.g., desirability as a marriage partner) of many young men drops, and, as a result, the costs of risky aggression decrease and the potential benefits increase (M. Wilson & Daly, 1985). In preindustrial cultures, expansion into neighboring territories—to acquire resources or to capture women—is one potential and apparently common response to these conditions (Mesquida & Wiener, 1996). However, the ability of achieving such expansion and the likelihood of being victimized during periods of expansion are related to the group's ecology, with geographically isolated groups in resource-poor ecologies being less frequently victimized than groups living in more accessible and resource-rich ecologies (D. R. White & Burton, 1988).

Wider social mores also appear to influence the dynamics of sexual selection, in particular, the formal rules for men's marriages (Alexander, 1979; MacDonald, 1995a; D. R. White & Burton, 1988). In Western culture, the most significant of these rules is the prohibition against polygynous marriages. As described earlier, the most important outcome of a polygynous marriage system is a sometimes dramatic difference in the number of children sired by different men—many men sire no children and a few men sire many children. A polygynous marriage system can thus increase the benefits of male–male competition for the winners and can have dramatic—lineage extinction—consequences for the losers (Daly & Wilson, 1988a). The net result is an increase in the intensity of male–male competition in societies that allow polygynous marriages, including, on average, a relatively high level of male-on-male aggression and a tendency for men to suppress female choice, among other things (e.g., Betzig, 1986; Chagnon, 1977, 1988; D. R. White & Burton, 1988). In these societies, polygynously married men are typically the most socially dominant and wealthiest men of the community and generally consist of less than 15% of the men in these communities (Murdock, 1981). The maintenance of polygyny is thus in the best interest of this minority of socially dominant men and generally not in the best interest of lower and middle-status men or, oftentimes, of women.

Western culture has a long history of monogamous marriages, but polygynous matings by powerful men; that is, high-status men often had a single wife—with whom legitimate heirs were sired—along with access to many other women (e.g., Betzig, 1986, 1992, 1995). In Western Europe, cultural prohibitions against polygynous matings evolved slowing during the Middle Ages, although the extent to which these prohibitions reduced the polygyny of powerful men is debated (see Betzig, 1995; MacDonald, 1995a). Nonetheless, in Western culture, a confluence of factors did eventually lead to a reduction in the ability of powerful men to mate polygynously. These factors appear to include the political activities of influential women and lower and middle-status men, the influence of the Christian church, and, perhaps, the need of high-status men to enlist the cooperation of lower and middle-status men for staging state-level wars and for supporting the infrastructure (e.g., through craft specialization) of the wider society (Alexander, 1979; Betzig, 1986; MacDonald, 1995a). The cooperation of lower and middle-status men is best achieved by providing a social system that levels the reproductive variance of men (i.e., a social system that enables nearly all men to reproduce). In this view, socially imposed monogamy reduces the costs and benefits—the reproductive differentials —of intense male–male competition, so that high levels of aggression do not benefit men in these societies in the same way that they do men in other societies. Also, as described earlier, socially imposed monogamy likely increases the intensity of female–female competition.

Of course, men in Western culture compete and are often violent. Polygynous matings are still achieved by some men through extramarital affairs and through serial relationships. Serial monogamy, for instance, is an alternative form of polygyny—and polyandry from the women's perspective—that appears to have important reproductive consequences for men but not women. In an extensive study of more than 900 Swedish women and men over the age of 40 years—and thus not likely to have more children—Forsberg and Tullberg (1995) found that men, but not women, who engaged in serial monogamy had more children than their same-sex peers who stayed monogamously married. Moreover, even with strictly monogamous marriages, men, and women, compete for the mates they find most attractive.

Several world wars and many smaller scale conflicts attest to the coalition-based aggression found in Western culture, as these conflicts have resulted in the death of about 100 million people in this century alone (Keeley, 1996). Nonetheless, if Western conflicts produced the same level of per capita war-related deaths as is found in many preindustrial societies, the estimated number killed as a result of modern wars jumps from 100 million to about 2 billion (Keeley, 1996). The cultural mores, such as the prohibition of polygynous marriages (and other factors as well, no doubt), associated with Western society appear to have mitigated the intensity of male aggression, but they have far from eliminated it.

Nonetheless, the implications of any such social–ideological influence on the dynamics of sexual selection are important. First, the pattern demonstrates that social mores can influence the expression of evolved social behaviors in humans (MacDonald, 1988, 1995a; D. S. Wilson & Sober, 1994), perhaps primarily by suppressing the expression of these proclivities. Second, the study of sex differences must involve a consideration of cultural and social influences in the way in which these differences are expressed (Rohner, 1976). For instance, the intensity of male-on-male physical aggression and, as a result, the sex difference in levels of aggression are expected to be lower in the middle and upper classes in Western societies than is found in many other contexts (M. Wilson & Daly, 1997). Indeed, laboratory-based social psychological studies, and many field studies, of the pattern of sex differences in aggression reveal only small-to-moderate differences, favoring men (C. A. Anderson & Bushman, 1997; Bettencourt & Miller, 1996; Eagly & Steffen, 1986).

However, such studies almost certainly underestimate the sex difference in the potential for aggression, given that they are typically conducted under controlled, low-cost conditions; that is, conditions that almost never have reproductive or long-term social-status consequences for the participants (see also Knight, Fabes, & Higgins, 1996). The fact that these studies are conducted with populations, college samples, that are socialized in a culture with both relatively mitigated levels of physical male–male competition and relatively heightened levels of female–female competition (because of socially imposed monogamy) also contributes to the small sex differences in these studies. For these samples, male–male competition, for instance, is more frequently expressed in terms of acquiring indicators of cultural success (e.g., a law degree) rather than in terms of physical competition and aggression.

SUMMARY AND CONCLUSION

When considered from a cross-cultural perspective, it is clear that human mate choices are influenced by a host of social, ecological, and personal factors. For instance, in societies characterized by fraternal or ideological coalitions, men tend to work to control the social and material resources of the society. If any such coalition gains control of the society's resources, then there is a tendency for the men that make up this coalition to use the resulting power as a means to actualize their reproductive preferences; that is, despotic regimes often emerge in such societies (see Betzig, 1986). Basically, in many of these societies, coalitions of high-status men achieve social control by means of violence or threats of violence and use this control to reproduce at the expense of lower and middle-status men and with little regard for the preferences of women. In these societies, the most salient feature of sexual selection is male–male competition, as this competition determines male status rank, as in other primates, and, in turn, this rank influences one's ability to exercise one's reproductive preferences (D. R. White & Burton, 1988).

The dynamics of sexual selection differ considerably in societies in which coalitions of men are not able to dominate the social dynamics of the society. The sharpest contrast appears to be between despotic societies and societies in which monogamy is either ecologically or socially imposed (Betzig, 1986; Flinn & Low, 1986); the latter are typically relatively democratic societies (Betzig, 1995). Whether monogamy is ecologically imposed or social ideologically imposed, the net result is the relative restriction of the sociopolitical power of elite men and, as a result, a reduction in the reproductive variance of men. A reduction in reproductive variance, in turn, reduces the costs and benefits of male–male competition. A monogamous mating system is thus generally associated with a decrease in the intensity and a change in the form of male–male competition, along with a fuller expression of female choice and a more intense level of male choice and female–female competition. Male–male competition in these societies essentially shifts from the use of physical violence to control the behavior of other people to the accumulation of indicators of cultural success (Irons, 1979; Keeley, 1996). Achieving cultural success is simply another means of achieving control and increasing one's ability to exercise one's reproductive preferences, but this influence is not achieved by force.

Rather, for men, cultural success increases the ability to exercise one's reproductive preferences, but the exercise of these preferences is moderated more by female choice than by direct male-on-male aggression (Pérusse, 1993). Female choice, in turn, is largely influenced by the social, material, and perhaps the genetic benefits that a marriage or mating partner can provide to a woman and her children. Moreover, with a relatively monogamous mating system, marriage restricts the man's parental investment to one woman, or at least one woman at a time, and her children. Relatively high levels of paternal investment, in turn, appear to result in men being rather more choosy than might otherwise be the case, with male choice largely focused on compatibility with a potential marriage partner and on indicators of the women's likely fecundity (Buss, 1994). The other side of this coin is that as men become more selective in their choice of marriage partners, competition among women for preferable marriage partners increases. Such competition involves enhancing indicators of fecundity (e.g., the use of makeup to produce a more youthful appearance) and derogating and socially excluding competitors.

As predicted by the parental investment model presented in chapter 2 (Trivers, 1972), a monogamous marriage system appears to reduce the social and behavioral differences between men and women, because such a system results in more equal levels of maternal and paternal investment than would otherwise be the case. In societies in which monogamy is not ecologically or socially imposed, the reproductive effort of most men is relatively more focused on mating effort than on parental effort, as is found with the males of nearly all other mammalian species and with most other species of primate (Clutton-Brock, 1989).

6

THE EVOLUTION AND DEVELOPMENT
OF THE HUMAN MIND

Now that a basic understanding of sex differences in reproductive activities has been achieved, the question becomes how are these sex differences related to the psychological and cognitive evolution of men and women? In other words, the sex differences in parental investment, the nature of intrasexual competition, and so forth will necessarily result in sex differences in any supporting motivational, emotional, cognitive, and brain systems and will potentially result in differences in the ways in which these systems develop in boys and girls (Gaulin, 1995). The goal of this chapter is to provide a framework for linking the behavioral and social sex differences described in chapter 4 and chapter 5 to sex differences in motivation, emotion, cognition, brain, and developmental patterns. Sex differences in motivational and emotional patterns are described in this chapter as the basic framework for linking reproductive behaviors with psychological and cognitive evolution is developed. The framework is then used to interpret the pattern of developmental and brain and cognitive sex differences in chapter 7 and in chapter 8, respectively.

The basic premise is that the mind is organized in terms of functional systems, systems designed—by selection pressures—to selectively process information related to survival and reproduction in the environments of our ancestors and to direct the behavior of the individual toward the achievement of survival and reproduction-related goals (Cosmides &

Tooby, 1994; Fodor, 1983; Geary, 1998; Heckhausen & Schulz, 1995; Tooby & Cosmides, 1995). These systems are made up of (a) a motivational component that channels the goal-directed activities of the individual, (b) an emotional component that provides feedback to the individual as to the effectiveness of their goal-directed activities, (c) a cognitive component that allows the individual to process goal-relevant information, and (d) a behavioral component that allows the individual to act on the environment and attempt to achieve the goal in question.

The relations among these components of functional systems are represented in Figure 6.1. The apex of the triangle represents the fundamental goal to attempt to achieve some level of control over the social, biological, and physical resources that support survival and reproduction. The midsection shows that emotional responses to control-related activities act to modify and to direct control-related behavioral strategies and the supporting psychological systems (e.g., fantasy). The base of the triangle represents the classes of cognitive module that have been designed by selection pressures to process control-related social, biological, and physical information. The general structure shown in Figure 6.1 should provide a useful conceptual frame for studying behavior and cognition across species, although the specifics (e.g., the types of information processed by the social modules)

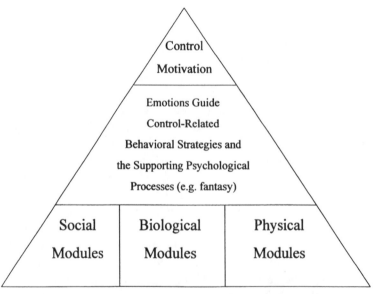

Figure 6.1. The motivation–emotion–cognition triangle. The apex represents the fundamental motivation to control the social, biological, and physical resources that support survival and reproduction. The midsection shows that emotional responses associated with control-related activities modify and direct control-related behavioral strategies and psychological processes. The base represents the classes of cognitive module that support the processing of information associated with the control motivation.

will of course differ from one species to the next. For humans, it is assumed that the basic structure of these functional systems is the same for women and men—for instance, both women and men have cognitive modules for processing facial expressions—and that these systems have largely been shaped by natural selection. Sexual selection would result in sex differences in the degree to which the associated competencies, such as the ability to interpret the emotions signaled by facial expressions, are elaborated in one sex or the other.

The first section below outlines the general motivational and emotional features of functional systems, and the second describes the domains for which functional cognitive modules appear to have evolved, along with the associated cognitive and behavioral architecture. The third and final section describes the ways in which functional systems might become elaborated during development.

THE MOTIVATION TO CONTROL

Human beings, and arguably all other complex organisms, appear to be fundamentally designed to attempt to achieve some level of control over the social, biological, and physical resources that support survival and reproduction (Geary, 1998). In fact, it can be argued that the desire to control is the fundamental motivation underlying the behavioral and psychological development of human beings (Heckhausen & Schulz, 1995; Schulz & Heckhausen, 1996). From this perspective, the emotional, cognitive, and behavioral systems of human beings—and all other complex organisms—have been designed by selection pressures to enable the individual to pursue the fundamental motivation to control or to organize the environments within which he or she lives and develops; Heckhausen and Schulz defined control as "bringing the environment into line with one's wishes" (p. 285).

Stated somewhat differently, Darwin's (1859) conceptualization of natural selection as resulting from a "struggle for life" (p. 115) is more precisely defined as a struggle for control of the resources that support life and that allow one to reproduce. In this view, the mind and the body of the organism have been fine-tuned by selection pressures to enable the organism to attempt to gain control of the social, biological, and physical resources in its habitat and to organize these resources in ways that facilitate survival and reproduction. If selection has in fact resulted in a fundamental motivation to control essential resources, then individual differences in skill at achieving control should be related to individual differences in morbidity, mortality, and reproductive outcomes. The first section below addresses this issue. The second section describes the psychological control mechanisms that support attempts to achieve environmental control, and the third section describes the relation between emotional patterns and motivation to control. As noted earlier, relevant sex differences in motivational and emotional patterns are discussed to illustrate essential concepts and to provide a foundation for the later (chapter 7) discussion of sex differences in social development.

Patterns of Control

The physical, social, and reproductive benefits of achieving some level of control over the resources that support survival and reproduction are overviewed in the first section below. The second section illustrates the different control-oriented strategies of women and men, with a discussion of the sex difference in the pattern of social motives.

Benefits of Control

The benefits of achieving some level of control over one's environment and one's behavior have been documented many times. "Hundreds of studies and dozens of books have been devoted to the theory, research, and applications of a variety of personal control strategies. . . . This body of work has demonstrated that people's ability to gain and maintain a sense of control is essential for evolutionary survival" (Shapiro, Schwartz, & Astin, 1996, p. 1213; see also S. C. Thompson, Armstrong, & Thomas, 1998). The thesis here is that the implicit focus of these control activities is to organize social, biological, and physical resources in ways that enhance survival and reproduction, as noted earlier, and that functional systems are the means by which this control is achieved. If this is the case, then, across species, the pattern of social conflict should reflect a struggle for control of the resources that support survival and reproduction when these resources are limited in supply or when the accumulation of additional resources provides additional physical or social benefits to the individual (e.g., additional wives or more surviving children; Borgerhoff Mulder, 1990).

The pattern of male–male competition in nonmonogamous primates (described in chapter 3 and in chapter 5) illustrates the main point. For instance, in nearly all cultures, men attempt to enhance their reproductive options by gaining control over the biological or physical resources that women need to raise their children (e.g., cattle and land; Borgerhoff Mulder, 1990). Intersexual and intrasexual conflict is essentially conflict of interest over the distribution and control of these resources. Unlike men, the males of most other primate species cannot easily control the food sources that females need to support their offspring. As a result, male–male competition in these species is not typically focused on the control of biological resources (i.e., food) but rather is focused on the control of social and sometimes physical (e.g., territory) resources. Male–male competition for the establishment and the maintenance of social dominance, for instance, is essentially a conflict over the control of reproductive resources, specifically the suppression of the sexual activities of male competitors and the self-serving control of the sexual activities of estrous females (e.g., Dixson et al., 1993).

These control-related activities benefit successful males in all primate species, including humans, as dominant males are typically healthier and typically sire more offspring than their less dominant peers (Altmann et al., 1996; Sapolsky, 1993). Similarly, in many primate species, socially dominant females are able to restrict the access of less dominant females to the biological resources—high-quality food (e.g., fruit)—necessary for survival; males probably do not attempt to gain control of these resources because they are often effectively controlled by coalitions of females (e.g., Wrangham, 1980). These dominant females and their offspring, in turn, are healthier and are more likely to survive from one year to the next than their subordinate peers and their offspring are (e.g., Pusey et al., 1997; Silk, 1987, 1993).

Goodall's (1986) studies of the chimpanzee (*Pan troglodytes*) provide a more specific example. For male chimpanzees, within-group conflict typically focuses on the control of the social and sexual behavior of other group members. The primary function of these activities, such as physical threats, is to gain control of sexually receptive females and, through this, reproductive outcomes. Conflict over biological resources, such as the leaves used as food, is less frequent and typically less intense, except for access over limited biological resources, such as meat obtained through hunting. Coalition-based, between-group conflict is over control of the physical territory that supports the social group and over control of young females. In all cases, the achievement of control almost certainly enhances the likelihood of survival and the reproductive options of the individual, often at the expense of other individuals.

Similar patterns are clearly evident in human beings. Within-group and between-group conflicts are inevitably over control of those social, biological, and physical resources that are needed to support survival and reproduction (Alexander, 1979; Chagnon, 1988; Keeley, 1996). As described by Betzig (1986, 1993), the first six human civilizations—ancient Mesopotamia, Egypt, Aztec, Inca, and imperial India and China—were controlled by coalitions of despotic men. The behavior of these despots is particularly enlightening because their activities were not constrained by social consequences. Despots can and typically do act with impunity, and, given this, their behavior provides a glimpse at the unrestrained motivations of men, at least men for whom the achievement of social dominance is a life goal (see Pratto, 1996). Across civilizations, the activities of despots are typically centered on diverting the material and social resources of the culture to themselves and to their kin. They live in opulence and almost always have exclusive access to scores, sometimes thousands, of women (Betzig, 1986, 1992). Regardless of how one might morally evaluate these activities, despots and their kin are typically better fed, are in better health, and have more children than their subjects (e.g., Betzig, 1992).

Of course, not all people are motivated to attempt to achieve absolute, despotic control over the community within which they live. As with other biological characteristics, it is almost certain that there are individual differences in the intensity of the motivation to control and individual differences in the manner in which it is expressed. Inherited personality differences might, in fact, reflect the evolution of different strategies for obtaining social and material resources (Buss, 1991; MacDonald, 1995b; McCrae & Costa, 1997; D. C. Rowe, 1994), with the desire for despotic control reflecting only one of many of these alternative strategies (D. S. Wilson, Near, & Miller, 1996). Moreover, in almost all contexts, the motivation to control is necessarily constrained by formal laws and informal social mores (enforced, for example, through gossip), and for many people, adherence to these laws and mores provides benefits, such as reciprocal exchanges, that are sufficient to avoid the risks associated with attempts to achieve despotic control (Barkow, 1992; Baron, 1997; H. A. Simon, 1990).

Nonetheless, gaining some level of control over the activities of daily life and important social and material resources appears to afford many of the same benefits, although on a much smaller scale, as those enjoyed by despots. As described in chapter 4, in nearly all societies, there is a linear relation between social status—the ability to influence other people (Fiske, 1993)—material wealth—the control of money, cows, and so forth—and physical health and life span (e.g., Adler et al., 1994), but not happiness or subjective evaluation of well-being (Diener & Diener, 1996; Lykken & Tellegen, 1996; Myers & Diener, 1995). Most important, in preindustrial societies, social status and wealth improve reproductive outcomes for both men and women (Borgerhoff Mulder, 1990; Chagnon, 1988; Irons, 1979), and for men in industrial societies, social status and wealth influence their desirability as mating partners (Pérusse, 1993).

Sex Differences

Given that social conflict over biological resources, physical territories, and reproductive activities is common in species in which there are few sex differences (Abbott, 1993), and thus little sexual selection, it is likely that the motivation to control has largely been shaped by natural selection. In this view, sex differences are not expected in the general motivation to control. For species in which sexual selection has operated, sex differences are expected in the focus of control activities and in the strategies used to achieve control. The relative degree of any such sex difference should be reflected in the relative emphasis of males and females on mating effort and parental effort (see the *Parental Care* section of chapter 2). In nonmonogamous mammalian species, for instance, the functional systems of males should be more strongly focused, in comparison to females, on the activities that enhance mating opportunities; whereas for females, these systems should be more strongly focused on the activities that enhance the likelihood of offspring survival. For humans, any such sex difference would be relative rather than absolute. This is so because men show some level of parental investment, though less so than women, on average, and women sometimes benefit from pursuing multiple mating partners, although less so than men.

Sex differences in the social motives of women and men illustrate how the motivation to control is reflected in reproduction-related activities; social motives reflect the way in which individuals would prefer, in the absence of constraints, to organize their social community. Both men and women value social relationships (Baumeister & Leary, 1995; Foley, 1996) but differ in the focus of social activities (see the *Social Development* section of chapter 7). Studies of personal values and interests reveal a consistent pattern of social sex differences, with women, more than men, valuing the development of altruistic, reciprocal relationships with other people, and men, more than women, being "interested primarily in power, competition, and struggle" (Willingham & Cole, 1997, p. 144), that is, politics; four out of five women value the development of reciprocal social relationships more than the average man does, whereas three out of four men value political activities more than the average woman does. These patterns are evident across historical periods and cultures, and the same pattern of sex differences in social relationships is found in chimpanzees (de Waal, 1993; Eibl-Eibesfeldt, 1989; Willingham & Cole, 1997). For humans, chimpanzees, and many other social species, these sex differences appear to be a reflection of the different reproductive strategies of males and females.

The relatively greater interest of men than women in political activities is a reflection of the sex difference in the general concern for the establishment and the maintenance of social dominance (Pratto, 1996). Politics is essentially about the control of other people and their resources and, across human cultures, is largely a manifestation of competition among coalitions of men (and in some societies, a few women). As noted earlier, gaining control over the group's resources often enhances the reproductive success of men (Betzig, 1986), as socially dominant men in many cultures typically have more wives and more children than their subordinates (e.g., Betzig & Turke, 1992; Chagnon, 1988). In most contexts, men thus have relatively more to gain—reproductively—than women by engaging in political activities. Indeed, for men, the desire to achieve social dominance is related to the desire for multiple mating partners and to less interest in parental investment, in keeping with the view that the motivation to achieve social dominance (i.e., engage in politics) is implicitly related to reproductive interests; socially dominant women, in contrast, are more interested in marrying high-status men than in finding multiple mates (see Pratto, 1996).

The tendency of women to value reciprocal social relationships more than men might reflect a more general motive of maintaining stability within the social community. As illustrated by the research of Flinn and his colleagues and others, unstable social relationships have adverse effects on the physical well-being of children (Flinn & England, 1997; Flinn et al., 1996), which will be of greater concern for women than for men, given the sex difference in parental investment (see chapter 4). Children living in unstable social environments tend to have abnormal (elevated or highly variable) cortisol profiles, are ill more frequently, and weigh less than children living in more stable households and communities. Under some conditions, social instability also increases child mortality rates (K. Hill & Hurtado, 1996). For individuals who survive to adulthood, growing up in a socially unstable environment appears to increase mortality risks at all ages in adulthood and, as a result, appears to shorten the life span (Friedman et al., 1995; Goodman & Armelagos, 1988; Tucker et al., 1997).

In preindustrial contexts, a shorter life span almost certainly reduces the number of children born to both men and women, although such costs are likely to be greater for women than for men. This is so because of the different reproductive potentials of women and men—men can have more children in a shorter period of time (through multiple mates)—and because a mother's death is associated with higher child mortality rates than a father's death is (see chapter 4). Within relatively small communities, stable social relationships can apparently be achieved by engaging in activities that suppress male–male competition, activities that result in a more-or-less equal distribution of resources (which results in a more stable food supply), and activities that promote cooperative child care and economic interdependence of women and men (Hewlett, 1992b; Irwin, 1990; Pratto, 1996; see the *Social Development* section of chapter 7).

These are, of course, relative and not absolute differences. Not all men are politically active or politically motivated, and many men, in many cultures, are more concerned with the well-being of their family than in achieving social power; these types of individual differences are expected and are possibly the reflection of situation-contingent reproductive strategies (i.e., men who do not achieve political power or acquire other forms of cultural success adopt a more monogamous and high paternal-investment reproductive strategy). In societies in which men do not actively suppress the political activities of women, many women seek and obtain political power. Even in societies in which the overt political activities of women are suppressed by men, women can often achieve social influence by influencing the political activities of their husband or male kin (Chagnon, 1977). However they are achieved, the political interests and activities of women and men tend to differ, on average. Men are more inclined, than women, to advocate political policies associated with dominance-oriented activities (e.g., military spending), and women are more inclined, than men, to advocate political policies that result in a more equitable distribution of social resources (e.g., higher taxes to pay for social welfare) and a greater investment in children (e.g., public day care; Pratto, 1996).

Stated more bluntly, there are consistent sex differences in the ways in which men and women would prefer to organize their social worlds and in the strategies they use to achieve this organization. These differences are reflected in the social motives and political interests and activities of men and women and appear to reflect the relative focus of men on mating effort and women on parental effort (see the *Parental Care* section of chapter 2). Men seek to achieve social dominance, because in most contexts—and almost certainly throughout the course of human evolution—the achievement of social dominance results in more wives and more children. Women, in contrast, cannot improve their reproductive success by gaining additional husbands, but they can improve their reproductive success by organizing the social community in a way that would enhance the well-being of their children. In other words, women who were able to maintain stability in the social lives of their children very likely had more surviving children (or at least more surviving grandchildren) than their peers who were not able to achieve this stability.

Stable communities are characterized by a low level of physical male–male competition and by a more-or-less equal distribution of social and material resources; in these communities, women would still be expected to compete among themselves to some extent for access to these resources, if they were in short supply. By advocating social policies that suppress male–male competition, women might be able to reduce the overall level of socially disruptive violence in the society, including male-on-female aggression; primate males and men often displace aggression stemming from male–male competition (see below) onto conspecific females and women, respectively (Smuts, 1985). In this view, the relatively greater reciprocity in the social motives and relationships of women, in comparison to men, is just as functionally self-serving as the dominance-oriented social motives of men (further discussion is provided in the *Social Development* section of chapter 7).

Psychological Control Mechanisms

In addition to behavioral strategies for attempting to achieve some level of control over the environment, people also have a system of supporting psychological processes (Dweck & Leggett, 1988; Heckhausen &

Schulz, 1995). These psychological control mechanisms are important, because the failure of these mechanisms appears to result in depression and behavioral inhibition; that is, a cessation of attempts to achieve environmental control (e.g., Seligman, 1991; Shapiro et al., 1996). In other words, one important function of these psychological mechanisms is to maintain control-oriented behaviors in the face of failure (see Heckhausen & Schulz, 1995). These mechanisms include attributions that allow people to interpret personal failure in ways that maintain their sense of self-efficacy; that is, their belief that they can in fact achieve the goal in question. Such interpretations might involve attributing failure to external causes ("It wasn't my fault") or maintaining an illusion of control by interpreting the outcome as predictable ("I knew that this would happen"). These same mechanisms are engaged with rituals, belief in psychic powers, and so forth and serve the function of attempting to predict and control potentially significant life events (e.g., finding a mate, health of kin, and so forth) and to mollify the fear and anxiety associated with not having complete control over these events.

Fantasy is another psychological control mechanism. The primary function of fantasy appears to be to create an illusionary world. Within this world, essential resources are typically controlled by the individual and are organized in ways that would enhance the well-being of this individual, if a similar level of control were achieved in the real world. In other words, fantasy provides a blueprint for later control-oriented activities and a platform for rehearsing the associated social strategies. Fantasy also provides an end point to be achieved, so that social strategies are rehearsed in such a way that—if successfully used in the real world—would reduce the difference between fantasized and actual outcomes (Heckhausen & Schulz, 1995). Under these conditions, selection would likely favor the evolution of psychological control mechanisms that mirrored activities that would enhance the likelihood of survival and enhance reproductive outcomes. In this view, fantasy and other psychological control mechanisms provide not only a blueprint for control-oriented activities but also a glimpse at the reality that people would create for themselves in the absence of social and psychological (e.g., guilt) constraints.

As mentioned in chapter 5 (see the *Female Choice* and *Male Choice* sections), the sex differences in sexual fantasy, in the content of personal ads, preferred fiction, and so forth all appear to engage the psychological control mechanisms involved in creating a world that would enhance reproductive outcomes (Buss, 1994; B. J. Ellis & Symons, 1990; Greenlees & McGrew, 1994; MacDonald, 1988; Whissell, 1996). From this perspective, the finding that nearly 1 out of 3 young men but less than 1 out of 10 young women report having fantasized about sexual relationships with more than 1,000 members of the opposite sex reflects the sex difference in the motivation to seek multiple sex partners. The sex difference in the motivation for sexual variety presumably evolved as a result of the sex difference in the reproductive benefits of obtaining multiple sex partners (B. J. Ellis & Symons, 1990; Symons, 1979). Fantasizing about multiple relationships is not only a reflection of this motive, but it would also influence the extent to which the individual actually sought multiple sexual relationships and would provide a means for rehearsing strategies for achieving these relationships. Men who had such fantasies and sought multiple relationships would, per force, leave more descendants than their less imaginative peers.

In this view, the reproductive motivation of despots and young college men is the same, although they clearly differ in the ability to realize their fantasies and in the strategies used to pursue their reproductive goal. Similarly, the content of popular fiction stories that women find more appealing, on average, than men appears to mirror the sexual fantasies of many women, as described in chapter 5 (*Female Choice* section). The realization of such a fantasy would result in the woman developing a long-term relationship with a physically attractive, socially dominant, and wealthy man. The development of such a relationship, in turn, would not only provide good genes to the woman's offspring but allow her to create a stable and resource-rich social and material environment within which to raise her children.

Emotional Mechanisms

The first section below provides a brief description of the function of emotions (for a more thorough treatment see M. Lewis & Haviland, 1993), whereas the second section provides discussion of the pattern of sex differences in emotional reactions.

The Function of Emotions

Although there is not a complete consensus, there is general agreement that there are a finite number of evolved emotional systems that are common to mammals (e.g., Darwin, 1872; Izard, 1993, 1994; Lazarus, 1991; Panksepp, 1989; Tooby & Cosmides, 1992). These basic systems appear to include foraging–expectancy (the basis for joy), anger–rage, fear–anxiety, separation–distress, and possibly social–play circuitry that are involved in "establishing, maintaining, or disrupting the relation between the organism and the environment on matters of significance" to the organism (Campos, Campos, & Barrett, 1989; p. 394; see also Ledoux, 1995). From an evolutionary perspective, matters of significance relate primarily to activities associated with the acquisition and retention of those resources needed to survive and reproduce. Emotional reactions provide feedback to the individual about the relative success and failure at acquiring and retaining these resources and act to modify the individual's behavioral strategies in ways that will increase the likelihood of achieving these goals (MacDonald, 1995b).

More basically, positive emotions (e.g., joy) are hypothesized to be directly linked to the acquisition of evolutionarily significant goals (e.g., finding a mate), and negative emotions (e.g., anger or sadness) to difficulties in the achievement of these goals or to the loss of important relationships or resources (Buss, 1996; MacDonald, 1988), as illustrated by the pouting expression of the chimpanzee shown in Figure 6.2. This facial expression was prompted by "an orange having been offered him, and then taken away. A similar protrusion or pouting of the lips, though to a much slighter degree, may be seen in sulky children" (Darwin, 1872, p. 140; see also Goodall, 1986). Pouting is often an effective strategy for getting desired resources, especially from one's parents (Trivers, 1974).

In most circumstances, the relation between emotions and behavior is more complex than the pouting associated with not getting what one wants (Lazarus, 1991). In many cases, there appears to be an innate relation between specific experiences, such as those that result in physical pain, and specific emotional reactions, such as anger (Campos et al., 1989). For instance, physical pain caused by another individual is likely to result in anger, which, in turn, will prompt a behavioral retaliation. Whether the individual actually retaliates will depend on the social context within which the pain was inflicted. In primates, when a subordinate attacks or

Figure 6.2. A disappointed and sulky chimpanzee (*Pan troglodytes*). From *The Expression of Emotions in Man and Animals* (p. 141), by C. Darwin, 1872, London: John Murray.

simply irritates a dominant group member, the dominant animal often behaviorally retaliates against the subordinate, which, in turn, suppresses the "unwanted" behavior of the subordinate (and any other subordinate that witnessed the retaliation). The situation is often different when a dominant group member attacks a subordinate animal. In this circumstance, displaced rather than direct behavioral aggression is common (Goodall, 1986). Displaced aggression—in which one primate will attack a lower status primate after a physical confrontation with a more dominant animal—appears to involve the expression of anger in a way that will not provoke further attack by the more dominant group member (Smuts, 1985).

The emotion of anger, along with other evolved emotions, is thus expressed in a way that is situationally adaptive for the individual (Izard, 1993; Lazarus, 1991): When provoked by a subordinate animal, anger and behavioral retaliation often result, but when provoked by a more-dominant animal, fear, anger, and displaced aggression often result, as shown in Figure 6.3. These relations most likely reflect an evolved system of emotional and

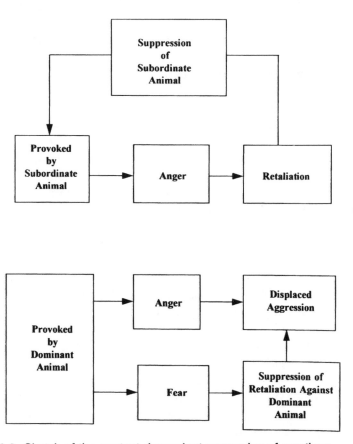

Figure 6.3. Sketch of the context-dependent expression of emotions.

behavioral responses that regulates the individual's behavior in dynamic social contexts. In fact, it appears that the emotional systems of humans and all other primates are especially sensitive to the costs and benefits of social relationships and are intimately involved in shaping the behaviors associated with the regulation and the maintenance of these relationships (Baumeister & Leary, 1995; Cosmides, 1989; Ekman, 1992; Foley, 1996; Mesquita & Frijda, 1992; Trivers, 1971). Stated otherwise, emotional reactions are elicited in social contexts to the extent that the current situation is relevant to the individual's control-oriented social strategies and result in the modification of the associated behaviors so that these behaviors are adaptively expressed in the current context.

In addition, emotional reactions can become associated with behaviors and resources that do not have an evolutionary history (Ledoux, 1995), as illustrated by the euphoria associated with winning the lottery. Money has no evolutionary significance per se but does enable one to acquire resources that do have an evolutionary significance (e.g., an increase in SES or social status; Adler et al., 1994). Along these same lines, the indicators of a man's social success often vary from one culture to the next. Nonetheless, the achievement of cultural success—whether this is the acquisition of money, cattle, or the heads of one's competitors (Irons, 1979)—almost always increases the reproductive options of men and almost certainly results in positive emotional reactions (e.g., joy) in these men (MacDonald, 1988). The activities associated with acquiring money or the head of a competitor are, in most cases, very different but can lead to similar emotional states because these activities have the same functional outcome, allowing one to gain greater control over the social, biological, or physical resources that support survival and reproduction. The positive emotions associated with achieving these goals are important because they signal that the behavioral strategy used by the individual was effective. A failure to achieve cultural success, in contrast, is more typically associated with anger or depression (Lazarus, 1991), and, more important, these negative emotional states will likely prompt a change in the individual's behavioral strategies for pursuing cultural success.

Emotional reactions thus shape niche-seeking activities, so that individuals pursue evolutionarily significant goals—such as finding a mate (or mates) or acquiring resources—in ways that are most adaptive for them (D. C. Rowe, 1994; Scarr & McCarthy, 1983). Adaptive niche seeking would require the individual to pursue goals in ways that capitalized on his or her social, cognitive, or behavioral strengths; that is, by using competencies for which he or she has an advantage over other people (e.g., Lubinski & Dawis, 1992). The use of these strengths is more likely to result in success, and the emotional reactions to success reinforce their use (Izard, 1993). Conversely, niches that require competencies for which one is at a disadvantage, such as an introvert in a contact-sales position, would result in relatively poor outcomes, and the associated emotional reactions (e.g., disappointment and frustration) would prompt the individual to seek another niche; that is, adopt a different social or behavioral strategy for acquiring cultural resources (in this example, finding a different job), finding a mate, and so forth.

Sex Differences

From a functional systems perspective, emotional patterns are expected to guide men and women to attempt to organize the social, biological, and physical resources in their environment in ways that have been adaptive throughout human evolution. Sex differences in the pattern of emotional responses are expected, and are often found, for those behaviors that are related to the different reproductive motives of men and women; that is, the relative focus of men on mating effort and women on parental effort (Buss, 1989a). For instance, for casual sexual relationships, more women than men develop unwanted feelings of social dependency and anxiety about their partner's emotional investment in them (Townsend et al., 1995); 69% of the young women in Townsend et al.'s study reported these feelings as compared with 21% of the young men. As described in chapter 5, an implicit concern of many women is the degree of their sexual partner's long-term commitment to them and their future children. That is, many women are implicitly focused on developing a relationship with a man who will provide resources to assist them in the raising of their children. Unwanted feelings of social dependency and anxiety guide, so to speak, women to develop sexual relationships with men who will make such an investment, as these feelings will prompt them to evaluate whether their partner is likely to provide a long-term investment and to avoid men who are not likely to make such an investment.

There are other sex differences in emotional patterns, as well. For instance, it appears that women experience positive and negative emotions, except perhaps anger, more intensely than men, on average, do (Diener, Sandvik, & Larsen, 1985; George, Ketter, Parekh, Herscovitch, & Post, 1996; Grossman & Wood, 1993; Gur et al., 1995; Larsen & Diener, 1987; G. E. Schwartz, Brown, & Ahern, 1980). The factors underlying this sex difference are not fully understood but might be related to the nature of the social relationships maintained by women and men. Women are generally more sensitive to nonverbal social communication signals than men are (e.g., facial expressions; Buck, Savin, Miller, & Caul, 1972) and tend to maintain a more complex network of intimate social relationships (Golombok & Fivush, 1994; B. F. Turner, 1982). In comparison to men, the greater emotional reactivity of women might then complement a greater sensitivity to the social cues and the nuances of social relationships. In combination, these competencies will provide women with a relative advantage in managing social relationships (see below). In keeping with this view is the finding that relative to men, women are better able to strategically inhibit social cues, such as facial expressions, especially when interacting with members of the opposite sex (Bjorklund & Kipp, 1996); this is a context-sensitive sex difference, however, as men are more likely to generally suppress all social cues (e.g., facial expressions) than women are (see the *Social Modules* section of chapter 6).

Stated somewhat differently, relatively intense emotional reactions, combined with a sensitivity to the social cues signaled by other people, and greater skill at strategically managing the expression of social cues would result in a greater overall sensitivity to and greater skill at controlling the subtleties of social dynamics in women than in men. Among other things, these sex differences might provide women with an advantage in their attempts to manage relationships with physically larger and potentially more aggressive men and might be useful in controlling the dynamics associated with the relational aggression that appears to characterize female–female competition (see chapter 5). At the same time, the greater sensitivity of women to social cues and their relatively more intense emotional reactions to these cues might facilitate social behaviors that maintain social stability, at least in the context of their relationships with friends and kin; more intense feelings of guilt, for instance, would reduce the likelihood of socially exploitative behaviors (see the *Social Modules* section of chapter 6 and the *Social Development* section of chapter 7).

Male–male competition might also contribute to the sex difference in the intensity with which emotions are experienced. Repression of certain emotional reactions, such as fear (Archer, 1996), would be one selected skill during intense male–male competition. This is so because such reactions would not only be disruptive in the heat of competition but they would—if expressed too openly—also diminish the man's status within his group of peers. In comparison to positive emotions, the sex difference in emotional intensity is indeed more pronounced for these negative emotions (e.g., fear and general emotional reactivity to stress); that is, those emotions that would be disruptive during periods of confrontation (Grossman & Wood, 1993; McGue, Bacon, & Lykken, 1993; Schwartz et al., 1980). Another possibility is that the ability to suppress negative emotions (e.g., guilt) and their less intense emotional reactions, in general, might enable men to more effectively engage in the form of social control that is often necessary to achieve social dominance (e.g., Betzig, 1986). More precisely, the relative lack of emotional intensity and the ability to suppress negative emotions appear to enable some men to depersonalize other people and to use more direct, sometimes brute force, methods in the exploitation of other people (Betzig, 1986; Mealey, 1995).

These are, of course, relative and not absolute differences. As implied previously, women are by no means nurturing and reciprocal in their relationships with sexual competitors (see the *Female–Female Competition* section of chapter 5), nor are they necessarily concerned with the social stability of out-groups (see below). For instance, Eisenberg and Lennon (1983) found that men and women did not differ in terms of physiological responsiveness to the distress of other people and, on the basis of this finding, suggested that there were no sex differences in emotional empathy. However, in the studies reviewed by Eisenberg and Lennon, these other people were almost always strangers (see also Rushton, 1988). On self-report measures—on which people typically indicate empathy toward the distress of friends—a very large sex difference is found for emotional empathy; four out of five women report sharing the emotional distress of their friends more frequently than the average man does (Hoffman, 1977; see also the *Infancy* section of chapter 7). Thus, despite Eisenberg and Lennon's conclusion, on the basis of self-report and behavioral measures (e.g., comforting), women at times do appear to experience greater empathy for the distress of strangers than men do, on average (Hoffman, 1977). The overall pattern suggests that the emotional empathy of women is directed primarily toward their social in-group, friends, and kin (Baumeister & Sommer, 1997). Empathetic reactions to in-group members are especially important, because these individuals typically constitute the social environment within which women raise their children, and heightened empathy for these individuals will likely facilitate the maintenance of a stable social group (e.g., less socially disruptive cheating and greater levels of social support during periods of stress).

Similarly, men, per force, cooperate in the development of coalitions, and these coalitions are very stable, once the within-coalition dominance hierarchy has been established (see the *Social Development* section of chapter 7). Moreover, given that only dominant men benefit from the establishment and the maintenance of a strict dominance hierarchy, it is expected that many men (especially middle- and low-ranking men) would advocate and pursue social and political activities that foster a more equitable distribution of resources (MacDonald, 1995a). That is, these men would be expected—because it is in their self-interest—to advocate social policies that redirect the resources of powerful men to the wider community and policies (e.g., that prohibit polygynous marriages) which would restrict the sexual behavior of these powerful men.

Finally, it appears that the magnitude of these sex differences might be influenced by socialization patterns (as discussed in the *Parenting* section of chapter 7) and by sex hormones and genetics. As noted in chapter 5, testosterone appears to be related to the desire for social dominance (Mazur & Booth, in press), and circulating testosterone levels have been found to be positively correlated with measures of aggression and negatively correlated with measures of prosocial behavior, such as altruism and emotional empathy (J. A. Harris et al., 1996); individual differences in both aggression and empathy are also moderately heritable (Finkel & McGue, 1997; Rushton, Fulker, Neale, Nias, & Eysenck, 1986; S. L. Sherman et al., 1997). Similarly, Collaer and Hines (1995) concluded that prenatal exposure to male hormones might increase aggressiveness and social detachment in girls and women. Nonetheless, the exact nature of the relations among genes, hormones, social motives, and emotional patterns is not well understood (Popp & Baum, 1989), as described in chapter 3 for other primates. For humans, it is almost certainly the case that hormones, reactivity to life events, social motives, emotional patterns, and genetic influences are related in complex and reciprocal ways (Sapolsky, 1993).

EVOLVED COGNITIVE DOMAINS

From a functional systems perspective, cognition is important to the extent to which it allows the individual to pursue the general goal of organizing social, biological, and physical resources in ways that enhance survival and reproduction. In other words, evolved cognitive domains are designed to focus the attention of the organism on those social and ecological resources that support survival and reproduction and that enable the processing of the relevant domain-specific information. Perhaps, needless to say, the argument that human cognition is largely the result of evolutionary selection is controversial in the behavioral and cognitive sciences (Tooby & Cosmides, 1992). Given this, brief discussion of current controversy in this area is presented in the first section below. The second and third sections outline the basic features of social and ecological modules, respectively, and the fourth and final section provides brief discussion of the cognitive and behavioral architecture of these modules. Additional discussion of the underlying brain systems is provided in chapter 8, along with the overview of sex differences in brain and cognition.

Current Controversy

One perspective is that the human mind is best understood in terms of domain-specific modules that have been shaped by natural selection to address specific and recurring problems of adaptation in ancestral environments (Cosmides & Tooby, 1994; Fodor, 1983; Tooby & Cosmides, 1989, 1990). For instance, the basic processes associated with language—such as those involved in processing language sounds (e.g., "ba," "da," and so forth)—are understood to have evolved from more rudimentary social communication systems and to have specifically been designed to support language production and comprehension (Gannon, Holloway, Broadfield, & Braun, 1998; Hauser, 1996; Kay, Cartmill, & Balow, 1998; Lenneberg, 1967; Pinker, 1994; Pinker & Bloom, 1990). An alternative view is that language and other domains of the mind are best understood as resulting from the operation of more general processing units that can construct domain-specific cognitive competencies, such as language, on the basis of the need to solve specific problems and on the basis of regularities in the input from the social and physical environments within which these problems are solved (e.g., Elman et al., 1996; Quartz & Sejnowski, 1998). Or stated otherwise, from this perspective, there is no particular need to invoke an innate architecture to explain domain-specific modules, as more general learning mechanisms, combined with a preference to attend to certain classes of information (e.g., faces), can account for the emergence of domain-specific competencies (see Bever, 1992; Müller, 1996; Piatelli-Palmarini, 1989, for related discussion).

Although it is clear that not all forms of cognition reflect evolved domain-specific competencies (e.g., reading; Geary, 1995a; Rozin, 1976), comparative research strongly supports the position that some domains of cognition have indeed been shaped by evolutionary selection and have a modular architecture (Moss & Shettleworth, 1996; see the *Summary and Conclusion* section for further discussion of modularity). Social communication systems, for instance, are evident across many species, serve the analogous function of regulating social relationships, and show common features in the associated developmental processes, such as a period early in life when the individual readily acquires the communication system (i.e., a sensitive period; Ball & Hulse, 1998; Hauser, 1996; Marler, 1970). Perhaps most important, these communication systems show a complexity of design that is most readily understood in terms of natural selection (Dennett, 1995; Mayr, 1983; Pinker, 1994; G. C. Williams, 1966): that sexual reproduction will result in subtle variations, across individuals, in the fidelity and in the architecture of the species' communication system and that selection will sufficiently act on this variability for the gradual evolutionary emergence of a highly complex communication system, such as human language (Pinker & Bloom, 1990).

Another line of comparative research that has been used to draw inferences about the evolution of the brain and mind involves comparison of the brain volume, or the volume of specific brain regions, of related species that occupy different habitats, show different foraging strategies, or live in different social structures (Barton, 1996; Barton, Purvis, & Harvey, 1995; Dunbar, 1993). If selection pressures have shaped the evolution of the brain and mind, then, across species, the volume of specific brain regions should vary systematically with variations in the habitats within which these species have evolved. As an example, there are two general classes of animal that store food: larder hoarders and scatter hoarders. Larder hoarders store all of their food in one or a few locations, whereas scatter hoarders store small quantities of food in many spatially dispersed locations (Healy, 1996). Larder storage places few memory demands on the animal but creates a resource that must be defended. Scatter storage, in contrast, obviates the need to defend the food store but creates a heavy demand on the memory system of the animal. Neurobiological studies indicate that the hippocampus, which is related to spatial memory and cognition, among other things (Poucet, 1993; Sherry et al., 1989), of scatter-storing bird species is larger than the hippocampus of evolutionarily related larder-storing species (Healy, 1996).

Analogously, the olfactory (smell) and visual systems of nocturnal and diurnal (awake during the day) primate species tend to differ (Barton et al., 1995). Nocturnal species tend to have better developed olfactory systems than their diurnal cousins that, in turn, tend to have relatively better developed visual systems. These differences in brain structure and presumably in the associated perceptual and cognitive systems appear to reflect the different foraging strategies that have evolved in nocturnal and diurnal primates. A similar analysis of primate species revealed that the size of the neocortex is independently related to social group size and to diet (Barton, 1996). After controlling for body size and evolutionary relatedness (i.e., common ancestors), Barton found that the size of the neocortex increases as the size of the species' social group increases and that the cortex of fruit-eating primates is larger than the cortex of leaf-eating primates; group size explained 33% of the variability in cortex size across primate species, and diet explained an additional 16% of the variability. The latter finding is likely to reflect the greater complexity of foraging for fruits (e.g., determining ripeness, remembering the location of fruit trees, and so forth) as opposed to leaves.

Of course, it might be argued that these species differences emerge from domain-general learning mechanisms operating on different patterns of experience. Indeed, for many species, the development of the neural, perceptual, and cognitive systems that allow them to function in their social and physical habitats is often dependent on experience (Healy, 1996; Knudesen, 1998). As noted in chapter 2, for many bird species, the emergence of song is dependent on early exposure to song. In other species, however, song emerges with or without early song exposure (Ball & Hulse, 1998; Marler, 1991). Moreover, the males of many species of bird selectively attend to the songs of conspecifics and learn these songs more readily than they learn the songs of evolutionarily related species (Marler, 1991). Domain-general learning mechanisms operating on a structured pattern of input cannot explain these patterns (see also J. L. Gould, 1996), nor can domain-general learning mechanisms explain the selective relation between exposure to sex hormones and changes in the neural, cognitive, and behavioral systems associated with many sexually selected traits, as described in chapter 2 (see chapter 9—Sex Differences in Academic Competencies—for further discussion).

The argument is not that there are no domain-general cognitive and neural systems, there almost certainly are (e.g., Bjorklund & Harnishfeger, 1995; Siegler & Crowley, 1994); for instance, the prefrontal cortex is involved in the regulation and inhibition of the functioning of a variety of more specific neural systems (Bjorklund & Harnishfeger, 1995). Rather, the position here is that evolutionary selection pressures have indeed shaped the organization of the human mind and that much of this organization can most readily be understood from a modular perspective (Fodor, 1983; Tooby & Cosmides, 1995). At the same time, it recognizes that not all cognitive domains are the end product of evolutionary processes. The focus of the sections below is on evolved, or biologically primary, domains of cognition (Geary, 1995a; Rozin, 1976); a discussion of culturally specific, or secondary, domains (e.g., reading), and any associated sex differences, is presented in chapter 9.

The comparative approach suggests that evolved cognitive domains are a reflection of the types of social and ecological information that must be processed for the animal to survive and to reproduce in its natural habitat, but the degree to which these domains reflect the operation of modules that are genetically fixed in structure and operation is not known (e.g., only respond to domain-specific information, not open to developmental input, and so forth; see *The Development of Functional Systems* section). What is important is that there is some a priori structure to the way in which the human mind processes information and that this structure reflects the evolutionary history of our species. In this view, the study of the human mind, or any other mind, can effectively be organized by considering cognition in terms of social and ecological modules (i.e., systems of neural, sensory, perceptual, and cognitive systems that enable the processing of the information that is relevant in the species' current habitat and throughout its evolution).

For humans, the social and ecological modules presented in Figure 6.4 are likely to capture the core features of the evolved mind, although there appear to be other modules as well, such as for the processing of basic numerical information and music (the latter appears to serve social and emotional functions; Geary, 1995a; Schellenberg & Trehub, 1996; see also Flinn, 1997). More precisely, the argument is that the human mind is hierarchically organized into domains of social and ecological modules. These broad domains can be subdivided into more specialized domains, each with an accompanying ensemble of submodules. The submodules, in turn, can further be decomposed into more specialized submodules, such as the production and comprehension features of the general language module, which, in turn, can be decomposed into even more specialized submodules, such as the sensory and perceptual mechanisms associated with the recognition and production of speech sounds. The neurobiological correlates of these, or any other, functional cognitive modules are not well understood, at this point, and are the focus of considerable scientific debate

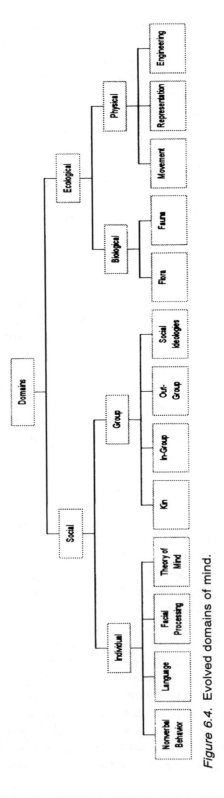

Figure 6.4. Evolved domains of mind.

(e.g., Elman et al., 1996; Müller, 1996). Nonetheless, some neurobiological possibilities seem more likely than others. For instance, it is almost certain that there is not a one-to-one correspondence between the modules represented in Figure 6.4 and circumscribed brain regions, although localized ensembles of cells that are specialized for the processing of domain-specific information seem likely (e.g., Brothers & Ring, 1992; Kemmerer, 1996; Moscovitch, Winocur, & Behrmann, 1997). Functional cognitive competencies might then be realized with the synchronized activities of systems of such cell ensembles, systems that are distributed throughout the brain.

The goal here is not to debate brain–cognition relations, but rather to provide a theoretically plausible—from a Darwinian perspective—organization of the vast literature on human cognition and in chapter 8 to apply this organization to the understanding of cognitive sex differences. It should be noted at the outset that the cognitive modules presented in the sections that follow are assumed to have been largely shaped by natural selection and in many cases modified by sexual selection. It follows from this that there will be considerable variability, or individual differences, in all of cognitive competencies associated with evolved modules, including an overlap in the distribution of competencies found in groups of men and women. The basic premise is that natural selection has resulted in the same structure of the human mind in women and men but that sexual section has acted to enhance differentially—through the outcome of male–male competition, female choice, and so forth—those cognitive competencies and the associated neural systems that are differentially related to the re-productive strategies of men and women (as discussed in chapter 8).

Social Modules

Barton's (1996) previously mentioned findings provide support for the view that the evolution of the brain and mind has been influenced by the size and complexity of the social group within which the species lives and presumably evolved (see also Alexander, 1990; Byrne, 1995; Dunbar, 1993; Foley, 1996; Humphrey, 1976). In fact, all but one—the orangutan (*Pongo pygmaeus*)—of the more than 175 primate species that have been identified and studied live in relatively complex social groups. Within these groups, "individuals associate with each other for extended periods, interact in patterned ways and form relationships than can be defined by their qualities and intensity" (Foley, 1996, p. 96). The pattern across primate species suggests that human sociality has at least a 25-to-35-million-year evolutionary history (the estimated age of the ancestor common to all extant primates). Moreover, Sawaguchi's (1997) analysis of the relation between neocortex size and intensity of intrasexual competition in primates suggests that the dynamics of sexual selection have been a potent aspect of social complexity and an influential pressure in the evolution of the associated cognitive modules (as described in chapter 8).

The sociality of humans, and probably of many other primates (Goodall, 1986; Smuts, 1985), involves developing and maintaining preferred relationships with other individuals and organizing conspecifics into social categories. These features of sociality, in turn, appear to reflect the evolution of individual-level and group-level modules (Premack & Premack, 1995), as described in the two respective sections below.

Individual-Level Modules

The function of individual-level modules is to control the dynamics of one-on-one social interactions, to develop and maintain long-term relationships with kin and friends, and to support attempts to obtain social and material resources from other people.

Kin-based relationships are found across many species, ranging from invertebrates to primates (e.g., Altmann et al., 1996; Hamilton, 1964), and are understood in terms of inclusive fitness. *Inclusive fitness* refers to an individual's overall genetic contribution to the next generation, which is represented by the combination of one's children and the children of kin (e.g., nephews). Natural selection would strongly favor individuals who aided kin in ways that facilitated their reproduction and survival, because the reproductive success of kin would per force increase the altruist's genetic contributions to the next generation (Hamilton, 1964, 1975). More simply, selection pressures will quickly favor individuals who selectively provide social and material support to their kin (see Daly & Wilson, 1995; T. Day & Taylor, 1997).

The primary distinction between the nature of the social relationships among kin and that among friends is reciprocity. Relationships with kin, especially parent–offspring relationships, are not always reciprocal, whereas long-term friendships are defined by reciprocity (Hartup & Stevens, 1997; Trivers, 1974). In fact, in a seminal contribution, Trivers (1971) argued that the evolution of the ability to develop long-term relationships with nonkin is per force dependent on social and emotional mechanisms that maintain reciprocity in the relationship; guilt, for instance, prompts reciprocation. More basically, Trivers argued that friends are friends because their relationship is mutually beneficial. Decades of empirical research on friendships in children, adolescents, and, more recently, adults confirm Trivers's position (Hartup & Stevens, 1997; Youniss, 1986). Of friends, Hartup and Stevens (1997) concluded that children "and adults of all ages consider these relationships to be marked by reciprocation, that is, *mutuality*—the giving and taking, and returning in kind or degree. On this basis, then we argue that the [friendship's] deep structure . . . is best described as 'symmetrical reciprocity'" (p. 356).

As shown in Figure 6.4, the core cognitive modules that appear to be involved in maintaining and regulating long-term social relationships, as well as managing the dynamics of one-on-one social interactions, are nonverbal communication, language, facial processing, and theory of mind (Baron-Cohen, 1995; Brothers & Ring, 1992; Ekman, 1992; Leslie, 1987; Moscovitch et al., 1997; Pinker, 1994; Premack & Woodruff, 1978; Wellman, 1990). Of central importance is theory of mind. Even though the specific mechanisms and processes, such as the degree of modularity, are currently debated, there is general agreement that theory of mind represents the ability of individuals to develop a mental model of the intentions, beliefs, and emotional states of other individuals (Gopnik & Wellman, 1994; Karmiloff-Smith et al., 1997; Karmiloff-Smith, Klima, Bellugi, Grant, & Baron-Cohen, 1995; Povinelli & Eddy, 1996). Although, across cultures, these states are not always attributed to the mind per se—sometimes they are seen as originating in the heart, for instance (Lillard, 1997, 1998). Either way, facial processing and processing of other nonverbal forms of communication (e.g., body posture), along with changes in vocal intonation and language itself, all appear to provide the basic information that feeds into these mental models.

These mental models, in turn, serve the pragmatic function of enabling one to predict the behavior of other individuals and to plan and implement complex social strategies (Baron-Cohen, 1995; Byrne, 1995; Gopnik & Wellman, 1994). For instance, the development and the maintenance of a friendship are dependent on the ability to predict the future behavior of any would-be friend, such as determining whether this individual is likely to reciprocate current favors, whether he or she will make a dependable social ally, and so forth. At the same time, these mental models support social manipulation, deception, and exploitation (Baron-Cohen, 1995; D. S. Wilson et al., 1996). In fact, theory of mind appears to represent the fundamental cognitive scaffolding that supports the earlier described motivation to organize and control the social resources that support survival and reproduction, regardless of whether one believes that social behavior is governed by the mind, the heart, or the forces of nature. As long as the behavior of other people can be predicted, theory of mind (or theory of heart) supports attempts to secure social or material resources from other people and to prevent other people from securing such resources from you.

Overall, given the highly social nature of human beings, there is little question that selection pressures resulted in the evolution of neural and cognitive systems—modules—that are specialized for the processing of social information (see Moscovitch et al., 1997, for an illustration for facial processing). Indeed, the finding that cortex size is strongly related to the size and complexity of the social group within which the species lives and presumably evolved (Barton, 1996; Dunbar, 1993; Sawaguchi, 1997) suggests that the threefold increase in brain volume from A. *afarensis* to modern humans (Figure 3.7) was driven in large part by increases in the complexity of hominid social relationships, including intrasexual and intersexual dynamics, and reflects the associated elaboration of social modules (Alexander, 1990; Humphrey, 1976). Comparisons of the chimpanzee—which might have a rudimentary understanding of intention (a proto theory of mind; Baron-Cohen, 1995; Byrne, 1995)—and human children suggest that the individual-level social modules showing the greatest evolutionary change are language and theory of mind (Pinker, 1994; Povinelli & Eddy, 1996).

Group-Level Modules

In addition to cognitive systems that are specialized for maintaining and regulating dyadic relationships and interactions, there are almost certainly complementary systems—the group-level modules shown in Figure 6.4—that are designed to divide and organize the social universe. The categorization of people into social groups appears to reflect the above-described categorical significance of kin, the formation of in-groups and out-groups, and an ideologically based social identification, as exemplified by gender roles (Alexander, 1979; Dunbar, 1993; Eagly, 1987; MacDonald, 1988).

In preindustrial cultures, and most likely during the course of human evolution, functional group size appears to be constrained by the number of individuals with whom human beings are able to maintain reciprocal relationships (i.e., recognize and engage in one-on-one social exchanges) without the existence of formal laws and a formal police force to enforce these laws (Dunbar, 1993). The size of such groups varies in response to the opportunities and demands of the local habitat that supports the group (Alexander, 1990; Chagnon, 1977; H. Kaplan & Hill, 1985) but typically does not exceed 150–200 individuals (Dunbar, 1993). The individuals that make up these groups are typically kin and share beliefs, such as origin myths, that not only distinguish them from other groups but that often, if not always, assign special significance to their group (Brown, 1991).

Cognitive constraints on the size of functional social groups, shared belief systems, and competition over limited resources appear to have set the stage for the evolution of an in-group/out-group social psychology (Alexander, 1979). In-groups and out-groups are defined by differing social and moral ideologies that favor in-group members (kin and friends) and, under extreme conditions, devalue and even dehumanize out-group members (see J. Hartung, 1995, for a discussion). In fact, one important condition for effective competition against an out-group is the disengagement of the emotional and moral mechanisms that appear to be designed to reduce conflict and to foster cooperation within in-groups. Although some level of in-group conflict is anticipated, especially when there are no cur-rent competing out-groups, it appears that emotional reactions, such as guilt and empathy, moderate this conflict in the service of mutually ben-eficial cooperative exchanges (Baumeister & Leary, 1995; Trivers, 1971), as does the belief that reciprocal relationships are often in one's best in-terest (Baron, 1997).

When directed toward out-groups, these same moderating emotional reactions would result in a competitive disadvantage. In other words, when the competition between groups affected reproduction and survival—as it likely did in many instances throughout the course of human evolution (Alexander, 1990; Chagnon, 1988; J. Hartung, 1995; Keeley, 1996)—in-dividuals who were able to dehumanize, in extreme cases, members of out-groups were likely at a competitive advantage. Stephan's (1985) review of the social psychology of intergroup relations supports this position, as do numerous studies on the social identification processes underlying group formation and competition (Abrams & Hogg, 1990; Messick & Mackie, 1989; Schaller, 1992; Sherif, Harvey, White, Hood, & Sherif, 1961). Hu-mans readily form in-groups and out-groups and process information about members of these groups in ways that are favorably biased toward the in-group, particularly when the comparisons are made between competing groups. Moreover, "anticipated competition caused in-group members to feel more hostility toward the out-group than did anticipated cooperation" (Stephan, 1985, p. 615; see Pettigrew, 1998, for related discussion); the seminal *Robbers cave* experiment nicely illustrates the process of in-group/out-group formation and intergroup competition (see Sherif et al., 1961).

An in-group/out-group social psychology that likely evolved in the context of competition between relatively small kin-based groups more likely than not provided the foundation for the evolution of social ideol-ogies (Alexander, 1990; Hirschfeld, 1994; MacDonald, 1988). These ide-ologies are particularly important, because they appear to be the basis for the formation of large nation states; that is, the social organization of in-dividuals who have never met, and never will, and thus are unable to develop one-on-one reciprocal relationships. Such ideologies define the mutual self-interest of individuals that make up groups that are larger than functional villages in preindustrial societies and are the basis for large-scale, between-group conflict. In fact, the competitive advantage associated with group size was the likely pressure that determined the evolution of human beings' tendency to form and to rally around such ideologies (Alexander, 1990; Goodall, 1986). In support of this view is the finding that people show an enhanced endorsement of in-group ideologies and a harsher eval-uation of out-group members under conditions that imply a threat to one's mortality (Arndt, Greenberg, Pyszczynski, & Solomon, 1997; Greenberg, Pyszczynski, Solomon, Simon, & Breus, 1994).

One relevant ideological category is gender. For all sexually reproducing species, there are, per force, cognitive systems involved in distinguishing one sex from the other. Indeed, it is clear that human beings socially categorize one another on the basis of biological sex (Kozlowski & Cutting, 1977; Kujawski & Bower, 1993; Maccoby, 1988). Kujawski and Bower, for instance, showed that infants as young as 10 months of age can distinguish—as measured by looking patterns—the sex of other infants on the basis of the movement pattern of these infants. Neuroimaging studies indicate that the brain regions involved in categorizing faces as male or female differ from the regions involved in categorizing objects and in facial recognition (Cabeza & Nyberg, 1997).

In addition, there is a system of beliefs—termed *gender roles*—associated with the behaviors, attitudes, social expectations and the social positions of men and boys and women and girls in any given society (Eagly, 1987, 1995; O'Brien, 1992). According to Eagly (1987), many sex differences in social behavior are directly related to differences between women and men on two important gender-role dimensions: communion and agency. Women are, on average, more communal than men, as "manifested by self-lessness, concern with others, and a desire to be at one with others" (Eagly, 1987, p. 16), whereas men are, on average, more agentic than women, as manifested by "self-assertion, self-expansion, and the urge to master" (Eagly, 1987, p. 16; see Cross & Madson, 1997, for a related model).

It is argued further that these differences arise from the different social and economic roles that men and women occupy in society; in particular, women's greater involvement in domestic activities, such as child care, and men's greater involvement in paid employment. In addition to the greater communal demands of domestic activities and the greater agency demands of employment-related activities, women and men tend to differ in social status, including a greater frequency of men than women in high-status occupations. From this perspective, the greater social status of men than women, on average, not only further reinforces the communal and agency roles of women and men, respectively, but also creates sex differences in those social behaviors associated with dominance and submission (Eagly, 1987). Although Eagly acknowledged that many factors contribute to these sex differences—"the requirements of the economy and social structure interact with the biological attributes of women and men and with the political ideologies of societies to produce differential role occupancy" (Eagly, 1987, p. 31)—the gist of the theory is that most sex differences are caused by socially imposed roles (Eagly & Wood, 1991).

The argument that sex differences are largely the result of socially imposed roles is appealing because such theories create an illusion of control, which, as described earlier in this chapter (*The Motivation to Control* section), is of fundamental importance to human beings. If the gender-role theory were largely correct, then all sex differences in social status, social behavior, and so forth could potentially be eliminated by modifying the social expectations for women and men. While appealing, strong versions of this view are almost certainly wrong (Archer, 1996). As described in chapter 3 and later in chapter 7 (*Social Development* section), the communal–agency distinction can probably be applied to all nonmonogamous primates (and nearly to all other species, as well), in that male–male competition to establish social dominance, or agency, is a salient feature of nearly all of these primate societies, as is the fact that most "domestic" activities, in particular the care of offspring, are the domain of females (Andersson, 1994; Whitten, 1987).

Moreover, the social roles of women and men differ in consistent ways across societies, even societies in which there are no explicit gender roles, such as the Batek of Malaysia (see Best & Williams, 1993; Endicott, 1992; Murdock, 1981). In fact, the same general pattern of sex differences in social activities emerges in societies that are socially isolated from one another, and, thus, similarities across these societies cannot be explained in terms of shared cultural ideologies about the gender roles of women and men (Brown, 1991; Eibl-Eibesfeldt, 1989; Murdock, 1981). In a review of sex differences in the division of labor across 224 societies, among many other differences, Daly and Wilson (1983) reported that weapon making, for instance, was an exclusively male activity in 121 of the 122 societies in which information on this activity was available (women assisted men in the 1 remaining society), whereas cooking was an exclusively female activity in 158 of the 201 societies surveyed; in 38 of the 43 remaining societies, men did some of the cooking.

Regardless, gender roles cannot be dismissed as an influence on the social behavior of men and women. As noted earlier, social ideologies can influence human behavior (MacDonald, 1988, 1995a), and there is no reason to expect that gender will be immune from such ideological influences. Steele (1997), for instance, has demonstrated that when mathematics tests are defined as being measures on which men generally outperform women, the performance of mathematically talented women on these tests is lower than the performance of similarly talented men (although sex differences do exist in certain areas of mathematics for nonmatched samples; see chapter 9 and Geary, 1996). When the same measures are defined as tests in which sex differences are not typically found, the average performance of talented women and similarly talented men does not differ. These findings suggest that when tasks are defined as favoring men, many women may not persist in their problem-solving efforts when the task becomes difficult. In other words, gender roles might exaggerate certain sex differences by affecting the psychological control mechanisms that maintain goal-directed behavior in the face of failure, so that goal-directed activities are abandoned more readily when the individual believes that she or he will not perform well, even with additional effort.

Pratto and her colleagues have also shown that a combination of factors influences the occupational differences that are prominent in Eagly's (1987) theory (Pratto, 1996; Pratto et al., 1997). In addition to stereotypes about the relative communal and agentic orientations of women and men, which do influence hiring practices, the distribution of women and men into different status-related occupations is related to self-selection, presumably by means of the earlier described niche seeking. When given a choice, many more men than women prefer dominance-oriented occupations, those emphasizing hierarchical social relationships and the control of other people. Many more women than men, in contrast, prefer to work in "hierarchy-attenuating" jobs, those that involve working with people, especially the disadvantaged and underprivileged (see Pratto et al., 1997). These differences are, of course, in keeping with the earlier described sex differences in social motives and are related to the sex difference reproductive strategies. In other words, gender roles largely reflect a description, not a causal agent, of biologically based sex differences, although ideological prescriptions might result in the exaggeration of some of these differences.

The construction of gender ideologies is also likely to reflect attempts at social and political manipulation. The tendency of some writers to describe girls and women as passive and boys and men as active might represent an implicit attempt to suppress female choice and to maintain the status quo (i.e., male control of social and material resources; Smuts, 1995). There is a sex difference, favoring males, in physical activity levels (chapter 7), but both men and women actively pursue their self-interests. Similarly, the ideological prescriptions of some feminist scholars appear to be implicitly designed to disrupt the formation of male coalitions, suppress male–male competition (i.e., suppress the establishment of dominance hierarchies), and, at the same time, increase female choice and female control of essential resources (e.g., G. C. H. Hall & Barongan, 1997). These ideological prescriptions reflect the extension and expression of sexual politics—conflict over the different reproductive preferences of men and women (chapter 5)—through human language; similar ideological debates would likely emerge in chimpanzees, for instance, if they were capable of humanlike language (Goodall, 1986; Smuts, 1995).

Ecological Modules

On the basis of the motivational structure described earlier, the human mind should not only function to organize and control social relationships but it should also enable the exploitation of biological and physical resources in local habitats in the service of survival and reproduction. Barton's (1996; Barton et al., 1995) earlier described research suggests that the foraging requirements of the species do indeed influence the evolution of brain and mind. In addition, there is little question that the activities associated with survival and reproduction require cognitive systems that enable organisms to act on and, in some cases, mentally represent the physical world (Gallistel, 1990; Shepard, 1994). The two sections below briefly outline the basic cognitive systems that appear to form the associated biological and physical modules, respectively.

Biological Modules

The issue here is whether the goal of attempting to control biological resources created selection pressures resulting in the evolution of cognitive modules that organize the processing of relevant biological information and that categorize the biological environment in ways enhancing reproduction and survival. Gathering, hunting, horticulture, and agriculture provide examples of such control-related activities. Deductively, it seems likely that natural selection would favor individuals who could categorize the universe in ways that enabled the exploitation of biological resources. This is not to say that human beings have an inherent categorical system of all the plants and animals found throughout the world, this is very unlikely (Malt, 1995). Rather, any biological module would bias the types of information that people processed (e.g., animate vs. inanimate) and the ways in which this information was organized (e.g., animate organisms further classified as flying vs. terrestrial). As shown in Figure 6.4, any such modules would be designed, at the most general level, to categorize and represent (e.g., behavior or growth patterns) the flora and fauna in local ecologies.

Although the origins of folk biological taxa are debated (Atran, 1994; Carey & Spelke, 1994), it is clear that humans categorize the flora and fauna in their local ecologies (Atran, 1994, in press; Berlin, Breedlove, & Raven, 1966; J. M. Diamond, 1966) and develop mental models of the behavior (e.g., growth patterns) of these plants and animals. Through ethnobiological studies, "it has become apparent that, while individual societies may differ considerably in their conceptualization of plants and animals, there are a number of strikingly regular structural principles of folk biological classification which are quite general" (Berlin, Breedlove, & Raven, 1973, p. 214). Moreover, the classification of plants and animals in preindustrial societies is similar to the scientific classification of these same organisms (Atran, 1994; Diamond, 1966), although the system within a particular culture is more or less elaborated, contingent on the social and biological significance of the plants or animals to people in the culture (see Atran, in press; Malt, 1995, for thorough reviews).

In preindustrial societies, the classification of flora and fauna is based on morphology, behavior, growth patterns, and ecological niche, which, in combination, represent the basic "essence" of the species (Atran, 1994; Malt, 1995). In effect, the essence is a mental model, or basic psychological representation of the salient characteristics of the species. The resulting mental models of biological organisms appear to be similar in many respects to people's theory of mind, in that these biological models would seem to be well suited for representing and predicting the likely behavior of organisms, just as theory of mind enables the representation of the intentions and therefore the prediction of the behavior of other people (Leslie, 1987). Moreover, this folk biological knowledge allows people to make reasonably accurate inferences about the essence of unfamiliar species. So, knowledge of one species of frog allows inferences to be drawn about the likely essence of other species of frog, but such knowledge tells little about the essence of birds. The ability to represent the behavior, growth cycles, and so forth of flora and fauna would seem to be an essential feature of any module that has been designed by selection pressures to organize and to control biological resources in the service of survival and reproduction (Atran, in press).

Atran's (1994) finding of a highly differentiated taxonomy of fauna for Itza-Maya (Guatemala) hunters is in keeping with the view that the function of this folk biological knowledge is, at least in part, survival related (but see below). This taxonomy was "related to features of behavior, habitat, diet, and functional relationships to people" (Atran, 1994, p. 331), which very likely facilitates the hunting of these animals. At the same time, knowledge of animals that were not regularly used for food was much more rudimentary, although still consistent with scientific taxonomies (Malt, 1995). Similarly, in preindustrial societies, knowledge about plants that serve as food, for instance, is much more highly differentiated—in terms of basic morphology, growth cycles, and so forth—than knowledge about nonfood plants (Berlin et al., 1966; Clement, 1995).

Nevertheless, the existence of well-developed biological taxonomies in all preindustrial societies in which the issue has been studied does not prove that these taxonomies reflect evolved cognitive modules. As described at the beginning of this section, it is possible that the taxonomies develop from general learning mechanisms that are applied to matters of importance (e.g., hunted species). However, research on Western children's formation of folk biological taxonomies, which are not survival related for them, suggests that the pan-cultural existence of these taxonomies might reflect an evolved module. Preschool children appear to have the basic skeletal knowledge from which these classification systems and mental models develop. For instance, preschool children have an implicit understanding of the basic essence of living and nonliving things, including an understanding that living things have "innards" that differ from the "innards" of nonliving things and are capable of self-initiated movement (Gelman, 1990; Hickling & Gelman, 1995; Premack & Premack, 1995). Later, children understand that animals must eat to survive and reproduce offspring that share characteristics with their parents (Carey & Spelke, 1994; Coley, 1995). As described later in the section on development, this type of skeletal knowledge appears to be a basic characteristic of at least some evolved cognitive modules (Gelman, 1990). Moreover, Malt (1995) and Atran's (in press) reviews of folk biology across preindustrial cultures indicate a structure and organization to the categorization of plants and animals that are not used as food sources or in cultural rituals, a categorization that is highly consistent with the scientific classification of these same species. These classification systems are not simply the result of domain-general learning mechanisms operating on problems of significance.

Using a somewhat different perspective on this issue, Crites and Cacioppo (1996) examined the pattern of event-related brain potentials associated with the evaluative (i.e., liked and not liked vegetables) and semantic (vegetable vs. nonvegetable) categorization of food items. They found that the evaluative categorization of food items engaged certain regions of the right hemisphere more strongly than the semantic categorization of these same food sources. Similarly, neuroimaging studies indicate that certain regions of the left-temporal cortex (see Figure 8.2) are involved in the nonevaluative classification of objects as living or nonliving and that different regions of the temporal cortex are engaged during other types of object classification tasks (e.g., making same–different judgments about two objects; Cabeza & Nyberg, 1997). The overall pattern is consistent with the view that the human brain/mind differentially categorizes living and nonliving things, is sensitive to the biological significance of living things, and provides organization to this biological universe, independent of the need to solve functional problems. Although it is not as yet certain, these findings implicate the operation of an evolved biological module rather than general learning mechanisms (see also Keil, 1992).

Physical Modules

Physical modules are designed to allow the organism to behaviorally engage the environment and, in some species, to develop mental representations of the structure of the environment and to use tools to manipulate (i.e., gain some level of control) this environment. The latter skills appear to be restricted to only a small number of species and thus will be considered after the discussion of the behavioral and representational functions of physical modules.

Conceptual models vary in the extent to which behavioral engagement and mental representation are emphasized, and there is some debate as to the exact nature of the neural and cognitive mechanisms underlying these functions (Andersen, Snyder, Bradley, & Xing, 1997; Gallistel, 1990; J. L. Gould, 1996; Poucet, 1993; Shepard, 1994; Ungerleider & Mishkin, 1982). Nonetheless, a useful conceptualization of physical modules is in terms of movement and representation, as shown in the rightmost portion of Figure 6.4. This conceptualization is based on Milner and Goodale's

(1995) framework for the functional and anatomical organization of the visual system, but similar functions are probably associated with other sensory systems, as illustrated by the bat's use of echolocation to guide movement in the external world (Moss & Simmons, 1996). Milner and Goodale argued—at least for the visual system—that movement and representational modules are functionally and anatomically distinct, although the two types of systems interact in many contexts (Kosslyn & Sussman, 1995).

Movement modules are almost certainly phylogenetically older than representation modules and are designed to allow the organism to track and behaviorally respond to current information in the external world. Milner and Goodale (1995) provided a number of examples for the visuomotor system, including prey location and capture, predator avoidance, navigating around obstacles, and so forth. Moreover, it appears that distinct pathways in the visual system underlie these distinct visuomotor functions, in keeping with the modular perspective (Milner & Goodale, 1995). Barton and Dean (1993), for instance, hypothesized that the function of one particular visual pathway is prey capture: the tectospinal pathway, with projections predominately originating in the superior colliculus–tectum, which, in turn, receives input from the lower half of the visual field. To test this hypothesis, they examined the relation between the number of neurons in this pathway, the size of the cell bodies of these neurons, and the predatory behaviors within four taxa of mammals: rodentia, primates, carnivora, and marsupiala. Within each of these taxa, species were classified as more (i.e., their diet was largely based on prey capture) or less (e.g., heavy reliance on fruits) predatory. Predatory species had more and larger neurons in this visual pathway than their less predatory relatives, but there were no cross-species differences in the volume of adjacent visual pathways that do not appear to be related to prey capture. Moreover, across primate species, a very strong relation was found ($r = .92$) between the percentage of diet based on prey capture and the number of neurons in this pathway. The greater the reliance on prey as a food source, the greater the number of neurons in this pathway.

In addition to prey capture and predator avoidance, the visuomotor system—as well as movement modules associated with other sensory systems—appears to include a navigational module, among others (Gallistel, 1990; Landau, Gleitman, & Spelke, 1981; Moss & Simmons, 1996; Shepard, 1994). Although the specific mechanisms are debated, one view is that the navigation module constructs a three-dimensional analog map of the environment that includes implicit knowledge of the geometric relations among features of this environment (Gallistel, 1990; Shepard, 1994; see Poucet, 1993, for a different interpretation). This map enables navigation by means of dead reckoning; that is, movement from one place to another on the basis of their geometric coordinates. For instance, J. L. Gould (1986) demonstrated that the common honeybee (*Apis mellifera*) can generate such a map and use it to navigate a novel route. In one study, bees were captured at a feeding site and were then displaced 160 meters to a novel location. If the bees relied on landmarks to navigate, then when released from the novel site, their flight trajectory would be random. In contrast, if they had a mental map of the geometric coordinates of this local environment, then they would fly directly back to the feeding site, which is exactly what they did.

In addition to movement modules, many species appear to have modules that allow them to represent features of the physical environment when they are not directly engaging the environment. These representational modules are "associated with memory, planning, and other more 'cognitive' processes . . . [and] . . . subserve an intermediate goal in the guidance of behavior, specifically the perceptual representations of objects and of their relationships" (Milner & Goodale, 1995, p. 19). These representations appear to engage the parietal cortex, the hippocampus, and several other brain systems (Andersen et al., 1997; Maguire, Frackowiak, & Frith, 1997) and appear to make up at least two relatively distinct systems: One is involved in generating a mental model of the physical layout of the habitat, and the other in remembering the relative location of objects within this habitat.

The former involves the generation of a cognitive representation of the large-scale physical environment (Gallistel, 1990; Helbing, Keltsch, & Molnár, 1997; Kosslyn, 1975; Matthews, 1992; Shepard, 1994). These representations appear to include an implicit understanding of the three-dimensional relationships among objects in the representation, including relative distance, direction, and Euclidean relations. For instance, glance at Figure 2.9 and then imagine the position of the primary objects in this figure. For many people, the generation of this type of image includes information on the relative distance of the rock, tree, and chimpanzee from one another, as well as information on the geometric coordinates of their relative positions (Gallistel, 1990). The triangle in Figure 2.9 illustrates the latter knowledge, conveying information on both distance and geometric position, as represented by the length of the line segments and the angles in the triangle, respectively. This knowledge is relatively abstract in that it conveys information about the relational features of major objects in the environment rather than information about the specific objects themselves.

Memory for the relative location of specific objects within the environment is dependent on a spatial memory system (or module) that appears to be distinct, in some respects, from the system that generates this abstract representation of three-dimensional space. In a neuroimaging study, Maguire and her colleagues contrasted the brain regions involved in navigating a complex route through London—taxi drivers imagined and described these routes while being imaged—with the brain regions associated with imagining highly salient landmarks (Maguire et al., 1997). The route and landmark tasks engaged many of the same brain systems, such as parts of the parietal cortex, but the route task also engaged the hippocampus, whereas the landmark task did not (see also Maguire, Frackowiak, & Frith, 1996). Furthermore, there is evidence that sex hormones differentially affect the use of navigation and landmark cues, which is consistent with the view that the systems supporting landmark memory and the geometric representation of physical space are distinct in at least some respects (C. L. Williams et al., 1990).

Although the origin of these systems is debated (see Matthews, 1992, for a discussion), the above-noted comparative studies suggest that these movement and representation systems are evolved modules in humans, as they are in other animals (Andersen et al., 1997; Milner & Goodale, 1995; see also the *Physical Modules* section of chapter 8). Landau et al. (1981), for instance, showed that a congenitally blind $2\frac{1}{2}$-year-old child was able to develop a maplike representation of the relative location of four objects in a room and use this representation to move from one object to the next. Moreover, the development of this maplike representation appeared to occur more or less automatically as the child explored her environment; across species, exploration appears to be the primary means for gathering the information needed to form mental representations of physical habitats (Poucet, 1993).

In another study of the ability to remember the specific location of arrays of 12 to 20 objects, Kearins (1981) demonstrated a consistent superiority of Australian Aboriginal children over White Australian children; on one task, 9 out of 10 Aboriginal children outperformed the average White Australian child. The superior spatial memory of Aboriginal children was evident whether or not they lived in seminatural tribal conditions or in settlements, where they spoke English, went to school, and lived in houses as their White peers did. In fact, the spatial memory of Aboriginal children living in seminatural conditions and on settlements did not differ, suggesting that rearing conditions were not responsible for the differences between the Aboriginal and White children. Kearins argued that the superior spatial memory of the Aboriginal children reflected an "important requirement of desert living—accurate memory for the spatial relationships between several environmental features" (p. 437). Consistent with this interpretation is the finding that the visual cortex is larger, relative to overall brain size, in Aborigines than in Whites (Klekamp, Riedel, Harper, & Kretschmann, 1987).

As noted earlier, the ability to use tools to manipulate and to better control the environment is evident in a few species, but most notably in humans. Pinker (1997) argued that the associated competencies represented an engineering module, as shown in Figure 6.4, which, in turn, is a reflection of the evolution of tool use in humans. Indeed, tools that are more sophisticated than the tools used by chimpanzees, such as stone flakes used in cutting, have been found in archaeological sites that are more than 2 million years old, and very sophisticated tools, such as hand axes, are evident from about 1.5 million years ago (Gowlett, 1992b; Trinkaus, 1992). These patterns indicate that relatively sophisticated, in comparison to extant nonhuman primates, tool use emerged with H. habilis, evolved further with H. erectus, and developed further still with modern humans (see Gowlett, 1992b, for an overview). Or stated otherwise, there is a long history of tool use in humans, a host of accompanying anatomical changes (e.g., the human thumb), and a clear selection advantage associated with their use (Trinkaus, 1992). The advantages associated with tool use include an increase in the range of foods available to the individual—such as with the use of stone hammers to extract marrow from bone—and an enhanced ability to control some physical resources, as in tools used to start fires. Given this, it is very likely that there is indeed an evolved system of skeletal knowledge—engineering modules—associated with the invention, construction, and use of tools (Gowlett, 1992a; Pinker, 1997), although at this point the associated cognitive competencies are not well understood.

Architecture

A detailed discussion of the architecture of cognitive modules is beyond the scope of this book, but two features merit brief consideration. The first involves the nature of the knowledge associated with cognitive modules, and the second involves the behavioral component of these modules, issues discussed in the two respective sections below.

Knowledge

When considering the architecture of a cognitive module, it is important to distinguish between *implicit* and *explicit* knowledge (Karmiloff-Smith, 1992; Mandler, 1992; Rozin, 1976). Explicit knowledge refers to information that can be communicated to other people, as through language or mathematical equations. Implicit knowledge is inferred by regularities in the behavior of organisms, but the principles governing these regularities cannot explicitly be articulated. In this section, the distinction between implicit and explicit knowledge is not in reference to the study of learning and memory as it is commonly done in cognitive psychology laboratories. These laboratory studies tend to use rather unnatural tasks (e.g., artificial grammar), and an implicit understanding of these tasks does not typically emerge until the individual has had repeated exposure to the material (see Stadler & Frensch, 1997, for examples). The implicit knowledge associated with evolved modules, in contrast, appears to guide the development of the associated behaviors (Mandler, 1992) rather than resulting from repeated exposure to experimental tasks. The former is discussed in *The Development of Functional Systems* section. The issue here is the apparently implicit nature of much of the knowledge associated with evolved cognitive modules.

As an example, many of the just-described movement and representation modules appear to capture the basic postulates of Euclidean geometry (Gallistel, 1990), as Euclidean geometry is an approximate mathematical representation of the organization of the physical universe, at least those features of the universe that our sensory and perceptual systems process. Given this, the perceptual and sensory systems that enable navigation in this universe must, per force, be sensitive to Euclidean features of physical space, such as angle and trajectory (Shepard, 1994). In this view, J. L. Gould's (1986) finding that honeybees move in a more-or-less straight trajectory when traveling from a novel location to their feeding site reflects an implicit understanding that the most efficient way to move from one location to the next is to go "as the crow flies," or to travel in a straight line. Euclid explicitly formalized this innate and implicit knowledge in his first postulate: A line can be drawn from any point to any point, that is, a line is a straight line (a straight line represents the shortest distance between two objects). Thus, some features of the implicit knowledge associated with the evolved navigation system are explicitly described by Euclid's postulates. The explicit articulation of these postulates was important in the development of mathematical geometry, but an awareness and an understanding of these postulates are not needed to navigate in physical space (Landau et al., 1981).

As another example, consider that children are able to form and maintain friendships on the basis of reciprocity, without having read Trivers's (1971) seminal article on the evolution of reciprocal altruism. Or stated otherwise, an explicit understanding of the reciprocal basis of long-term friendships is not needed to develop and maintain friendships. However, the social behavior of children indicates an implicit understanding of the importance of reciprocity in long-term social relationships—children who do not reciprocate are socially rejected (Newcomb, Bukowski, & Pattee, 1993; Youniss, 1986). In this view, social behaviors are more or less automatically constrained by an implicit understanding of the costs and benefits of reciprocal relationships, as well as by the pattern of emotional reactions to these relationships (e.g., anger resulting from nonreciprocation prompts social rejection), but the explicit understanding of these same principles was only achieved through considerable scientific effort (e.g., Cosmides, 1989; Hartup & Stevens, 1997; Trivers, 1971).

Although it is not certain, it appears that this implicit knowledge is represented in terms of the organization of the associated neurobiological systems and the types of information to which these systems respond. For instance, Barton and Dean's (1993) earlier described study suggests that the prey–capture module of mammals is, at least in part, supported by one specific pathway in the visual system. Cells in this system are likely to be sensitive to the movement patterns of prey species and enable the coordination of the behaviors necessary to capture this prey. In other words, the functioning of this module reflects an implicit understanding of how to catch prey. The organization of prey-catching behavior indicates some form of knowledge, and this knowledge is represented in the structure and functioning of the underlying neural systems.

From this perspective, much of human behavior is guided by knowledge that is implicit in the organization and functioning of evolved modules. Nevertheless, human behavior—and the behavior of most other organisms—is not reflexively driven by the operation of such modules. When a potential meal catches the attention of the prey–capture module, animals do not reflexively catch and eat this prey (Milner & Goodale, 1995). Rather, this module is only operational under specific conditions: when the animal is hungry, is in a relatively safe environment, and is not engaged in other behaviors (e.g., mate seeking). Similarly, human behavior is very context sensitive. In fact, evolved modules are probably designed to operate in specific contexts and under specific conditions (e.g., Geary et al., 1995).

In addition, human behavior can be guided by explicit belief systems, such as social ideologies (MacDonald, 1995a). Social ideologies appear to function by inhibiting some evolved tendencies, such as aggression, and by enhancing others, such as reciprocal altruism. Moreover, humans are able to use evolved competencies in ways that other species cannot, as described in chapter 9. Nonetheless, it is important to realize that much of human behavior is guided by neural, emotional, and cognitive systems that operate without our explicit awareness and that these systems are functional because they represent an implicit understanding of how to get along with other people, how to categorize and secure food (in preindustrial contexts), how to get from one place to another, and so forth.

Behavior

As was just mentioned, the suggestion that much of human behavior is guided by the operation of evolved cognitive modules must not be interpreted as indicating that people respond to the environment in a fixed stimulus–response manner. Variability and adaptiveness in people's strategic approaches to meeting short-term and long-term goals are the norm, not the exception (see Siegler, 1989, 1996). In fact, rigid behavioral responses to environmental events would quickly be eliminated by selection pressures. For instance, if prey-catching behaviors were rigidly executed whenever a potential meal triggered the associated module, then any adjustment in the prey species' strategies for avoiding capture would quickly eliminate them from the diet of the would-be predator. In other words, selection pressures would favor individuals who could adjust prey-catching behaviors to accommodate the inevitable variability in the prey species' predator-avoidance strategies, variability that will be found across individuals—resulting, in part, from sexual reproduction (see chapter 2)—and within individuals. Intraindividual variability appears to be a natural feature of evolved modules and functions to allow the individual to learn from experience. Siegler aptly described the gist of this. Strategic variability "is important for promoting change because it provides opportunities to learn which activities are most effective in achieving goals" (Siegler, 1996, p. 17).

Indeed, Siegler (1996) argued that intraindividual variability in behavioral strategies and in ways of understanding and representing the world appear to be the norm, with the associated processes acting in ways analogous to natural selection. The consequences, including emotional reactions, that these varying approaches produce are the selection mechanism acting on individual strategies, just as differential reproduction is the selection mechanism acting on individual organisms. Just as natural selection results in changes in gene frequencies across generations, selection processes that act on strategic variability result in a form of inheritance: change in memory patterns, knowledge about strategies, and so forth. These cognitive changes, in turn, appear to result in a form of strategy selection, so that behavioral strategies are more-or-less automatically fine-tuned to local contexts. The fine-tuning, so to speak, results in the most adaptive approach available being used in any given situation by the individual (Siegler, 1996).

Although Siegler's (1996) model is based largely on studies in human cognition—including both evolved (e.g., language and social interaction) and nonevolved (e.g., spelling) competencies—the basic principles might well be applicable to all complex organisms. As described in chapter 3, the social behavior of chimpanzees, and probably of all other primates, is clearly strategic, adaptive, and variable (de Waal, 1982; Smuts, 1985). For instance, Goodall's (1986; Riss & Goodall, 1977) studies of the Gombe chimpanzee indicate that most males attempt to improve their positions in the dominance hierarchy but that the strategies used to achieve this goal vary considerably. In their attempts to achieve social dominance, some individuals primarily rely on brute strength and intimidation, and others primarily form coalitions. Most individuals, however, use a combination of individual and coalition-based strategies in pursuit of this goal, depending on the social conditions at the time. At least one of these chimpanzees, Mike, used a completely novel social strategy to achieve social dominance. Mike incorporated large, empty tin cans into his social displays and by banging these cans together was able to achieve the alpha position by frightening his competitors (Riss & Goodall, 1977).

From this perspective, the life goal of organisms—attempting to achieve some level of control over the social, biological, and physical resources that support survival and reproduction—is invariant. However, the mechanisms that allow for the pursuit of this goal produce variability in the organisms' goal-directed activities (see Siegler, 1996, and Bjorklund, 1997, for an engaging discussion). Thus, evolved modules do not result in fixed systems of behavior that reflexively respond to environmental contingencies but rather are designed to produce behavioral and cognitive variability, which, in turn, enables the individual to adaptively adjust its goal-related activities to situational demands.

The issue of variability and adaptive change within individual life spans is especially important for understanding human behavior. This is so because humans are clearly able to develop adaptive strategies (e.g., housing and clothing) for adjusting to a wide range of biological and physical (e.g., from the tropics to the Arctic) habitats and because such flexibility is needed to respond to our most formidable competitor—other people. Moreover, unlike most other species, humans are able to pursue evolutionarily significant goals by using behavioral strategies that do not have an evolutionary history. A Western boy's fascination with guns provides an example. It is very unlikely that humans have an evolved affinity for guns per se. Nonetheless, in contexts in which guns are available and demonstrated (e.g., on television), their utility for achieving power and dominance is readily recognized, and, in many cases, they are incorporated by boys and men into their dominance-oriented social strategies, just as Mike incorporated cans into his social displays.

THE DEVELOPMENT OF FUNCTIONAL SYSTEMS

Although it appears that the desire to exert some level of control over the social, biological, and physical environments within which we live and develop is universal (Heckhausen & Schulz, 1995), the specifics of these environments vary considerably from one culture and context to the next. As described in the previous section, social and ecological variability creates pressures for the evolution of cognitive systems that can adapt themselves, so to speak, to changing circumstances (B. K. Hall, 1992; Siegler, 1996; Tooby & Cosmides, 1990). The ontogenetic adaptation of an evolved cognitive system to local conditions appears to reflect the operation of what Mayr (1974) called an *open genetic program*, as contrasted with a *closed genetic program*. A closed program results in a perceptual, cognitive, or behavioral trait that cannot be affected by experience. With an open genetic program, "new information acquired through experience is inserted into the translated program in the nervous system" (Mayr, 1974, p. 651), although an "open program is by no means tabula rasa; certain types of information are more easily inserted than others" (Mayr, 1974, p. 652). Of particular importance in the evolution of open programs is the length of the developmental period of the species.

> The longer the life span of an individual, the greater will be the selection premium on replacing or supplementing closed genetic programs by open ones. . . . A subsidiary factor favoring the development of an open program is prolonged parental care. When the young of a species grow up under the guidance of their parents, they have a long period of opportunity to learn from them—to fill their open programs with useful information on enemies, food, shelter, and other important components of their immediate environment. (Mayr, 1974, p. 657)

Mayr's (1974) description of an open program is entirely consistent with the views of many developmental researchers: that many of the early competencies of infants and young children reflect innate but skeletal knowledge (Gelman, 1990; Karmiloff-Smith, 1992; Mandler, 1992; Premack & Premack, 1995; Spelke, Breinlinger, Macomber, & Jacobson, 1992; see Knudsen, 1998, for an example in a nonhuman species). Such knowledge is skeletal because it only provides the initial structure of evolved cognitive competencies (Gelman, 1990). These competencies are fleshed out as the child processes domain-relevant information and engages the environment. In other words, innate skeletal knowledge biases the types of information that infants and children attend to, influences the ways in which this information is processed and represented, and motivates infants and children to engage and to learn about their local ecologies. For the latter, an inherent motivation to seek out environments that correspond to the evolved modules represented in Figure 6.4 is expected. Indeed, there is evidence that infants and children have a skeletal understanding of folk psychology (engaging social modules), folk biology (engaging biological modules), and naive physics (engaging physical modules) and that they elaborate this knowledge through their self-initiated play and exploratory behavior (Geary, 1995a; Gelman, 1990; Keil, 1992; Spelke et al., 1992; Wellman, 1990).

Thus, many of the modules and associated submodules represented in Figure 6.4 are likely to be the product of open genetic programs, although some of these modules are more open than others. The early skeletal structure of the system defines the types of information to which the system will respond, and the early experience of the child determines which features of this biological space are elaborated and which features are not (Greenough, 1991; Greenough, Black, & Wallace, 1987; see also the *Play* section of chapter 7). The net result of a constellation of such open systems is that the essential aspects of what it is to be a human being (e.g., to intuitively know about other people) are necessarily universal, but, at the same time, the specifics of these systems can be tailored to local conditions.

In this view, one purpose of development is to fine-tune evolved functional systems to the social, biological, and physical habitats in which the individual must survive and ultimately must attempt to reproduce. Many of these systems may be open to experience in adulthood as well, although the sensitivity of these systems to environmental experiences appears to be greater earlier, rather than later, in life.

The interaction between infants' language perception and their early exposure to language provides one example of how early environmental input appears to shape the biological space of an evolved module; see Acredolo (1988) and Pick, Montello, and Somerville (1988) for examples associated with the elaboration of physical modules. Infants born into all cultures can respond to the same basic phonemes, even those that are not in their parents' native language, and can discriminate these language sounds from other categories of sound, such as musical notes (Kuhl, 1994; Molfese, Freeman, & Palermo, 1975; Stager & Werker, 1997). The neural, perceptual, and cognitive systems that allow infants to respond to the phonemes of all human languages define the biological space that will eventually support the comprehension and production features of the language module. This space is, in turn, "trimmed" by language exposure during the first year of life (Kuhl et al., 1997). The net result is that the functional features of the system (i.e., the language sounds that can be comprehended and produced) correspond to the local language.

For language perception, it is very likely that the biological space—the sounds to which the associated neural ensembles respond—is genetically predetermined (Pinker, 1994) and that experience acts to activate and deactivate (i.e., turn on or off; Tooby & Cosmides, 1990) features of this system. It seems likely that the basic organization of some other modules is much more skeletal than language perception. As noted earlier, it is very unlikely that an ability to categorize flora and fauna is as preset as language perception. Natural language sounds are finite, and, thus, the neural systems that respond to all of these sound can genetically be predetermined. However, the variety and number of biological species to which humans are exposed are much greater than the number of natural language sounds, and, given this, it is unlikely that all features of the associated biological modules are genetically predetermined, with experience determining which features are activated or deactivated. Rather, is more likely that the modules for representing flora and fauna are, as described earlier, initially skeletal in nature and that extensive experience is needed to develop rich classification systems of flora and fauna.

Either way, experience appears to influence the expression and development of most evolved modules (see the *Summary and Conclusion* section). For any such adaptive shaping to occur, however, the child must be biased to seek the types of information that can be "inserted into" or that can shape the system; it appears that shaping results, at least in part, from the child's pattern of experience influencing which neurons and neuron ensembles survive and which do not (Greenough et al., 1987). In this view, the self-directed, or niche-seeking, activities of the child are not random but rather are an essential feature of functional systems—such systems must include a component that motivates the child to seek the pattern of experiences necessary to shape these systems to local ecologies. The first section below provides several examples of how children's self-directed play and exploratory behavior might influence the development of evolved modules, and the second section provides a discussion of the potential relation between parenting and the development of these modules.

Children's Play and Exploration

The position here is that children's natural play and exploratory behavior are essential developmental features of evolved modules, in that play and exploration result in the experiences necessary for shaping the module to local ecologies (Geary, 1992, 1995a).

As one example of the potential relation between play and the development of evolved social competencies—although not everyone would agree that these competencies represent the operation of modules (Walker-Andrews, 1997)—consider the early social behavior and activities of infants and preschool children (see the *Play* section of chapter 7). Initially, infants have a number of skeletal competencies that support social interactions, including an implicit conceptual understanding of the difference between people and nonpeople and a rudimentary understanding of the emotions signaled by facial expressions, as well as behaviors that enable social interactions (Baldwin & Moses, 1996; Baron-Cohen, 1995; Bower, 1982; Walker-Andrews, 1997). These behaviors would include the visual tracking of human movement and smiling at familiar people, among others. The net result of these competencies is that infants orient themselves to the social environment, such as human faces, and respond to social stimulation with positive affect (Bower, 1982; McGuinness & Pribram, 1979). The positive affect associated with social stimulation presumably motivates continued engagement with other people (Campos et al., 1989), which, in turn, produces the experiences that are needed for the continued development of the infant's social and emotional competencies.

The argument is that all of these behaviors, and many others, reflect the basic skeletal competencies of the individual-level social modules (e.g., language and facial processing), which appear to be further elaborated as children engage in social play (Baumeister & Leary, 1995). Sociodramatic play, for instance, appears to be an important vehicle for elaborating children's social competencies, particularly for learning the implicit scripts that choreograph many social interactions and for elaborating their emerging theory of mind (Baron-Cohen, 1995; Wellman, 1990). Beginning at around

3 years of age, children practice social scripts in the context of their play (Rubin, Fein, & Vandenberg, 1983). Initially, this type of play involves the use of dolls or other toys to act out everyday social experiences (e.g., dinner). Later, particularly between the ages of 4 to 6 years, children rehearse and then expand on these scripts with groups of other children (Rubin et al., 1983) and engage in activities, such as social role playing, that almost certainly elaborate their theory of mind (Leslie, 1987). Thus, from 3 to 6 years of age, children's play activities involve increasingly complex patterns of social interaction, patterns that build on and elaborate the initial skeletal structures associated with many, if not all, of the individual-level social modules. Moreover, it is very likely that a similar pattern of play and exploratory behavior is involved in the elaboration of the group-level social modules, as illustrated by the increasing tendency of children to form cliques as they mature, and the biological and physical modules shown in Figure 6.4 (see chapter 7 for additional examples).

Parenting

Research conducted in the United States and in other Western nations indicates that the relation between parenting and the social, psychological, and cognitive development of children is considerably weaker than many people assume (J. R. Harris, 1995; Lytton & Romney, 1991; Plomin, Fulker, Corley, & DeFries, 1997; D. C. Rowe, 1994; Scarr, 1992), although, as described in chapter 4, parents have a profound influence on the physical well-being of children. Nonetheless, cross-cultural comparisons do suggest that parenting can systematically affect the social and psychological development of children, although the magnitude of these effects appears to be small to moderate (Low, 1989).

In particular, child-rearing practices, such as the degree of parent–child warmth, appear to vary in ways that prepare the child for adult responsibilities (Low, 1989; MacDonald, 1988; Whiting & Whiting, 1975). These child-rearing practices appear to be a reflection of parental knowledge of the demands of adult life, as well as of more subtle, implicit influences. For instance, in Western culture, parents in secure bureaucratic jobs tend to have relatively permissive child-rearing practices and lay "greater stress on the development of interpersonal skills; by contrast . . . [parents] working in entrepreneurial settings were found to be more concerned with individual achievement and striving" (Bronfenbrenner, 1986, p. 728); genetic influences on both economic niche-seeking and parenting practices might account for this pattern as well. More subtle influences might include the degree of job-related stress, which appears to influence parental responsiveness to children (Belsky et al., 1991; see also the *Parenting* section of chapter 7).

When viewed from a cross-cultural perspective, parenting practices appear to provide an adaptive link between the demands of the adult world and the children's developing competencies. The assumption here is that there are certain universal demands, such as finding a mate, obtaining resources, and developing a social network, that can be addressed in a variety of ways. Cultural parameters, such as the economic and social (e.g., stratified or nonstratified society) systems of the society, determine the most adaptive way in which these demands can be approached, and parental practices might be one means of fine-tuning the associated modules to these demands (MacDonald, 1988, 1992). For instance, MacDonald argued that the degree of parental warmth modifies the neurobiological systems that support emotional reactions to social interactions, much like language input modifies the language module. These modifications result in children becoming more-or-less emotionally sensitive to other people (e.g., feeling empathy to their distress), which, in turn, appears to influence the extent to which their behavior is relatively self-serving or relatively cooperative. Harsh treatment, such as physical beatings, is thought to "shut down" the emotional systems that facilitate empathy and social cooperation, resulting in a relatively self-serving social style, which, in turn, appears to be adaptive in certain highly competitive, polygynous societies (MacDonald, 1988).

In other words, it appears that parental warmth moderates the relative sensitivity of the emotional systems associated with at least some of the social modules shown in Figure 6.4; there are almost certainly genetic influences on the sensitivity of these modules as well. What is not clear is whether these socialization practices also influence the development and functioning of the associated perceptual and cognitive systems, although it is possible that parental treatment, for instance, will influence the ways in which people process social information (Crick & Dodge, 1994). For instance, harsh treatment might result in one being less sensitive to the emotion cues (e.g., facial expressions) of other people and in one being more likely to interpret the behavior of others as being hostile. Although these particular examples might or might not be correct, it seems likely— as Mayr (1974) implied—that parenting practices will have some influence on the development of at least some evolved functional systems, although any such influences are likely to involve the amplification or suppression of biological biases in a child's behavior and not to involve the creation of social behaviors from "scratch" (Dunne et al., 1997; Scarr, 1992).

SUMMARY AND CONCLUSION

The basic assumption of this chapter is that human beings—and all other organisms—are designed to attempt to achieve some level of control over the social, biological, and physical resources that support survival and reproduction (Heckhausen & Schulz, 1995) and that the human brain/mind is the organ that directs this motivation to control. On the basis of this motivation to control, a one-to-one correspondence between the types of social, biological, and physical resources that have supported survival and reproduction throughout the course of human evolution and the organization of the human mind is expected (Cosmides & Tooby, 1994). If gaining some level of control over the dynamics of social discourse, for instance, provided survival and reproductive benefits throughout the course of human evolution, and it almost certainly did, then selection would favor the emergence of sociocognitive competencies that process the associated information. The processing of information is necessary but not sufficient to ensure adaptive responses to local habitats, however. To be functional, the systems that process this information must also include emotional and behavioral components. Emotional components provide feedback to the individual about her or his relative success at gaining some level of control over essential resources, and behavioral components enable the individual to attempt to actually achieve survival and reproductive goals.

As an example, one-on-one social discourse is typically imbued with some emotional tone, which, in turn, moderates the dynamics of the social engagement. Such discourse also involves the processing of social information, such as facial expressions; the development of a mental model of the emotional state, intentions, and likely future behavior of the individual; and, at times, the attempts to elicit information from this other person or to change his or her behavior (Baron-Cohen, 1995; Ekman, 1992). The latter is typically achieved through language, which is a behavioral as well as a cognitive competency; language is considered a behavioral competency to the extent that language can actually change the social environment (Pinker & Bloom, 1990). The individual-level modules shown in Figure 6.4 thus constitute a functional system that regulates one-on-one social discourse and that enables the pursuit of social strategies related to survival and reproduction.

The specific architecture of the cognitive modules that are features of such functional systems is not completely clear, although it is likely that many of these modules are the product of open genetic programs (Mayr, 1974). An open program allows the neurobiological systems that support the cognitive modules to be influenced by contextual factors, particularly during childhood (Karmiloff-Smith et al., 1995). If language perception is representative of the architecture of cognitive modules in general, then an open program determines the biological space, so to speak, of the system, and early experience trims this space, so that the system is fined-tuned to local conditions. For language perception, it appears that the biological space is represented by those neurobiological systems, presumably ensembles of neurons, that respond to the natural sounds of all human languages (Kuhl, 1994; Kuhl et al., 1997). The language sounds to which the infant is exposed determine which ensembles of neurons survive and which do not; that is, which ensembles remain active and responsive to the environment and which are switched off. The net result is that the perceptual system that later supports language comprehension and production is tailored to the local language.

It seems unlikely, however, that all modules are constrained to the same extent as is apparently the case with the language perception module. Such constraints would require that the biological space of the flora and fauna modules shown in Figure 6.4, for instance, includes the representation of all plants and animals found throughout the world, which is highly unlikely (Malt, 1995). An alternative is that many modules consist of skeletal features that guide the processing of domain-relevant information and bias the ways in which this information is categorized and represented, but they are otherwise relatively open systems (Gelman, 1990; Karmiloff-Smith et al., 1995; Mandler, 1992; Spelke et al., 1992). For instance, early in development, such skeletal structures would result in infants implicitly categorizing objects as alive and not alive and gradually developing complex representations of the essence—behavior, growth patterns, and so forth—of those objects that are categorized as alive (Premack & Premack, 1995). These skeletal constraints on the ways in which biological information is categorized and represented, combined with a general motivation to seek information about biological organisms, would result in regularities of folk taxonomies across cultures but, at the same time, would allow for the development of taxonomies that are well suited to local conditions.

In this view, many cognitive modules are relatively more open to environmental input than the language perception module. The relatively greater openness of these modules must, per force, be accompanied by a relatively long period of development; that is, a period of time during which the system is readily modified by environmental information (Mayr, 1974). In fact, there is likely to be a strong relation between the developmental period during which the module can be modified and the degree to which it is open. The language perception module appears to be open to modification until about the age of 8 months (Kuhl, 1994; Stager & Werker, 1997) and is closed after this point. Many other competencies, such as theory of mind and other language skills (e.g., comprehension of complex utterances), have a much longer developmental period and might therefore be considered relatively more open than the language perception module (Lenneberg, 1967; Wellman, 1990).

One function of human development is thus to provide the experiences necessary to adapt relatively open cognitive modules, and the associated emotional and behavioral components, to local conditions. In other words, the play and exploratory behavior of children should be focused on providing the experiences needed to elaborate and adapt the social, biological, and physical modules shown in Figure 6.4 to local ecologies. In terms of sex differences, the play and exploratory behavior of boys and girls should be designed to provide the experiences necessary for the emergence of those cognitive sex differences associated with the different reproductive strategies of men and women described in chapter 5. Chapter 7 provides consideration of these developmental sex differences, and chapter 8 provides an overview of the associated sex differences in brain and cognition.

7

DEVELOPMENTAL SEX DIFFERENCES

Is sexual selection related to differences in the physical, social, and psychological development of boys and girls? The goal of this chapter is to address this question by examining the pattern of sex differences across a variety of domains and by relating these sex differences to adult sex differences in the nature of intrasexual competition, parental investment, and so forth. Developmental sex differences in the pattern of physical development, infancy, play patterns, social development, and parenting influences are described in the respective sections that follow. The pattern that emerges across these sections is consistent with the view that many developmental sex differences are indeed related to sexual selection and are involved in a largely self-directed preparation for engaging in the reproductive activities described in chapter 4 and in chapter 5. In keeping with the position presented in chapter 6, this self-directed preparation is manifested in terms of differences in the types of activities in which girls and boys prefer to engage in and results in an adaptation of functional systems to local conditions.

PHYSICAL DEVELOPMENT

With any consideration of the relation between sexual selection and developmental sex differences, the first question that must be addressed is evolutionary change in the developmental period. This is so because selection will always favor early maturation and therefore faster reproduction unless delayed reproduction results in considerable reproductive advantages. In chapter 6, it was argued that one important function of development is to provide the experiences needed to elaborate the basic skeletal knowledge associated with evolved competencies, so that these competencies are tailored to local conditions (Mayr, 1974). In other words, a period of immaturity allows the individual to flesh out the skeletal competencies that appear to make up evolved cognitive modules and to develop the associated behavioral and social skills needed to function in adulthood, including those skills associated with intrasexual competition and parenting.

For any given species, a relatively long developmental period suggests the need for relatively sophisticated social, cognitive, and behavioral skills for adequate functioning in adulthood; relatively open genetic programs supporting these skills; and, on the basis of Sawaguchi's (1997) analysis, intense intrasexual competition (see the sections that follow and the *Social Modules* section of chapter 6). The first section below addresses the issue of evolutionary change in the length of the developmental period, and the second section provides discussion of sex differences in the pattern of physical development and physical competencies.

Evolutionary Change

On the basis of the strong relation between adult size and age of physical maturity, McHenry (1994a) estimated that the age of maturation for *A. afarensis*, *A. africanus*, and *H. habilis* was very similar to that found in the modern chimpanzee (*Pan troglodytes*); that is, 9 to 10 years (see also Conroy & Kuykendall, 1995). The estimated age of maturation for *H. erectus*, in contrast, was between 12 and 13 years. The roughly 3-year delay in the maturation of *H. erectus*, and a relatively large brain size (see Figure 3.7), suggest a significant increase, relative to their ancestors, in the complexity of the social, cognitive, and behavioral competencies needed to function in adulthood (see McKinney, 1998, for a general discussion).

The evolutionary trend is extended further in modern humans, in which physical maturation is achieved as late as the early 20s (Garai & Scheinfeld, 1968; Tanner, 1990) and brain volume increased 50% relative to *H. erectus*. Moreover, in comparison to other primates, Leigh (1996) found that human physical development is characterized by a distinct period of relatively slow growth, especially between about 6 to 10 years of age, but that it is unexceptional in other respects (e.g., the sex difference in the growth spurt; Leigh, 1995, 1996). Leigh's (1996) findings, combined with the overall evolutionary pattern, suggest that the relatively long maturational period of modern humans is largely due to an increase in the length of childhood—the period between birth and puberty—and that childhood is the period in the life span in which basic social, behavioral, and cognitive competencies are elaborated and adapted to local ecologies.

Comparative studies also reveal a strong relation between the length of the juvenile period, the size of the neocortex, and the complexity of the species' social system. These patterns suggest that the acquisition and refinement of social competencies are especially important during childhood (Joffe, 1997) and that the more refined social competencies that can be achieved during a longer as opposed to a shorter developmental period provided a strong selection advantage, especially in H. erectus and H. sapiens. Moreover, the finding that neocortical size in primates is related, in part, to the intensity of intrasexual competition suggests that sexual selection contributed to the evolution of a long developmental period in humans (Sawaguchi, 1997).

Sex Differences

Two general issues associated with physical sex differences are reviewed in the two sections below. In the first section, the pattern of sex differences in physical development and physical competencies is discussed; whereas in the second section, discussion of the sex difference in vulnerability to illness and developmental difficulties is provided.

Physical Development

For many species, including humans, physical dimorphisms are smaller before puberty than after puberty. As noted in chapter 2, the development of secondary sexual characteristics is often costly, especially for males (as discussed later). Such costs include suppressed immune functions and increased risk of predation (e.g., for brightly colored males), among others. The increased cost associated with the development of secondary sexual characteristics will result in natural selection favoring the delay of the emergence of physical dimorphisms until the individual has gained the social, behavioral, cognitive, or physical (e.g., weight) competencies needed for successful intrasexual competition. Among other things, this view suggests that the maturational period reflects the portion of the life span during which sex-specific skills—those related to intrasexual competition and reproductive strategies in general (e.g., degree of parental investment)—are refined, as suggested earlier. Puberty, in turn, results in the physical changes associated with adult reproduction, as well as those physical changes that directly facilitate intrasexual competition or that influence mate choice (e.g., an increase in body size for male–male competition or the acquisition of bright plumage for female choice), as described by Darwin more than 125 years ago:

> There is ... a striking parallelism between mammals and birds in all their secondary sexual characteristics, namely in their weapons for fighting with rival males, in their ornamental appendages, and in their colours. In both classes, when the male differs from the female, the young of both sexes almost always resemble each other, and in a large majority of cases resemble the adult female. In both classes the male assumes the characters proper to his sex shortly before the age for reproduction. (Darwin, 1871, Vol. II p. 297)

Studies of the northern elephant seal (*Mirounga angustirostris*) and the satin bowerbird (*Ptilonorhynchus violaceus*), described in chapter 2, provide examples of the relation between sex differences in the maturational period and sexual selection. Male northern elephant seals mature at around 8 years of age, as compared with 3 years of age for females (Clinton & Le Boeuf, 1993). Among other things, the males' relatively long maturational period allows them to gain the body mass needed to compete for a harem. Male satin bowerbirds do not achieve the full-adult blue plumage until they are 7 years old, many years after conspecific females have sexually matured (Collis & Borgia, 1992). Before this point, young males maintain a green plumage and do not differ significantly in appearance from young and adult females. During this period of immaturity, "young males spend a great deal of time observing older males at their bower, and practice bower building and display behaviors when the owner is absent from the bower site" (Collis & Borgia, 1992, p. 422; see Figure 2.6). Young males also engage in agonistic encounters with their same-age peers, which appears to provide the experience needed for dominance-related encounters in adulthood. Thus, in addition to the development of larger body sizes, delayed maturation also allows for the refinement of those social, behavioral, and presumably cognitive skills associated with intrasexual competition.

Sex differences in human physical development are characterized by the same general features described by Darwin (1871); that is, the most prominent physical dimorphisms emerge during puberty, although there are some earlier differences. Basically, "girls grow up faster than boys: that is, they reach 50% of their adult height at an earlier age ..., enter puberty earlier and cease earlier to grow.... At birth the difference corresponds to 4 to 6 weeks of maturation and at the beginning of puberty to 2 years" (Tanner, 1990, p. 56; see also Garai & Scheinfeld, 1968; Hutt, 1972). The slower maturation of boys appears to heighten their risk for early mortality (discussed later) but contributes to their adult height. For instance, the slower maturation of boys results in longer legs, relative to overall body height, than would otherwise be the case, which, in turn, contributes to the larger overall size of men relative to women (Tanner, 1990).

The most prominent sex differences to emerge during puberty are a widening of the hips and pelvis in girls and a widening of the width of the shoulders in boys. During puberty, which can last from 1.5 to 5 years, boys also "develop larger hearts as well as larger skeletal muscles, larger lungs, higher systolic blood pressure, lower resting heart-rate, a greater capacity for carrying oxygen in the blood, and a greater power of neutralizing the chemical products of muscular exercise. . . . In short, the male becomes more adapted at puberty for the tasks of hunting, fighting and manipulating all sorts of heavy objects" (Tanner, 1990, p. 74). Other sex differences include greater changes in the facial features of boys than of girls and greater increases in body fat in girls than in boys. The former reflects the emergence of those facial features that members of the opposite sex find attractive; that is, a masculine jaw in men and a youthful appearance (i.e., less change from childhood to adulthood) in women (see Figure 5.1 and Figure 5.3).

These changes in physical structure are accompanied by marked changes in physical competencies. The longer legs of men, relative to overall body height, allow for faster running and running for longer distances than women, on average. There are, in addition, some sex differences in physical competencies before puberty, although these differences are not typically as marked as those associated with pubertal changes. During childhood, there are small-to-moderate sex differences, favoring boys, in tasks such as grip strength, jumping distance, and running speeds, with large differences emerging during puberty (Thomas & French, 1985); by 17 years of age, more than 9 out of 10 men outperform the average woman in these areas. Infant boys are also more physically active than infant girls—about 3 out of 5 boys are more active than the average girl—and, again, this difference becomes more pronounced with maturation; by adolescence, just over 7 out of 10 boys are more active than the average girl (Eaton & Enns, 1986; Eaton & Yu, 1989). Girls, on the other hand, show greater physical flexibility and fine-eye motor coordination (e.g., as in threading a needle) than boys. The advantage of girls in these areas does not appear to vary with age and is modest in size (about 3 out of 5 girls outperform the average boy; Thomas & French, 1985); Kimura (1987) argued that the advantage of girls and women in this area might be related to manipulating objects "within personal space, or within arm's reach, such as food and clothing preparation and child care" (p. 145).

By far, the largest documented sex differences in physical competencies are for throwing distance and throwing velocity (Thomas & French, 1985). As early as 4 to 7 years of age, more than 9 out of 10 boys show a higher throwing velocity than the average same-age girl, despite the fact that girls are physically more mature at this age. By 12 years of age, there is little overlap in the distribution of the throwing velocities of boys and girls; the very best girls show throwing velocities that are comparable to the throwing velocities of the least skilled boys. The sex difference is somewhat larger for throwing distance. By 2 to 4 years of age, more than 9 out of 10 boys can throw farther than the average girl; by 17 years of age, only the very best girls can throw as far as the least skilled boys. At this age, men also have moderate-to-large advantages in visual acuity, in throwing accuracy, and in the ability to track and intercept (i.e., block) objects thrown at them; about 3 out of 4 men outperform the average woman in these areas (Jardine & Martin, 1983; Kolakowski & Malina, 1974; Law, Pellegrino, & Hunt, 1993; Velle, 1987; Watson & Kimura, 1991; see the *Physical Modules* section of chapter 8).

The finding of large sex differences in throwing skills as early as 2 years of age indicates that it is very unlikely that these differences result from the differential socialization of boys and girls (see the *Parenting* section of this chapter). In fact, these sex differences are almost certainly related, at least in part, to differences in the structure of the skeletal system that supports throwing. For instance, relative to overall body height, boys have a longer ulna and radius (i.e., forearm), on average, than girls do—a difference that emerges in utero (Gindhart, 1973; Tanner, 1990). For neonates, the radii of 3 out of 4 boys are longer than the radii of the average girl; whereas for 18-year-olds, the radii of more than 19 out of 20 men are longer than the radii of the average woman. There are also sex differences in the timing and pattern of skeletal ossification in the elbow and in the length and robustness of the humerus (i.e., upper arm; Benfer & McKern, 1966; Frisancho & Flegel, 1983; Tanner, 1990).

These differences in skeletal structure and the associated throwing competencies, combined with the large male advantage in arm and upper body strength, indicate strong selection pressures for these physical competencies in men. In fact, these sex differences are consistent with the view that the evolution of male–male competition in humans was influenced by the use of projectile (e.g., spears) and blunt force (e.g., clubs) weapons (Keeley, 1996; see also the *Physical Modules* section of chapter 8); during agonistic encounters, male chimpanzees often use projectile weapons (e.g., stones) and sticks as clubs and do so much more frequently than female chimpanzees do (Goodall, 1986). The finding that men have a higher threshold and a greater tolerance for physical pain than women do, on average, is also in keeping with the view that male–male competition is related to human physical dimorphisms, given that success at such competition is almost certainly facilitated by the ability to endure physical pain (Berkley, 1997; Velle, 1987); of course, women can endure considerable pain under some circumstances, such as childbirth.

Nonetheless, it might be argued that these physical sex differences have emerged from a sex difference in the division of labor, such as hunting, rather than in direct male–male competition (e.g., Frost, 1998; Kolakowski & Malina, 1974). Although the sexual division of labor contributes to the differential mortality of men and women in preindustrial societies and might influence the reproductive variance of men, comparative studies of the relation between physical dimorphisms and male–male competition suggest that the sexual division of labor is not likely to be the primary cause of these physical dimorphisms (see also *The Evolution of Sex Differences and the Sexual Division of Labor* section of chapter 3). Recall that for primates and many other species, there is a consistent relation between the physical sex differences and the nature of intrasexual competition (see chapter 3). For monogamous primates—those with little direct male–male competition over access to mating partners—there are little or no differences in the physical size or in the pattern of physical development of females and males (Leigh, 1995). For nonmonogamous primates—those characterized by direct male–male competition over access to mating partners—males are consistently larger than females, and this difference in physical size is consistently related, across species, to the intensity of physical male–male competition and not to the foraging strategy of the species (Clutton-Brock et al., 1977; Mitani et al., 1996; Plavcan & van Schaik, 1997b).

Across these nonmonogamous species, there is also a characteristic pattern of female and male growth. In those species in which females have growth spurts, the female pubertal growth spurt begins at an earlier age, reaches its peak more quickly, and lasts for a shorter period of time than that found in male conspecifics (Leigh, 1996). The pattern of human sex differences in physical development fits this general pattern (Leigh, 1996; Tanner, 1990; Weisfeld & Berger, 1983), a pattern that is consistent with the position that physical sex differences in humans have evolved largely by means of sexual selection (Tanner, 1992). Of course, some physical dimorphisms, such as the wider pelvic region in women, have likely emerged through natural selection. Nonetheless, once this difference emerged—creating the WHR (recall, waist-to-hip ratio) that men find attractive—it appears to have influenced mate choice and is thus also influenced by sexual selection (see the *Male Choice* section of chapter 5).

In other cases, it is likely that some physical sex differences are largely due to natural selection, as noted in chapter 3 (see *The Evolution of Sex Differences and the Sexual Division of Labor* section). Female and male chimpanzees, for instance, have different foraging strategies, which, in turn, can result in the evolution of sex differences independent of sexual selection. Goodall (1986) noted that "females not only crack nuts more frequently than males, [they also] show more dexterity in their manipulation of hammer stones" (p. 564); whether the advantage of girls and women in fine motor dexterity is related to a sex difference in the foraging strategies of our ancestors is not known.

Vulnerability

The delayed maturation of boys relative to girls and the general tendency for male hormones to suppress immune functions appear to put boys and men at risk for a wider array of illnesses and for premature death than same-age girls and women (Davis & Emory, 1995; McEwen et al., 1997; Tanner, 1990). In addition, boys and men have higher basal metabolic rates and higher activity levels than girls and women, on average, which, in turn, results in higher caloric requirements for boys than for girls for normal development to occur (Aiello, 1992). The net result of these differences appears to be a greater sensitivity of developing boys than developing girls to poor environmental conditions, such as poor nutrition or inadequate health care (see Stinson, 1985, for related discussion). In fact, a greater sensitivity of males than females to environmental conditions is often found in species in which physical sex differences appear to have been shaped through sexual selection (Clutton-Brock et al., 1985; McDonald, 1993; Møller, 1994a; Potti & Merino, 1996; Rowe & Houle, 1996). As described in chapter 2, the greater environmental sensitivity of males appears to reflect, at least in some cases, the evolution of condition-dependent secondary sexual characteristics, so that these characteristics are only fully developed in the most healthy males (see the *Sex Hormones and Parasites* section).

Whether a similar process is operating in humans is not currently known, but this is a distinct possibility (Thornhill & Møller, 1997). For instance, there is some evidence that boys and men respond to social and other stressors differently than girls and women. M. Davis and Emory (1995), as an example, found that newborn boys showed an increase in cortisol levels after exposure to mild but prolonged stressors, but newborn girls showed no such increase, although they did show a larger increase in heart rate than boys did. It is likely that any such sex differences in the nature of stressor-related physiological responses vary across social and other contexts (Flinn et al., 1996; Sapolsky, 1993). Nonetheless, an overall sex difference in cortisol responses, among other factors, would make boys and men more susceptible to growth disorders and other diseases—through suppression of immune functions and growth hormones—than girls and women and might contribute to the higher mortality rates in boys and men relative to same-age girls and women (McEwen et al., 1997; Tanner, 1990).

As an example, Martorell and his colleagues followed the physical, intellectual, and educational development of 249 rural Guatemalans from early childhood to 26 years of age (Martorell, Rivera, Kaplowitz, & Pollitt, 1992). Growth failure at age 3 years, because of an inadequate diet and a high rate of infection, was related to stunted physical and educational development for both men and women in adulthood. Men, however, were more severely affected, as a group, than women on a number of dimensions, including the proportion of lean muscle mass, years of education, and literacy scores. For instance, of those individuals showing early growth failure, nearly 1 out of 3 men, but only 1 out of 10 women, exhibited reading difficulties in adulthood. In contrast, for individuals showing normal growth at age 3 years, more men than women passed the literacy test.

No doubt there are other physiological and social mechanisms involved in the apparent sex difference in sensitivity and reactivity to environmental conditions (see, for example, Gualtieri & Hicks, 1985). Stinson (1985), for instance, suggested that in many preindustrial cultures, parents might compensate for the greater sensitivity of boys through a preferential treatment of boys, such as providing them with more calories relative to girls. Whatever the mechanisms, these sex differences also appear to result in greater variability across many characteristics within groups of boys and men relative to groups of girls and women (Hedges & Nowell, 1995), as would be expected for condition-dependent traits (implications are discussed in chapter 9). In other words, poor environmental conditions appear to more adversely affect larger numbers of boys than girls, whereas more boys than girls might benefit from more optimal rearing conditions. However, it is not known whether the greater variability within groups of boys and men extends to most domains (e.g., physical and cognitive development) or whether girls and women are more susceptible than boys and men in some areas. The finding that female–female competition and male choice have operated during the course of human evolution suggests that sex-specific sensitivities to poor environments are possible and, in fact, are expected (Thornhill & Møller, 1997; see the *Social Modules* section of chapter 6).

INFANCY

The study of sex differences in infancy is inherently more difficult than the study of sex differences in older children, because the behavior of infants is more variable than the behavior of older children (which would obscure many sex differences) and because there are fewer methods that can be used to study infants than to study older children (Maccoby & Jacklin, 1974). As a result, the pattern of sex differences in infants has not been as systematically assessed, at least in recent years, as the pattern in older children. Given these limitations, many of the sex differences described in this section need to be interpreted with some caution.

With the study of developmental sex differences, it is often assumed that biologically influenced sex differences will manifest themselves early in development, whereas sex differences that are largely influenced by cultural factors, such as gender roles, will manifest themselves later in development and as a result of the cumulative effects of socializing agents (e.g., parents' stereotyped interactions with girls and boys; see Adamson & McArthur, 1995; Serbin, Powlishta, & Gulko, 1993; Whiting & Edwards, 1973). As noted earlier, this assumption is incorrect. In species in which sexual selection has resulted in the evolution of sex differences, such differences are often not manifested until puberty (Darwin, 1871). In this view, infant boys and girls are expected to be more similar than different, and this appears to be the case (Hsu, Soong, Stigler, Hong, & Liang, 1981; Maccoby & Jacklin, 1974; Rothbart, 1989).

In theory, those sex differences that are found in infancy should reflect the seeds of the later described sex differences in play and social development, which, in turn, should provide the experience and practice needed to acquire the behavioral, social, and cognitive competencies associated with the sex difference in reproductive activities, such as differences in the nature of intrasexual competition (see chapter 5). There are indeed several patterns in the infancy literature suggesting that the skeletal structure of sex differences in social and play activities is evident in the in first year or two of life and in some cases in the first few days of life (J. H. Block, 1976; Cohen & Gelber, 1975; Davis & Emory, 1995; Fagan, 1972; Gunnar & Donahue, 1980; Gunnar & Stone, 1984; Haviland & Malatesta, 1981; Kujawski & Bower, 1993; W. D. Rosen, Adamson, & Bakeman, 1992; Simner, 1971; Zahn-Waxler, Radke-Yarrow, Wagner, & Chapman, 1992; Zahn-Waxler, Robinson, & Emde, 1992).

One of the more consistent of these differences is the general orientation of boys and girls toward other people (Freedman, 1974; Garai & Scheinfeld, 1968; Haviland & Malatesta, 1981; McGuinness & Pribram, 1979). For infants, the degree of orientation toward other people has been measured in terms of the duration of eye contact, empathic responses to the distress of other people, recognition of faces, and time spent looking at faces, among other behaviors. In a review of sex differences in nonverbal behavior, Haviland and Malatesta (1981) noted that "there is no doubt that girls and women establish and maintain eye contact more than boys and men. The earliest age for which this is reported is one day" (p. 189). In addition, boys and men gaze-avert much more frequently than girls and women, a sex difference that has been found as early as 6 months of age. In the first few days of life, it appears that girls orient themselves to faces and voices more frequently, on average, than boys do (Haviland & Malatesta, 1981), and, by least at 6 months of age, girls might have a better memory for faces and might be more skilled than boys in discriminating between two similar faces (e.g., Fagan, 1972); these latter differences, however, are not found as consistently in infants as they are in older individuals (J. A. Hall, 1984; Haviland & Malatesta, 1981; Maccoby & Jacklin, 1974; McGuinness & Symonds, 1977).

A number of other studies suggest that infant girls react with greater empathy to the distress of other people than infant boys do (Hoffman,

1977). Simner (1971), for instance, found that infant girls cried longer than infant boys when exposed to the cry of another infant, but no sex difference in reflexive crying was found when the infants were exposed to artificial noise of the same intensity as infant crying. More recently, Zahn-Waxler and her colleagues found a sex difference in the responses of 12- to 20-month-olds to the distress of other people (Zahn-Waxler, Radke-Yarrow, et al., 1992; Zahn-Waxler, Robinson, & Emde, 1992). In both studies, girls responded to the distress of other people with greater empathic concern than boys did, which is defined as "emotional arousal that appears to reflect sympathetic concern for the victim . . . manifested in facial or vocal expressions (e.g., sad looks, sympathetic statements . . .) or gestures" (Zahn-Waxler, Radke-Yarrow, et al., 1992, p. 129). In one of the studies, girls also responded to the distressed individual with more prosocial behavior (e.g., comforting) and engaged in more information-seeking behaviors (e.g., "What's wrong?") than boys did. Boys, in contrast, were unresponsive or affectively indifferent to the victim's distress more frequently than girls were.

However, these differences were only found for distress that was witnessed and not caused by the child. In other words, girls did not show more empathy than boys when they caused the distress in another individual (e.g., in the course of some conflict), although boys behaved more aggressively (e.g., hit) than girls in these situations. Moreover, the magnitude of the sex differences in empathic concern and indifference was modest. At 20 months of age, about three out of five girls responded with greater empathic concern to the distress of another person than the average boy did, whereas two out of three boys showed more affective indifference than the average girl did. Finally, both empathic concern and affective indifference were found to have moderate genetic influences for both 14- and 20-month-olds, suggesting that these social behaviors are influenced by a mix of biological, social, and contextual factors; between 29% and 35% of the individual differences in these social behaviors appear to be heritable at these ages (Zahn-Waxler, Robinson, & Emde, 1992).

The results of several studies of the nature and quality of social interactions between parents and infants are also consistent with the view that infant girls are more responsive, and perhaps more sensitive, to social cues than infant boys are (Freedman, 1974; Gunnar & Donahue, 1980; Gunnar & Stone, 1984; W. D. Rosen et al., 1992). Gunnar and Stone found that in ambiguous situations—such as in the presence of an unfamiliar and potentially threatening toy (i.e., a monkey)—12-month-olds of both sexes would approach the unfamiliar object if their mother signaled positive emotions (e.g., smiling) in reference to this object. W. D. Rosen et al. found the same pattern, as well as a sex difference when mothers signaled fear in response to the unfamiliar object. In this situation, girls tended to withdraw from the object, whereas boys tended to approach the object. Independent coders rated the intensity of the mothers' fear signal and judged that these signals were more intense when directed toward boys than when directed toward girls, suggesting that the difference in the reaction of boys and girls was not likely to be due to the behavior of their mother. Rather, the tendency of boys to approach unfamiliar objects more frequently than girls, on average, might be one early manifestation of the sex difference in risk taking, mentioned later (*Social Development* section), and the mothers' more intense signals to boys might be a reflection of their prior experiences with unresponsive sons (see Adamson & McArthur, 1995, for an alternative explanation).

In a related study with 6- to 12-month-olds, Gunnar and Donahue (1980) found that mothers were just as likely to attempt to initiate social interactions with their sons as with their daughters, but daughters were much more responsive than sons to their mother's verbal requests; Whiting and Edwards (1988) found the same pattern with older children, across cultures. For instance, for 12-month-olds, girls responded to 52% of their mother's verbal requests to engage in some form of social interaction, as compared with a 25% response rate in same-age boys. In contrast, boys and girls were equally responsive to their mother when she used a toy to attempt to initiate a social interaction. In addition, girls initiated about 30% more social interactions with their mother than boys did, on average. Gunnar and Donahue's results suggest that the occasional finding that mothers sometimes interact more with their daughters than with their sons (e.g., Klein & Durfee, 1978) might stem from a sex difference, favoring girls, in social responsiveness and the degree to which social interactions are initiated, rather than a maternal preference for girls per se (Freedman, 1974).

Although girls appear to orient themselves more to other people and show greater sensitivity to some social cues than boys do, boys appear to orient themselves more to physical information and show greater sensitivity to certain physical cues, such as geometric shape, than girls do (Cohen & Gelber, 1975; Freedman, 1974; McGuinness & Pribram, 1979). When "differences are found, males from 4–6 months onwards respond preferentially to blinking lights, geometric patterns, colored photographs of objects and three-dimensional objects" (McGuinness & Pribram, 1979, p. 19). A similar conclusion was drawn by Cohen and Gelber, which was based on a review of research on infants' visual memory. On the basis of this review, they argued that "males and females are processing and storing different kinds of information about repeatedly presented [visual] stimuli. Males appear to be more likely to store information about the various components of a repeatedly presented stimulus, for example, its form and color ... [while] females, unlike males, are more likely to store information about the consequences of orienting" (Cohen & Gelber, 1975, p. 382). In short, it appears that by about 4 months of age, boys selectively attend to the physical properties of objects, such as shape, whereas girls selectively attend to the consequences of orienting to objects in their environment, rather than to the objects themselves (except when these objects are people); *consequences* refer, for instance, to how the objects might be related to the behavior of other people (e.g., whether their behavior changes when the objects are present).

In all, the pattern of sex differences in infancy suggests that girls and boys orient, process, and react to certain social and physical cues differently. These sex differences, in turn, appear to reflect early differences in the skeletal competencies underlying the sex differences in certain social and physical cognitive modules (as described in chapter 8) as well as the precursors to some of the differences in the play styles and social development of boys and girls (as described below). In other words, infant boys and girls appear to be differentially biased in the ways in which they process information associated with individual-level social modules and certain physical modules (as described in chapter 6), and their attentional and processing biases, along with the activity differences described below, appear to be related to many of the cognitive sex differences described in chapter 8 (McGuinness & Pribram, 1979).

PLAY

To illustrate the apparent functions of play, the first section focuses on nonhuman species. The second section focuses on human sex differences in play-related activities.

The Functions of Play

Play in one form or another is found in most mammalian species and in some species of bird, but generally not in fishes, reptiles, or insects (Fagen, 1981). Across mammalian species, play is typically categorized as social, locomotor, or object oriented (Aldis, 1975; Fagen, 1981), and it is often assumed that play provides delayed benefits to the individual (see Archer, 1992; Fagen, 1995, for discussion). "The consensus that emerges from the scores of definitions is that play incorporates many physical components of adult behavior patterns, such as those used in aggression, but without their immediate functional consequences" (J. R. Walters, 1987, p. 360). The delayed benefits of play are in terms of practicing those behaviors that are important for survival and reproduction in adulthood. In addition, Barber (1991) hypothesized that play resulted in a number of more immediate benefits, although this interpretation is debated (Archer, 1992).

For instance, play increases body temperature, which, in turn, can enhance resistance to infections.

In mammals, play often occurs in social contexts and very frequently involves rough-and-tumble play and chasing (Archer, 1992; Panksepp, Siviy, & Normansell, 1984; J. R. Walters, 1987). Rough-and-tumble play or play fighting appears to be especially common in species in which social conflict in adulthood is resolved through physical contests (e.g., elephant seals), and, given this, it has been proposed that these play activities provide the practice needed to develop social–competitive skills (Pellis, Field, Smith, & Pellis, 1997; P. K. Smith, 1982). Moreover, across those mammalian species in which it has been studied, rough-and-tumble play is generally more common and more vigorous in males than in females and appears to occur relatively more frequently and more vigorously with males of polygynous species—those characterized by physical male–male competition—than with males of monogamous species (Aldis, 1975; P. K. Smith, 1982). One apparent exception is for carnivores, in which both males and females hunt, defend territory, and engage in physical competition with conspecifics. In these species, it appears that both juvenile males and females regularly engage in rough-and-tumble play (Aldis, 1975; Fagen, 1981).

Extensive experimental studies of rough-and-tumble play have been conducted with the laboratory rat and the rhesus macaque (*Macaca mulatta*; e.g., Meaney & Stewart, 1981; Panksepp, 1981; Panksepp et al., 1984; Pellis et al., 1997; Wallen, 1996). These studies indicate that the expression of rough-and-tumble play is influenced by a mix of hormonal, social rearing, and contextual factors. For the polygynous rhesus macaque, males consistently show more rough-and-tumble play than females, although the magnitude of this sex difference varies somewhat with rearing environment (Wallen, 1996). In comparison to males reared in typical male–female social groups, males reared only with other males show relatively more rough-and-tumble play, whereas males reared in isolation show relatively less rough-and-tumble play when introduced to their peers. Neonatal castration and other manipulations that suppress androgens after the male is born have little effect on the frequency of rough-and-tumble play. For females, prolonged prenatal exposure to androgens significantly increases the frequency of rough-and-tumble play, regardless of rearing environment. On the basis of these results, it appears that, at least for the rhesus macaque, the frequency of rough-and-tumble is primarily influenced by prenatal exposure to androgens (Wallen, 1996), although prenatal exposure to estrogens, and social and contextual factors, also appears to be important for the expression of this form of play in some other species (Panksepp et al., 1984; Pellis et al., 1997).

It appears that chasing and associated behaviors such as stalking, rushing, and pawing are related to the development of prey capture or predator avoidance skills (P. K. Smith, 1982). Sex differences in these behaviors have not been as systematically studied as the sex difference in rough-and-tumble play, although there is some indication that, at least for some species, this form of play might be relatively more common in females than in males (Fagen, 1981).

Another form of social play that is more common in females than in males is alloparenting, or play parenting, although this form of play can occur in both sexes (Nicolson, 1987; Pryce, 1992, 1993, 1995). In primates, play parenting is most frequently observed in young females that have not yet had their first offspring. In a number of these species, early play parenting (e.g., caring for siblings) is associated with higher survival rates of the firstborn, and sometimes later born, offspring (Nicolson, 1987). For instance, across five primate species, it was found that firstborn survival rates were two to more than four times higher for mothers with early experience with infant care, obtained through play parenting, than for mothers with no such experience (Pryce, 1993). As noted in chapter 4 (*Hormonal Influences* section), maternal care is also influenced by the hormonal changes that occur during pregnancy and the birthing process, so that a combination of early play parenting and these hormonal changes contributes to the adequacy of female caregiving in many primate species (P. C. Lee & Bowman, 1995; Pryce, 1995).

In contrast to social play, which involves dyads and sometimes larger groups, locomotor play is typically a solitary activity and often involves an exaggeration of those movements involved in common functional activities, such as predator avoidance (Fagen, 1981; P. K. Smith, 1982). Byers and Walker (1995) have recently argued that early locomotor play results in long-term changes in the synaptic organization of the cerebellum, which is involved in the coordination of complex motor movements, and in the distribution of fast and slow muscle fibers. In this view, locomotor play results in neural and muscular changes that support complex functional activities in adulthood. As an example, with the Siberian ibex (*Capra sibirica*), a species of mountain goat, "social play is equally likely on flat and sloped terrains, but solitary locomotor play was much more frequent on sloped terrain, despite the greater dangers of falling" (P. K. Smith, 1982, p. 142). From the perspective introduced by Byers and Walker, the ibex kids' play on sloped terrain would result in neural and muscular adaptations, thus facilitating later locomotion in mountainous terrain.

Object play occurs relatively infrequently in primates, except for chimpanzees and humans, and involves the nonfunctional manipulation of objects, such as throwing them, banging them, and so forth (Byrne, 1995; Fagen, 1981). The function of this type of play appears to be to learn about the different ways in which various objects in the environment can be used, which, in turn, appears to facilitate later tool use and perhaps later problem-solving skills as related to tool use (Byrne, 1995; P. K. Smith, 1982). Goodall (1986) provided an example with the chimpanzee:

> Youngsters utilize many objects during solitary play, demonstrating the extent to which infants make use of the objects in their environment—sometimes in a very inventive way. Fruit-laden twigs, strips of skin and hair from an old kill, or highly prized pieces of cloth may be draped over the shoulders or carried along in the neck or groin pocket (that is, tucked between the neck and shoulder or thigh and belly); stones or small fruits may be hit about on the ground, from one hand to the other, or thrown short distances into the air and retrieved. (p. 559)

At times, these play episodes result in important discoveries. For Gombe chimpanzees, sticks are often used to fish for termites. On one occasion, "a juvenile male, Wilkie, poked his stick into an ant nest, causing a stream of fierce black ants to emerge. Wilkie avoided them. His mother, who had been watching, immediately approached and ate the ants" (Goodall, 1986, p. 563). Chimpanzees that lack this type of object-oriented play in their childhood are "poor at problem-solving later in life with tasks that involve objects" (Byrne, 1995, p. 86). Stated otherwise, these individuals do not use common chimpanzee tools, such as the stick used by Wilkie, to solve everyday problems, such as getting food.

In summary, play provides a pattern of early experience that results in the fine-tuning of a number of social and physical competencies associated with survival and reproduction in adulthood. For instance, these experiences appear to result in long-term neural and muscular adaptations associated with the facile execution of essential behavioral competencies, such as predator avoidance. In some species, it also appears that early play—object-oriented play in particular—results in learning about the potential usefulness of objects in the local ecology, which, in turn, appears to be related to later tool use. It also seems likely that social play influences the development of social–cognitive competencies, such as those associated with theory of mind, at least to the extent that the particular species, such as the chimpanzee, develops a theory of mind.

Sex Differences

Sex differences in play activities are a universal feature of children's behavior, and the study of these differences has generally focused on three relatively independent components: gender schemes, knowledge about the sex-typed activities of girls and women and boys and men; child-initiated activities, such as rough-and-tumble play; and formation of same-sex play groups (Aldis, 1975; Boulton & Smith, 1992; Brown, 1991; Lever, 1978; Maccoby, 1988; Maccoby & Jacklin, 1974; Pitcher & Schultz, 1983; Sandberg & Meyer-Bahlburg, 1994; Weisfeld & Berger, 1983; Whiting & Edwards, 1973, 1988). Children's gender schemes are only very weakly related to the actual play and social activities of girls and boys (Serbin et al., 1993; Turner & Gervai, 1995). Moreover, girls and boys play in same-sex groups, regardless of the degree to which their activities are sex typed (Maccoby, 1988). Boys who engage in high levels of rough-and-tumble play, for instance, spend most of their play time with other boys, as do boys who do not engage in high levels of rough-and-tumble play.

The focus of this section is primarily on child-initiated play activities; a discussion of the social styles of girls and boys, including the formation of same-sex play groups, is presented in the section below, and discussion of parental influences, or a lack thereof, on children's social development is presented in the last section of the chapter. As is the case with many other mammals, the pattern of human sex differences in child-initiated play activities appears to be influenced by a mix of hormonal, social, and contextual factors and involves at least six different forms of play: rough-and-tumble, locomotor, exploratory, parenting, object oriented, and fantasy (Berenbaum & Hines, 1992; Berenbaum & Snyder, 1995; Boulton, 1996; Collaer & Hines, 1995; DiPietro, 1981; Hines & Kaufman, 1994; Loy & Hesketh, 1995; Maccoby, 1988; Serbin, Connor, & Citron, 1981). Sex differences in the pattern and the frequency of engagement in each of these forms of play are described in the respective sections that follow.

Rough-and-Tumble Play

One of the more consistently found child-initiated sex differences, favoring boys, is in the frequency and the nature of rough-and-tumble play; although sex differences are not always found for all components of this form of play, and the nature of rough-and-tumble play can vary from one culture to the next (Boulton, 1996; Whiting & Edwards, 1988). As noted earlier, females of many primates species engage in rough-and-tumble play but do so less frequently and less vigorously than conspecific males (Aldis, 1975; P. K. Smith, 1982). Similarly, female-on-female aggression frequently occurs in these primates, typically over access to food, but results in severe injury and death much less frequently than male-on-male aggression does (see the *Female–Female Competition and Male Choice* section of chapter 3). The same pattern is found in humans: Rough-and-tumble play is not an exclusively male activity, but it occurs much more frequently and more vigorously with boys than with girls and parallels the sex difference in the intensity of physical intrasexual competition (see chapter 5).

Across contexts, sex differences in rough-and-tumble play are most evident with groups of three or more boys and in the absence of adult supervision (Maccoby, 1988; Pellegrini, 1995); adults often discourage this type of play. In situations in which play activities are not monitored by adults and in contexts in which their activities are not otherwise restricted (e.g., a play area that is too small), groups of boys engage in various forms of rough-and-tumble play—including playful physical assaults and wrestling—three to six times more frequently than groups of same-age girls do (DiPietro, 1981; Maccoby, 1988). As an example, in an analysis of the activities of triads of same-sex 4-year-olds who did not know that they were being observed, DiPietro found that boys engaged in playful physical assaults—including hitting, pushing, and tripping—four and one-half times more frequently than girls; biting is not typically a feature of this form of play (see the *Sexual Dimorphisms* section of chapter 3 for related discussion). Research conducted in the United States indicates that the sex difference in playful physical assaults and other forms of rough-and-tumble play begins to emerge by about 3 years of age (Maccoby, 1988), and the same general pattern is found in other industrial, as well as in many preindustrial, societies, although the magnitude of the sex difference in this form of play varies across these cultures (Eibl-Eibesfeldt, 1989; Whiting & Edwards, 1973, 1988).

The nature of boys' rough-and-tumble play also varies somewhat across cultures. In societies characterized by relatively high levels of adult male-on-male physical aggression, the play fighting of boys tends to be rougher than the play fighting found in societies with relatively less male-on-male physical aggression. For instance, intergroup aggression is a pervasive feature of Yanomamö society (Chagnon, 1988; see the *Male–Male Competition* section of chapter 5), and young Yanomamö boys often play fight with clubs or bows and arrows, practices that are typically discouraged in settings in which male-on-male physical aggression occurs infrequently (N. A. Chagnon, personal communication, July 1997). Loy and Hesketh (1995) provided a number of other examples in their analysis of the war-related games of the Native American warrior societies of the central plains. "Evidence suggests that all Plains Indian tribes were, to greater or lesser degrees, involved in a wide range of warring activities . . . confined primarily to small war parties, raids, forays; that is, conflicts which were brief and usually indecisive" (Loy & Hesketh, 1995, p. 80). For the Sioux, and for many other Indian tribes, the activities of young boys were designed to encourage aggression—both one-on-one and coalition based—and physical endurance (Culin, 1902/1903; Hassrick, 1964).

> Games for the Sioux frequently were contrived life-situations in miniature. They ran the gamut from the more complex diversion of the Moccasin Game enjoyed by adults to the raucously rough Swing-Kicking Game played by young boys. . . .
>
> The Swing-Kicking Game took first place as a rugged conditioner, and there was no pretense at horseplay. Here two rows of boys faced each other, each holding his robe over his left arm. The game was begun only after the formality of the stock question, "Shall we grab them by the hair and knee them in the face until they bleed?" Then

using their robes as a shield, they all kicked at their opponents, endeavoring to upset them. There seems to have been no rules, for the boys attacked whoever was closest, often two boys jumping one. Kicking from behind the knees was a good way of throwing an opponent, and once down he was grabbed at the temples with both hands and kneed in the face.

Once released, the bloody victims would fight on, kicking and kneeing and bleeding until they could fight no longer. . . . As Iron Shell explained, "Some boys got badly hurt, but afterwards we would talk and laugh about it. Very seldom did any fellows get angry. . . ."

Throw at Each Other with Mud was a slightly more gentle spring pastime where teams of boys attacked [each other] with mud balls which they threw from the tips of short springy sticks. Each boy carried several sticks and an arsenal of mud as he advanced. "It certainly hurt when you got hit, so you must duck and throw as you attack." Sometimes live coals were embedded in the mud balls to add zest to the game. (Hassrick, 1964, pp. 127–130)

Similar types of play fighting are evident even in cultures in which most men do not engage in intergroup aggression or physical one-on-one competition. For instance, in several large-scale studies of the play activities of boys and girls in the United States, consistent sex differences, favoring boys, in one-on-one and coalition-based play fighting and intrasexual competition have been found (Lever, 1978; Sandberg & Meyer-Bahlburg, 1994; Willingham & Cole, 1997); see Sherif et al. (1961) for an engaging illustration of social–competitive play in boys. These sex differences have changed little from one decade to the next and are evident whether observations, questionnaires, interviews, or diaries of leisure activities are used to assess play behavior. As an example, Lever asked 181 10- and 11-year-old children to record their after-school activities during the course of 1 week, resulting in 895 cases of social play. An analysis of sex differences in social play indicated that boys participated in group-level competitive activities, such as football and basketball, three times as frequently as girls. Observation of the spontaneous (i.e., not organized by adults) play activities of these same children confirmed the pattern noted in diaries and indicated that boys' social play involves larger groups, on average, than girls' social play does and greater role differentiation within these groups.

> More often, boys compete as members of teams and must simultaneously coordinate their actions with those of their teammates while taking into account the action and strategies of their opponents. Boys interviewed expressed finding gratification in acting as a representative of a collectivity; the approval or disapproval of one's teammates accentuates the importance of contributing to a group victory. (Lever, 1978, p. 478)

A more recent questionnaire-based assessment of the play activities of 355 6- to 10-year-old girls and 333 same-age boys revealed the same pattern (Sandberg & Meyer-Bahlburg, 1994). For 6-year-olds, 44% of the boys regularly played football, compared with 2% of the girls. For 10-year-olds, 70% of the boys regularly played football, compared with 15% of the girls. The magnitude of the sex difference was smaller, although still substantial, for basketball; 85% and 86% of the 6- and 10-year-old boys, respectively, played regularly, as compared with 25% and 36% of the same-age girls. These differences, along with many other sex differences, were essentially the same as those found three decades earlier by Sutton-Smith and his colleagues (Sutton-Smith, Rosenberg, & Morgan, 1963).

The sex difference in one-on-one and group-level competitive play is related, at least in part, to prenatal exposure to androgens. Indeed, the "clearest evidence for hormonal influences on human behavioral development comes from studies of childhood play. Elevated androgen in genetic females . . . is associated with masculinized and defeminized play" (Collaer & Hines, 1995, p. 92). For example, Berenbaum and Snyder (1995) administered the same questionnaire used by Sandberg and Meyer-Bahlburg (1994) to boys and girls who were prenatally exposed to excess levels of androgens (i.e., CAH; recall, congenital adrenal hyperplasia), unaffected children, and their parents. On the bases of parental and self-reports, girls affected by CAH engaged in more athletic competition than their unaffected peers—between 7 and 8 out of every 10 girls affected by CAH engaged in athletic competition more frequently than the average unaffected girl. This difference, however, was not as large as the difference between unaffected boys and unaffected girls; more than 9 out of 10 unaffected boys reported engaging in athletic competition more frequently than the average unaffected girl.

In an observational study, Hines and Kaufman (1994) found that girls affected by CAH engaged in more playful physical assaults, physical assaults on objects, wrestling, and rough-and-tumble play in general than unaffected girls, but none of these differences was statistically significant. The lack of significance was possibly due to the testing arrangements used in this study. Here, most of the girls affected by CAH were observed as they played with one unaffected girl, a situation (two girls), as noted earlier, that does not typically facilitate rough-and-tumble play (Maccoby, 1988).

In all, the cross-cultural pattern of sex differences in rough-and-tumble play and group-level competition, combined with the finding that at least some components of this type of play are influenced by prenatal exposure to androgens, is consistent with the view that these activities represent fundamental differences in the way in which the typical boy and the typical girl play. Moreover, this form of play appears to serve the function of developing the component competencies associated with intrasex-

Figure 7.1. A game similar to lacrosse played by the Menomini Indians of Wisconsin. The aim is to catch and carry the ball to the opponent's goal. From *Games of the North American Indians* (between pages 568–569), by S. Culin, 1902/1903, Washington, DC, Bureau of American Ethnology.

ual competition in adulthood. Boulton (1996), for instance, found that the component behaviors associated with rough-and-tumble play, such as hitting, were the same as those involved in actual one-on-one physical fights. Play fighting also provides the practice of those component skills associated with coalition-based intergroup warfare.

As an example, consider the game of baseball played in modern America and the game of Throw at Each Other with Mud played by Sioux Indians 200 hundred years ago; similar games were common throughout Native American tribes (Culin, 1902/1903), as shown in Figure 7.1, and are found in many other parts of the world as well (Eibl-Eibesfeldt, 1989). Both of these games, as well as most if not all other forms of athletic competition, require many of the same physical, social, and cognitive competencies involved in coalition-based warfare (Geary, 1995b). Both baseball and Throw at Each Other with Mud require the formation of in-groups and out-groups, the strategic coordination of the activities of in-group members as related to competition with the out-group, the throwing of projectiles (baseballs and mud balls) at specific targets, and the tracking and reacting to the movement of these projectiles (to catch the baseball or to avoid being hit by the mud ball).

The latter activities are in keeping with the earlier described sex differences, favoring boys and men, in throwing distance, velocity, and accuracy, as well as skill at intercepting thrown objects (Thomas & French, 1985; Watson & Kimura, 1991). These component skills, along with the male advantage in upper body strength and length of the forearm (Tanner, 1990), are the same competencies involved in the use of—and in the avoidance of being hit by—projectile weapons. Or stated differently, the rough-and-tumble play and fighting games of boys appear to provide the activities needed to fine-tune the competencies associated with physical one-on-one and coalition-based male–male competition, and, given this, they have likely evolved by means of sexual selection (Darwin, 1871).

Moreover, the finding that the nature of play fighting is influenced by cultural factors (Whiting & Edwards, 1988), in particular the intensity and frequency of intergroup warfare, supports the position that the function of childhood is to adapt evolved traits to local conditions (Loy & Hesketh, 1995). In many cases, the form of play fighting—such as club fights or spear throwing—mirrors the actual form of male-on-male aggression in adulthood and thus provides direct practice of the associated component skills (Eibl-Eibesfeldt, 1989). In addition to providing the practice of those social, cognitive, and behavioral competencies associated with primitive warfare, it is also likely that the intensity of the play fighting results in changes in the sensitivity of the associated emotional systems (MacDonald, 1988). For instance, the physical pain that was associated with playing the Swing-Kicking Game almost certainly resulted in more aggressive boys than would otherwise be the case, as well as boys who were less sensitive to the distress of other people and who were better able to suppress their fear and their reaction to physical pain (see the *Parenting* section).

Locomotor and Exploratory Play

In addition to rough-and-tumble play, boys also engage in gross locomotor play more frequently than girls, a sex difference that has been found in industrial as well as in many preindustrial societies (Eibl-Eibesfeldt, 1989; R. L. Munroe & Munroe, 1971; Whiting & Edwards, 1988). The sex difference in locomotor play is related in part to the different types of activities in which boys and girls engage. As noted earlier, boys engage in group-level competitive play, such as football or soccer, about three times as frequently as girls do, and engagement in this type of play results in a sex difference in gross locomotor activities, in particular, running (Eaton & Enns, 1986; Lever, 1978). Boys also engage in competitive running games, such as relay races, more frequently than girls do, but the sex difference in these activities is not nearly as large as the sex difference in the frequency of engagement in group-level competitive play (Sandberg & Meyer-Bahlburg, 1994). Nonetheless, on the basis of Byers and Walker's (1995) model, it appears that the sex difference in gross locomotor activities creates neuromuscular changes that will result in men, relative to women, being better adapted for running and traveling long distances on foot. In addition to any such neuromuscular adaptations, the sex difference in gross locomotor activities results in larger play ranges for boys than for girls. Within these ranges, boys not only engage in these locomotor activities more frequently than girls do but they also explore and manipulate (e.g., build things, such as forts) the environment much more frequently than girls do (Matthews, 1992; R. L. Munroe & Munroe, 1971). The sex difference in the size of the play range and in the associated exploratory play is potentially important because these factors appear to be related to the development of certain spatial competencies, and, given this, might be one factor contributing to the sex differences in the elaboration of certain physical modules (described in chapter 8; Matthews, 1992). There are two associated issues related to developmental sex differences: the extent to which the play ranges of boys and girls differ and any associated sex difference in the ability to represent these ranges mentally.

The sex difference in the play-range area appears to be related, at least in part, to greater parental restrictions on the ranges of girls than of boys. However, a sex difference in the size of the play range is found in the absence of any such restrictions and has been found in both industrial and in some preindustrial societies (Matthews, 1992; R. L. Munroe & Munroe, 1971); girls appear to be more cautious than boys with respect to exploring unfamiliar territory (Sherry & Hampson, 1997). In studies of the exploratory play of children in suburban England, for instance, Matthews (1992) found that younger children, both boys and girls, tended to play within close proximity of one or both of their parents (see also Whiting & Edwards, 1988). Older children, in contrast, were more likely to play away from home, and, at this point, a sex difference in the area making up the play range emerges. For 8- to 11-year-olds, the unrestricted play range of boys was found to cover from one and one-half to nearly three times the unrestricted play-range area of same-age girls. Whiting and Edwards (1988) reported a similar sex difference for older children in three separate groups in Kenya, as well as for children in Peru and Guatemala. Nonetheless, the age at which this sex difference emerges appears to vary with the ecology of the group. For the Ache, who live in a dense tropical rain forest, the size of the play range of boys and girls does not typically diverge until adolescence (K. Hill & Hurtado, 1996).

Research on the exploratory behavior of animals suggests that, among other things, this activity allows for the development of cognitive representations of the local ecology, such as a mental map of the relative position of major landmarks. These cognitive representations, in turn, appear to support navigation within this ecology (Poucet, 1993; see the *Physical Modules* section of chapter 6). Similar conclusions have been drawn about the relation between the size of children's play ranges and their spatial representations of local environments (Matthews, 1992). In a review of the relation between childhood experiences and cognitive abilities, Matthews concluded that exploration of the physical environment improved children's ability to represent this environment mentally, as assessed, for instance, by the ability to later draw a map of the environment.

Nonetheless, overall research on the relation between children's play activities and spatial and other abilities has yielded mixed results. Sometimes relations between play activities and cognitive competencies are found, and sometimes they are not (e.g., Matthews, 1987; R. H. Munroe, Munroe, & Brasher, 1985; Rubin et al., 1983; Serbin & Connor, 1979; Webley, 1981). In fact, it is very likely that the relation between play experiences and the development of physical, social, and cognitive competencies is very specific and thus is difficult to assess. For instance, it is likely that the relation between locomotor play in ibex kids, described earlier, and any associated neuromuscular changes that result from this form of play is specific to movement in mountainous terrain and thus is not evident for other types of motor behaviors (Byers & Walker, 1995). Similarly, it appears that environmental exploration improves the ability to generate mental maps of physical environments but is not consistently related to other forms of spatial cognition (e.g., the ability to copy geometric figures; see R. H. Munroe et al., 1985).

Matthews's (1987) study of the relation between exposure to a novel environment and the pattern of sex differences in the spatial representations of this environment illustrates the basic point. Here, 8- to 11-year-old boys and girls were taken on a 1-hour tour of an unfamiliar area in suburban England. In one condition, the children were given a map of the entire area and were then taken on the tour, with the guide pointing out various environmental features. In the second more-difficult condition, another group of children was given a map of one half of the area and their tour was interrupted for 30 minutes at the halfway point, although the same environmental features were pointed out to the children; these conditions placed greater memory demands on the children when later asked to draw a map of this environment. At the end of the tour, the children were asked to draw a map of the entire area. Various features of these maps, such as the inclusion of landmarks and the clustering and relative orientation of these landmarks, were then analyzed to make inferences about the ways in which boys and girls mentally represented this unfamiliar environment.

The maps of boys and girls did not differ in the overall amount of information provided, but sex differences did emerge for other map features. For the first group, that taken on the uninterrupted tour, the only difference was that girls included more landmarks in their maps and that boys included more routes (e.g., roads). Under the more difficult conditions, with the interrupted tour, boys outperformed girls on a number of map features. At all ages, but especially for 10- and 11-year-olds, "boys showed a keener appreciation of the juxtaposition of places" (Matthews, 1987, p. 84). Boys were also better able than girls to integrate clusters of environmental features in ways that reflected their actual topographical positions, and they showed significantly fewer topographical distortions than girls. Moreover, "some of the older boys . . . managed to show a euclidean grasp of space" (Matthews, 1987, p. 86). In other words, under conditions with fewer supports—such as one half versus one entire map of the area—boys were better able than girls, on average, in mentally reconstructing the topography of an unfamiliar environment, thus retaining general orientation, clustering, and Euclidean (e.g., relative direction) relations among important environmental features. Under conditions with many supports, an entire map of the area and an uninterrupted tour, girls and boys remembered different features of the environment (landmarks vs. routes) but did not differ in the complexity of the maps that they later drew of this environment.

The pattern found by Matthews (1987) suggests that the relation between childhood play experiences and later competencies is very complex. Studies that assess only global play activities and global physical, social, or cognitive competencies are not likely to find a strong relation between early experiences and later competencies, even when these relations do in fact exist (e.g., Greenough et al., 1987; Resnick, Berenbaum, Gottesman, & Bouchard, 1986). In this case, the sex of the child and the types of experiences they received interacted in complex ways in the expression of certain types of spatial competencies, so that sex differences for mentally representing an unfamiliar environment were only found with experiences that did not provide many external supports (e.g., a map). The sex difference in the ability to generate accurate mental maps of unfamiliar environments was evident under some, but not all, experiential conditions and appears to affect only specific types of spatial cognitions (see, for example, Grimshaw, Sitarenios, & Finegan, 1995). More important, Matthews's (1987) findings suggest that under natural play conditions (i.e., no map or tour), boys develop much more accurate mental representations of unfamiliar territory than girls do.

Indeed, the sex difference in skill at generating cognitive representations of unfamiliar environments (see also the *Physical Modules* section of chapter 8), the earlier described sex difference in physical activity levels, and the finding that in prehistoric and preindustrial contexts men traveled farther from the home village than women indicate stronger selection pressures on men than on women for the competencies associated with traveling in unfamiliar territories; for prehistoric fossils, patterns of bone wear indicate that men walked and ran more frequently than women (Ruff, 1987). Across preindustrial societies, men travel farther from the home village than women, on average, for a number of reasons, including finding mates, developing alliances with the men of neighboring villages, hunting, and participating in intergroup warfare (Chagnon, 1977; K. Hill & Hurtado, 1996; K. Hill & Kaplan, 1988; Symons, 1979).

As described in chapter 5, many of these activities—especially finding mates and participating in intergroup warfare—are an important feature of male–male competition. Given this, the just-mentioned sex differences, along with the associated play patterns, have likely been shaped by means of sexual selection (S. T. Parker, 1984). In this view, the sex differences in size of the play area, in gross locomotor activity levels, and in exploratory behavior within these ranges function to make the neuromuscular adaptations that are associated with running and traveling long distances on foot and to provide the experiences that will later facilitate the generation of cognitive maps of unfamiliar ecologies. All of these competencies are associated with intergroup warfare, as well as other sex-typed activities (e.g., hunting).

Play Parenting

In contrast to rough-and-tumble play and size of the play range, both of which favor boys, play parenting occurs much more frequently with girls (Lever, 1978; Pitcher & Schultz, 1983; Sandberg & Meyer-Bahlburg, 1994; Sutton-Smith et al., 1963). The sex difference in play parenting is related, in part, to the fact that girls are assigned child-care roles, especially for infants, much more frequently than boys are throughout the world (Whiting & Edwards, 1988). In addition, girls seek out and engage in child care, play parenting, and other domestic activities (e.g., playing house)—with younger children or child substitutes, such as dolls—much more frequently than same-age boys (Pitcher & Schultz, 1983), as is the case with many other species of primate (Nicolson, 1987).

Nevertheless, as with most other social sex differences, the magnitude of these differences varies across age and context (Berman, 1980; Whiting & Edwards, 1988). Before about 6 years of age, both girls and boys are generally responsive to infants, but after this age, and continuing into adulthood, girls are more responsive, on average, to infants and younger children than boys are (P. W. Berman, 1986; P. W. Berman, Monda, & Myerscough, 1977; Edwards & Whiting, 1993; Fogel, Melson, & Mistry, 1986). The emergence of this sex difference is related to a significant drop in the frequency with which older boys attend to and interact with infants and younger children (e.g., P. W. Berman, 1986) and to an increase in girls' interest in children after menarche (S. Goldberg, Blumberg, & Kriger, 1982). The latter finding suggests that girls' interest in play parenting is heightened as a result of the hormonal changes associated with puberty, as is the case with many other species of primate (Nicolson, 1987). Nonetheless, the sex difference in the nature and frequency of interactions with infants and younger children varies with the relationship between the child caregiver and the infant and with whether the caregiving is an assigned responsibility or not. Generally, the sex difference, favoring girls, is largest when a girl is caring for a sibling and when she has been assigned this role by an adult (Berman, 1986).

Studies of children's self-initiated play activities and the relation between these activities and prenatal exposure to androgens suggest that the sex difference in caregiving and play parenting is not simply due to a sex difference in socially assigned roles (but see Fogel et al., 1986), in keeping with the just-mentioned changes associated with menarche (S. Goldberg et al., 1982). Studies conducted in the United States, for instance, have consistently found that girls engage in play parenting much more frequently than same-age boys. Sandberg and Meyer-Bahlburg (1994) found that nearly 99% of 6-year-old girls frequently played with dolls, as compared with 17% of same-age boys (it was not clear if this included play with "action figures" such as G. I. Joe). By 10 years of age, 92% of girls frequently played with dolls, as compared with 12% of same-age boys. Similar differences were found 30 years earlier, despite significant changes in the social roles of men and women in the United States (Sutton-Smith et al., 1963; see also Lever, 1978). Moreover, sex differences in play parenting have been documented across many preindustrial societies, such as the Yanomamö, the !Ko Bushman of the central Kalahari (see Figure 7.2), and the Himba of Southwest Africa (Eibl-Eibesfeldt, 1989). Eibl-Eibesfeldt (1995) described a Himba girl using a sandal as a child substitute. While holding and cuddling the sandal, she sings, "This is also a human being, this is my child, this is my child." Toward the end of the sequence, she punishes the "child" by beating it with a leather string, and after this she blows on the sandal to reduce the pain and then comforts her "child" (I. Eibl-Eibesfeldt, personal communication, September 1997); play parenting, like actual parenting, involves nurturance and discipline.

Research on children affected by CAH suggests that engagement in play parenting is influenced, at least in part, by prenatal exposure to androgens (Berenbaum & Hines, 1992; Berenbaum & Snyder, 1995; Collaer & Hines, 1995). As noted earlier, prenatal exposure to androgens is associated with a defeminization of play activities, including significantly less play with dolls and less interest in infants (Collaer & Hines, 1995). In a study involving the direct observation of the play activities of 5- to 8-year-old boys and girls affected with CAH and unaffected same-sex relatives, Berenbaum and Hines found that unaffected girls played with dolls and kitchen supplies two and one-half times longer than girls affected by CAH. These girls, in turn, played with boys' toys (e.g., toy cars) nearly two and one-half times longer than unaffected girls. The same pattern was found in a follow-up study 3 to 4 years later (Berenbaum & Snyder, 1995). With this latter study, the children were also allowed to choose a toy to take home, after the assessment was complete. Unaffected girls most frequently chose a set of markers or a doll to take home, whereas girls affected by CAH most frequently chose a transportation toy (e.g., toy car) or a ball

Figure 7.2. A !Ko girl using a melon as a doll substitute. Photo from *Human Ethology* (p. 590), by I. Eibl-Eibesfeldt, 1989, New York: Aldine de Gruyter. Copyright 1989 by I. Eibl-Eibesfeldt. Reprinted with permission.

to take home; 7% of the girls affected by CAH chose a doll, as compared with 28% of the unaffected girls.

In summary, a sex difference in play parenting, favoring girls, is found in both industrial and preindustrial societies and, in fact, many other species of primate (Eibl-Eibesfeldt, 1989; Nicolson, 1987). For children, this sex difference is related, in part, to the fact that child-care responsibilities are assigned more frequently to girls than to boys throughout the world (Whiting & Edwards, 1988); of course, girls might be assigned these roles because they are more attentive to their siblings than boys are, on average (Edwards & Whiting, 1993). Even in the absence of assigned roles, girls engage in play parenting much more frequently than boys do, a pattern that is a precursor of the later sex difference in the level of parental investment (see chapter 4). Moreover, the finding that early play parenting substantially improves the survival rate of firstborn offspring, in many species of primate, suggests that this form of play has evolved by means of natural, as contrasted with sexual, selection and serves the function of providing experiences that result in the improvement of later caretaking competencies (Nicolson, 1987; Pryce, 1993).

Object-Oriented Play

In keeping with the earlier described sex difference in the general orientation of infant girls to people and infant boys to objects, object-oriented play occurs much more frequently with boys than with girls (Eibl-Eibesfeldt, 1989; Freedman, 1974; Goodenough, 1957; Sandberg & Meyer-Bahlburg, 1994; Sutton-Smith et al., 1963). However, the sex difference in this form of play cannot simply be described as play with things versus play with people. Girls, in fact, engage more frequently than boys in the broader category of construction play, including play with puzzles, markers, clay, and so forth (Christie & Johnsen, 1987; Jennings, 1977; Rubin et al., 1983). It appears that boys more frequently engage in a more restricted category of play with things, in particular, inanimate mechanical objects (such as toy cars), and in construction play that involves building (such as with blocks; Garai & Scheinfeld, 1968; Hutt, 1972). Moreover, boys, more than girls, frequently engage in the experimental manipulation of these objects, such as taking them apart and trying to put them back together (Hutt, 1972).

The degree to which boys are interested in play with inanimate mechanical objects is illustrated by the earlier described Sandberg and Meyer-Bahlburg (1994) study. Here, it was found that 97% of 6-year-old boys frequently played with toy vehicles (e.g., cars), as compared with 51% of same-age girls. At 10 years of age, 94% of boys frequently played with toy vehicles, but only 29% of girls did so. Sutton-Smith et al. (1963) found the same sex difference 30 years earlier, and Eibl-Eibesfeldt (1989) described a similar pattern with !Ko children. Here, an analysis of 1,166 drawings revealed that boys drew technical objects, such as wagons and airplanes, 10 times more frequently than girls did (20% vs. 2%). The same pattern has in fact been found in the drawings of children in the United States, Japan, Hong Kong, Bali, Ceylon, India, and Kenya (Freedman, 1974).

Moreover, studies of children affected by CAH suggest that an interest in mechanical objects and the associated play style is influenced, in part, by prenatal exposure to androgens (Berenbaum & Hines, 1992; Berenbaum & Snyder, 1995; Collaer & Hines, 1995). As noted earlier, girls affected by CAH played with boys' toys (a helicopter, two cars, and a fire engine) nearly two and one-half times longer than unaffected girls, and they played with these boys' toys more than three times longer than with girls' toys, such as a doll (Berenbaum & Hines, 1992). When given an opportunity to take a toy home, 43% of the girls affected by CAH chose a toy car or an airplane, whereas none of the unaffected girls chose these items; boys affected by CAH and unaffected boys chose these items 57% and 61% of the time, respectively.

As with the chimpanzee, it appears that object-oriented play helps children to learn about the physical properties of objects and the different ways in which these objects can be used and classified (Jennings, 1975; Rubin et al., 1983). Jennings, for instance, found that the free-play activities of preschool children could be classified as largely people oriented or object oriented. An analysis of the relation between the focus of play activities and the pattern of cognitive abilities indicated that children whose play was object oriented "performed better on tests of ability to organize and classify physical materials" (Jennings, 1975, p. 515), as assessed by tests of spatial cognition (e.g., the ability to represent and manipulate geometric designs mentally) and by the ability to sort objects on the basis of, for example, color and shape. In other words, manipulative and exploratory play with objects appears to be involved in the elaboration of the engineering modules described in chapter 6 (Jennings, 1975; Rubin et al., 1983), which, in turn, appears to be related to the evolution of tool use in humans (Byrne, 1995; Pinker, 1997).

If this is the case, then—given the sex difference in object-oriented play—the construction and use of tools would have occurred more frequently with our male ancestors than with our female ancestors, or at least the range of tool use would have varied more for men than for women. In support of this argument is the finding that men work with a wider range of objects than women do across preindustrial societies (Daly & Wilson, 1983; Murdock, 1981). The activities that are performed exclusively or primarily by men include metalworking; weapon making; manufacturing musical instruments; working with wood, stone, bone, and shells; boatbuilding; manufacturing ceremonial objects; and net making (Daly & Wilson, 1983). Across cultures, nearly 92% of those activities that appear to be most similar to the likely toolmaking activities of H. *habilis* and H. *erectus* (weapon making and working with wood, stone, bone, and shells) are performed exclusively by men; just over 1% of these activities are performed exclusively by women, and about 7% are performed by both men and women (Daly & Wilson, 1983; Gowlett, 1992b). At the same time, there are no object-working activities—at least of those recorded—that show the same degree of exclusivity for women, although across cultures women engage in pottery making, basket making, and weaving much more frequently than men do (Murdock, 1981).

From this perspective, the sex difference in manipulative and exploratory object-oriented play reflects an evolved bias in children's activities, so that boys, more than girls, play in ways that elaborate the skeletal competencies associated with the engineering modules and later tool use. As noted in chapter 6, natural selection would favor the evolution of tool use to the extent that its use afforded greater control over the biological resources in the group's ecology, such as expanding the array of foods available to the individual (e.g., stone hammers can be used to extract bone marrow), and greater control over physical resources (e.g., tools for starting a fire; Gowlett, 1992a). To the extent that some tools—such as stones used as projectile weapons or spears—provided an advantage in male-on-male aggression, their use, along with any associated play patterns, was likely influenced by sexual selection. Given this, the sex difference in manipulative and exploratory object-oriented play is likely to be the result of a combination of natural and sexual selection, with the former potentially related to an early difference in the foraging strategies of male and female hominids and the latter to male–male competition.

Fantasy Play

Finally, there is also a sex difference in the fantasy elements of children's sociodramatic play (Pitcher & Schultz, 1983; Rubin et al., 1983; Ruble & Martin, 1997). Recall that sociodramatic play involves groups of children enacting some social episode—often with great flair and emotion—centered on an everyday or imaginary theme, such as dinner or dragon slaying (Rubin et al., 1983; see the *Children's Play and Exploration* section of chapter 6). This form of play appears to be involved in the rehearsal and the development of social and social–cognitive (e.g., theory of mind) competencies (Leslie, 1987). Both boys and girls regularly engage in sociodramatic play but differ in the associated themes and the roles they tend to adopt, as noted by Pitcher and Schultz (1983):

> Boys play more varied and global roles that are more characterized by fantasy and power. Boys' sex roles tend to be functional, defined by action plans. Characters are usually stereotyped and flat with habitual attitudes and personality features (cowboy, foreman, Batman, Superman). Girls prefer family roles, especially the more traditional roles of daughter and mother. Even at the youngest age, girls are quite knowledgeable about the details and subtleties in these roles. . . . From a very early age girls conceive of the family as a system of relationships and a complex of reciprocal actions and attitudes. (p. 79)

In other words, the sociodramatic play of boys focuses, more often than not, on themes associated with power, dominance, and aggression, as in enacting conflicts between cowboys and Indians; whereas the sociodramatic play of girls focuses, more often than not, on family-related themes, such as taking care of children. These activities, of course, reflect the same sex differences found in rough-and-tumble play and play parenting, respectively. In addition to practicing the behaviors associated with physical male–male competition and child care (i.e., parental investment), the fantasy element of sociodramatic play might also be involved in the development of the psychological control mechanisms described in chapter 6. More precisely, the fantasy component of this form of play might provide practice at using fantasy to rehearse later social strategies and to provide a vehicle for the expression of the motivational and emotional mechanisms associated with adult activities. For instance, in this view, Freud's Oedipus and Electra complexes (i.e., fantasy about replacing the same-sex parent) are an early manifestation of intrasexual competition and provide early experiences in coping with the emotional features of this competition, such as sexual jealousy (Daly & Wilson, 1988a; Freud, 1923/1957).

SOCIAL DEVELOPMENT

The first section below provides a description of the tendency of boys and girls to segregate into same-sex social groups, and the second section provides discussion of the different social styles and motives that are manifest within these groups. The third and final section presents an evolutionary consideration of the patterns described in the first two sections.

Segregation

One of the most consistently found features of the social behavior of children is the formation of same-sex play and social groups (Maccoby, 1988; Moller & Serbin, 1996; Strayer & Santos, 1996; Whiting & Edwards, 1988). The formation of these groups is evident by the time children are about 3 years of age and becomes increasingly frequent through childhood. For instance, in a longitudinal study of children in the United States, Maccoby and Jacklin (1987) found that 4- to 5-year-old children spent 3 hours playing with same-sex peers for every single hour they spent playing in mixed-sex groups. By the time these children were 6 to 7 years old, the ratio of time spent in same-sex versus mixed-sex groups was 11:1. Strayer and Santos found a similar pattern for French Canadian children, as did Turner and Gervai (1995) for children in England and Hungary and Whiting and Edwards for children in Kenya, Mexico, the Philippines, Japan, India, and the United States, although the degree of segregation varied across these societies. It appears that children's social segregation is most common in situations that are not monitored by adults; that is, situations in which the children are free to form their own social groups (Maccoby, 1988; Strayer & Santos, 1996).

The tendency of children to segregate themselves into same-sex groups appears to be related, in part, to the different play and social styles of girls and boys (Maccoby, 1988; Serbin et al., 1993). Girls and boys not only play differently (e.g., in terms of rough-and-tumble play), as described earlier, but they also tend to use different social strategies to attempt to gain control over desired resources (e.g., toys) or to influence group activities. For instance, in situations in which access to a desired object—such as a movie viewer that can be watched by only one child at a time—is limited, boys and girls use different strategies, on average, for gaining access to this object (Charlesworth & Dzur, 1987). More often than not, boys gain access to this object by playfully shoving and pushing other boys out of the way, whereas girls gain access by means of verbal persuasion (e.g., polite suggestions to share) and sometimes verbal commands (e.g., "It's my turn now!").

On the basis of these and other studies, Maccoby (1988) argued that segregated social groups emerge primarily because children are generally unresponsive to the play and social-influence styles of the opposite sex. Boys, for instance, sometimes try to initiate rough-and-tumble play with girls, but most girls withdraw from these initiations, whereas most other boys readily join the fray. Similarly, girls often attempt to influence the behavior of boys through verbal requests and suggestions, but boys, unlike other girls, are generally unresponsive to these requests (Charlesworth & LaFrenier, 1983). In this view, children form groups on the bases of mutual interests and the ability to influence group activities, and sex-segregation results, at least in part, from the sex differences in play interests and styles of social influence. There are also peer pressures that promote this segregation, such as teasing about "cooties" if one interacts with a member of the opposite sex (Maccoby, 1988).

In addition, studies of children affected by CAH suggest that the tendency to segregate into same-sex groups might be moderated by the categorization of other children as boys or girls and by a tendency to congregate with children in the same social category (Berenbaum & Snyder, 1995). In keeping with this view, most girls affected by CAH prefer other girls as playmates, even though their play activities tend to be masculinized (Berenbaum & Hines, 1992). However, the same-sex segregation occurs before many children consistently label themselves and other children as a boy or a girl, indicating that the categorization of children as boys and girls is not likely to be a sufficient explanation for this phenomenon (Maccoby, 1988; Moller & Serbin, 1996). In addition, many girls affected by CAH do in fact prefer boys as playmates, consistent with Maccoby's (1988) position. Hines and Kaufman (1994), for instance, found that 44% of the girls affected by CAH in their study indicated that their most frequent playmates were boys, as compared with 11% of their unaffected peers and compared with more than 80% of the boys affected by CAH and unaffected boys. Girls affected by CAH thus show a pattern intermediate to that found in unaffected boys and unaffected girls. A substantial minority of these girls do tend to play in boys' groups, whereas the majority of similarly affected girls tend to play in girls' groups.

At this point, it appears that a combination of sex-differences play and social styles, and social categorization, are the proximate mechanisms underlying the segregation of boys and girls into same-sex groups. The net result is that boys and girls spend much of their childhood in distinct peer cultures (J. R. Harris, 1995; Maccoby, 1988). Also, it is in the context of these cultures that differences in the social styles and preferences of boys and girls congeal, as described in the next section (see J. R. Harris, 1995, for a more general discussion).

Social Behavior and Motives

In those communities in which there are enough same-age children to form peer groups, children and adolescents throughout the world form these groups and spend much of their free time engaged in social discourse within these groups. Within these groups, the nature of the social relationships that develop among boys and among girls differs in a number of important ways. Most generally, the social relationships that develop among girls are more consistently communal—manifesting greater empathy, more concern for the well-being of other girls, more nurturing, intimacy, social–emotional support, and so forth—than the relationships that develop among boys; whereas relationships among boys are more consistently instrumental or agentic—more concern for the establishment of dominance, control of group activities, task orientation, and greater risk taking (Ahlgren & Johnson, 1979; Alfieri, Ruble, & Higgins, 1996; Archer, 1992, 1996; J. H. Block, 1976; Charlesworth & Dzur, 1987; Feingold, 1994; Ginsburg & Miller, 1982; Jarvinen & Nicholls, 1996; Jones & Costin, 1995; Knight & Chao, 1989; Maccoby, 1988; D. C. Miller & Byrnes, 1997; Ryff, 1995; Savin-Williams, 1987; Strough, Berg, & Sansone, 1996).

These sex differences are evident with the use of direct observation of social behavior, self-report measures, personality tests, tasks that involve the allocation or control of desired resources, and, depending on how they are assessed, moral judgments about the "rights and wrongs" of social behavior (Carlo, Koller, Eisenberg, Da Silva, & Frohlich, 1996; Charlesworth & Dzur, 1987; Feingold, 1994; Knight & Chao, 1989; Petrinovich, O'Neill, & Jorgensen, 1993; Whiting & Edwards, 1988; Woods, 1996). The sex differences in social behavior, in turn, appear to be a reflection of the sex differences in social motives described in chapter 6 (*The Motivation to Control* section). Recall that men are more concerned with the establishment and the maintenance of social dominance than women are, on average, whereas women are more motivated than men to develop and to maintain a reciprocal and socially stable system of interpersonal relationships—relationships that are characterized by a relatively equal distribution of resources and less obvious social hierarchies.

As described earlier, sex differences in some of the associated component competencies—such as girls' greater sensitivity to social cues (e.g., facial expression) and their greater empathy to the distress of others—are found during infancy. Differences in the social relationships that form within groups of boys and groups of girls are evident as earlier as 3 years of age and are found at every age thereafter, although the magnitude of these differences is relatively larger during puberty and relatively smaller during old age (Ahlgren & Johnson, 1979; Alfieri et al., 1996; Knight & Chao, 1989; Maccoby, 1988, 1990; B. F. Turner, 1982). The sex differences in social behaviors and motives are also found across industrial and pre-industrial societies (e.g., Feingold, 1994; Whiting & Edwards, 1988). As an example, in their study of the social development of children in Liberia, Kenya, India, Mexico, the Philippines, Japan, and the United States (with less extensive observations in Peru and Guatemala), Whiting and Edwards (1988) concluded the following:

> Of the five major categories of interpersonal behavior explored in [these studies]—nurturance, dependency, prosocial dominance, egoistic dominance, and sociability—two emerge as associated with sex differences. Across the three older age groups (knee, yard, and school-age children) girls on average are more nurturant than boys in all dyad types . . . while boys are more egoistically dominant than girls. (p. 270)

The same pattern is evident for adolescents and adults. In one associated analysis, Feingold (1994) focused on the pattern of sex differences on personality tests normed in the United States. The analysis of test norms is especially informative, given that these involve large and oftentimes nationally representative samples (Feingold's analysis included the scores of 105,742 people). Across tests, he found moderate-to-large sex differences for "tender-mindedness" (i.e., nurturance and empathy), favoring women, and assertiveness (e.g., dominance-related activities), favoring men; about 6 out of 7 women scored higher than the average man on measures of tender mindedness, whereas about 7 out of 10 men scored higher than the average woman on measures of assertiveness. The magnitude of these differences varied little for samples assessed from the 1940s to the 1990s and varied little across groups drawn from high schools, colleges, or the general population. Multiple (i.e., greater than one) studies of sex differences in personality were also available for adults from Canada, Finland, Germany, and Poland, and these studies revealed the same pattern as was found in the United States, although the magnitude of the sex differences varied across these nations.

Ahlgren and Johnson (1979) found a similar pattern in the social motives of 2nd to 12th graders. The social motives of these children and adolescents were captured by two salient themes: cooperation (e.g., "I like to learn by working with other students") and competition (e.g., "I like to do better work than my friends"). At all grade levels, girls endorsed cooperative social behaviors more frequently than boys did, whereas boys endorsed competitive social behaviors more frequently than girls did. A more recent study of 250 14-year-olds revealed the same pattern (Jarvinen & Nicholls, 1996). Here, boys' social goals were largely focused on the achievement of dominance and leadership, whereas girls' social goals were largely focused on the establishment of intimate and nurturing relationships, a pattern that did not differ across the academic track (i.e., low, average, or high achieving) of these students. The largest sex differences were for the establishment of intimacy—more than 4 out of 5 girls rated this goal as being more important than the average boy did—and dominance—3 out of 4 boys rated this goal as being more important than the average girl did.

Knight and Chao (1989) found the same pattern in the rules that 3- to 12-year-olds use to distribute a valuable resource among themselves and their social group (money in this case). The associated studies were designed to determine whether the children had preferences for *equality* (minimizing differences between oneself and others), *group enhancement* (enhancing the overall resources of the group, regardless of how this affects one's own resources), *superiority* (trying to maximize one's resources relative to other group members), or *individualism* (enhancing one's resources independent of peer resources). Self-interest was evident in the resource distributions of 3- to 5-year-old boys and girls, as about 50% of these children showed an individualism preference. At the same time, 25% of the girls, but none of the boys, showed an equality preference, whereas 19% of the boys, but only 5% of the girls, showed a superiority preference. By 6 years of age, the majority of boys showed a superiority preference, whereas the girls were largely split between the individualism and the equality preferences. For instance, for 9- to 12-year-olds, 75% of the boys showed a superiority preference, as compared with 20% of the girls. The remaining girls were split evenly (40% each) between the individualism and the equality preferences; only 7% of the boys showed an equality preference. Parallel sex differences are often, but not always, found in the moral judgments of boys and girls and men and women (Gilligan, 1982; Petrinovich et al., 1993; Woods, 1996). For instance, girls and women more consistently than boys and men endorse a moral ethos that espouses equality in social relationships and an avoidance of harm to others (e.g., Gilligan, 1982).

Qualitative differences in the nature of the social relationships that form within groups of boys and groups of girls are nicely illustrated by Savin-Williams's (1987) ethological study of adolescent social groups. Here, the social relationships that developed during the course of a 5-week summer camp were systematically observed and documented for groups of 12- to 16-year-old boys and girls assigned to the same cabin. These observations revealed a number of similarities in the social behaviors that emerged within these same-sex groups. Both boys and girls formed dominance hierarchies and frequently used ridicule to establish social dominance, such as name calling ("homo" or "perverted groin") or gossiping. For both sexes, the establishment of social dominance resulted in greater access to desired resources (e.g., larger desserts) and greater control over the activities of the group, relative to lower status peers. At the same time, there were sex differences in the stability of the social hierarchies, the degree to which dominance displays were direct or indirect, the use of physical strength and skills to establish dominance, and the benefits of achieving dominance, among others.

In some groups, boys began their bid for social dominance within hours of arriving in the cabin, whereas most of the girls were superficially polite for the first week and then began to exhibit dominance-related behaviors. For boys, dominance-related behaviors included ridicule, as noted earlier, as well as directives ("Get my dessert for me"), counterdominance statements ("Eat me"), and physical assertion (e.g., play wrestling, pillow fights, and so forth and sometimes actual physical fights). More than 90% of the time, these behaviors were direct and overt; that is, they were visible to all group members, clearly directed at one other boy, and were essentially attempts to establish some type of control over this individual.

Girls used ridicule, recognition, and verbal directives to establish social dominance, but they used physical assertion only one third as frequently as boys did. Unlike boys, more than one half of the girls' dominance-related behaviors were indirect. For instance, a girl might suggest to another girl that she "take her napkin and clean a piece of food off of her face," whereas under the same conditions a boy would simply call his less-kept peer a "pig" and then try to enlist other boys in a group-wide ridicule session of this boy; once he was "down," lower status boys would typically use this opportunity to attempt to establish individual dominance over this peer. Moreover, girls, in contrast with boys, often overtly recognized the leadership of another girl. In fact, recognition was the second-most frequently used form of dominance-related behavior with girls, but it occurred infrequently with boys (23% vs. 6% of the dominance-related behaviors for girls and boys, respectively). In these cases, less dominant girls would approach their more dominant peers for advice, social support, grooming (e.g., having her hair combed), and so forth.

Boys' dominance hierarchies were also much more stable across situations and across time than girls' hierarchies were. By the end of summer camp, the boys' groups showed greater stability and cohesiveness relative to the first week of camp, whereas most of the girls' groups were on the verge of splintering or had already split into "status cliques based on popularity, beauty, athletics, and sociability" (Savin-Williams, 1987, p. 124). In some cases, dominant girls disengaged from the cabin group and spent most of their free time with one or two friends, consistent with the finding that girls' groups often comprise dyads or triads (Lever, 1978). During this free time, the girls would typically walk and talk. Dominant boys, in contrast, never disengaged from the group and spent most of their free time directing the group in competitive athletic activities against other groups. In other words, dominant boys more actively and more successfully controlled group activities than dominant girls did, as illustrated by the following flag-making exercise:

> Andy [the alpha male] immediately grabbed the flag cloth and penciled a design; he turned to Gar for advice, but none was given. Otto [low ranking] shouted several moments later, "I didn't say you could do it!" Ignoring this interference, Andy wrote the tribal name at the top of the flag. Meanwhile, Delvin and Otto were throwing sticks at each other with Gar watching and giggling. SW [the counselor] suggested that all should participate by drawing a design proposal on paper and the winning one, as determined by group vote, would be drawn on the flag. . . . Andy, who had not participated in the "contest," now drew a bicentennial sunset; it was readily accepted by the others. Without consultation, Andy drew his design as Gar and Delvin watched. Gar suggested an alteration but Andy told him "Stupid idea," and continued drawing. Otto, who had been playing in the fireplace, came over and screamed, "I didn't tell ya to draw that you Bastard Andy!" Andy's reply was almost predictable, "Tough shit, boy!" (Savin-Williams, 1987, p. 79)

Andy's mode of domination was more physically assertive and verbally aggressive than the social style of the dominant boys in some of the other cabins. The result was the same, however. The dominant boys got first choice of what to eat (e.g., they almost always got the largest desserts), where to sleep, and what to do during free time. Across cabins, dominant girls also differed in their social styles. Although some girls were physically assertive and direct in their attempts to dominate other girls, the most influential girls (over the course of the 5 weeks) were much more subtle, as exemplified by Anne.

> [Her] style of authority [was] subtle and manipulative, she became the cabin's "mother." She instructed the others on cleanup jobs, corrected Opal's table manners ("Dottie, pass Opal a napkin so she can wipe the jelly off her face."), and woke up the group in the morning. . . . Anne became powerful in the cabin by first blocking Becky's [the beta female] dominance initiations through refusing and shunning and then through ignoring her during the next three weeks. By the fifth week of camp Anne effectively controlled Becky by physical assertion, ridicule, and directive behaviors. (Savin-Williams, 1987, p. 92)

For both boys and girls, the achievement of social dominance was related to athletic ability, pubertal maturity, and leadership. Dominant girls were more socially popular than many of the dominant boys—Andy was not well liked by his cabin-mates but they followed his directives nonetheless—and physical attractiveness was more important for achieving social dominance within boys' groups than within girls' groups. Moreover, other studies suggest that risk taking is more frequently used by boys than by girls in their attempts to achieve social status, with high risk takers being afforded a higher social status, on average, than their risk-avoiding peers (MacDonald, 1988; D. C. Miller & Byrnes, 1997). In all, the boys described ideal leaders as instrumental, "determined and tries hard at what he does, considerate in tolerating underlings, organizes activities, and knows what to do and makes the right decisions. The [girls'] groups emphasized expressive attributes: relates to my problems, friendly, outgoing, patient, considerate in respecting the needs and feelings of others" (Savin-Williams, 1987, p. 127).

Ethological and other studies suggest that these social patterns congeal as adolescents approach physical maturation (Ahlgren & Johnson, 1979; J. Block, 1993; Savin-Williams, 1987). Ahlgren and Johnson, for instance, found that at about the time of puberty, girls' social motives become more cooperative and less competitive than their younger peers. Savin-Williams found that by the end of adolescence, there was a significant reduction in ridicule, "backbiting, bickering, and cattiness" (Savin-Williams, 1987, p. 150) in girls' interpersonal relationships, compared with early adolescence. By late adolescence, girls' relationships also showed greater stability (i.e., less changing of "best friends"), more recognition, greater sensitivity to the needs and emotions of their friends, more helping behavior, and fewer attempts at establishing dominance (i.e., the relationships were more often among equals) than were found during early adolescence.

Boys' relationships changed, as well. By late adolescence, boys' group-level games were characterized by greater focus and organization, with fewer within-group negative criticisms and more encouragement than was found with younger boys (Savin-Williams, 1987). At the same time, during their dominance-related encounters, older boys used physical assertion less frequently and used recognition more frequently than their younger peers. Under some conditions, however, male dominance encounters can become very physically aggressive and even deadly by late adolescence (sometimes earlier; M. Wilson & Daly, 1985).

Social Development and Evolution

When viewed from the perspective of human evolution in general, children's relationships within the above-described social groups provide one mechanism through which the individual- and group-level cognitive modules, along with the associated motivational and emotional components, become elaborated and adapted to the group's social structure and customs (see chapter 6). For instance, the nature of the play fighting that emerges within boys' groups appears to be related, in part, to the nature of male–male competition in adulthood, and the intensity of this play fighting likely contributes to the preparation of these boys, as described earlier, for later participation in the adult community; they learn, for instance, how to achieve cultural success (Irons, 1979; see *the Male–Male Competition* section of chapter 5). Moreover, social relationships within these groups likely allow children and adolescents to refine those social skills that will later be used to influence other people and to garner important resources. They learn which social strategies work well for them and which do not (e.g., social persuasion vs. attempts to physically dominate; MacDonald, 1996).

When viewed from the perspective of sexual selection in particular, the tendency of children to segregate themselves into same-sex groups and to manifest a different pattern of social behavior and motives within these groups follows, at least in part, from the sex differences in reproductive strategies (described in chapter 4 and in chapter 5). In other words, the types of social competencies needed to compete with members of the same sex or to raise children successfully differ for men and women, and, given this, the developmental experiences that support the refinement of these competencies should differ as well. In this view, one important function of children's relationships within peer groups is to develop the social competencies that will later be used in the context of intrasexual competition and to refine those social competencies that will later be used to attempt to organize and control other people; examples of attempts to organize the social world were provided in chapter 6, with the description of the sex difference social motives (*The Motivation to Control* section).

Any evolutionary interpretation of the specific sex differences described earlier must be based on a consideration of the social groups within which our female and male ancestors likely lived (Foley & Lee, 1989; Rodseth et al., 1991). Of particular importance is the fact that men, and our male ancestors, are the philopatric sex for humans; that is, men tend to stay in the birth group and women tend to emigrate to a different group, although women often maintain contact with their kin (Pasternak et al., 1997; Rodseth et al., 1991). These social patterns indicate that as adults our female and male ancestors lived in very different social worlds. Our male ancestors, more often than not, lived in the same community as their male kin; whereas our female ancestors, more often than not, lived in a community with nonkin. As described in chapter 6 (*Social Modules* section), social relationships with kin and nonkin often differ. Relationships with friends are characterized by higher levels of reciprocity than relationships with kin (Hartup & Stevens, 1997; Trivers, 1971). Moreover, as described in chapter 3 (*Male–Male Competition* section), whether males or females are the philopatric sex influences coalition formation and the nature of intergroup relationships, with the philopatric sex being more likely to form same-sex coalitions and more likely to engage in intergroup coalition-based competition (e.g., Rodseth et al., 1991; Wrangham, 1980).

From an evolutionary perspective, coalition-based intrasexual competition is therefore expected and, in fact, does occur more frequently in men than in women (as described in chapter 5). From a developmental perspective, the social culture that emerges within boys' groups should provide a context for refining individual-level, dominance-related competencies and an opportunity to develop the competencies necessary to form and to maintain cohesive and effective large-scale coalitions. The latter activities would be designed to improve one's position within the coalition, and the former for competition against other coalitions. The finding that boys, in relation to girls, are more concerned with achieving social dominance and that they more frequently organize themselves into relatively large and cohesive groups, which compete against other groups of boys, is entirely consistent with this view (i.e., these activities involve a preparation for later coalition-based male–male competition). The findings that the striving for social dominance, the tendency to engage in group-level athletic competition, and the physical competencies associated with male-on-male aggression (e.g., upper body strength) are all related to exposure to sex hormones (Collaer & Hines, 1995; Mazur & Booth, in press; Tanner, 1990) further support the position that the social behavior within boys' groups has been shaped by sexual selection and involves a preparation for later male–male competition.

As with other primate species in which males are the philopatric sex, girls and women do not form coalitions to compete against groups of other girls or women—bonobo females form coalitions but not for the purpose of intergroup aggression (de Waal & Lanting, 1997)—nor are they as concerned as boys and men about establishing social dominance. Nonetheless, some form of one-on-one dominance-related behaviors is expected for girls and women, given that social dominance results in greater access to important resources and because, across primate species, access to these resources (especially food) often has reproductive consequences (see the *Female–Female Competition and Male Choice* section of chapter 3; Pusey et al., 1997). Moreover, for those species in which males provide some level of postnatal parental investment, which includes humans (chapter 4), some level of female–female competition is expected (e.g., G. A. Parker & Simmons, 1996), although the intensity (e.g., risk of injury or death) of intrasexual competition should be lower for females than for males, as described in previous chapters (e.g., chapter 2 and chapter 5); males generally benefit more than females by intense and risky competition (e.g., by gaining additional mates), and physical injury can be particularly costly to females because any such injury will reduce their ability to care for offspring (Campbell, in press).

Adolescent girls and women do indeed develop relatively subtle dominance relationships (Björkqvist, Osterman, & Lagerspetz, 1994). The achievement of dominance within these relationships is probably important for securing important resources and for controlling the social behavior of other people (e.g., Grotpeter & Crick, 1996) and is likely to be related, in part, to female–female competition. Although in many societies and presumably during the course of human evolution (Hrdy, 1997), men often attempt to control the marriage and sexuality of their daughters and other women, female–female competition could readily manifest itself in the context of polygynous marriages (i.e., conflict between co-wives) and in the context of less formal and furtive social and sexual relationships (Betzig, 1986; Daly & Wilson, 1983; K. Hill & Hurtado, 1996). Within polygynous marriages, for instance, the first and usually dominant wife typically has more children than her younger peers (Daly & Wilson, 1983), although it is not known, at this point, if dominant women somehow suppress the reproduction of their co-wives (e.g., through creating social stress).

Across contexts, female–female competition often involves relational aggression, in which girls and women attempt to exclude their competitors from the social group, by means of gossiping, shunning, and so forth. These, of course, are exactly the forms of dominance-related behaviors that are manifested in the social groups of adolescent and sometimes younger girls (Savin-Williams, 1987; see the *Female–Female Competition* section of chapter 5). Thus, as with boys, social behavior within girls' groups appears to provide experience in using the social strategies associated with later intrasexual competition. The particular form of intrasexual competition in girls and women follows from the sex difference in the valuation of intimate and reciprocal relationships. As described later, the formation of these relationships provides an important source of social support for women, and, given this, relational aggression would be particularly effective in competing against other women. This is so because relational aggression disrupts the ability of potential competitors to develop these relationships. As noted in chapter 5 (*Female–Female Competition* section), the disruption of social relationships often reduces fertility in females, at least in some primate species (e.g., Abbott, 1993). Given this, this form of competition could very well have influenced reproductive outcomes in women and could represent a form of female-on-female aggression that has been shaped by sexual selection. The finding that these social behaviors are influenced by hormonal and genetic factors further supports the position that these are biologically based aspects of girls' and women's social relationships (Skuse et al., 1997; Van Goozen et al., 1995).

As noted earlier, it is likely that female hominids more frequently than male hominids transferred into groups in which they were not genetically related to other individuals in the group. Under these circumstances, female hominids were more likely to be socially isolated and thus at greater risk for exploitation than male hominids (Pasternak et al., 1997). The greater attentiveness of girls and women to social cues (e.g., facial expressions), their greater positive social signaling (e.g., smiling), their skill at strategically using emotion cues in social contexts, and their general

motivation to develop intimate social relationships as an end in itself—
rather than as a means to compete as is the case with boys and men—
might reflect an adaptation to these social conditions (Bjorklund & Kipp,
1996; Freedman, 1974). For instance, in adulthood, about 7 out of 10
women smile more frequently in noncompetitive social situations than the
average man and direct these smiles more frequently to other women than
to men (J. A. Hall, 1984; see the *Social Modules* section of chapter 6).

Any such adaptation, shaped by natural selection, might reflect the
evolutionary elaboration of the social and emotional systems that support
friendships (i.e., relationships with nonkin). Or stated differently, kin bias
would more or less automatically provide men with a system of social support, but no such kin-based support system would be available for immi-
grant women. Under the latter conditions, intimate relationships would
provide an important social resource in a potentially hostile social environment. In keeping with this view, girls and women are indeed more
concerned than boys and men about the nuances of interpersonal relationships (e.g., the other person's feelings), and they use these relationships as
a source of social and emotional support more frequently than boys and
men do (Brodzinsky et al., 1992; Causey & Dubow, 1992; A. Simon &
Ward, 1982; Strough et al., 1996).

Alternatively, it might be argued that the sex difference in the motivation to develop intimate relationships is related to the sex difference
in parental investment, so that girls' intimate relationships provide practice
for the later development of intimate family relationships. Of course, this
is possible. However, for children and adolescents, these relationships develop with same-age (not younger) peers, and the social behaviors that
emerge with peer relationships differ from play parenting. The distinction
between peer relationships and play parenting suggests that the development of these intimate relationships is not simply practice for later
parent–child relationships, although in adulthood these peer relationships
might provide a source of social support and assistance in child rearing
(e.g., through alloparenting, such as baby-sitting). In addition, such relationships would also provide an important support system for dealing
with the dynamics of adult-on-adult social relationships, such as providing
social support in the context of male-on-female aggression (Smuts, 1992,
1995).

PARENTING

The study of parental influences on developing children is complicated because in most families parents provide their children with genes
and a rearing environment (Scarr, 1992; Scarr & McCartney, 1983). As a

result, the often-found correlation between parental characteristics and the characteristics of young children, which are often assumed to be due to parental socialization, might well result from the overlapping genes between parents and children, socialization, or differences in the ways in which children with different genotypes react to similar rearing environments (Maccoby & Martin, 1983; Reiss, 1995; Scarr, 1992). Indeed, behavioral–genetic and other studies suggest that parental influences on individual differences in children's personality, social behavior, intelligence, and so forth are much weaker than many people believe, or would like to believe (J. R. Harris, 1995; Plomin et al., 1997; D. C. Rowe, 1994; Scarr, 1992). This is not to say that parents are not important. They are. As described in chapter 4, parental investment can have a profound—sometimes life or death—effect on the physical and physiological development of children (Flinn et al., 1996; K. Hill & Hurtado, 1996; Sapolsky, 1997).

Moreover, behaviors outside of the range that naturally occurs in parent–child relationships, such as severe neglect, can adversely affect the social and psychological development of children (Scarr, 1992), just as neglectful parenting can adversely affect offspring development in other primates (Goodall, 1986). Most parents, however, provide a level of investment that allows for normal development, and variations within this normal range do not appear to be systematically related to variations in child outcomes. Stated differently, parents provide an evolutionarily expected rearing environment for the infant and child, including exposure to language, synchronized parent–child interactions, and so forth, that provides the experiences that begin to flesh out the skeletal competencies of evolved modules, in particular the individual–social modules (Kuhl et al., 1997; MacDonald, 1993; Papoušek & Papoušek, 1995). Experiences that go above and beyond these evolutionarily expected experiences, in contrast, do not appear to have strong influences on the developing child (Scarr, 1992).

In a similar vein, studies conducted in Western nations indicate that parents, on average, treat boys and girls in very similar ways—with a few exceptions noted later—and given this, the earlier described sex differences in infancy, play, and social development are not likely to be the result of parental treatment (Lytton & Romney, 1991; Maccoby & Jacklin, 1974). The most comprehensive assessment, involving 172 studies and 27,836 participants, of the parental treatment of boys and girls was conducted by Lytton and Romney. In this meta-analysis, parental treatment was assessed across eight broad socialization areas, including amount of interaction, achievement encouragement, warmth and nurturance, encouragement of dependency, restrictiveness, disciplinary strictness, encouragement of sex-typed activities, and clarity of communication directed toward the child. For studies conducted in North America, there were very few differences in the ways in which parents treated girls and boys, as assessed by observation, parental report, and child report.

One exception was for encouragement of sex-typed activities, although the difference was relatively small; for about two out of three boys, parents encouraged sex-typed activities more frequently than they did with the average girl. This result appears to largely reflect an active discouragement of boys, especially by fathers, from playing with girls' toys, such as dolls. Doll play in boys appears to prompt concerns of sexual orientation (Maccoby & Jacklin, 1974). Studies conducted in Western nations outside of North America indicated that boys received more physical discipline than girls, but again the difference was small. A more recent meta-analysis revealed some differences in the ways in which parents talk to boys and girls (Leaper, Anderson, & Sanders, 1998). Mothers, for instance, talked more and provided more encouraging speech to their daughters than to their sons.

Lytton and Romney (1991) suggested that even these differences might result from parental reactions to differences in the behavior of girls and boys. The greater use of physical punishment with boys, relative to girls, might be a reflection of the tendency of boys to be less responsive to verbal requests than girls. Similarly, paternal concerns over doll play might be a reaction to the fact that such play occurs relatively infrequently in boys (Sandberg & Meyer-Bahlburg, 1994) and is, in fact, correlated with later gay sexual orientation (Green, 1987). Similarly, the difference in the ways in which parents talk to boys and girls likely reflects the earlier described (*Infancy* section) differences in the social responsiveness and behavior of boys and girls.

It is not likely that the sex differences described in this chapter are due to children's selective imitation of the same-sex parent or other same-sex people. On the basis of a review of 23 studies of children's imitative behavior, Maccoby and Jacklin (1974) tentatively concluded "that early sex typing is not a function of a child's having selectively observed, and selectively learned, the behavior of same-sex, rather than opposite-sex, models" (p. 299). Barkley and his colleagues reached the same conclusion, after reviewing 81 relevant studies (Barkley, Ullman, Otto, & Brecht, 1977). Moreover, in an empirical study of their own, they found that girls tended to imitate traditionally feminine behavior, such as playing house, whether these behaviors were enacted by a male or female model and that boys tended to imitate traditionally masculine behavior, such as play fighting, regardless of the sex of the model (Barkley et al., 1977).

It is not likely that these findings result from children only imitating behavior that is considered to be sex appropriate. As noted earlier, children's knowledge of gender roles is only weakly related to the actual behavioral differences that are observed between boys and girls (Serbin et al., 1993; P. J. Turner & Gervai, 1995), and many of the sex differences described in this chapter emerge before children know that they are a boy or a girl or before they have any knowledge of what is "expected" of boys and men or girls and women (Maccoby, 1988). Rather, in keeping with the sex differences described in the *Infancy* section, it is more likely that boys and girls selectively attend to and find more attractive or engaging behaviors that are traditionally defined as sex typed, although young boys who label themselves as boys and understand that they will someday be men do attend to men more frequently than boys who do not yet understand that one's biological sex is constant through time (Slaby & Frey, 1975).

In other words, boys and girls selectively attend to different types of behaviors in adults, although for very young children this selective attention does appear to be related to knowledge of their biological sex. Endicott provided an illustration of the selective attention of boys, with her description of the play of Batek children in Malaysia; the Batek are a relatively egalitarian hunter–gatherer society in which "no gender distinctions are made in the terms for children, siblings, cousins, and grandchildren" (Endicott, 1992, p. 282). Endicott's example of selective attention is as follows:

> Playgroup activities range from pretending to move camp to imitating monkeys to play-practicing economic skills such as blowpipe-hunting, digging tubers, collecting rattan, and fishing. Fathers sometimes intervene in the activities of children to offer advice about how to perform these skills. For example, when several children were pretending that they were harvesting honey by smoking bees out of a hive high in a tree in the middle of camp, a father who often participated in honey collecting showed the children how to properly construct rattan ladders to use for climbing up to the hive. It was the older boys, in the 10- to 12-year-old range, *who paid closest attention to this informal lesson.* (emphasis added; Endicott, 1992, p. 288)

Although studies conducted in Western nations suggest that parenting does not strongly influence the personality and social behavior of children, as noted above, cross-culture comparisons do find a relation between parenting and child development (Low, 1989; MacDonald, 1992; Rohner, 1976). These seemingly contradictory findings are due, in part, to differences in how the relation between parenting and child outcomes is measured in these studies. For within-culture studies, individual differences in children's behavior are related to individual differences in parenting style, whereas cross-cultural studies involve comparisons of average differences across groups of people from different societies. Moreover, within- and cross-culture studies often yield different results because the range of parenting behaviors is larger when assessed across rather than within cultures (MacDonald, 1992).

To illustrate, in societies characterized by high levels of intergroup aggression, parenting practices for both boys and girls tend to be harsher, including more physical discipline, less responsiveness to the child's emotional state and so forth, than parenting practices found in more peaceful societies (Bonta, 1997; MacDonald, 1993; M. M. West & Konner, 1976). One apparent result of these differences in the modal style of parenting is a cross-cultural difference in the average level of aggression found in societies with relatively harsh as opposed to relatively warm parenting styles (MacDonald, 1992). At the same time, the pattern of sex differences remains within cultures, although girls or women from one culture might be more aggressive, on average, than boys and men from another culture. The cross-cultural pattern suggests that parenting can in fact accentuate or attenuate the expression of certain social behaviors (e.g., frequency of physical aggression), but these effects largely result in cross-cultural differences in the behavior of same-sex children and not in the creation of sex differences in one culture but not in another.

The largest cross-cultural analysis of the relation between child-rearing practices and children's social behavior was conducted by Low (1989). In this analysis of 93 cultures, child-rearing practices were examined as they were related to social structure (i.e., stratified vs. nonstratified societies and group size) and marriage system (i.e., polygynous vs. monogamous). In nonstratified polygynous societies, in which men can improve their social status and thus increase the number of women they can marry, the socialization of boys focuses on fortitude, aggression, and industriousness; traits that will likely influence economic and thus reproductive success in adulthood. Moreover, for these nonstratified societies, there was a very strong linear relation between the socialization of competitiveness in boys and the maximum harem size allowed within the society. The larger the maximum harem size, the more the competitiveness of boys was emphasized in parental socialization.

In contrast, for stratified societies, in which men cannot improve their social status, boys are not strongly socialized to exhibit aggression and fortitude, although industriousness is still important. For girls, there was a relation between the amount of economic and political power held by women in the society and socialization practices. In societies in which women could inherit property and hold political office, girls were socialized to be less obedient, more aggressive, and more achievement oriented relative to girls who lived in societies in which men had more or less complete control over economic and political resources. On the basis of these patterns, Low (1989) concluded that "there is thus some evidence that patterns of child training across cultures vary in ways predictable from evolutionary theory, differing in specifiable ways between the sexes, and varying with group size, marriage system, and stratification" (p. 318).

These differences in socialization patterns appear to reflect differences in the ways in which social, economic, and reproductive success can be achieved in different cultures, and the associated child-rearing practices appear to prepare the child, in terms of social scripts, emotional reactions to social relationships, and so forth, for the social environment that he or she will experience as an adult (MacDonald, 1992). These parenting practices, however, appear to largely amplify or suppress, rather than create, the pattern of sex differences described in this chapter, with parents tending to emphasize those characteristics that will enhance the reproductive opportunities of their children (boys and girls) and thus increase the likelihood that they will have grandchildren. In this view, the earlier described cross-cultural differences in the intensity of boys' play fighting result from the differences in parental disciplinary techniques (e.g., punishment that results in physical pain appears to result in relatively angry and aggressive children) and the extent to which parents encourage or discourage boys' natural play fighting.

SUMMARY AND CONCLUSION

The period between birth and puberty appears to represent the portion of the life span during which the skeletal competencies associated with those cognitive, social, and behavioral skills that support survival and reproduction are elaborated and tailored to the local ecology. The length of this development period has increased considerably during the course of hominid evolution (McHenry, 1994a), and it appears that much of this change is related to an increase in the complexity of human social systems (Dunbar, 1993; Joffe, 1997). The complexity of these systems, in turn, is related, in part, to the reproductive concerns and strivings of human beings (Chagnon, 1988; Symons, 1979). From this perspective, one important function of childhood is to provide the experiences needed to refine those competencies that are associated with intrasexual competition and other reproductive activities (e.g., parental investment) in adulthood.

On the bases of the sex differences in parental investment (chapter 4), the nature of intrasexual competition (chapter 5), and the mate-choice criteria (chapter 5) in adulthood, sex differences in the self-initiated developmental experiences of boys and girls are expected and are found. Although there are, of course, many similarities in the childhood experiences of boys and girls, there are also considerable differences. Girls and boys show different patterns of physical development (Tanner, 1990), different play interests and styles, as well as different social behaviors and motives, and many of these differences can readily be understood in terms of sexual selection in general and intrasexual competition in particular (Darwin, 1871).

As an example, the delayed physical maturation of boys, relative to girls, and the sex difference in the timing, duration, and intensity of the pubertal growth spurt follow the same pattern as is found in other non-monogamous primates (Leigh, 1995, 1996). Across these primate species, the sex differences in these features of physical maturation are consistently related to the intensity of physical male–male competition, as contrasted with any sex differences in foraging strategy (Mitani et al., 1996). The sex difference in the pattern of human physical competencies, such as a longer forearm and greater upper body strength in men than in women, is also readily explained in terms of selection for male-on-male aggression, selection that involved the use of projectile and blunt force weapons (Keeley, 1996). Stated more directly, the sex differences in physical development and physical competencies have almost certainly been shaped by sexual selection, and the majority of these differences have resulted from male–male competition over access to mates (Tanner, 1992); of course, some physical sex differences, such as the wider pelvis in women, have been shaped by natural selection.

It is very likely that many of the sex differences in play interests and social behaviors have also been shaped by sexual selection. The sex differences in rough-and-tumble play, exploratory behavior and size of play range, tendency of boys to form coalitions in their competitive activities with other boys, and formation of within-coalition dominance hierarchies also are patterns that are associated with male–male competition in other primates, particularly primates in which males are the philopatric sex (Goodall, 1986; P. K. Smith, 1982). In this view, all of these features of boys' play and social behavior involve a preparation for later within-group dominance striving and coalition formation for intergroup aggression. Through parenting practices, such as degree of physical discipline, the selective imitation of competitive activities, and actual experiences within same-sex groups, boys learn how to best achieve within-group social dominance and how to practice the specific competencies associated with male–male competition in their particular culture. They learn how to achieve cultural success (e.g., by leading raids on other villages or becoming a star football player).

Not all developmental sex differences are related to male–male competition, however. For instance, the relational aggression that is common in girls' groups might be a feature of female–female competition, and a number of other physical and behavioral sex differences that become evident during development have likely been shaped by natural selection or mate choice. The sex difference, favoring boys, in manipulative and exploratory object-oriented play appears to be related to the evolution of tool use and a sex difference, favoring men, in the range of tool-related activities in adulthood. Although it is not certain, these sex differences have likely been shaped, in part, by natural selection (e.g., through a sex difference in the foraging strategies of our ancestors). Similarly, the sex difference in play parenting, favoring girls, reflects the later sex difference in parental investment, favoring women, and has almost certainly been shaped by natural selection (Pryce, 1995). Finally, many of the physical changes associated with puberty, such as development of a masculine jaw in men and relatively large breasts in women, have likely been shaped by the mate-choice preferences of the opposite sex and might be condition-dependent indictors of physical and genetic health (Thornhill & Møller, 1997) and thus influenced by sexual selection.

8

SEX DIFFERENCES IN BRAIN AND COGNITION

Throughout this century, the question of sex differences in brain and cognition has captured the attention of the general public and has been an area of intensive and often contentious scientific study. Today, the existence of sex differences in the pattern of cognitive ability and in the structure and functioning of certain regions of the brain is not questioned by most scientists, although the origin of these differences is debated (D. F. Halpern, 1992, 1997; Pakkenberg & Gundersen, 1997; Rushton & Ankney, 1996; Shaywitz et al., 1995). At least for some domains, there is little question that the development and the expression of the sex differences in brain and cognition are influenced by exposure to sex hormones (Arnold, 1996; K. F. Berman et al., 1997; Kimura, 1996; Volkow et al., 1997). The relation between exposure to sex hormones and sex differences in brain and cognition suggests that many, but not necessarily all, of these sex differences have been shaped by sexual selection (see the *Proximate Mechanisms and Consequences of Sexual Selection* section of chapter 2). In fact, the driving assumption of this chapter is that many of the sex differences in the organization of the mind and brain directly mirror the sex differences in reproductive strategies that have been described throughout this book (Gaulin, 1995).

At the same time, it is also assumed that the basic structure of the human mind and brain has largely evolved by means of natural selection

259

(G. C. Williams, 1966), and, as a result, the minds and brains of women and men are likely to be more similar than different (Gur et al., 1995; Kimura, 1996). In this view, sexual selection acts to create sex differences in the pattern of cognitive ability and in the supporting brain systems to the extent that different cognitive competencies differentially support the ability of men and women to pursue their reproductive interests (Gaulin, 1995). As an example, the tendency of men to form coalitions in the context of male–male competition and the tendency of women to form more reciprocal one-on-one relationships than men create the potential for selection pressures to elaborate the group-level social modules more in men than in women and the individual-level social modules more in women than in men. As described in chapter 1, any such selection pressure would result in the accompanying ability distributions shifting in one direction or the other for women or men. The net result of any such shift is that sex differences in the average competencies of men and women would be found, as would differences in the numbers of women and men at the high and low end of the distributions (see Figure 1.1 and *Intrasexual Variability* section of chapter 9). The theoretical expectation is that there should also be overlap in the cognitive-ability distributions of men and women, an expectation that has been confirmed for all ability domains in which average sex differences are found (D. F. Halpern, 1992).

Following these basic assumptions, the proposed system of evolved cognitive modules presented in chapter 6 (Figure 6.4) is used as the organizing framework for attempting to make sense of the sex differences in brain and cognitive functioning. The use of this framework provides theoretical coherence across chapters but also results in some redundancies in the material presented. The presentation of these redundancies seemed preferable to presenting all of the material in this chapter and in chapter 6 in one very long chapter.

The first section below presents an overview of the sex differences in the cognitive competencies associated with the social modules, along with discussion of any accompanying differences in brain structure and function, when such information is available. The second section provides a discussion of the sex differences in the cognitive competencies, and associated brain systems, that make up the ecological modules; a brief discussion of sex differences in cognitive competencies, such as reading, that are culturally specific, or nonevolved, is provided in chapter 9 (Geary, 1995a). The third and final section provides an evolutionary interpretation of the cognitive sex differences described in the first two sections.

SOCIAL DOMAINS

Following the structure of the *Evolved Cognitive Domains* section of chapter 6, the first section provides discussion of the pattern of sex differences in individual-level social modules, such as facial processing, whereas the second section presents an overview of the pattern of sex differences in group-level social modules, such as the dynamics of in-group and out-group relationships.

Individual-Level Modules

The discussion of the pattern of sex differences in individual-level social modules, those involved in one-on-one dyadic interactions, follows the organization shown in Figure 6.4. The first section that follows provides discussion of sex differences in language-related competencies, whereas the second and third sections focus on facial processing/nonverbal behavior and theory of mind, respectively.

Language

It is not the case that girls and women outperform boys and men on all tests of verbal ability (D. F. Halpern, 1992). In fact, there are no sex differences on many such tests, such as the verbal section of the Scholastic Achievement Test (SAT-V; Hyde & Linn, 1988). However, tests such as the SAT-V are too complex (the associated items require many different types of cognitive processes) to make judgments one way or the other about the language-related competencies of women and men. In addition to this, performance on such tests has little direct relevance to any discussion of potential sex differences in evolved language-related skills (Geary, 1995a; Rozin, 1976). As noted in the introductory statements, of particular importance in this and the following sections is the pattern of sex differences in cognitive competencies that appears to have evolved. For language, these competencies would include language production (e.g., speed of articulating words), language comprehension, and pragmatics of language (i.e., how language is used in social contexts). When considered at this level, many sex differences are found, some as early as 16 months of age (D. F. Halpern, 1992, 1997; Hampson, 1990a; Hyde & Linn, 1988; Molfese, 1990; Shaywitz et al., 1995; P. M. Smith, 1985; Tallal, 1991).

One of the more noticeable sex differences is in the ways girls and women and boys and men use language to influence and attempt to control the dynamics of social relationships (Maccoby, 1990; P. M. Smith, 1985). Basically, boys and men and girls and women use language in ways that mirror their social motives (described in chapter 6) and their social relationships (described in chapter 7). For instance, boys and men more than girls and women use language to attempt to assert their social dominance (i.e., boys and men often use language as a form of status display in the context of male–male competition); Andy's statements (described in the *Social Behavior and Motives* section of chapter 7) provide one example.

"Boys in their groups are more likely than girls in all-girl groups to interrupt one another; use commands, threats, or boasts of authority; refuse to comply with another child's command; give information; heckle a speaker; . . . top someone else's story; or call another child names" (Maccoby, 1990, p. 516).

In comparison to boys and men, girls and women more frequently show socially enabling language; that is, language that provides equal time to all members of the group and that allows other girls and women to express their thoughts and feelings. In all-girl groups, they "are more likely than boys to express agreement with what another speaker has just said, pause to give another girl a chance to speak, or when starting a speaking turn, acknowledge a point previously made by another speaker. . . . Among girls, conversation is a more socially binding process" (Maccoby, 1990, p. 516) than among boys. For girls and women, language is a skill that is used for the development and the maintenance of intimate and reciprocal relationships with other girls and women (see the *Social Behavior and Motives* section of chapter 7).

Nonetheless, this is not the whole story. Language also appears to be a much more central feature of female–female competition than it is in male–male competition. Recall that boys and men more often than not ignore the commands, directives, and requests of other people, except for those of clearly dominant boys or men (see, for example, the *Infancy* section of chapter 7). As a result, in all-male groups, language, in and of itself, is not often an effective means of achieving social dominance. One exception might be politicians who use language to organize the social behavior (e.g., to stage war parties) of large numbers of other people (Pinker & Bloom, 1990). For the most part, however, boys and men more typically compete physically or through the attainment of socially prized resources, such as money or the heads of one's competitors, which they then brag about to other boys or men (see the *Male–Male Competition* section of chapter 5). Girls and women, on the other hand, compete by attempting to disrupt the social relationships of their competitors, and this competition is largely expressed through language. As features of this relational aggression, girls gossip about other girls, spread lies and rumors about their sexual behavior, tell secrets in attempts to control other girls' social behavior, and so forth (Campbell, 1995; Crick et al., 1997; Grotpeter & Crick, 1996; Savin-Williams, 1987).

The importance of language as a means by which girls and women compete with one another sets the stage for selection to elaborate basic language competencies more in women than in men, in much the same way that physical male–male competition has resulted in larger and physically stronger men than women. As noted earlier, language is also an important means for the establishment and the maintenance of the intimate and reciprocal relationships that are important to girls and women, and it might also provide a means to control the dynamics of their relationships with larger and potentially aggressive men; like many other primates, men often use physical force to control the behavior of the women in their life, but most women do not have this option. For all of these reasons, women should not only use language differently than men but they should also show relatively better developed basic language competencies.

Indeed, relative to boys and men, girls and women have advantages for a number of basic language-related skills, including the length and quality of utterances (e.g., in their utterances women show standard grammatical structure and correct pronunciation of language sounds more frequently than do men), the ease and speed of articulating complex words, the ability to generate strings of words, the speed of retrieving individual words from long-term memory, and the skill at discriminating basic language sounds (e.g., consonants and vowels) from one another (R. A. Block, Arnott, Quigley, & Lynch, 1989; D. F. Halpern, 1992, 1997; D. F. Halpern & Wright, 1996; Hampson, 1990a; Hunt, Lunneborg, & Lewis, 1975; Hyde & Linn, 1988). Girls and women also show fewer pauses (e.g., filled with "uhh") in their utterances than boys and men (J. A. Hall, 1984), and, at the same time, boys and men manifest language-related disorders, such as stuttering, two to four times more frequently than girls and women (D. F. Halpern, 1992; Tallal, 1991).

The relative advantage of girls and women in these areas ranges from small to very large. For speech production, such as the number of words produced in a given period of time, about 2 out of 3 women outproduce the average man (D. F. Halpern & Wright, 1996; Hyde & Linn, 1988). Similarly, about 3 out of 4 women commit fewer speech errors (e.g., retrieving the wrong word) than the average man (J. A. Hall, 1984). One study found that 9 out of 10 women outperformed the average man in the ability to discriminate among basic language sounds (i.e., determination of consonant–vowel sequences; R. A. Block et al., 1989), and an analysis of sex differences in speech pauses across many different studies indicated that nearly 9 out of 10 men had more frequent pauses in their utterances than the average woman (J. A. Hall, 1984). These latter findings represent some of the largest cognitive sex differences ever documented.

There is some evidence to suggest that prenatal exposure to sex hormones contributes to the just-described sex differences, with prenatal exposure to testosterone, in particular, potentially suppressing the development of the neural systems that support these skills (Geschwind & Galaburda, 1987; Witelson, 1991). The latter relationship is not certain, however. Inconsistent with this model is the finding that girls and women affected by CAH (recall, CAH is associated with prenatal exposure to androgens) do not differ, on average, from their unaffected peers on measures of verbal fluency (Collaer & Hines, 1995; Resnick et al., 1986). However, girls and women affected by CAH have not systematically been compared with their unaffected peers on all of the language competencies for

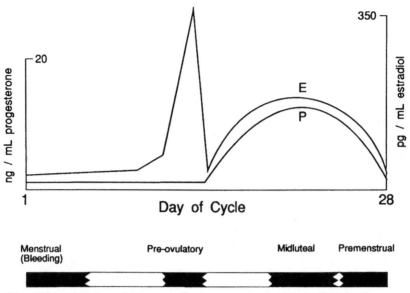

Figure 8.1. Variations in serum concentrations of estradiol (E) and progesterone (P) across the menstrual cycle. From "Cognitive Pattern in Men and Women Is Influenced by Fluctuations in Sex Hormones," by D. Kimura and E. Hampson, 1994, *Current Directions in Psychological Science, 3*, p. 58. Copyright 1994 by Cambridge University Press. Reprinted with permission.

which sex differences are found, and, given this, the finding of no differences between girls and women affected by CAH and their unaffected peers on some verbal fluency measures does not rule out the possibility that prenatal exposure to androgens affects some language competencies.

Either way, circulating hormone levels do appear to be related to certain language competencies (Hampson, 1990a; Kimura & Hampson, 1994), although circulating estrogens (e.g., estradiol) appear to be more strongly related to these competencies than circulating androgens do (Gouchie & Kimura, 1991; Kimura & Hampson, 1994; Moffat & Hampson, 1996b). One method that is often used to assess the relation between circulating estrogens, such as estradiol, and the pattern of cognitive ability is to evaluate the cognitive performance of women at different points in their menstrual cycle. As shown in Figure 8.1, estrogens are at their lowest levels during menstruation. Estradiol levels increase after menstruation and then peak at around the time of ovulation, after which progesterone levels begin to increase (M. S. Smith & Ryan, 1987). Because these hormonal changes are an integral part of the menstrual cycle, inferences can be drawn about the relative influence of estrogens on cognitive performance, by comparing the cognitive performance of women during menstruation with their performance at, for instance, the midluteal phase of their cycle (Kimura & Hampson, 1994).

Some of the better controlled studies in this area have been conducted by Hampson and her colleagues (Hampson, 1990a, 1990b). With these studies, it has been found that the speed of articulating words is at its highest during the midluteal phase of the menstrual cycle (i.e., when estradiol and progesterone levels are high); it appears that these effects are primarily related to estradiol and not to progesterone (Gaulin, Silverman, et al., 1997). For articulation speed, such as speed of articulating syllables, performance is about 5% to 10% higher during the midluteal phase than during menstruation (e.g., Hampson, 1990a). Skill at generating words has also been found to vary across the menstrual cycle, but this pattern is found less consistently than the pattern for articulation speed.

In a similar vein, Kimura and Hampson (1994) reported that estrogen replacement therapy is associated with improved performance on a word articulation task, as did Henderson, Watt, and Buckwalter (1996) for performance on a task that assesses skill at naming objects. In a related study, Van Goozen and her colleagues examined the pattern of change in social behavior and in cognitive performance for female-to-male transsexuals and for male-to-female transsexuals before and during hormonal treatments (Van Goozen et al., 1995). The female-to-male transsexuals were treated with testosterone, whereas the male-to-female transsexuals were treated with a combination of androgen-suppressing drugs and estrogens. After 3 months of hormonal treatments, the female-to-male transsexuals scored significantly lower (by 30% to 34%) on two measures of verbal fluency: one assessing the ability to generate words, and one the ability to generate sentences. For the male-to-female transsexuals, performance decreased slightly (6%) on the word fluency test but improved significantly (22%) for the sentence fluency test.

There is little question that for most individuals—the pattern varies somewhat for right- and left-handers—the majority of the above-described language-related competencies are supported by a number of areas of the left hemisphere of the brain (i.e., the left cortex) and that men and women differ to some degree in the brain regions that support these competencies (Cabeza & Nyberg, 1997; Corballis & Morgan, 1978; Fitch, Miller, & Tallal, 1997; Geschwind & Behan, 1982; Geschwind & Levitsky, 1968; Kimura, 1987; Lenneberg, 1967; Levy, 1969; Moffat & Hampson, 1996b; Molfese, 1990; Shaywitz et al., 1995). In a now classic study, Geschwind and Levitsky (1968) demonstrated that part (the planum temporale) of Wernicke's area—traditionally associated with speech comprehension, among other things—in the left-temporal cortex is physically larger than the comparable area in the right cortex for about two out of three people (see Figure 8.2; see also Gannon et al., 1998). Moreover, some studies have found that this asymmetry (i.e., left larger than right) is less pronounced or sometimes reversed in more women than men (McGlone, 1980; Wada, Clark, & Hamm, 1975).

These findings, among other factors, such as fewer language disorders

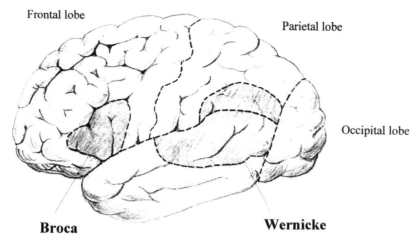

Frontal lobe

Parietal lobe

Occipital lobe

Broca

Wernicke

Temporal lobe

Figure 8.2. Major areas in the cortex. Illustration by Christopher Nadolski.

associated with left-hemispheric damage in women than in men, led McGlone (1980) to conclude that language functions are differentially represented in the left and right hemispheres (i.e., left and right cortex) for women and men. More precisely, it appears that many basic language skills are represented in both the left and the right hemispheres for many women but that these functions are largely represented in the left hemisphere for most men, although these patterns also vary with whether the individual is left- or right-handed and might vary across the menstrual cycle for women; the sex differences are most evident with comparisons of right-handed men and women (Annett, 1985; Hampson, 1990a). Several recent neuroimaging studies are consistent with McGlone's position; that is, that both the left and the right hemispheres are involved in the processing of language sounds for many women but that only the left hemisphere is involved with many men, although these sex differences are not as clear-cut as suggested by McGlone.

In one of these studies, Shaywitz and his colleagues found that certain regions of the frontal cortex, including Broca's area (which is traditionally associated with language production and other language competencies), were differentially involved in the processing of language sounds for women and men (Pugh, Shaywitz, Shaywitz, Constable, et al., 1996; Shaywitz et al., 1995). These differences were evident when men and women were asked to determine if a pair of words read off a computer screen rhymed (e.g., *GOOZ–REWS*); that is, they had to base their judgments on the sounds associated with the words. In this study, about one half of the women showed a strong activation of both the left and the right hemispheres while processing these sounds, but none of the men showed any significant activation of the right hemisphere (i.e., all of their processing was apparently confined to the left hemisphere). Several follow-up studies have confirmed this pattern, but with smaller overall sex differences (Pugh et al., 1997). In one of these studies, the original pattern found by Shaywitz et al. was confirmed when men and women simply listened to speech sounds (Pugh, Shaywitz, Shaywitz, Fulbright, et al., 1996). While listening to speech sounds, both men and women, as a group, engaged Broca's area in the left and right hemispheres, but men showed relatively greater engagement of the left hemisphere than the right hemisphere, whereas women showed the opposite pattern. As suggested by McGlone (1980), there do appear to be sex differences in the representation of some language competencies in the left and right hemispheres, but these are relative and not absolute differences.

Moreover, there appear to be sex differences in the regions supporting language competencies even within the left hemisphere, as suggested by Kimura's (1987) analysis of the relation between brain injury (e.g., stroke) and patterns of language-related disorders (i.e., aphasia). These patterns revealed that damage to many different regions of the left hemisphere—including the frontal, temporal, parietal, and occipital cortices—could result in aphasia in men. For women, in contrast, only damage to the frontal and temporal cortices, corresponding roughly to Broca's and Wernicke's areas, resulted in aphasia. The highest incidence of aphasia was associated with damage to the frontal cortex for women and to the parietal and temporal cortices for men. On the basis of these patterns, Kimura concluded that language functions were diffusely represented in the left hemisphere for men but were focally represented for women.

In addition to sex differences in the areas of the brain that support language competencies, there is also some evidence to suggest that the size and shape of certain regions of the corpus callosum—the neuronal axons that connect the two hemispheres—differ for women and men, although the existence of this potential sex difference is not at all certain (Allen & Gorski, 1992; Allen, Richey, Chai, & Gorski, 1991; de Lacoste-Utamsing & Holloway, 1982; Holloway, Anderson, Defendini, & Harper, 1993; Witelson, 1985). The mixed findings in this area appear to be related, in part, to whether the absolute or relative size of the corpus callosum is assessed. When absolute comparisons are made between men and women, there are few sex differences in the size of the corpus callosum (e.g., Allen et al., 1991; Witelson, 1985). However, when overall brain size is controlled—men have larger brains than women (Pakkenberg & Gundersen, 1997)—women are sometimes found to have a relatively larger corpus callosum than men (see Bishop & Wahlsten, 1997; Holloway et al., 1993, for reviews and different interpretations of these studies). Although the functional significance of any such difference is not currently known, it has been suggested that the relatively larger corpus callosum of women allows the language centers of the left and right hemispheres to communicate with one another (e.g., Allen et al., 1991; but see Bishop & Wahlsten, 1997).

In summary, it is clear that in social contexts boys and men and girls and women use language differently and that girls and women have an advantage over boys and men for a number of basic language-related competencies. It is likely that these sex differences are related, in part, to prenatal and circulating hormone levels, although the precise nature of these relationships is not yet known. Similarly, it is very likely that the sex differences in language-related competencies reflect a sex difference in the distribution of brain regions that support these competencies, as well as differences in the ways in which the development and functioning of these regions are affected by sex hormones.

Facial Processing and Nonverbal Behavior

In this section, sex differences in the ability to interpret and send nonverbal social messages are overviewed, including differences in processing facial expressions, interpreting body posture, and changes in vocal intonation independent of what is actually said. Significant sex differences are found in many of these areas, and most of these differences favor girls and women, in keeping with the position that many individual-level social modules are more highly elaborated in girls and women than in boys and men (Buck et al., 1972; Dimberg & Öhman, 1996; Erwin et al., 1992; Gur, Skolnick, & Gur, 1994; J. A. Hall, 1978, 1984; Rosenthal, Hall, DiMatteo, Rogers, & Archer, 1979; Rotter & Rotter, 1988; H. L. Wagner, Buck, & Winterbotham, 1993; H. L. Wagner, MacDonald, & Manstead, 1986).

The most ambitious and comprehensive assessment of sex differences in the processing of nonverbal information was conducted by Rosenthal et al. (1979). The overall goal of this project was to develop a standardized test that assessed an individual's sensitivity to the nonverbal emotion cues signaled by another individual, including visual (e.g., facial expressions and body posture), auditory (e.g., emotional tone conveyed in utterances), and combined (i.e., including both visual and auditory information) cues—the Profile of Nonverbal Sensitivity (PONS). The test involves watching a 45-minute film that consists of 220 short segments of a woman's nonverbal behavior, including facial expressions, body posture, and content-filtered speech (i.e., speech in which the individual words cannot be identified, but the emotional tone can), as well as segments that include combinations of these cues. The PONS was initially administered to 492 high school students, but in follow-up studies, the entire PONS or portions of it were administered to more than 4,000 other individuals, including elementary and junior high school students, college students, and older adults from a variety of occupations. Testing was also done with three or more samples of individuals from Australia, Canada, Israel, and New Guinea, and smaller numbers of individuals were assessed in Northern Ireland, Mexico, New Zealand, Hong Kong, West Germany, and Singapore.

Across all samples, girls and women showed an advantage over boys and men for accuracy in judging emotion cues on the bases of facial expressions, body posture, and vocal intonation. The magnitude of the overall advantage of girls and women did not vary with age and was moderate in size; about two out of three girls and about two out of three women outperformed the average same-age boy or man on the PONS (Rosenthal et al., 1979). The advantage of girls and women was found in all nations in which three or more samples were obtained (Australia, Canada, the United States, Israel, and New Guinea) and was of the same general magnitude in all of these nations (J. A. Hall, 1984). Moreover, the advantage of girls and women remained significant, although somewhat smaller, when the sex difference in the tendency to gaze-avert was controlled, a finding that suggests that the superior emotion-decoding skills of girls and women are not simply because of the sex difference in the tendency to attend to other people; recall that boys and men gaze-avert much more than girls and women (see the *Infancy* section of chapter 7).

The pattern of sex differences differed, however, for visual, auditory, and combined cues. On the basis of Rosenthal et al.'s (1979) findings and related studies, J. A. Hall (1984) concluded that the advantage of girls and women in the decoding of nonverbal messages "is most pronounced for facial cues, less pronounced for body cues, and least pronounced for vocal cues" (p. 27). However, when all nonverbal cues were provided, the advantage of girls and women over boys and men was larger than for each of these cues alone. For combined cues, which represent a more accurate assessment of nonverbal decoding skills in "real-world" settings, about 17 out of 20 girls and women were more accurate at decoding the emotion cues of another individual than the average same-age boy or man (J. A. Hall, 1978).

Nonetheless, the sex difference in skill at decoding nonverbal cues appears to vary with social context and the particular emotions being signaled. For instance, Buck et al. (1972) found that pairs of women were more effective in expressing and in reading the emotion cues of the other member of the pair, as signaled by changes in facial expression, than pairs of men were. Similarly, H. L. Wagner et al. (1993) found that women were relatively more accurate in judging the emotion cues of other women than the emotion cues of men. These findings appear to reflect the greater sensitivity of women to the emotion cues signaled by facial expressions and other nonverbal behaviors, combined with a greater expressiveness on the part of women than men. Roughly 17 out of 20 women, for instance, are judged to convey more information in their facial expressions than the average man, and nearly 3 out of 4 women engage in social smiling and maintain eye contact more consistently than the average man (J. A. Hall,

1984). These patterns appear to be related, in part, to a sex difference in the tendency to suppress social cues. In situations with emotional overtones, both men and women show physiological arousal, but men tend to suppress social indicators of their emotional state, whereas women tend to signal socially (e.g., through facial expressions) their emotional state (Buck et al., 1972).

Although women are, on average, better at decoding the facial expressions of other people (J. A. Hall, 1984), there is some evidence to suggest that men are more sensitive to negative emotion cues signaled by other men, especially anger, than they are to the same cues signaled by women or to more positive emotion cues signaled by men (Rotter & Rotter, 1988; H. L. Wagner et al., 1993). In two large-scale studies involving more than 1,100 people, Rotter and Rotter found that women were consistently more accurate than men in judging the emotion cues signaled by the facial expressions (shown by means of photographs) of other women and men, when these expressions conveyed the emotions of disgust, fear, or sadness. Women were also more accurate than men in detecting an angry expression on the face of other women. Men, in contrast, were more accurate than women in detecting an angry expression on the face of other men. At the same time, men were less accurate in detecting disgust, fear, and sadness in the facial expressions of other men than they were in detecting these cues in the facial expressions of women; several more recent studies, however, suggest that men might be particularly insensitive to women's sad facial expressions (Erwin et al., 1992; Gur, Skolnick, et al., 1994).

Relatedly, on the basis of a review of psychophysiological responses to facial information, Dimberg and Öhman (1996) concluded that men are more sensitive to the angry expressions of other men than they are to the angry expressions of women, especially when these anger-signaling cues are expressed in adult men as contrasted with adolescents and when the expressions are directed toward the individual (e.g., with eye contact). Women, in contrast, appear to be equally sensitive to angry expressions in men and in other women. The finding that men might be especially sensitive to angry expressions in other men is consistent with Rosenthal et al.'s (1979) findings that relative to other emotion cues, men were especially sensitive to negative dominance-related emotional cues. In other words, women were found to be more sensitive than men in detecting nonverbal indicators of negative emotional states, but the gap was smaller for aggression- and dominance-related themes, such as jealous anger or threatening someone, in relation to other themes, such as talking about a friend's death.

The brain systems involved in the processing of emotion-laden information include a number of subcortical (e.g., the amygdala) and cortical regions (e.g., Halgren & Marinkovic, 1995). The processing of specific emotion-signaling facial expressions appears to especially engage the right-parietal cortex, although the left hemisphere appears to be involved in the processing of certain emotion cues, especially more positive cues (Dimberg & Öhman, 1996; Gur, Skolnick, et al., 1994). Sex differences in the pattern of brain activity associated with the processing of nonverbal emotion cues have not been as systematically studied as sex differences in the processing of language-related information, although at least one such study has been conducted (Gur, Skolnick, et al., 1994). Here, men and women were asked to judge whether photographs of actors' faces were displaying a happy, sad, or neutral expression. Relative to neutral faces, the processing of happy and sad faces was associated with relatively higher activation of the right hemisphere, particularly in the region of the parietal cortex, although increased activation of the left-frontal cortex was also found. Both men and women showed the same pattern of brain activation while processing these facial expressions, but women showed higher overall cortical activity than men did.

There is also evidence to suggest that facial processing is influenced by circulating hormone levels, but again this relation has not been as systematically studied as the relation between hormone levels and language processing (R. Diamond, Carey, & Back, 1983; Heister, Landis, Regard, & Schroeder-Heister, 1989). In one study, women were tachistoscopically presented a series of pictures of normal faces and pictures in which the major features of the faces were scrambled; for instance, the mouth was placed on the forehead (Heister et al., 1989). The tachistoscope was used to present briefly the faces to the right or left visual field, which effectively results in the information being initially presented to the left hemisphere or to the right hemisphere, respectively. The task was simply to determine whether the presented face was real or scrambled. In addition, the women were tested across four phases of their menstrual cycle, including the menstrual and midluteal phases shown in Figure 8.1.

The overall procedure allowed these researchers to determine if the left hemisphere or the right hemisphere is relatively better at processing faces and whether any such advantage varies across the menstrual cycle (Heister et al., 1989). In keeping with other studies, faces that were initially presented to the right hemisphere were processed faster and more accurately than faces that were initially presented to the left hemisphere, except during the premenstrual phase (i.e., when estradiol and progesterone levels are declining). At this point, the processing of faces was relatively slow and inaccurate, whether the faces were initially presented to the left hemisphere or to the right hemisphere. The results also showed that whether they were initially presented either to the left hemisphere or to the right hemisphere, the processing of faces was the fastest and most accurate during the point in the menstrual cycle when estradiol and progesterone levels were near their peak.

In a related study, Skuse et al. (1997) assessed the social–cognitive skills of girls and women affected by Turner's syndrome. Turner's syndrome is a genetic disorder in which the girl or woman has received only a single X chromosome instead of the two X chromosomes found in genetically normal women. For about 7 out of 10 women affected by Turner's syndrome, their single X chromosome comes from their mother, with the X chromosome coming, of course, from their father for the remaining women. Whether the X chromosome comes from their mother or their father is theoretically important, because in a number of other mammals the same gene can be expressed differently when it is received from the mother as compared with the father—this difference is called *genomic imprinting* (see, for example, Barlow, 1995). The question with this study was whether receiving the X chromosome from their mother or father was related to their social–cognitive skills, including skills at interpreting body language and general sensitivity to the emotion cues of other people.

In keeping with the findings reviewed previously, genetically normal girls and women outscored genetically normal boys and men on a test of social–cognitive skills (Skuse et al., 1997); about 7 out of 10 girls and women scored higher than the average boy or man on this test. Of the girls and women affected by Turner's syndrome, those individuals who received their X chromosome from their father scored significantly better than those individuals who received their X chromosome from their mother; the girls and women in the former category scored about as well as the genetically normal boys and men but worse than the genetically normal girls and women. Moreover, 72% of the girls and women who received their X chromosome from their mother had a significant history of social problems, relative to 29% of the girls and women who received their X chromosome from their father. The overall findings suggest that genes on the X chromosome provided by an individual's father, but not by an individual's mother, are related to the development and expression of certain social–cognitive competencies, including skill at decoding nonverbal communication signals, and these genes might contribute to the sex differences described in this section, given that boys and men necessarily receive their single X chromosome from their mother.

Theory of Mind

In the previous section, the focus was on the ability to "read" emotion cues, such as sensitivity to the emotions signaled by facial expressions. Theory of mind goes at least one step beyond this ability. Among other things (e.g., making inferences about the intentions of other people), theory of mind represents the ability to infer whether the emotions signaled by these facial expressions are an accurate reflection of the actual emotional state of the individual. In other words, people often signal or suppress emotion cues independent of their actual emotional state (e.g., with social deception). Given this, sensitivity to the social and emotion cues signaled by nonverbal behavior and the ability to make inferences about the underlying emotional state of another individual are two relatively distinct classes of ability. Sex differences in the latter ability—theory of mind—are the focus of this section.

On the basis of the argument that girls and women have better developed individual-level social competencies than boys and men, the expectation is that a sex difference, favoring girls and women, will be found for at least some aspects of theory of mind. Unfortunately, relatively little research has been conducted on this issue (J. Astington, personal communication, August 1997; H. M. Wellman, personal communication, August 1997). The few studies that have been conducted have focused on children and do indeed suggest that by 3 years of age girls have a more sophisticated theory of mind than same-age boys (Banerjee, 1997; Bosacki, 1998; Happé, 1995), although considerably more research will be needed before any such sex difference is fully understood.

The most comprehensive of these studies was conducted by Banerjee (1997). In this study, 3-, 4-, and 5-year-old boys and girls were administered two theory-of-mind tests. The tests assessed their ability to distinguish between real and apparent emotional states and their understanding of the display rules that moderate how emotions are expressed in specific social contexts. In short, the first test assessed how well the children understood that the expression of emotion cues could differ from the individual's actual emotional state; children who do not understand this distinction believe, for instance, that if another individual "looks happy," then he or she must feel happy. The second test assessed the children's understanding of display rules: that emotion signals should be suppressed in certain situation, so as, for example, not to "hurt another persons feelings." Both of these competencies were assessed by presenting the child with a series of stories, some with positive emotional themes (e.g., a happy main character) and others with negative emotional themes (e.g., a sad main character), in which the child character was motivated to hide his or her emotional state, as illustrated by the following:

> Diana has a brother named Bill. Bill wasn't very nice to Diana today so Diana wants to hide his favorite toy. That's what she does—she hides his favorite toy. When Bill comes home he can't find his toy anywhere. Diana is really happy because Bill can't find his toy anywhere. But, Diana doesn't want Bill to see how she feels, because then Bill will shout at her. So, Diana tries to hide how she feels. (Banerjee, 1997, p. 115)

After hearing each story, the children were asked a number of questions to ensure that they remembered and understood the story plot. They were then presented with a series of facial drawings depicting happy, sad, and neutral expressions—the children were introduced to these drawings before hearing the stories—and were asked, "Show me the picture for how Diana really feels. How does Diana really feel when Bill can't find his favorite toy? (Banerjee, 1997, p. 116). After this, the children were asked to point to the picture for how Diana was trying to look. A similar procedure was used to assess their understanding of display rules.

The results showed that even many 3-year-olds have some understanding of the difference between apparent and real emotional states and some understanding of display rules, although both of the these competencies were more fully developed in 5-year-olds than in 3-year-olds. For the test that assessed an understanding of apparent–real emotional states, girls understood this distinction for both positive and negative stories, whereas boys were more sensitive to this distinction for negative stories (e.g., when the character is sad) than for positive stories (e.g., when the character is happy); girls had higher average scores than boys for positive and negative stories. For the test that assessed an understanding of display rules, both boys and girls understood that emotion signals should be suppressed in some situations (e.g., so as not to "hurt someone's feelings"). In situations in which it is appropriate to display emotions (e.g., happiness during a birthday party), boys more frequently than girls stated that emotion displays should be suppressed. The overall results suggest that preschool girls have a clearer understanding of the difference between the apparent and real emotional states of other people, and in terms of display rules they "seem more attuned to the social context" (Banerjee, 1997, p. 127) than preschool boys.

The few neuroimaging studies that have been conducted in this area indicate that portions of the frontal cortex, in both the left and the right hemispheres, are engaged during the processing of certain theory-of-mind tasks (Baron-Cohen et al., 1994; Frith et al., 1996). In the study conducted by Baron-Cohen and his colleagues, the brain activity of men was monitored as they made judgments about mind-related words and body-related words. For the former list, the men were presented with a series of words, such as *think, car, pretend,* and so forth. For each word, the men had to determine if it was mind related (something the mind could do) or not. For mind-related words, but not for body-related words or for filler words (e.g., car), portions of the frontal cortex, especially in the right hemisphere, were preferentially activated, suggesting that this area of the brain is involved in at least certain aspects of theory of mind.

Again, it is unfortunate that sex differences have not been assessed in these studies (U. Frith, personal communication, November 1997). The finding that there are sex differences in functioning of the frontal cortices associated with a number of other cognitive competencies (e.g., in the degree to which context influences the tendency to respond to certain types of information) suggests that sex differences in functioning of these cortices during theory-of-mind tasks might be found with future neuroimaging studies (Cowell et al., 1994; E. Goldberg, Podell, Harner, Riggio, & Lovell, 1994). Similarly, studies of the relation among prenatal exposure to androgens (e.g., with CAH), circulating hormone levels (e.g., across the menstrual cycle), and performance on theory-of-mind tasks would be very informative.

Group-Level Modules

In comparison to research on sex differences in individual-level social competencies, there has been little sex-differences research on the pattern of cognitive competencies associated with the group-level modules proposed in chapter 6. Nonetheless, some sex-differences research has been conducted on the dynamics of in-group and out-group formation and on the pattern of kin relationships that develop in women and men. The first section that follows provides a brief consideration of the sex differences in the pattern of kin bias, whereas the second section overviews research on the dynamics of in-group and out-group relationships.

Kin Bias

Both men and women show a preferential treatment of kin (Hamilton, 1975), although the pattern of kin relationships is moderated by a host of social and ecological factors, such as whether the group is engaged in frequent intergroup conflict or whether women migrate to new groups or not. Despite these variations, the most consistent pattern (across cultures) of kin relationships is found between women and their young children (Whiting & Edwards, 1988), reflecting the sex difference in parental investment described in chapter 4.

For men, the pattern of kin relationships appears to be more strongly influenced by contextual factors than is the case with women. For instance, in societies characterized by intense male–male competition and frequent intergroup conflict, the activities of men tend to be relatively more centered on relationships among adult-male kin than on relationships with their children (Draper & Harpending, 1988; Pasternak et al., 1997). In fact, relatively cohesive male kin groups are often found in preindustrial societies that are frequently engaged in intergroup conflict, although this pattern is most common in economically midlevel societies, such as agricultural societies without a central government (Pasternak et al., 1997). In societies with ecologically or socially imposed monogamy, in contrast, men often focus more on their families (i.e., wife and children) than on the larger network of male kin (Flinn & Low, 1986; MacDonald, 1988).

At this point, little is known about the brain systems involved in the classification of kin versus nonkin, and relatively little is known about how hormones might influence the structure and functioning of any such brain regions and associated social patterns. The only exception is for certain social relationships. Recall that a relation among prenatal exposure to male hormones, circulating hormone levels, and relative interest in interacting with infants and children has been found (Collaer & Hines, 1995; Lee & Bowman, 1995; Pryce, 1995), although these relations are moderated by contextual factors (see the *Hormonal Influences* section of chapter 4).

In-Groups and Out-Groups

On the basis of the prediction that coalition-based male–male competition has been an important feature of sexual selection during the course of human evolution (e.g., see the *Evolutionary Models* section of chapter 3), sex differences in the dynamics of in-group and out-group formation are expected, especially during periods of conflict. However, relative and not absolute differences are expected in this area, given that the consequences of losing a conflict to an out-group can have life-changing consequences for both men and women. Unfortunately, sex-differences research in this area is meager, in comparison to the quantity of studies on individual-level social sex differences. The research that has been conducted suggests that boys and girls and men and women are indeed more similar than different (L. E. Davis, Cheng, & Strube, 1996; Jackson, Sullivan, Harnish, & Hodge, 1996; M. Rogers, Hennigan, Bowman, & Miller, 1984; Schaller, 1992; Towson, Lerner, & de Carufel, 1981).

Both boys and girls, as well as men and women, readily form in-groups and out-groups and generally make judgments about in-group members that are more favorable than their judgments about out-group members (e.g., Schaller, 1992). Under conditions that implicitly or explicitly provide a reminder of one's mortality (e.g., being exposed to issues associated with death), both men and women show a marked increase in their endorsement of the in-group's social ideology and show more negative attitudes toward people who question this ideology (J. Arndt, personal communication, October 1997; Arndt et al., 1997; Greenberg et al., 1994). Nonetheless, it appears that sex differences in the dynamics of in-group and out-group formations do emerge under some conditions (e.g., L. E. Davis et al., 1996).

One potential early manifestation of this sex difference is the degree to which children's social and play activities are segregated by sex, although any such difference needs to be considered in light of the different types of social groups formed by boys and girls. Recall that to engage in intergroup competition, such as competitive sports activities, boys tend to form larger groups than girls (see the *Play and Social Development* sections of chapter 7). Their larger size often makes boys' groups more accessible to boys who might otherwise be considered as members of an out-group. For instance, M. Rogers et al. (1984) showed that under some conditions Black boys and White boys were more likely to play together than were Black girls and White girls, who showed a strong tendency to self-segregate into same-race groups. The greater integration of the boys groups was largely due to the competitive play of these boys, that is, "because black and white boys need each other to form complete sports teams" (M. Rogers et al., 1984, p. 215). Even so, the formation of mixed-race teams is to compete against another group of boys, who, by definition, form an out-group. Once an in-group and an out-group have been formed, there is some indication that boys exert more social pressure than girls on other in-group members to conform to group-sanctioned activities (Sherif et al., 1961).

As described in chapter 7 (*Social Development* section), boys and girls segregate themselves into same-sex social groups and manifest different types of social behavior within these groups. Recall that the formation of same-sex groups appears to be influenced by the different play and social styles of boys and girls and by the categorization of other children as girls or boys combined with a tendency to congregate with people in the same social category (Maccoby, 1988). In addition, boys and girls exert social pressures on other same-sex children to stay away from members of the opposite sex, lest they become infected with "cooties" or with other such maladies. Both boys and girls exert this pressure on their same-sex peers, but this pressure appears to be stronger within boys groups than within girls groups. Boys, for instance, show a greater concern for and teasing about cooties than girls do (Maccoby, 1988).

In addition, the play patterns of boys are more rigidly stereotyped than the play patterns of girls. In comparison to boys, girls can more easily engage in activities that are more typical of the opposite sex, without parental and peer concerns about their sexual orientation, for instance (Lytton & Romney, 1991; Maccoby & Jacklin, 1974). As an example, cross-over play, such as girls playing competitive sports or boys playing with dolls, occurs much more frequently with girls than with boys. As described in chapter 7, one of the largest sex differences in play activities, favoring girls, involves playing with dolls, with nearly all girls between the ages of 6 to 10 years frequently engaging in this form of play (Sandberg & Meyer-Bahlburg, 1994). From 6 to 10 years of age, boys' doll play reaches its peak at age 7 years and then declines considerably over the next 3 years; at 7 years of age, about 28% of boys regularly played with dolls—it was not clear whether this included play with "action figures," such as G. I. Joe— but only 12% did so at age 10 years. The participation of girls in competitive sports, in contrast, increases over this same age range. In Sandberg and Meyer-Bahlburg's (1994) study, the most dramatic change was found for participation in basketball, in which the participation of girls increased sixfold from 6 to 10 years of age (6% vs. 36%).

Although it is far from certain, these patterns suggest that peer pressures for the segregation of social groups and adherence to group mores are stronger within boys groups than within girls groups. In other words, boys appear to exert more social pressure on other boys to stay away from out-group members (girls, in this case) and to engage in activities that are valued by the in-group and avoid activities that are valued by the out-group. A similar pattern may in fact be evident with adults, as exemplified by attitudes toward gay men and lesbians (Whitley & Kite, 1995). Men and women appear to have similar attitudes toward lesbians, but "men's attitudes toward homosexuality are particularly negative when the target is a gay man rather than a lesbian" (Whitley & Kite, 1995, p. 147); in this meta-analysis, Whitley and Kite found that about 7 out of 10 men had more negative attitudes toward gay men than the average woman did. A similar pattern is found with the Ache (K. Hill & Hurtado, 1996). In this society, men who take on a feminine role and feminine behaviors are called *panegi* (*pane* means unlucky in hunting). "Men who are *panegi* generally do not hunt, but instead collect plant resources and insect larvae. They weave baskets, mats . . . and other female handicrafts. [These men] were low status and not always treated well. They were forced to do menial chores . . . and were also often the butt of jokes and off-color sexual humor" (K. Hill & Hurtado, 1996, pp. 276–277).

Although not enough research has been conducted to draw firm conclusions, the results of several experimental studies are also consistent with the view that there are some sex differences in the dynamics of in-group/out-group relationships, particularly when these relations involve direct competition or distribution of resources (L. E. Davis et al., 1996; Towson et al., 1981). In one study, fifth- and sixth-grade children watched videos of boys and girls working in low- (working to meet individual goals) and high-competition settings. In the high-competition setting, the workers were described as being members of a boys' team or a girls' team, thus creating a same-sex in-group and an opposite-sex out-group. The children's task was to determine how much each worker was to be paid. In the low-competition setting, both boys and girls paid the more productive worker more than his or her less productive peer (60% vs. 40%), regardless of the sex of the workers. However, when the more productive worker was a girl in the high-competition setting, boys paid her significantly less than when she was the more productive worker in the low-competition setting. Girls, in contrast, showed the opposite pattern. Girls paid productive boys the same amount in the high- and low-competition settings, but they substantially favored productive girls in the high-competition setting. In short, during periods of competition, boys discriminated against the out-group, whereas girls "boosted" the in-group.

More recently, L. E. Davis et al. (1996) studied the behavior of same-sex groups that differed in racial composition, thus implicitly creating a same-race in-group and an other-race out-group. Each group included four individuals: two White individuals and two Black individuals, three White individuals and one Black individual, or three Black individuals and one White individual. Each group was provided with a brief description of 10 people (no information was provided on race). The groups were then "given the hypothetical scenario that war had been declared and that an existing fallout shelter could support only six individuals. Thus, four individuals must be excluded from the shelter so that six could live to rebuild a new society" (L. E. Davis et al., 1996, p. 159). The task of the group was to reach a consensus as to which four people would be excluded from the shelter.

The task was potentially contentious and thus useful for testing several hypotheses about group relationships. One hypothesis is that when in-groups and out-groups are equal in size, intergroup tensions increase. Consistent with this hypothesis was the finding that group atmosphere was rated as significantly lower (e.g., relatively cold and unpleasant) for groups that contained two White individuals and two Black individuals, in comparison to groups that contained three individuals of one race. This pattern was found for both men and women. However, sex differences emerged for overall satisfaction with the group decision. For women, the racial composition of the group did not influence their overall satisfaction with the group's final decision, as most women were satisfied with this decision. For men, the highest levels of satisfaction were found for groups in which one race (Black or White) was in the majority, but significantly lower levels of satisfaction were found when the group consisted of two Black individuals and two White individuals. The pattern suggests that women were able to reach a consensus that was supported by all of the group members, regardless of group composition. Men reached a consensus in groups in which the in-group had a numerical majority, but they did not reach a satisfactory consensus in groups in which the in-group and out-group were equal in size. In other words, intergroup cooperation was lower for men, but not for women, when the in-group and the out-group were equally matched.

In summary, both boys and girls and men and women readily form in-groups and out-groups and generally favor in-group members to out-group members. However, relative to girls and women, boys and men appear to exert more intense social pressures on in-group members to adhere to group ideologies and typical group behaviors, and they also appear to develop relatively more negative attitudes about out-group members during periods of competition and conflict. In other words, in comparison to girls and women, boys and men appear to be relatively intolerant of in-group members who deviate from group norms, and they more readily develop agonistic attitudes and behaviors toward out-group members. These sex differences, in turn, would result in relatively cohesive all-male groups and groups that are easily provoked into coalition-based competition. At this point, little is known about the brain mechanisms underlying these sex differences or the degree to which these sex differences are related to exposure to sex hormones.

ECOLOGICAL DOMAINS

The first section that follows provides a summary of the pattern of sex differences in biological modules, whereas the second section provides a consideration of the pattern of sex differences in physical modules.

Biological Modules

In chapter 3, it was argued that the pattern of physical, social, behavioral, and cognitive sex differences is more readily understood in terms of sexual selection than in terms of the sexual division of labor (see the *Sexual Selection and Human Evolution* section). Nonetheless, in many preindustrial societies, the sexual division of labor—in particular, hunting by men and gathering by women—results in higher mortality in rates in men than in women and can have an important influence on the number of offspring sired by individual men and an influence on the ability of individual women to keep their children alive (Blurton Jones et al., 1997; Frost, in press; K. Hill & Hurtado, 1996; Silverman & Eals, 1992; Symons, 1979). Given this, it is likely that hunting and gathering skills have contributed to individual differences in survival rates and reproductive outcomes, and, given this, it is likely that any associated cognitive competencies, such as folk biological knowledge, have been subject to selection pressures (see the *Biological Modules* section of chapter 6).

To the extent that folk biological knowledge actually influenced skills at gathering and hunting, the evolution of sex differences in the cognitive and brain systems that support (a) the ease with which this knowledge is acquired and (b) the complexity of this knowledge once it has been acquired is possible. As an example, if the development of mental models of the behavior of hunted animals facilitated actual hunting skills, then, all other things being equal, men who excelled in this area would have had more reproductive options and more surviving children, as a result of greater hunting success, than their less knowledgeable peers. Under these conditions, a sex difference in the interest in or the ability to develop complex knowledge systems of fauna could evolve.

Unfortunately, the issue of sex differences in folk biological knowledge has not systematically been assessed by either ethnobiologists—who study classification systems in preindustrial societies—or developmental psychologists—who study children's intuitive understanding of the behavior and growth of plants and animals (e.g., Berlin, Breedlove, & Raven, 1966; Keil, 1992). On the basis of the little systematic research that has been conducted, it appears that the folk biological knowledge of boys and girls and men and women is more similar than different (S. Atran, personal communication, July 1997; F. C. Keil, personal communication, July 1997), although some differences have been found.

There is some indication that boys attend to potentially dangerous and wild animals more often than girls do, on average. For instance, Eibl-Eibesfeldt noted that boys growing up in a kibbutz "often identified in their symbolic games with animals, such as horses, dogs, snakes, frogs, and wolves, and not with those surrounding them, like cows, lambs, sheep or chickens" (Eibl-Eibesfeldt, 1989, p. 282). Similarly, in the drawings of !Ko children (mentioned in chapter 7), boys depicted domestic and wild animals about three times more frequently than girls did. Blurton Jones et al. (1997) have documented a related sex difference in the self-initiated activities of Hadza children older than 10 years of age; the Hadza are a hunter–gatherer group in northern Tanzania. Before this age, both boys and girls forage. After this age, boys generally restrict their activities to hunting, despite the fact that their hunting returns—in terms of calories —are much lower than would be the case if they continued to forage.

For adults, the most extensive assessment of sex differences in folk biological knowledge was conducted with the Aguaruna, a forest-dwelling tribe in northern Peru (Berlin, Boster, & O'Neill, 1981; Boster, 1985). The subsistence activities of the Aguaruna include gardening, fishing, hunting, and collecting foods in the forest. As in many other preindustrial societies, gardening is primarily done by women and hunting by men (Daly & Wilson, 1983). To assess the classification system of local birds, some of which are hunted with blowguns, Berlin et al. (1981) asked groups of men and women to name and classify (i.e., put related species together) more than 150 specimens of local species. As a group, the classification system of men was more highly differentiated and showed more consistency across raters than the classification system of women. Moreover, for many species, the men's classification system was very similar to the corresponding taxonomy developed by Western biologists (also men, for the most part).

Atran (1994) found a similar sex difference in the folk biological knowledge of the Itza-Maya (Guatemala). Men and women showed similar taxonomies for local animals but differed considerably in their level of expertise. In their classifications, women were more likely to rely on static morphological features of the animal, such as color or body shape, than men were, whereas men relied "more on complexly related features of behavior, habitat, diet, and functional relationship to people" (Atran, 1994, p. 331) than women did. In contrast, Boster (1985) found a sex difference, favoring women, in the Aguaruna classification system of plants grown in local gardens. As a group, women showed more agreement among themselves and greater complexity in the overall classification system of these plants than men did. Similarly, Figueiredo, Leitão-Filho, and Begossi (1993,

1997) found that for groups of South American Indians residing at the Sepetiba Bay region in Brazil, women showed greater knowledge of medicinal plants than men did; many of these plants are used to treat sick children (e.g., earaches).

The origin of these sex differences is not at all clear, however. These differences could simply result from the different activities of men and women, so that these activities result in a sex difference in the knowledge of flora and fauna without any inherent sex differences in the ways in which folk biological knowledge is organized or learned (e.g., Boster, 1985). Alternatively, there could be an inherent bias in the ecological features to which boys and girls attend to, which would eventually result in a sex difference in the degree to which knowledge of these features is relatively more elaborated in one sex or the other. The suggestion that boys attend to wild and potentially dangerous animals more frequently than girls do might reflect such an attentional bias (Blurton Jones et al., 1997; Eibl-Eibesfeldt, 1989).

At this point, however, not enough is known about the extent of these sex differences and the factors that moderate their expression to draw any firm conclusions one way or the other. For instance, if attention to and learning about wild animals was moderated by exposure to sex hormones, then this would suggest that there might be biologically based differences in the ways in which boys and girls and men and women organize folk biological knowledge. However, unfortunately, no such studies have been conducted. Nor is it known whether there are any sex differences in the brain systems that support the categorization of biological knowledge, even though such studies can be conducted. For instance, specific regions of the left-temporal cortex appear to be involved in categorizing objects as living or nonliving, but it is not known whether men and women engage these regions differently during such categorizations (Cabeza & Nyberg, 1997).

Physical Modules

Following the framework presented in Figure 6.4, the first section that follows overviews research on the pattern of sex differences in the ability to act on and respond to the physical environment, whereas the second section provides discussion of the pattern of sex differences in the ability to represent the physical environment mentally; little is known about the cognitive competencies associated with the proposed engineering modules (but see Wynn, 1993), and thus the issue of sex differences is not considered. Studies that have examined the relation between the cognitive competencies supporting movement and representation indicate that these two classes of skill are related to one another—above-average performance in one area tends to be associated with above-average performance in the other—but only weakly. The overall pattern suggests that the cognitive and brain systems making up the competencies that support movement and representation differ to some extent (e.g., Schiff & Oldak, 1990; Watson & Kimura, 1991), as suggested in chapter 6 (see the *Physical Modules* section).

Movement

Although people can use both auditory (e.g., the sounds produced by oncoming objects, such as cars) and visual information to track the movement of objects in physical space, people tend to focus more on visual information than on auditory information when tracking any such object. In addition, people are generally more accurate in their judgments of the movement of objects on the basis of visual as compared with auditory information (Schiff & Oldak, 1990). Thus, the focus of this section is on the visuomotor competencies that are associated with acting on and responding to the physical world. In chapter 6, several examples of such visuomotor systems were provided, such as those involved in prey capture and predator avoidance (Barton & Dean, 1993; Milner & Goodale, 1995). The specific issue addressed in this section is whether there are sex differences in the visuomotor systems that support the ability to act on and respond to the physical world.

As briefly noted in chapter 7, there are indeed significant sex differences, favoring boys and men, in at least some visuomotor systems. Recall that during infancy, boys and girls selectively attend to different types of information in their environment. Boys, on average, orient themselves more to physical objects (e.g., colored lights) and to physical space more than girls do, whereas girls orient themselves more to people (Cohen & Gelber, 1975; McGuinness & Pribram, 1979). Men show a number of advantages associated with the visual system as well, even though women have more sensitive sensory systems in the areas of touch, smell, taste, and hearing (Velle, 1987). Men have sharper vision than women do and are better at detecting the orientation and the relative movement of single objects within an array of objects (Linn & Petersen, 1985; Velle, 1987; Voyer, Voyer, & Bryden, 1995). The sex differences in skill at detecting the relative orientation and the relative movement of objects are often found before puberty and appear to be similar to skill at detecting the movement of animals or other people in a forest. Before puberty, about 3 out of 5 boys show better skills in these areas than the average girl; whereas in adulthood, about 7 out of 10 men outperform the average woman (Linn & Petersen, 1985; Voyer et al., 1995).

Men show complementary advantages in the ability to judge the velocity of moving objects and in the ability to estimate when an object moving directly toward them will make contact, that is, hit them (Law et al., 1993; Schiff & Oldak, 1990). In a set of experiments, Law et al. asked men and women to judge the relative distance traveled by two objects and the relative velocity of two moving objects. No sex differences were found in the ability to judge which object had traveled farther, but men showed a moderate-to-large advantage in the ability to judge object velocity. In one of the studies, more than four out of five men were more sensitive to relative velocity than the average woman was. Moreover, it was found that practice and feedback (i.e., telling the participants if their choice was correct or incorrect after every trial) improved the performance of both men and women, but the magnitude of the men's advantage did not change. In another series of experiments, Schiff and Oldak demonstrated that men were more accurate than women in judging time of arrival (i.e., judging when an object moving toward them would either hit them or pass them). For objects that could only be seen, about three out of four men were more accurate at judging time of arrival than the average woman was. Men were also more accurate, on average, at judging time of arrival for objects that could only be heard, despite the fact that women have more sensitive hearing than men (Velle, 1987).

In a similar vein, Watson and Kimura (1991) found that about 3 out of 4 men could block targets that were thrown at them—actually, tennis balls shot from launching devices—with both their right and their left hand with greater skill than the average woman could. In fact, as a group, men successfully blocked an average of 26 of the 30 tennis balls shot at them, suggesting that the task was too easy for men and thus that the magnitude of the sex difference in blocking skill had been underestimated. As mentioned in chapter 7, the throwing accuracy of men is also higher than that of women. Watson and Kimura again found that about 3 out of 4 men outperformed the average woman in this area. Jardine and Martin (1983) found even larger sex differences in throwing accuracy. For adolescents, about 7 out of 8 boys threw more accurately than the average same-age girl, whereas 9 out of 10 fathers threw more accurately than mothers.

As described in the next section, there is a considerable amount of research on the relation between performance on spatial ability tests and prenatal exposure to sex hormones and circulating hormone levels. Unfortunately, the relation between hormonal exposure and performance in the above-described areas has not been as systematically assessed. There is, however, some very preliminary findings suggesting that the ability to throw accurately might be related to prenatal exposure to sex hormones or to more direct genetic influences (J. A. Y. Hall & Kimura, 1995; Kimura, 1996) and that the ability to determine the relative orientation of single objects might be related, in part, to circulating hormone levels (Hampson, 1990b; Hampson & Kimura, 1988). A complete understanding of these relationships must, however, await further research. Similarly, although the brain systems that support some of these competencies have been studied

(Andersen et al., 1997; Milner & Goodale, 1995), sex differences in the structure and functioning of these regions have not systematically been assessed.

Nonetheless, the just-described sex differences complement the sex differences in the structure of the forearm and humerus, as well as the male advantage in upper body strength (see the *Physical Development* section of chapter 7), and are consistent with the argument that the use of projectile weapons has been an important feature in the evolution of male–male competition. Of course, the sex difference for many of these same competencies, such as throwing accuracy, might have evolved as a consequence of the sexual division of labor (in particular, as a result of hunting in men), as is often argued (Frost, 1998; Jardine & Martin, 1983; Kimura, 1996; Kolakowski & Malina, 1974). However, the male advantages in the ability to judge when a moving object would make contact with them and in the ability to block thrown objects are competencies that would not influence hunting skills but would be important defensive skills in the context of male–male competition that involved the use of projectile weapons, such as stones (see Isaac, 1992); as described in chapter 7, boys' play, as with the Sioux game of Throw at Each Other with Mud, often involves the practice of such skills.

Representation

Although the previous section focused on sex differences in the ability to act on and respond to certain features of the physical environment, this section focuses on sex differences in the ability to form mental representations (e.g., images of the local ecology) of this environment. Sex differences in many of these visuospatial skills have extensively been studied for many decades, and the pattern that has emerged with these studies is complex. Boys and men do not simply outperform girls and women in all spatial domains (e.g., Stumpf & Eliot, 1995). For instance, men typically outperform women on tests that involve the representation and rotation of images in three-dimensional, and sometimes two-dimensional, space; whereas there are often small or no sex differences in the ability to perform other types of spatial tasks, such as mentally folding sheets of paper (Collins & Kimura, 1997; Delgado & Prieto, 1997; D. F. Halpern, 1992; Johnson & Meade, 1987; Liben, 1991; Linn & Petersen, 1985; Masters & Sanders, 1993; McGee, 1979; Voyer et al., 1995). As with some language competencies, the pattern is complicated further by some findings suggesting that certain spatial abilities vary for right- and left-handers and even for right-handers with and without left-handed parents (Casey & Brabeck, 1989; Casey, Colón, & Goris, 1992; McKeever, 1995). The development of spatial abilities is also influenced by engagement in spatial-related activities, activities that differ for boys and girls (Baenninger & Newcombe, 1995;

Gilger & Ho, 1989). Moreover, recent studies (described below) indicate that women have a considerable advantage over men in at least one form of visuospatial memory (Herlitz, Nilsson, & Bäckman, 1997; Silverman & Eals, 1992; Stumpf & Eliot, 1995).

Despite these complications, a consistent pattern of sex differences has emerged for certain forms of spatial cognition (see Caplan, Mac-Pherson, & Tobin, 1985, for an alternative view). Of particular theoretical importance is the pattern of sex differences for those spatial abilities that are potentially related to the different reproductive and foraging activities of men and women in preindustrial societies and, presumably, during the course of human evolution. The associated competencies include the ability to generate mental representations of the large-scale physical environment, which appears to be related to skill at navigating within this environment; the ability to manipulate or transform three-dimensional representations mentally, which appears to engage the same cognitive systems used to represent three-dimensional space and thus might also be related to navigation (Just & Carpenter, 1985; Moffat, Hampson, & Hatzipantelis, 1998; Shepard, 1994); and memory for the location of specific objects in the environment, which might be related to foraging activities (Gaulin, 1995; Silverman & Eals, 1992).

The sex difference in the ability to generate mental representations (e.g., a map) of a novel environment was discussed in chapter 7 (*Play* section). Recall that under conditions that do not provide many external supports to facilitate children's memory, boys were found to be more skilled than same-age girls in the ability to reconstruct mentally the topography of an unfamiliar environment that was visited once (Matthews, 1987, 1992). Relative to the average girl, the map of the average boy showed a more accurate clustering of environmental features and provided a more accurate representation of the geometric relations among these features (e.g., that the relative position of one environmental feature is northeast of another). One analysis classified maps according to the overall organization of environmental features, ranging from a highly unorganized (Level I) to a highly organized and accurate representation of the geometric relations among features (Level III). The maps were scored by two independent judges who were not aware of the age or sex of the mapmakers. Across ages, 29% of the boys' maps were classified as Level III, compared with 7% of the girls' maps. Conversely, 23% of the girls' maps were classified as Level I, compared with 6% of the boys' maps. A related analysis revealed that 43% of the girls' maps contained significant distortions in the placement of important environmental features, but only 10% of the boys' maps showed such distortions. Boys and girls also differed in the extent to which they focused on landmarks (e.g., specific buildings) or routes (e.g., roadways) in their maps, with girls focusing on the former and boys on the latter.

Figure 8.3. A sample item from the Mental Rotation Test (Vandenberg & Kuse, 1978). When rotated, two of the items to the right are identical to the comparison item on the left.

Galea and Kimura (1993) found a similar pattern with adults, as did Holding and Holding (1989), Bever (1992), L. K. Miller and Santoni (1986), and Dabbs, Chang, Strong, and Milun (1998). As an example, in Galea and Kimura's study, men and women were asked to study a map of an unfamiliar, fictitious town. They were then tested on their ability to learn a route within this town, as well as on their reliance on geometric knowledge to navigate this route and their memory for landmarks on and off the route. Men learned the route more quickly—in less time and in fewer practice trials—than women and made fewer errors during this learning. As found by Matthews (1987), women remembered more landmarks than men did, whereas men had better geometric or directional knowledge of the map than women did. For both men and women, overall route-learning scores were significantly related to geometric knowledge of the map and to performance on a test that assesses the ability to generate and rotate three-dimensional geometric figures mentally, as illustrated by the Vandenberg Mental Rotation Test (MRT) shown in Figure 8.3 (Vandenberg & Kuse, 1978), but this ability was not related to landmark knowledge (but see Choi & Silverman, 1996).

The potential relation between performance on the route-learning task and skill at mentally rotating three-dimensional images is theoretically important, because skill at rotating these images represents one of the largest and most consistently identified sex difference in spatial cognition, favoring men (Linn & Petersen, 1985; Masters & Sanders, 1993; Vandenberg & Kuse, 1978; Voyer et al., 1995). The advantage of boys and men in the ability to generate and rotate three-dimensional images is found at the earliest age at which the test can reliably be administered (early adolescence) and is found at every age thereafter (Linn & Petersen, 1985; Stumpf & Eliot, 1995; Voyer et al., 1995). Between 15 and 20 years of age, about four out of five boys and men are better able to generate and manipulate three-dimensional images mentally than the average girl or woman, and between 20 and 35 years of age, about six out of seven men outperform the average woman in this area (Linn & Petersen, 1985; Masters & Sanders, 1993).

In an extensive analysis of the cognitive processes supporting the ability to generate and rotate these images, Just and Carpenter (1985) concluded that "the cognitive coordinate system within which the figures are represented is the standard environmentally defined one" (p. 165). Or stated differently, it appears that the ability to generate and rotate three-dimensional images is dependent, to some extent, on the same cognitive system involved in generating three-dimensional representations of large-scale physical space (Moffat et al., 1998; Shepard, 1994), although there is not a perfect one-to-one relation between these competencies (Galea & Kimura, 1993). For instance, both processing of three-dimensional images, such as those shown in Figure 8.3, and route learning appear to engage the hippocampus as well as the parietal cortex, although processing of three-dimensional images and route learning appear to engage different regions of the parietal cortex (Cabeza & Nyberg, 1997; Maguire et al., 1997; Tagaris et al., 1997); unfortunately sex differences have not been assessed in these neuroimaging studies.

In contrast, it appears that the tasks that require locating objects in an array (described below) do not engage the hippocampus, at least with small-scale experimental tasks (Cabeza & Nyberg, 1997). Thus, as suggested earlier, these findings are consistent with the view that the MRT taps, at least to some extent, the ability to generate three-dimensional representations of physical space, which, in turn, appears to facilitate navigation in unfamiliar environments (see also Moffat et al., 1998). Moreover, it appears that these spatial competencies are distinct from the ability to locate specific objects within this space (Geary, 1995b; Maguire et al., 1997), as suggested in chapter 6 (*Physical Modules* section).

The advantage of boys and men over girls and women in the ability to generate accurate representations of novel environments and to manipulate three-dimensional images mentally stands in sharp contrast to an advantage of girls and women in certain forms of visuospatial memory (Eals & Silverman, 1994; James & Kimura, 1997; McBurney, Gaulin, Devineni, & Adams, 1997; Silverman & Eals, 1992; Stumpf & Eliot, 1995). On the basis of the sexual division of labor, Silverman and Eals (1992) proposed that "spatial specializations associated with foraging should have ... evolved in females. Food plants are immobile, but they are embedded within complex arrays of vegetation. Successful foraging, then, would require locating food sources within such arrays and finding them in ensuing growing seasons" (p. 535). In this view, women should have an advantage over men in the ability to remember objects and their relative locations.

To test this hypothesis, Silverman and Eals (1992) asked women and men to examine the objects in the array shown in Figure 8.4 for 1 minute, and they then presented them with two additional sheets of objects. The first test sheet included all of the objects shown in Figure 8.4 and a number of additional items, whereas the second test sheet showed the same items as shown in the figure, but some of the items were moved to a different location. The first test required the participants to circle all of the items that were on the original sheet and to put a cross through the new items,

Figure 8.4. Example of a stimulus array used for tests of object memory and location memory. From *The Adapted Mind: Evolutionary Psychology and the Generation of Culture*, edited by Jerome H. Barkow, Leda Cosmides, and John Tooby. Copyright © 1992 by Oxford University Press, Inc. Used by permission of Oxford University Press, Inc.

whereas the second test required them to circle the objects that were in the same location and to put a cross through those objects that were moved. Thus, the former test assessed object memory, and the latter location memory. The results showed that women outperformed men on both the object memory and the location memory tests. Three additional studies confirmed this pattern and found that 8- to 13-year-old girls outperformed same-age boys on object memory tests. For location memory tests, a sex difference, favoring girls, was only found in the older groups, suggesting that the superior location memory of girls and women does not emerge until puberty.

Follow-up studies have found that the pattern of sex differences in object memory and location memory is somewhat more complex than originally proposed by Silverman and Eals (1992); an alternative explanation is that women have better episodic memories (e.g., memories of personal experiences) than men (Herlitz et al., 1997). The advantage of women on object memory tasks has not consistently been replicated (Eals & Silverman, 1994; McBurney et al., 1997), but several studies have now replicated the finding that women have superior memories for the location of objects than men do, an advantage that has been demonstrated with paper-and-pencil tests, computer-based tasks, memory games, and in more natural settings (Eals & Silverman, 1994; James & Kimura, 1997; McBurney et al., 1997). Across these different conditions, about four out of five women outperform the average man. Nonetheless, the magnitude of the sex difference for location memory varies with the participants' familiarity with the objects and learning conditions, in particular whether the participants are directly asked to remember the location of the objects (directed learning) or not (incidental learning). With common objects, women outperform men in both directed and incidental learning conditions, but with uncommon objects, women outperform men only under incidental learning conditions. The latter finding suggests that women, more than men, implicitly attend to novel environmental objects and more-or-less automatically remember their location.

The just-described pattern of sex differences in spatial cognition appears to be related to a combination of experiential and hormonal influences, although these sex differences do not appear to be related in any simple way to spatial-related experience or to hormonal exposure (Baenninger & Newcombe, 1995; Gilger & Ho, 1989; J. A. Sherman, 1967). The relation between experiential and hormonal influences on the development of cognitive sex differences, including the differences in spatial cognition, is discussed in *The Evolution and Development of Cognitive Sex Differences* section. The remainder of this section focuses on the relation between exposure to sex hormones and the just-described sex differences in spatial cognition, along with discussion of the associated brain systems.

One of the clearest demonstrations of the relation between prenatal exposure to androgens and spatial cognition was provided by Resnick et al. (1986). In this study, women and men affected with CAH and unaffected women and men were administered an IQ test and a series of spatial, verbal, and perceptual tests. There were no differences between the women affected with CAH and the unaffected women in IQ, verbal ability, or perceptual abilities, but the women affected with CAH outscored the unaffected women on all five tests of spatial cognition (one of the differences was not statistically significant, however). On the MRT, the women affected with CAH substantially outperformed unaffected women and scored only slightly lower than the men affected with CAH and unaffected men (who did not differ from one another); more than four out of five CAH women had spatial test scores that were above the average of unaffected women (see Berenbaum, Korman, & Leveroni, 1995; Sherry & Hampson, 1997, for reviews).

Although not every study has found a relation between circulating hormone levels and spatial cognition (e.g., Gordon & Lee, 1993), many studies, using different experimental techniques, have found such a relation (Hampson, 1990a, 1990b; Hampson & Kimura, 1988; McKeever, 1995; Moffat & Hampson, 1996a, 1996b; Shute, Pellegrino, Hubert, & Reynolds, 1983; Silverman & Phillips, 1993; Van Goozen, Cohen-Kettenis, Gooren, Frijda, & Van de Poll, 1994). For spatial tests on which men typically outperform women, several studies have found a linear relation between circulating testosterone levels and right-handed women's performance on these tests. The higher the testosterone levels, the higher the spatial test performance (Gouchie & Kimura, 1991; Moffat & Hampson, 1996a, 1996b); the relation between hormone levels and spatial cognition is not as well understood for left-handed men or women. With men, the pattern is more complicated, but, generally, lower testosterone levels, especially for right-handers, are associated with higher spatial test performance (e.g., Moffat & Hampson, 1996a, 1996b); men with relatively low testosterone levels still have significantly more circulating testosterone than women with relatively high testosterone levels. At the same time, testosterone levels are not consistently correlated with performance on tests of verbal ability (Gouchie & Kimura, 1991), indicating that the relation between circulating testosterone levels and cognitive ability is selective.

Most, but not all, studies of changes in cognitive performance across the menstrual cycle suggest that high circulating levels of female hormones (e.g., estradiol and progesterone) might suppress certain spatial abilities, especially those spatial abilities for which men typically show an advantage over women (Choi & Silverman, 1996; Gaulin, Silverman, et al., 1997; Gordon & Lee, 1993; Hampson, 1990a, 1990b; Hampson & Kimura, 1988; Ho, Gilger, & Brink, 1986; K. Phillips & Silverman, 1997; Sherry & Hampson, 1997). As noted earlier, the best controlled studies in this area have been conducted by Hampson and her colleagues. With these studies, it has been shown that performance on a variety of spatial ability tests is at its highest during menstruation (i.e., when estradiol and progesterone levels are relatively low). At the same time, spatial performance is relatively low during the time when estradiol and progesterone levels are relatively high (i.e., during the midluteal phase; e.g., Hampson, 1990a); see Figure 8.1.

However, Peters et al. (1995) failed to find a relation between phase of the menstrual cycle and performance on the MRT, although Silverman and Phillips (1993) documented changes in MRT performance across the menstrual cycle in four separate studies (see also K. Phillips & Silverman, 1997). Across these studies, women scored between 16% and 89% higher during menstruation than during the midluteal phase of their cycle. The strongest evidence for a relation between the hormonal fluctuations associated with the menstrual cycle and the spatial abilities assessed by the MRT comes from the performance of the same women during different points of the menstrual cycle. Here, Silverman and Phillips (Study 2) found that the MRT scores of women were 40% to 49% higher, although still not as high as the average score of men, during menstruation as compared with the midluteal phase. Hampson (1990a) found the same pattern for a battery of spatial tests—performance on each of these tests typically favors men—although the magnitude of change across the menstrual cycle was not as large as that found by Silverman and Phillips.

There is preliminary evidence that MRT performance varies seasonally with men (Kimura & Hampson, 1994), just as the spatial abilities of males vary seasonally in some other species (Galea et al., 1994; Gaulin, 1992; Gaulin & Fitzgerald, 1986; Sherry & Hampson, 1997; see the *Sex Hormones, Cognition, and Brain Development* section of chapter 2). In the northern hemisphere, testosterone levels tend to be higher in men in autumn than in spring. "If lower testosterone levels within the normal range are associated with better spatial ability, one might expect men's scores on spatial tasks to be higher in spring than in fall. This indeed turned out to be the case" (Kimura & Hampson, 1994, p. 59). Although men outperformed women on the MRT in both fall and spring, the magnitude of their fall advantage was about one half of the size of their advantage in spring. In the earlier described study of female-to-male transsexuals, Van Goozen et al. (1994) found a relation between androgen administration and performance on a spatial ability measure, although they did not administer the MRT. Here, performance on a test of the ability to rotate images in a two-dimensional space, which typically shows smaller sex differences than the MRT, improved 19%, on average, comparing performance before androgen treatment to performance 3 months after the initiation of treatment; 77% of these individuals showed improved spatial abilities after androgen treatment.

The relation between circulating hormone levels and performance on route-learning tests and tests of location memory has only been assessed in a few human studies (Choi & Silverman, 1996; Gaulin, Silverman, et al., 1997). Gaulin and his colleagues found no consistent relation between menstrual phase and performance on either the object memory test or the object location test (which were described earlier), although, in keeping with the studies described previously, women scored higher on the MRT during menstruation than during other parts of their cycle. Similarly, Choi and Silverman found no relation between menstrual phase and performance on tests of object location memory—a different test than originally used by Silverman and Eals (1992)—or spatial map learning. However, inconsistent with most previous studies, there were no sex differences on either of these tasks, although men tended to use Euclidean information and women tended to use landmarks to describe routes on the map. The lack of significant sex differences on these particular tests suggests that they are not sensitive to the sex differences in map generation, favoring men, or location memory, favoring women. Given this, the lack of relation between hormonal status and performance on these measures should be interpreted with caution.

Similarly, for humans, little is known about the relation between prenatal exposure to sex hormones and navigational abilities and location memory. Nonetheless (as described in chapter 2), C. L. Williams et al. (1990) found that, at least for the laboratory rat, prenatal exposure to androgens—normal males and hormonally treated females—was associated with faster maze learning with fewer errors during this learning. Moreover, it was found that normal males and hormonally treated females used geometric or directional knowledge to navigate these mazes, whereas castrated males and normal females used a combination of geometric knowledge and landmark cues; the use of landmark cues was associated with poorer maze learning. It remains to be seen whether the earlier mentioned tendency of girls and women to focus on landmarks and boys and men to use geometric or directional knowledge to navigate is related to prenatal exposure to androgens. To the extent that performance on the MRT taps the cognitive and brain systems associated with the use of three-dimensional geometric cues for navigating, a relation between tests of route learning and prenatal exposure to androgens is likely to be found (Moffat et al., 1998).

Neuroimaging studies suggest that both the left and the right sides of the brain—including the cortex and some subcortical areas—support spatial abilities, although the right side appears to be preferentially involved in some spatial tasks, such as route learning (Cabeza & Nyberg, 1997; Gur et al., 1982; Gur, Ragland, et al., 1994; Maguire et al., 1997). Unfortunately, the pattern of sex differences in the brain regions involved in spatial processing has not systematically been assessed in these neuroimaging studies. As a result, inferences about differences in the brains of men and women, as related to spatial cognition, are necessarily based on less direct measures, including studies of the effects of brain damage on cognitive performance and performance on cognitive tasks that appear to differentially engage the right and left hemispheres (e.g., McGlone, 1980). Despite the use of these indirect measures, there is ample evidence to support the conclusion that there are sex differences in the structure and functioning of the brain systems that support at least some spatial abilities, and there is reason to believe that these differences are influenced by prenatal exposure to sex hormones (Breedlove, 1994; Geschwind & Galaburda, 1987; Gur et al., 1982; Kimura, 1987, 1996; McGlone, 1980; Witelson, 1976, 1991). The complexity of these relations is illustrated by studies conducted by Witelson (1976) and Gur et al. (1982).

In Witelson's (1976) developmental study, objects formed into meaningless shapes were presented to 200 6- to 12-year-old right-handed girls and boys. The children were asked to manipulate several of these objects one at a time but could not see the objects. For each trial, they were then asked to identify the shape from a visual display containing the manipulated object and five other objects. Because the perception of objects manipulated by the left hand is largely mediated by the right hemisphere and because the perception of objects manipulated by the right hand is largely mediated by the left hemisphere, this procedure provides an assessment of whether the right hemisphere (left hand) or the left hemisphere (right hand) is more sensitive to shape perception. The results indicated that at all ages, boys were significantly better at identifying shapes with their left hand (right hemisphere) than with their right hand (left hemisphere). Girls, in contrast, were equally skilled with their left and right hands. Boys and girls did not differ in overall identification accuracy, although the boys' use of their left hand resulted in the highest overall accuracy scores, whereas the use of their right hand resulted in the lowest overall accuracy scores; the left- and right-handed scores of girls fell in between these extremes. On the basis of this pattern, Witelson (1976) concluded "that for boys of at least 6 [years of age] the right hemisphere is more specialized than the left for spatial processing; in girls, however, there is a bilateral representation at least until adolescence" (p. 426).

Gur et al. (1982) used neuroimaging techniques to examine the pattern of blood flow, and by inference brain activity, associated with the processing of verbal and spatial (determining the orientation of lines) information. Brain activity was higher in the left hemisphere during the verbal task and higher in the right hemisphere during the spatial task. The pattern varied across men and women and right- and left-handers, however. For left-handers, the differences between the two hemispheres were generally smaller than for right-handers, suggesting that for many of the left-handers both the left and the right hemispheres were engaged during both tasks; left-handed men, however, tended to engage the right hemisphere more than the left hemisphere for the spatial task. Moreover, for this spatial task, right-handed women showed a greater relative activation of the right hemisphere than right-handed men did, a pattern opposite to that found by Witelson (1976).

These different findings are not too surprising, given that the pattern of brain activity associated with spatial processing is likely to vary with the specific type of spatial processing involved in the task and with the participant's familiarity with the task materials (Cabeza & Nyberg, 1997; Kimura, 1987). Despite these moderating factors, both the Witelson (1976) and the Gur et al. (1982) studies, as well as other studies (see Kimura, 1987; McGlone, 1980; Witelson, 1991, for reviews), suggest that women and men engage different brain regions during the processing of some forms of spatial information. One possibility is that the right hemisphere—and presumably any associated subcortical areas (e.g., the hippocampus)—of right-handed men is more strongly specialized for some spatial abilities than the right hemisphere of women or even left-handed men; these patterns also vary with whether one or both of the participant's parents are left-handed (Annett, 1985; McGlone, 1980; Witelson, 1991).

In other words, a similar pattern emerges for spatial competencies as was described for language competencies. For right-handed boys and men, some spatial competencies might be more focally represented in the right hemisphere, with the same competencies being represented in both sides of the brain in girls and women and in many left-handed boys and men, although this does not appear to be the case for all spatial skills (see Kimura, 1996). Another possibility is that the right hemisphere is largely specialized for the processing of complex spatial information for both men and women but that different regions within the right hemisphere support this processing for men and women (Kimura, 1987, 1996).

The resolution of these issues will require neuroimaging studies of the pattern of brain regions engaged in the processing of theoretically interesting spatial tasks, such as route learning, three-dimensional rotations, and object location memory. During the processing of these tasks, it will be particularly interesting to determine if men and women differ in the pattern of laterality (right hemisphere vs. left hemisphere) and in the relative engagement of the parietal cortex and the hippocampus (Andersen et al., 1997; Maguire et al., 1997). The results of Maguire et al., for instance, suggest that sex differences might emerge in the degree to which the right hippocampus is engaged during route learning.

THE EVOLUTION AND DEVELOPMENT OF COGNITIVE SEX DIFFERENCES

In the first section that follows, the just-described pattern of cognitive sex differences is considered in terms of selection pressures, whereas the second section provides discussion of the developmental influences on the expression of these differences.

Evolution

The advantage of girls and women for individual-level social competencies is pervasive, including many basic language skills, skill at decoding nonverbal emotion cues, and apparently theory-of-mind, in particular, skill at making inferences about the emotional state of other people. All of these differences are consistent with the view that the competencies associated with one-on-one dyadic interactions are more highly elaborated in girls and women than in boys and men. From an evolutionary perspective, the advantage of girls and women for individual-level social competencies can be understood in terms of female–female competition, residence patterns of our ancestors, and dynamics of female–male relationships.

As described earlier, female–female competition is focused on disrupting the social networks of potential competitors, which, in turn, is largely achieved by means of individual-level social competencies, such as language-based gossiping and spreading rumors. Given that this form of competition has likely influenced the relative reproductive success of women during the course of human evolution (e.g., Pusey et al., 1997; see the *Female–Female Competition* sections of chapter 3 and chapter 5), selection pressures would result in the associated cognitive competencies, such as language, becoming more highly elaborated in women than in men, just as physical male–male competition has resulted in larger males than females. Nonetheless, female–female competition is not likely to be the only source of the advantage of girls and women in individual-level social competencies, given that some of these advantages do not appear to be well suited to this competition. In particular, the greater frequency of social smiling, the use of language to develop and maintain reciprocal relationships, and the greater social expressiveness of girls and women, relative to boys and men, appear to be more focused on building than on disrupting social relationships.

As argued in chapter 7 (*Social Development and Evolution* section), these sex differences might be understandable in terms of the likely residence patterns of our male and female ancestors. Recall that in the great apes, including humans, males tend to stay in their birth group and females tend to reside in the birth group of their mate (e.g., Foley & Lee, 1989). Under these conditions, most men will have a social network of kin, whereas most women will not, although many of these women will maintain contact with their kin. Because stable social relationships and social support are important for the health and well-being of these women and their children (see the *Paternal Investment and the Well-Being of Children* section of chapter 4), selection pressures would favor those women who were skilled at developing and maintaining such relationships. Moreover, because these relationships would be developed with nonkin, they would require greater reciprocity and equity in the context of the relationship than would be necessary for relationships with kin. Relationships with nonkin (i.e., friends) cannot be maintained without this reciprocity and equity (Hartup & Stevens, 1997). In this view, the social motives (e.g., equality) and social behaviors (e.g., reciprocity) of girls and women, as well as many of their advantages over men in social skills (e.g., social smiling and expressiveness), are, in part, a reflection of these selection pressures.

In addition to female–female competition and residence patterns, the dynamics of female–male relationships would also favor the evolution of relatively sophisticated individual-level social competencies in women. Throughout the world—and in many other primate species (see chapter 3)—many men attempt to control the social and sexual activities of the women in their life by means of physical force or threat of physical force, a tactic that often works because of the strength and size advantage that men have over women (e.g., Smuts, 1995). On the basis of the assumption that all organisms have a fundamental desire to exert some level of control over their environment (see chapter 6), strategies that counter the tendency of some men to attempt to control the social and sexual behavior of their partners would be expected to evolve in women. In other words, social competencies that enabled women to better control the dynamics of female–male relationships would be favored by selection. These competencies would clearly involve those skills related to one-on-one relationships, such as decoding nonverbal emotion cues, given that these female–male dynamics are per force manifested in the context of one-on-one relationships.

Despite the general advantage of girls and women over boys and men in most individual-level social competencies, the gap is smaller and possibly reversed for some of these competencies. In particular, it appears that boys and men are relatively more sensitive to those social cues and emotional overtones that would be associated with male–male competition than to other types of social cues (e.g., those that signal positive emotions). More precisely, Rotter and Rotter's (1988) finding that men are more sensitive than women to the anger-related emotion cues of other men—especially adult men and when these cues are directed toward them (e.g., with eye contact, as contrasted with a side view of the face)—is readily understood in terms of male–male competition, as is the finding that boys and men are more sensitive to dominance- and aggression-related emotion cues than to other emotion cues (Rosenthal et al., 1979). The apparent sex differences in the pattern of in-group and out-group relationships can also be understood in terms of male–male competition. Both (a) the tendency of boys and men to exert more conformity-related social pressures on in-group members than girls and women and (b) the apparently greater agonistic attitudes of boys and men toward out-group members during periods of competition would facilitate coalition-based male–male competition.

Most of the other cognitive sex differences that favor boys and men are also readily understood in terms of male–male competition; in particular, competition that involved the use of projectile weapons (Keeley, 1996). For instance, the advantage of boys and men in many of the movement-related physical modules—such as throwing accuracy, skill at blocking objects thrown at them, and ability to judge time of arrival—would facilitate the use of or defense against projectile weapons. Moreover, as noted earlier, these cognitive competencies complement many of the physical sex differences described in chapter 7 (*Physical Development* section), such as the relatively longer forearm of boys and men, the sex difference in the shape of the humerus, and the advantage of men in upper body strength (Tanner, 1990). All of these physical differences contribute to two of the largest sex differences ever documented—the advantage of boys and men over girls and women in throwing distance and throwing velocity (Thomas & French, 1985). No interpretation other than selection for the use of projectile weapons in the context of male–male competition can provide a more elegant or parsimonious explanation of these patterns; as argued earlier, hunting does not provide an explanation for the above-mentioned defensive skills, such as the ability to block thrown objects.

The advantage of boys and men in certain representation-related physical modules can also be understood in terms of male–male competition. The advantage of boys and men in this area appears to be largely related to their ability to generate an accurate cognitive representation of the large-scale three-dimensional environment. In other words, boys and men are more skilled than girls and women in generating mental maps of the environment, especially novel environments. In other species, such mental representations are related to navigation within this environment, and there is no reason to believe that this is not the case for people (Gallistel, 1990; J. L. Gould, 1996; Maguire et al., 1996; Poucet, 1993). As described in the *Locomotor and Exploratory Play* section of chapter 7, in preindustrial societies, men travel farther into relatively unknown territories than women do for a number of reasons, including hunting, finding mates, and conducting raids on neighboring groups (often with the intent of capturing women; Chagnon, 1977; Keeley, 1996). The two latter activities are directly related to male–male competition, and, given this, the advantage of boys and men in the just-mentioned representational competencies have likely been shaped, at least in part, by sexual selection (see also Sherry & Hampson, 1997).

Just as girls and women do not appear to have an advantage over boys and men in all individual-level social competencies, boys and men do not have an advantage over girls and women in all of the competencies associated with the representation of the physical environment. It appears that girls and women have an advantage over boys and men in the ability to remember landmarks and the location of objects, both of which appear to be associated with foraging activities (James & Kimura, 1997). Silverman and Eals (1992) argued that the advantage of girls and women in these apparently foraging-related competencies is related to the sexual division of labor (i.e., gathering in women). Another possibility is that the sex difference in these abilities is related to a sex difference in the foraging strategies of our male and female ancestors before the emergence of long-term pair-bonding and the sexual division of labor.

As described in chapter 3 (*The Evolution of Sex Differences and the Sexual Division of Labor* section), such a pattern is evident in the chimpanzee (*Pan troglodytes*). Recall that there is very little direct paternal investment by male chimpanzees, and, thus, there is no reproduction-related sexual division of labor. There is, however, a clear sex difference in foraging strategies (Goodall, 1986). Males hunt much more frequently than females do, whereas females obtain a much higher proportion of their total calories from fixed food sources, such as termite mounds, than males do. Under these conditions, natural selection could easily result in the evolution of a female advantage in location memory and in the tendency to remember landmarks implicitly without a sexual division of labor. Nevertheless, any sex difference that existed before the emergence of a sexual division of labor would still be open to further selection if the associated activities (i.e., gathering and hunting) influenced reproductive outcomes (Frost, 1998). As noted earlier, it is likely that the sexual division of labor has been one factor that has contributed to individual differences in the reproductive success of both men and women (see, for example, Blurton Jones et al., 1997). Thus, even if the sexual division of labor is not the initial source of the advantage of girls and women in location memory or, for instance, the apparent advantage of boys and men in folk biological knowledge of fauna, these activity differences could still influence the evolution of any associated cognitive competencies and increase the magnitude of the sex differences in these competencies.

Development

In the *Development of Functional Systems* section of chapter 6, it was argued that many evolved cognitive competencies are skeletal early in life and are then fleshed out, or more fully developed, with experiences during childhood (e.g., Gelman, 1990). It was argued further that the niche-seeking activities of children are not random but rather are essential features of the biological systems that support evolved cognitive competencies. The initial structure of fundamental cognitive competencies, such as human language, is inherent, but these competencies become tailored to local conditions, such as the specific language of the group, on the basis of early experiences, such as social discourse, that children are biologically prepared to seek.

It is very likely that a similar process contributes to many of the cognitive sex differences described in this chapter. In this view, sex hormones, or perhaps more direct genetic influences (e.g., Skuse et al., 1997), not only influence the development and functioning of the brain but also result in differences in the types of information to which boys and girls attend to and in the types of niches boys and girls create for themselves (Scarr, 1992). These differences in attentional patterns and environmental niche seeking likely contribute to the earlier described sex differences in brain functioning and the associated differences in the pattern of cognitive ability. From this perspective, the sex differences described in chapter 7 are viewed as a manifestation of the different niche-seeking activities of girls and boys, which, in turn, appear to contribute to the sex differences in brain and cognitive functioning described in this chapter. As an example, the tendencies of infant boys to attend to environmental cues more frequently than same-age girls do and for infant girls to attend to social cues more frequently than same-age boys do are likely to be early manifestations of the sex differences in individual-level social competencies, favoring girls, and environmental representation, favoring boys (McGuinness & Pribram, 1979).

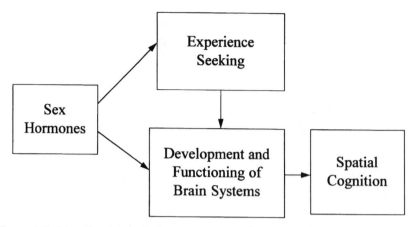

Figure 8.5. Hypothesized relations among sex hormones (prenatal and circulating), spatial-related experience, and the development and functioning of the brain systems supporting spatial cognition.

The basic model can be illustrated more fully with a consideration of the sex differences in spatial cognition. The sex differences in spatial abilities, such as skill at generating cognitive maps, appear to result from a combination of experiential and hormonal influences or rather from their interaction (D. F. Halpern, 1992; Matthews, 1992). For instance, Peters and his colleagues found that the repeated administration of alternative forms of the MRT (see Figure 8.3) resulted in improved performance for both men and women but that the relative advantage of men remained constant across practice sessions (Peters et al., 1995). On the other hand, there is some indication that the tendency of boys to engage in more exploration of their environment than girls contributes to the sex difference, favoring boys, in the ability to represent this environment mentally; girls who explore the environment also have an enhanced ability to represent this environment mentally (Matthews, 1992; R. L. Munroe & Munroe, 1971). These results suggest that spatial abilities improve with experience for both boys and girls and that differences in the spatial-related experiences of boys and girls contribute to the advantage of boys and men in certain spatial domains (Baenninger & Newcombe, 1995). However, simple experience-dependent explanations of spatial sex differences cannot explain the earlier described relation among prenatal exposure to sex hormones, circulating sex hormone levels, and spatial abilities.

A full explanation of the sex differences in spatial cognition thus requires consideration of both experiential and hormonal factors, as shown in Figure 8.5. From this perspective, prenatal exposure to sex hormones biases the play and social activities of boys and girls (as described in chapter 7) and might result in a sex difference in the sensitivity of the supporting brain systems to these experiences. Assuming a relatively stress-free rearing environment, early biases in the types of information to which girls and boys attend to, such as objects versus people, and their later experiences with the physical world, such as exploration of local environments, might interact with hormonally induced differences in the brain systems that support spatial cognition. The net result of these interactions, combined with the later influence of circulating sex hormones, would be the earlier described sex differences in spatial cognition (McGuinness & Pribram, 1979).

Indeed, for some other species, prenatal exposure to sex hormones interacts with environmental rearing conditions to produce sex differences in brain structure and spatial cognition, rather than simply affecting the structure and functioning of the brain and any associated cognitive competencies (DeVoogd, 1991; Juraska, 1991; see chapter 2, the *Sex Hormones, Cognition, and Brain Development* section). For instance, with studies of the laboratory rat, Juraska found that the male advantage on spatial-learning tasks and in the size and complexity of some of the supporting brain systems is more consistently found when males and females are reared under socially and environmentally complex conditions, as contrasted with being reared in social isolation (but see Seymoure et al., 1996); sex differences in brain structure are less pronounced when males are reared in social isolation.

Although it is not certain, this pattern suggests that spatial learning in males might be a condition-dependent trait, with restricted environmental experiences or prolonged exposure to stress hormones damaging the hippocampus and thus suppressing certain spatial abilities (Sapolsky, 1986; Xu, Anwyl, & Rowan, 1997). In this view, the simple presence of androgens does not result in a sex difference in the brain systems that support navigation, for instance, but rather results in these systems being sensitive to navigation-related experiences, such as environmental exploration; one possibility is that prenatal exposure to androgens elaborates the brain systems associated with navigation but that experience is needed to maintain this elaborated system (Greenough et al., 1987). Only the combination of environmental exploration and brain systems that are sensitive to the associated experiences results in a male advantage in the ability to navigate in novel environments.

SUMMARY AND CONCLUSION

As noted in the introductory statements, there is little question that men and women differ to some degree in the pattern of cognitive competencies and in the structure and functioning of many of the brain systems that underlie these competencies. Furthermore, there is little question that the development and expression of many of these cognitive sex differences are moderated by exposure to sex hormones, although many of these differences are also influenced by the different experiences of boys and girls and men and women. Most generally, these sex differences reflect a greater elaboration of those cognitive competencies associated with one-on-one social relationships in girls and women and a relatively greater elaboration of those cognitive competencies associated with representing and acting on the large-scale physical environment in boys and men; of course, there are specific exceptions, such as gathering in women and monitoring for signs of aggression in other men in men.

These sex differences, in turn, are a reflection of the different reproductive strategies and social motives of men and women. Recall that it was proposed in chapter 6 that the fundamental but implicit motivation of many women is to create a socially stable community within which to raise their children. For women, the development of such a community involves developing and maintaining a social support network, as well as developing and maintaining a relationship with a mate who is willing and able to invest in their children (Buss, 1994). In other words, the primary control motivation of many women is focused on developing and maintaining a network of relationships to provide the social support and resources necessary for the growth and development of their children. The achievement of this goal necessarily requires that women manage the dynamics of many one-on-one social relationships, relationships with other women, their mate, and with their own children. Given this, during the course of human evolution, women who had relatively sophisticated individual-level social competencies were almost certainly more successful in raising their children than their less competent peers were.

The implicit motivation of many men, in contrast, is to achieve and maintain social dominance over other people, especially other men. During the course of human evolution and in many preindustrial (and sometimes industrial) societies today, the achievement of social dominance very often involves physical male–male competition, as is the case with most other primates (see the *Male–Male Competition* sections of chapter 3 and chapter 5). On the basis of patterns found in preindustrial societies and in the chimpanzee, the achievement of this goal was almost certainly facilitated —during the course of human evolution—by coalition-based male–male competition and competition that eventually relied on the use of projectile weapons (Keeley, 1996). In this view, the sex differences in throwing distance, throwing accuracy, judging time to arrival, the social dynamics of in-group and out-group relationships, and so forth emerged as men pursued the fundamental motivation to control the social and sexual behavior of other people.

Similarly, the advantage of boys and men in the ability to represent the large-scale physical environment is also a reflection of this fundamental motivation. The achievement of social dominance by means of male–male competition quite often involves coalition-based warfare between neighboring groups (Chagnon, 1977; Keeley, 1996; Knauft, 1987). Such conditions would favor men who could readily generate cognitive maps of the large-scale environment—maps that were not dependent on the use of landmarks—because the associated raids often involve movement in unfamiliar territory and then returning to one's home camp.

The advantage of boys and men over girls and women in the generation of these geometry-based maps is only indirectly related to this warfare, however. Any activity that involves navigation in an unfamiliar large-scale physical environment will result in the elaboration of these competencies, as is found with female brown-headed cowbirds (*Molothrus ater ater*); recall that females in this species use the home range in more complex ways than conspecific males because the females are brood parasites and must locate the nests of potential hosts (Sherry et al., 1993; see the *Sex Hormones, Cognition, and Brain Development* section of chapter 2). Intergroup warfare—as well as other male-dominated activities such as hunting—requires navigation in the large-scale environment and, thus, over the course of human evolution would eventually result in an advantage of boys and men over girls and women in the ability to represent this environment mentally.

Now, of course, many of the social conditions that are evident in preindustrial societies, and almost certainly during the course of human evolution, are very different from the day-to-day experiences of most people living in modern industrial societies. For instance, men do not generally stage war parties—except symbolically, in the form of sports teams—for raids on neighboring communities, nor do they kill one another at the same rates found in many preindustrial societies (Keeley, 1996; Knauft, 1987). Similarly, in modern industrial societies, central governments generate laws and provide a professional police force to enforce these laws. The net result in most cases is a degree of social stability that is not enjoyed in many other contexts (see, for example, Chagnon, 1988). The wider society provides much of the social stability that appears to be fundamentally important to women. Or stated otherwise, many of the sex differences in social, physical, behavioral, and cognitive competencies that have supported the different reproductive strategies of men and women throughout human evolution are no longer important in many societies today. Nevertheless, many of the sex differences described in this chapter and throughout this book are still reflected in the cognitive patterns, social interests, and so forth of the boys and girls and the men and women in these societies, the implications of which are discussed in the next chapter.

9

SEX DIFFERENCES IN MODERN SOCIETY

For most of us, the advantage of boys and men over girls and women in throwing distance and throwing velocity is no longer relevant to our day-to-day lives, except in the context of sports activities (Thomas & French, 1985). Nonetheless, these sex differences and many other evolved sex differences are still manifested in technologically advanced societies and almost certainly will continue to be found in these societies for many generations to come (A. R. Rogers & Mukherjee, 1992). Moreover, it is likely that many of the sex differences that have directly been shaped by sexual selection have an indirect influence on the expression of sex differences in many evolutionarily novel domains, such as performance on the mathematics section of the SAT (SAT-M; Geary, 1996). The focus of this chapter is on such indirect influences of sexual selection, as they are manifested in modern society.

It should be stated at the outset that for nearly all of the sex differences described throughout this book, there is an overlap in the distribution of girls and boys and women and men. As a result, none of the implications described in this chapter (or in earlier chapters) can be used to make judgments about any individual boy, girl, man, or woman. The patterns described in this book are nonetheless useful for understanding a number of broader social patterns, as illustrated in the sections that follow. In these sections, sex differences in academic competencies, behavioral and psychological domains, and occupational interests and achievement are discussed.

SEX DIFFERENCES IN ACADEMIC COMPETENCIES

Girls consistently receive higher grades than boys in nearly all, if not all, academic subjects (e.g., Kimball, 1989). Girls receive higher grades than boys for a number of reasons, including greater compliance with teacher requests, fewer missed school days, greater frequency of turning in assignments, and so forth, and not because of a sex difference in general academic competency. When scores are averaged across all areas, there is no sex difference in the academic competency of boys and girls, as measured by performance on standardized achievement tests (Willingham & Cole, 1997). There are, however, consistent sex differences in performance on a number of more specific academic achievement tests, including tests in the areas of reading, writing, mathematics, and science (Hedges & Nowell, 1995). The largest sex difference in these key areas favors girls and involves several writing competencies, including spelling, correct use of grammar, and so forth; about 7 out of 10 girls outperform the average boy in overall writing performance. Girls also have an advantage over boys in reading achievement, with about 3 out of 5 girls outperforming the average boy. Boys in contrast have small-to-moderate performance advantages on mathematics and science achievement tests, with about 3 out of 5 boys outperforming the average girl.

However, the sex differences on academic achievement tests are not always the best indicator of sex differences in academic competencies. Academic achievement tests involve the averaging of performance across items that tap many different cognitive skills. The result of this averaging is to obscure some sex differences on components of these tests. For instance, on mathematics achievement tests, girls often (at least in the United States) outperform boys on arithmetic items, and boys typically outperform girls on items that involve three-dimensional geometry and word-problem solving (Geary, 1996). For the two latter domains, the advantage of boys is about twice as large as that found for overall (i.e., averaged across different types of items) performance on mathematics achievement tests; about 7 out of 10 boys outperform the average girl in these areas.

Despite the difficulty in interpreting sex differences on standardized achievement tests—it is not always clear which test items yield sex differences and which do not—such differences are consistently found and therefore merit consideration. The first three sections below provide discussion regarding this consideration and focus on several factors that are potentially related to the sex differences in performance on many academic achievement tests (i.e., general intelligence, academic patterns, and intrasexual variability). The implications of the patterns described in the first three sections are discussed in the final section.

General Intelligence

The first issue addressed in this section concerns the relation between general intelligence and evolution, and the second issue concerns whether there is a sex difference in general intelligence.

General Intelligence and Evolution

General intelligence, or *g*, is typically measured by means of standardized IQ tests, shows moderate-to-high heritability estimates (i.e., individual differences in IQ are related, in part, to genetics), and is a good predictor of a number of activities that are important in modern society, including academic achievement, years of schooling completed, and performance in occupational settings, among many other things (Bouchard et al., 1990; Ceci & Williams, 1997; Gottfredson, 1997; Herrnstein & Murray, 1994; Hunter & Hunter, 1984; Jensen, 1998; Neisser et al., 1995; Plomin et al., 1997; Plomin & Petrill, 1997; Schmidt & Hunter, 1992). The advantages of general intelligence are especially evident in contexts that involve dealing with complex (e.g., having to manage multiple tasks) and constantly changing situations; that is, contexts that involve learning new skills and dealing with multiple demands (see Gottfredson, 1997, for a thorough review).

Moreover, the finding that men and women throughout the world base their mate-choice decisions, in part, on a prospective partner's intelligence suggests that *g* is also important in nonindustrial contexts and has been important throughout the course of human evolution (Bouchard et al., 1990; Buss, 1989b; Geary, 1996). The benefit of *g* in such contexts is not currently known, but it might facilitate adapting to changing ecological conditions and dealing with the complexities of social life (Legree, 1995; Rosenthal et al., 1979). In an analysis of the relation between *g* and occupational performance, Gottfredson (1997) concluded that some of the more intellectually demanding jobs in industrial societies involve dealing with people and that intelligent individuals have an advantage in these occupations; "other individuals are among the most complex, novel, changing, active, demanding, and unpredictable objects in our environments. Living and working with others is a complicated business" (Gottfredson, 1997, p. 107), and *g* predicts one's skill at negotiating these social complexities. It is very likely that the advantage that *g* provides in dealing with social complexities in the industrial workplace is also found in nonindustrial settings.

Legree (1995), for instance, examined the relations between performance on measures of *g* and performance on a series of measures of social intelligence in a sample of 400 adults. The measures of social intelligence appeared to assess theory of mind and sensitivity to nuances in social behavior across a variety of settings. The results showed that some aspects of social intelligence were distinct from *g* but that performance on tests of *g* and tests of social intelligence were highly related. This pattern indicates that there are aspects of social intelligence, such as the ability to decode emotion cues, that are distinct from whatever cognitive processes underlie *g* but that a high level of general intelligence is associated with high performance in at least some social domains. Legree's findings and Gottfredson's (1997) analysis indicate that *g* not only predicts the ability to learn in evolutionarily novel contexts, such as school, but it also appears to be related to the ability to acquire those cognitive competencies that have been important throughout our evolutionary history; in particular, those competencies associated with managing interpersonal dynamics.

As noted previously, general intelligence also facilitates learning in nonsocial domains, including most domains taught in school. For these school-taught domains, it appears that *g* reflects the ability to use evolved, or biologically primary, cognitive competencies in ways that are unrelated to their evolutionary function; the *g*-related cognitive competencies that likely support this ability include working memory (i.e., the ability to manipulate information mentally) and the basic speed with which the mind processes information (e.g., Fry & Hale, 1996; Hunt et al., 1975; Rozin, 1976). For instance, reading involves co-opting (i.e., the use of an ability for a nonevolved purpose) many of the same cognitive and brain systems involved in language comprehension and production (see below; Pugh et al., 1997). As an example, the brain and cognitive systems that are engaged during the processing of phonemes or basic language sounds are engaged also during reading. R. K. Wagner, Torgesen, and Rashotte (1994) reported that individual differences in the fidelity of kindergarten children's phonological processing systems are strongly predictive of the ease with which basic reading abilities (e.g., word decoding; that is, the ability to sound out unfamiliar words) are acquired in first grade. In this view, reading involves the acquisition of cognitive competencies, such as word decoding, that are biologically secondary with respect to the more primary language systems that support these competencies; the evolution of these primary systems was not related to reading, but they nonetheless can be used for secondary or nonevolved purposes, such as reading.

Reading and language acquisition thus share some of the same brain and cognitive systems, but learning to read printed words, unlike learning a spoken vocabulary, is generally a slow, effortful process, and for many children it requires direct and deliberate instruction. General intelligence predicts how quickly individual children will respond to this instruction and thus indexes, to some extent, the relative ease with which individual children can adapt, or co-opt, evolved cognitive competencies for use in evolutionarily novel ways (Bailey, 1987; Geary, 1995a; Rozin, 1976). In this example, IQ predicts the ease with which children co-opt the language-based phonological systems for making the letter–sound correspondences involved in reading.

The acquisition of evolutionarily novel, or biologically secondary, cognitive competencies, such as reading, is thus dependent on (a) the fidelity of the biologically primary cognitive systems that support the biologically secondary competencies and (b) the ease with which these systems can be co-opted for use in novel tasks. The latter being related to *g*. From this perspective, sex differences in biologically secondary academic competencies, such as reading, writing, and much of mathematics, can result from sex differences to the degree in which the underlying primary cognitive systems are developed or are from a sex difference in *g*. The latter possibility is addressed in the section on sex differences in general intelligence, whereas the former is addressed in the section on academic patterns.

Sex Differences in General Intelligence

Echoing a debate that occurred more than 100 years ago, several scientists have recently argued that boys and men, as a group, have slightly higher average IQ scores than girls and women (the issue of variability is discussed later; Lynn, 1994; Rushton & Ankney, 1996). For instance, an analysis of performance on two widely used IQ measures (the Wechsler Adult Intelligence Scale—Revised and the Wechsler Intelligence Scale for Children—Revised [Wechsler, 1974, 1981]) revealed that the overall IQ score of boys and men was about 2 points higher than that of girls and women, on average (Collaer & Hines, 1995). However, the pattern varied across the different subtests of these IQ measures. Boys and men consistently outperformed girls and women on measures of general knowledge and spatial abilities, there were no sex differences or a slight advantage for girls on a test of memory span, and girls and women consistently outperformed boys and men on a test that assesses the speed of matching arbitrary symbols to numbers.

If a measure of sensitivity to nonverbal social cues, such as the PONS (Rosenthal et al., 1979), were incorporated as a subtest on these IQ measures, then a different pattern might emerge. Girls and women would almost certainly outperform boys and men on any such measure (see the *Social Modules* section of chapter 6). With the incorporation of this performance into the overall IQ score, the IQ gap between boys and girls and men and women on these IQ tests would necessarily narrow and would likely be eliminated. In other words, the subtests used on these IQ measures will necessarily influence overall IQ scores. If subtests that generally favored girls and women were added to these measures, then the advantage of boys and men over girls and women in average IQ might well disappear.

In keeping with this view is the finding that there appear to be no average sex differences on another widely used IQ test—the Raven's Progressive Matrices—that provides just one overall measure of *g*, as contrasted with being a composite of many more specialized competencies (Raven, Court, & Raven, 1993). For this test, Raven and his colleagues reported that there are no sex differences in average IQ, on the basis of scores from a variety of standardization samples from different countries. Geary and his colleagues found no sex differences in performance on the Raven's Progressive Matrices for groups of children, adolescents, or adults from the United States or mainland China (Geary et al., 1997). Similarly, an analysis of the cognitive performance of nearly 100,000 randomly selected high school students from Project Talent—a nationwide (United States) study conducted in 1960—revealed no substantive sex difference in average IQ scores (Lubinski & Humphreys, 1990).

The overall pattern suggests that there are no sex differences, or only a very small and unimportant advantage of boys and men, in average IQ scores (but see the *Intrasexual Variability* section that follows). Given this, the above-described sex difference in the pattern of academic competencies is more readily understood in terms of cognitive sex differences (as described in chapter 8) than in terms of any potential sex difference in general intelligence.

Academic Patterns

The goal of this section is to provide several illustrations of the potential relation between the sex differences in brain and cognition (as described in chapter 8) and the sex differences in the pattern of academic competencies. A thorough treatment of this issue is beyond the scope of this book, but the utility of this approach is briefly illustrated in the sections below for reading and mathematics.

Reading

Large-scale studies based on nationally (United States) representative samples indicate that girls and women outperform boys and men on measures of general reading ability in elementary school, middle school, high school, and in the general population of adults (Willingham & Cole, 1997). The magnitude of the advantage of girls and women over boys and men in reading abilities is relatively constant across these groups and has changed little from the 1960s through the 1990s (Hedges & Nowell, 1995; Willingham & Cole, 1997).

When viewed in terms of the more primary cognitive sex differences (as described in chapter 8), the advantage of girls and women in reading abilities can be understood as being related to their advantage in language competencies (see the *Social Modules* section of chapter 6). In particular, the tendency for more women than men to process language sounds in both the left and the right hemispheres and the tendency for more men than women to process language sounds only in the left hemisphere (e.g., Shaywitz et al., 1995) might contribute to the sex difference in average reading scores, as well as the sex differences, favoring girls and women, in spelling and writing performance. In support of this suggestion is Pugh et al.'s (1997) findings that the representation of language sounds in both the left and the right hemispheres is strongly associated with the skill of making correspondences between letters and the associated sounds. In other words, individuals, men and women, who processed language sounds in both the left and the right hemispheres were more skilled at matching letters to their correct English pronunciations than individuals who processed language sounds only in the left hemisphere. If this same pattern is found in childhood (comparable neuroimaging studies have not yet been conducted with children), then those children who process language sounds in both the left and the right hemispheres, which will presumably include more girls than boys, will likely show an advantage in learning the associations between English letters and the associated language sounds; a similar relation would likely be found for other languages as well. The skill of making such associations should facilitate reading acquisition, especially word decoding, as well as performance in the areas of spelling and writing.

The apparent advantage of girls and women in theory of mind might also contribute to their advantage in reading comprehension (V. Frith & Happé, 1996). For instance, Willingham and Cole (1997) reported that the largest advantage for girls and women in reading comprehension is for literary novels, poems, and dramas; about 7 out of 10 girls and women outperform the average boy or man in these areas. In many cases, comprehension of these passages involves making inferences about the nuances of social relationships. In contrast, the smallest sex differences in reading comprehension are for passages that do not involve people (e.g., in the physical sciences or city planning). The overall pattern suggests that the potential sex difference in theory of mind might contribute to the sex difference in overall reading comprehension scores. Any such relation might stem from a sex difference, favoring girls and women, in the ability to develop mental models of the plots and subplots associated with reading passages that involve social themes.

In addition to theory of mind and other cognitive sex differences, the advantage of girls and women in reading comprehension might be related to the sex difference in social motives. For instance, the comprehension advantage of girls and women for novels, poetry, and drama might result from their reading these materials more frequently than boys and men. These reading-experience differences, in turn, might be understood in terms of differences in the degree to which girls and women and boys and men find the social themes represented in these materials attractive. In other words, some combination of cognition and motivation likely contributes to the sex difference in reading comprehension as well as to many of the other sex differences in academic competencies; motivation will not result in a cognitive competency but will influence the extent to which one engages in the activities needed to develop the competency.

Mathematics

As noted earlier, the pattern of sex differences in mathematical competencies is complex. Girls and women sometimes outperform boys and men in some domains (e.g., complex arithmetic), boys and men typically outperform girls and women in other domains (e.g., the solving of word problems), whereas there appear to be no sex differences in still other domains (e.g., use of geometric theorems; see Geary, 1996, for a thorough discussion). The focus of this section is on the two areas that most consistently—across nations and historical cohorts—favor boys and men, the solving of complex multistep word problems and geometry (but not theorems).

Geary (1996) argued that the advantage of boys and men in the solving of arithmetical and algebraic word problems is related to their advantage in the spatial abilities associated with navigation (see the *Physical Modules* section of chapter 8). In particular, boys and men appear to be more skilled than girls and women in co-opting these spatial abilities to diagram or to represent the quantitative relations in complex word problems spatially. A. B. Lewis and Mayer (1987) showed that word problems that involve the relative comparison of two quantities are especially difficult to solve. For example, consider the following problem from Geary (1994): "Amy has two candies. She has one candy less than Mary. How many candies does Mary have?" The solution of this problem requires only simple addition, that is, 2 + 1. However, many children and adults often subtract rather than add to solve this type of problem. The key word "less" appears to prompt subtraction. The structure of the second sentence also leads individuals to conclude that Amy has more candy than Mary. A. B. Lewis (1989) showed that one way to reduce the frequency of errors that are common with these types of relational statements is to diagram (i.e., spatially represent) the relative quantities in the statements (in this example, the number of both Amy's and Mary's candies).

In an analysis of the sex difference, favoring men, in the ability to solve algebraic word problems, E. S. Johnson (1984) found that providing diagrams of the quantitative relations described in the word problems significantly improved the performance of women but not that of men; the advantage of men was reduced by about one half when diagrams were provided. In a set of studies, Casey and her colleagues demonstrated that the advantage of adolescent boys on the SAT-M (about 7 out of 10 boys outperform the average girl on this measure) was meditated in large part by their advantage in three-dimensional spatial abilities, as measured by the MRT (recall, Mental Rotation Test; see Figure 8.3). In one study, math self-confidence, which favored boys, also contributed to this sex difference, but to a lesser degree than the sex difference in three-dimensional spatial abilities (M. B. Casey, Nuttall, & Pezaris, 1997; M. B. Casey, Nuttall, Pezaris, & Benbow, 1995). These patterns suggest that boys and men more than girls and women represent mathematical problems in terms of spatial relationships, as in diagramming the relationships, and that this sex difference contributes to the advantage of boys and men in certain mathematical domains, including the solving of word problems.

Geary (1996) also argued that the brain and cognitive systems that support navigation in three-dimensional space include an implicit understanding of Euclidean geometry (see the *Architecture* section of chapter 6). In other words, the advantage of boys and men in the ability to represent the physical world mentally, as described in chapter 8 (*Physical Modules* section), is associated with an implicit understanding of Euclidean relationships (i.e., relative direction, angle, and so forth). The combination of the tendency to represent mathematical problems spatially and to understand implicitly some features of geometry provides one explanation for the finding that mentally gifted junior high school boys outperform similarly gifted girls on the SAT-M, which includes many geometry and word problem items, before formal instruction on the types of problems found on the SAT-M (see Benbow, 1988). In other words, the cognitive and neural systems that support the ability to generate representations of the three-dimensional environment are more elaborated in boys and men than in girls and women, on average, and these systems provide an intuitive understanding of geometry.

Intrasexual Variability

Differences in the average scores of boys and girls and men and women sometimes belie rather important differences in the numbers of high- and low-ability boys and girls and men and women in many academic and cognitive domains (Halpern, 1997). In most of these domains, boys and men are more variable as a group than girls and women are (Willingham & Cole, 1997). One result of this sex difference in intrasexual variability is that for most academic and cognitive domains, especially domains in which the average performance of boys and men exceeds the average performance of girls and women, there are more boys and men than girls and women among the highest scoring and among the lowest scoring individuals.

The most comprehensive assessment of this pattern was provided by

Hedges and Nowell (1995); this meta-analysis is particularly important because it included the assessment of multiple, nationally (United States) representative samples (the issue of intrasexual variability can only be adequately assessed with representative samples). In this analysis, greater intrasexual variability was found within groups of boys and men as compared with groups of girls and women for all of the cognitive and academic tests assessed, including ability measures in the domains of reading, vocabulary, mathematics, science, social studies, nonverbal reasoning, associative memory, spatial ability, mechanical reasoning, electronics information, and auto and shop information.

Similar results were reported by Feingold (1992b). An analysis of performance on the California Achievement Tests revealed greater variability in the scores of boys than girls in elementary school and in high school. The same pattern was evident for both the 1956 and 1985 standardization samples and for all academic domains assessed: vocabulary, reading comprehension, language, spelling, and arithmetic. In another analysis, sex differences in intrasexual variability were examined across four standardization samples (from 1947 to 1980) of the Differential Aptitude Tests, a battery of cognitive ability measures. From the 8th through 12th grade and for all four standardization samples, there was greater variability in boys' scores than girls' scores for tests of mechanical reasoning, numerical ability, and spatial ability. From the 10th through 12th grade and again for all four samples, the boys' scores were also more variable than the girls' scores on spelling tests, although there was a tendency for girls to be more variable on tests of verbal abilities in the 8th and 9th grades.

These sex differences in intrasexual variability have very important implications for understanding sex differences in the numbers of high- and low-achieving children. As an example, Hedges and Nowell (1995) calculated the ratio of girls to boys at the high and low end of all of the above-described measures. Across five measures of reading comprehension, more boys than girls scored in the lowest 10%; there are three boys for every two girls with reading comprehension scores in the lowest 10%. In contrast, for two of the studies reviewed by Hedges and Nowell slightly more girls than boys were in the top 5%. Another study found an equal number of boys and girls in the top 5%, and a fourth study found more boys than girls in the top 5%. Thus, although girls and women obtain higher average reading scores than boys and men and more boys and men than girls and women are found among the poorest readers, roughly equal numbers of boys and men and girls and women are found among the very best readers.

The consequences of the sex differences in intrasexual variability are more dramatic for mathematics than for reading and are most extreme in samples of highly gifted people (Benbow, 1988; Benbow & Stanley, 1980, 1983; Stanley, 1993). In the 1970s, Stanley began a project designed to identify mathematically precocious adolescents (called *Study of Mathematically Precocious Youth* [SMPY]). To achieve this end, Stanley invited children who scored in the top 2% to 5% on standardized mathematics achievement tests in the 7th grade to take the SAT. Those 12- and 13-year-olds who scored above the mean for high school girls on the SAT-M were considered to be mathematically gifted (i.e., in the top 1% of mathematical ability). For these gifted adolescents, there were 3 boys to every 2 girls at the lower end of SAT-M scores. For scores greater than 700, there were as many as 13 boys for every girl. The overrepresentation of boys at the high end of SAT-M performance is not limited to SMPY samples (Dorans & Livingston, 1987; Moore & Smith, 1987). Dorans and Livingston, for example, found that across two administrations of the SAT to high school seniors, 19 out of every 20 perfect scores (i.e., 800) were obtained by boys.

An especially controversial issue is whether there is more variability in the IQ scores of boys and men than in scores of girls and women (e.g., Fausto-Sterling, 1985). This issue was not addressed in the analysis conducted by Hedges and Nowell (1995), but Feingold (1992b) did provide an analysis of intrasexual variability on the WAIS–R (Wechsler, 1981) and its predecessor, the WAIS (Wechsler, 1955). Across these two standardization samples, the performance of men was more variable than that of women for 10 of the 11 subtests. The pattern was roughly the same comparing the 1955 to 1981 samples for 6 subtests, the sex differences declined (and was reversed for 1 subtest) for 4 subtests and increased for the final subtest. Lubinski and Humphrey's (1990) analysis of the Project Talent data also revealed greater variability in IQ scores within groups of adolescent boys than within groups of adolescent girls. The overall pattern suggests that there is greater variability in general intelligence within groups of boys and men than within groups of girls and women; that is, there are more boys and men than girls and women among groups of both low-IQ and high-IQ people.

Implications

The suggestion that many of the sex differences in academic competencies are indirectly related to sexual selection should not be taken to mean that these differences are immutable. In fact, a complete understanding of the nature and sources of these sex differences, even if the sources are largely biological in origin, in academic competencies will likely facilitate the development of instructional techniques that can narrow the gap in many domains: Equal outcomes may require unequal treatments (Geary, 1996). For instance, E. S. Johnson's (1984) earlier mentioned study suggests that the sex difference in the skill of solving multistep arithmetical and algebraic word problems can be cut by about one half by providing girls and women with diagrams of the quantitative relations conveyed in the problems. The implication is that girls would benefit more than boys with direct instruction on spatially representing quantitative information.

Similarly, the finding that the bilateral processing of language sounds facilitates the generation of correspondences between letters and sounds should not be taken to mean that boys can never, on average, read as well as girls (Pugh et al., 1997). In fact, in the Pugh et al. study, men who processed language sounds only in the left hemisphere could read as quickly and as accurately as women and men who processed language sounds in both hemispheres. In other words, the bilateral processing of language sounds might facilitate learning the letter–sound associations that are important in the beginning stages of learning how to read, but it does not imply that the ultimate level of reading and related skills, such as spelling and writing, that can be acquired by boys and men and girls and women will necessarily differ. The implication is that girls will have a head start in learning how to read, but with added instruction and experience most boys will become proficient readers. In this view, boys would benefit more than girls from additional instruction in the areas of reading, writing, and spelling; whether boys would need to be instructed differently than girls is not known.

The implications of the sex differences in intrasexual variability are much more complicated. As suggested in chapter 7 (*Physical Development* section) and in chapter 8 (*The Evolution and Development of Cognitive Sex Differences* section), the greater variability within groups of boys and men than within groups of girls and women might reflect, to some extent, condition-dependent variability. In other words, sexual selection can result in certain traits being more sensitive to environmental conditions in one sex than in the other, and across species, this greater sensitivity is more frequently found in males than in females (e.g., Møller, 1994a). The result is that males as a group are more readily affected by environmental conditions than females are, which, in turn, creates more variability within groups of males than within groups of females.

Whether this is the case for people is not known, but it should be considered. For instance, if a portion of the sex difference in intrasexual variability in academic and cognitive domains is related to a greater sensitivity of boys than girls to early environmental conditions, then the numbers of boys and girls at the high and low ends of the accompanying ability distributions will vary across contexts. In difficult contexts (e.g., poor health care, inadequate nutrition, and so forth), the prediction is that many more boys will adversely be affected than girls, which, in turn, will result in an overrepresentation of boys among the lowest scoring individuals and an underrepresentation of boys among the highest scoring individuals. In more optimal conditions, a more equal number of boys and girls will be found among the lowest scoring individuals, and boys will be overrepresented among the highest scoring individuals. Martorell et al.'s (1992) earlier described study of rural Guatemalans would seem to support these predictions. Recall that for a number of physical and academic domains, men were more severely affected, as a group, than women were by early physical stressors (e.g., poor nutrition), whereas men benefited more than women in more optimal rearing environments (see the *Vulnerability* section of chapter 7). Boys also show greater sensitivity than girls to a variety of physical and social stressors in industrial societies (e.g., Eme & Kavanaugh, 1995). Given this, the above-described sex differences in intrasexual variability might well reflect the evolution of condition-dependent functioning in boys and men.

BEHAVIORAL AND PSYCHOLOGICAL SEX DIFFERENCES

The two sections below provide several illustrations of how an understanding of the principles of sexual selection can be useful for understanding sex differences in a number of behavioral and psychological domains. The behavioral section focuses on activities that are directed toward the outer world, including other people, whereas the psychological section focuses on processes (e.g., depression) and activities that largely involve the individual.

Behavioral Sex Differences

The sections that follow focus on sex differences in violence and in the pattern of accidental injuries. Boys and men exceed girls and women in the frequency of engaging in both classes of activity, and in both cases, this sex difference can be understood, at least in part, in terms of male–male competition (Eme & Kavanaugh, 1995; C. M. Hartung & Widiger, 1998; Leadbeater, Blatt, & Quinlan, 1995; Rosen & Peterson, 1990; Rushton, 1996).

Violence

There is little question that threats, physical assaults, and homicides have been a central feature of male–male competition throughout much of human evolution (Daly & Wilson, 1988a; Keeley, 1996). As described in chapter 5 (*Male–Male Competition* section), men throughout the world compete for the attainment of social status and for the control of those resources that support reproduction. Across preindustrial societies, almost one in three young men is killed during the course of this competition and "having killed is a decided social asset in many, perhaps most, prestate societies" (Daly & Wilson, 1988a, p. 129). In the Yanomamö, for instance, roughly two out of five men have participated in the murder of at least one other person, and those men who have killed have a higher social status and more wives and children than men who have not killed (Chagnon, 1988).

Daly and Wilson's (1988a, 1990) seminal study of homicide patterns clearly supports the view that men's violence is related, at least in part, to male–male competition. "There is no known human society in which the level of lethal violence among women even approaches that among men" (Daly & Wilson, 1988a, p. 146). In other words, in relation to competition among women, competition among men is much more likely to escalate to homicide or to serious but nonlethal physical assaults, as is the case with most, if not all, other primates (Smuts, 1987a). In an analysis of same-sex homicide rates across a variety of industrial and preindustrial settings, and including homicide records dating from more than 700 years ago, Daly and Wilson (1988a) found that male-on-male homicide occurs between 30 and 40 times more frequently than female-on-female homicide. Male-on-male homicide occurs most frequently during the initial mate-finding stage of the life span (i.e., late teens through mid-20s) and more frequently among unmarried than married men (M. Wilson & Daly, 1985). Moreover, roughly two out of three male-on-male homicides occur as a result of social conflict, rather than being crime specific (e.g., during the course of a robbery), and more than one half of the homicides are associated with "matters of status competition and the maintenance of face" (Daly & Wilson, 1988a, p. 175). Stated somewhat differently, men kill other men during jealousy disputes over relationships with women and in the course of their attempts to improve their relative social dominance or to prevent other men from achieving dominance over them—a pattern that is no different than that described in chapter 3 for other polygynous primates (Male–Male Competition section).

Men not only kill each other much more frequently than women do, but they also kill women much more frequently than women kill men. This form of male-on-female violence, as well as serious nonlethal assaults, often stems from mate guarding; that is, men's attempts to control the sexual behavior of the women in their life (Daly & Wilson, 1988a, 1988b; Flinn, 1988a). In fact, "male sexual proprietariness is the dominant issue in marital violence. In studies of 'motives' of spousal homicide, the leading identified substantive issue is 'jealousy'" (Daly & Wilson, 1988b, p. 521). For instance, between 1974 and 1983, 1,060 spousal homicides were investigated in Canada (Daly & Wilson, 1988a). In three out of four cases, the victim was the wife, and in the vast majority of these cases, the motives were classified as "argument" or "jealousy." Of the 214 homicides that were classified as jealousy related, 195 (91%) were committed by men. It is likely that many of the homicides classified as argument related were in fact jealousy related, and about 7 out of 10 of these homicides were committed by men. These patterns are not unique to Canada. They are found throughout the world (see M. I. Wilson & Daly, 1992, for a related discussion). For instance, one study revealed that 42 of 90 homicides among the Basoga (a polygynous, horticultural society in Uganda) involved a man killing a woman, usually his wife. Motives could be discerned for 32 of these homicides, and 21 of them occurred after the wife's adultery, her desertion of her husband, or her refusal to have sex with her husband (Daly & Wilson, 1988a).

In all, most homicides are committed by men, and the majority of these homicides, as well as serious nonlethal assaults, result from male–male competition for social status or from more direct disputes over relationships with women. Similarly, when men kill women, it is often related to the man's reproductive concerns (e.g., sexual jealousy).

Accidents

As soon as children can walk and extending throughout the life span, boys and men are injured and killed by accidents much more frequently than are same-age girls and women (Arnett, 1995; B, N. Rosen & Peterson, 1990). In a comprehensive assessment of childhood injuries and deaths in the United States, B. N. Rosen and Peterson documented a much higher frequency of accidental death and injury in boys than in girls. Boys experience near drowning nearly twice as frequently as girls and die as a result of drowning almost four times as frequently as girls. Boys are injured and killed more frequently than girls while riding bicycles, playing on recreational equipment, and during unorganized (i.e., not supervised by adults) sports activities. For every girl that is injured on a playground, four boys are injured. For every girl who sustains a serious burn, three boys sustain an equally serious burn (e.g., while playing with fireworks). B. N. Rosen and Peterson concluded that the sex differences in accidental injury and death rates were related to the sex differences in activity levels, risk taking, and frequency of engagement in rough-and-tumble and competitive play.

As described in chapter 7, all of these childhood activities involve a preparation for later one-on-one and coalition-based male–male competition. As an example, D. C. Miller and Byrnes (1997) examined the social and personality factors associated with risk taking in third-, fifth-, and seventh-grade boys and girls; in this study, risk taking involved making decisions about engaging in activities that had a high chance of failure but that provided enhanced benefits if successful. In keeping with previous studies (Ginsburg & Miller, 1982), boys engaged in greater risk-taking activities than girls did, but only when peers were present. Girls' decisions were more conservative than boys' and did not vary as a function of whether their peers would be aware of their choices. A second study revealed that children who are high risk takers tend to be competitive, tend to enjoy engaging in physical activities that entail some risk of injury, and tend to be boys. Risk taking is thus related to general competitiveness and often involves a form of social display (i.e., these risks are taken in full view of their peers) for boys but not for girls. Risk-taking displays, in turn, serve the function of enhancing the boy's status within the peer group, and for boys and men, activities that are related to enhancing one's social status are typically related to male–male competition (see chapter 5 *Male–Male Competition* section).

Psychological Sex Differences

In this section, the potential relations among sexual selection, reproductive concerns, and several psychological disorders that affect girls and women more frequently than boys and men—anxiety, depression, and eating disorders—are described.

Anxiety and Depression

Roughly twice as many girls and women suffer from socially important levels of anxiety and depression (i.e., levels that can disrupt social relationships) than same-age boys and men, although these sex differences do not typically emerge until adolescence (Cicchetti & Toth, 1998; C. M. Hartung & Widiger, 1998; Kashani & Orvaschel, 1990; Keenan & Shaw, 1997; Leadbeater et al., 1995; Nolen-Hoeksema, 1987; see Mineka, Watson, & Clark, 1998, for a discussion of anxiety, depression, and their interrelationship). In one study, 210 randomly selected 8-, 12-, and 17-year-olds participated in a semistructured clinical interview designed to detect anxiety disorders and were administered several standardized anxiety measures (Kashani & Orvaschel, 1990). More girls than boys exhibited clinically significant levels of anxiety at all age levels. Across age levels, about 13% of the boys were identified as showing some form of anxiety-related difficulty (e.g., social phobia) as compared with nearly 29% of the girls.

In a comprehensive review of sex differences in depression, Nolen-Hoeksema (1987) found that in the United States about twice as many women as men experience symptoms of depression (e.g., lethargy, guilt, and sleep problems), and about twice as many women as men seek treatment for depression. Greater numbers of women than men are also treated for depression in Denmark, Scotland, England, Australia, Canada, Iceland, and Israel. Across these countries, the overall ratio of depressed women to men was 2.4:1 and ranged from 1.7:1 (England) to 3.8:1 (Denmark). Community-based assessments have found that more women than men report symptoms of depression in Sweden, Denmark, Iceland, Australia, Uganda, Kenya, and Iran; the only exception was for a sample from Nigeria, in which equal numbers of women and men reported symptoms of depression. The factors underlying the sex differences in the experience of anxiety-

and depression-related symptoms and disorders are not yet fully understood and are, no doubt, many and varied (Keenan & Shaw, 1997; Nolen-Hoeksema, 1987).

There are at least two ways in which implicit reproductive concerns might contribute to these sex differences. First, it was argued earlier that development of reciprocal and intimate relationships is more important for women than for men, because across preindustrial societies and almost certainly throughout the course of human evolution women have resided in groups with nonkin more frequently than men have (see the *Social Development and Evolution* section of chapter 7). Under these conditions, development of such relationships would provide not only a system of personal support for women but also a more stable social environment for the rearing of their children. In this view, girls and women should not only value the development of reciprocal and intimate relationships more than boys and men but should also react more strongly to the disruption of these relationships, especially during their reproductive years; recall that it was argued in chapter 6 (*Emotional Mechanisms* section) that negative affect—anxiety and depression—is expected to result from the loss of evolutionarily significant resources, both social and material (Buss, 1996; MacDonald, 1988).

A recent analysis of the life events that trigger depressive symptoms in adolescent boys and girls supports this position (Leadbeater et al., 1995). Both adolescent boys and girls often experience symptoms of depression (e.g., sad affect or lack of self-worth) after personal failure, such as poor grades. A significant sex difference is found, however, in reactivity to negative interpersonal events, such as "threats to intimacy and closeness in relationships" (Leadbeater et al., 1995, p. 12). Adolescent girls and women are much more likely to experience symptoms of depression after interpersonal conflict or loss of a significant relationship than same-age boys and men. In addition, adolescent girls and women often experience symptoms of depression when negative life events affect their family or friends, whereas boys and men typically do not. In fact, it appears that adolescent girls are four times more likely than same-age boys to experience anxiety and depression as a result of disrupted interpersonal relationships, and, as noted in chapter 5 (the *Female–Female Competition* section), the disruption of these relationships is often the goal of female–female competition (Crick & Bigbee, 1998). In other words, female–female competition likely contributes to the higher levels of anxiety and depression in adolescent girls and in women compared with same-age boys and men.

The second way in which implicit reproductive concerns might contribute to the sex differences in anxiety and depression is through marital instability (Lampert & Friedman, 1992). As described in chapter 4, women throughout the world show higher levels of parental investment than men, and one manifestation of this sex difference is that men abandon their children in much higher frequencies than women do in both industrial and preindustrial societies (e.g., Furstenberg & Nord, 1985; K. Hill & Hurtado, 1996). In situations in which biparental care benefits children, women are thus more vulnerable to desertion than men are and thus might show greater concerns about abandonment. Lampert and Friedman tested this hypothesis with a sample of 258 adults living in socially egalitarian kibbutzim in Israel; both parents worked, and equal participation in child care was expected. Despite the norm of equality, for every couple with children, the mother reported high levels of parental investment (e.g., in terms of time, educational instruction, and so forth) than the father did. Mothers who invested the most in their children and who had younger children (less than 12 years of age) were more vulnerable—"apprehension of being deserted and the feeling of dependency on the partner" (Lampert & Friedman, 1992, p. 66)—than lower investing mothers, mothers with older children (greater than 12 years of age), or married women with no children. Women in each of these three categories reported higher levels of vulnerability than their husbands, but the magnitude the sex difference was relatively small for women without children and for women with older children but was large for women with younger children. Feelings of vulnerability, in turn, were related to high levels of anxiety and depression, among other things.

A recent longitudinal study of the relation between marital satisfaction and depression further supports the view that women are more emotionally vulnerable in this relationship than men are (Fincham, Beach, Harold, & Osborne, 1997). Levels of marital adjustment (e.g., level of satisfaction with the relationship, conflict, and so forth) and depressive symptoms were assessed twice in 150 newlyweds. The first assessment was 3 to 8 months after the marriage, and the second was 18 months after the first assessment. Marital satisfaction and depressive symptoms were related to each other, but differently for men and women. For men, depression at the first assessment was associated with poorer marital satisfaction at the second assessment. The opposite pattern was found for women: Dissatisfaction with the marital relationship at the first assessment was related to depressive symptoms at the second assessment. In other words, depression disrupts the marital relationship for men but seems to result from a disrupted relationship in women (see Gottman, 1998, for further discussion).

Thus, even though both men and women generally benefit (physically and psychologically) from marriage (Mastekaasa, 1994; Wyke & Graeme, 1992), women are more likely than men to experience anxiety and depression after marital conflict (Fincham et al., 1997; Lampert & Friedman, 1992). The greater reactivity—in terms of symptoms of anxiety and depression—of women to marital conflict, in turn, appears to be related, at least in part, to an implicit concern over paternal investment. It might be argued that this position is inconsistent with the finding that in industrial societies, women are much more likely to initiate divorce than men are (e.g., Buckle et al., 1996). The counterargument is that the evolution of paternal investment was probably more strongly related to child mortality than to the child's social well-being. In industrial societies, paternal investment is no longer needed to keep children alive, and, given this, women are no longer in a position in which they must tolerate the behavior of some men (e.g., jealousy-related mate guarding) to ensure paternal investment. In more difficult situations, however, paternal investment can significantly reduce child mortality rates, and it is under conditions such as these that an implicit concern about paternal investment and the accompanying vulnerability could evolve (K. Hill & Hurtado, 1996; see the *Paternal Investment and the Well-Being of Children* section of chapter 4).

Eating Disorders

In many Western societies, more adolescent girls and women suffer from eating disorders than same-age boys and men (Rolls, Fedoroff, & Guthrie, 1991). In fact, for every adolescent boy or man with an eating disorder, there are at least nine same-age girls and women with a similar disorder (C. M. Hartung & Widiger, 1998). These eating disorders often manifest themselves as anorexia nervosa (self-starvation to stay thin) or bulimia nervosa (binge eating, followed by fasting or vomiting) and can be fatal if untreated. The factors that contribute to these eating disorders appear to be multiple and not fully understood but likely involve a combination of social (e.g., family dynamics), psychological, and cultural processes. The principles of sexual selection might provide an additional and potentially useful perspective from which the etiology and treatment of these disorders can be approached (Buss, 1994).

As noted in chapter 5, physical characteristics are more important to men than to women in making mate-choice decisions, and, given this, it is not surprising that one way in which women compete with one another is to enhance their physical appearance. Such competition is likely to be especially important in cultures with socially imposed monogamy, given that male choice appears to be more stringent in these cultures than in other cultures (Gaulin & Boster, 1990). Moreover, at this point in history, relatively high-status men choose to marry relatively slim women, at least in Western industrialized nations (Argyle, 1994); an attraction to relatively slim women is not necessarily inherent (although the preference for a 0.7 WHR appears to be inherent) and, in fact, appears to vary across contexts (Feingold & Mazzella, 1998)—relatively heavier women might be preferred in contexts in which food is in short supply and all but the wealthy are thin. These patterns suggest that the concern that many adolescent girls and women have about their weight might be driven, in part, by male choice (Joiner, Schmidt, & Singh, 1994).

The other side of the male-choice coin is, of course, female–female competition. In fact, Rozin and Fallon (1988) found that "mothers and daughters believed that men (of their own generation) prefer much thinner women than these men actually prefer" (Rozin & Fallon, 1988, p. 342). In other words, many men do in fact prefer relatively thin marriage partners, but many women place more of an emphasis on being thin than men do. The greater focus of women than men on weight is potentially related to female–female competition, which, in the case of eating disorders, has been taken to an extreme (perhaps an analogous process in men is the taking of steroids to increase muscle mass). One potential contributing factor to this female–female competition is the prevalence of unusually thin fashion models; pictures of these models are found more frequently in female-targeted magazines than in male-targeted magazines. These models might represent symbolic competitors (especially if men attend to them) or might be misperceived as having the "ideal" body shape for attracting a high-status mate; Rozin and Fallon's study suggests that most men would rate most fashion models as too thin. At the same time, many of these models have a body weight that is below the biological optimum for women and is thus not at all "ideal."

Implications

The section on violence should not be taken to mean that men, as a group, are biologically destined to engage in physical assaults and homicides. Men are biologically destined to compete with each other for social status and for the attainment of cultural success, but this competition need not be expressed physically. Social and cultural factors have an important influence on how men compete with each other and on the level of violence in the society. For instance, homicide rates have steadily dropped over the past 700 years in England (Daly & Wilson, 1988a) and are lower in industrialized than in many preindustrialized societies (Keeley, 1996). One important influence on the level of male violence in the culture is the way in which cultural success is achieved. In many societies with high levels of male violence, having murdered is one way to achieve cultural success (e.g., Chagnon, 1988). In mainstream Western culture, in contrast, success is gauged in terms of relative control of resources, such as income, and most men compete accordingly, typically by obtaining an education and later through striving for occupational success (see next section).

Violence often results from the unequal distribution of culturally valued resources (see M. Wilson & Daly, 1997). Thus, one prediction is that much of the violence in Western culture will be expressed by men who, for whatever reason, cannot compete in culturally valued ways, especially men who are in the initial mate-finding phase of the life span (in which intrasexual competition tends to be the most intense). M. Wilson and Daly's

(1985) analysis suggests that this is indeed the case. In this study, murderers and their victims tended to be young men and tended to be unemployed and unmarried. One implication is that improved educational outcomes and employment opportunities, and thus a more equal distribution of resources among men in the society, will reduce the level of violence in these segments of the population (M. Wilson & Daly, 1997). In other words, employment provides an alternative means of competing with other men and will likely make these men better marriage prospects, in terms of female choice.

Leadbeater et al.'s (1995) conclusion that the sex difference in depression is related to the sex difference in interpersonal concerns has important implications, whether the associated evolutionary interpretation is correct. The most obvious implication is that social support groups (e.g., in junior high school and high school) might provide an effective method of reducing levels of anxiety and depression in adolescent girls. On the basis of the social development patterns described in chapter 7, these groups might be most effective if they were relatively small and included same-age peers (perhaps monitored by an adult), as contrasted with one-on-one counseling with an adult or relatively large peer groups; it might be difficult for many girls to develop feelings of intimacy in larger groups. Similar support groups would almost certainly be beneficial for women as well, especially women who are otherwise socially isolated, experiencing marital conflict, or both. The evolutionary theme presented by Lampert and Friedman (1992) suggests that an underlying concern for women in conflicted marriages is not only for their own well-being but also for the well-being of their children. On the basis of this perspective, the effectiveness of marital therapy might be enhanced if such concerns were explicitly introduced and discussed (i.e., feelings of being vulnerable, concerns of abandonment, and so forth).

If eating disorders are in fact related in one way or another to competition for desirable mates—no doubt other factors are involved as well (Rolls et al., 1991)—then Rozin and Fallon's (1988) findings suggest that one aspect of treatment might focus on the difference between the affected women's ideal weight and the heavier ideal preferred by men. And, if women do implicitly or explicitly perceive models as competitors or as a reflection of what desirable men prefer (although most models appear to be thinner than what many men prefer), then the inclusion of heavier models in magazines and other sources might be helpful.

SEX DIFFERENCES IN OCCUPATIONAL INTERESTS AND ACHIEVEMENT

Sex differences in occupational interests and achievement are socially important, because these differences contribute greatly to the wage and social status advantage that men enjoy in most, if not all, industrialized nations (e.g., Paglin & Rufolo, 1990; Pratto, 1996). Many of these sex differences appear to be indirectly related to sexual selection, through the sex differences in orientation toward people, status striving, and cognitive pattern, among others.

As an example, across occupations, "evidence consistently suggests that despite comparable educational qualifications, tenure, and occupational attitudes, women have not achieved occupational status comparable to that of men" (S. D. Phillips & Imhoff, 1997, p. 46). The sex difference in occupational achievement has been attributed to a host of factors, including bias against women (e.g., the "glass ceiling"). Any such bias is not the whole story, however. As a group, men tend to be more focused on occupational achievement (e.g., they work longer hours, engage in more status-enhancing risk taking, and so forth) than women and are more likely than women to value such achievement more highly than they value family and other interpersonal relationships (Browne, 1995; Pratto, 1996).

In Western culture, occupational success is synonymous with cultural success, and, for men, the associated status striving is a manifestation of male–male competition. In other words, the sex difference in occupational achievement is related, in part, to the striving of men to achieve cultural success, which not only increases their status with respect to other men but it also improves their mating and marriage prospects (Buss, 1996; Pérusse, 1993). The finding that the mating and marriage prospects of men improve as their incomes and occupational status improve indicates that the sex difference in status striving is also related to female choice (Buss, 1996; Kenrick et al., 1993). All other things being equal, most women prefer well-educated and occupationally successful marriage partners, which, in turn, intensifies male–male competition for the attainment of occupational status.

The sex differences in cognitive pattern and social interests also contribute to the sex differences in occupational interests and outcomes. Although a comprehensive treatment of these issues is beyond the scope of this book, the indirect relations between cognitive and social sex differences that have been shaped by sexual selection and occupational outcomes are illustrated in the sections that follow on math-intensive occupations; see Browne (1984, 1995, 1997) for a thorough discussion of associated legal issues. The focus is on math-intensive careers—engineering, physical sciences, mathematics, and computer science—because in modern society these occupations command higher salaries than language-intensive occupations (e.g., journalism). Men enter these high-paying occupations in much higher frequencies than women do, which, in turn, contributes to the overall wage advantage enjoyed by men (see Paglin & Rufolo, 1990).

Cognitive Influences

The attainment of the educational credentials that allow access to a high-paying career in a math-intensive area, such as engineering, is made easier by a number of cognitive factors. In particular, an above-average level of general intelligence and an above-average level of spatial, mathematical, and mechanical competencies (Gottfredson, 1997; Humphreys, Lubinski, & Yao, 1993; Lubinski & Dawis, 1992; Paglin & Rufolo, 1990). Sex differences in the former (spatial, mathematical, and mechanical) competencies contribute to the sex difference in the proportion of men and women entering math-intensive fields. For instance, individuals who enter math-intensive fields tend to have SAT-M and Graduate Record Examination—Quantitative scores that are in the 600–800 range (500 is average and 800 is the top score), and the ratio of men to women with scores in this range is between 2:1 to more than 5:1 (Paglin & Rufolo, 1990). The ratio is even larger at the very high end of mathematical performance. As noted earlier, 95% of the top scores on the SAT-M (i.e., 800) are earned by men (Dorans & Livingston, 1987).

Similarly, there are more men than women who receive top scores (i.e., 700–800) on the math-intensive achievement tests that are sometimes taken as part of the SAT or other college entrance examinations. The ratio of top-scoring men to women on physics tests is nearly 3:1 and about 2.5:1 on chemistry tests (Stanley, 1993). A similar pattern is evident for advanced placement tests (i.e., tests taken in high school for college credit), including tests in all areas of physics and chemistry (e.g., electricity and magnetism, mechanics, and so forth; Stanley, Benbow, Brody, Dauber, & Lupkowski, 1992). In other words, many more men than women have the minimal spatial, mathematical, and mechanical competencies needed to succeed in many math-intensive fields.

As described in the *Academic Patterns* section, at least some of these sex differences appear to be related to the sex difference, favoring boys and men, in evolved spatial–navigational competencies and are thus indirectly related to sexual selection (Geary, 1996). It is likely that the sex difference, favoring boys and men, in object-oriented interests and activities also contributes to some of these sex differences (e.g., in mechanical competencies), although it is not currently known how engagement in these activities affects cognitive development and any associated cognitive sex differences (see the *Play* section of chapter 7).

Social Influences

Social sex differences appear to be relatively more important than the just-described cognitive sex differences for understanding the disparity in the proportion of women and men that enter math-intensive fields. For societies in which women and men are relatively free to choose their own careers, the occupational interests and choices of men and women have been found to differ consistently from each other. On vocational interest tests, "young women [score] higher than young men on domestic, artistic, writing, social service, and office service vocational interests and young men [score] higher than young women on business, law, politics, mathematics, science, agriculture, athletics, and mechanical interests" (Willingham & Cole, 1997, p. 178). The sex difference in vocational interests is especially striking among the earlier mentioned SMPY youth. When they are in their 20s, for every mathematically gifted SMPY woman who is working toward or who aspires to earn an advanced degree in mathematics, engineering, or physical sciences, there are eight equally talented men (Lubinski & Benbow, 1994).

For these gifted individuals, the sex difference in the pursuit of an advanced education in math-intensive areas cannot be attributed to cognitive factors, given that nearly all of these women have the mathematical competencies necessary to succeed in these careers, nor can the difference be attributed solely to a bias against women. For example, gifted women, as a group, do not view mathematics as a "male" occupation and are not discouraged from pursuing math-intensive careers (Lubinski & Humphreys, 1990; Raymond & Benbow, 1986). Rather, the sex difference in the pursuit of math-intensive careers appears to stem largely from the occupational and social interests of these gifted men and women.

People—men and women—who enter math-intensive fields tend to have a relatively "low need for people contact" (Lubinski, Benbow, & Sanders, 1993, p. 701) and tend to prefer occupations that involve a high degree of theoretical and investigative activities (i.e., abstract disciplines that involve some form of discovery). Mathematically gifted SMPY men who enter these fields do indeed show this pattern of occupational and social interests. As a group, mathematically gifted SMPY women, in contrast, "are more socially and esthetically oriented and have interests that are more evenly divided among investigative, social and artistic pursuits" (Lubinski et al., 1993, p. 702). In short, many mathematically gifted women choose not to enter math-intensive fields because they have broader social and occupational interests than their equally gifted male peers and therefore more frequently pursue occupations outside of these math-intensive areas.

Geary (1996) argued that many of the sex differences in occupational interests are indirectly related to sexual selection. For instance, the tendency for girls and women to value the development and maintenance of intimate and reciprocal social relationships more than boys and men appears to have an evolutionary history, as described earlier (see also the *Social Development and Evolution* section of chapter 7). In modern society, this sex difference appears to contribute to the sex difference in the relative attractiveness of math-intensive careers. More generally, it appears that gifted women are more interested in careers that involve living things (e.g., biology and medicine) as opposed to inorganic things (e.g., physics and engineering), whereas gifted men show the opposite pattern, on average. These sex differences would appear to be a continuation of the object versus people orientation that emerges in infancy and that is evident in the play patterns and social interests of boys and girls (chapter 7), as well as in the social motives of men and women (chapter 6). In short, the sex differences in occupational pursuits are a reflection, at least in part, of the different reproductive motives, such as status striving and interest in people, of men and women (see the *Patterns of Control* section of chapter 6).

There are other ways in which an evolutionary perspective might be useful in understanding these patterns. For instance, men also appear to be more focused in their occupational interests than women are (i.e., men are more likely to specialize than women are). Mathematically gifted women, for instance, "enroll in courses in math/science and English/foreign language in essentially equal proportions, whereas [men] were approximately six times more likely to enroll in math/science areas than in English/foreign languages" (Lubinski et al., 1993, p. 702). Although it is not certain, the tendency of men to specialize might be a reflection of relatively more intense male–male than female–female competition, given that the tendency to specialize is often associated with intense competition (Dawkins & Krebs, 1979; Weiner, 1995).

Implications

The most obvious implication of the patterns described in this section is that the sex differences in occupational interests and achievement cannot reflexively be attributed to some form of bias, such as the glass ceiling, against women (Browne, 1995). This is not to say that such bias does not sometimes occur. Rather, the factors that contribute to the sex differences in occupational interests and status are very complex and are not fully understood (S. D. Phillips & Imhoff, 1997). The position here is that sex differences that have been shaped by sexual selection, such as men's concern for the attainment of cultural success (i.e., male–male competition), indirectly contribute to some of these occupation-related sex differences. Even so, it does not necessarily follow that these sex differences are immutable.

For instance, on the basis of the sex differences described throughout this book (e.g., in social development, chapter 7), the participation of gifted women in math-intensive careers might be increased by changing the work environment, or at least the perceptions thereof, associated with these occupations. As noted earlier, men who choose these careers tend to have a lower than average need for social affiliation (see also Roe, 1956).

Working with individuals who have a relatively low need for social affiliation and thus do not seek social contact as frequently as many other people might be perceived by many women as being rejecting or hostile, given the value that many women place on more intimate social relationships and given the fact that the relational aggression associated with female–female competition (see chapter 5) involves a similar type of behavior (i.e., shunning or social isolation). If this is the case, then the nature of the social environments in which math-intensive work occurs, or is perceived to occur, likely contributes to the relatively low interest of gifted women in these occupations.

One implication is that changing the perception of these occupations—much of the work in these areas involves collaborative projects, the work contributes to the well-being of other people, and so forth—might make the fields more attractive to young women. Once they enter math-intensive occupations, the development of social supports might be more important for young women than for young men. In other words, employers might be more successful at attracting and retaining women in these areas if they encouraged the development of peer support groups (this would require hiring more than one woman, of course) and work teams that were stable (i.e., not reconfigured for each new project) and relatively small in size.

SUMMARY AND CONCLUSION

The primary goal of this chapter was to explore some of the ways in which an understanding of sexual selection can be used to comprehend many of the sex differences that are predominant in modern society. At the broadest level, there are both scientific and social benefits that can be accrued by using sexual selection as a framework for understanding sex differences in modern society (Geary, 1996). Scientifically, sexual selection provides a broader perspective to the study of sex differences than is typically the case with psychological studies of social, emotional, cognitive, and behavioral sex differences. Given this, a knowledge of the principles of sexual selection will allow for a more complete understanding of human sex differences than is now the case. Socially, a more complete understanding of human sex differences will allow for better control of those differences that are socially (e.g., violence) and individually (e.g., eating disorders) harmful.

Unfortunately, many laypersons and members of the scientific community incorrectly assume that human sex differences that have biological origins are unchangeable. The belief that these sex differences are immutable appears to create a psychological resistance to even a thoughtful consideration of biological influences, such as hormonal influences, in general and evolution in particular. As described in chapter 6 (*The Motivation to Control* section), this resistance appears to stem from the fundamental human desire to control things that are important to us (Heckhausen & Schulz, 1995). Or stated otherwise, the desire to control people, things, and events that are important to us appears to have resulted in an uncritical acceptance of psychological theories that focus on constructs, such as gender roles (Eagly, 1987), that create an illusion of control over sex differences.

The position here is that such control will never be achieved until an understanding of all of the processes that create sex differences are fully known. An understanding of all of these processes is not possible without a consideration of the direct and indirect ways in which sexual selection has influenced sex differences that are important in modern society. Several illustrations were provided in this chapter as to how an understanding of sexual selection can not only provide a more complete scientific comprehension of sex differences but can also be used to change the associated sex differences in ways that are socially and individually beneficial. Just as research in the biological and medical sciences has reduced the pain and suffering that were an integral part of our evolutionary past (e.g., infectious diseases), biologically informed psychological research on social, emotional, behavioral, and cognitive processes that have been shaped by evolutionary selection can result in strategies for changing the ways in which these evolved biases are expressed in modern society. This is not to say that all of the sex differences that are directly or indirectly related to sexual selection, such as the advantage of boys and men in throwing distance and throwing velocity, can be eliminated. Rather, an understanding of sexual selection can be useful for designing interventions that can reduce the magnitude of many of the associated sex differences, such as the advantage of boys and men in solving mathematical word problems, and for understanding and therefore more effectively treating behavioral (e.g., violence) and psychological (e.g., depression) difficulties that differentially affect boys and men and girls and women.

REFERENCES

Abbott, D. H. (1993). Social conflict and reproductive suppression in marmoset and tamarin monkeys. In W. A. Mason & S. P. Mendoza (Eds.), *Primate social conflict* (pp. 331–372). Albany: State University of New York Press.

Abrams, D., & Hogg, M. A. (Eds.). (1990). *Social identity theory: Constructive and critical advances.* New York: Springer-Verlag.

Acredolo, L. P. (1988). From signal to "symbol": The development of landmark knowledge from 9 to 13 months. *British Journal of Developmental Psychology, 6,* 369–372.

Adamson, L. B., & McArthur, D. (1995). Joint attention, affect, and culture. In C. Moore & P. J. Dunham (Eds.), *Joint attention: Its origins and role in development* (pp. 205–221). Hillsdale, NJ: Erlbaum.

Adler, N. E., Boyce, T., Chesney, M. A., Cohen, S., Folkman, S., Kahn, R. L., & Syme, S. L. (1994). Socioeconomic status and health: The challenge of the gradient. *American Psychologist, 49,* 15–24.

Ahlgren, A., & Johnson, D. W. (1979). Sex differences in cooperative and competitive attitudes from the 2nd to the 12th grades. *Developmental Psychology, 15,* 45–49.

Aiello, L. C. (1992). Body size and energy requirements. In S. Jones, R. Martin, & D. Pilbeam (Eds.), *The Cambridge encyclopedia of human evolution* (pp. 41–45). New York: Cambridge University Press.

Aiello, L. C. (1994). Variable but singular. *Nature, 368,* 399–400.

Aldis, O. (1975). *Play fighting.* New York: Academic Press.

Alexander, R. D. (1979). *Darwinism and human affairs.* Seattle: University of Washington Press.

Alexander, R. D. (1990). *How did humans evolve? Reflections on the uniquely unique species.* Ann Arbor: Museum of Zoology (Special Publication No. 1), University of Michigan.

Alexander, R. D., Hoogland, J. L., Howard, R. D., Noonan, K. M., & Sherman, P. W. (1979). Sexual dimorphisms and breeding systems in pinnipeds, ungulates, primates, and humans. In N. A. Chagnon & W. Irons (Eds.), *Evolutionary biology and human social behavior: An anthropological perspective* (pp. 402–435). North Scituate, MA: Duxbury Press.

Alfieri, T., Ruble, D. N., & Higgins, E. T. (1996). Gender stereotypes during adolescence: Developmental changes and the transition to junior high school. *Developmental Psychology, 32,* 1129–1137.

Allen, L. S., & Gorski, R. A. (1992). Sexual orientation and the size of the anterior commissure in the human brain. *Proceedings of the National Academy of Sciences USA, 89,* 7199–7202.

Allen, L. S., Richey, M. F., Chai, Y. M., & Gorski, R. A. (1991). Sex differences in the corpus callosum of the living human being. *Journal of Neuroscience, 11,* 933–942.

Altmann, J. (1980). *Baboon mothers and infants.* Cambridge, MA: Harvard University Press.

Altmann, J., Alberts, S. C., Haines, S. A., Dubach, J., Muruthi, P., Coote, T., Geffen, E., Chessman, D. J., Mututua, R. S., Saiyalel, S. N., Wayne, R. K., Lacy, R. C., & Bruford, M. W. (1996). Behavior predicts genetic structure in a wild primate group. *Proceedings of the National Academy of Sciences, USA, 93,* 5797–5801.

Amato, P. R., & Booth, A. (1996). A prospective study of divorce and parent–child relationships. *Journal of Marriage and the Family, 58,* 356–365.

Amato, P. R., & Keith, B. (1991). Parental divorce and the well-being of children: A meta-analysis. *Psychological Bulletin, 110,* 26–46.

Andersen, R. A., Snyder, L. H., Bradley, D. C., & Xing, J. (1997). Multimodal representation of space in the posterior parietal cortex and its use in planning movements. *Annual Review of Neuroscience, 20,* 303–330.

Anderson, C. A., & Bushman, B. J. (1997). External validity of "trivial" experiments: The case of laboratory aggression. *Review of General Psychology, 1,* 19–41.

Andersson, M. (1982). Sexual selection, natural selection and quality advertisement. *Biological Journal of the Linnean Society, 17,* 375–393.

Andersson, M. (1994). *Sexual selection.* Princeton, NJ: Princeton University Press.

Annett, M. (1985). *Left, right, hand and brain: The right shift theory.* Hillsdale, NJ: Erlbaum.

Apanius, V., Penn, D., Slev, P. R., Ruff, L. R., & Potts, W. K. (1997). The nature of selection on the major histocompatibility complex. *Critical Reviews in Immunology, 17,* 179–224.

Archer, J. (1991). The influence of testosterone on human aggression. *British Journal of Psychology, 82,* 1–28.

Archer, J. (1992). *Ethology and human development.* Savage, MD: Barnes & Noble Books.

Archer, J. (1994). Testosterone and aggression. In M. Hillbrand & N. J. Pallone (Eds.), *The psychobiology of aggression* (pp. 3–35). New York: Haworth Press.

Archer, J. (1996). Sex differences in social behavior: Are the social role and evolutionary explanations compatible? *American Psychologist, 51,* 909–917.

Argyle, M. (1994). *The psychology of social class.* New York: Routledge.

Armelagos, G. J., & Van Gerven, D. P. (1980). Sexual dimorphism and human evolution: An overview. *Journal of Human Evolution, 9,* 437–446.

Arndt, J., Greenberg, J., Pyszczynski, T., & Solomon, S. (1997). Subliminal exposure to death-related stimuli increases defense of the cultural worldview. *Psychological Science, 8,* 379–385.

Arnett, J. (1995). The young and the reckless: Adolescent reckless behavior. *Current Directions in Psychological Science, 4,* 67–71.

Arnold, A. P. (1996). Genetically triggered sexual differentiation of brain and behavior. *Hormones and Behavior, 30,* 495–505.

Arnold, A. P., & Gorski, R. A. (1984). Gonadal steroid induction of structural sex differences in the central nervous system. *Annual Review of Neuroscience, 7,* 413–442.

Arsuaga, J. L., Carretero, J. M., Lorenzo, C., Gracia, A., Martínez, I., Bermúdez de Castro, J. M., & Carbonell, E. (1997). Size variation in middle Pleistocene humans. *Science, 277,* 1086–1088.

Atran, S. (1994). Core domains versus scientific theories: Evidence from systematics and Itza-Maya folkbiology. In L. A. Hirschfeld & S. A. Gelman (Eds.), *Mapping the mind: Domain specificity in cognition and culture* (pp. 316–340). New York: Cambridge University Press.

Atran, S. (in press). Folk biology and the anthropology of science: Cognitive universals and cultural particulars. *Behavioral and Brain Sciences.*

Bachmann, C., & Kummer, H. (1980). Male assessment of female choice in hamadryas baboons. *Behavioral Ecology and Sociobiology, 6,* 315–321.

Baenninger, M., & Newcombe, N. (1995). Environmental input to the development of sex-related differences in spatial and mathematical ability. *Learning and Individual Differences, 7,* 363–379.

Bailey, K. G. (1987). *Human paleopsychology: Applications to aggression and pathological processes.* Hillsdale, NJ: Erlbaum.

Baker, R. (1996). *Sperm wars: The science of sex.* New York: Basic Books.

Baldi, R., Campagna, C., Pedraza, S., & Le Boeuf, B. J. (1996). Social effects of space availability on the breeding behavior of elephant seals in Patagonia. *Animal Behaviour, 51,* 717–724.

Baldwin, D. A., & Moses, L. J. (1996). The ontogeny of social information gathering. *Child Development, 67,* 1915–1939.

Ball, G. F., & Hulse, S. H. (1998). Birdsong. *American Psychologist, 53,* 37–58.

Banerjee, M. (1997). Hidden emotions: Preschoolers' knowledge of appearance-reality and emotion display rules. *Social Cognition, 15,* 107–132.

Barber, N. (1991). Play and energy regulation in mammals. *Quarterly Review of Biology, 66,* 129–147.

Barber, N. (1995). The evolutionary psychology of physical attractiveness: Sexual selection and human morphology. *Ethology and Sociobiology, 16,* 395–424.

Bard, K. A. (1995). Parenting in primates. In M. H. Bornstein (Ed.), *Handbook of parenting, Vol. 2: Biology and ecology of parenting* (pp. 27–58). Hillsdale, NJ: Erlbaum.

Barkley, R. A., Ullman, D. G., Otto, L., & Brecht, J. M. (1977). The effects of sex typing and sex appropriateness of modeled behavior on children's imitation. *Child Development, 48,* 721–725.

Barkow, J. H. (1992). Beneath new culture is old psychology: Gossip and social stratification. In J. H. Barkow, L. Cosmides, & J. Tooby (Eds.), *The adapted mind: Evolutionary psychology and the generation of culture* (pp. 627–637). New York: Oxford University Press.

Barlow, D. P. (1995). Gametic imprinting in mammals. *Science, 270,* 1610–1613.

Baron, J. (1997). The illusion of morality as self-interest: A reason to cooperate in social dilemmas. *Psychological Science, 8,* 330–335.

Baron-Cohen, S. (1995). *Mindblindness: An essay on autism and theory of mind.* Cambridge, MA: MIT Press/Bradford Books.

Baron-Cohen, S., Ring, H., Moriarty, J., Schmitz, B., Costa, D., & Ell, P. (1994). Recognition of mental state terms: Clinical findings in children with autism and a functional neuroimaging study of normal adults. *British Journal of Psychiatry, 165,* 640–649.

Bartlett, T. Q., Sussman, R. W., & Cheverud, J. M. (1993). Infant killing in primates: A review of observed cases with specific reference to the sexual selection hypothesis. *American Anthropologist, 95,* 958–990.

Barton, R. A. (1996). Neocortex size and behavioural ecology in primates. *Proceedings of the Royal Society of London B, 263,* 173–177.

Barton, R. A., & Dean, P. (1993). Comparative evidence indicating neural specialization for predatory behaviour in mammals. *Proceedings of the Royal Society of London B, 254,* 63–68.

Barton, R. A., Purvis, A., & Harvey, P. H. (1995). Evolutionary radiation of visual and olfactory systems in primates, bats and insectivores. *Philosophical Transactions of the Royal Society of London B, 348,* 381–392.

Bateman, A. J. (1948). Intra-sexual selection in *drosophila. Heredity, 2,* 349–368.

Baumeister, R. F., & Leary, M. R. (1995). The need to belong: Desire for interpersonal attachments as a fundamental human motivation. *Psychological Bulletin, 117,* 497–529.

Baumeister, R. F., & Sommer, K. L. (1997). What do men want? Gender differences in two spheres of belongingness: Comment on Cross and Madson (1997). *Psychological Bulletin, 122,* 38–44.

Beck, G., & Habicht, G. S. (1996, November). Immunity and the invertebrates. *Scientific American, 275,* 60–66.

Beck, S. P., Ward-Hull, C. I., & McClear, P. M. (1976). Variables related to women's somatic preferences of the male and female body. *Journal of Personality and Social Psychology, 34,* 1200–1210.

Bell, G., & Maynard Smith, J. (1987). Short-term selection for recombination among mutually antagonistic species. *Nature, 328,* 66–68.

Bellis, M. A., & Baker, R. R. (1990). Do females promote sperm competition? Data for humans. *Animal Behaviour, 40,* 997–999.

Belsky, J. (1993). Etiology of child maltreatment: A developmental–ecological analysis. *Psychological Bulletin, 114,* 413–434.

Belsky, J. (1997). Attachment, mating, and parenting: An evolutionary interpretation. *Human Nature, 8,* 361–381.

Belsky, J., Gilstrap, B., & Rovine, M. (1984). The Pennsylvania infant and family development project. I: Stability and change in mother–infant and father–infant interaction in a family setting at one, three, and nine months. *Child Development, 55,* 692–705.

Belsky, J., Rovine, M., & Fish, M. (1989). The developing family system. In M. R. Gunnar & E. Thelen (Eds.), *Systems and development: The Minnesota Symposia on Child Psychology* (Vol. 22, pp. 119–166). Hillsdale, NJ: Erlbaum.

Belsky, J., Steinberg, L., & Draper, P. (1991). Childhood experience, interpersonal development, and reproductive strategy: An evolutionary theory of socialization. *Child Development, 62,* 647–670.

Benbow, C. P. (1988). Sex differences in mathematical-reasoning ability in intellectually talented preadolescents: Their nature, effects, and possible causes. *Behavioral and Brain Sciences, 11,* 169–232.

Benbow, C. P., & Stanley, J. C. (1980). Sex differences in mathematical ability: Fact or artifact? *Science, 210,* 1262–1264.

Benbow, C. P., & Stanley, J. C. (1983). Sex differences in mathematical reasoning ability: More facts. *Science, 222,* 1029–1031.

Benfer, R. A., & McKern, T. W. (1966). The correlation of bone robusticity with the perforation of the coronoid-olecranon septum in the humerus of man. *American Journal of Physical Anthropology, 24,* 247–252.

Berard, J. D., Nürnberg, P., Epplen, J. T., & Schmidtke, J. (1993). Male rank, reproductive behavior, and reproductive success in free-ranging rhesus macaques. *Primates, 34,* 481–489.

Bercovitch, F. B. (1986). Male rank and reproductive activity in savanna baboons. *International Journal of Primatology, 7,* 533–550.

Bercovitch, F. B., & Nuernberg, P. (1996). Socioendocrine and morphological correlates of paternity in rhesus macaques (*Macaca mulatta*). *Journal of Reproduction and Fertility, 107,* 59–68.

Bereczkei, T., & Csanaky, A. (1996). Mate choice, marital success, and reproduction in a modern society. *Ethology and Sociobiology, 17,* 17–35.

Berenbaum, S. A., & Hines, M. (1992). Early androgens are related to childhood sex-typed toy preferences. *Psychological Science, 3,* 203–206.

Berenbaum, S. A., Korman, K., & Leveroni, C. (1995). Early hormones and sex differences in cognitive abilities. *Learning and Individual Differences, 7,* 303–321.

Berenbaum, S. A., & Snyder, E. (1995). Early hormonal influences on childhood sex-typed activity and playmate preferences: Implications for the development of sexual orientation. *Developmental Psychology, 31,* 31–42.

Berkley, K. J. (1997). Sex differences in pain. *Behavioral and Brain Sciences, 20,* 371–380.

Berlin, B., Boster, J. S., & O'Neill, J. P. (1981). The perceptual bases of ethnobiological classification: Evidence from Aguaruna Jívaro ornithology. *Journal of Ethnobiology, 1,* 95–108.

Berlin, B., Breedlove, D. E., & Raven, P. H. (1966). Folk taxonomies and biological classification. *Science, 154,* 273–275.

Berlin, B., Breedlove, D. E., & Raven, P. H. (1973). General principles of classification and nomenclature in folk biology. *American Anthropologist, 75,* 214–242.

Berman, K. F., Schmidt, P. J., Rubinow, D. R., Danaceau, M. A., Van Horn, J. D., Esposito, G., Ostrem, J. L., & Weinberger, D. R. (1997). Modulation of cognition-specific cortical activity by gonadal steroids: A positron–emission tomography study in women. *Proceedings of the National Academy of Sciences, USA, 94,* 8836–8841.

Berman, P. W. (1980). Are women more responsive than men to the young? A review of developmental and situational variables. *Psychological Bulletin, 88,* 668–695.

Berman, P. W. (1986). Young children's responses to babies: Do they foreshadow differences between maternal and paternal styles? In A. Fogel & G. F. Melson (Eds.), *Origins of nurturance: Developmental, biological, and cultural perspectives on caregiving* (pp. 25–51). Hillsdale, NJ: Erlbaum.

Berman, P. W., Monda, L. C., & Myerscough, R. P. (1977). Sex differences in young children's responses to an infant: An observation within a day-care setting. *Child Development, 48,* 711–715.

Bermúdez de Castro, J. M., Arsuaga, J. L., Carbonell, E., Rosas, A., Martinez, I., & Mosquera, M. (1997). A hominid from the lower pleistocene of Atapuerca, Spain: Possible ancestor to Neanderthals and modern humans. *Science, 276,* 1392–1395.

Bernstein, H., Hopf, F. A., & Michod, R. E. (1989). The evolution of sex: DNA repair hypothesis. In A. E. Rasa, C. Vogel, & E. Voland (Eds.), *The sociobiology of sexual and reproductive strategies* (pp. 3–18). London: Chapman & Hall.

Best, D. L., & Williams, J. E. (1993). A cross-cultural viewpoint. In A. E. Beall & R. J. Sternberg (Eds.), *The psychology of gender* (pp. 215–248). New York: Guilford Press.

Bettencourt, B. A., & Miller, N. (1996). Gender differences in aggression as a function of provocation: A meta-analysis. *Psychological Bulletin, 119,* 422–447.

Betzig, L. L. (1986). *Despotism and differential reproduction: A Darwinian view of history.* New York: Aldine de Gruyter.

Betzig, L. (1989). Causes of conjugal dissolution: A cross-cultural study. *Current Anthropology, 30,* 654–676.

Betzig, L. (1992). Roman polygyny. *Ethology and Sociobiology, 13,* 309–349.

Betzig, L. (1993). Sex, succession, and stratification in the first six civilizations: How powerful men reproduced, passed power on to their sons, and used power to defend their wealth, women, and children. In L. Ellis (Ed.), *Social stratification and socioeconomic inequality, Vol. 1: A comparative biosocial analysis* (pp. 37–74). Westport, CT: Praeger.

Betzig, L. (1995). Medieval monogamy. *Journal of Family History, 20,* 181–216.

Betzig, L. (1997). Introduction: People are animals. In L. Betzig (Ed.), *Human nature: A critical reader* (pp. 1–17). New York: Oxford University Press.

Betzig, L., & Turke, P. (1992). Fatherhood by rank on Ifaluk. In B. S. Hewlett (Ed.), *Father–child relations: Cultural and biosocial contexts* (pp. 111–129). New York: Aldine de Gruyter.

Bever, T. (1992). The logical and extrinsic sources of modularity. In M. R. Gunnar & M. Maratsos (Eds.), *Modularity and constraints in language and cognition: The Minnesota Symposia on Child Psychology* (Vol. 25, pp. 179–212). Hillsdale, NJ: Erlbaum.

Birkhead, T. R., & Møller, A. P. (1996). Monogamy and sperm competition in birds. In J. M. Black (Ed.), *Partnerships in birds: The study of monogamy* (pp. 323–343). New York: Oxford University Press.

Bishop, K. M., & Wahlsten, D. (1997). Sex differences in the human corpus callosum: Myth or reality? *Neuroscience and Biobehavioral Reviews, 21,* 581–601.

Bjorklund, D. F. (1997). The role of immaturity in human development. *Psychological Bulletin, 122,* 153–169.

Bjorklund, D. F., & Harnishfeger, K. K. (1995). The evolution of inhibition mechanisms and their role in human cognition and behavior. In F. N. Dempster & C. J. Brainerd (Eds.), *New perspectives on interference and inhibition in cognition* (pp. 141–173). New York: Academic Press.

Bjorklund, D. F., & Kipp, K. (1996). Parental investment theory and gender differences in the evolution of inhibition mechanisms. *Psychological Bulletin, 120,* 163–188.

Björkqvist, K., Lagerspetz, K. M. J., & Kaukiainen, A. (1992). Do girls manipulate and boys fight? Developmental trends in regard to direct and indirect aggression. *Aggressive Behavior, 18,* 117–127.

Björkqvist, K., Osterman, K., & Lagerspetz, K. M. J. (1994). Sex differences in covert aggression among adults. *Aggressive Behavior, 20,* 27–34.

Black, J. M. (Ed.). (1996). *Partnerships in birds: The study of monogamy*. New York: Oxford University Press.

Block, J. (1993). Studying personality the long way. In D. C. Funder, R. D. Parke, C. Tomlinson-Keasey, & K. Widaman (Eds.), *Studying lives through time: Personality and development* (pp. 9–41). Washington, DC: American Psychological Association.

Block, J. H. (1976). Issues, problems, and pitfalls in assessing sex differences: A critical review of *The psychology of sex differences*. *Merrill-Palmer Quarterly, 22*, 283–308.

Block, R. A., Arnott, D. P., Quigley, B., & Lynch, W. C. (1989). Unilateral nostril breathing influences lateralized cognitive performance. *Brain and Cognition, 9*, 181–190.

Blurton Jones, N. G., Hawkes, K., & O'Connell, J. F. (1997). Why do Hadza children forage? In N. L. Segal, G. E. Weisfeld, & C. C. Weisfeld (Eds.), *Uniting psychology and biology: Integrative perspectives on human development* (pp. 279–313). Washington, DC: American Psychological Association.

Böer, M., & Sommer, V. (1992). Evidence for sexually selected infanticide in captive *Cercopithecus mitis, Cercocebus torquatus*, and *Mandrillus leucophaeus. Primates, 33*, 557–563.

Bonta, B. D. (1997). Cooperation and competition in peaceful societies. *Psychological Bulletin, 121*, 299–320.

Borgerhoff Mulder, M. (1988). Kipsigis bridewealth payments. In L. Betzig, M. Borgerhoff Mulder, & P. Turke (Eds.), *Human reproductive behaviour: A Darwinian perspective* (pp. 65–82). Cambridge, England: Cambridge University Press.

Borgerhoff Mulder, M. (1990). Kipsigis women's preferences for wealthy men: Evidence for female choice in mammals? *Behavioral Ecology and Sociobiology, 27*, 255–264.

Borgerhoff Mulder, M. (1997). Marrying a married man: A postscript. In L. Betzig (Ed.), *Human nature: A critical reader* (pp. 115–117). New York: Oxford University Press.

Borgia, G. (1985a). Bower destruction and sexual competition in the satin bower bird *(Ptilonorhynchus violaceus). Behavioral Ecology and Sociobiology, 18*, 91–100.

Borgia, G. (1985b). Bower quality, number of decorations and mating success of male satin bower birds *(Ptilonorhynchus violaceus)*: An experimental analysis. *Animal Behaviour, 33*, 266–271.

Borgia, G. (1986). Satin bowerbird parasites: A test of the bright male hypothesis. *Behavioral Ecology and Sociobiology, 19*, 355–358.

Borgia, G. (1995a). Complex male display and female choice in the spotted bowerbird: Specialized functions for different bower decorations. *Animal Behaviour, 49*, 1291–1301.

Borgia, G. (1995b). Threat reduction as a cause of differences in bower architecture, bower decoration and male display in two closely related bowerbirds *Chlamydera nuchalis* and *C. maculata. Emu, 95*, 1–12.

Borgia, G., & Collis, K. (1989). Female choice for parasite-free male satin bowerbirds and the evolution of bright male plumage. *Behavioral Ecology and Sociobiology, 25*, 445–454.

Borgia, G., Kaatz, I. M., & Condit, R. (1987). Flower choice and bower decoration in the satin bowerbird *Ptilonorhynchus violaceus*: A test of hypotheses for the evolution of male display. *Animal Behaviour, 35*, 1129–1139.

Borgia, G., & Mueller, U. (1992). Bower destruction, decoration stealing and female choice in the spotted bowerbird *Chlamydera maculata. Emu, 92*, 11–18.

Borgia, G., & Wingfield, J. C. (1991). Hormonal correlates of bower decoration and sexual display in the satin bowerbird *(Ptilonorhynchus violaceus). Condor, 93*, 935–942.

Bosacki, S. (1998). *Theory of mind in preadolescents: Relationships among social understanding, self-concept and social relations*. Unpublished doctoral dissertation, University of Toronto, Ontario, Canada.

Boster, J. S. (1985). "Requiem for the omniscient informant": There's life in the old girl yet. In J. W. D. Dougherty (Ed.), *Directions in cognitive anthropology* (pp. 177–197). Urbana: University of Illinois Press.

Bouchard, T. J., Jr., Lykken, D. T., McGue, M., Segal, N. L., & Tellegen, A. (1990). Sources of human psychological differences: The Minnesota study of twins reared apart. *Science, 250,* 223–228.

Boulton, M. J. (1996). A comparison of 8- and 11-year-old girls' and boys' participation in specific types of rough-and-tumble play and aggressive fighting: Implications for functional hypotheses. *Aggressive Behavior, 22,* 271–287.

Boulton, M. J., & Smith, P. K. (1992). The social nature of play fighting and play chasing: Mechanisms and strategies underlying cooperation and compromise. In J. H. Barkow, L. Cosmides, & J. Tooby (Eds.), *The adapted mind: Evolutionary psychology and the generation of culture* (pp. 429–444). New York: Oxford University Press.

Bower, T. G. R. (1982). *Development in infancy* (2nd ed.). San Francisco: Freeman.

Brace, C. L., & Ryan, A. S. (1980). Sexual dimorphism and human tooth size differences. *Journal of Human Evolution, 9,* 417–435.

Breedlove, S. M. (1994). Sexual differentiation of the human nervous system. *Annual Review of Psychology, 45,* 389–418.

Brodzinsky, D. M., Elias, M. J., Steiger, C., Simon, J., Gill, M., & Hitt, M. C. (1992). Coping scale for children and youth: Scale development and validation. *Journal of Applied Developmental Psychology, 13,* 195–214.

Bronfenbrenner, U. (1986). Ecology of the family as a context for human development: Research perspectives. *Developmental Psychology, 22,* 723–742.

Brothers, L., & Ring, B. (1992). A neuroethological framework for the representation of minds. *Journal of Cognitive Neuroscience, 4,* 107–118.

Brown, D. E. (1991). *Human universals.* Philadelphia: Temple University Press.

Brown, D. E., & Hotra, D. (1988). Are prescriptively monogamous societies effectively monogamous? In L. Betzig, M. Borgerhoff Mulder, & P. Turke (Eds.), *Human reproductive behavior: A Darwinian perspective* (pp. 153–159). New York: Cambridge University Press.

Browne, K. R. (1984). Biology, equality, and the law: The legal significance of biological sex differences. *Southwestern Law Journal, 38,* 617–702.

Browne, K. R. (1995). Sex and temperament in modern society: A Darwinian view of the glass ceiling and the gender gap. *Arizona Law Review, 37,* 971–1106.

Browne, K. R. (1997). An evolutionary perspective on sexual harassment: Seeking roots in biology rather than ideology. *Journal of Contemporary Legal Issues, 8,* 5–77.

Brunelli, S. A., Wasserman, G. A., Rauh, V. A., Alvarado, L. E., & Caraballo, L. R. (1995). Mothers' reports of paternal support: Associations with maternal child-rearing attitudes. *Merrill-Palmer Quarterly, 41,* 152–171.

Buchanan, C. M., Maccoby, E. E., & Dornbusch, S. M. (1992). Adolescents and their families after divorce: Three residential arrangements compared. *Journal of Research on Adolescence, 2,* 261–291.

Buck, R. W., Savin, V. J., Miller, R. E., & Caul, W. F. (1972). Communication of affect through facial expression in humans. *Journal of Personality and Social Psychology, 23,* 362–371.

Buckle, L., Gallup, G. G., Jr., & Rodd, Z. A. (1996). Marriage as a reproductive contract: Patterns of marriage, divorce, and remarriage. *Ethology and Sociobiology, 17,* 363–377.

Bugos, P. E., & McCarthy, L. M. (1984). Ayoreo infanticide: A case study. In G. Hausfater & S. B. Hrdy (Eds.), *Infanticide: Comparative and evolutionary perspectives* (pp. 503–520). New York: Aldine de Gruyter.

Bulmer, M. (1994). *Theoretical evolutionary ecology.* Sunderland, MA: Sinauer.

Buss, D. M. (1988). From vigilance to violence: Tactics of mate retention in American undergraduates. *Ethology and Sociobiology, 9,* 291–317.

Buss, D. M. (1989a). Conflict between the sexes: Strategic interference and the evocation of anger and upset. *Journal of Personality and Social Psychology, 56,* 735–747.

Buss, D. M. (1989b). Sex differences in human mate preferences: Evolutionary hypothesis tested in 37 cultures. *Behavioral and Brain Sciences, 12,* 1–49.

Buss, D. M. (1991). Evolutionary personality psychology. *Annual Review of Psychology, 42,* 459–491.

Buss, D. M. (1994). *The evolution of desire: Strategies of human mating.* New York: Basic Books.

Buss, D. M. (1996). The evolutionary psychology of human social strategies. In E. T. Higgins & A. E. Kruglanski (Eds.), *Social psychology: Handbook of basic principles* (pp. 3–38). New York: Guilford Press.

Buss, D. M., Haselton, M. G., Shackelford, T. K., Bleske, A. L., & Wakefield, J. C. (1998). Adaptations, exaptations, and spandrels. *American Psychologist, 53,* 533–548.

Buss, D. M., Larsen, R. J., & Westen, D. (1996). Sex differences in jealousy: Not gone, not forgotten, and not explained by alternative hypotheses. *Psychological Science, 7,* 373–377.

Buss, D. M., Larsen, R. J., Westen, D., & Semmelroth, J. (1992). Sex differences in jealousy: Evolution, physiology, and psychology. *Psychological Science, 3,* 251–255.

Buss, D. M., & Schmitt, D. P. (1993). Sexual strategies theory: An evolutionary perspective on human mating. *Psychological Review, 100,* 204–232.

Buss, D. M., & Shackelford, T. K. (1997). From vigilance to violence: Mate retention tactics in married couples. *Journal of Personality and Social Psychology, 72,* 346–361.

Byers, J. A., & Walker, C. (1995). Refining the motor training hypothesis for the evolution of play. *American Naturalist, 146,* 25–40.

Bygott, J. D. (1979). Agnostic behavior, dominance, and social structure in wild chimpanzees of the Gombe National Park. In D. A. Hamburg & E. R McCown (Eds.), *The great apes* (pp. 405–427). Menlo Park, CA: Benjamin/Cummings Publishing Co.

Byrne, R. (1995). *The thinking ape: Evolutionary origins of intelligence.* New York: Oxford University Press.

Cabeza, R., & Nyberg, L. (1997). Imaging cognition: An empirical review of PET studies with normal subjects. *Journal of Cognitive Neuroscience, 9,* 1–26.

Campbell, A. (1995). A few good men: Evolutionary psychology and female adolescent aggression. *Ethology and Sociobiology, 16,* 99–123.

Campbell, A. (in press). Staying alive: Evolution, culture and women's intra-sexual aggression. *Behavioral and Brain Sciences.*

Campos, J. J., Campos, R. G., & Barrett, K. C. (1989). Emergent themes in the study of emotional development and emotion regulation. *Developmental Psychology, 25,* 394–402.

Caplan, P. J., MacPherson, G. M., & Tobin, P. (1985). Do sex-related differences in spatial abilities exist? A multilevel critique with new data. *American Psychologist, 40,* 786–799.

Carey, S., & Spelke, E. (1994). Domain-specific knowledge and conceptual change. In L. A. Hirschfeld & S. A. Gelman (Eds.), *Mapping the mind: Domain specificity in cognition and culture* (pp. 169–200). New York: Cambridge University Press.

Carlo, G., Koller, S. H., Eisenberg, N., Da Silva, M. S., & Frohlich, C. B. (1996). A cross-national study on the relations among prosocial moral reasoning, gender role orientations, and prosocial behaviors. *Developmental Psychology, 32,* 231–240.

Carranza, J. (1996). Sexual selection for male body mass and the evolution of litter size in mammals. *American Naturalist, 148,* 81–100.

Carroll, L. (1871). *Through the looking-glass and what Alice found there.* London: Macmillan.

Carson, J., Burks, V., & Parke, R. D. (1993). Parent–child physical play: Determinants and consequences. In K. MacDonald (Ed.), *Parent–child play: Descriptions & implications* (pp. 197–220). Albany: State University of New York Press.

Carter, C. S., & Getz, L. L. (1993, June). Monogamy and the prairie vole. *Scientific American, 268*, 100–106.

Casey, M. B., & Brabeck, M. M. (1989). Exceptions to the male advantage on a spatial task: Family handedness and college major as factors identifying women who excel. *Neuropsychologia, 27*, 689–696.

Casey, M. B., Colón, D., & Goris, Y. (1992). Family handedness as a predictor of mental rotation ability among minority girls in a math–science training program. *Brain and Cognition, 18*, 88–96.

Casey, M. B., Nuttall, R. L., & Pezaris, E. (1997). Mediators of gender differences in mathematics college entrance test scores: A comparison of spatial skills with internalized beliefs and anxieties. *Developmental Psychology, 33*, 669–680.

Casey, M. B., Nuttall, R., Pezaris, E., & Benbow, C. P. (1995). The influence of spatial ability on gender differences in mathematics college entrance test scores across diverse samples. *Developmental Psychology, 31*, 697–705.

Cashdan, E. (1993). Attracting mates: Effects of paternal investment on mate attraction strategies. *Ethology and Sociobiology, 14*, 1–24.

Casimir, M. J., & Rao, A. (1995). Prestige, possessions, and progeny: Cultural goals and reproductive success among the Bakkarwal. *Human Nature, 6*, 241–272.

Causey, D. L., & Dubow, E. F. (1992). Development of a self-report coping measure for elementary school children. *Journal of Clinical Child Psychology, 21*, 47–59.

Ceci, S. J., & Williams, W. M. (1997). Schooling, intelligence, and income. *American Psychologist, 52*, 1051–1058.

Chagnon, N. A. (1974). *Studying the Yanomamö.* New York: Holt, Rinehart & Winston.

Chagnon, N. A. (1977). *Yanomamö, the fierce people.* New York: Holt, Rinehart & Winston.

Chagnon, N. A. (1979). Is reproductive success equal in egalitarian societies? In N. A. Chagnon & W. Irons (Eds.), *Evolutionary biology and human social behavior: An anthropological perspective* (pp. 374–401). North Scituate, MA: Duxbury Press.

Chagnon, N. A. (1988). Life histories, blood revenge, and warfare in a tribal population. *Science, 239*, 985–992.

Charlesworth, B. (1993). The evolution of sex and recombination in a varying environment. *Journal of Heredity, 84*, 345–350.

Charlesworth, W. R., & Dzur, C. (1987). Gender comparisons of preschoolers' behavior and resource utilization in group problem-solving. *Child Development, 58*, 191–200.

Charlesworth, W. R., & LaFrenier, P. (1983). Dominance, friendship utilization and resource utilization in preschool children's groups. *Ethology and Sociobiology, 4*, 175–186.

Cherlin, A. J., Furstenberg, F. F., Jr., Chase-Lansdale, P. L., Kiernan, K. E., Robins, P. K., Morrison, D. R., & Teitler, J. O. (1991). Longitudinal studies of effects of divorce on children in Great Britain and the United States. *Science, 252*, 1386–1389.

Cherry, M. I. (1993). Sexual selection in the raucous toad, *Bufo rangeri. Animal Behaviour, 45*, 359–373.

Choi, J., & Silverman, I. (1996). Sexual dimorphism in spatial behaviors: Applications to route learning. *Evolution and Cognition, 2*, 165–171.

Choudhury, S., & Black, J. M. (1993). Mate-selection behaviour and sampling strategies in geese. *Animal Behaviour, 46*, 747–757.

Christensen, A., & Heavey, C. L. (1990). Gender and social structure in the demand/ withdraw pattern of marital conflict. *Journal of Personality and Social Psychology, 59*, 73–81.

Christie, J. F., & Johnsen, E. P. (1987). Reconceptualizing constructive play: A review of the empirical literature. *Merrill-Palmer Quarterly, 33*, 439–452.

Cicchetti, D., & Toth, S. L. (1998). The development of depression in children and adolescents. *American Psychologist, 53,* 221–241.

Clement, D. (1995). Why is taxonomy utilitarian? *Ethnobiology, 15,* 1–44.

Clinton, W. L., & Le Boeuf, B. J. (1993). Sexual selection's effects on male life history and the pattern of male mortality. *Ecology, 74,* 1884–1892.

Clutton-Brock, T. H. (1988). Reproductive success. In T. H. Clutton-Brock (Ed.), *Reproductive success: Studies of individual variation in contrasting breeding systems* (pp. 472–485). Chicago: University of Chicago Press.

Clutton-Brock, T. H. (1989). Mammalian mating systems. *Proceedings of the Royal Society of London B, 236,* 339–372.

Clutton-Brock, T. H. (1991). *The evolution of parental care.* Princeton, NJ: Princeton University Press.

Clutton-Brock, T. H., Albon, S. D., & Guinness, F. E. (1981). Parental investment in male and female offspring in polygynous mammals. *Nature, 289,* 487–489.

Clutton-Brock, T. H., Albon, S. D., & Guinness, F. E. (1985). Parental investment and sex differences in juvenile mortality in birds and mammals. *Nature, 313,* 131–133.

Clutton-Brock, T. H., Albon, S. D., & Guinness, F. E. (1988). Reproductive success in male and female red deer. In T. H. Clutton-Brock (Ed.), *Reproductive success: Studies of individual variation in contrasting breeding systems* (pp. 325–343). Chicago: University of Chicago Press.

Clutton-Brock, T. H., Harvey, P. H., & Rudder, B. (1977). Sexual dimorphism, socionomic sex ratio and body weight in primates. *Nature, 269,* 797–800.

Clutton-Brock, T., & McComb, K. (1993). Experimental tests of copying and mate choice in fallow deer (*Dama dama*). *Behavioral Ecology, 4,* 191–193.

Clutton-Brock, T. H., & Vincent, A. C. J. (1991). Sexual selection and the potential reproductive rates of males and females. *Science, 351,* 58–60.

Coe, C. L., Mendoza, S. P., & Levine, S. (1979). Social status constrains the stress response in the squirrel monkey. *Physiology and Behavior, 23,* 633–638.

Cohen, L. B., & Gelber, E. R. (1975). Infant visual memory. In L. B. Cohen & P. Salapatek (Eds.), *Infant perception: From sensation to cognition* (pp. 347–403). New York: Academic Press.

Coley, J. D. (1995). Emerging differentiation of folkbiology and folkpsychology: Attributions of biological and psychological properties of living things. *Child Development, 66,* 1856–1874.

Collaer, M. L., & Hines, M. (1995). Human behavioral sex differences: A role for gonadal hormones during early development? *Psychological Bulletin, 118,* 55–107.

Collins, D. W., & Kimura, D. (1997). A large sex difference on a two-dimensional mental rotation task. *Behavioral Neuroscience, 111,* 845–849.

Collis, K., & Borgia, G. (1992). Age-related effects of testosterone, plumage, and experience on aggression and social dominance in juvenile male satin bowerbirds (*Ptilonorhynchus violaceus*). *Auk, 109,* 422–434.

Colmenares, F. (1992). Clans and harems in a colony of hamadryas and hybrid baboons: Male kinship, familiarity and the formation of brother-teams. *Behaviour, 121,* 61–94.

Conroy, G. C., & Kuykendall, K. (1995). Paleopediatrics: Or when did human infants really become human? *American Journal of Physical Anthropology, 98,* 121–131.

Corballis, M. C., & Morgan, M. J. (1978). On the biological basis of human laterality: I. Evidence for a maturational left–right gradient. *Behavioral and Brain Sciences, 2,* 261–336.

Corter, C. M., & Fleming, A. S. (1995). Psychobiology of maternal behavior in human beings. In M. H. Bornstein (Ed.), *Handbook of parenting, Vol. 2: Biology and ecology of parenting* (pp. 87–116). Hillsdale, NJ: Erlbaum.

Cosmides, L. (1989). The logic of social exchange: Has natural selection shaped how humans reason? Studies with the Wason selection task. *Cognition, 31,* 187–276.

Cosmides, L., & Tooby, J. (1994). Origins of domain specificity: The evolution of functional organization. In L. A. Hirschfeld & S. A. Gelman (Eds.), *Mapping the mind: Domain specificity in cognition and culture* (pp. 85–116). New York: Cambridge University Press.

Cowell, P. E., Turetsky, B. I., Gur, R. C., Grossman, R. I., Shtasel, D. L., & Gur, R. E. (1994). Sex differences in aging of the human frontal and temporal lobes. *Journal of Neuroscience, 14,* 4748–4755.

Cowlishaw, G., & Dunbar, R. I. M. (1991). Dominance rank and mating success in male primates. *Animal Behaviour, 41,* 1045–1056.

Cox, C. R., & Le Boeuf, B. J. (1977). Female incitation of male competition: A mechanism of sexual selection. *American Naturalist, 111,* 317–335.

Cox, M. J., Owen, M. T., Lewis, J. M., & Henderson, V. K. (1989). Marriage, adult adjustment, and early parenting. *Child Development, 60,* 1015–1024.

Crano, W. D., & Aronoff, J. (1978). A cross-cultural study of expressive and instrumental role complementarity in the family. *American Sociological Review, 43,* 463–471.

Crick, N. R., & Bigbee, M. A. (1998). Relational and overt forms of peer victimization: A multiinformant approach. *Journal of Consulting and Clinical Psychology, 66,* 337–347.

Crick, N. R., Casas, J. F., & Mosher, M. (1997). Relational and overt aggression in preschool. *Developmental Psychology, 33,* 579–588.

Crick, N. R., & Dodge, K. A. (1994). A review and reformulation of social information-processing mechanisms in children's social adjustment. *Psychological Bulletin, 115,* 74–101.

Crick, N. R., & Wellman, N. E. (1997, April). *Social information-processing mechanisms in relational and overt aggression.* Paper presented at the biennial meeting of the Society for Research in Child Development, Washington, DC.

Crites, S. L., & Cacioppo, J. T. (1996). Electrocortical differentiation of evaluative and nonevaluative categorizations. *Psychological Science, 7,* 318–321.

Cronin, H. (1991). *The ant and the peacock.* New York: Cambridge University Press.

Cross, S. E., & Madson, L. (1997). Models of the self: Self-construals and gender. *Psychological Bulletin, 122,* 5–37.

Crow, J. F. (1997). The high spontaneous mutation rate: Is it a health risk? *Proceedings of the National Academy of Sciences, USA, 94,* 8380–8386.

Culin, S. (1902/1903). *Games of the North American Indians.* Washington, DC: Bureau of American Ethnology.

Cunningham, M. R. (1986). Measuring the physical in physical attractiveness: Quasi-experiments on the sociobiology of female beauty. *Journal of Personality and Social Psychology, 50,* 925–935.

Cunningham, M. R., Barbee, A. P., & Pike, C. L. (1990). What do women want? Facialmetric assessment of multiple motives in the perception of male facial physical attractiveness. *Journal of Personality and Social Psychology, 59,* 61–72.

Dabbs, J. M., Jr., Chang, E.-L., Strong, R. A., & Milun, R. (1998). Spatial ability, navigation strategy, and geographic knowledge among men and women. *Evolution and Human Behavior, 19,* 89–98.

Daly, M. (1996). Evolutionary adaptation: Another biological approach to criminal and antisocial behaviour. In G. R. Bock & J. A. Goode (Eds.), *Genetics of criminal and antisocial behavior* (pp. 183–191). New York: Wiley.

Daly, M., & Wilson, M. (1981). Abuse and neglect of children in evolutionary perspective. In R. D. Alexander & D. W. Tinkle (Eds.), *Natural selection and social behavior* (pp. 405–416). New York: Chiron Press.

Daly, M., & Wilson, M. (1983). *Sex, evolution and behavior* (2nd ed.). Boston: Willard Grant.

Daly, M., & Wilson, M. (1985). Child abuse and other risks of not living with both parents. *Ethology and Sociobiology, 6*, 155–176.

Daly, M., & Wilson, M. (1988a). *Homicide*. New York: Aldine de Gruyter.

Daly, M., & Wilson, M. (1988b). Evolutionary social psychology and family homicide. *Science, 242*, 519–524.

Daly, M., & Wilson, M. (1990). Killing the competition: Female/female and male/male homicide. *Human Nature, 1*, 81–107.

Daly, M., & Wilson, M. (1995). Discriminative parental solicitude and the relevance of evolutionary models to the analysis of motivational systems. In M. S. Gazzaniga (Ed.), *The cognitive neurosciences* (pp. 1269–1286). Cambridge, MA: Bradford Books/MIT Press.

Daly, M., Wilson, M., & Weghorst, S. J. (1982). Male sexual jealousy. *Ethology and Sociobiology, 3*, 11–27.

Darwin, C. (1859). *On the origins of species by means of natural selection*. London: John Murray.

Darwin, C. (1871). *The descent of man, and selection in relation to sex*. London: John Murray.

Darwin, C. (1872). *The expression of emotions in man and animals*. London: John Murray.

Davies, P. T., & Cummings, E. M. (1994). Marital conflict and child adjustment: An emotional security hypothesis. *Psychological Bulletin, 116*, 387–411.

Davis, L. E., Cheng, L. C., & Strube, M. J. (1996). Differential effects of racial composition on male and female groups: Implications for group work practice. *Social Work Research, 20*, 157–166.

Davis, M., & Emory, E. (1995). Sex differences in neonatal stress reactivity. *Child Development, 66*, 14–27.

Dawkins, R. (1989). *The selfish gene* (2nd ed.). New York: Oxford University Press.

Dawkins, R., & Krebs, J. R. (1979). Arms races between and within species. *Proceedings of the Royal Society of London B, 205*, 489–511.

Day, M. H. (1994). The origin and evolution of man. In E. E. Bitter & N. Bittar (Eds.), *Evolutionary biology* (pp. 321–351). Greenwich, CT: JAI Press.

Day, T., & Taylor, P. D. (1997). Hamilton's rule meets the Hamiltonian: Kin selection on dynamic characteristics. *Proceedings of the Royal Society of London B, 264*, 639–644.

Deater-Deckard, K., Scarr, S., McCartney, K., & Eisenberg, M. (1994). Paternal separation anxiety: Relationships with parenting stress, child-rearing attitudes, and maternal anxieties. *Psychological Science, 5*, 341–346.

de Lacoste-Utamsing, C., & Holloway, R. L. (1982). Sexual dimorphism in the human corpus callosum. *Science, 216*, 1431–1432.

Delgado, A. R., & Prieto, G. (1997). Mental rotation as a mediator for sex-differences in visualization. *Intelligence, 24*, 405–416.

Delson, E. (Ed.). (1985). *Ancestors: The hard evidence*. New York: Alan R. Liss.

Dennett, D. C. (1995). *Darwin's dangerous idea: Evolution and the meaning of life*. New York: Touchstone.

de Ruiter, J. R., & Inoue, M. (1993). Paternity, male social rank, and sexual behavior. *Primates, 34*, 553–555.

de Ruiter, J. R., & van Hooff, J. A. R. A. M. (1993). Male dominance rank and reproductive success in primate groups. *Primates, 34*, 513–523.

de Ruiter, J. R., van Hooff, J. A. R. A. M., & Scheffrahn, W. (1994). Social and genetic aspects of paternity in wild long-tailed macaques (*Macaca fascicularis*). *Behaviour, 129*, 203–224.

DeSteno, D. A., & Salovey, P. (1996). Evolutionary origins of sex differences in jealousy? Questioning the fitness of the model. *Psychological Science, 7*, 367–372.

de Vlaming, V. L. (1979). Actions of prolactin among the vertebrates. In E. J. W. Barrington (Ed.), *Hormones and evolution* (pp. 561–642). New York: Academic Press.

DeVoogd, T. J. (1991). Endocrine modulation of the development and adult function of the avian song system. *Psychoneuroendocrinology, 16*, 41–66.

de Waal, F. B. M. (1982). *Chimpanzee politics: Power and sex among apes*. New York: Harper & Row.

de Waal, F. (1989). *Peacemaking among primates*. Cambridge, MA: Harvard University Press.

de Waal, F. B. M. (1993). Sex differences in chimpanzee (and human) behavior: A matter of social values? In M. Hechter, L. Nadel, & R. E. Michod (Eds.), *The origin of values* (pp. 285–303). New York: Aldine de Gruyter.

de Waal, F. B. M. (1996). Macaque social culture: Development and perpetuation of affiliative networks. *Journal of Comparative Psychology, 110*, 147–154.

de Waal, F., & Lanting, F. (1997). *Bonobo: The forgotten ape*. Berkeley: University of California Press.

Diamond, J. (1992). *The third chimpanzee: The evolution and future of the human animal*. New York: HarperPerennial.

Diamond, J. M. (1966). Zoological classification system of a primitive people. *Science, 151*, 1102–1104.

Diamond, M. C. (1991). Hormonal effects on the development of cerebral lateralization. *Psychoneuroendocrinology, 16*, 121–129.

Diamond, M. C., Johnson, R. E., Young, D., & Singh, S. S. (1983). Age-related morphologic differences in the rat cerebral cortex and hippocampus: Male–female; right–left. *Experimental Neurology, 81*, 1–13.

Diamond, R., Carey, S., & Back, K. J. (1983). Genetic influences on the development of spatial skills during early adolescence. *Cognition, 13*, 167–185.

Dickemann, M. (1981). Paternal confidence and dowry competition: A biocultural analysis of purdah. In R. D. Alexander & D. W. Tinkle (Eds.), *Natural selection and social behavior* (pp. 417–438). New York: Chiron Press.

Diener, E., & Diener, C. (1996). Most people are happy. *Psychological Science, 7*, 181–185.

Diener, E., Sandvik, E., & Larsen, R. J. (1985). Age and sex effects for emotional intensity. *Developmental Psychology, 21*, 542–546.

Dimberg, U., & Öhman, A. (1996). Behold the wrath—Psychophysiological responses to facial stimuli. *Motivation & Emotion, 20*, 149–182.

DiPietro, J. A. (1981). Rough and tumble play: A function of gender. *Developmental Psychology, 17*, 50–58.

Dixson, A. F. (1993). Sexual selection, sperm competition and the evolution of sperm length. *Folia Primatologica, 61*, 221–227.

Dixson, A. F., Bossi, T., & Wickings, E. J. (1993). Male dominance and genetically determined reproductive success in the mandrill (*Mandrillus sphinx*). *Primates, 34*, 525–532.

Dorans, N. J., & Livingston, S. A. (1987). Male–female differences in SAT-verbal ability among students of high SAT-mathematical ability. *Journal of Educational Measurement, 24*, 65–71.

Draper, P. (1989). African marriage systems: Perspectives from evolutionary ecology. *Ethology and Sociobiology, 10*, 145–169.

Draper, P., & Harpending, H. (1988). A sociobiological perspective on the development of human reproductive strategies. In K. B. MacDonald (Ed.), *Sociobiological perspectives on human development* (pp. 340–372). New York: Springer-Verlag.

Dugatkin, L. A. (1992). Sexual selection and imitation: Females copy of the mate choice of others. *American Naturalist, 139*, 1384–1389.

Dugatkin, L. A. (1996). Interface between culturally based preferences and genetic preferences: Female mate choice in *Poecilia reticulata*. *Proceedings of the National Academy of Sciences, USA, 93*, 2770–2773.

Dugatkin, L. A., & Godin, J.-G. J. (1992). Reversal of female mate choice by copying in the guppy (*Poecilia reticulata*). *Proceedings of the Royal Society of London B, 249,* 179–184.

Dugatkin, L. A., & Godin, J.-G. J. (1993). Female mate copying in the guppy (*Poecilia reticulata*): Age-dependent effects. *Behavioral Ecology, 4,* 289–292.

Dunbar, R. I. M. (1984). *Reproductive decisions: An economic analysis of gelada baboon social strategies.* Princeton, NJ: Princeton University Press.

Dunbar, R. I. M. (1986). The social ecology of the gelada baboons. In D. I. Rubenstein & R. W. Wrangham (Eds.), *Ecological aspects of social evolution: Birds and mammals* (pp. 332–351). Princeton, NJ: Princeton University Press.

Dunbar, R. I. M. (1993). Coevolution of neocortical size, group size and language in humans. *Behavioral and Brain Sciences, 16,* 681–735.

Dunne, M. P., Martin, N. G., Statham, D. J., Slutske, W. S., Dinwiddie, S. H., Bucholz, K. K., Madden, P. A. F., & Heath, A. C. (1997). Genetic and environmental contributions to variance in age at first sexual intercourse. *Psychological Science, 8,* 211–216.

Dweck, C. S., & Leggett, E. L. (1988). A social–cognitive approach to motivation and personality. *Psychological Review, 95,* 256–273.

Eagly, A. H. (1987). *Sex differences in social behavior: A social-role interpretation.* Hillsdale, NJ: Erlbaum.

Eagly, A. H. (1995). The science and politics of comparing women and men. *American Psychologist, 50,* 145–158.

Eagly, A. H., & Steffen, V. J. (1986). Gender and aggressive behavior: A meta-analytic review of the social psychological literature. *Psychological Bulletin, 100,* 309–330.

Eagly, A. H., & Wood, W. (1991). Explaining sex differences in social behavior: A meta-analytic perspective. *Personality and Social Psychology Bulletin, 17,* 306–315.

Eals, M., & Silverman, I. (1994). The hunter–gatherer theory of spatial sex differences: Proximate factors mediating the female advantage in recall of object arrays. *Ethology and Sociobiology, 15,* 95–105.

Eaton, W. O., & Enns, L. R. (1986). Sex differences in human motor activity level. *Psychological Bulletin, 100,* 19–28.

Eaton, W. O., & Yu, A. P. (1989). Are sex differences in child motor activity level a function of sex differences in maturational status? *Child Development, 60,* 1005–1011.

Edwards, C. P., & Whiting, B. B. (1993). "Mother, older sibling and me": The overlapping roles of caregivers and companions in the social world of two- to three-year-olds in Ngeca, Kenya. In K. MacDonald (Ed.), *Parent–child play: Descriptions & implications* (pp. 305–329). Albany: State University of New York Press.

Eibl-Eibesfeldt, I. (1989). *Human ethology.* New York: Aldine de Gruyter.

Eibel-Eibesfeldt, I. (1995). *Die Biologie des menschlichen Verhaltens: Grundriß der Humanethologie* [The biology of human behavior: An architecture of human ethology] (3rd ed.). Munich, Germany: Piper.

Eisenberg, N., & Lennon, R. (1983). Sex differences in empathy and related capacities. *Psychological Bulletin, 94,* 100–131.

Ekman, P. (1992). Facial expressions of emotion: New findings, new questions. *Psychological Science, 3,* 34–38.

Ellis, B. J., & Symons, D. (1990). Sex differences in sexual fantasy: An evolutionary psychological approach. *Journal of Sex Research, 27,* 527–555.

Ellis, L. (Ed.). (1993). *Social stratification and socioeconomic inequality, Vol. 1: A comparative biosocial analysis.* Westport, CT: Praeger.

Ellis, L. (1995). Dominance and reproductive success among nonhuman animals: A cross-species comparison. *Ethology and Sociobiology, 16,* 257–333.

Elman, J. L., Bates, E. A., Johnson, M. H., Karmiloff-Smith, A., Parisi, D., & Plunkett, K.

(1996). *Rethinking innateness: A connectionist perspective on development*. Cambridge, MA: Bradford Books/MIT Press.

Ely, J., Alford, P., & Ferrell, R. E. (1991). DNA "fingerprinting" and the genetic management of a captive chimpanzee population (*Pan-troglodytes*). *American Journal of Primatology, 24,* 39–54.

Ember, C. R. (1978). Myths about hunter–gatherers. *Ethnology, 17,* 439–448.

Eme, R. F., & Kavanaugh, L. (1995). Sex differences in conduct disorder. *Journal of Clinical Child Psychology 24,* 406–426.

Emery, R. E. (1988). *Marriage, divorce, and children's adjustment*. Newbury Park: CA. Sage.

Emlen, S. T. (1995). An evolutionary theory of the family. *Proceedings of the National Academy of Sciences, USA, 92,* 8092–8099.

Emlen, S. T., & Oring, L. W. (1977). Ecology, sexual selection, and the evolution of mating systems. *Science, 197,* 215–223.

Endicott, K. (1992). Fathering in an egalitarian society. In B. S. Hewlett (Ed.), *Father–child relations: Cultural and biosocial contexts* (pp. 281–295). New York: Aldine de Gruyter.

Erwin, R. J., Gur, R. C., Gur, R. E., Skolnick, B., Mawhinney-Hee, M., & Smailis, J. (1992). Facial emotion discrimination: I. Task construction and behavioral findings in normal subjects. *Psychiatry Research, 42,* 231–240.

Essock-Vitale, S. M., & McGuire, M. T. (1988). What 70 million years hath wrought: Sexual histories and reproductive success of a random sample of American women. In L. Betzig, M. Borgerhoff Mulder, & P. Turke (Eds.), *Human reproductive behaviour: A Darwinian perspective* (pp. 221–235). Cambridge, England: Cambridge University Press.

Fagan, J. F., III. (1972). Infants' recognition memory for faces. *Journal of Experimental Child Psychology, 14,* 453–476.

Fagen, R. M. (1981). *Animal play behavior*. New York: Oxford University Press.

Fagen, R. (1995). Animal play, games of angels, biology, and Brian. In A. D. Pellegrini (Ed.), *The future of play theory: A multidisciplinary inquiry into the contributions of Brian Sutton-Smith* (pp. 23–44). Albany: State University of New York Press.

Fairbanks, L. A. (1993). What is a good mother? Adaptive variation in maternal behavior of primates. *Current Directions in Psychological Science, 2,* 179–183.

Fairbanks, L. A., & McGuire, M. T. (1995). Maternal condition and the quality of maternal care in vervet monkeys. *Behaviour, 132,* 733–754.

Farber, S. L. (1981). *Identical twins reared apart: A reanalysis*. New York: Basic Books.

Fausto-Sterling, A. (1985). *Myths of gender*. New York: Basic Books.

Feingold, A. (1990). Gender differences in effects of physical attractiveness on romantic attraction: A comparison across five research paradigms. *Journal of Personality and Social Psychology, 59,* 981–993.

Feingold, A. (1992a). Gender differences in mate selection preferences: A test of the parental investment model. *Psychological Bulletin, 112,* 125–139.

Feingold, A. (1992b). Sex differences in variability in intellectual abilities: A new look at an old controversy. *Review of Educational Research, 62,* 61–84.

Feingold, A. (1994). Gender differences in personality: A meta-analysis. *Psychological Bulletin, 116,* 429–456.

Feingold, A., & Mazzella, R. (1998). Gender differences in body image are increasing. *Psychological Science, 9,* 190–195.

Feldesman, M. R., Kleckner, J. G., & Lundy, J. K. (1990). Femur–stature ratio and estimates of stature in mid and late Pleistocene fossil hominids. *American Journal of Physical Anthropology, 83,* 359–372.

Feldman, S. S., Nash, S. C., & Aschenbrenner, B. G. (1983). Antecedents of fathering. *Child Development, 54,* 1628–1636.

Figueiredo, G. M., Leitão-Filho, H. F., & Begossi, A. (1993). Ethnobotany of Atlantic forest coastal communities: Diversity of plant used in Gamboa. *Human Ecology, 21,* 419–430.

Figueiredo, G. M., Leitão-Filho, H. F., & Begossi, A. (1997). Ethnobotany of Atlantic forest coastal communities: II. Diversity of plant uses at Sepetiba Bay (SE Brazil). *Human Ecology, 25,* 353–360.

Figueredo, A. J., & McCloskey, L. A. (1993). Sex, money, and paternity: The evolutionary psychology of domestic violence. *Ethology and Sociobiology, 14,* 353–379.

Fincham, F. D., Beach, S. R. H., Harold, G. T., & Osborne, L. N. (1997). Marital satisfaction and depression: Different causal relationships for men and women? *Psychological Science, 8,* 351–357.

Finkel, D., & McGue, M. (1997). Sex differences in nonadditivity in heritability of the Multidimensional Personality Questionnaire scales. *Journal of Personality and Social Psychology, 72,* 929–938.

Fisher, H. E. (1982). *The sex contract: The evolution of human behavior.* New York: Morrow.

Fisher, H. E. (1989). Evolution of human serial pairbonding. *American Journal of Physical Anthropology, 78,* 331–354.

Fisher, R. A. (1958). *The genetical theory of natural selection* (2nd ed.). New York: Dover.

Fiske, S. T. (1993). Controlling other people: The impact of power on stereotyping. *American Psychologist, 48,* 621–628.

Fitch, R. H., Miller, S., & Tallal, P. (1997). Neurobiology of speech perception. *Annual Review of Neuroscience, 20,* 331–351.

Fleming, A. S., Corter, C., & Steiner, M. (1995). Sensory and hormonal control of maternal behavior in rat and human mothers. In C. R. Pryce, R. D. Martin, & D. Skuse (Eds.), *Motherhood in human and nonhuman primates: Biosocial determinants* (pp. 106–114). Basel, Switzerland: Karger.

Fleming, A. S., Ruble, D., Krieger, H., & Wong, P. Y. (1997). Hormonal and experiential correlates of maternal responsiveness during pregnancy and the puerperium in human mothers. *Hormones and Behavior, 31,* 145–158.

Fleming, A. S., Steiner, M., & Corter, C. (1997). Cortisol, hedonics, and maternal responsiveness in human mothers. *Hormones and Behavior, 32,* 85–98.

Flinn, M. V. (1988a). Mate guarding in a Caribbean village. *Ethology and Sociobiology, 9,* 1–28.

Flinn, M. V. (1988b). Parent–offspring interactions in a Caribbean village: Daughter guarding. In L. Betzig, M. Borgerhoff Mulder, & P. Turke (Eds.), *Human reproductive behaviour: A Darwinian perspective* (pp. 189–200). Cambridge, England: Cambridge University Press.

Flinn, M. V. (1992). Paternal care in a Caribbean village. In B. S. Hewlett (Ed.), *Father–child relations: Cultural and biosocial contexts* (pp. 57–84). New York: Aldine de Gruyter.

Flinn, M. V. (1997). Culture and the evolution of social learning. *Evolution and Human Behavior, 18,* 23–67.

Flinn, M. V., & England, B. (1995). Childhood stress and family environment. *Current Anthropology, 36,* 854–866.

Flinn, M. V., & England, B. G. (1997). Social economics of childhood glucocorticoid stress response and health. *American Journal of Physical Anthropology, 102,* 33–53.

Flinn, M. V., & Low, B. S. (1986). Resource distribution, social competition, and mating patterns in human societies. In D. I Rubenstein & R. W. Wrangham (Eds.), *Ecological aspects of social evolution: Birds and mammals* (pp. 217–243). Princeton, NJ: Princeton University Press.

Flinn, M. V., Quinlan, R. J., Decker, S. A., Turner, M. T., & England, B. G. (1996). Male–female differences in effects of parental absence on glucocorticoid stress response. *Human Nature, 7,* 125–162.

Fodor, J. A. (1983). *The modularity of mind: An essay on faculty psychology.* Cambridge, MA: MIT Press.

Fogel, A., Melson, G. F., & Mistry, J. (1986). Conceptualizing the determinants of nurturance: A reassessment of sex differences. In A. Fogel & G. F. Melson (Eds.), *Origins of nurturance: Developmental, biological, and cultural perspectives on caregiving* (pp. 53–67). Hillsdale, NJ: Erlbaum.

Foley, R. (1995). Evolution and adaptive significance of hominid maternal behavior. In C. R. Pryce, R. D. Martin, & D. Skuse (Eds.), *Motherhood in human and nonhuman primates: Biosocial determinants* (pp. 27–36). Basel, Switzerland: Karger.

Foley, R. A. (1996). An evolutionary and chronological framework for human social behavior. *Proceedings of the British Academy, 88,* 95–117.

Foley, R. A., & Lee, P. C. (1989). Finite social space, evolutionary pathways, and reconstructing hominid behavior. *Science, 243,* 901–906.

Folstad, I., & Karter, A. J. (1992). Parasites, bright males, and the immunocompetence handicap. *American Naturalist, 139,* 603–622.

Folstad, I., & Skarstein, F. (1997). Is male germ line control creating avenues for female choice? *Behavioral Ecology, 8,* 109–112.

Formby, D. (1967). Maternal recognition of infant's cry. *Developmental Medicine & Child Neurology, 9,* 293–298.

Forsberg, A. J. L., & Tullberg, B. S. (1995). The relationship between cumulative number of cohabiting partners and number of children for men and women in modern Sweden. *Ethology and Sociobiology, 16,* 221–232.

Fossey, D. (1984). *Gorillas in the mist.* Boston, MA: Houghton Mifflin.

Fox, G. L. (1995). Noncustodial fathers following divorce. *Marriage & Family Review, 20,* 257–282.

Frayer, D. W. (1980). Sexual dimorphism and cultural evolution in the late Pleistocene and Holocene of Europe. *Journal of Human Evolution, 9,* 399–415.

Frayer, D. W., & Wolpoff, M. H. (1985). Sexual dimorphism. *Annual Review of Anthropology, 14,* 429–473.

Freedman, D. G. (1974). *Human infancy: An evolutionary perspective.* New York: Wiley.

Freud, S. (1957). The ego and the id. In J. Rickman (Ed.), *A general selection from the works of Sigmund Freud* (pp. 210–235). Garden City, NY: Doubleday Anchor Books. (Original work published 1923)

Friedman, H. S., Tucker, J. S., Schwartz, J. E., Tomlinson-Keasey, C., Martin, L. R., Wingard, D. L., & Criqui, M. H. (1995). Psychosocial and behavioral predictors of longevity: The aging and death of the "Termites." *American Psychologist, 50,* 69–78.

Frisancho, A. R., & Flegel, P. N. (1983). Elbow breadth as a measure of frame size for U.S. males and females. *American Journal of Clinical Nutrition, 37,* 311–314.

Frith, C. B., Borgia, G., & Frith, D. W. (1996). Courts and courtship behaviour of Archbold's bowerbird *Archboldia papuensis* in Papua New Guinea. *Ibis, 138,* 204–211.

Frith, U., & Happé, F. (1996). Mary has more: Sex differences, autism, coherence, and theory of mind. *Behavioral and Brain Sciences, 19,* 253–254.

Frodi, A. M., Lamb, M. E., Leavitt, L. A., Donovan, W. L., Neff, C., & Sherry, D. (1978). Fathers' and mothers' responses to the faces and cries of normal and premature infants. *Developmental Psychology, 14,* 490–498.

Frost, P. (1998). Sex differences may indeed exist for 3-D navigational abilities. But was sexual selection responsible? *Behavioral and Brain Sciences, 21,* 443–444.

Fry, A. F., & Hale, S. (1996). Processing speed, working memory, and fluid intelligence: Evidence for a developmental cascade. *Psychological Science, 7,* 237–241.

Furedy, J. J., Fleming, A. S., Ruble, D., Scher, H., Daly, J., Day, D., & Loewen, R. (1989). Sex differences in small-magnitude heart-rate responses to sexual and infant-related stimuli: A psychophysiological approach. *Physiology and Behavior, 46,* 903–906.

Furlow, F. B., Armijo-Prewitt, T., Gangestad, S. W., & Thornhill, R. (1997). Fluctuating asymmetry and psychometric intelligence. *Proceedings of the Royal Society of London B*, *264*, 823–829.

Furstenberg, F. F., Jr. (1990). Divorce and the American family. *Annual Review of Sociology*, *16*, 379–403.

Furstenberg, F. F., Jr., Morgan, S. P., & Allison, P. D. (1987). Paternal participation and children's well-being after marital dissolution. *American Sociological Review, 52*, 695–701.

Furstenberg, F. F., Jr., & Nord, C. W. (1985). Parenting apart: Patterns of childrearing after marital disruption. *Journal of Marriage and the Family, 47*, 893–904.

Furstenberg, F. F., Jr., Peterson, J. L., Nord, C. W., & Zill, N. (1983). The life course of children of divorce: Marital disruption and parental contact. *American Sociological Review, 48*, 656–668.

Furstenberg, F. F., Jr., & Teitler, J. O. (1994). Reconsidering the effects of marital disruption. *Journal of Family Issues, 15*, 173–190.

Furuichi, T. (1989). Social interactions and the life history of female *Pan paniscus* in Wamba. *International Journal of Primatology, 10*, 173–197.

Furuichi, T., & Ihobe, H. (1994). Variation in male relationships in bonobos and chimpanzees. *Behaviour, 130*, 211–228.

Gagneux, P., Woodruff, D. S., & Boesch, C. (1997). Furtive mating in female chimpanzees. *Nature, 387*, 358–359.

Galea, L. A. M., Kavaliers, M., Ossenkopp, K.-P., Innes, D., & Hargreaves, E. L. (1994). Sexually dimorphic spatial learning varies seasonally in two populations of deer mice. *Brain Research, 635*, 18–26.

Galea, L. A. M., & Kimura, D. (1993). Sex differences in route-learning. *Personality and Individual Differences, 14*, 53–65.

Galen, B. R., & Underwood, M. K. (1997). A developmental investigation of social aggression among children. *Developmental Psychology, 33*, 589–600.

Gallistel, C. R. (1990). *The organization of learning.* Cambridge, MA: MIT Press/Bradford Books.

Gangestad, S. W. (1993). Sexual selection and physical attractiveness. *Human Nature, 4*, 205–235.

Gangestad, S. W., & Buss, D. M. (1993). Pathogen prevalence and human mate preferences. *Ethology and Sociobiology, 14*, 89–96.

Gangestad, S. W., & Simpson, J. A. (1990). Toward an evolutionary history of female sociosexual variation. *Journal of Personality, 58*, 69–96.

Gangestad, S. W., & Thornhill, R. (1997). The evolutionary psychology of extrapair sex: The role of fluctuating asymmetry. *Evolution and Human Behavior, 18*, 69–88.

Gangestad, S. W., Thornhill, R., & Yeo, R. A. (1994). Facial attractiveness, developmental stability, and fluctuating asymmetry. *Ethology and Sociobiology, 15*, 73–85.

Gannon, P. J., Holloway, R. L., Broadfield, D. C., & Braun, A. R. (1998). Asymmetry of chimpanzee planum temporale: Humanlike pattern of Wernicke's brain language area homolog. *Science, 279*, 220–222.

Garai, J. E., & Scheinfeld, A. (1968). Sex differences in mental and behavioral traits. *Genetic Psychology Monographs, 77*, 169–299.

Gaulin, S. J. C. (1992). Evolution of sex differences in spatial ability. *Yearbook of Physical Anthropology, 35*, 125–151.

Gaulin, S. J. C. (1995). Does evolutionary theory predict sex differences in the brain? In M. S. Gazzaniga (Ed.), *The cognitive neurosciences* (pp. 1211–1225). Cambridge, MA: Bradford Books/MIT Press.

Gaulin, S. J. C., & Boster, J. S. (1990). Dowry as female competition. *American Anthropologist, 92*, 994–1005.

Gaulin, S. J. C., & Boster, J. S. (1992). Human marriage systems and sexual dimorphism in stature. *American Journal of Physical Anthropology, 89*, 467–475.

Gaulin, S. J. C., & Fitzgerald, R. W. (1986). Sex differences in spatial ability: An evolutionary hypothesis and test. *American Naturalist, 127*, 74–88.

Gaulin, S. J. C., & Fitzgerald, R. W. (1989). Sexual selection for spatial-learning ability. *Animal Behaviour, 37*, 322–331.

Gaulin, S. J. C., McBurney, D. H., & Brakeman-Wartell, S. L. (1997). Matrilateral biases in the investment of aunts and uncles: A consequence and measure of paternity uncertainty. *Human Nature, 8*, 139–151.

Gaulin, S. J. C., & Sailer, L. D. (1984). Sexual dimorphism in weight among the primates: The relative impact of allometry and sexual selection. *International Journal of Primatology, 5*, 515–535.

Gaulin, S. J. C., Silverman, I., Phillips, K., & Reiber, C. (1997). Activational hormonal influences on abilities and attitudes: Implications for evolutionary theory. *Evolution and Cognition, 3*, 191–199.

Geary, D. C. (1992). Evolution of human cognition: Potential relationship to the ontogenetic development of behavior and cognition. *Evolution and Cognition, 1*, 93–100.

Geary, D. C. (1994). *Children's mathematical development: Research and practical applications.* Washington, DC: American Psychological Association.

Geary, D. C. (1995a). Reflections of evolution and culture in children's cognition: Implications for mathematical development and instruction. *American Psychologist, 50*, 24–37.

Geary, D. C. (1995b). Sexual selection and sex differences in spatial cognition. *Learning and Individual Differences, 7*, 289–301.

Geary, D. C. (1996). Sexual selection and sex differences in mathematical abilities. *Behavioral and Brain Sciences, 19*, 229–284.

Geary, D. C. (1998). Functional organization of the human mind: Implications for behavioral genetic research. *Human Biology, 70*, 185–198.

Geary, D. C., Hamson, C. O., Chen, G.-P., Liu, F., Hoard, M. K., & Salthouse, T. A. (1997). Computational and reasoning abilities in arithmetic: Cross-generational change in China and the United States. *Psychonomic Bulletin & Review, 4*, 425–430.

Geary, D. C., Rumsey, M., Bow-Thomas, C. C., & Hoard, M. K. (1995). Sexual jealousy as a facultative trait: Evidence from the pattern of sex differences in adults from China and the United States. *Ethology and Sociobiology, 16*, 355–383.

Geen, R. G. (1990). *Human aggression.* Pacific Grove, CA: Brooks/Cole Publishing Co.

Gelman, R. (1990). First principles organize attention to and learning about relevant data: Number and animate–inanimate distinction as examples. *Cognitive Science, 14*, 79–106.

George, M. S., Ketter, T. A., Parekh, P. I., Herscovitch, P., & Post, R. M. (1996). Gender differences in regional cerebral blood flow during transient self-induced sadness or happiness. *Biological Psychiatry, 40*, 859–871.

Geschwind, N., & Behan, P. (1982). Left-handedness: Association with immune disease, migraine, and developmental learning disorder. *Proceedings of the National Academy of Sciences, USA, 79*, 5097–5100.

Geschwind, N., & Galaburda, A. M. (1987). *Cerebral lateralization: Biological mechanisms, associations, and pathology.* Cambridge, MA: MIT Press/Bradford Books.

Geschwind, N., & Levitsky, W. (1968). Human brain: Left–right asymmetries in temporal speech region. *Science, 161*, 186–187.

Ghiglieri, M. P. (1987). Sociobiology of the great apes and the hominid ancestor. *Journal of Human Evolution, 16*, 319–357.

Ghiselin, M. T. (1974). *The economy of nature and the evolution of sex.* Berkeley: University of California Press.

Ghiselin, M. T. (1996). Differences in male and female cognitive abilities: Sexual selection or division of labor? *Behavioral and Brain Sciences, 19,* 254–255.

Gilger, J. W., & Ho, H.-Z. (1989). Gender differences in adult spatial information processing: Their relationship to pubertal timing, adolescent activities, and sex-typing of personality. *Cognitive Development, 4,* 197–214.

Gilliard, E. T. (1969). *Birds of paradise and bower birds.* London: Weidenfeld and Nicolson.

Gilligan, C. (1982). *In a difference voice: Psychological theory and women's development.* Cambridge, MA: Harvard University Press.

Gindhart, P. S. (1973). Growth standards for the tibia and radius in children aged one month through eighteen years. *American Journal of Physical Anthropology, 39,* 41–48.

Ginsburg, H. J., & Miller, S. M. (1982). Sex differences in children's risk-taking behavior. *Child Development, 53,* 426–428.

Goldberg, E., Podell, K., Harner, R., Riggio, S., & Lovell, M. (1994). Cognitive bias, functional cortical geometry, and the frontal lobes: Laterality, sex, and handedness. *Journal of Cognitive Neuroscience, 6,* 276–296.

Goldberg, S., Blumberg, S. L., & Kriger, A. (1982). Menarche and interest in infants: Biological and social influences. *Child Development, 53,* 1544–1550.

Goldizen, A. W. (1987). Tamarins and marmosets: Communal care of offspring. In B. B. Smuts, D. L. Cheney, R. M. Seyfarth, R. W. Wrangham, & T. T. Struhsaker (Eds.), *Primate societies* (pp. 34–43). Chicago: University of Chicago Press.

Goldschmidt, T., Bakker, T. C. M., & Feuth-De Bruijn, E. (1993). Selective copying of mate choice of female sticklebacks. *Animal Behaviour, 45,* 541–547.

Golombok, S., & Fivush, R. (1994). *Gender development.* New York: Cambridge University Press.

Goodall, J. (1986). *The chimpanzees of Gombe: Patterns of behavior.* Cambridge, MA: Belknap Press of Harvard University Press.

Goodall, J., Bandora, A., Bergmann, E., Busse, C., Matama, H., Mpongo, E., Pierce, A., & Riss, D. (1979). Inter-community interactions in the chimpanzee population of the Gombe National Park. In D. A. Hamburg & E. R. McCown (Eds.), *The great apes* (pp. 13–53). Menlo Park, CA: Benjamin/Cummings Publishing Co.

Goodenough, E. W. (1957). Interest in persons as an aspect of sex differences in the early years. *Genetic Psychology Monographs, 55,* 287–323.

Goodman, A. H., & Armelagos, G. J. (1988). Childhood stress and decreased longevity in a prehistoric population. *American Anthropologist, 90,* 936–944.

Gooren, L. J. G. (1987). Androgen levels and sex functions in testosterone-treated hypogonadal men. *Archives of Sexual Behavior, 16,* 463–473.

Gopnik, A., & Wellman, H. M. (1994). The theory theory. In L. A. Hirschfeld & S. A. Gelman (Eds.), *Mapping the mind: Domain specificity in cognition and culture* (pp. 257–293). New York: Cambridge University Press.

Gordon, H. W., & Lee, P. (1993). No difference in cognitive performance between phases of the menstrual cycle. *Psychoneuroendocrinology, 18,* 521–531.

Gottfredson, L. S. (1997). Why g matters: The complexity of everyday life. *Intelligence, 24,* 79–132.

Gottman, J. M. (1998). Psychology and the study of marital processes. *Annual Review of Psychology, 49,* 169–197.

Gouchie, C., & Kimura, D. (1991). The relationship between testosterone levels and cognitive ability patterns. *Psychoneuroendocrinology, 16,* 323–334.

Gould, E., Woolley, C. S., & McEwen, B. S. (1991). The hippocampal formation: Morphological changes induced by thyroid, gonadal and adrenal hormones. *Psychoneuroendocrinology, 16,* 67–84.

Gould, J. L. (1986). The locale map of the honey bee: Do insects have cognitive maps? *Science, 232,* 861–863.

Gould, J. L. (1996). Specializations in honey bee learning. In C. F. Moss & S. J. Shettleworth (Eds.), *Neuroethological studies of cognitive and perceptual processes* (pp. 11–30). Boulder, CO: Westview Press.

Gould, J. L., & Gould, C. G. (1996). *Sexual selection: Mate choice and courtship in nature.* New York: Scientific American Library.

Gould, S. J., & Vrba, E. S. (1982). Exaptation—A missing term in the science of form. *Paleobiology, 8,* 4–15.

Gowlett, J. A. J. (1992a). Early human mental abilities. In S. Jones, R. Martin, & D. Pilbeam (Eds.), *The Cambridge encyclopedia of human evolution* (pp. 341–345). New York: Cambridge University Press.

Gowlett, J. A. J. (1992b). Tools—The Paleolithic record. In S. Jones, R. Martin, & D. Pilbeam (Eds.), *The Cambridge encyclopedia of human evolution* (pp. 350–360). New York: Cambridge University Press.

Grammer, K., & Thornhill, R. (1994). Human (*Homo sapiens*) facial attractiveness and sexual selection: The role of symmetry and averageness. *Journal of Comparative Psychology, 108,* 233–242.

Grant, B. R., & Grant, P. R. (1989). Natural selection in a population of Darwin's finches. *American Naturalist, 133,* 377–393.

Grant, B. R., & Grant, P. R. (1993). Evolution of Darwin's finches caused by a rare climatic event. *Proceedings of the Royal Society of London B, 251,* 111–117.

Gray, J. P. (1985). *Primate sociobiology.* New Haven, CT: Hraf Press.

Graziano, W. G., Jensen-Campbell, L. A., Shebilske, L. J., & Lundgren, S. R. (1993). Social influence, sex differences, and judgments of beauty: Putting the *interpersonal* back in interpersonal attraction. *Journal of Personality and Social Psychology, 65,* 522–531.

Green, R. (1987). *The "sissy boy syndrome" and the development of homosexuality.* New Haven, CT: Yale University Press.

Greenberg, J., Pyszczynski, T., Solomon, S., Simon, L., & Breus, M. (1994). Role of consciousness and accessibility of death-related thoughts in mortality salience effects. *Journal of Personality and Social Psychology, 67,* 627–637.

Greenlees, I. A., & McGrew, W. C. (1994). Sex and age differences in preferences and tactics of mate attraction: Analysis of published advertisements. *Ethology and Sociobiology, 15,* 59–72.

Greenough, W. T. (1991). Experience as a component of normal development: Evolutionary considerations. *Developmental Psychology, 27,* 14–17.

Greenough, W. T., Black, J. E., & Wallace, C. S. (1987). Experience and brain development. *Child Development, 58,* 539–559.

Greenstein, T. N. (1996). Husbands' participation in domestic labor: Interactive effects of wives' and husbands' gender ideologies. *Journal of Marriage and the Family, 58,* 585–595.

Griffin, P. B., & Griffin, M. B. (1992). Fathers and childcare among the Cagayan Agta. In B. S. Hewlett (Ed.), *Father–child relations: Cultural and biosocial contexts* (pp. 297–320). New York: Aldine de Gruyter.

Grimshaw, G. M., Sitarenios, G., & Finegan, J.-A. K. (1995). Mental rotation at 7 years: Relations with prenatal testosterone levels and spatial play experiences. *Brain and Cognition, 29,* 85–100.

Grossman, M., & Wood, W. (1993). Sex differences in intensity of emotional experience: A social role interpretation. *Journal of Personality and Social Psychology, 65,* 1010–1022.

Grotpeter, J. K., & Crick, N. R. (1996). Relational aggression, overt aggression and friendship. *Child Development, 67,* 2328–2338.

Gualtieri, T., & Hicks, R. E. (1985). An immunoreactive theory of selective male affliction. *Behavioral and Brain Sciences, 8,* 427–441.

Gunnar, M. R., & Donahue, M. (1980). Sex differences in social responsiveness between six and twelve months. *Child Development, 51,* 262–265.

Gunnar, M. R., & Stone, C. (1984). The effects of positive maternal affect on infant responses to pleasant, ambiguous, and fear-provoking toys. *Child Development, 55,* 1231–1236.

Gur, R. C., Gur, R. E., Obrist, W. D., Hungerbuhler, J. P., Younkin, D., Rosen, A. D., Skolnick, B. E., & Reivich, M. (1982). Sex and handedness differences in cerebral blood flow during rest and cognitive activity. *Science, 217,* 659–661.

Gur, R. C., Mozley, L. H., Mozley, P. D., Resnick, S. M., Karp, J. S., Alavi, A., Arnold, S. E., & Gur, R. E. (1995). Sex differences in regional cerebral glucose metabolism during a resting state. *Science, 267,* 528–531.

Gur, R. C., Ragland, J. D., Resnick, S. M., Skolnick, B. E., Jaggi, J., Muenz, L., & Gur, R. E. (1994). Lateralized increases in cerebral blood flow during performance of verbal and spatial tasks: Relationship with performance level. *Brain and Cognition, 24,* 244–258.

Gur, R. C., Skolnick, B. E., & Gur, R. E. (1994). Effects of emotional discrimination tasks on cerebral blood flow: Regional activation and its relation to performance. *Brain and Cognition, 25,* 271–286.

Guttentag, M., & Secord, P. (1983). *Too many women?* Beverly Hills, CA: Sage.

Haley, M. P., Deutsch, C. J., & Le Boeuf, B. J. (1994). Size, dominance and copulatory success in male northern elephant seals, *Mirounga angustirostris. Animal Behaviour, 48,* 1249–1260.

Halgren, E., & Marinkovic, K. (1995). Neurophysiological networks integrating human emotions. In M. S. Gazzaniga (Ed.), *The cognitive neurosciences* (pp. 1137–1151). Cambridge, MA: Bradford Books/MIT Press.

Hall, B. K. (1992). *Evolutionary developmental biology.* London: Chapman & Hall.

Hall, G. C. H., & Barongan, C. (1997). Prevention of sexual aggression: Sociocultural risk and protective factors. *American Psychologist, 52,* 5–14.

Hall, J. A. (1978). Gender effects in decoding nonverbal cues. *Psychological Bulletin, 85,* 845–857.

Hall, J. A. (1984). *Nonverbal sex differences: Communication accuracy and expressive style.* Baltimore: Johns Hopkins University Press.

Hall, J. A. Y., & Kimura, K. (1995). Sexual orientation and performance on sexually dimorphic motor tasks. *Archives of Sexual Behavior, 24,* 395–407.

Halpern, C. T., Udry, J. R., Campbell, B., & Suchindran, C. (1993). Relationships between aggression and pubertal increases in testosterone: A panel analysis of adolescent males. *Social Biology, 40,* 8–24.

Halpern, D. F. (1992). *Sex differences in cognitive abilities* (2nd ed.). Hillsdale, NJ: Erlbaum.

Halpern, D. F. (1997). Sex differences in intelligence and their implications for education. *American Psychologist, 52,* 1091–1102.

Halpern, D. F., & Wright, T. M. (1996). A process-oriented model of cognitive sex differences. *Learning and Individual Differences, 8,* 3–24.

Hames, R. (1992). Variation in paternal care among the Yanomamö. In B. S. Hewlett (Ed.), *Father–child relations: Cultural and biosocial contexts* (pp. 85–110). New York: Aldine de Gruyter.

Hames, R. (1996). Costs and benefits of monogamy and polygyny for Yanomamö women. *Ethology and Sociobiology, 17,* 181–199.

Hamilton, W. D. (1964). The genetical evolution of social behavior. II. *Journal of Theoretical Biology, 7,* 17–52.

Hamilton, W. D. (1975). Innate social aptitudes of man: An approach from evolutionary genetics. In R. Fox (Ed.), *Biosocial anthropology* (pp. 133–155). New York: Wiley.

Hamilton, W. D. (1980). Sex versus non-sex versus parasite. *Oikos, 35,* 282–290.

Hamilton, W. D. (1990). Mate choice near or far. *American Zoologist, 30,* 341–352.

Hamilton, W. D., Axelrod, R., & Tanese, R. (1990). Sexual reproduction as an adaptation to resist parasites (A review). *Proceedings of the National Academy of Sciences, USA, 87,* 3566–3573.

Hamilton, W. D., & Zuk, M. (1982). Heritable true fitness and bright birds: A role for parasites? *Science, 218,* 384–387.

Hampson, E. (1990a). Estrogen-related variations in human spatial and articulatory-motor skills. *Psychoneuroendocrinology, 15,* 97–111.

Hampson, E. (1990b). Variations in sex-related cognitive abilities across the menstrual cycle. *Brain and Cognition, 14,* 26–43.

Hampson, E., & Kimura, D. (1988). Reciprocal effects of hormonal fluctuations on human motor and perceptual–spatial skills. *Behavioral Neuroscience, 102,* 456–459.

Happé, F. G. E. (1995). The role of age and verbal ability in the theory of mind task performance of subjects with autism. *Child Development, 66,* 843–855.

Happé, F., Ehlers, S., Fletcher, P., Frith, U., Johansson, M., Gillberg, C., Dolan, R., Frackowiak, R., & Frith, C. (1996). "Theory of mind" in the brain: Evidence from a PET scan study of Asperger-snydrome. *NeuroReport, 8,* 197–201.

Harkness, S., & Super, C. M. (1992). The cultural foundations of fathers' roles: Evidence from Kenya and the United States. In B. S. Hewlett (Ed.), *Father–child relations: Cultural and biosocial contexts* (pp. 191–211). New York: Aldine de Gruyter.

Harris, C. R., & Christenfeld, N. (1996). Gender, jealousy, and reason. *Psychological Science, 7,* 364–366.

Harris, J. A., Rushton, J. P., Hampson, E., & Jackson, D. N. (1996). Salivary testosterone and self-report aggressive and pro-social personality characteristics in men and women. *Aggressive Behavior, 22,* 321–331.

Harris, J. R. (1995). Where is the child's environment? A group socialization theory of development. *Psychological Review, 102,* 458–489.

Hartung, C. M., & Widiger, T. A. (1998). Gender differences in the diagnosis of mental disorders: Conclusions and controversies of the *DSM–IV. Psychological Bulletin, 123,* 260–278.

Hartung, J. (1995). Love thy neighbor: The evolution of in-group morality. *Skeptic, 3,* 86–99.

Hartup, W. W., & Stevens, N. (1997). Friendships and adaptation in the life course. *Psychological Bulletin, 121,* 355–370.

Harvey, P. H., Kavanagh, M., & Clutton-Brock, T. H. (1978a). Canine tooth size in female primates. *Nature, 276,* 817–818.

Harvey, P. H., Kavanagh, M., & Clutton-Brock, T. H. (1978b). Sexual dimorphism in primate teeth. *Journal of Zoology, 186,* 475–485.

Hassrick, R. B. (1964). *The Sioux: Life and customs of a warrior society.* Norman: University of Oklahoma Press.

Hatfield, E., & Sprecher, S. (1995). Men's and women's preferences in marital partners in the United States, Russia, and Japan. *Journal of Cross-Cultural Psychology, 26,* 728–750.

Hauser, M. D. (1996). *The evolution of communication.* Cambridge, MA: MIT Press/Bradford Books.

Haviland, J. J., & Malatesta, C. Z. (1981). The development of sex differences in nonverbal signals: Fallacies, facts, and fantasies. In C. Mayo & N. M. Henley (Eds.), *Gender and nonverbal behavior* (pp. 183–208). New York: Springer-Verlag.

Hayaki, H., Huffman, M. A., & Nishida, T. (1989). Dominance among male chimpanzees in the Mahale Mountains National Park, Tanzania: A preliminary study. *Primates, 30,* 187–197.

Healy, S. D. (1996). Ecological specialization in the avian brain. In C. F. Moss & S. J.

Shettleworth (Eds.), *Neuroethological studies of cognitive and perceptual processes* (pp. 84–110). Boulder, CO: Westview Press.

Heckhausen, J., & Schulz, R. (1995). A life-span theory of control. *Psychological Review, 102*, 284–304.

Hedges, L. V., & Nowell, A. (1995). Sex differences in mental scores, variability, and numbers of high-scoring individuals. *Science, 269*, 41–45.

Hedrick, P. W., & Black, F. L. (1997). HLA and mate selection: No evidence in South Amerindians. *American Journal of Human Genetics, 61*, 505–511.

Heister, G., Landis, T., Regard, M., & Schroeder-Heister, P. (1989). Shift of functional cerebral asymmetry during the menstrual cycle. *Neuropsychologia, 27*, 871–880.

Helbing, D., Keltsch, J., & Molnár, P. (1997). Modelling the evolution of human trail systems. *Nature, 388*, 47–50.

Henderson, V. W., Watt, L., & Buckwalter, J. G. (1996). Cognitive skills associated with estrogen replacement in women with Alzheimer's disease. *Psychoneuroendocrinology, 21*, 421–430.

Herlitz, A., Nilsson, L.-G., & Bäckman, L. (1997). Gender differences in episodic memory. *Memory & Cognition, 25*, 801–811.

Herrnstein, R. J., & Murray, C. (1994). *The bell curve: Intelligence and class structure in American life.* New York: Free Press.

Herz, R. S., & Cahill, E. D. (1997). Differential use of sensory information in sexual behavior as a function of gender. *Human Nature, 8*, 275–286.

Hewlett, B. S. (1988). Sexual selection and paternal investment among Aka pygmies. In L. Betzig, M. Borgerhoff Mulder, & P. Turke (Eds.), *Human reproductive behaviour: A Darwinian perspective* (pp. 263–276). Cambridge, England: Cambridge University Press.

Hewlett, B. S. (Ed.). (1992a). *Father–child relations: Cultural and biosocial contexts.* New York: Aldine de Gruyter.

Hewlett, B. S. (1992b). Husband–wife reciprocity and the father–infant relationship among Aka pygmies. In B. S. Hewlett (Ed.), *Father–child relations: Cultural and biosocial contexts* (pp. 153–176). New York: Aldine de Gruyter.

Hickling, A. K., & Gelman, S. A. (1995). How does your garden grow? Early conceptualization of seeds and their place in the plant growth cycle. *Child Development, 66*, 856–876.

Hill, A. V. S., Allsopp, C. E. M., Kwiatkowski, D., Anstey, N. M., Twumasi, P., Rowe, P. A., Bennett, S., Brewster, D., McMichael, A. J., & Greenwood, B. M. (1991). Common West African HLA antigens are associated with protection from severe malaria. *Nature, 352*, 595–560.

Hill, D. A., & van Hooff, J. A. R. A. M. (1994). Affiliative relationships between males in groups of nonhuman primates: A summary. *Behaviour, 130*, 143–149.

Hill, G. E. (1991). Plumage coloration is a sexually selected indicator of male quality. *Nature, 350*, 337–339.

Hill, K. (1982). Hunting and human evolution. *Journal of Human Evolution, 11*, 521–544.

Hill, K., & Hurtado, A. M. (1996). *Ache life history: The ecology and demography of a foraging people.* New York: Aldine de Gruyter.

Hill, K., & Kaplan, H. (1988). Tradeoffs in male and female reproductive strategies among the Ache: Part 1. In L. Betzig, M. Borgerhoff Mulder, & P. Turke (Eds.), *Human reproductive behaviour: A Darwinian perspective* (pp. 277–289). Cambridge, England: Cambridge University Press.

Hill, R. (1945). Campus values in mate selection. *Journal of Home Economics, 37*, 554–558.

Hillgarth, H., Ramenofsky, M., & Wingfield, J. (1997). Testosterone and sexual selection. *Behavioral Ecology, 8*, 108–109.

Hines, M., & Kaufman, F. R. (1994). Androgens and the development of human sex-typical behavior: Rough-and-tumble play and sex of preferred playmates in children with congenital adrenal hyperplasia (CAH). *Child Development, 65,* 1042–1053.

Hirschfeld, L. A. (1994). Is the acquisition of social categories based on domain-specific competence or knowledge transfer? In L. A. Hirschfeld & S. A. Gelman (Eds.), *Mapping the mind: Domain specificity in cognition and culture* (pp. 201–233). New York: Cambridge University Press.

Ho, H.-Z., Gilger, J. W., & Brink, T. M. (1986). Effects of menstrual cycle on spatial information-processes. *Perceptual and Motor Skills, 63,* 743–751.

Hoffman, M. L. (1977). Sex differences in empathy and related behaviors. *Psychological Bulletin, 84,* 712–722.

Holding, C. S., & Holding, D. H. (1989). Acquisition of route network knowledge by males and females. *Journal of Genetic Psychology, 116,* 29–41.

Holliday, T. W. (1997). Body proportions in late Pleistocene Europe and modern human origins. *Journal of Human Evolution, 32,* 423–447.

Holloway, R. L., Anderson, P. J., Defendini, R., & Harper, C. (1993). Sexual dimorphism of the human corpus callosum from three independent samples: Relative size of the corpus callosum. *American Journal of Physical Anthropology, 92,* 481–498.

Howard, J. C. (1991). Disease and evolution. *Nature, 352,* 565–567.

Howell, F. C. (1978). Hominidae. In V. J. Maglio & H. B. S. Cooke (Eds.), *Evolution of African mammals* (pp. 154–248). Cambridge, MA: Harvard University Press.

Howes, P., & Markman, H. J. (1989). Marital quality and child functioning: A longitudinal investigation. *Child Development, 60,* 1044–1051.

Hrdy, S. B. (1979). Infanticide among animals: A review, classification, and examination of the implications for the reproductive strategies of females. *Ethology and Sociobiology, 1,* 13–40.

Hrdy, S. B. (1997). Raising Darwin's consciousness: Female sexuality and the prehominid origins of patriarchy. *Human Nature, 8,* 1–49.

Hsu, C., Soong, W., Stigler, J. W., Hong, C., & Liang, C. (1981). The temperamental characteristics of Chinese babies. *Child Development, 52,* 1337–1340.

Huffman, M. A. (1992). Influences of female partner preference on potential reproductive outcomes in Japanese macaques. *Folia Primatologica, 59,* 77–88.

Humphrey, N. K. (1976). The social function of intellect. In P. P. G. Bateson & R. A. Hinde (Eds.), *Growing points in ethology* (pp. 303–317). New York: Cambridge University Press.

Humphreys, L. G., Lubinski, D., & Yao, G. (1993). Utility of predicting group membership and the role of spatial visualization in becoming an engineer, physical scientist, or artist. *Journal of Applied Psychology, 78,* 250–261.

Hunt, E., Lunneborg, C., & Lewis, J. (1975). What does it mean to be high verbal? *Cognitive Psychology, 7,* 194–227.

Hunter, J. E., & Hunter, R. F. (1984). Validity and utility of alternative predictors of job performance. *Psychological Bulletin, 96,* 72–98.

Hurtado, A. M., & Hill, K. R. (1992). Paternal effect on offspring survivorship among Ache and Hiwi hunter–gatherers: Implications for modeling pair-bond stability. In B. S. Hewlett (Ed.), *Father–child relations: Cultural and biosocial contexts* (pp. 31–55). New York: Aldine de Gruyter.

Hutt, C. (1972). Sex differences in human development. *Human Development, 15,* 153–170.

Hyde, J. S., & Linn, M. C. (1988). Gender differences in verbal ability: A meta-analysis. *Psychological Bulletin, 104,* 53–69.

Ihobe, H. (1992). Male–male relationships among wild bonobos *Pan paniscus* at Wamba Republic of Zaire. *Primates, 33,* 163–179.

Inoue, M., Mitsunaga, F., Nozaki, M., Ohsawa, H., Takenaka, A., Sugiyama, Y., Shimizu,

K., & Takenaka, O. (1993). Male dominance rank and reproductive success in an enclosed group of Japanese macaques: With special reference to post-conception mating. *Primates, 34*, 503–511.

Inoue, M., Takenaka, A., Tanaka, S., Kominami, R., & Takenaka, O. (1990). Paternity discrimination in a Japanese macaque group by DNA fingerprinting. *Primates, 31*, 563–570.

Irons, W. (1979). Cultural and biological success. In N. A. Chagnon & W. Irons (Eds.), *Natural selection and social behavior* (pp. 257–272). North Scituate, MA: Duxbury Press.

Irons, W. (1988). Parental behavior in humans. In L. Betzig, M. Borgerhoff Mulder, & P. Turke (Eds.), *Human reproductive behaviour: A Darwinian perspective* (pp. 307–314). Cambridge, England: Cambridge University Press.

Irons, W. (1993). Monogamy, contraception and the cultural and reproductive success hypothesis. *Behavioral and Brain Sciences, 16*, 295–296.

Irwin, C. (1990). The Inuit and the evolution of limited group conflict. In J. van der Dennen & V. Falger (Eds.), *Sociobiology and conflict: Evolutionary perspectives on competition, cooperation, violence and warfare* (pp. 189–226). London: Chapman & Hall.

Isaac, B. (1992). Throwing. In S. Jones, R. Martin, & D. Pilbeam (Eds.), *The Cambridge encyclopedia of human evolution* (p. 358). New York: Cambridge University Press.

Ives, A. R. (1996). Evolution of insect resistance to *Bacillus thuringiensis*—Transformed plants. *Science, 273*, 1412–1413.

Iwasa, Y., & Pomiankowski, A. (1994). The evolution of mate preferences for multiple sexual ornaments. *Evolution, 48*, 853–867.

Izard, C. E. (1993). Organizational and motivational functions of discrete emotions. In M. Lewis & J. M. Haviland (Eds.), *Handbook of emotions* (pp. 631–641). New York: Guilford Press.

Izard, C. E. (1994). Innate and universal facial expressions: Evidence from developmental and cross-cultural research. *Psychological Bulletin, 115*, 288–299.

Jackson, L. A., Sullivan, L. A., Harnish, R., & Hodge, C. N. (1996). Achieving positive social identity: Social mobility, social creativity, and permeability of group boundaries. *Journal of Personality and Social Psychology, 70*, 241–254.

Jacobs, L. F., Gaulin, S. J. C., Sherry, D. F., & Hoffman, G. E. (1990). Evolution of spatial cognition: Sex-specific patterns of spatial behavior predict hippocampal size. *Proceedings of the National Academy of Sciences, USA, 87*, 6349–6352.

Jaffe, K., Urribarri, D., Chacon, G. C., Diaz, G., Torres, A., & Herzog, G. (1993). Sex-linked strategies of human reproductive behavior. *Social Biology, 40*, 61–73.

Jain, A., Belsky, J., & Crnic, K. (1996). Beyond fathering behaviors—Types of dads. *Journal of Family Psychology, 10*, 431–442.

James, T. W., & Kimura, D. (1997). Sex differences in remembering the locations of objects in an array: Location-shifts versus local exchanges. *Evolution and Human Behavior, 18*, 155–163.

Jamieson, I. (1995). Do female fish prefer to spawn in nests with eggs for reasons of mate choice copying or egg survival? *American Naturalist, 145*, 824–832.

Jardine, R., & Martin, N. G. (1983). Spatial ability and throwing accuracy. *Behavior Genetics, 13*, 331–340.

Jarvinen, D. W., & Nicholls, J. G. (1996). Adolescent's social goals, beliefs about the causes of social success, and satisfaction in peer relations. *Developmental Psychology, 32*, 435–441.

Jennings, K. D. (1975). People versus object orientation, social behavior, and intellectual abilities in preschool children. *Developmental Psychology, 11*, 511–519.

Jennings, K. D. (1977). People versus object orientation in preschool children: Do sex differences really occur? *Journal of Genetic Psychology, 131*, 65–73.

Jensen, A. R. (1998). *The g factor: The science of mental ability*. Westport, CT: Praeger.

Joffe, T. H. (1997). Social pressures have selected for an extended juvenile period in primates. *Journal of Human Evolution, 32*, 593–605.

Johnson, E. S. (1984). Sex differences in problem solving. *Journal of Educational Psychology, 76*, 1359–1371.

Johnson, E. S., & Meade, A. C. (1987). Developmental patterns of spatial ability: An early sex difference. *Child Development, 58*, 725–740.

Johnson, L. S., Kermott, L. H., & Lein, M. R. (1994). Territorial polygyny in house wrens: Are females sufficiently compensated for the cost of mate sharing? *Behavioral Ecology, 5*, 98–104.

Johnstone, R. A., Reynolds, J. D., & Deutsch, J. C. (1996). Mutual mate choice and sex differences in choosiness. *Evolution, 50*, 1382–1391.

Joiner, T. E., Jr., Schmidt, N. B., & Singh, D. (1994). Waist-to-hip ratio and body dissatisfaction among college women and men: Moderating role of depressed symptoms and gender. *International Journal of Eating Disorders, 16*, 199–203.

Jones, D. (1995). Sexual selection, physical attractiveness, and facial neoteny. *Current Anthropology, 36*, 723–748.

Jones, D. C., & Costin, S. E. (1995). Friendship quality during preadolescence and adolescence: The contributions of relationship orientations, instrumentality, and expressivity. *Merrill-Palmer Quarterly, 41*, 517–535.

Jones, D., & Hill, K. (1993). Criteria of facial attractiveness in five populations. *Human Nature, 4*, 271–296.

Juraska, J. M. (1986). Sex differences in developmental plasticity of behavior and the brain. In W. T. Greenough & J. M. Juraska (Eds.), *Developmental neuropsychobiology* (pp. 409–422). San Diego, CA: Academic Press.

Juraska, J. M. (1991). Sex differences in "cognitive" regions of the rat brain. *Psychoneuroendocrinology, 16*, 105–119.

Juraska, J. M., Henderson, C., & Müller, J. (1984). Differential rearing experience, gender, and radial maze performance. *Developmental Psychobiology, 17*, 209–215.

Just, M. A., & Carpenter, P. A. (1985). Cognitive coordinate systems: Accounts of mental rotation and individual differences in spatial ability. *Psychological Review, 92*, 137–172.

Kalick, S. M., Zebrowitz, L. A., Langlois, J. H., & Johnson, R. M. (1998). Does human facial attractiveness honestly advertise health? Longitudinal data on an evolutionary question. *Psychological Science, 9*, 8–13.

Kano, T. (1980). Social behavior of wild pygmy chimpanzees (*Pan paniscus*) of Wamba: A preliminary report. *Journal of Human Evolution, 9*, 243–260.

Kano, T. (1992). *The last ape: Pygmy chimpanzee behavior and ecology.* Stanford, CA: Stanford University Press.

Kano, T., & Mulavwa, M. (1984). Feeding ecology of the pygmy chimpanzee (*Pan paniscus*) of Wamba. In R. L. Susman (Ed.), *The pygmy chimpanzee: Evolutionary biology and behavior* (pp. 233–284). New York: Plenum.

Kaplan, H., & Hill, K. (1985). Food sharing among Ache foragers: Tests of explanatory hypotheses. *Current Anthropology, 26*, 223–246.

Kaplan, H. S., Lancaster, J. B., Bock, J. A., & Johnson, S. E. (1995). Does observed fertility maximize fitness among New Mexican men? A test of an optimality model and a new theory of parental investment in the embodied capital of offspring. *Human Nature, 6*, 325–360.

Kaplan, J. R. (1977). Patterns of fight interference in free-ranging rhesus monkeys. *American Journal of Physical Anthropology, 47*, 279–288.

Karmiloff-Smith, A. (1992). *Beyond modularity: A developmental perspective on cognitive science.* Cambridge, MA: Bradford Books/MIT Press.

Karmiloff-Smith, A., Grant, J., Berthoud, I., Davies, M., Howlin, P., & Udwin, O. (1997).

Language and Williams syndrome: How intact is "intact"? *Child Development, 68,* 246–262.

Karmiloff-Smith, A., Klima, E., Bellugi, U., Grant, J., & Baron-Cohen, S. (1995). Is there a social module? Language, face processing, and theory of mind in individuals with Williams syndrome. *Journal of Cognitive Neuroscience, 7,* 196–208.

Kashani, J. H., & Orvaschel, H. (1990). A community study of anxiety in children and adolescents. *American Journal of Psychiatry, 147,* 313–318.

Katz, M. M., & Konner, M. J. (1981). The role of the father: An anthropological perspective. In M. E. Lamb (Ed.), *The role of the father in child development* (2nd ed., pp. 155–186). New York: Wiley.

Kawanaka, K. (1982). Further studies of predation by chimpanzees of Mahale Mountains. *Primates, 23,* 364–384.

Kay, R. F., Cartmill, M., & Balow, M. (1998). The hypoglossal canal and the origin of human vocal behavior. *Proceedings of the National Academy of Sciences, USA, 95,* 5417–5419.

Kearins, J. M. (1981). Visual spatial memory in Australian Aboriginal children of desert regions. *Cognitive Psychology, 13,* 434–460.

Keeley, L. H. (1996). *War before civilization: The myth of the peaceful savage.* New York: Oxford University Press.

Keenan, K., & Shaw, D. (1997). Developmental and social influences on young girls' early problem behavior. *Psychological Bulletin, 121,* 95–113.

Keightley, P. D., & Caballero, A. (1997). Genomic mutation rates for lifetime reproductive output and lifespan in *Caenorhabditis elegans. Proceedings of the National Academy of Sciences, USA, 94,* 3823–3827.

Keil, F. C. (1992). The origins of an autonomous biology. In M. R. Gunnar & M. Maratsos (Eds.), *Modularity and constraints in language and cognition: The Minnesota Symposia on Child Psychology* (Vol. 25, pp. 103–137). Hillsdale, NJ: Erlbaum.

Kemmerer, D. (1996). Innateness, autonomy, universality, and the neurobiology of regular and irregular inflectional morphology. *Behavioral and Brain Sciences, 19,* 639–641.

Kenrick, D. T., Groth, G. E., Trost, M. R., & Sadalla, E. K. (1993). Integrating evolutionary and social exchange perspectives on relationships: Effects of gender, self-appraisal, and involvement level on mate selection criteria. *Journal of Personality and Social Psychology, 64,* 951–969.

Kenrick, D. T., & Keefe, R. C. (1992). Age preferences in mates reflect sex differences in human reproductive strategies. *Behavioral and Brain Sciences, 15,* 75–133.

Kenrick, D. T., Keefe, R. C., Gabrielidis, C., & Cornelius, J. S. (1996). Adolescents' age preferences for dating partners: Support for an evolutionary model of life-history strategies. *Child Development, 67,* 1499–1511.

Kenrick, D. T., Sadalla, E. K., Groth, G., & Trost, M. R. (1990). Evolution, traits, and the stages of human courtship: Qualifying the parental investment model. *Journal of Personality, 58,* 97–116.

Kerig, P. K., Cowan, P. A., & Cowan, C. P. (1993). Marital quality and gender differences in parent–child interaction. *Developmental Psychology, 29,* 931–939.

Kimball, M. M. (1989). A new perspective on women's math achievement. *Psychological Bulletin, 105,* 198–214.

Kimura, D. (1987). Are men's and women's brains really different? *Canadian Psychology, 28,* 133–147.

Kimura, D. (1996). Sex, sexual orientation and sex hormones influence human cognitive function. *Current Opinion in Neurobiology, 6,* 259–263.

Kimura, D., & Hampson, E. (1994). Cognitive pattern in men and women is influenced by fluctuations in sex hormones. *Current Directions in Psychological Science, 3,* 57–61.

Kirkpatrick, M. (1996). Genes and adaptation: A pocket guide to the theory. In M. R. Rose & G. V. Lauder (Eds.), *Adaptation* (pp. 125–146). San Diego, CA: Academic Press.

Kirkpatrick, M., & Dugatkin, L. A. (1994). Sexual selection and the evolutionary effects of copying mate choice. *Behavioral Ecology and Sociobiology, 34,* 443–449.

Kirkpatrick, M., & Ryan, M. J. (1991). The evolution of mating preferences and the paradox of the lek. *Nature, 350,* 33–38.

Klein, R. P., & Durfee, J. T. (1978). Effects of sex and birth order on infant social behavior. *Infant Behavior and Development, 1,* 106–117.

Klekamp, J., Riedel, A., Harper, C., & Kretschmann, H. J. (1987). A quantitative study of Australian Aboriginal and Caucasian brains. *Journal of Anatomy, 150,* 191–210.

Klindworth, H., & Voland, E. (1995). How did the Krummhörn elite males achieve above-average reproductive success? *Human Nature, 6,* 221–240.

Kluwer, E. S., Heesink, J. A. M., & Vandevliert, E. (1996). Marital conflict about the division of labor and paid work. *Journal of Marriage and the Family, 58,* 958–969.

Knauft, B. M. (1987). Reconsidering violence in simple human societies: Homicide among the Gebusi of New Guinea. *Current Anthropology, 28,* 457–500.

Knight, G. P., & Chao, C.-C. (1989). Gender differences in the cooperative, competitive, and individualistic social values of children. *Motivation and Emotion, 13,* 125–141.

Knight, G. P., Fabes, R. A., & Higgins, D. A. (1996). Concerns about drawing causal inferences from meta-analyses: An example in the study of gender differences in aggression. *Psychological Bulletin, 119,* 410–421.

Knudsen, E. I. (1998). Capacity for plasticity in the adult owl auditory system expanded by juvenile experience. *Science, 279,* 1531–1533.

Kolakowski, D., & Malina, R. M. (1974). Spatial ability, throwing accuracy and man's hunting heritage. *Nature, 251,* 410–412.

Kondrashov, A. S. (1988). Deleterious mutations and the evolution of sexual reproduction. *Nature, 336,* 435–440.

Kondrashov, A. S., & Crow, J. F. (1991). Haploidy or diploidy: Which is better? *Nature, 351,* 314–315.

Koopman, P., Gubbay, J., Vivian, N., Goodfellow, P., & Lovell-Badge, R. (1991). Male development of chromosomally female mice transgenic for Sry. *Nature, 351,* 117–121.

Kosslyn, S. M. (1975). Information representation in visual images. *Cognitive Psychology, 7,* 341–370.

Kosslyn, S. M., & Sussman, A. L. (1995). Roles of imagery in perception: Or, there is no such thing as immaculate perception. In M. S. Gazzaniga (Ed.), *The cognitive neurosciences* (pp. 1035–1042). Cambridge, MA: Bradford Books/MIT Press.

Kozlowski, L. T., & Cutting, J. E. (1977). Recognizing the sex of a walker from a dynamic point-light display. *Perception & Psychophysics, 21,* 575–580.

Kuhl, P. K. (1994). Learning and representation in speech and language. *Current Opinion in Neurobiology, 4,* 812–822.

Kuhl, P. K., Andruski, J. E., Chistovich, I. A., Chistovich, L. A., Kozhevnikova, E. V., Ryskina, V. L., Stolyarova, E. I., Sundberg, U., & Lacerda, F. (1997). Cross-language analysis of phonetic units in language addressed to infants. *Science, 277,* 684–686.

Kujawski, J. H., & Bower, T. G. R. (1993). Same-sex preferential looking during infancy as a function of abstract representation. *British Journal of Developmental Psychology, 11,* 201–209.

Kusmierski, R., Borgia, G., Uy, A., & Crozier, R. H. (1997). Labile evolution of display traits in bowerbirds indicates reduced effects of phylogenetic constraint. *Proceedings of the Royal Society of London B, 264,* 307–313.

Lamb, M. E. (1981). The development of father–infant relationships. In M. E. Lamb (Ed.), *The role of the father in child development* (pp. 459–488). New York: Wiley.

Lamb, M. E., & Elster, A. B. (1985). Adolescent mother–infant–father relationships. *Developmental Psychology, 21*, 768–773.

Lamb, M. E., Frodi, A. M., Hwang, C.-P., & Frodi, M. (1982). Varying degrees of paternal involvement in infant care: Attitudinal and behavioral correlates. In M. E. Lamb (Ed.), *Nontraditional families: Parenting and child development* (pp. 117–137). Hillsdale, NJ: Erlbaum.

Lamb, M. E., Pleck, J. H., & Levine, J. A. (1986). Effects of paternal involvement on fathers and mothers. *Marriage & Family Review, 9*, 67–83.

Lampert, A., & Friedman, A. (1992). Sex differences in vulnerability and maladjustment as a function of parental investment: An evolutionary approach. *Social Biology, 39*, 65–81.

Lancaster, J. B. (1989). Evolutionary and cross-cultural perspectives on single-parenthood. In R. W. Bell & N. J. Bell (Eds.), *Interfaces in psychology: Sociobiology and the social sciences* (pp. 63–72). Lubbock: Texas Tech University Press.

Landau, B., Gleitman, H., & Spelke, E. (1981). Spatial knowledge and geometric representations in a child blind from birth. *Science, 213*, 1275–1278.

Larsen, R. J., & Diener, E. (1987). Affect intensity as an individual difference characteristic: A review. *Journal of Research in Personality, 21*, 1–39.

Law, D. J., Pellegrino, J. W., & Hunt, E. B. (1993). Comparing the tortoise and the hare: Gender differences and experience in dynamic spatial reasoning tasks. *Psychological Science, 4*, 35–40.

Lazarus, R. S. (1991). *Emotion and adaptation*. New York: Oxford University Press.

Leadbeater, B. J., Blatt, S. J., & Quinlan, D. M. (1995). Gender-linked vulnerabilities to depressive symptoms, stress, and problem behaviors in adolescents. *Journal of Research on Adolescence, 5*, 1–29.

Leakey, M., & Walker, A. (1997, June). Early hominid fossils from Africa. *Scientific American, 276*, 74–79.

Leaper, C., Anderson, K. J., & Sanders, P. (1998). Moderators of gender effects on parents' talk to their children: A meta-analysis. *Developmental Psychology, 34*, 3–27.

Le Boeuf, B. J. (1974). Male–male competition and reproductive success in elephant seals. *American Zoologist, 14*, 163–176.

Le Boeuf, B. J., & Peterson, R. S. (1969). Social status and mating activity in elephant seals. *Science, 163*, 91–93.

Le Boeuf, B. J., & Reiter, J. (1988). Lifetime reproductive success in northern elephant seals. In T. H. Clutton-Brock (Ed.), *Reproductive success: Studies of individual variation in contrasting breeding systems* (pp. 344–362). Chicago: University of Chicago Press.

Ledoux, J. E. (1995). In search of an emotional system in the brain: Leaping from fear to emotion and consciousness. In M. S. Gazzaniga (Ed.), *The cognitive neurosciences* (pp. 1049–1061). Cambridge, MA: Bradford Books/MIT Press.

Lee, P. C., & Bowman, J. E. (1995). Influence of ecology and energetics on primate mothers and infants. In C. R. Pryce, R. D. Martin, & D. Skuse (Eds.), *Motherhood in human and nonhuman primates: Biosocial determinants* (pp. 47–58). Basel, Switzerland: Karger.

Legree, P. J. (1995). Evidence for an oblique social intelligence factor established with a Likert-based testing procedure. *Intelligence, 21*, 247–266.

Leigh, S. R. (1995). Socioecology and the ontogeny of sexual size dimorphism in anthropoid primates. *American Journal of Physical Anthropology, 97*, 339–356.

Leigh, S. R. (1996). Evolution of human growth spurts. *American Journal of Physical Anthropology, 101*, 455–474.

Leighton, D. R. (1987). Gibbons: Territoriality and monogamy. In B. B. Smuts, D. L. Cheney, R. M. Seyfarth, R. W. Wrangham, & T. T. Struhsaker (Eds.), *Primate societies* (pp. 135–145). Chicago: University of Chicago Press.

Lenneberg, E. H. (1967). *Biological foundations of language*. New York: Wiley.

Lenz, N. (1994). Mating behaviour and sexual competition in the regent bowerbird *Sericulus chrysocephalus*. *Emu, 94*, 263–272.

Leslie, A. M. (1987). Pretense and representation: The origins of "theory of mind." *Psychological Review, 94*, 412–426.

Lever, J. (1978). Sex differences in the complexity of children's play and games. *American Sociological Review, 43*, 471–483.

Levy, J. (1969). Possible basis for the evolution of lateral specialization of the human brain. *Nature, 224*, 614–615.

Lewis, A. B. (1989). Training students to represent arithmetic word problems. *Journal of Educational Psychology, 81*, 521–531.

Lewis, A. B., & Mayer, R. E. (1987). Students' misconceptions of relational statements in arithmetic word problems. *Journal of Educational Psychology, 79*, 363–371.

Lewis, M., & Haviland, J. M. (Eds.). (1993). *Handbook of emotions.* New York: Guilford Press.

Liben, L. S. (1991). The Piagetian water-level task: Looking beneath the surface. *Annals of Child Development, 8*, 81–144.

Lillard, A. S. (1997). Other folks' theories of mind and behavior. *Psychological Science, 8*, 268–274.

Lillard, A. (1998). Ethnopsychologies: Cultural variations in theory of mind. *Psychological Bulletin, 123*, 3–32.

Linn, M. C., & Petersen, A. C. (1985). Emergence and characterization of sex differences in spatial abilities: A meta-analysis. *Child Development, 56*, 1479–1498.

Lovejoy, C. O. (1981). The origin of man. *Science, 211*, 341–350.

Lovejoy, C. O., Kern, K. F., Simpson, S. W., & Meindl, R. S. (1989). A new method for estimation of skeletal dimorphism in fossil samples with an application to *Australopithecus afrarensis*. In G. Giacobini (Ed.), *Hominidae* (pp. 103–108). Milano, Italy: Jaka Books.

Low, B. S. (1988). Pathogen stress and polygyny in humans. In L. Betzig, M. Borgerhoff Mulder, & P. Turke (Eds.), *Human reproductive behaviour: A Darwinian perspective* (pp. 115–127). Cambridge, England: Cambridge University Press.

Low, B. S. (1989). Cross-cultural patterns in the training of children: An evolutionary perspective. *Journal of Comparative Psychology, 103*, 311–319.

Low, B. S. (1990). Marriage systems and pathogen stress in human societies. *American Zoologist, 30*, 325–339.

Loy, J. W., & Hesketh, G. L. (1995). Competitive play on the plains: An analysis of games and warfare among Native American warrior societies, 1800–1850. In A. D. Pellegrini (Ed.), *The future of play theory: A multidisciplinary inquiry into the contributions of Brian Sutton-Smith* (pp. 73–105). Albany: State University of New York Press.

Lubinski, D., & Benbow, C. P. (1994). The study of mathematically precocious youth: The first three decades of a planned 50-year study of intellectual talent. In R. F. Subotnik & K. D. Arnold (Eds.), *Beyond Terman: Contemporary longitudinal studies of giftedness and talent* (pp. 255–281). Norwood, NJ: Ablex.

Lubinski, D., Benbow, C. P., & Sanders, C. E. (1993). Reconceptualizing gender differences in achievement among the gifted. In K. A. Heller, F. J. Monks, & A. H. Passow (Eds.), *International handbook of research and development of giftedness and talent* (pp. 693–707). London: Pergamon Press.

Lubinski, D., & Dawis, R. V. (1992). Aptitudes, skills, and proficiencies. In M. D. Dunnette & L. M. Hough (Eds.), *The handbook of industrial/organizational psychology* (2nd ed., pp. 1–59). Palo Alto, CA: Consulting Psychologists Press.

Lubinski, D., & Humphreys, L. G. (1990). A broadly based analysis of mathematical giftedness. *Intelligence, 14*, 327–355.

Lykken, D., & Tellegen, A. (1996). Happiness is a stochastic phenomenon. *Psychological Science, 7,* 186–189.

Lynn, R. (1994). Sex differences in intelligence and brain size: A paradox resolved. *Personality and Individual Differences, 17,* 257–271.

Lytton, H., & Romney, D. M. (1991). Parents' differential socialization of boys and girls: A meta-analysis. *Psychological Bulletin, 109,* 267–296.

Maccoby, E. E. (1988). Gender as a social category. *Developmental Psychology, 24,* 755–765.

Maccoby, E. E. (1990). Gender and relationships: A developmental account. *American Psychologist, 45,* 513–520.

Maccoby, E. E., Buchanan, C. M., Mnookin, R. H., & Dornbusch, S. M. (1993). Postdivorce roles of mothers and fathers in the lives of their children. *Journal of Family Psychology, 7,* 24–38.

Maccoby, E. E., & Jacklin, C. N. (1974). *The psychology of sex differences.* Stanford, CA: Stanford University Press.

Maccoby, E. E., & Jacklin, C. N. (1987). Gender segregation in childhood. In E. H. Reese (Ed.), *Advanced in child development and behavior* (Vol. 20, pp. 239–287). New York: Academic Press.

Maccoby, E. E., & Martin, J. A. (1983). Socialization in the context of the family: Parent–child interaction. In E. M. Hetherington (Ed.), *Handbook of child psychology: Vol. 4. Socialization, personality, and social development* (4th ed., pp. 1–101). New York: Wiley.

MacDonald, K. (1988). *Social and personality development: An evolutionary synthesis.* New York: Plenum.

MacDonald, K. (1992). Warmth as a developmental construct: An evolutionary analysis. *Child Development, 63,* 753–773.

MacDonald, K. (1993). Parent–child play: An evolutionary perspective. In K. MacDonald (Ed.), *Parent–child play: Descriptions and implications* (pp. 113–143). Albany: State University of New York Press.

MacDonald, K. (1995a). The establishment and maintenance of socially imposed monogamy in Western Europe. *Politics and the Life Sciences, 14,* 3–46.

MacDonald, K. (1995b). Evolution, the five-factor model, and levels of personality. *Journal of Personality, 63,* 525–567.

MacDonald, K. (1996). What do children want? A conceptualisation of evolutionary influences on children's motivation in the peer group. *International Journal of Behavioral Development, 19,* 53–73.

Maguire, E. A., Frackowiak, R. S. J., & Frith, C. D. (1996). Learning to find your way: A role for the human hippocampal formation. *Proceedings of the Royal Society of London B, 263,* 1745–1750.

Maguire, E. A., Frackowiak, R. S. J., & Frith, C. D. (1997). Recalling routes around London: Activation of the right hippocampus in taxi drivers. *Journal of Neuroscience, 17,* 7103–7110.

Malt, B. C. (1995). Category coherence in cross-cultural perspective. *Cognitive Psychology, 29,* 85–148.

Mandler, J. M. (1992). How to build a baby: II. Conceptual primitives. *Psychological Review, 99,* 587–604.

Manning, J. T., & Chamberlain, A. T. (1993). Fluctuating asymmetry, sexual selection and canine teeth in primates. *Proceedings of the Royal Society of London B, 251,* 83–87.

Manning, J. T., Koukourakis, K., & Brodie, D. A. (1997). Fluctuating asymmetry, metabolic rate and sexual selection in human males. *Evolution and Human Behavior, 18,* 15–21.

Manning, J. T., Scutt, D., Whitehouse, G. H., & Leinster, S. J. (1997). Breast asymmetry and phenotypic quality in women. *Evolution and Human Behavior, 18,* 223–236.

Manson, J. H. (1996). Male dominance and mount series duration in Cayo Santiago rhesus macaques. *Animal Behaviour, 51,* 1219–1231.

Manson, J. H., & Wrangham, R. W. (1991). Intergroup aggression in chimpanzees and humans. *Current Anthropology, 32,* 369–390.

Marler, P. (1970). Bird song and speech development: Could there be parallels? *American Scientist, 58,* 669–673.

Marler, P. (1991). The instinct to learn. In S. Carey & R. Gelman (Eds.), *The epigenesis of mind: Essays on biology and cognition* (pp. 37–66). Hillsdale, NJ: Erlbaum.

Marshall, W. A. (1978). Puberty. In F. Falkner & J. M. Tanner (Eds.), *Human growth 2: Postnatal growth* (pp. 141–181). New York: Plenum Press.

Martorell, R., Rivera, J., Kaplowitz, H., & Pollitt, E. (1992). Long-term consequences of growth retardation during early childhood. In M. Hernández & J. Argente (Eds.), *Human growth: Basic and clinical aspects* (pp. 143–149). Amsterdam: Elsevier.

Mastekaasa, A. (1994). Marital status, distress, and well-being: An international comparison. *Journal of Comparative Family Studies, 25,* 183–205.

Masters, M. S., & Sanders, B. (1993). Is the gender difference in mental rotation disappearing? *Behavior Genetics, 23,* 337–341.

Matthews, M. H. (1987). Sex differences in spatial competence: The ability of young children to map "primed" unfamiliar environments. *Educational Psychology, 7,* 77–90.

Matthews, M. H. (1992). *Making sense of place: Children's understanding of large-scale environments.* Savage, MD: Barnes & Noble Books.

Maynard Smith, J. (1977). Parental investment: A prospective analysis. *Animal Behaviour, 25,* 1–9.

Mayr, E. (1974). Behavior programs and evolutionary strategies. *American Scientist, 62,* 650–659.

Mayr, E. (1983). How to carry out the adaptationist program? *American Naturalist, 121,* 324–334.

Mazur, A., & Booth, A. (in press). Testosterone and dominance in men. *Behavioral and Brain Sciences.*

McBurney, D. H., Gaulin, S. J. C., Devineni, T., & Adams, C. (1997). Superior spatial memory of women: Stronger evidence for the gathering hypothesis. *Evolution and Human Behavior, 18,* 165–174.

McCardle, P., & Wilson, B. E. (1990). Hormonal influence on language development in physically advanced children. *Brain and Language, 38,* 410–423.

McClintock, M. K., & Herdt, G. (1996). Rethinking puberty: The development of sexual attraction. *Current Directions in Psychological Science, 5,* 178–183.

McCrae, R. R., & Costa, P. T., Jr. (1997). Personality trait structure as a human universal. *American Psychologist, 52,* 509–516.

McDonald, D. B. (1993). Demographic consequences of sexual selection in the long-tailed manakin. *Behavioral Ecology, 4,* 297–309.

McEwen, B. S., Biron, C. A., Brunson, K. W., Bulloch, K., Chambers, W. H., Dhabhar, F. S., Goldfarb, R. H., Kitson, R. P., Miller, A. H., Spencer, R. L., & Weiss, J. M. (1997). The role of adrenocorticoids as modulators of immune function in health and disease: Neural, endocrine and immune interactions. *Brain Research Reviews, 23,* 79–133.

McGee, M. G. (1979). Human spatial abilities: Psychometric studies and environmental, genetic, hormonal, and neurological influences. *Psychological Bulletin, 86,* 889–918.

McGinnis, P. R. (1979). Sexual behavior in free-living chimpanzees: Consort relationships. In D. A. Hamburg & E. R McCown (Eds.), *The great apes* (pp. 429–439). Menlo Park, CA: Benjamin/Cummings Publishing Co.

McGlone, J. (1980). Sex differences in human brain asymmetry: A critical survey. *Behavioral and Brain Sciences, 3,* 215–263.

McGrew, W. C. (1992). *Chimpanzee material culture: Implications for human evolution*. New York: Cambridge University Press.

McGue, M., Bacon, S., & Lykken, D. T. (1993). Personality stability and change in early adulthood: A behavioral genetic analysis. *Developmental Psychology, 29*, 96–109.

McGuinness, D., & Pribram, K. H. (1979). The origins of sensory bias in the development of gender differences in perception and cognition. In M. Bortner (Ed.), *Cognitive growth and development: Essays in memory of Herbert G. Birch* (pp. 3–56). New York: Brunner/Mazel.

McGuinness, D., & Symonds, J. (1977). Sex differences in choice behavior: The object–person dimension. *Perception, 6*, 691–694.

McHenry, H. M. (1991). Sexual dimorphism in *Australopithecus afarensis. Journal of Human Evolution, 20*, 21–32.

McHenry, H. M. (1992). Body size and proportions in early hominids. *American Journal of Physical Anthropology, 87*, 407–431.

McHenry, H. M. (1994a). Behavioral ecological implications of early hominid body size. *Journal of Human Evolution, 27*, 77–87.

McHenry, H. M. (1994b). Tempo and mode in human evolution. *Proceedings of the National Academy of Sciences, USA, 91*, 6780–6786.

McKeever, W. F. (1995). Hormone and hemisphericity hypotheses regarding cognitive sex differences: Possible future explanatory power, but current empirical chaos. *Learning and Individual Differences, 7*, 323–340.

McKinney, M. L. (1998). The juvenilized ape myth—Our "overdeveloped" brain. *BioScience, 48*, 109–116.

McLoyd, V. C. (1989). Socialization and development in a changing economy: The effects of paternal job and income loss on children. *American Psychologist, 44*, 293–302.

Mealey, L. (1995). The sociobiology of sociopathy: An integrated evolutionary model. *Behavioral and Brain Sciences, 18*, 523–599.

Meaney, M. J., & Stewart, J. (1981). Neonatal androgens influence the social play of prepubescent rats. *Hormones and Behavior, 15*, 197–213.

Menken, J., Trussell, J., & Larsen, U. (1986). Age and infertility. *Science, 233*, 1389–1394.

Mesquida, C. G., & Wiener, N. I. (1996). Human collective aggression: A behavioral ecology perspective. *Ethology and Sociobiology, 17*, 247–262.

Mesquita, B., & Frijda, N. H. (1992). Cultural variations in emotion: A review. *Psychological Bulletin, 112*, 179–204.

Messick, D. M., & Mackie, D. M. (1989). Intergroup relations. *Annual Review of Psychology, 40*, 45–81.

Miller, D. C., & Byrnes, J. P. (1997). The role of contextual and personal factors in children's risk taking. *Developmental Psychology, 33*, 814–823.

Miller, E. M. (1994). Paternal provisioning versus mate seeking in human populations. *Personality and Individual Differences, 17*, 227–255.

Miller, L. K., & Santoni, V. (1986). Sex differences in spatial abilities: Strategic and experiential correlates. *Acta Psychologica, 62*, 225–235.

Milner, A. D., & Goodale, M. A. (1995). *The visual brain in action*. New York: Oxford University Press.

Mineka, S., Watson, D., & Clark, L. A. (1998). Comorbidity of anxiety and unipolar mood disorders. *Annual Review of Psychology, 49*, 377–412.

Mitani, J. C., Gros-Louis, J., & Richards, A. F. (1996). Sexual dimorphism, the operational sex ratio, and the intensity of male competition in polygynous primates. *American Naturalist, 147*, 966–980.

Moffat, S. D., & Hampson, E. (1996a). A curvilinear relationship between testosterone and spatial cognition in humans: Possible influence of hand preference. *Psychoneuroendocrinology, 21*, 323–337.

Moffat, S. D., & Hampson, E. (1996b). Salivary testosterone levels in left- and right-handed adults. *Neuropsychologia, 34*, 225–233.

Moffat, S. D., Hampson, E., & Hatzipantelis, M. (1998). Navigation in a "virtual" maze: Sex differences and correlation with psychometric measures of spatial ability in humans. *Evolution and Human Behavior, 19*, 73–87.

Molfese, D. L. (1990). Auditory evoked responses recorded from 16-month-old human infants to words they did and did not know. *Brain and Language, 38*, 345–363.

Molfese, D. L., Freeman, R. B., & Palermo, D. S. (1975). The ontogeny of brain lateralization for speech & nonspeech stimuli. *Brain and Language, 2*, 356–368.

Moller, L. C., & Serbin, L. A. (1996). Antecedents of gender segregation—Cognitive consonance, gender-typed toy preferences and behavioral compatibility. *Sex Roles, 35*, 445–460.

Møller, A. P. (1988). Female choice selects for male sexual tail ornaments in the monogamous swallow. *Nature, 332*, 640–642.

Møller, A. P. (1989). Viability costs of male tail ornaments in a swallow. *Nature, 339*, 132–135.

Møller, A. P. (1990a). Effects of a haematophagous mite on the barn swallow (*HIRUNDO RUSTICA*): A test of the Hamilton and Zuk hypothesis. *Evolution, 44*, 771–784.

Møller, A. P. (1990b). Parasites and sexual selection: Current status of the Hamilton and Zuk hypothesis. *Journal of Evolutionary Biology, 3*, 319–328.

Møller, A. P. (1991). Sexual selection in the monogamous barn swallow (*HIRUNDO RUSTICA*). I. Determinants of tail ornament size. *Evolution, 45*, 1823–1836.

Møller, A. P. (1993). Patterns of fluctuating asymmetry in sexual ornaments predict female choice. *Journal of Evolutionary Biology, 6*, 481–491.

Møller, A. P. (1994a). *Sexual selection and the barn swallow*. New York: Oxford University Press.

Møller, A. P. (1994b). Symmetrical male sexual ornaments, paternal care, and offspring quality. *Behavioral Ecology, 5*, 188–194.

Møller, A. P. (1997). Immune defence, extra-pair paternity, and sexual selection in birds. *Proceedings of the Royal Society of London B, 264*, 561–566.

Møller, A. P., Saino, N., Taramino, G., Galeotti, P., & Ferrario, S. (1998). Paternity and multiple signaling: Effects of secondary sexual character and song on paternity in the barn swallow. *American Naturalist, 151*, 236–242.

Møller, A. P., Soler, M., & Thornhill, R. (1995). Breast asymmetry, sexual selection, and human reproductive success. *Ethology and Sociobiology, 16*, 207–219.

Møller, A. P., & Tegelström, H. (1997). Extra-pair paternity and tail ornamentation in the barn swallow *Hirundo rustica*. *Behavioral Ecology and Sociobiology, 41*, 353–360.

Møller, A. P., & Thornhill, R. (1998). Bilateral symmetry and sexual selection: A meta-analysis. *American Naturalist, 151*, 174–192.

Molleson, T. (1994, November). The eloquent bones of Abu Hureyra. *Scientific American, 271*, 70–75.

Moore, E. G., & Smith, A. W. (1987). Sex and ethnic group differences in mathematics achievement: Results from the national longitudinal study. *Journal for Research in Mathematics Education, 18*, 25–36.

Mori, A., Watanabe, K., & Yamaguchi, N. (1989). Longitudinal changes of dominance rank among females of the Koshima group of Japanese monkeys. *Primates, 30*, 147–173.

Moscovitch, M., Winocur, G., & Behrmann, M. (1997). What is special about face recognition? Nineteen experiments on a person with visual object agnosia and dyslexia but normal face recognition. *Journal of Cognitive Neuroscience, 9*, 555–604.

Moss, C. F., & Shettleworth, S. J. (Eds.). (1996). *Neuroethological studies of cognitive and perceptual processes.* Boulder, CO: Westview Press.

Moss, C. F., & Simmons, J. A. (1996). Perception along the axis of target range in the echolocating bat. In C. F. Moss & S. J. Shettleworth (Eds.), *Neuroethological studies of cognitive and perceptual processes* (pp. 253–279). Boulder, CO: Westview Press.

Mountain, J. L., Lin, A. A., Bowcock, A. M., & Cavalli-Sforza, L. L. (1993). Evolution of modern humans: Evidence from nuclear DNA polymorphisms. In M. J. Aitken, C. B. Stringer, & P. A. Mellars (Eds.), *The origins of modern humans and the impact of chronometric dating* (pp. 69–83). Princeton, NJ: Princeton University Press.

Muller, H. J. (1964). The relation of recombination to mutational advance. *Mutation Research, 1,* 2–9.

Müller, R.-A. (1996). Innateness, autonomy, universality? Neurobiological approaches to language. *Behavioral and Brain Sciences, 19,* 611–675.

Munroe, R. H., Munroe, R. L., & Brasher, A. (1985). Precursors of spatial ability: A longitudinal study among the Logoli of Kenya. *Journal of Social Psychology, 125,* 23–33.

Munroe, R. L., & Munroe, R. H. (1971). Effect of environmental experience on spatial ability in an East African society. *Journal of Social Psychology, 83,* 15–22.

Murdock, G. P. (1981). *Atlas of world cultures.* Pittsburgh: University of Pittsburgh Press.

Myers, D. G., & Diener, E. (1995). Who is happy? *Psychological Science, 6,* 10–19.

Nei, M., & Hughes, A. L. (1991). Polymorphism and evolution of the major histocompatibility complex loci in mammals. In R. K. Selander, A. G., Clark, & T. S. Whittam (Eds.), *Evolution at the molecular level* (pp. 222–247). Sunderland, MA: Sinauer.

Neisser, U., Boodoo, G., Bouchard, T. J., Jr., Boykin, A. W., Brody, N., Ceci, S. J., Halpern, D. F., Loehlin, J. C., Perloff, R., Sternberg, R. J., & Urbina, S. (1995). *Intelligence: Knowns and unknowns.* Washington, DC: American Psychological Association.

Newcomb, A. F., Bukowski, W. M., & Pattee, L. (1993). Children's peer relations: A meta-analytic review of popular, rejected, neglected, controversial, and average sociometric status. *Psychological Bulletin, 113,* 99–128.

Nicolson, N. A. (1987). Infants, mothers, and other females. In B. B. Smuts, D. L. Cheney, R. M. Seyfarth, R. W. Wrangham, & T. T. Struhsaker (Eds.), *Primate societies* (pp. 330–342). Chicago: University of Chicago Press.

Nishida, T. (1979). The social structure of chimpanzees of the Mahale Mountains. In D. A. Hamburg & E. R McCown (Eds.), *The great apes* (pp. 73–121). Menlo Park, CA: Benjamin/Cummings Publishing Co.

Nishida, T., & Hiraiwa-Hasegawa, M. (1987). Chimpanzees and bonobos: Cooperative relationships among males. In B. B. Smuts, D. L. Cheney, R. M. Seyfarth, R. W. Wrangham, & T. T. Struhsaker (Eds.), *Primate societies* (pp. 165–177). Chicago: University of Chicago Press.

Nolen-Hoeksema, S. (1987). Sex differences in unipolar depression: Evidence and theory. *Psychological Bulletin, 101,* 259–282.

Nottebohm, F. (1970). Ontogeny of bird song. *Science, 167,* 950–956.

Nottebohm, F. (1971). Neural lateralization of vocal control in a Passerine bird: 1. Song. *Journal of Experimental Zoology, 177,* 229–262.

Nottebohm, F. (1980). Testosterone triggers growth of brain vocal control nuclei in adult female canaries. *Brain Research, 189,* 429–436.

Nottebohm, F. (1981). A brain for all seasons: Cyclical anatomical changes in song-control nuclei of the canary brain. *Science, 214,* 1368–1370.

Ober, C., Elias, S., Kostyu, D. D., & Hauck, W. W. (1992). Decreased fecundability in Hutterite couples sharing HLA-DR. *American Journal of Human Genetics, 50,* 6–14.

Ober, C., Weitkamp, L. R., Cox, N., Dytch, H., Kostyu, D., & Elias, S. (1997). HLA and mate choice in humans. *American Journal of Human Genetics, 61,* 497–504.

O'Brien, M. (1992). Gender identity and sex roles. In V. B. Van Hasselt & M. Hersen

(Eds.), *Handbook of social development: A lifespan perspective* (pp. 325–345). New York: Plenum Press.

Ohsawa, H., Inoue, M., & Takenaka, O. (1993). Mating strategy and reproductive success of male patas monkeys (*Erythrocebus patas*). *Primates, 34,* 533–544.

Oliver, M. B., & Hyde, J. S. (1993). Gender differences in sexuality: A meta-analysis. *Psychological Bulletin, 114,* 29–51.

Oring, L. W., Lank, D. B., & Maxson, S. J. (1983). Population studies of the polyandrous spotted sandpiper. *Auk, 100,* 272–285.

Owens, I. P. F., Burke, T., & Thompson, D. B. A. (1994). Extraordinary sex roles in the Eurasian dotterel: Female mating arenas, female–female competition, and female mate choice. *American Naturalist, 144,* 76–100.

Owens, I. P. F., & Hartley, I. R. (1998). Sexual dimorphism in birds: Why are there so many different forms of dimorphism? *Proceedings of the Royal Society of London B, 265,* 397–407.

Packer, C., Herbst, L., Pusey, A. E., Bygott, J. D., Hanby, J. P., Cairns, S. J., & Mulder, M. B. (1988). Reproductive success of lions. In T. H. Clutton-Brock (Ed.), *Reproductive success: Studies of individual variation in contrasting breeding systems* (pp. 363–383). Chicago: University of Chicago Press.

Packer, C., & Pusey, A. E. (1997, May). Divided we fall: Cooperation among lions. *Scientific American, 276,* 52–59.

Paglin, M., & Rufolo, A. M. (1990). Heterogeneous human capital, occupational choice, and male–female earnings differences. *Journal of Labor Economics, 8,* 123–144.

Pakkenberg, B., & Gundersen, J. G. (1997). Neocortical neuron number in humans: Effect of sex and age. *Journal of Comparative Neurology, 384,* 312–320.

Panksepp, J. (1981). The ontogeny of play in rats. *Developmental Psychobiology, 14,* 327–332.

Panksepp, J. (1989). The neurobiology of emotions: Of animal brains and human feelings. In H. Wagner & A. Manstead (Eds.), *Handbook of social psychophysiology* (pp. 5–26). New York: Wiley.

Panksepp, J., Siviy, S., & Normansell, L. (1984). The psychobiology of play: Theoretical and methodological perspectives. *Neuroscience & Biobehavioral Reviews, 8,* 465–492.

Papoušek, H., & Papoušek, M. (1995). Intuitive parenting. In M. H. Bornstein (Ed.), *Handbook of parenting, Vol. 2: Biology and ecology of parenting* (pp. 117–136). Hillsdale, NJ: Erlbaum.

Parish, A. R. (1996). Female relationships in bonobos (*Pan paniscus*): Evidence for bonding, cooperation, and female dominance in a male-philopatric species. *Human Nature, 7,* 61–96.

Parke, R. D. (1995). Fathers and families. In M. H. Bornstein (Ed.), *Handbook of parenting, Vol. 3: Status and social conditions of parenting* (pp. 27–63). Hillsdale, NJ: Erlbaum.

Parker, G. A., & Simmons, L. W. (1996). Parental investment and the control of selection: Predicting the direction of sexual competition. *Proceedings of the Royal Society of London B, 263,* 315–321.

Parker, S. T. (1984). Playing for keeps: An evolutionary perspective on human games. In P. K. Smith (Ed.), *Play in animals and humans* (pp. 271–293). Oxford, England: Basil Blackwell.

Pasternak, B., Ember, C. R., & Ember, M. (1997). *Sex, gender, and kinship: A cross-cultural perspective.* Upper Saddle River, NJ: Prentice Hall.

Paterson, S., & Pemberton, J. M. (1997). No evidence for major histocompatibility complex-dependent mating patterns in a free-living ruminant population. *Proceedings of the Royal Society of London B, 264,* 1813–1819.

Paul, A., Kuester, J., Timme, A., & Arnemann, J. (1993). The association between rank, mating effort, and reproductive success in male barbary macaques (*Macaca sylvanus*). *Primates, 34,* 491–502.

Paul, L., & Hirsch, L. R. (1996). Human male mating strategies: II. Moral codes of "quality" and "quantity" strategies. *Ethology and Sociobiology, 17,* 71–86.

Peck, J. R., & Eyre-Walker, A. (1997). The muddle about mutations. *Nature, 387,* 135–136.

Pedersen, F. A. (1991). Secular trends in human sex ratios: Their influence on individual and family behavior. *Human Nature, 2,* 271–291.

Pellegrini, A. D. (1995). Boys' rough-and-tumble play and social competence: Contemporaneous and longitudinal relations. In A. D. Pellegrini (Ed.), *The future of play theory: A multidisciplinary inquiry into the contributions of Brian Sutton-Smith* (pp. 107–126). Albany: State University of New York Press.

Pellis, S. M., Field, E. F., Smith, L. K., & Pellis, V. C. (1997). Multiple differences in the play fighting of male and female rats. Implications for the causes and functions of play. *Neuroscience and Biobehavioral Reviews, 21,* 105–120.

Perloe, S. I. (1992). Male mating competition, female choice and dominance in a free ranging group of Japanese macaques. *Primates, 33,* 289–304.

Perper, T. (1989). Theories and observations on sexual selection and female choice in human beings. *Medical Anthropology, 11,* 409–454.

Pérusse, D. (1993). Cultural and reproductive success in industrialized societies: Testing the relationship at the proximate and ultimate levels. *Behavioral and Brain Sciences, 16,* 267–322.

Pérusse, D. (1994). Mate choice in modern societies: Testing evolutionary hypotheses with behavioral data. *Human Nature, 5,* 255–278.

Pérusse, D., Neale, M. C., Heath, A. C., & Eaves, L. J. (1994). Human parental behavior: Evidence for genetic influence and potential implication for gene-culture transmission. *Behavior Genetics, 24,* 327–335.

Peters, M., Laeng, B., Latham, K., Jackson, M., Zaiyouna, R., & Richardson, C. (1995). A redrawn Vandenberg and Kuse mental rotations test: Different versions and factors that affect performance. *Brain and Cognition, 28,* 39–58.

Petrie, M. (1983). Female moorhens compete for small fat males. *Science, 220,* 413–415.

Petrie, M. (1994). Improved growth and survival of offspring of peacocks with more elaborate trains. *Nature, 371,* 598–599.

Petrie, M., Halliday, T., & Sanders, C. (1991). Peahens prefer peacocks with elaborate trains. *Animal Behavior, 41,* 323–331.

Petrinovich, L., & Baptista, L. F. (1987). Song development in the white crowned sparrow: Modification of learned song. *Animal Behaviour, 35,* 961–974.

Petrinovich, L., O'Neill, P., & Jorgensen, M. (1993). An empirical study of moral intuitions: Toward an evolutionary ethics. *Journal of Personality and Social Psychology, 64,* 467–478.

Pettigrew, T. F. (1998). Intergroup contact theory. *Annual Review of Psychology, 49,* 65–85.

Phares, V., & Compas, B. E. (1993). Fathers and developmental psychopathology. *Current Directions in Psychological Science, 2,* 162–165.

Phillips, K., & Silverman, I. (1997). Differences in the relationship of menstrual cycle phase to spatial performance on two- and three-dimensional tasks. *Hormones and Behavior, 32,* 167–175.

Phillips, S. D., & Imhoff, A. R. (1997). Women and career development: A decade of research. *Annual Review of Psychology, 48,* 31–59.

Piatelli-Palmarini, M. (1989). Evolution, selection and cognition: From "learning" to parameter setting in biology and the study of language. *Cognition, 31,* 1–44.

Pick, H. L., Jr., Montello, D. R., & Somerville, S. C. (1988). Landmarks and the coordination and integration of spatial information. *British Journal of Developmental Psychology*, 6, 372–375.

Pierce, C. A. (1996). Body height and romantic attraction: A meta-analytic test of the male-taller norm. *Social Behavior and Personality*, 24, 143–150.

Pinker, S. (1994). *The language instinct*. New York: Morrow.

Pinker, S. (1997). *How the mind works*. New York: Norton.

Pinker, S., & Bloom, P. (1990). Natural language and natural selection. *Behavioral and Brain Sciences*, 13, 707–784.

Pitcher, E. G., & Schultz, L. H. (1983). *Boys and girls at play: The development of sex roles*. South Hadley, MA: Bergin & Garvey Publishers.

Plavcan, J. M., & van Schaik, C. P. (1992). Intrasexual competition and canine dimorphism in anthropoid primates. *American Journal of Physical Anthropology*, 87, 461–477.

Plavcan, J. M., & van Schaik, C. P. (1997a). Interpreting hominid behavior on the basis of sexual dimorphism. *Journal of Human Evolution*, 32, 345–374.

Plavcan, J. M., & van Schaik, C. P. (1997b). Intrasexual competition and body weight dimorphism in anthropoid primates. *American Journal of Physical Anthropology*, 103, 37–68.

Plavcan, J. M., van Schaik, C. P., & Kappeler, P. M. (1995). Competition, coalitions and canine size in primates. *Journal of Human Evolution*, 28, 245–276.

Ploegh, H. L. (1998). Viral strategies of immune evasion. *Science*, 280, 248–253.

Plomin, R., Fulker, D. W., Corley, R., & DeFries, J. C. (1997). Nature, nurture, and cognitive development from 1 to 16 years: A parent–offspring adoption study. *Psychological Science*, 8, 442–447.

Plomin, R., & Petrill, S. A. (1997). Genetics and intelligence: What's new? *Intelligence*, 24, 53–77.

Pomiankowski, A., & Iwasa, Y. (1998). Runaway ornament diversity caused by Fisherian sexual selection. *Proceedings of the National Academy of Sciences, USA*, 95, 5106–5111.

Popp, K., & Baum, A. (1989). Hormones and emotions: Affective correlates of endocrine activity. In H. Wagner & A. Manstead (Eds.), *Handbook of social psychophysiology* (pp. 99–120). New York: Wiley.

Potthoff, R. F., & Whittinghill, M. (1965). Maximum-likelihood estimation of the proportion of nonpaternity. *American Journal of Human Genetics*, 17, 480–494.

Potti, J., & Merino, S. (1996). Parasites and the ontogeny of sexual size dimorphism in a passerine bird. *Proceedings of the Royal Society of London B*, 263, 9–12.

Potts, W. K., Manning, C. J., & Wakeland, E. K. (1991). Mating patterns in seminatural populations of mice influenced by MHC genotype. *Nature*, 352, 619–621.

Poucet, B. (1993). Spatial cognitive maps in animals: New hypotheses on their structure and neural mechanisms. *Psychological Review*, 100, 163–182.

Povinelli, D. J., & Eddy, T. J. (1996). What young chimpanzees know about seeing. *Monographs of the Society for Research in Child Development*, 61(Serial No. 247).

Pratto, F. (1996). Sexual politics: The gender gap in the bedroom, the cupboard, and the cabinet. In D. M. Buss & N. M. Malamuth (Eds.), *Sex, power, conflict: Evolutionary and feminist perspectives* (pp. 179–230). New York: Oxford University Press.

Pratto, F., Stallworth, L. M., Sidanius, J., & Siers, B. (1997). The gender gap in occupational role attainment: A social dominance approach. *Journal of Personality and Social Psychology*, 72, 37–53.

Premack, D., & Premack, A. J. (1995). Origins of human social competence. In M. S. Gazzaniga (Ed.), *The cognitive neurosciences* (pp. 205–218). Cambridge, MA: Bradford Books/MIT Press.

Premack, D., & Woodruff, G. (1978). Does the chimpanzee have a theory of mind? *Behavioral and Brain Sciences*, 1, 515–526.

Pribil, S., & Picman, J. (1996). Polygyny in the red-winged blackbird: Do females prefer monogamy or polygamy? *Behavioral Ecology & Sociobiology, 38*, 183–190.

Pruett-Jones, S., & Pruett-Jones, M. (1994). Sexual competition and courtship disruptions: Why do male bowerbirds destroy each other's bowers? *Animal Behaviour, 47*, 607–620.

Pryce, C. R. (1992). A comparative systems model of the regulation of maternal motivation in mammals. *Animal Behaviour, 43*, 417–441.

Pryce, C. R. (1993). The regulation of maternal behaviour in marmosets and tamarins. *Behavioural Processes, 30*, 201–224.

Pryce, C. R. (1995). Determinants of motherhood in human and nonhuman primates: A biosocial model. In C. R. Pryce, R. D. Martin, & D. Skuse (Eds.), *Motherhood in human and nonhuman primates: Biosocial determinants* (pp. 1–15). Basel, Switzerland: Karger.

Pugh, K. R., Shaywitz, B. A., Shaywitz, S. E., Constable, R. T., Skudlarski, P., Fulbright, R. K., Bronen, R. A., Shankweiler, D. P., Katz, L., Fletcher, J. M., & Gore, J. C. (1996). Cerebral organization of component processes in reading. *Brain, 119*, 1221–1238.

Pugh, K. R., Shaywitz, B. A., Shaywitz, S. E., Fulbright, R. K., Byrd, D., Skudlarski, P., Shankweiler, D. P., Katz, L., Constable, R. T., Fletcher, J., Lacadie, C., Marchione, K., & Gore, J. C. (1996). Auditory selective attention: An MRI investigation. *Neuroimage, 4*, 159–173.

Pugh, K. R., Shaywitz, B. A., Shaywitz, S. E., Shankweiler, D. P., Katz, L., Fletcher, J. M., Skudlarski, P., Fulbright, R. K., Constable, R. T., Bronen, R. A., Lacadie, C., & Gore, J. C. (1997). Predicting reading performance from neuroimaging profiles: The cerebral basis of phonological effects in printed word identification. *Journal of Experimental Psychology: Human Perception and Performance, 23*, 299–318.

Pusey, A., Williams, J., & Goodall, J. (1997). The influence of dominance rank on the reproductive success of female chimpanzees. *Science, 277*, 828–831.

Quartz, S. R., & Sejnowski, T. J. (1998). The neural basis of cognitive development: A constructivist manifesto. *Behavioral and Brain Sciences, 20*, 537–596.

Raleigh, M. J., & McGuire, M. T. (1989). Female influences on male dominance acquisition in captive vervet monkeys, *Cercopithecus aethiops sabaeus. Animal Behaviour, 38*, 59–67.

Rasika, S., Nottebohm, F., & Alvarez-Buylla, A. (1994). Testosterone increases the recruitment and-or survival of new high vocal center neurons in adult female canaries. *Proceedings of the National Academy of Sciences, USA, 91*, 7854–7858.

Raven, J. C., Court, J. H., & Raven, J. (1993). *Manual for Raven's Progressive Matrices and Vocabulary Scales.* London: H. K. Lewis.

Ray, J. C., & Sapolsky, R. M. (1992). Styles of male social behavior and their endocrine correlates among high-ranking wild baboons. *American Journal of Primatology, 28*, 231–250.

Raymond, C. L., & Benbow, C. P. (1986). Gender differences in mathematics: A function of parental support and student sex typing? *Developmental Psychology, 22*, 808–819.

Read, A. F. (1987). Comparative evidence supports the Hamilton and Zuk hypothesis on parasites and sexual selection. *Nature, 328*, 68–70.

Read, A. F. (1988). Parasites. *Trends in Ecology & Evolution, 3*, 97–102.

Read, A. F., & Weary, D. M. (1990). Sexual selection and the evolution of bird song: A test of the Hamilton–Zuk hypothesis. *Behavioral Ecology and Sociobiology, 26*, 47–56.

Rees, E. C., Lievesley, P., Pettifor, R. A., & Perrins, C. (1996). Mate fidelity in swans: An interspecific comparison. In J. M. Black (Ed.), *Partnerships in birds: The study of monogamy* (pp. 118–137). New York: Oxford University Press.

Reinisch, J. M. (1981). Prenatal exposure to synthetic progestins increases potential for aggression in humans. *Science, 211*, 1171–1173.

Reiss, D. (1995). Genetic influences on family systems: Implications for development. *Journal of Marriage and the Family, 57,* 543–560.

Resnick, S. M., Berenbaum, S. A., Gottesman, I. I., & Bouchard, T. J., Jr. (1986). Early hormonal influences on cognitive functioning in congenital adrenal hyperplasia. *Developmental Psychology, 22,* 191–198.

Reynolds, J. D. (1987). Mating system and nesting biology of the red-necked phalarope *Phalaropus lobatus:* What constrains polyandry? *Isis, 129,* 225–242.

Reynolds, J. D., & Székely, T. (1997). The evolution of parental care in shorebirds: Life histories, ecology, and sexual selection. *Behavioral Ecology, 8,* 126–134.

Reznick, D. N., Shaw, F. H., Rodd, F. H., & Shaw, R. G. (1997). Evaluation of the rate of evolution in natural populations of guppies (*Poecilia reticulata*). *Science, 275,* 1934–1937.

Richmond, B. G., & Jungers, W. L. (1995). Size variation and sexual dimorphism in *Australopithecus afarensis* and living hominoids. *Journal of Human Evolution, 29,* 229–245.

Ridley, M. (1993). *The red queen: Sex and the evolution of human nature.* New York: Penguin Books.

Riss, D., & Goodall, J. (1977). The recent rise to the alpha-rank in a population of free-living chimpanzees. *Folia Primatologica, 27,* 134–151.

Ritchie, M. G. (1996). The shape of female mating preferences. *Proceedings of the National Academy of Sciences, USA, 93,* 14628–14631.

Robinson, J. G. (1982). Intrasexual competition and mate choice in primates. *American Journal of Primatology Supplement, 1,* 131–144.

Rodman, P. S., & Mitani, J. C. (1987). Orangutans: Sexual dimorphism in a solitary species. In B. B. Smuts, D. L. Cheney, R. M. Seyfarth, R. W. Wrangham, & T. T. Struhsaker (Eds.), *Primate societies* (pp. 146–164). Chicago: University of Chicago Press.

Rodseth, L., Wrangham, R. W., Harrigan, A. M., & Smuts, B. B. (1991). The human community as a primate society. *Current Anthropology, 32,* 221–254.

Roe, A. (1956). *Psychology of occupations.* New York: Wiley.

Rogers, A. R., & Mukherjee, A. (1992). Quantitative genetics of sexual dimorphism in human body size. *Evolution, 46,* 226–234.

Rogers, M., Hennigan, K., Bowman, C., & Miller, N. (1984). Intergroup acceptance in classroom and playground settings. In N. Miller & M. B. Brewer (Eds.), *Groups in contact: The psychology of desegregation* (pp. 213–227). Orlando, FL: Academic Press.

Rohner, R. P. (1976). Sex differences in aggression: Phylogenetic and enculturation perspectives. *Ethos, 4,* 57–72.

Rolls, B. J., Fedoroff, I. C., & Guthrie, J. F. (1991). Gender differences in eating behavior and body weight regulation. *Health Psychology, 10,* 133–142.

Rosen, B. N., & Peterson, L. (1990). Gender differences in children's outdoor play injuries: A review and an integration. *Clinical Psychology Review, 10,* 187–205.

Rosen, W. D., Adamson, L. B., & Bakeman, R. (1992). An experimental investigation of infant social referencing: Mothers' messages and gender differences. *Developmental Psychology, 28,* 1172–1178.

Rosenblatt, J. S. (1995). Hormonal basis of parenting in mammals. In M. H. Bornstein (Ed.), *Handbook of parenting, Vol. 2: Biology and ecology of parenting* (pp. 3–25). Hillsdale, NJ: Erlbaum.

Rosenthal, R., Hall, J. A., DiMatteo, M. R., Rogers, P. L., & Archer, D. (1979). *Sensitivity to nonverbal communication: The PONS test.* Baltimore: Johns Hopkins University Press.

Rothbart, M. K. (1989). Temperament and development. In G. A. Kohnstamm, J. E. Bates, & M. K. Rothbart (Eds.), *Temperament in childhood* (pp. 187–247). New York: Wiley.

Rothbaum, F., & Weisz, J. R. (1994). Parental caregiving and child externalizing behavior in nonclinical samples: A meta-analysis. *Psychological Bulletin, 116,* 55–74.

Rotter, N. G., & Rotter, G. S. (1988). Sex differences in the encoding and decoding of negative facial emotions. *Journal of Nonverbal Behavior, 12,* 139–148.

Rowe, D. C. (1994). *The limits of family influence: Genes, experience, and behavior.* New York: Guilford Press.

Rowe, L., & Houle, D. (1996). The lek paradox and the capture of genetic variance by condition dependent traits. *Proceedings of the Royal Society of London B, 263,* 1415–1421.

Rozin, P. (1976). The evolution of intelligence and access to the cognitive unconscious. In J. M. Sprague & A. N. Epstein (Eds.), *Progress in psychobiology and physiological psychology* (Vol. 6, pp. 245–280). New York: Academic Press.

Rozin, P., & Fallon, A. (1988). Body image, attitudes to weight, and misperceptions of figure preferences of the opposite sex: A comparison of men and women in two generations. *Journal of Abnormal Psychology, 97,* 342–345.

Rubin, K. H., Fein, G. G., & Vandenberg, B. (1983). Play. In P. Mussen & E. M. Hetherington (Eds.), *Handbook of child psychology: Socialization, personality, and social development* (4th ed., Vol. 4, pp. 693–774). New York: Wiley.

Ruble, D. N., & Martin, C. L. (1997). Gender development. In N. Eisenberg (Ed.), *Handbook of child psychology: Social, emotional, and personality development* (5th ed., Vol. 3, pp. 933–1016). New York: Wiley.

Ruff, C. (1987). Sexual dimorphism in human lower limb bone structure: Relationship to subsistence strategy and sexual division of labor. *Journal of Human Evolution, 16,* 391–416.

Ruff, C. B., Trinkaus, E., & Holliday, T. W. (1997). Body mass and encephalization in Pleistocene *Homo. Nature, 387,* 173–176.

Rushton, J. P. (1988). Epigenetic rules in moral development: Distal–proximal approaches to altruism and aggression. *Aggressive Behavior, 14,* 35–50.

Rushton, J. P. (1996). Self-report delinquency and violence in adult twins. *Psychiatric Genetics, 6,* 87–89.

Rushton, J. P., & Ankney, C. D. (1996). Brain size and cognitive ability: Correlations with age, sex, social class, and race. *Psychonomic Bulletin & Review, 3,* 21–36.

Rushton, J. P., Fulker, D. W., Neale, M. C., Nias, D. K. B., & Eysenck, H. J. (1986). Altruism and aggression: The heritability of individual differences. *Journal of Personality and Social Psychology, 50,* 1192–1198.

Russell, G. (1982). Shared-caregiving families: An Australian study. In M. E. Lamb (Ed.), *Nontraditional families: Parenting and child development* (pp. 139–171). Hillsdale, NJ: Erlbaum.

Ryan, M. J., & Keddy-Hector, A. (1992). Directional patterns of female mate choice and the role of sensory biases. *American Naturalist, 139,* S4–S35.

Ryff, C. D. (1995). Psychological well-being in adult life. *Current Directions in Psychological Science, 4,* 99–104.

Sade, D. S. (1967). Determinants of dominance in a group of free-ranging rhesus monkeys. In S. A. Altmann (Ed.), *Social communication among primates* (pp. 99–114). Chicago: Chicago University Press.

Saino, N., Bolzern, A. M., & Møller, A. P. (1997). Immunocompetence, ornamentation, and viability of male barn swallows (*Hirundo rustica*). *Proceedings of the National Academy of Sciences, USA, 94,* 549–552.

Saino, N., Galeotti, P., Sacchi, R., & Møller, A. P. (1997). Song and immunological condition in male barn swallows (*Hirundo rustica*). *Behavioral Ecology, 8,* 364–371.

Saino, N., & Møller, A. P. (1994). Secondary sexual characteristics, parasites and testosterone in the barn swallow, *Hirundo rustica. Animal Behaviour, 48,* 1325–1333.

Saino, N., Møller, A. P., & Bolzern, A. M. (1995). Testosterone effects on the immune system and parasite infestations in the barn swallow (*Hirundo rustica*): An experimental test of the immunocompetence hypothesis. *Behavioral Ecology, 6,* 397–404.

Saino, N., Primmer, C. R., Ellegren, H., & Møller, A. P. (1997). An experimental study of paternity and tail ornamentation in the barn swallow (*Hirundo rustica*). *Evolution, 51,* 562–570.

Sandberg, D. E., & Meyer-Bahlburg, H. F. L. (1994). Variability in middle childhood play behavior: Effects of gender, age, and family background. *Archives of Sexual Behavior, 23,* 645–663.

Sandnabba, N. K. (1996). Selective breeding for isolation-induced intermale aggression in mice: Associated responses and environmental influences. *Behavior Genetics, 26,* 477–488.

Sapolsky, R. M. (1986). Glucocorticoid toxicity in the hippocampus: Reversal by supplementation with brain fuels. *Journal of Neuroscience, 6,* 2240–2244.

Sapolsky, R. M. (1991). Testicular function, social rank and personality among wild baboons. *Psychoneuroendocrinology, 16,* 281–293.

Sapolsky, R. M. (1993). The physiology of dominance in stable versus unstable social hierarchies. In W. A. Mason & S. P. Mendoza (Eds.), *Primate social conflict* (pp. 171–204). Albany: State University of New York Press.

Sapolsky, R. M. (1997). The importance of a well-groomed child. *Science, 277,* 1620–1621.

Savin-Williams, R. C. (1987). *Adolescence: An ethological perspective.* New York: Springer-Verlag.

Sawaguchi, T. (1997). Possible involvement of sexual selection in neocortical evolution of monkeys and apes. *Folia Primatologica, 68,* 95–99.

Scarr, S. (1992). Developmental theories of the 1990s: Developmental and individual differences. *Child Development, 63,* 1–19.

Scarr, S., & McCartney, K. (1983). How people make their own environments: A theory of genotype → environment effects. *Child Development, 54,* 424–435.

Scarr, S., Phillips, D., & McCartney, K. (1989). Working mothers and their families. *American Psychologist, 44,* 1402–1409.

Schaal, B., Tremblay, R. E., Soussignan, R., & Susman, E. J. (1996). Male testosterone linked to high social dominance but low physical aggression in early adolescence. *Journal of the American Academy of Child and Adolescent Psychiatry, 35,* 1322–1330.

Schaller, M. (1992). In-group favoritism and statistical reasoning in social inference: Implications for formation and maintenance of group stereotypes. *Journal of Personality and Social Psychology, 63,* 61–74.

Schellenberg, E. G., & Trehub, S. E. (1996). Natural musical intervals: Evidence from infant listeners. *Psychological Science, 7,* 272–277.

Scher, A., & Mayseless, O. (1994). Mothers' attachment with spouse and parenting in the first year. *Journal of Social and Interpersonal Relationships, 11,* 601–609.

Schiff, W., & Oldak, R. (1990). Accuracy of judging time to arrival: Effects of modality, trajectory, and gender. *Journal of Experimental Psychology: Human Perception and Performance, 16,* 303–316.

Schlupp, I., Marler, C., & Ryan, M. J. (1994). Benefit to male sailfin mollies of mating with heterospecific females. *Science, 263,* 373–374.

Schmidt, F. L., & Hunter, J. E. (1992). Development of a causal model of processes determining job performance. *Current Directions in Psychological Science, 1,* 89–92.

Schmitt, D. P., & Buss, D. M. (1996). Strategic self-promotion and competitor derogation: Sex and context effects on the perceived effectiveness of mate attraction tactics. *Journal of Personality and Social Psychology, 70,* 1185–1204.

Schoech, S. J., Mumme, R. L., & Wingfield, J. C. (1996). Prolactin and helping behaviour in the cooperatively breeding Florida scrub-jay, *Aphelocoma c. coerulescens. Animal Behaviour, 52,* 445–456.

Schulz, R., & Heckhausen, J. (1996). A life span model of successful aging. *American Psychologist, 51,* 702–714.

Schwartz, G. E., Brown, S.-L., & Ahern, G. L. (1980). Facial muscle patterning and subjective experience during affective imagery: Sex differences. *Psychophysiology, 17,* 75–82.

Schwartz, J. E., Friedman, H. S., Tucker, J. S., Tomlinson-Keasey, C., Wingard, D. L., & Criqui, M. H. (1995). Sociodemographic and psychosocial factors in childhood as predictors of adult mortality. *American Journal of Public Health, 85,* 1237–1245.

Scutt, D., & Manning, J. T. (1996). Symmetry and ovulation in women. *Human Reproduction, 11,* 2477–2480.

Secord, P. F. (1983). Imbalanced sex ratios: The social consequences. *Personality and Social Psychology Bulletin, 9,* 525–543.

Seehausen, O., van Alphen, J. J. M., & Witte, F. (1997). Cichlid fish diversity threatened by eutrophication that curbs sexual selection. *Science, 277,* 1808–1811.

Segal, N. L., & MacDonald, K. B. (1998). Behavior genetics and evolutionary psychology: A unified perspective on personality research. *Human Biology, 70,* 159–184.

Segesser, F. V., Scheffrahn, W., & Martin, R. D. (1994). Parentage analysis within a semi-free-ranging group of Barbary macaques *Macaca sylvanus. Molecular Ecology, 3,* 115–120.

Seligman, M. E. P. (1991). *Learned optimism.* New York: Knopf.

Serbin, L. A., & Connor, J. M. (1979). Sex typing of children's play preferences and patterns of cognitive performance. *Journal of Genetic Psychology, 134,* 315–316.

Serbin, L. A., Connor, J. M., & Citron, C. C. (1981). Sex-differentiated free play behavior: Effects of teacher modeling, location, and gender. *Developmental Psychology, 17,* 640–646.

Serbin, L. A., Powlishta, K. K., & Gulko, J. (1993). The development of sex typing in middle childhood. *Monographs of the Society for Research in Child Development, 58* (No. 2, Serial No. 232).

Seymoure, P., Dou, H., & Juraska, J. M. (1996). Sex differences in radial maze performance: Influence of rearing environment and room cues. *Psychobiology, 24,* 33–37.

Shackelford, T. K., & Larsen, R. J. (1997). Facial asymmetry as an indicator of psychological, emotional, and physiological distress. *Journal of Personality and Social Psychology, 72,* 456–466.

Shapiro, D. H., Jr., Schwartz, C. E., & Astin, J. A. (1996). Controlling ourselves, controlling our world: Psychology's role in understanding positive and negative consequences of seeking and gaining control. *American Psychologist, 51,* 1213–1230.

Shaywitz, B. A., Shaywitz, S. E., Pugh, K. R., Constable, R. T., Skudlarski, P., Fulbright, R. K., Bronen, R. A., Fletcher, J. M., Shankweiler, D. P., Katz, L., & Gore, J. C. (1995). Sex differences in the functional organization of the brain for language. *Nature, 373,* 607–609.

Sheldon, B. C., Merilä, J., Qvarnström, A., Gustafsson, L., & Ellegren, H. (1997). Paternal genetic contribution to offspring condition predicted by size of male secondary sexual character. *Proceedings of the Royal Society of London B, 264,* 297–302.

Shepard, R. N. (1994). Perceptual–cognitive universals as reflections of the world. *Psychonomic Bulletin & Review, 1,* 2–28.

Sherif, M., Harvey, O. J., White, B. J., Hood, W. R., & Sherif, C. W. (1961). *Intergroup conflict and cooperation: The Robbers Cave experiment.* Norman: Institute of Group Relations, University of Oklahoma.

Sherman, J. A. (1967). Problem of sex differences in space perception and aspects of intellectual functioning. *Psychological Review, 74,* 290–299.

Sherman, S. L., DeFries, J. C., Gottesman, I. I., Loehlin, J. C., Meyer, J. M., Pelias, M. Z., Rice, J., & Waldman, I. (1997). Recent developments in human behavioral genetics:

Past accomplishments and future directions. *American Journal of Human Genetics, 60,* 1265–1275.

Sherry, D. F., Forbes, M. R. L., Khurgel, M., & Ivy, G. O. (1993). Females have a larger hippocampus than males in the brood-parasitic brown-headed cowbird. *Proceedings of the National Academy of Sciences, USA, 90,* 7839–7843.

Sherry, D. F., & Hampson, E. (1997). Evolution and the hormonal control of sexually-dimorphic spatial abilities in humans. *Trends in Cognitive Sciences, 1,* 50–56.

Sherry, D. F., Vaccarino, A. L., Buckenham, K., & Herz, R. S. (1989). The hippocampal complex of food-storing birds. *Brain, Behavior & Evolution, 34,* 308–317.

Sherwin, B. B. (1988). A comparative analysis of the role of androgen in human male and female sexual behavior: Behavioral specificity, critical thresholds, and sensitivity. *Psychobiology, 16,* 416–425.

Shute, V. J., Pellegrino, J. W., Hubert, L., & Reynolds, R. W. (1983). The relationship between androgen levels and human spatial abilities. *Bulletin of the Psychonomic Society, 21,* 465–468.

Siegler, R. S. (1989). Mechanisms of cognitive development. *Annual Review of Psychology, 40,* 353–379.

Siegler, R. S. (1996). *Emerging minds: The process of change in children's thinking.* New York: Oxford University Press.

Siegler, R. S., & Crowley, K. (1994). Constraints on learning in nonprivileged domains. *Cognitive Psychology, 27,* 194–226.

Sigg, H., Stolba, A., Abegglen, J.-J., & Dasser, V. (1982). Life history of hamadryas baboons: Physical development, infant mortality, reproductive parameters and family relationships. *Primates, 23,* 473–487.

Silk, J. B. (1987). Social behavior in evolutionary perspective. In B. B. Smuts, D. L. Cheney, R. M. Seyfarth, R. W. Wrangham, & T. T. Struhsaker (Eds.), *Primate societies* (pp. 318–329). Chicago: University of Chicago Press.

Silk, J. B. (1993). The evolution of social conflict among female primates. In W. A. Mason & S. P. Mendoza (Eds.), *Primate social conflict* (pp. 49–83). Albany: State University of New York Press.

Silverman, I., & Eals, M. (1992). Sex differences in spatial abilities: Evolutionary theory and data. In J. H. Barkow, L. Cosmides, & J. Tooby (Eds.), *The adapted mind: Evolutionary psychology and the generation of culture* (pp. 533–549). New York: Oxford University Press.

Silverman, I., & Phillips, K. (1993). Effects of estrogen changes during the menstrual cycle on spatial performance. *Ethology and Sociobiology, 14,* 257–270.

Silverstein, L. B. (1991). Transforming the debate about child care and maternal employment. *American Psychologist, 46,* 1025–1032.

Simner, M. L. (1971). Newborn's response to the cry of another infant. *Developmental Psychology, 5,* 136–150.

Simon, A., & Ward, L. O. (1982). Sex-related patterns of worry in secondary school pupils. *British Journal of Clinical Psychology, 21,* 63–64.

Simon, H. A. (1990). A mechanism for social selection and successful altruism. *Science, 250,* 1665–1668.

Simons, R. L., & Johnson, C. (1996). The impact of marital and social network support on quality of parenting. In G. R. Pierce, B. R. Sarason, & I. G. Sarason (Eds.), *Handbook of social support and the family* (pp. 269–287). New York: Plenum Press.

Singh, D. (1993a). Adaptive significance of female physical attractiveness: Role of waist-to-hip ratio. *Journal of Personality and Social Psychology, 65,* 293–307.

Singh, D. (1993b). Body shape and women's attractiveness: The critical role of waist-to-hip ratio. *Human Nature, 4,* 297–321.

Singh, D. (1995a). Female health, attractiveness, and desirability for relationships: Role of breast asymmetry and waist-to-hip ratio. *Ethology and Sociobiology, 16,* 465–481.

Singh, D. (1995b). Female judgment of male attractiveness and desirability for relationships: Role of waist-to-hip ratio and financial status. *Journal of Personality and Social Psychology, 69,* 1089–1101.

Singh, D., & Luis, S. (1995). Ethnic and gender consensus for the effect of waist-to-hip ratio on judgment of women's attractiveness. *Human Nature, 6,* 51–65.

Singh, D., & Young, R. K. (1995). Body weight, waist-to-hip ratio, breasts, and hips: Role in judgments of female attractiveness and desirability for relationships. *Ethology and Sociobiology, 16,* 483–507.

Skuse, D. H., James, R. S., Bishop, D. V. M., Coppin, B., Dalton, P., Aamodt-Leeper, G., Bacarese-Hamilton, M., Creswell, C., McGurk, R., & Jacobs, P. A. (1997). Evidence from Turner's syndrome of an imprinted X-linked locus affecting cognitive function. *Nature, 387,* 705–708.

Slaby, R. G., & Frey, K. S. (1975). Development of gender constancy and selective attention to same-sex models. *Child Development, 46,* 849–856.

Small, M. F. (1992). The evolution of female sexuality and mate selection in humans. *Human Nature, 3,* 133–156.

Smith, D. G. (1993). A 15-year study of the association between dominance rank and reproductive success of male rhesus macaques. *Primates, 34,* 471–480.

Smith, D. G. (1994). Male dominance and reproductive success in a captive group of rhesus macaques (*Macaca mulatta*). *Behaviour, 129,* 225–242.

Smith, M. S., & Ryan, K. D. (1987). The estrous and menstrual cycle, neuroendocrine control. In G. Adelman (Ed.), *Encyclopedia of neuroscience* (Vol. 1, pp. 407–409). Boston: Birkhauser.

Smith, P. K. (1982). Does play matter? Functional and evolutionary aspects of animal and human play. *Behavioral and Brain Sciences, 5,* 139–184.

Smith, P. M. (1985). *Language, the sexes and society.* Oxford, England: Basil Blackwell.

Smuts, B. B. (1985). *Sex and friendship in baboons.* New York: Aldine de Gruyter.

Smuts, B. B. (1987a). Gender, aggression, and influence. In B. B. Smuts, D. L. Cheney, R. M. Seyfarth, R. W. Wrangham, & T. T. Struhsaker (Eds.), *Primate societies* (pp. 400–412). Chicago: University of Chicago Press.

Smuts, B. B. (1987b). Sexual competition and mate choice. In B. B. Smuts, D. L. Cheney, R. M. Seyfarth, R. W. Wrangham, & T. T. Struhsaker (Eds.), *Primate societies* (pp. 385–399). Chicago: University of Chicago Press.

Smuts, B. (1992). Male aggression against women: An evolutionary perspective. *Human Nature, 3,* 1–44.

Smuts, B. (1995). The evolutionary origins of patriarchy. *Human Nature, 6,* 1–32.

Smuts, B. B., Cheney, D. L., Seyfarth, R. M., Wrangham, R. W., & Struhsaker, T. T. (Eds.). (1987). *Primate societies.* Chicago: University of Chicago Press.

Smuts, B., & Gubernick, D. J. (1992). Male–infant relationships in nonhuman primates: Paternal investment or mating effort? In B. S. Hewlett (Ed.), *Father–child relations: Cultural and biosocial contexts* (pp. 1–30). New York: Aldine de Gruyter.

Smuts, B., & Nicolson, N. (1989). Reproduction in wild female olive baboons. *American Journal of Primatology, 19,* 229–246.

Sorci, G., Morand, S., & Hugot, J.-P. (1997). Host–parasite coevolution: Comparative evidence for covariation of life history traits in primates and oxyurid parasites. *Proceedings of the Royal Society of London B, 264,* 285–289.

Spelke, E. S., Breinlinger, K., Macomber, J., & Jacobson, K. (1992). Origins of knowledge. *Psychological Review, 99,* 605–632.

Sprecher, S., Sullivan, Q., & Hatfield, E. (1994). Mate selection preferences: Gender differences examined in a national sample. *Journal of Personality and Social Psychology, 66,* 1074–1080.

Stadler, M. A., & Frensch, P. A. (Eds.). (1997). *Handbook of implicit learning.* Thousand Oaks, CA: Sage.

Stager, C. L., & Werker, J. F. (1997). Infants listen for more phonetic detail in speech perception than in word-learning tasks. *Nature, 388,* 381–382.

Stanley, J. C. (1993). Boys and girls who reason well mathematically. In G. R. Bock & K. Ackrill (Eds.), *The origins and development of high ability* (pp. 119–138). New York: Wiley.

Stanley, J. C., Benbow, C. P., Brody, L. E., Dauber, S., & Lupkowski., A. E. (1992). Gender differences on eighty-sex nationally standardized aptitude and achievement tests. In N. Colangelo, S. G. Assouline, & D. L. Ambroson (Eds.), *Talent development: Proceedings from the 1991 Henry B. and Jocelyn Wallace National Research Symposium on talent development* (pp. 42–65). Unionville, NY: Trillium Press.

Steele, C. M. (1997). A threat in the air: How stereotypes shape intellectual identity and performance. *American Psychologist, 52,* 613–629.

Stephan, W. G. (1985). Intergroup relations. In G. Lindzey & E. Aronson (Eds.), *Handbook of social psychology: Vol. II: Special fields and applications* (pp. 599–658). New York: Random House.

Sterck, E. H. M., Watts, D. P., & van Schaik, C. P. (1997). The evolution of female social relationships in nonhuman primates. *Behavioral Ecology and Sociobiology, 41,* 291–309.

Stevenson, M. R., & Black, K. N. (1988). Paternal absence and sex-role development: A meta-analysis. *Child Development, 59,* 793–814.

Stinson, S. (1985). Sex differences in environmental sensitivity during growth and development. *Yearbook of Physical Anthropology, 28,* 123–147.

Strait, D. S., Grine, F. E., & Moniz, M. A. (1997). A reappraisal of early hominid phylogeny. *Journal of Human Evolution, 32,* 17–82.

Strayer, F. F., & Santos, A. J. (1996). Affiliative structures in preschool peer groups. *Social Development, 5,* 117–130.

Strough, J., Berg, C. A., & Sansone, C. (1996). Goals for solving everyday problems across the life span: Age and gender differences in the salience of interpersonal concerns. *Developmental Psychology, 32,* 1106–1115.

Stumpf, H., & Eliot, J. (1995). Gender-related differences in spatial ability and the *k* factor of general spatial ability in a population of academically talented students. *Personality and Individual Differences, 19,* 33–45.

Sugiyama, Y., Kawamoto, S., Takenaka, O., Kumazaki, K., & Miwa, N. (1993). Paternity discrimination and inter-group relationships of chimpanzees at Bossou. *Primates, 34,* 545–552.

Susman, E. J., Inoff-Germain, G., Nottelmann, E. D., Loriaux, D. L. Cutler, G. B., Jr., & Chrousos, G. P. (1987). Hormones, emotional dispositions, and aggressive attributes in young adolescents. *Child Development, 58,* 114–134.

Sutton-Smith, B., Rosenberg, B. G., & Morgan, E. F., Jr. (1963). Development of sex differences in play choices during preadolescence. *Child Development, 34,* 119–126.

Swisher, C. C., III, Rink, W. J., Antón, S. C., Schwarcz, H. P., Curtis, G. H., Suprijo, A., & Widiasmoro. (1996). Latest *Homo erectus* of Java: Potential contemporaneity with *Homo sapiens* in Southeast Asia. *Science, 274,* 1870–1874.

Symons, D. (1979). *The evolution of human sexuality.* New York: Oxford University Press.

Symons, D. (1980). Précis of *The evolution of human sexuality. Behavioral and Brain Sciences, 3,* 171–214.

Tagaris, G. A., Kim, S.-G., Strupp, J. P., Andersen, P., Ugurbil, K., & Georgopoulos, A. P. (1997). Mental rotation studied by functional magnetic resonance imaging at high field (4 tesla): Performance and cortical activation. *Journal of Cognitive Neuroscience, 9*, 419–432.

Takahata, N., & Nei, M. (1990). Allelic genealogy under overdominant and frequency-dependent selection and polymorphism of major histocompatibility complex loci. *Genetics, 124*, 967–978.

Tallal, P. (1991). Hormonal influences in developmental learning disabilities. *Psychoneuroendocrinology, 16*, 203–211.

Tanner, J. M. (1990). *Foetus into man: Physical growth from conception to maturity.* Cambridge, MA: Harvard University Press.

Tanner, J. M. (1992). Human growth and development. In S. Jones, R. Martin, & D. Pilbeam (Eds.), *The Cambridge encyclopedia of human evolution* (pp. 98–105). New York: Cambridge University Press.

Tassinary, L. G., & Hansen, K. A. (1998). A critical test of the waist-to-hip ratio hypothesis of female physical attractiveness. *Psychological Science, 9*, 150–155.

Temrin, H., & Tullberg, B. S. (1995). A phylogenetic analysis of the evolution of avian mating systems in relation to altricial and precocial young. *Behavioral Ecology, 6*, 296–307.

Thomas, J. R., & French, K. E. (1985). Gender differences across age in motor performance: A meta-analysis. *Psychological Bulletin, 98*, 260–282.

Thompson, C. W., Hillgarth, N., Leu, M., & McClure, H. E. (1997). High parasite load in house finches (*Carpodacus mexicanus*) is correlated with reduced expression of a sexually selected trait. *American Naturalist, 149*, 270–294.

Thompson, S. C., Armstrong, W., & Thomas, C. (1998). Illusions of control, underestimations, and accuracy: A control heuristic explanation. *Psychological Bulletin, 123*, 143–161.

Thornhill, R., & Gangestad, S. W. (1993). Human facial beauty: Averageness, symmetry, and parasite resistance. *Human Nature, 4*, 237–269.

Thornhill, R., & Gangestad, S. W. (1994). Human fluctuating asymmetry and sexual behavior. *Psychological Science, 5*, 297–302.

Thornhill, R., Gangestad, S. W., & Comer, R. (1995). Human female orgasm and mate fluctuating asymmetry. *Animal Behaviour, 50*, 1601–1615.

Thornhill, R., & Møller, A. P. (1997). Developmental stability, disease and medicine. *Biological Reviews of the Cambridge Philosophical Society, 72*, 497–548.

Tooby, J., & Cosmides, L. (1989). Evolutionary psychology and the generation of culture, Part I: Theoretical considerations. *Ethology and Sociobiology, 10*, 29–49.

Tooby, J., & Cosmides, L. (1990). On the universality of human nature and the uniqueness of the individual: Role of genetics and adaptation. *Journal of Personality, 58*, 17–67.

Tooby, J., & Cosmides, L. (1992). The psychological foundation of culture. In J. H. Barkow, L. Cosmides, & J. Tooby (Eds.), *The adapted mind: Evolutionary psychology and the generation of culture* (pp. 19–136). New York: Oxford University Press.

Tooby, J., & Cosmides, L. (1995). Mapping the evolved functional organization of mind and brain. In M. S. Gazzaniga (Ed.), *The cognitive neurosciences* (pp. 1185–1197). Cambridge, MA: Bradford Books/MIT Press.

Townsend, J. M., Kline, J., & Wasserman, T. H. (1995). Low-investment copulation: Sex differences in motivations and emotional reactions. *Ethology and Sociobiology, 16*, 25–51.

Towson, S. M. J., Lerner, M. J., & de Carufel, A. (1981). Justice rules or ingroup loyalties: The effects of competition on children's allocation behavior. *Personality and Social Psychology Bulletin, 7*, 696–700.

Travis, C. B., & Yeager, C. P. (1991). Sexual selection, parental investment, and sexism. *Journal of Social Issues, 47*, 117–129.

Trinkaus, E. (1992). Evolution of human manipulation. In S. Jones, R. Martin, & D. Pilbeam (Eds.), *The Cambridge encyclopedia of human evolution* (pp. 346–349). New York: Cambridge University Press.

Trivers, R. L. (1971). The evolution of reciprocal altruism. *Quarterly Review of Biology, 46,* 35–57.

Trivers, R. L. (1972). Parental investment and sexual selection. In B. Campbell (Ed.), *Sexual selection and the descent of man 1871–1971* (pp. 136–179). Chicago: Aldine.

Trivers, R. L. (1974). Parent–offspring conflict. *American Zoologist, 14,* 249–264.

Trivers, R. L. (1985). *Social evolution.* Menlo Park, CA: Benjamin/Cummings Publishing Co.

Tucker, J. S., Friedman, H. S., Schwartz, J. E., Criqui, M. H., Tomlinson-Keasey, C., Wingard, D. L., & Martin, L. R. (1997). Parental divorce: Effects on individual behavior and longevity. *Journal of Personality and Social Psychology, 73,* 381–391.

Turner, B. F. (1982). Sex-related differences in aging. In B. B. Wolman (Ed.), *Handbook of developmental psychology* (pp. 912–936). Englewood Cliffs, NJ: Prentice Hall.

Turner, P. J., & Gervai, J. (1995). A multidimensional study of gender typing in preschool children and their parents: Personality, attitudes, preferences, behavior, and cultural differences. *Developmental Psychology, 31,* 759–772.

Tutin, C. E. G. (1979). Mating patterns and reproductive strategies in a community of wild chimpanzees (*Pan troglodytes schweinfurthii*). *Behavioral Ecology and Sociobiology, 6,* 29–38.

Ungerleider, L. G., & Mishkin, M. (1982). Two cortical visual systems. In D. J. Ingle, M. A. Goodale, & R. J. W. Mansfield (Eds.), *Analysis of visual behavior* (pp. 549–586). Cambridge, MA: MIT Press.

Vandenberg, S. G., & Kuse, A. R. (1978). Mental rotations, a group test of three-dimensional spatial visualization. *Perceptual and Motor Skills, 47,* 599–604.

Van Goozen, S. H. M., Cohen-Kettenis, P. T., Gooren, L. J. G., Frijda, N. H., & Van de Poll, N. E. (1994). Activating effects of androgens on cognitive performance: Causal evidence in a group of female-to-male transsexuals. *Neuropsychologia, 32,* 1153–1157.

Van Goozen, S. H. M., Cohen-Kettenis, P. T., Gooren, L. J. G., Frijda, N. H., & Van de Poll, N. E. (1995). Gender differences in behaviour: Activating effects of cross-sex hormones. *Psychoneuroendocrinology, 20,* 343–363.

van Hooff, J. A. R. A. M., & van Schaik, C. P. (1994). Male bonds: Affiliative relationships among nonhuman primate males. *Behaviour, 130,* 309–337.

van Lawick-Goodall, J. (1971). *In the shadow of man.* Boston: Houghton Mifflin.

Van Valen, L. (1973). A new evolutionary law. *Evolutionary Theory, 1,* 1–30.

Velle, W. (1987). Sex differences in sensory functions. *Perspectives in Biology and Medicine, 30,* 490–522.

Vining, D. R., Jr. (1986). Social versus reproductive success: The central theoretical problem of human sociobiology. *Behavioral and Brain Sciences, 9,* 167–216.

Voland, E. (1988). Differential infant and child mortality in evolutionary perspective: Data from late 17th to 19th century Ostfriesland (Germany). In L. Betzig, M. Borgerhoff Mulder, & P. Turke (Eds.), *Human reproductive behaviour: A Darwinian perspective* (pp. 253–261). Cambridge, England: Cambridge University Press.

Volkow, N. D., Wang, G.-J., Fowler, J. S., Hitzemann, R., Pappas, N., Pascani, K., & Wong, C. (1997). Gender differences in cerebellar metabolism: Test–retest reproducibility. *American Journal of Psychiatry, 154,* 119–121.

vom Saal, F. S., & Howard, L. S. (1982). The regulation of infanticide and parental behavior: Implications for reproductive success in male mice. *Science, 215,* 1270–1272.

von Schantz, T., Göransson, G., Andersson, G., Fröberg, I., Grahn, M., Helgée, A., & Wittzell, H. (1989). Female choice selects for a viability-based male trait in pheasants. *Nature, 337,* 166–169.

von Schantz, T., Grahn, M., & Göransson, G. (1994). Intersexual selection and reproductive success in the pheasant *Phasianus colchicus. American Naturalist, 144*, 510–527.

von Schantz, T., Wittzell, H., Göransson, G., Grahn, M., & Persson, K. (1996). MHC genotype and male ornamentation: Genetic evidence for the Hamilton–Zuk model. *Proceedings of the Royal Society of London B, 263*, 265–271.

Voyer, D., Voyer, S., & Bryden, M. P. (1995). Magnitude of sex differences in spatial abilities: A meta-analysis and consideration of critical variables. *Psychological Bulletin, 117*, 250–270.

Vrba, E. S. (1985). Ecological and adaptive changes associated with early hominid evolution. In E. Delson (Ed.), *Ancestors: The hard evidence* (pp. 63–71). New York: Alan R. Liss.

Vrijenhhoek, R. C. (1993). The origin and evolution of clones versus the maintenance of sex in Poeciliopsis. *Journal of Heredity, 84*, 388–395.

Wada, J., Clark, R., & Hamm, A. (1975). Cerebral hemisphere asymmetry in humans. *Archives of Neurology, 32*, 239–246.

Wagner, H. L., Buck, R., & Winterbotham, M. (1993). Communication of specific emotions: Gender differences in sending accuracy and communication measures. *Journal of Nonverbal Behavior, 17*, 29–53.

Wagner, H. L., MacDonald, C. J., & Manstead, A. S. R. (1986). Communication of individual emotions by spontaneous facial expressions. *Journal of Personality and Social Psychology, 50*, 737–743.

Wagner, R. K., Torgesen, J. K., & Rashotte, C. A. (1994). Development of reading-related phonological processing abilities: New evidence of bidirectional causality from a latent variable longitudinal study. *Developmental Psychology, 30*, 73–87.

Walker-Andrews, A. S. (1997). Infants' perception of expressive behaviors: Differentiation of multimodal information. *Psychological Bulletin, 121*, 437–456.

Wallace, A. R. (1892). Note on sexual selection. *Natural Science, 1*, 749–750.

Wallen, K. (1996). Nature needs nurture: The interaction of hormonal and social influences on the development of behavioral sex differences in rhesus monkeys. *Hormones and Behavior, 30*, 364–378.

Walters, J. R. (1987). Transition to adulthood. In B. B. Smuts, D. L. Cheney, R. M. Seyfarth, R. W. Wrangham, & T. T. Struhsaker (Eds.), *Primate societies* (pp. 358–369). Chicago: University of Chicago Press.

Walters, S., & Crawford, C. B. (1994). The importance of mate attraction for intrasexual competition in men and women. *Ethology and Sociobiology, 15*, 5–30.

Watson, N. V., & Kimura, D. (1991). Nontrivial sex differences in throwing and intercepting: Relation to psychometrically-defined spatial functions. *Personality and Individual Differences, 12*, 375–385.

Waxman, D., & Peck, J. R. (1998). Pleiotropy and the preservation of perfection. *Science, 279*, 1210–1213.

Weatherhead, P. J. (1994). Mixed mating strategies by females may strengthen the sexy son hypothesis. *Animal Behaviour, 47*, 1210–1211.

Webley, P. (1981). Sex differences in home range and cognitive maps in eight-year-old children. *Journal of Environmental Psychology, 1*, 293–302.

Wechsler, D. (1955). *Manual for the Wechsler Adult Intelligence Scale*. San Antonio, TX: Psychological Corporation.

Wechsler, D. (1974). *Manual for the Wechsler Intelligence Scale for Children—Revised (WISC–R)*. San Antonio, TX: Psychological Corporation.

Wechsler, D. (1981). *Manual for the Wechsler Adult Intelligence Scale—Revised (WAIS–R)*. San Antonio, TX: Psychological Corporation.

Wedekind, C. (1992). Detailed information about parasites revealed by sexual ornamentation. *Proceedings of the Royal Society of London B, 247*, 169–174.

Wedekind, C., Seebeck, T., Bettens, F., & Paepke, A. J. (1995). MHC-dependent mate preferences in humans. *Proceedings of the Royal Society of London B, 260*, 245–249.

Weiner, J. (1995). *The beak of the finch.* New York: Vintage Books.

Weisfeld, G. E., & Berger, J. M. (1983). Some features of human adolescence viewed in evolutionary perspective. *Human Development, 26*, 121–133.

Wellman, H. M. (1990). *The child's theory of mind.* Cambridge, MA: MIT Press/Bradford Books.

West, M. J., & King, A. P. (1980). Enriching cowbird song by social deprivation. *Journal of Comparative and Physiological Psychology, 94*, 263–270.

West, M. M., & Konner, M. J. (1976). The role of father: An anthropological perspective. In M. E. Lamb (Ed.), *The role of the father in child development* (pp. 185–217). New York: Wiley.

Westneat, D. F., & Sherman, P. W. (1997). Density and extra-pair fertilizations in birds: A comparative analysis. *Behavioral Ecology and Sociobiology, 41*, 205–215.

Whissell, C. (1996). Mate selection in popular women's fiction. *Human Nature, 7*, 427–447.

White, D. R. (1988). Rethinking polygyny: Co-wives, codes, and cultural systems. *Current Anthropology, 29*, 529–572.

White, D. R., & Burton, M. L. (1988). Causes of polygyny: Ecology, economy, kinship, and warfare. *American Anthropologist, 90*, 871–887.

White, F. J., & Burgman, M. A. (1990). Social organization of the pygmy chimpanzee (*Pan paniscus*): Multivariate analysis of intracommunity associations. *American Journal of Physical Anthropology, 83*, 193–201.

Whiting, B. B., & Edwards, C. P. (1973). A cross-cultural analysis of sex differences in the behavior of children aged three through 11. *Journal of Social Psychology, 91*, 171–188.

Whiting, B. B., & Edwards, C. P. (1988). *Children of different worlds: The formation of social behavior.* Cambridge, MA: Harvard University Press.

Whiting, B. B., & Whiting, J. W. M. (1975). *Children of six cultures: A psycho-cultural analysis.* Cambridge, MA: Harvard University Press.

Whitley, B. E., Jr., & Kite, M. E. (1995). Sex differences in attitudes toward homosexuality: A comment on Oliver and Hyde (1993). *Psychological Bulletin, 117*, 146–154.

Whitten, P. L. (1987). Infants and adult males. In B. B. Smuts, D. L. Cheney, R. M. Seyfarth, R. W. Wrangham, & T. T. Struhsaker (Eds.), *Primate societies* (pp. 343–357). Chicago: University of Chicago Press.

Wickings, E. J., Bossi, T., & Dixson, A. F. (1993). Reproductive success in the mandrill, *Mandrillus sphinx*: Correlations of male dominance and mating success with paternity, as determined by DNA fingerprinting. *Journal of Zoology, 231*, 563–574.

Wiesenfeld, A. R., & Klorman, R. (1978). The mother's psychophysiological reactions to contrasting affective expressions by her own and an unfamiliar infant. *Developmental Psychology, 14*, 294–304.

Wilcockson, R. W., Crean, C. S., & Day, T. H. (1995). Heritability of a sexually selected character expressed in both sexes. *Nature, 374*, 158–159.

Wiley, R. H., & Poston, J. (1996). Indirect mate choice, competition for mates, and co-evolution of the sexes. *Evolution, 50*, 1371–1381.

Williams, C. L., Barnett, A. M., & Meck, W. H. (1990). Organizational effects of early gonadal secretions on sexual differentiation in spatial ability. *Behavioral Neuroscience, 104*, 84–97.

Williams, C. L., & Meck, W. H. (1991). The organizational effects of gonadal steroids on sexually dimorphic spatial ability. *Psychoneuroendocrinology, 16*, 155–176.

Williams, G. C. (1966). *Adaptation and natural selection: A critique of some current evolutionary thought.* Princeton, NJ: Princeton University Press.

Williams, G. C. (1975). *Sex and evolution.* Princeton, NJ: Princeton University Press.

Williams, G. C., & Mitton, J. B. (1973). Why reproduce sexually? *Journal of Theoretical Biology, 39,* 545–554.

Willingham, W. W., & Cole, N. S. (1997). *Gender and fair assessment.* Hillsdale, NJ: Erlbaum.

Wilson, D. S., Near, D., & Miller, R. R. (1996). Machiavellianism: A synthesis of the evolutionary and psychological literatures. *Psychological Bulletin, 119,* 285–299.

Wilson, D. S., & Sober, E. (1994). Re-introducing group selection to the human behavioral sciences. *Behavioral and Brain Sciences, 17,* 585–654.

Wilson, E. O. (1975). *Sociobiology: The new synthesis.* Cambridge, MA: Harvard University Press.

Wilson, G. D. (1997). Gender differences in sexual fantasy: An evolutionary analysis. *Personality and Individual Differences, 22,* 27–31.

Wilson, M., & Daly, M. (1985). Competitiveness, risk taking, and violence: The young male syndrome. *Ethology and Sociobiology, 6,* 59–73.

Wilson, M. I., & Daly, M. (1992). Who kills whom in spouse killing? On the exceptional sex ratio of spousal homicides in the United States. *Criminology, 30,* 189–215.

Wilson, M., & Daly, M. (1997). Life expectancy, economic inequality, homicide, and reproductive timing in Chicago neighbourhoods. *British Medical Journal, 314,* 1271–1274.

Winslow, J. T., Hastings, N., Carter, C. S., Harbaugh, C. R., & Insel, T. R. (1993). A role for central vasopressin in pair bonding in monogamous prairie voles. *Nature, 365,* 545–548.

Witelson, S. F. (1976). Sex and the single hemisphere: Specialization of the right hemisphere for spatial processing. *Science, 193,* 425–427.

Witelson, S. F. (1985). The brain connection: The corpus callosum is larger in left-handers. *Science, 229,* 665–668.

Witelson, S. F. (1991). Neural sexual mosaicism: Sexual differentiation of the human temporo-parietal region for functional asymmetry. *Psychoneuroendocrinology, 16,* 131–153.

Wolfe, L. D., & Gray, J. P. (1982). Subsistence practices and human sexual dimorphism of stature. *Journal of Human Evolution, 11,* 575–580.

Wolpoff, M. H. (1973). Posterior tooth size, body size, and diet in south African gracile australopithecines. *American Journal of Physical Anthropology, 39,* 375–394.

Wolpoff, M. H. (1976). Some aspects of the evolution of early hominid sexual dimorphism. *Current Anthropology, 17,* 579–606.

Wood, B. (1992). Origin and evolution of the genus *Homo. Nature, 355,* 783–790.

Wood, J. W. (1994). *Dynamics of human reproduction: Biology, biometry, and demography.* New York: Aldine de Gruyter.

Woods, C. J. P. (1996). Gender differences in moral development and acquisition: A review of Kohlberg's and Gilligan's models of justice and care. *Social Behavior and Personality, 24,* 375–384.

Wrangham, R. W. (1979). Sex differences in chimpanzee dispersion. In D. A. Hamburg & E. R McCown (Eds.), *The great apes* (pp. 481–489). Menlo Park, CA: Benjamin/Cummings Publishing Co.

Wrangham, R. W. (1980). An ecological model of female-bonded primate groups. *Behaviour, 75,* 262–300.

Wrangham, R. W. (1986). Ecology and social relationships in two species of chimpanzee. In D. I. Rubenstein & R. W. Wrangham (Eds.), *Ecological aspects of social evolution: Birds and mammals* (pp. 352–378). Princeton, NJ: Princeton University Press.

Wrangham, R. W. (1997). Subtle, secret female chimpanzees. *Science, 277,* 774–775.

Wrangham, R., & Peterson, D. (1996). *Demonic males.* New York: Houghton Mifflin.

Wyke, S., & Graeme, F. (1992). Competing explanations for associations between marital status and health. *Social Science & Medicine, 34,* 523–532.

Wynn, T. (1993). Layers of thinking in tool behavior. In K. R. Gibson & T. Ingold (Eds.), *Tools, language and cognition in human evolution* (pp. 389–406). Cambridge, England: Cambridge University Press.

Xu, L., Anwyl, R., & Rowan, M. J. (1997). Behavioral stress facilitates the induction of long-term depression in the hippocampus. *Nature, 387,* 497–500.

Youniss, J. (1986). Development in reciprocity through friendship. In C. Zahn-Waxler, E. Cummings, & R. Iannotti. (Eds.), *Altruism and aggression: Biological and social origins* (pp. 88–106). New York: Cambridge University Press.

Zaadstra, B. M., Seidell, J. C., Van Noord, P. A. H., Te Velde, E. R., Habbema, J. D. F., Vrieswijk, B., & Karbaat, J. (1993). Fat and female fecundity: Prospective study of effect of body fat distribution on conception rates. *British Medical Journal, 306,* 484–487.

Zahavi, A. (1975). Mate selection—A selection for a handicap. *Journal of Theoretical Biology, 53,* 205–214.

Zahn-Waxler, C., Radke-Yarrow, M., Wagner, E., & Chapman, M. (1992). Development of concern for others. *Developmental Psychology, 28,* 126–136.

Zahn-Waxler, C., Robinson, J. L., & Emde, R. N. (1992). The development of empathy in twins. *Developmental Psychology, 28,* 1038–1047.

Zeh, J. A., & Zeh, D. W. (1997). The evolution of polyandry. II: Post-copulatory defences against genetic incompatibility. *Proceedings of the Royal Society of London B, 264,* 69–75.

Zuk, M. (1996). Disease, endocrine–immune interactions, and sexual selection. *Ecology, 77,* 1037–1042.

Zuk, M., Johnsen, T. S., & Maclarty, T. (1995). Endocrine–immune interactions, ornaments and mate choice in red jungle fowl. *Proceedings of the Royal Society of London B, 260,* 205–210.

Zuk, M., & McKean, K. A. (1996). Sex differences in parasite infections—Patterns and processes. *International Journal for Parasitology, 26,* 1009–1023.

Zuk, M., Thornhill, R., & Ligon, J. D. (1990). Parasites and mate choice in red jungle fowl. *American Zoologist, 30,* 235–244.

INDEX

United States, 99–102, 152, 226, 227, 235

Van Goozen, S. H. M., 265, 292
van Schaik, C. P., 85
Van Valen, L., 19
Vasopressin, 53
Verbal ability, 261, 310–312
Violence, 317–319. *See also* Male–male competition
Visuomotor system, 192, 283
Voland, E., 143
Vole (*Microtus*), 48–51
von Schantz, T., 33
Vulnerability, and physical development, 216–217

WAIS–R, 315
Waist-to-hip-ratio (WHR), 131, 150–151, 215, 323
Walker, C., 223
Wallace, A. R., 30
Walters, J. R., 221

Watson, N. V., 284
Weiner, J., 7
Wernicke's area, 267
West, M. M., 108
Whiting, B. B., 99, 220, 243
Whitley, B. E., Jr., 278
Whitten, P. L., 105, 106
WHR. *See* Waist-to-hip-ratio
William, C. L., 292–293
Williams, G. C., 18, 22
Willingham, W. W., 328
Wilson, M., 110–111, 318, 324–325
Witelson, S. F., 293–294
Wrangham, R., 85

Yanomamö Indians, 126, 140, 226, 317–318

Zahn-Waxler, C., 219
Zuk, M., 32–33
Zulu, 127

ABOUT THE AUTHOR

David C. Geary is currently a professor of psychology and an adjunct professor of anthropology at the University of Missouri—Columbia. He received his PhD in 1986 in developmental psychology from the University of California, Riverside and from there held faculty positions at the University of Texas at El Paso and the University of Missouri—Rolla before moving to the Columbia campus. Geary has wide-ranging research interests including individual and developmental differences in numerical and arithmetical cognition, cognitive aging, and more recently evolutionary psychology—as related to children's cognitive development and to sex differences. In 1992 he received an award for excellence in intelligence research from the Mensa Education and Research Foundation, and in 1996 he received the Chancellor's Award for Outstanding Research and Creative Activity in the Behavioral and Social Sciences from the University of Missouri—Columbia.